THE RAILROAD THAT BUILT AN EMPIRE

Linda S. Daugherty Reynolds
115 N. Hickory Lane
Kokomo, Ind.

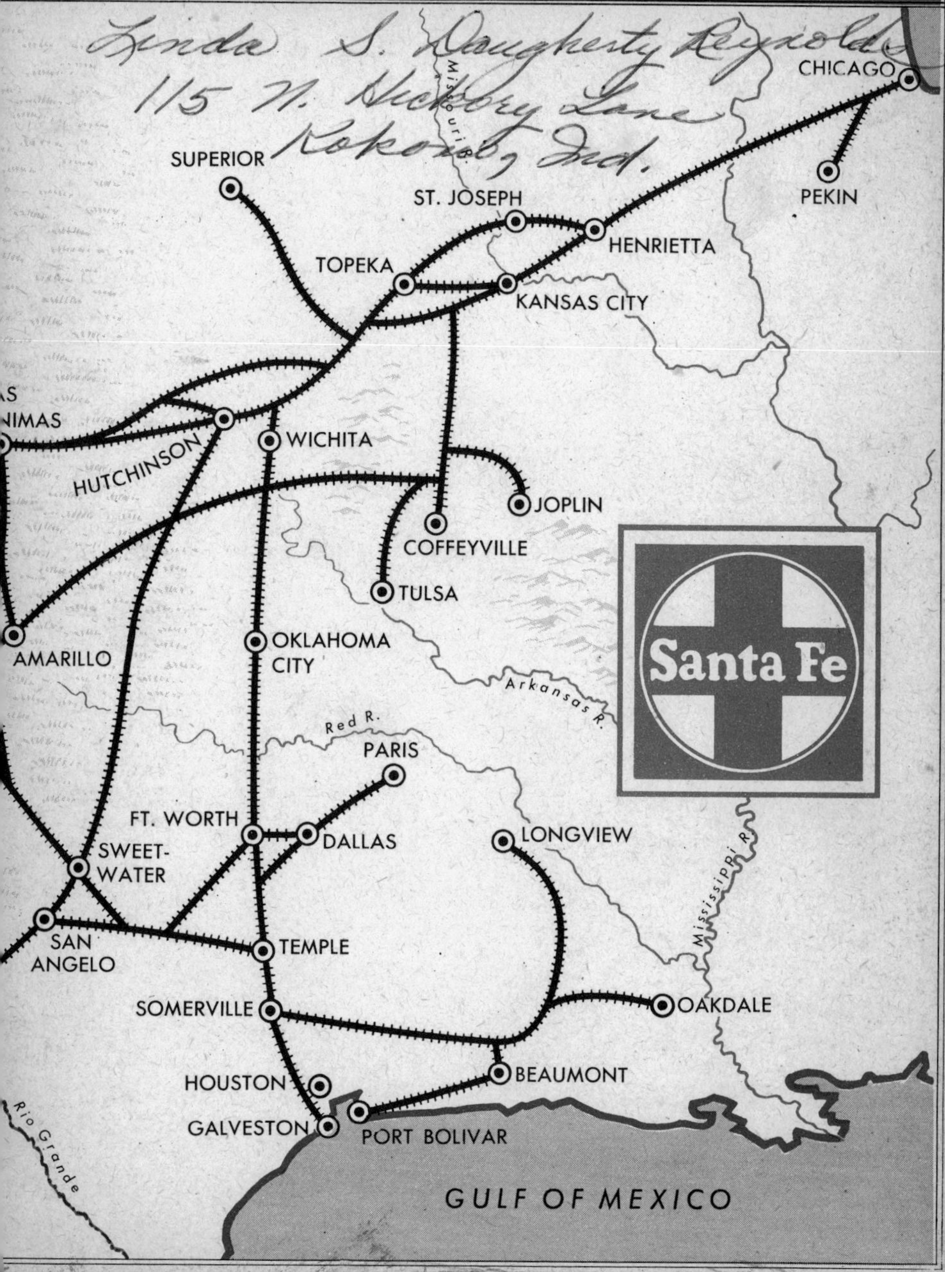

CHICAGO
PEKIN
SUPERIOR
ST. JOSEPH
HENRIETTA
TOPEKA
KANSAS CITY
Missouri R.
AS
NIMAS
HUTCHINSON
WICHITA
JOPLIN
COFFEYVILLE
TULSA
AMARILLO
OKLAHOMA CITY
Arkansas R.
Red R.
PARIS
Santa Fe
FT. WORTH
DALLAS
LONGVIEW
SWEET-WATER
SAN ANGELO
TEMPLE
Mississippi R.
SOMERVILLE
OAKDALE
HOUSTON
BEAUMONT
GALVESTON
PORT BOLIVAR
Rio Grande
GULF OF MEXICO

SANTA FE

The Railroad that Built an Empire

SANTA FE

THE RAILROAD THAT BUILT AN EMPIRE

BY JAMES MARSHALL

RANDOM HOUSE, NEW YORK

THIRD PRINTING

Published simultaneously in Canada by Random House of Canada Limited

Designed by Robert Josephy

MANUFACTURED IN THE UNITED STATES OF AMERICA

For Peg, my wife
and Lee, my friend

ACKNOWLEDGMENTS

FOR ASSISTANCE in preparing this history, the author is indebted to the following:

Dr. L. L. Waters, University of Kansas, for thorough and painstaking research.

Voluminous "Splinters" of Santa Fe history compiled by the late Joseph Weidel, formerly valuation engineer of the Santa Fe System.

The Story of the Santa Fe by Glenn D. Bradley (The Gorham Press, Boston, copyright, 1920, by Richard G. Badger).

The Kansas Historical Quarterly (Kansas State Historical Society, Topeka, Kans.).

Files of the *Santa Fe Magazine.*

The Reorganization of the American Railroad System by E. G. Campbell, Ph.D. (Columbia University Press, New York, 1938).

A History of Texas Railroads by S. G. Reed (St. Clair Publishing Company, Houston, Texas, 1941).

Sucker's Progress, a History of Gambling in America by Herbert Asbury (Dodd, Mead and Company, New York, 1938).

The News Bureau, Southern Pacific Company, San Francisco, California.

Guidebook of the Western United States, Part C, The Santa Fe Route, by N. H. Darton and others. U. S. Geological Survey, 1916.

Harry E. Maule, for valuable editorial advice, maps, picture layouts and captions.

The files of newspapers quoted in the text.

Many manuscript records by Santa Fe employees.

The Crowell-Collier Publishing Company, New York, for permission to reprint and adapt certain material from *Collier's Magazine.*

Research departments of the New York and Los Angeles Public Libraries.

Louise Kellam Smithies and Katherine Kellam Burpee, granddaughters of Col. Holliday.

My wife, for invaluable help in preparation of the manuscript.

CONTENTS

		PAGE
I.	TRAILS TO TREASURE LANDS	3
II.	THE DIRT FLIES AT LAST	13
III.	COLONEL HOLLIDAY HEADS WEST	22
IV.	STEEL ACROSS THE PRAIRIE	42
V.	INTO THE ROCKIES	64
VI.	THE PRAIRIE BLOOMS	81
VII.	THE COMING OF FRED HARVEY	97
VIII.	HEADED FOR TROUBLE	114
IX.	"SEIZE AND HOLD THAT PASS!"	127
X.	GUNS IN ROYAL GORGE	144
XI.	UNLOCKING AN EMPIRE	159
XII.	CALIFORNIA, HERE WE COME!	176
XIII.	THE INVASION OF CHICAGO	196
XIV.	NORTH FROM THE GULF	212
XV.	OKLAHOMA!	229
XVI.	SLOW! ROUGH TRACK!	242
XVII.	DOWN THROUGH ARIZONA	262
XVIII.	MR. RIPLEY FIGHTS IT THROUGH	286
XIX.	THE COMING OF THE DIESELS	300
XX.	TALES ALONG THE TRACK	316
XXI.	THE TRAIL THAT IS ALWAYS NEW	330

APPENDIX

I.	*Who, When and Where*	349
II.	*Santa Fe Town Names*	351

III. *Railroad Slang* 360
IV. *Santa Fe Departments* 377
V. *Trains* 379
VI. *Some Santa Fe Firsts* 384
VII. *Financial* 386
VIII. *Chronological Development of the Atchison, Topeka and Santa Fe Railway System* 396
IX. *Santa Fe Presidents* 450
Index 451

PHOTOGRAPHS

Following Page 224

A Glance at Santa Fe History in
32 Pages of Pictures

Cyrus K. Holliday
Bo-o-a-rd!
First Train to Run on the Santa Fe
Motive Power For the Santa Fe Trail
Fred G. Gurley
Santa Fe Engine # 1
A Far Cry From the Engineering Problems of '68
Groomed and Ready For the Run
The Old Trail, and the New
Drill You Tarriers, Drill
End of Rail, Hutchinson, Kansas in 1872
Construction Problems
A Respite From Dealing Them Off the Arm
Alvarado Hotel, Albuquerque
Harvey Lunchroom, Colorado Springs, Today
Harvey Lunchroom in the 80's
La Fonda at Santa Fe, Today
Old Drawing of La Fonda Before the Railroad Came
Across the Plains
Git Along Little Dogies . . .
First Depot at Dodge City
First Building, Dodge City
Indian Trading Post at Diablo Canyon
In Santa Fe Country
Early View of Dodge City
The Oklahoma Land Run
The Santa Fe Enters San Francisco
Death Valley Scotty's Record-Making Run

Fred Harvey, the Provider
Albert Alonzo Robinson
Edward P. Ripley
William B. Storey
Samuel T. Bledsoe
Edward J. Engel
The Petrified Forest, Arizona
An Indian Trading Post, Arizona
A Navajo Wickiup, New Mexico
Pullman Car Service—Now and Then
Courteous Service in Pullman Palace Sleeping Cars
"Everything's Up to Date in Kansas City"
Happy Days Are Here Again
California and a Well-Earned Rest
An Oasis in the Desert
The Santa Fe at War
The Grand Canyon
Development of the Locomotive, 1881-1945

MAPS

PROGRESS OF CONSTRUCTION	PAGE
The Fight for the Royal Gorge	129
Across Raton Pass and Down Through New Mexico	133
The Route Across Arizona	169
Early Attempts to Reach the Pacific Coast	173
Into California at Last	183
Illustrating the Battles in California	185
Down to the Gulf of Mexico	218
To Tidewater on San Francisco Bay	257

STATE RESOURCES	OPPOSITE PAGE
Kansas	94
Colorado	126
New Mexico	150
California	178
Illinois	198
Missouri	204
Iowa	210
Texas	214
Louisiana	226
Oklahoma	230
Arizona	262

FOREWORD

....NOW READY ON TRACK ONE

In the 1940's the most romantic call in America still was "'Booo-ard!" It was sung every day by a thousand conductors, echoed by ten thousand trainmen and Pullman porters, re-echoed by half a million passengers. It was almost the oldest call in the country and to most people it still meant adventure and hope and new horizons.

It meant a surging rush over singing steel, the wail of a chime whistle and the rhythmic click of the rail joints. It conjured up pictures of the west wind whipping waves across prairie grass and grain, of white clouds drifting across blue sky, of snowpeaks and tawny deserts, echoing canyons and lush, timbered valleys. As a creator of pleasant images of things to come it had no equal in all the world.

The Southwestern United States was built by tough, daring men who bound her leagues together, first by foot trails and wheel trails in the sod, and then with steel track. Over this track they sent people and goods rolling back and forth, more and more, faster and faster. . . . Trappers in buckskin, Indians in breechclouts, explorers in shining armor, soldiers in crimson and gold and blue: these led the way.

But men in denim and leather built the empire with timber and iron, the hiss of steam and the whirr of wheels.

This great empire, from the Missouri and Mississippi to the South Pacific Coast, from the Arkansas River to the Mexican border, was built by railroads—and the greatest builder of all was the

Santa Fe. It started as a tiny between-settlements stem in Kansas; it grew to be the longest system in the West. In 1945 it still was growing—because a railroad must grow, or die.

This is the story of the Santa Fe: its battles and its defeats; its heartaches and its triumphs; its smiles and tears and laughter. Here are the men who imagined and planned it, fought for it and built it and ran it. Here is how they did it, the sort of men they were, the sort of fighting they did.

Because of these men and their railroad a new empire grew swiftly out of wastelands that lay idle and almost worthless until they were awakened by the whistle blasts of the locomotive and the old familiar cry—in the mountains, on the plains and in roaring cities—"'Booo-ard!"

SANTA FE

The Railroad that Built an Empire

CHAPTER ONE

TRAILS TO TREASURE LANDS

WHERE TRAILS END there is a little romantic sadness and the feeling of farewell. Where trails meet and cross there is shouting and laughter and the hot quick words of man against man, the sound of bells and the clink of coins, the pad of feet and the rumble of wheels rolling and the hard breathing of driven things; the smells of cooking fires and new bread, of silks and spices, of dust and sweat.

For centuries there had been trails to the old pueblo where, in the dim future, swart men in sand-scoured armor would come roaring in from across the sea to build mud and timber palaces, bodegas, forts, and squat white cathedrals. They would dedicate this great new pueblo to a great holy one: San Francisco de Santa Fe.

But long before this the trails were old. In many places they were worn ankle-deep, knee-deep in the lava rock by the bare brown feet which shuffled endlessly north and south, east and west across the timeless land.

The first pueblo grew in a high valley. By some strange chance, here were tossed together the things men needed to live by. There was water, and the mountains walled out the blizzards. There were clay and wood for building, buffalo and antelope to kill and eat. There was earth from which to tease a little food. It was a place, too, that might be defended against warrior tribes marauding through the hills. Here the tall brown men and their families set up their mud houses. Carriers came from other tribes, bearing strange things to trade, plodding across the leagues of desert and mountain.

West the trails ran, through the chill, windy passes, across the dry wastelands and down to the warm beaches of the Pacific Ocean. Eastward they climbed the lava rock and on across the great rolling plains to the rivers beyond. North they twisted into the gorges and high silent valleys where the bear and the beaver lived and the precious salt and blue turquoise lay buried. South they crossed the hot deserts where shifting sands erased the track and men died with blackened tongues.

The little trails came first, then longer ones, as the short ones linked together.

The beach Indians passed along their shells to a tribe in the Coast Range, and these in turn carried them a few miles farther east. From the plains, the mountains and the deserts it was the same story: find and carry and trade. So at last the little trails between settlements a few miles apart became long trails that never ended, but lengthened into the swirling wakes of tall ships plowing through blue water.

At first the Indians moved around little. The salt people, the fur people and the turquoise people, the feather gatherers and the shell finders covered only short sections of the long trails. Their needs were few, their desires fewer. Millions of them lived and died knowing nothing of any world outside the valley or mesa top where they lived. There was no common language by which one tribe could exchange ideas with another.

They got about on their own two legs. It never occurred to them to tame the antelope or the buffalo and make carriers and haulers out of them. Then, into their lives came strange creatures—men welded to tall, four-legged beasts that walked and ran swiftly. At first these were one; then the creature split and here was a man and something he called a *caballo,* which was not part of the man at all but a separate animal.

The horse changed everything.

Cortez' *caballeros* came storming up from the south with mares and stallions—and in a few years the face of the land was different. The Indians, learning to ride, hunted farther afield; they could follow the *cibola* herds and the antelope. For a few years the horse was almost priceless; then, as their numbers grew, the price dropped and every tribe had enough and to spare. Distances between trail-trading places lengthened.

From the north, the salt, fur and turquoise trail came down to the old pueblo where the creek headed. The turquoise went west to meet the shells, southward turquoise and salt traveled to Chihuahua and so on to Vera Cruz on the sun-drenched Spanish Main. From Southern Mexico the traders came north with blue, red and white plumes from parrots and macaws.

The first wheels rolled up from Mexico in 1591 in the form of thick cross-sections of cottonwood logs. They supported heavy ox-carts which were driven by one Castaño de Sosa. This enterprising gentleman had no royal license to trade, but evidently got by with his effort very nicely.

Southward now the wagons began to roll, creaking under the familiar loads of salt, copper, fur, turquoise and gold. Northbound, they began to bring the loot of half the world—embroidered shawls from Canton via Manila; sugar, wine and silk from Italy; tobacco from Turkey; gewgaws from Madrid.

In 1536 a Spanish wanderer named Cabeza de Vaca turned up in Mexico City after a roundabout nine-year trip from Florida, via the mountain trails and pueblos, and touched off the first gold rush. Since Spanish officials in Mexico City demanded tales of vast riches, Cabeza supplied them. Up North, he said, people lived in terraced houses, the doors of which were encrusted with gems; they dressed in white wool and were heavily laden with golden beads, blue turquoise and silver chains.

Four years later Francisco Vasquez Coronado, brave in shining armor inlaid with gold, led 300 treasure seekers up the Chihuahua trail and into the Santa Fe country. At a settlement called Tiguex near the present Albuquerque they burned a large number of Indians alive, some accounts said 200, and started a death feud that lasted in one form or another for literally hundreds of years. They discovered the Grand Canyon and forayed as far north and east as Kansas seeking treasure.

After three years they returned to Mexico City, ruined, but leaving behind three friars. The body of one of them, Father Juan de Padilla, is buried at Isleta. Every twenty years, according to tradition, it rises briefly from its resting place in a hollowed cottonwood log, surveys the changing scene, and blesses, with thin brown fingers, those who witness the resurrection, while a few yards away the silver flash of a streamliner and the wail of a locomotive whistle wake the echoes of the tramp of Coronado's steeds.

Coronado left behind him a few horses and a band of sheep. More than 300 years later the descendants of these sheep, driven to the California valleys to feed a new gold rush, would provide a man named Wootton with the money to build a wagon road over the Santa Fe trail across Raton Mountain.

Up the long trail in Mexico in 1598 came the freight and emigrant train of Don Juan de Oñate, financed by the silver his peons dug from the mines around Zacatecas in Mexico. At the head of Don Juan's train rode his twelve-year-old son on a great white stallion draped with scarlet and gold. Then came the *caballeros* in red, purple and white silk, hat plumes waving, jeweled garters glinting in the yellow sunshine. A league north of their starting place, the *caballeros* changed to scarred armor and Don Juan put away his silks and jewels in a great silver bathtub jouncing along in a *carreta.*

After the horsemen rolled the trade wagons, eighty-three of them, and 130 colonists driving 7,000 sheep and cattle into the new wonderland of the north. It took them six months. They drove through the northern passes into the broad valley of El Rio Grande del Norte, looking, as usual, for the Seven Cities. In the valley they stopped three years, while the peons tended flocks and herds, scratched the earth and irrigated from the ancient *acequias* of the pueblo people.

The *caballeros* ranged the country and fought the Indians. There was no peace in the land. At a famous battle at Acoma, seventy Spaniards slew 600 to 900 Indians and beat the survivors into submission. Afterward, Don Juan and his *caballeros* went northwest, missing the pueblo that was to be Santa Fe, and explored far and wide. His precise route is not known. When he returned a year later, it was to the pueblo San Francisco de Santa Fe.

Here his new palace, fort and 'dobe cathedral erased the crumbling ruins of the old buildings. As the years passed, the wagon trains grew, the peon-driven mules hauling in dried oysters from the Caribbean, preserved fruits from the tropics, copper bells for the churches, silks and laces for the senoras and senoritas, nails, axes, tools and sacred paintings. The wagon trains ran on schedule now: nine months northbound; nine months layover for trading, refitting and reloading; nine months south again. From the West Coast the traders brought Digger Indian girls they had captured, to be *peonas* and concubines.

So, at the beginning of the seventeenth century, the white man's trade came to Santa Fe; then the great eastern trail opened up and met the westing path from the New England settlements beyond the rivers. Men began to know it as the Santa Fe Trail. Out over its rutted track came cotton, clocks and ingenious mechanical things from the factories of Connecticut and Massachusetts. Some of the American goods went on, up the old Spanish Trail northward to cross the Colorado near what is now Moab, Utah, then through the Wasatch canyons, over the desert and the Coast Range and down to the little Pueblo of Our Lady, Queen of the Angels. To the American trade goods were added gay wool serapes and the inevitable silver and turquoise.

Now the trail was complete from ocean to ocean.

The first wagons from Missouri rolled westward in 1821, led by Captain W. H. Becknell, wheels creaking, covers bellying in the prairie gale, taking six months for the trip. Three thousand dollars worth of American stuffs sold in Santa Fe for $15,000. In the spring of '23, the wagons lumbered back to tell their story—and the rush was on. The next train numbered twenty-five wagons and eighty-one men, dragging $30,000 worth of trade goods to the new bonanza. The train rolled east with $10,000 worth of furs and $180,000 in new gold, Spanish gold, Mexican gold.

From Mexico came roars of protest and angry threats. American goods were ousting native wares from the market.

The Mexicans outsmarted themselves by levying a tax of $750 on each American wagon and its load. So, at Arroyo Hondo, a few miles from Santa Fe, the contents of 100 wagons were repacked into sixty, and forty mule-teams were divided among the sixty to haul the bulging carts, with a flourish, into the plaza. The extra wagons, which had cost around $150 at the Missouri, brought $500 in Santa Fe; if they couldn't be sold they were cached in some hidden arroyo, to be picked up on the homeward journey. The Yankee traders figured in the $750 tax with the price of their cargoes, added $100 or more for good measure and sold out. In the end Mexicans paid their own tax and something more.

The province lost money every time a train arrived from the Missouri.

So the trails met at Santa Fe, and around the plaza milled tall Yankees, bronzed Mexicans and dark, silent Indians. The same old trails, but new trade goods, new faces and new methods of transportation.

East, west, north and south the trails grew broader. Scouts and traders, homeward bound down the Arkansas River and across to the Missouri at Westport Landing spread the story in Kansas, Missouri and back through Illinois, Ohio and Iowa until the youngsters were fired with romance, and the course of empire.

Texas broke away from Mexico and set up as an independent republic. Free Texans, roaring out their new liberty, got Stephen F. Austin to write a manifesto to the New Mexicans in Spanish and English: "Throw off the shackles; come in with us!" A party of Texans galloped west with the manifesto in 1841 and, in the plaza at San Miguel, Manuel Armijo, the shepherd boy who had risen to be governor of the province, laughed at them and threw them into a stinking 'dobe jail. Then he marched them, sick and half starved, on a 1,500-mile *jornado del muerto* to Mexico City.

The men of San Jacinto and the Alamo, the Pecos and the Canadian, would not soon forget that.

In July, 1846, Gen. Stephen W. Kearny led his ragtag army west, captured Las Vegas without firing a shot, and marched on to Santa Fe through Apache Pass, Armijo running before him. On August 18, 1846, the Mexican flag came down and the Stars and Stripes went up above the governor's palace, while thirteen Spanish guns boomed a salute. Kearny stayed a few weeks and then, led by a blue-eyed, wiry mountain man named Kit Carson, surged on westward to the Pacific. The flag snapped from the staff of the presidio at Monterey, as Commodore John Drake Sloat raised it on July 7, 1846—never to come down again.

That was empire building in mid-nineteenth century. Trails and trade were captured at guns' point. The dark blood in the dust dried in the sunshine and blew away in the wind. The rolling wheels leveled the little mounds over the shallow graves.

Two years later Mexico formally handed over huge sweeps of territory, out to the far Pacific, north into the Rockies, south into the mesquite plains. Now the flag flew free from coast to coast.

The Spaniards had looked for gold in the Rockies for 300 years—but the Californians found it in a far coastal valley, in 1848. San Francisco grew crazily on a sandflat. Sheepmen from New Mexico drove bands of wool-on-the-hoof over the mountains down to the diggings, and came home rich. They bought old Spanish land grants and lived like princes in the Cimarron and Rio Grande valleys, and spent their wealth in Las Vegas and Santa Fe. By that time Santa Fe had been almost forgotten. It was merely an overnight halt on the trail to the gold country. Then it became known that the Oregon Trail to the north was a little faster, and windjammers could freight more tonnage for less money, even if it took them 100 days around the Horn. Santa Fe dimmed to a memory—but only for a while.

In 1850 New Mexico came into the Union as a free soil territory—and went on buying and selling slaves as of old, calling them *peons* and *peonas*. Federal troops moved in and garrisoned frontier forts until war broke out between the states. Then the Texans came rampaging west and whipped the bluecoats at Pidgin's Ranch in the Glorietas. The Butternut Boys marched shouting into Santa Fe, flaunted the Stars and Stripes for a month, and marched out again. But the flag snapped in the mountain breeze once more from the old palace.

The war went on.

The railroads with one exception stopped far to the east, across the Missouri. This was the Union Pacific, a wobbly iron ribbon weaving uncertainly across Nebraska, inching ahead to join another ribbon, the Central Pacific, climbing the Sierra and clamping itself nervously to the desert. The stagecoach still rolled to Santa Fe: two weeks from Independence, Missouri, fare $250. The pony express raced back and forth. Could the steam engine replace the horse?

Well, look, it replaced the horse between New York and Washington and Philadelphia, and Chicago and St. Joe didn't it? Yes, well, didn't Francis Xavier Aubrey race on relays of horses from Santa Fe to the Missouri in five days, sixteen hours? Try beating that with your iron horse.

In Topeka, the capital of Kansas, there was a man who told the people there'd be a railroad to Santa Fe, just as there soon would be one out to Ogden and beyond. And in Topeka, which had grown from a ferry landing on the Kaw to a capital city in fifteen years, people talked that evening of October 28th, 1868, about the help-wanted ad in the day's *Record*. Dan Blush, the contractor, was offering $1.75 a day for railroad graders, and needed five hundred of them. It looked like Colonel Holliday's railroad might be getting started at last.

And high time, too. The Colonel had been talking about it long enough.

He'd been talking about it for ten years, in fact, between battling the Border Ruffians, who came ravaging into Kansas from Missouri, and writing fiery editorials against slavery, going back and forth to New York and Washington trying to get land grants and money, holding political office and being adjutant-general of Kansas.

A remarkable man, this young Colonel Holliday. He'd helped stake out Topeka, made it the capital and served as its first mayor. He had made money as a farmer, land-seller and lawyer ever since he'd arrived in Kansas in the summer of '54, with a few hundred dollars, part of a shrewd railroad deal he had made in his home state of Pennsylvania.

The war between the states was over, but the bitterness lingered on. Out in Western Kansas, the Indians still whooped, galloped and scalped. Cheyennes and Arapahoes blazed away, up and down the Solomon Valley, and General Phil Sheridan, in August, 1868, reported twenty valley settlers killed and many wounded. Five companies of cavalry were organized in September to guard the frontier and Governor Crawford, himself, was getting ready to resign and take command of the Nineteenth Regiment. General Sheridan had lately expressed the conviction that the only good Indians were dead Indians. All in all, it looked like a bad time to start a railroad west.

The prairie rolled and swelled and the streams ran bright from the ranges, spreading down to the Gulf and the Big River. Beyond the mountains, piled against the sunset, the desert valleys lay grim and sunbaked. Beyond them lay more ranges. Across these again, were greener and fatter lands sloping down to the blue Pacific washing at the feet of old 'dobe missions and the new, raw lumber buildings of the Californians.

Out there, somewhere, was Santa Fe in New Mexico. To down-to-earth Topekans, it was far away and fabulous. The study class of the American Home Missionary Society read about it and listened to returning members tell of its wickedness. Cy Holliday was always talking about Santa Fe. He was going to build a railroad to Santa Fe; he called it the Atchison & Topeka Rail Road. The missionaries smiled and shook their heads wisely. It would mean, they said, pulling trains more than 7,000 feet into the air to get through the passes. . . .

Topeka men, talking in the hotel lobby after supper—family style, fifty cents—discussed the building of the first transcontinental road. Far to the north and west Union Pacific's gangs of "Irish Terriers" were racing for Utah. From the west, up into the Sierra and across Nevada, 14,000 Chinese coolies—"Crocker's Pets"—were grading and laying track a mile a day or more, assisted by 2,000 whites and 6,000 horses and mules. Confederate and Unionist veterans sweated, shoveled, swore and drank and muleskinned side by side and Vice-President Thomas C. Durant of Union Pacific had bet Charles Crocker of Central Pacific that his terriers could lay more track in a day than the Westerner's Orientals.

Durant was right. General G. M. Dodge harangued the gangs, promised them more lashings of beer if they won, and set a day. The terriers spat on horny palms, and from pre-dawn to after dusk one day laid ten miles, fifty-six yards of track on the prairie. Good enough, admitted Crocker, and paid up. That was railroading.

It would take some time, said the lobby talkers, for Colonel Holliday's gangs to lick that record. Somebody laughed. A quiet, strong man named Tom Peter swore fluently and said, "Well, all you skeptics laugh if you want to and be damned to you, eh, John?"

"Sure, Tom," replied Captain John R. Ellinwood. He had just got back to town after surveying a line for Holliday's railroad southward up the creek toward Pauline and Wakarusa.

For a thousand miles and half as far again to the southwest the fat lands lay almost idle, the rivers brawling down the mountainsides, flowing placidly across the plains. The bunch grass greened and died as it had greened and died for centuries. Seventy-five million buffalo roamed the spaces and, only a year before, the cattle drives had started, up from Texas, across the Red River to new markets opening in the Middle West.

During the war, herds had grown vastly and now cattlemen wanted to get their money out. Then they found that the rich grass of Kansas, Southern Nebraska and Eastern Colorado would put beef on longhorns fast. So the trail herds started north that year of '67, their dust-clouded progress disputed by the buffalo and by Red Cloud's painted Sioux.

A railroad west and south, Holliday figured, would intercept thousands of beef cattle and so provide revenue for the young line as it crept westward. The Union Pacific, farther north, already was doing this. Holliday's line in the south might catch the herds first. It was shrewd reasoning—and correct. For twenty years the herds would come pounding up the trails to be loaded on the cars at Newton, Wichita, Dodge City, Kinsley and a dozen other roaring man-for-breakfast railroad towns across Kansas.

Out into the sea of grass, already little trickles of humanity were making their way to form tiny pools, linked by trails and rough roads. Plows tore through the buffalo sod and the grain came up, strong and green and full in the ear. In the years to come old stockmen would stamp and swear and curse the sodbusters for flouting God's will. God built the prairie for stock; He took centuries to build the sod. The nesters ruined His work in a year. God would surely punish them.

CHAPTER TWO

THE DIRT FLIES AT LAST

IRON TO SANTA FE was a dream, or worse. The big, lumbering Conestoga wagons still streamed out from Independence as they had been streaming before and during the war. Willing to let North and South fight it out, scores of thousands of Easterners and Southerners had lined out for Oregon, New Mexico, California, for the rich, hidden valleys of the Rockies. Santa Fe trail wagons still rumbled and squealed westward with calico, hardware and the gewgaws of civilization and came back, lighter and faster, with furs, buffalo hides, wool and some smuggled gold and silver.

The stirring land was larger than Europe. The crack of bullwhips, the groan of wagon wheels, the prayers and shouts of the trailers were waking it slowly. In all Kansas, Nebraska, California, New Mexico, Arizona and Texas there were fewer than 2,000,000 people—two to the square mile.

In all America there were not 50,000 miles of iron track and, of this, almost all was east of the Big River. Topeka, in '68, knew nothing of the great names in railroading that were to be. There were rumors of the "Erie Wars," led by Jay Gould and Jim Fisk. Gould, less than ten years before, had, at twenty-three, been the Boy Wonder of Wall Street. Ed Harriman, twenty, was managing clerk in the brokerage house of D. C. Hays, his Homeric battles with Jim Hill in the Pacific Northwest far in the future. Hill, thirty, was St. Paul agent for a small line called the St. Paul & Pacific, and, as the line ran along the Mississippi, he was agent for the Northwestern Packet Line as well. No one had yet thought of calling him an Empire Builder.

Out in the Pacific Southwest there was talk already of a quartet called the Big Four. They were Leland Stanford, Charles Crocker, Collis P. Huntington and Mark Hopkins. A few years before, they had all made a living in Sacramento—Stanford as a grocer, Crocker as a drygoods merchant, Huntington and Hopkins as partners in a hardware business. Now they were building the Central Pacific east. There was also a young engineer, Theodore D. Judah.

Holliday knew him slightly. They had met in Washington when Judah was there fighting for Central Pacific subsidies while Holliday fought for land grants. At first neither had much success, but finally Judah won his subsidy. Holliday had to build with what cash he and his associates could scrape together, along with money-promises from several Kansas counties, and a few thousand dollars from sales of land.

In Topeka people talked over the coming election. The diamonds and silks of Kate Chase Sprague, the reigning society matron of the day, had failed at the Democratic convention to win the nomination for her august father, Salmon Portland Chase, Chief Justice of the United States Supreme Court—and so, ironically, saved him from defeat at the hands of General Grant, who was to win over Lawyer Horatio Seymour. Topeka and Kansas were heavily for Grant and little Schuyler (Smiler) Colfax. In a few days the polls would show the score: Grant 31,000, Seymour 14,000.

In the White House, President Andrew Johnson, weary from his battles with Ben Wade and Congress, played out the last act of the mean, spiteful drama, still President by one vote. The one vote that saved him from impeachment had been cast by Senator Edmund G. Ross, a stern abolitionist, Kansas editor, warrior, and friend of Cy Holliday.

Holliday, just back from New York where he had been on a money-raising expedition, met Ross in the Capital Hotel lobby in Topeka, and asked him if he would make a short speech at the first dirt turning for the new railroad.

"When, Colonel?"

"Day or two."

"I've no heart for speeches," said the Senator. "They're blaming me for saving Johnson. I've resigned from the Senate, you know. But if you want a speech . . ."

Times were tough in the East, Holliday told Ross. The "Suffering Sixties" people called them. But the West seemed to be roaring on, as it had done during the war. In 1864 more than 150,000 people had moved out from the Missouri across the plains. Half of them went through Omaha, with 30,000 horses and 75,000 head of cattle. California welcomed hosts of them, boasting that California gold pouring into the national treasury was worth a dozen Union generals.

The Indian wars, still on, had started a few months after Fort Sumter. They continued for twenty-five years, and more than 1,000 battles were fought. Much of the trouble stemmed from the Chivington massacre of a band of Chief Black Kettle's Cheyennes at Sand Creek, out near Fort Lyon in 1864. An Indian peace commission had just said this orgy of blood by Colonel Chivington's Colorado Cavalry, "put to shame the savages of Africa." Custer denounced it. General Nelson A. Miles called it "the foulest and most unjustifiable crime in the annals of America." It started a war that still went on and that, ere it ended, was to cost the United States $30,000,000 and 15,000 lives.

Out in Mora, New Mexico, old Ceran St. Vrain lay dying at eighty. He was the partner of William Bent. Their fort, twelve miles from Las Animas, Colorado, had been a major trading center of the old trail and a gathering place for white traders from Independence; for Cheyennes, Utes, Arapahoes, Pawnees and Mexicans. Kit Carson and a youngster named Dick Wootton hunted meat for the fort and its guests.

Now in 1868 the remains of the old fort made a station for the Barlow & Sanderson stages. The government had offered Bent $12,000 for it in '52; he had held out for $16,000 and, when the government would not come to his figure, had moved out and blown it to bits. Kit Carson had died May 23rd, at Fort Lyon—some said by being shot through the shoulder by an arrow and thrown from his horse. He died, murmuring, "Doctor, *compadre, adios*!"

Trapper, scout, Indian fighter, guide to John Charles Frémont, Carson was one of the most romantic figures of the old West.

He was born in Kentucky and went through life, a mild, curly-haired little man, almost beardless, soft-spoken and saying much with his steel-blue eyes. Among his survivors was a youngster, his nephew, William Kit Carson, son of his brother Will. We shall meet him again, out in the Valley of Content in that fabled Las Animas country. In Will's day it was a valley of fear—and death.

More than a third of the country—about 1,300,000 square miles—was held by a few thousand men: trappers, emigrants, cowboys and soldiers. In the fall of 1868, Custer was leading the Seventh Cavalry against the Indians in various parts of the West, Kansas and what is now Oklahoma. Custer had heard of a stream named the Little Bighorn, away to the north, but it was, to him, just another creek. On June 25, 1876, it would become world-famous—and so would Custer.

Santa Fe, toward which Holliday was headed, had been American for twenty-two years, having been captured in '46, when Holliday was twenty. The famous old trail from the Missouri to Santa Fe was about 850 miles long and in most places 250 feet wide.

The first traders had made a trip a year, starting in late spring from Independence, Missouri, or some near-by town, and traveling southwest to meet the Arkansas River near what now is Hutchinson, Kansas. They followed the river for 350 miles or more, then bore south over Raton Mountain, and finally to Santa Fe. As the years passed, several cutoffs were graded and the line of the trail grew shorter and easier. Five thousand horses and oxen were hauling 500 wagons over the trail. Four tons to a wagon; eighty days west; forty days east.

Over in Missouri, Holliday heard from the gossips that the people had voted a $1,000,000 bond issue to build the Chillicothe & Omaha Air Line Railroad. Other enterprisers were planning to lay iron from Atchison to Leavenworth to connect with "The Central Road" and thence to Fort Kearney and the Union Pacific. Holliday told, with a chuckle, how surveyors for Union Pacific and Central Pacific, running lines west and east, had passed each other and lined out routes only a few feet apart.

End-of-survey on the Central Pacific was far to the east of end-of-survey on the Union Pacific, the cause being the fact that the more mileage either road built, the more land it would get. A commission finally decided the lines must meet at Promontory, north of the Great Salt Lake. They did, on May 10, 1869—with hammer blows carried to Washington by telegraph. Forever after, people would say the lines met at Promontory Point, which is miles away and wasn't founded until the Lucin Cutoff in the early 1900's.

Holliday commented to Ross that at least his new railroad would have no one building against it from the west, and Ross pointed out another item. This one read that the Pacific Mail Line of ships was being sued by the State of California for bringing in 5,000 Chinese laborers "without tax or permission." The line maintained the tax was unconstitutional.

"That," said the Senator, "is another problem you won't have."

But early railroad builders and operators had troubles besides those of raising money, getting land grants and arguing with skeptics. One minor attempt to try a new form of transportation in the Southwest had blown up only a year before.

In 1855, Congress, bemused by imaginative promoters, had laid out $30,000 for a herd of camels. In 1856, thirty-two of these strange beasts had been landed on the Texas coast, complete with native cameleers. There was some argument over which smelled worse. Next year forty more camels were landed. They loped around the desert for some years, but were so unpopular with the desert mule skinners that two years after Appomattox, the remaining thirty or forty were turned loose near Fort Yuma, Arizona.

Camels, though, were a minor headache—but a dreamer named Lorenzo Sherwood was something else again. Sherwood, who had served in both New York and Texas legislatures, was the sponsor of the Anti-Monopoly Cheap Freight League, and he had enough popular support to call a national convention to put over his scheme. This was, briefly, for the government to put up $200,000,000 to build seven doubletrack rail systems with a total length of 4,000 miles. Trains were to proceed at eight miles an hour in deference to millions of prudent, God-fearing folk who saw Satan's handiwork in the rash twenty-mile-an-hour dashings-about of some Eastern expresses.

Sherwood's system was at first to charge tolls, but when the cost had been paid off, the roads would run "free for all." There might, of course, be a small matter of taxes to take care of operating expenses. Horace Greeley, Roscoe Conkling and 198 other friends of the proletariat heartily endorsed this plan. Sherwood opened a campaign for the presidency on the Anti-Monopoly Cheap Freight ticket and railroad builders from Maine to Missouri worried quite a bit about him.

Providence, however, stepped in. Just before the convention, a yellow-fever epidemic hit Texas; the meeting was postponed; the scheme died a-borning.

Outside of this, there were hordes of inventors of wind-engines, mule-power railroads and tracklaying devices—and the minor fact that, between Topeka and the Kansas-Colorado line there were fewer than 5,000 people to support a railroad. Furthermore, no one quite knew just where the Kansas-Colorado line was.

There were the sneerers, wits and doubters, too. If camels couldn't make money carrying freight, how could a railroad? What would happen to unlucky trainloads of passengers marooned by prairie blizzards, maybe for weeks? As people later were to laugh at automobiles and flying machines, both "obviously impossible," so they laughed in the '60s at railroads. Every pike was sneered at as "two streaks of rust." A road's initials might mean Greytown, Rushville & Western to its harassed owners, but to the wits they stood for Grunt, Rattle & Wheeze.

There were curious ideas everywhere about land, of which the United States owned a great deal, most of it worth little or nothing at the moment. However our title to all of California, Nevada, Utah, Arizona, New Mexico and part of Colorado, was less than twenty years old and we got all this land for $26,800,000. The land over which many miles of the Santa Fe were to be built was part of the Louisiana Purchase, and these "magnificent and valuable lands" which the government "gave away" to the railroads had cost the nation four cents an acre.

At that time this was four cents more than most of it was worth. Without transportation, the spreading miles were just about as valuable for agriculture and industry then as so many square miles of the Pacific Ocean.

"Dandy Tom" Fletcher, who drove the big stage (built by Abbott & Downing in Concord, New Hampshire) between Topeka and Fort Riley, Kansas, sat in a corner of the lobby of the hotel in Topeka smoking a cigar. Like the other stage drivers, he was magnificently clad in broadcloth and silk, his hat, shoes and gloves shining brilliantly, a turquoise-and-silver pin from Santa Fe decorating his cravat.

Tom laughed tolerantly as Holliday and Ross, talking about railroads, glanced his way.

"How would you like to drive a steam engine across the plains, Mr. Fletcher?" asked Holliday.

"Reckon it'd be too dirty a job for me, Colonel," drawled the driver. "Give me my six bays any time."

Stage drivers were a great breed, and few of them ever took to railroading. They maintained, on their great thoroughbrace coaches, a strict code of etiquette. No passenger might sit on the rear seat on top—reserved for the guard—unless especially invited by the driver. In case of a hold-up, passengers' lives were to be protected but they were responsible for their own money. The coach and team also were to be saved at all costs, including sacrifice of passengers' gold watches, diamond stickpins and loose change, if necessary to placate the bandits.

When a coach tongue broke, as occasionally happened, it was the custom of these remarkable men to descend, catch a rattlesnake, entice it onto the broken tongue and then, by masterly use of profanity, so madden the serpent that it coiled tightly around the broken tongue, holding it firmly until repairs could be made. This practice is attested by the signatures and solemn oaths of several stage drivers in Western Kansas, the affidavits being on view to serious students, at various historical societies.

Holliday said good night to Senator Ross, nodded to the lobby crowd and started for home down the broad silent streets of the prairie capital. You could, he noted, run a railroad up the middle of any of them without seriously interfering with traffic. Then, as now, when visitors commented admiringly on the width of the roadways, Topekans grinned and explained the streets were laid out that way to allow a couple of Kansas windstorms to operate independently anywhere in town.

Passing the old Statehouse, the Colonel wondered what might, in the future, happen there to help or hinder his dream. He had some experience in the legislature. Also he had read history, and he remembered that, for centuries, there had been grim battles between those who built channels along which commerce might flow, and those who got themselves into positions from which, legitimately or not, they could block this commerce unless made partners in the profits.

A familiar early American example of the evils of power to block transportation was the old Spanish Camino Real from Nacogdoches to Austin, Texas, over which the French in Louisiana and the Spanish in Texas traded. This trade was forbidden by Spain, so the traders bribed the post commanders along the route. The commanders suitably paid, not only opened the road, but provided armed escorts against the Indians. It was an old, old story but always new.

Mainly, early day legislatures were composed of honest men but always there were one or two shady characters, seeking to profit by damming transportation channels or threatening to pass laws to dam them. Well, that would be a problem to tackle when it arose. One thing Holliday promised himself: there would be no bribery; he would fight out every obstacle honestly and aboveboard. He walked on home, and went to bed.

The next afternoon he went around to Joe Blush's office.

"Getting any men, Joe?" he asked.

"Twenty-five, thirty—enough to start with."

"Good. Tell them to be down on Washington Street between Fourth and Fifth tomorrow morning and we'll put them to work."

October 30, 1868, opened with a blustery wind and shortly before noon, a few townspeople, overcoated and mildly interested, gathered on Washington Street a few blocks from the river. The reporters from the *Weekly Leader* and *State Record* came together. Some of the newly hired grading hands stood around, leaning on shovels, waiting. Colonel Holliday and Senator Ross drove up in a livery hack with Joe Blush. Joe pulled a new shovel out of the rig and stabbed it into the hard, brown earth.

Clearing his throat the Senator made a short speech. After four years in the Union Army and three in the Senate at Washington he was glad to be home on this auspicious occasion—a day they'd been waiting for for ten years. Obstacles overcome . . . Now the fruition of their efforts . . . Big plans for the future, of which his friend, Colonel Holliday, known to all of you, will now tell you more. Colonel Holliday!

The Colonel mounted the livery hack and in fancy took his railroad out of Topeka, across the prairies to Santa Fe to the west, to Kansas City to the east. (Smiles, including a broad one from Major Tom Anderson, agent for the Kansas Pacific. This road ran from just across the river to Kansas City.)

Those present would live, continued the Colonel, to see the line head far down into Mexico, and meet the broad Pacific on the Gulf of California. (Grins) And into the Rocky Mountains, with their hidden mineral wealth . . . (The Colonel's going good, eh Neighbor?) And now, if the Senator would take the shovel . . .

The Senator took the shovel, bore down on it with one foot, heaved up a chunk of brown earth and handed the tool to Holliday. The Colonel heaved up a shovelful. Then Joe Blush heaved up *his* shovelful. The crowd gave a small cheer with a touch of irony in it. The graders moved in as the people went home to dinner, and Tom Peter, who was in charge of construction, ripped out a swear word or two, and got the dirt flying. The reporters returned to their offices. Holliday watched awhile as the dirt slowly piled up in the street.

The Santa Fe was on its way.

CHAPTER THREE

COLONEL HOLLIDAY HEADS WEST

BUT FOR THE MOMENT, Colonel Holliday's railroad headed, not for Atchison or Santa Fe, but north to the Kaw River, a few hundred yards from its starting point on Washington Street. To get material to build the road a connection first had to be made with the Kansas Pacific, which ran along the north bank of the river. So the winter was spent building a pile and trestle bridge.

Holliday, muffled in his greatcoat, walked briskly down to the bridge site every day, watching the piledriver thumping and the carpenters hammering and adzing away. Topekans, watching him, often grinned knowingly and asked, "How's your railroad coming, Colonel?" or commented, "Never get to Santa Fe by heading across the Kaw."

The Colonel took it goodnaturedly, as a man sure of himself, willing to let the scoffers laugh now, and all winter if they liked.

He would laugh later.

The idea of a railroad over the trail to Santa Fe might be novel and slightly incredible to the burghers of Topeka, but he had lived with it and believed passionately in it for years—ever since that evening back home in Pennsylvania in the early '50s when he and his Mary had sat around the lamp, poring over the old Atlas. . . .

He was born in Carlisle, Pennsylvania, April 3, 1826, the fifth of seven children of Mr. and Mrs. David Holliday, his father being an accountant at a local ironworks.

Very early in his boyhood he took a dislike to both his given names and at college began to be called simply "H." This carried on into his married life and, though people who did not know him well often tried "Cy," they got no encouragement. To most he was always "Mr." and "Colonel," for he was a man of dignity and reserve and on a first-name basis with but a few friends.

He was graduated as a lawyer when he was twenty-six from Allegheny College at Meadville, Pennsylvania, and married a school-sweetheart, Miss Mary Dillon Jones and, by all accounts, she was the belle of Meadville and the prettiest girl for miles around. For all that she was a practical young person, full of commonsense and understanding of her husband's adventurous journeys into the twin worlds of the West and of ideas about railroads.

Holliday, in turn, put much store in her judgment and, during absences, faithfully reported his doings in frequent letters.

A few days after his graduation from college, he hung out his shingle and was going after legal business. Almost at once, some local promoters, planning a railroad through Meadville, hired the youngster to draw up a charter. They chose Holliday because, to get a start, he would work cheaply and, like most promoters, they hadn't much money. Holliday went to work and, with some sweating over law books, produced a charter for the Pittsburgh & Erie road.

As he worked he grew interested in the line. Studying its location, he figured that with a connection with the Atlantic & Great Western, it ought to make money. He went to the promoters:

"That fee you promised me for drawing up your charter . . ."

"Yes, yes—you'll get paid all right, Holliday."

"I know—but if you don't mind, I'd just as soon take my fee in stock," he replied.

"Stock, eh? You must have faith in the scheme."

"I have. You know I've just got married, and I need money. But I figure I'll make more by waiting and selling my stock, than what you agreed to pay me."

So it was settled. The line was built and, after operating a few months was sold to the Atlantic & Great Western. Holliday hurried home an evening or so after the sale, a check in his pocket and a mysterious smile on his lips.

He chuckled teasingly all through supper, and, after the meal, put on his velvet "smoking jacket," his carpet slippers, and, with a sigh of satisfaction, settled himself in his favorite armchair. He was twenty-eight—and a capitalist. Mary knitted diligently in the circle of yellow light thrown by the lamp. Holliday watched her for a moment.

"I've got news for you, Mary—great news. You remember that railroad stock I took a year or more ago for drawing the Pittsburgh & Erie charter—you should, you thought I should have taken cash. . . . Well, everything's come out all right. I've sold the stock and we're rich, Mary, rich!"

"I'm glad, H. You've always had faith in railroads, haven't you?"

"Sure, and they've hardly got started yet. D'you know how much money I've got right here in my wallet? Twenty thousand dollars, Mary!"

"It's a lot of money, dear," said Mary, with a little gasp, "an awful lot. What are you going to do with it?"

"I had thought of going out west to Kansas," replied Holliday. "There'll be railroads to organize out there. The Emigrant Aid Societies are sending out hundreds of good settlers. A capable lawyer and $20,000 ought to be able to make a fortune—and help hold Kansas for the Union, too."

"But it's so wild out there, H. The Indians . . . Where would you build your railroad? There are no settlements and the stagecoaches and wagon trains carry on all the business. There's hardly anything, I've been told, between the river settlements and Santa Fe."

"Santa Fe! That's it, Mary. A railroad from the Missouri River to Santa Fe. Follow the old Santa Fe Trail. Trains will beat wagons; we can haul freight for half, a quarter of the present rates. There'll be new settlements all along the line, too."

He went to the bookshelf and from between Blackstone and the *Revised Statutes of Pennsylvania*, drew out an atlas. He opened it, laid it on the table before his wife and, with his forefinger, traced the line of the old trail westward.

"I hear Santa Fe is an ungodly place, H."

She was right. Santa Fe, at the time, was headquarters for gambling in the wild, half-lawless Southwest, although challenged by

El Paso, a village of 400 people. Half a hundred master American gamblers piled their tables with silver coins and play ran high as the traders tossed away their rich profits of the overland trade. Monte banks ran in every *fonda.* Everyone gambled, even the little Mexican children, playing with three-cent coins called *quartillas.* Ten faro layouts operated around the plaza. Hardly a night went by without a shooting—or the flash of a silver knife that suddenly became red. Yes, Santa Fe was an ungodly place, despite the golden tones of the great bells of the old cathedral.

"It's like that in all frontier settlements, Mary," said Holliday. "It's not to get to Santa Fe to gamble at cards and dice that I propose. It is the trade—all that trade going across the prairies."

On the map he traced out the old trail, up along the winding Arkansas River, over Raton Mountain and down through the Spanish grants to Gallina Creek. Mary, watching him, sighed—and knew his mind was made up. She was accustomed to these enthusiasms; once her husband was set on something, nothing could turn him from it.

"Very well, H," she said, sticking the long needles through the ball of wool and putting aside her knitting. "But leave most of your money here. Put it into bonds and let me send you cash as you need it, from the sale of them. No use risking all we have in that wild country. When will you leave?"

Kansas in those days was no place to take a young wife who was expecting a baby in four months. Holliday kissed her good-bye and set out, via Erie. Here he bought a ticket to St. Louis for $20, changing cars at Cleveland, Toledo and Chicago, and keeping a sharp lookout for footpads, card sharps and other evildoers who, in that era, lay in wait for travelers at junction points. At Alton, the young man took a boat for St. Louis, and from there bought a ticket for eleven dollars. He steamed up the river aboard the *F. X. Aubrey* about 450 miles to Kanzas City, as it then was spelled. The boat was loaded to the guards with emigrants, and there was a large Pennsylvania contingent. Kanzas City, founded two years before, already boasted 500 people.

Holliday had taken little cash with him. He had, as Mary had advised, prudently invested most of his $20,000 in bonds, leaving them with her. She was to send him cash in fifty- and hundred-dollar batches as he wrote for it.

Holliday first took up residence in Lawrence, going to that small settlement on the Kaw, fifty miles west of Kansas City by coach. Here he slept in a pole-and-brush hut with a dirt floor, atop a buffalo robe and under two heavy blankets. A great urge was then descending on many people to start new towns—and this urge caught Holliday.

With a new-found friend, Enoch Chase, and a few other men, he set out up the Kaw River in the fall of '54. The party finally arrived at a place called Papan's Ferry, a link on a western emigrant trail. It was operated by a family of French-Canadians, who were considerably surprised when Chase, Holliday and company announced a new town was to spring up there. There was some argument whether it should be on the north or south bank, but the south bank won. There were no surveying instruments in the party, but one of them had a watch-charm compass, and with this, and some twine, the town was laid out.

With customary optimism, young Holliday set aside twenty acres for a state capitol, having decided when the place was three days old that it should become the capital of Kansas Territory. This statesmanlike idea so impressed the party that he was unanimously elected president of the place, and for a few days presided at town meetings seated on a sack of flour. There wasn't a stick of furniture, or much of anything else in the town. After some discussion, it was decided to name the place Topeka, "The Potato Patch"—because the Indians used to dig edible roots there. The inevitable Western romanticism has since translated Topeka into "A good place to dig potatoes." Strangely enough, it is.

Just to confound the scoffers, within six years Topeka *was* the capital, largely through Holliday's efforts. He was then a member of the legislature which operated in Lawrence as a temporary capital. On January 1, 1855, however, Holliday sat on the ground in his new townsite, writing on a trunk and telling Mary that "There is neither bed, chair nor table in the entire city limits of Topeka." He added that he had taken a city lot and a farm claim.

Word of the new town got around and a few emigrants stopped there after coming across the river on Papan's ferry. Many of them were Pennsylvanians. Among them was the Reverend Samuel A. Lum, who had been sent out as a missionary to darkest Kansas by the American Home Missionary Society. This cared for the spiritual needs of the village; the material things were harder to come by. It was almost impossible to get lumber and hardware, except at high prices, plus higher freight charges.

The Reverend and the Pennsylvanians were all Abolitionists and fervidly anti-slavery, and so was Holliday. Across the Missouri border, however, most of the people were pro-slavery, and it wasn't long before the Border Ruffians were invading Free Soil Kansas. A band of them roared in in April, 1855, while an election was being held, drove off the Free Soilers and prevented Holliday from being elected as a representative from the third district. He heard, almost on the same day, that he had become a father. The baby's name, Mary wrote, was Lillie. She had been born on March 18th.

What really was civil war now started in Eastern Kansas. It was fought with horse, foot and artillery, with the Border Ruffians invading, killing, burning and looting, and the Free Soilers retaliating as best they could. Lawrence became a fortified town where 1,000 embattled Abolitionists stood off 900 "enemy troops" for several days.

Times were wild and uncertain, with the slavery fight burning at white heat and pitched battles being fought. Through all this sea of bitterness and bloodshed there flowed a tide of emigrants to the West, the white tops of prairie schooners pitching and blowing in the gale, sides tar-daubed with "Pike's Peak or Bust!" Some Americans might kill and burn for slavery, or against it, but thousands of their fellow-citizens looked on the whole thing as a nonsensical brawl and would have none of it. Until long after the Civil War, and all through it, the pioneers went shouting, singing, praying, cursing, roaring out into the sunset of the free-land trails.

The pull of the North was strong, the pull of the South was powerful. But the magnet of the West outpulled them both.

As the turmoil waxed and waned, Holliday alternately sent for Mary and Lillie, and warned them against coming. More and more he was drawn into the whirlpool of the Free Soil fight. By the fall of 1855 he was writing most of the *Kansas Freeman*, an Abolitionist paper. At the siege of Lawrence in December he was made a colonel and placed in command of the Second Kansas Regiment. He ran, too, for Secretary of State and was defeated.

Six weeks later, when the Border Ruffians came storming again across the line, the young Colonel was promoted to Brigadier-General and led his Kansans against the invading Missourians. He was three months short of thirty. The enemy repulsed, perhaps only temporarily, he turned to making a living and soon wrote Mary that he had planted thirty-five acres in corn and beans. That he found this none too easy we can guess from a letter he wrote home late in March of '56, in which he said, "It is now raining, hailing, snowing, blowing, thundering and lightning all at the same time. A great country!"

In mid-May the Border Ruffians roared in again threatening to burn and ravage Topeka. Holliday, writing to Meadville, grew pessimistic. "I fear," he told Mary, "that the days of our Union are numbered."

In June there was another battle. The Missourians were driven out and Free State troops held the border. Holliday now had become enmeshed in the political fight and, impelled by this and by a desire to see Mary and Lillie, turned over his Topeka holdings to friends and went back to Pennsylvania to campaign for General John C. Frémont, running against James Buchanan. Pennsylvania cast 400,000 votes and gave Buchanan only 1,000 majority.

"A moral victory," decided the Kansas Colonel. He went back to Topeka, promising his family he'd bring them out when times calmed down a little. He accomplished this some time later, when an express company accepted Mrs. Holliday and the baby for shipment. Express companies frequently did this in early days, but the practice was discontinued in 1878.

Back in Topeka two legislatures met—one a Free Soil congress, the other a pro-slavery affair. Holliday, rampant on the Free Soil side, watched bitterly while troops, sent in by President Franklin Pierce dispersed the Abolitionist meeting. But he kept up his interest in politics, at the same time making a living by farming and a little legal work. He was a member of the legislature and led a battle between Topeka and Tecumseh, a rival village, for the county seat. A few weeks later he capitalized on this victory and saw Topeka not only the government center of Shawnee County, but of Kansas.

Already the war clouds were billowing angrily on the horizon. Still the wagons streamed west from the frontier towns, St. Joseph and Westport Landing on the Missouri; from Independence, a few miles east of Westport, and from the Kaw crossing at Topeka. They lined out through Olathe, twenty-five miles southwest of the Missouri ferry at Westport on the long trail to free land and the sunny Pacific coast. Here and there, west of the Big River, little bits of railroads began creeping across the prairie, heading north, south, east and west. Just where and when Holliday was re-fired with the idea of building a railroad, no one now knows, but it would have been remarkable if he wasn't. Everyone was projecting railroads on paper. Merchants in towns twenty miles apart met and planned iron links between their communities.

"Capitalists" with four or five hundred dollars apiece got together and started grading. Other enterprisers denounced them as monopolists and organized "People's Railroads," in opposition. Counties voted bond issues to build track. Towns voted bonuses of land and cash for terminals, roundhouses, shops and offices. The curious fact is that most of these bond issues were paid off on the nail from the revenue created mainly by the roads they financed. A village of 100 people would float a bond issue for $50,000 to get a railroad; the road would be built; a train or two would sway and clatter over it and presto! the town had 1,000 people, 2,000, 10,000. Business boomed, real-estate prices soared, farms started, taxes flowed in. It was a game in which, honestly played, everybody won.

Even the railroads.

But Kansas still bled. The fury mounted as slaveryites and Free Soil Jayhawkers fought back and forth across the prairie. The death toll grew. A score of settlements could show the blackened ruins of homes and stores, and tell their grim stories of bloodshed and death by violence.

In 1859 Topeka already had been burned down once and rebuilt. It now boasted 1,200 people and a three-story building. Holliday's legislative work and the unsettled state of affairs didn't help his income and he had almost reached the bottom of the little stack of bonds he had bought with his first $20,000. What capital he had was in land and buildings and any day the fury of war might destroy what he had.

Up in his home state of Pennsylvania a railroad man had struck it rich—but not at railroading. That would be "Crazy Ed" Drake, a 75-dollar-a-month conductor on the New Haven, who had hired "Uncle Billy" Smith and Smith's son to dig for oil at Titusville. Uncle Billy struck it, sixty-nine feet down, on Saturday, August 27th—the first oil well in America. Holliday, hearing about it, gave it little thought. Trains ran on wood, coal, water—and mutton tallow.

After his successful fight to make Topeka the capital, the Colonel decided he had to make some money, and remembering his early success with the Pittsburgh & Erie, wrote a charter for a railroad from Topeka to Atchison, on the Missouri River, fifty miles to the northeast. He had had a small part in one other line, projected to St. Joseph, Missouri, but the unsettled times had prevented anything happening. He had, too, considered lines to Leavenworth, Independence, even to Kansas City. A scheme greater than the present modest Atchison & Topeka line grew in Holliday's mind.

Kansas City to Santa Fe—as he had boasted to Mary—that was it. Go the whole hog. All or nothing. The Colonel took pen in hand and wrote the charter. "Every word of it," he insisted years later when half a dozen "Fathers of the Santa Fe" showed up. The charter started the line at Atchison, took it through Topeka and carried it west and south over the old buffalo grounds "To such a point on the southern or western boundary of Kansas Territory in the direction of Santa Fe as may be convenient and suitable."

That was taking in a lot of territory. Might as well take in some more. He bit the end of his pen, thought a minute, and wrote himself permission to run a branch "To any points on the southern boundary of Kansas Territory in the direction of the Gulf of Mexico."

In this fabulous enterprise both Texans and Atchisonians joined. Political differences were forgotten. The advertised capital was $1,500,000, but if the promoters could raise $5,000 in cash on $50,000 in stock subscriptions, that was all they needed to organize. Some of the original incorporators dropped out; others came in. Among them was Edmund G. Ross, then editor of the *Kansas Tribune* whom we've met. Joel Huntoon came in, and Judge R. H. Weightman, who had been attorney-general over in Missouri. Another partner was J. H. Stringfellow of Atchison, editor of *Squatter Sovereignty*; still another from Atchison was the redoubtable Luther Challis, who later was to outshine many a Wall Street financier. There was P. T. Abell of the Atchison Town Company, and State Senator S. C. Pomeroy. They were able men—but they had very little cash to put into anything.

It was an explosive mixture, too. Challis, Stringfellow and some others were hot for the South and slavery; Ross, Holliday and a few more were stern Abolitionists. But they managed to keep the peace somehow. They got together a few thousand dollars and prepared to start building.

And in June, 1859, the Great Drought hit Kansas.

For months the sun blazed down from a flawless sky. A shower now and then hardly dampened the ground. The land dried up and blew away. Crops burned. People went hungry. In Shawnee County it took eight acres to produce one bushel of wheat. In the spring of 1860 the wagons began creaking back from the west, sun-bleached and misery-laden, oxen groaning for water, gaunt men and women riding listlessly. And on the covers "Pike's Peak—and Bust!"—"In God We Trusted—in Kansas We Busted!" Summer came and went. Fall went by, dry and parched. In November, 1860, it started to rain again, too late.

Kansas in '59 and '60 was no place to build a railroad. A railroad out into that desert! Don't make me laugh! Holliday stopped talking about it, but the idea never left his mind. The charter still stood. Drought could not last forever. He almost went broke, as did the others. Along toward the end of the summer of 1860 he walked down to Editor Ross' office and they came to a decision.

They got together a little money, borrowed a scrub team and wagon from a Topeka liveryman, and, with three or four other die-hards who were stockholders in the railroad, drove to Atchison. They took two days to make the trip, sleeping on the dry prairie at night. In Atchison they rounded up a few partners and, between September 15th and 17th, organized their company, Holliday being elected president. In all, thirteen men were included in the first board of directors. Each subscribed for $4,000 worth of stock. It was lucky that, under the charter, only ten per cent of this had to be paid in, because all of them had trouble in raising even the $400 in cash. The Topekans drove back home, talking about the best way to get a land grant, which would give them a basis for starting construction. There didn't seem to be much hope.

Kansas was a desert and so advertised throughout the East. The onrushing war monopolized public interest. No one was going to put up money to build a railroad into a desert in war time. Even the rains, coming late in '60, didn't help much to restore faith. Kansas became a state, and James H. Lane and Samuel C. Pomeroy went to Washington as Senators. The Pacific Railroad Bill came up—for a railroad, not to open up a new country, but as a military line to tie together East and West. Lane and Pomeroy could talk all they wanted about Colonel Holliday's road. Lincoln's "one war at a time" carried over into "one railroad at a time," in the still unfinished national capital.

But in 1863, with things still black for the Union, Pomeroy and Lane got through a bill by which the federal government handed over to the State of Kansas the odd-numbered sections of land for ten miles on each side of a projected railroad. Kansas, in turn, might turn over the land to reliable railroad builders. The national government very cannily doubled the price of the lands it had left and so, in monetary value, gave away nothing.

On November 24, 1863, when the Civil War seemed swinging to the Union side, and it looked feasible to revive the railroad project, some of the Atchison & Topeka's stockholders met at the Chase

House in Topeka. Colonel Holliday rose and said that now seemed a good time to begin expanding and hadn't they better figure on the little inter-town road going west?

"Well, where to, Colonel?" was asked.

They named over the only towns anyone knew anything about beyond the mountains: Tucson, Salt Lake, San Diego, San Francisco —Santa Fe.

"Santa Fe!" exclaimed Holliday, suddenly. The romance of the name still fired his imagination—the crossing of the trails, silver and turquoise, wool, copper, beef and mutton flowing east; men, cotton and machines flowing west to produce wheat and corn to flow east to buy more cotton, silk, furniture and machinery to flow west . . .

"Move we change the name of our line to the 'Atchison, Topeka & Santa Fe Rail Road,'" suggested Senator Pomeroy, home from Washington.

"Second the motion," said Luther Challis.

Everybody said "Aye."

A few weeks later, anxious to go east and raise money, Holliday, enthusiastic as ever, turned over the presidency to Senator Pomeroy, and, as secretary, set out for New York. Under Pomeroy's leadership, a group in the state legislature fought for and won a law permitting counties to float bond issues to help build railroads.

In New York, where the bankers were still scared half to death by the war situation, the Colonel got lots of promises—and practically no money. The war continued, bloody and implacable. Yet only part of the country seemed vitally interested.

But the call of the far places was strong. From both North and South, thousands of people pulled stakes, seeing only ruin in the wake of battle, and plodded grimly westward to try to get a new start where brother wasn't fighting brother and flame and sword did not rule. Here and there, still, iron was laid, slowly, across the prairie. Union Pacific forged ahead toward Promontory, and from the Coast, Central Pacific's coolie gangs fought up into the Sierra with rails and material carried around the Horn by a fleet of ships to San Francisco and Sacramento.

Here and there the new Santa Fe company collected a few hundred dollars, and by August, 1865, Holliday and his associates had enough in the treasury to order 3,000 tons of fifty-six pound iron rails, at $100 a ton, from England.

The first engineer was Otis Berthoude Gunn, who served in the Union Army in '65 and '66 and made the first surveys of the line between Topeka and Atchison—unbuilt for some years after the original track went south instead of north. He quit before the project got started and his line was resurveyed by A. A. Robinson, under Tom Peter. Major Gunn had been stationed near Kansas City during the war, in charge of army supplies; before that he had been chief engineer for the Kansas Pacific; after serving the Santa Fe he went to the Katy as chief engineer. The Katy was organized in 1870 from the Union Pacific (Southern Branch).

Late in November, Gunn started running surveys south and, by January, 1866, had reached Emporia, sixty-one miles southwest of Topeka and 111 miles from Atchison. Then everything stopped again.

Cash was scarce; land grants seemed to have no attraction as collateral. The rail contract was torn up. In June, 1866, things got to such a pass that Senator Pomeroy, back in Washington, tried to get a bill through the Senate to allow the Santa Fe to build without rails. It was to be just a graded roadway over which steam tractors would haul flat-wheeled cars at six miles an hour. If the Senate would permit this, Pomeroy promised the road would accept three sections of land to the mile instead of ten. The Senate said no. Out in Kansas, Holliday went doggedly ahead once more trying to raise money.

He turned now to the counties—Atchison, Osage, Lyon, Shawnee—holding meetings, organizing elections, promising, planning, prophesying. Time was running out. The road, to collect its land grants, had to be built far to the west by the spring of 1873.

Shawnee County went to the polls and voted $250,000 in seven percent bonds, and with the bond money—not $250,000 by any means—got stock in the Santa Fe. Holliday and his partners drove around the country, talking to farmers in their fields, knocking on doors, addressing meetings. Atchison County voted bonds. So did Lyon, Jefferson, Osage. Now there were funds in the treasury to get started. A contractor was hired. He spent some weeks surveying the situation—but gave it up as hopeless.

On June 20, 1868, there appeared on the scene Thomas J. Peter, a Cincinnatian, who, too, had studied the project—and had faith in it. He was to build the first mileage of the Santa Fe, and create a curious reputation. A member of the Ohio firm of Dodge, Lord & Company, he was a staunch Prohibitionist and non-smoker; he swore like a trooper and disdained paper work. He carried the grades and curves of the line in his head, shouted orders to his assistants, and dressed them down unmercifully if, weeks later, they had departed an inch from his plans. There are, today, very few construction records concerning the first few score miles of the system.

Peter put his own money into the road. He had spent some time riding about Kansas and the Arkansas Valley and had decided that if the land would support millions of buffalo it might just support a few thousand people. While he was getting under way, Lord, along with General A. E. Burnside of Rhode Island, Henry Keyes of Boston, and a handful of Kansas folk, formed a construction concern known as the Atchison Associates. Pomeroy stepped out; Lord became president of the Santa Fe. They were ready to go again.

Money ran low once more—and then for once the Santa Fe got a break. On the Pottawatomie Indian Reservation, 340,000 acres had been set aside for the Leavenworth, Pawnee & Western Railroad. The line hadn't held up its end of the deal. Lord dickered for the land and bought 114,401.76 acres of it for $1 an acre—a few thousand down, six years to pay, five percent interest. Five percent in times when twenty was normal.

These Indian lands now became a basis for raising money, and coupled with the bond money from half a dozen counties, provided a pool of cash to finance construction. Holliday, enthusiastic and triumphant after ten years of worry and defeat, wrote from New York to the Topeka *State Record*:

"Let the capital city rejoice. The A. T. & S. F. Road will be built beyond peradventure. Please inform the good people of Topeka and Shawnee County. Work will begin immediately . . ."

The day was October 7, 1868. Holliday followed his letter home.

It was no easy journey. From New York the Colonel took a ferry to Jersey, and, climbing aboard the wooden cars of the New Jersey Railroad, ambled down to Philadelphia where he changed to the Philadelphia, Wilmington & Baltimore for Baltimore. Here he took the Baltimore & Ohio for Parkersburg, and there changed again to the Marietta & Cincinnati, for Cincinnati. He was now well started. Another train took him over the Ohio and Mississippi, a six-foot gauge line, to St. Louis. From here to Kansas City he rode the Pacific Railway, which had been opened in 1866. He then took a Kansas Pacific train to North Topeka, ferrying across. It was a tiresome journey, occupying some sixty hours.

Holliday at this time was forty-two, a sturdily built man, five feet ten and a half inches tall, with a pleasant face and the side-whiskers of the period. He was nearly bald. A man of great enthusiasms, he was hard to swerve from a course, once he had settled on it. He managed his home life with the same attention to detail he gave to his railroad enterprise. In later years, for all his success, he never lost the common touch, and, up to a few years ago, many a Santa Fe oldtimer recalled how the Colonel pumped with the section gangs on handcars, rode locomotives and prowled about roundhouses all over the system.

Colonel Holliday was, as always, meticulously dressed—striped gray trousers, Prince Albert coat and stovepipe hat, as befitted a frontier legislator and retired soldier. The pants, of heavy wool, were uncreased—creased pants having been popularized only in the late 1890's by Edward, Prince of Wales, later King of England. The Colonel's high boots were handmade, and, unlike some frontiersmen, he wore them soberly inside his trousers.

Even in his pioneering days, H. kept himself as neat and clean as possible, sometimes noting in letters to Mary, his wife, that he had had to wear a shirt several days, or even a week, and getting a daily bath was a problem.

In speech he was a purist, phrasing his sentences carefully and never employing slang. He has been quoted, in some histories, as a swashbuckling fellow, in hip boots, swearing at his truck gangs, tossing off modern railroad slang. All such stories are imaginary. He invariably called employees "mister" and was hardly ever on a first-name basis with anyone.

His love of good things made him generous with Mary. Everything she had, from lace curtains to diamonds, was of the best. Once, in later years, the Colonel bought her a bedroom set that had taken first prize at the Philadelphia Exposition.

He was fond of other growing things besides railroads. In Topeka he planted elms and fruit trees and in droughts watered them from barrels laboriously rolled from a well to the orchard.

In his earlier years he was quite a religious man and his letters of the Kansas period are full of references to God's will, and hope for Divine blessing. He was deeply in love with his Mary, but this didn't stop him from venturing on what she thought were wild schemes far out in the wilderness—a wilderness to which, for her own safety and comfort, he was, for a long time, unwilling to bring his wife.

Because of its early history, all projects in Kansas, including railroads, tended to become crusades. In days ahead, the state was to bring forth scores of crusaders—Carry Nation, Sockless Jerry Simpson, Susan B. Anthony—to mention but three. When Kansas became the prize in a contest between slavery and anti-slavery factions, the North, having more money, managed not only to populate the territory with Free Soilers, but sent enough capital to maintain them and get them started.

To the far west, went the adventurous, often broke, often neurotic. But to Kansas went mature, settled people from Eastern farms and cities, with a definite purpose: to establish themselves, prosper—and hold Kansas for the Union. Back of this movement were the New England Emigrant Aid Society of Boston, The Vegetarian Settlement Company, The New York-Kansas League, The Octagon Settlement Company, The American Settlement Company, and a dozen others.

They selected stouthearted folks, with records for thrift and hard work, and sent them west across the river. Kansas was the only territory in which capital and labor arrived simultaneously in sizable quantities with a definite goal in mind.

This human foundation of the Kansas Commonwealth had an immense influence on early railroads—which partook of the character of crusades for civilization. The young roads, including the Santa Fe, were not promoters' dreams or speculative adventures, as they were in many eastern sections—they were down-to-earth projects, financed by men who knew the value of money and calculated the chances.

Construction and operation of pioneer transcontinental railroads, have, in history books and imaginative writings, become either a magnificent feat by miraculously gifted supermen, or a dark chapter of graft, skullduggery and betrayal of the public. They were neither. They took place simply from the desire on the part of a great many better-than-average Americans to make a living—and maybe add a spice of adventure to the making.

It was an era of large, free-flowing ideas. Men's minds had wide, almost limitless sweeps of territory to play with. Acres by the million lay wild and waiting, there to the southwest. Span them with steel, carry men and women by the thousand out there to break the sod, grow corn, dig for gold and silver, hew down the forests and create a rich new empire where the Indians, the Spaniards and the Mexicans had failed because they could not invent cheap enough or reliable enough transportation.

Nothing could save and develop this empire for America unless the railroad spread swiftly across it, to make it part of the United States. Holliday and his partners saw that. It fired their imaginations and outpulled, many a time, the urge to make a fortune.

There must have been, after all, some satisfaction in seeing iron-and-steel track creep relentlessly across the prairie, climb mountains, wind along friendly rivers—and in seeing, as the trains rolled, the land blossom and the new towns roar into prosperity. The men who imagined and built the railroads shared in that prosperity—and why not? Without them there would have been no prosperity.

It was ironical that the very people for whom the railroad builders opened up new opportunities often were the people from whom came the votes that gave a few rabblerousers and fanatics in state legislatures the power to "regulate" the roads almost to the point of unworkability. Cheap transportation was the lifeblood of the prairies, and the roads sold it. Without it, the land would have reverted in a few years to the buffalo and the Indians. The people who had to have this transportation, whose economic lives depended upon it, often were the very ones, incredibly enough, who put into power the bitter, and usually ne'er-do-well and ignorant men who lay awake nights thinking up new ways to make railroad operation harder and more expensive. They were not many in number, these obstructionists, but they were noisy and active.

Out of the lawyers, merchants and farmers who dreamed, built and operated it, the Santa Fe made not a single millionaire. But, like other granger roads, it created enough wealth out of almost nothing to make thousands of people wealthy and millions prosperous. For years it was the greatest corporation of the plains with which settlers, traders, workers came in contact. For the clarion-throated vote hunters, it became, naturally, a whipping-boy. It could be accused of everything from overcharging to mayhem—and was.

The Santa Fe's builders were not inspired idealists, nor did they build the system to carry the torch of civilization into the West. It was a business for some, and an investment for others. Some of them made money, some didn't. But they all gambled their time, their money and their brains in an era when it wasn't even certain the Union would keep on existing. They went through years of heartache and grim disappointment. The engineers and surveyors lived hard, tough, dangerous lives in wild country. Construction crews took their chances with Indian raiders, bad water and the rabble that followed the track. Train crews, operators, station agents lived and worked in peril, not only from evil men, but from cloudburst, blizzard and buffalo herd.

Three weeks after Holliday got back to Topeka, the first shovelfuls of dirt had been thrown. Up at Atchison, there was some discontent. The town, originally, had been chosen for the start. Now the new line wasn't even headed that way. It was headed up Shunganunga Creek, almost due south.

It headed that way because coal deposits had been discovered around Carbondale; these would provide not only fuel for the new road, but some freight tonnage. So Atchison would have to wait.

Meanwhile, as the grading crews worked slowly south during the winter, the Kaw bridge was going in. This bridge was built by D. E. "Jersey" Hogbin and J. D. Criley, who later made some tracklaying records for the system. Hogbin was a veteran of the First New Jersey Cavalry. He got to Topeka, November 23, 1868, with two cars of bridge material. Criley had borrowed an old piledriver from the U. P. and now Hogbin built another on the north bank of the Kaw, from what lumber he could scrape up. About thirty men were put to work.

Lumber came in over the K.P. track and was hauled half a mile by ox teams to the bridge site, where two 150-foot Howe trusses were built. Building went on through the winter snows, and by March 31, 1869, the span was ready. Waiting on a K.P. sidetrack was a small locomotive lettered "C. K. Holliday" and figured "No. 1." This kettle had been bought from the old Ohio & Mississippi road, a six-foot gauge pike, cut down to standard and hauled to the end of Santa Fe track by the K. P. She was now steamed up, all the carpenters and bridge men piled aboard and the engine ran over the bridge, everybody cheering like mad.

Topekans thought the Indians had cut loose again.

This was the first train movement over the road. It was made at 6 P.M. March 31st. The bridge seemed safe, the engine backed over it into North Topeka, Hogbin chocked the wheels with cordwood and mounted guard over the machine all night, getting in some overtime, so that his paycheck for the day was $7.50.

When the frost was out of the ground, and the line graded up the small hill toward Pauline, the Kansas Pacific began delivering material to the Santa Fe, at North Topeka.

There was some opposition by property owners around Pauline. Soon after the track had been laid over the bridge, five miles from

Topeka, a few diehards built a stone wall across the right of way. Three kids, riding down the grade on a handcar, hit the obstruction. One died.

The first locomotive was built by the Niles Machine Works of Cincinnati, and bought on the advice of Tom Peter.*

A day coach was bought from the Indianapolis & Cincinnati Railroad, now part of the Big Four, for a few hundred dollars. It was numbered "12." Barney & Smith, of Dayton, Ohio, supplied a dozen flat cars, each of which would carry about ten tons. There was a handcar made in Chicago. And that was all.

With this equipment the road was built up over the hill and down toward Wakarusa. As the wheat greened the black prairie soil the time seemed ripe for some celebration. A story in the *Weekly Record* said there'd be a picnic at Wakarusa Grove. Ride free on the steam cars of the Atchison, Topeka & Santa Fe Rail Road. Come one, come all!

* The first locomotive to appear during the construction of the original line was the first No. 1, a 4-4-0 type which is stated to have been obtained from the Ohio and Mississippi Railroad early in 1869. The engine had 16 x 20" cylinders and 60" drivers. In the roster of 1881, it was replaced by a second No. 1 and redesignated by letter "A." The next locomotive owned by the company was the first No. 2, likewise a 4-4-0 type. This engine bore the name "Gov. Burnside" and was built at the Rhode Island Works, Providence, in 1869, construction number 122. It had 14 x 22" cylinders and 54" drivers. Both locomotives disappeared from the records about 1882.

From—LOCOMOTIVES OF THE ATCHISON, TOPEKA & SANTA FE SYSTEM, The Railway and Locomotive Historical Society, Inc., Baker Library, Harvard Business School, Boston, Massachusetts.

CHAPTER FOUR

STEEL ACROSS THE PRAIRIE

CONDUCTOR W. W. FAGAN gave a highball, Fireman Brit Craft checked his fire, Brakemen Bill Bartling and Al Dugan released the brakes and Engineer George Beach cracked the throttle. The Santa Fe's first train—the Wakarusa Picnic Special—started to roll.

Over iron rail spiked to oak and walnut ties the Topeka picnickers traveled up the creek faster than holidaymakers ever had rolled that route before. It took thirty minutes to reach end-of-track, seven miles out, the "C. K. Holliday" shooting sparks and smoke and tossing the white plume of her whistle into the clear air. The cars—the Santa Fe's own—and one borrowed from the neighborly Kansas Pacific—lurched over the high centers and low joints. The passengers, already started on beer and soda biscuits that were standard picnic fare, walked through to congratulate Colonel and Mrs. Holliday and to say what a fine, big girl Lillie was getting to be. It was April 26, 1869.

Just along for the ride were Superintendent Ed Noble of the Kansas Pacific, and Major Tom Anderson, its station agent at North Topeka. Reporters for the *State Record* and *Weekly Leader* kept time with large silver watches, once announcing the speed as approaching twenty-five miles an hour—on an upgrade, too. Noble congratulated Holliday and Tom Peter, the builder, on the state of the track. Tom Anderson, a confirmed wit and heckler, said the Santa Fe might some day be as good as the old K. P.

This Anderson, who later worked for the Santa Fe for many years.

was a remarkable fellow. He was almost bald, with a flowing waterfall mustache that hid his mouth, and long sidewhiskers cascading down over his lapels. Peter, a stern disciplinarian, had tried to keep liquor off the train, but the Major had managed to smuggle some aboard and several of the Topekans carried medicinal draughts in bottles. Kansas was not to go dry until 1881.

At the end of track the brakeman set his brakes and brought the special to a stop. Everybody piled out, got into rigs and drove five miles south, along the new roadbed, to Wakarusa Grove beside Wakarusa Creek, over which a new bridge had just been built for the trains. It was now mid-afternoon and after some eating and drinking of creek-cooled beer, someone called on the Colonel for a speech. Never having to be urged a great deal to talk about railroads, Holliday soon was in full flight in all directions, building the Santa Fe north, south, east and west. He was cheered on by Tom Anderson, high and ironical on beer and sunshine.

Holliday built his road into Kansas City, Chicago and St. Louis. He took it down to the Gulf and out to the Pacific Coast. The *Record's* reporter, quoted him as saying, "See! There rolls the broad Pacific and on its bosom are the ships of the Santa Fe, riding proudly in from the Orient."

Through the years a legend has grown up that Holliday, at this and other railroad pep-rallies, "faced the southwest and crossed his arms in the form of a horizontal X at a level with his shoulders" and then announced: "Fellow Citizens! Imagine, if you please, my right hand as Chicago, my left as St. Louis. Eventually the railroad we contemplate will reach these cities, and, crossing at Topeka—the intersection of my arms—will extend to Galveston, the City of Mexico and San Francisco."

Like so many legends, this doesn't make sense. If Holliday had stood facing southwest, with the intersection of his crossed arms representing Topeka, one shoulder might have represented Chicago and the other St. Louis, but his left hand would have represented San Francisco and his right might have pointed to Mexico City, Topolobampo or Los Angeles, or, with a little imagination, to Galveston. But Los Angeles hardly was likely, the entire population of

Kansas in those days being in almost complete ignorance of the Pueblo of the Angels' Queen—a defect overwhelmingly remedied in later years.

The Colonel's imaginative oratory, at any rate, was too much for Tom Anderson. "The damn old fool!" he announced loudly, adding that if any road ever went to all those places it would be the good old Kansas Pacific. The meticulous reporters wrote down a couple of the Major's further comments: "You're taking in too much territory, H!" and "Oh, Lord, give us a rest!" This concluded the Major's part of the occasion, and, after he had been ssh'd, everyone drove down to end-of-track and climbed aboard the cars again. The train backed down the hill into Topeka.

Tom Peter's gang continued to make grade and lay track. In a few weeks the road was operating down to Carbondale, where some shallow mines not only provided fuel for the locomotive, but, as Holliday had anticipated, created a little freight revenue. A paying passenger—James Pratt of Wakarusa—appeared and was given a note testifying to his priority. For many years he was interviewed regularly on anniversaries on how it felt to be the first paying passenger of the Santa Fe. His invariable reply was that he had slipped one over on those Topeka boys—and it felt fine.

On September 18th, the line was opened down to Burlingame, twenty-six miles from Topeka. Only six years before—in '63—with most of Burlingame's men away fighting for the Union, Quantrell's Raiders had menaced the place. Its women, building a stone fort, had held off the enemy for six weeks until a Union detachment came riding to the rescue. The road, now for the first time, hit the old Santa Fe Trail, which came in from Olathe on the east and lined out to the west, thirty miles to Council Grove. The grade and the iron moved over the old trail, cutting it forever.

The Carbondale business had put a little cash into the treasury and the road now bought twenty-four coal cars, a dozen boxcars, another coach, a baggage car and a second locomotive. This was the *General A. E. Burnside*, which went into service July 3rd.

The Burnside No. 2, was a very light engine; it made the Topeka-Burlingame round trip with four or five cars every day. Southbound, a stop was made at Wakarusa Creek for water. South of this there was a hill up onto the prairie. The train made the grade by backing up about a mile north of the creek and making a run for it. It usually just managed to get over the top, with the passengers holding their breaths.

In a short time the road had six engines at work. No. 3 was the *Tom Peter*, No. 4 was the *Thomas Sherlock*, No. 5 was the *Thomas Nickerson* and No. 6 was the *Joseph Nickerson*. Sherlock and the Nickersons were directors and workers on the road in its early stages.

With this equipment the system handled its freight and put on two passenger trains daily, except Sunday. The schedule, Topeka to Burlingame, twenty-six miles, was two hours, thirty-five minutes.

The Santa Fe had no telegraph line. Trains ran by smoke and headlight, which was all right except that, at night, trainmen often couldn't see the smoke and the headlight rarely shone more than a block ahead. However, by running the passenger trains up and down in daylight and the freights at night, things worked pretty smoothly. There came a time, however, when traffic grew so that a wire from Topeka to the end-of-track became necessary. So one was strung along a pole line and connected to the Kansas Pacific's line at North Topeka, where the redoubtable Major Anderson still reigned. In fact, he sent the first test message:

TOPEKA, KS.

HUNKADORA

T. J. ANDERSON

The Santa Fe's new operator in Topeka was equally succinct:

T. J. ANDERSON, NORTH TOPEKA

O. K.

M. L. SARGENT, GEN. FRT. AGT.

Terseness of the first messages was typical of the operators' sending. In later years many a wayside station or siding was given a short four-or-five-letter name, for the operators' benefit. They had to write out and transmit train orders with speed and accuracy.

That is why many Western stations are still Hicks, Nero, Bell and Agra and not Ossapotawamie or Hassayavaipampa. Names of larger, established places, of course, were reduced to two-letter code combinations.

Early in 1869 somebody on the board of directors in New York grew tired of the name Atchison, Topeka & Santa Fe Rail Road and got through a motion to change it to National Pacific. This change lasted only five weeks, when the board thought better of it and resumed the old name. The line, in those days, had no money to waste repainting names on cars and stations or in getting new stationery printed. The name of the system, was, in later years, to be changed once—but that was merely from Rail Road to Railway. But that's a future story.

As the line was built across Kansas every new settlement reached was an excuse for another celebration. At Carbondale, the road had crossed the boundary of Shawnee County and so became eligible for some of the money raised by the county bond issue. This cash—although the bonds were badly discounted—together with surplus over earnings, went into more rail and material, and pushed the road ahead.

Things boomed in towns along its path and even before the line reached a prairie settlement, the people there profited immensely from increases in real-estate values and from better business brought in by land speculators and town lot investors. On June 15, 1869, months before it was reached, Emporia held a bond election to vote aid to the road, the bonds carrying by a large majority. This ensured the Santa Fe some cash when it built across Lyons County—and it also ensured that Lyons County citizens would make money hand over fist long before the road arrived.

"Things are lively here," wrote one "Citizen of Emporia" to a Topeka paper. "Lots that went begging at $500 are readily gobbled up at $1,000 now. About a hundred men with money are here awaiting the coming of the railroad."

"The goose," wrote another enthusiast, "was never more loftily suspended." This gentleman signed himself "Coeur de Lion," indicating that there might still be a faint heart or two loose on the plains.

It was true Emporia was filled with strangers with cash eager to get land and lots. Train service started from Topeka sixty-two miles away, in midsummer, 1870. Everybody made money except Atchison Associates, the construction concern that up to then had built the line. The company had to take county bonds for its fee, and these had to be accepted at face value, although they were selling, usually, at a generous discount. The Associates paid their workmen and their material bills but they were steadily losing money. They bowed out.

From then on the Santa Fe was on its own. President Henry Lord left. Henry Keyes, a kindly and upright Connecticut Yankee, took over.

The road went on, built by brawn. There was little or no machinery. Picks and shovels cut through the hills; horse-drawn scrapers made the fills. There were no railbending machines. On sharp curves the rails were hacked into short lengths and the curve built from these.

Ahead of iron and behind the surveyors came the grading camps. They were manned mainly by farm boys with a sprinkling of war veterans from both the North and South. The farm boys were known, inelegantly as "sorghum lappers." They drove mules and horses hitched to breaking plows that tore through the buffalo sod. After them came the scraper gangs which piled dirt on the right of way, cleaned out cuts and built up fills.

It was a rough, tough life, in tents or in shacks thrown together from scrap lumber. The life of a grading settlement was only a few weeks. Often the men boarded themselves in groups, living on beans, salt pork, bread and sorghum. On Sundays, when no railroad work was done, there were special treats: dried apples or peaches, store bread and black coffee with sugar. On such days all the men had to do was wash clothes, tend teams and mend harness. If they had any time off they wrote letters, or drifted back to the nearest end-of-track town to get drunk.

The camps sometimes were headed up by a boarding contractor

obsessed with the idea that his wife's place sixteen hours a day was within two feet of a cookstove. Some camps had sleeping tents for as many as a hundred men, whose beds were soft pine boards or straw mattresses held down by stakes driven into the ground. There were awnings to serve as stables, and a tent for the blacksmith. Irish workers were called "Jerries"; everyone else was a dago, regardless of nationality.

Special arrangements had to be made for the day after the pay car arrived. This usually was signalized by the non-cooking of the cook—cooks being notorious drunks. Bonuses were offered and paid for sober cooks and occasionally one was found. No track or grading work was done the day after pay day, or, if it was, contractors counted themselves lucky to get a few hundred yards, instead of the customary mile. If the blacksmith and his helpers were reasonably sober, the horses and mules were shod, but this seldom happened, as blacksmithing was a very thirsty occupation, especially in summer on the Kansas prairie.

Train crews generally were a soberer breed, although in those days there was no Rule G which forbids railroad men, from president to water boy, to imbibe while on duty. An exception to the rule seems to have been young Rhody Peter, brother of Tom Peter, then chief engineer. Rhody started as a brakeman, advanced to conductor and slid back to brakeman; he just couldn't stand prosperity. A jovial lad, it was his custom to stand atop boxcars when a little high, twisting up the brakewheel and singing the first Santa Fe song ever written:

"Just winding up business for the old Santa Fe . . ."

The telegrapher too, was often a source of annoyance. No train could leave without him and in the early days it was frequently necessary to hold everything for hours because of the brass pounder's tardiness. If he showed up drunk, there was another delay until he could be sobered up.

The line went on through Doyle Creek, which was renamed Florence, and finally into Newton, which was almost 135 miles from Topeka. On April 13, 1871, two pioneers got to the site of Newton in a bullteam wagon, out-spanned and put up a shack.

There was a rumor around that the Santa Fe would build through or near the place which the firstcomers named for Newton, Massachusetts. Six weeks later, when the road announced its coming, there were 2,000 people there. There were 6,000 when the grading gangs arrived, with twenty gambling tents going full blast on Main Street, one of them accommodating 600 people.

A few weeks before Senator Ross had spaded up the first shovelful of dirt in Topeka, a tall, gray-eyed and still blackhaired old plainsman had camped on the Canadian River, eaten a hearty meal of bear steaks—and died in pain. In the years to come, his name would be remembered along with those of Coronado and Kit Carson, Cortez and Becknell, Kearny and the other brave ones who first beat out the pathways across the Southwest. He was the son of a Scots father and a Cherokee girl.

His name was Jesse Chisholm, and his monument is the Chisholm Trail of song and story. It ran, in its heyday, from Corpus Christi in Texas up to Abilene, Kansas, and over it a million longhorns plodded northward in the great drives that started after the war between the states. Later, Holliday's railroad would follow the old trail across the plains to the Gulf, as it followed the old trace out to the Pacific.

Chisholm, who spoke fourteen Indian dialects, Spanish and English, came north to the mouth of the Little Arkansas near the present town of Wichita, Kansas, when Southern troops drove Unionist-minded tribes out of Indian Territory at the beginning of the war. This was the old Black Beaver Trail, named for a Delaware scout. After the war, Chisholm and a partner, James R. Mead, built up the trail. Intercepting the Santa Fe wagons along the Arkansas, they bought trade goods. These they toted down the trail into the Indian country, returning north with a few cattle. Thus the trail grew until the Santa Fe got to Newton in Harvey County, in 1871, and met its sod with iron rail.

After that there was no Chisholm Trail north of the track.

But for a month in the spring of '44 cattle moved up the old Trail from Texas and from winter pastures in New Mexico and Old Mexico, some to packing houses, some to feed lots. But most of them moved into a great tract of nearly 4,000,000 acres from the 36th parallel in Oklahoma, 200 miles north to the Kaw River. In Kansas this feed belt is called the Flint Hills; in Oklahoma, the Osage Hills.

In this rich grass country, the average steer puts on from 250 to 400 pounds of beef, feeding through the bluestem that grows as tall as a man. It takes twenty acres to pasture a cow in Western Texas, but only five in the bluegrass.

It would have astonished old Jesse Chisholm, half Cherokee and brother-in-law of Sam Houston, who first broke the long trail and picked out the river crossings all the way from Texas up to Abilene, Kansas, and the Union Pacific. In 1945 the cattle still came to Wichita, Kansas, and boarded the Santa Fe for their last ride, as they had done for seventy years. Not the old longhorns—but the whitefaces, chunky, steaky, bluebloods, little like the critters of the '70s.

Santa Fe's president in the early '70s was a former Massachusetts stage-line owner, with the curious name of Ginery Twitchell. He was a mild, honest little man who seemed—but was not—quite unsuited to boss the rough-and-tumble job of battling a railroad across the plains. He stayed with the line until May, 1873, and then went back to railroading in Massachusetts, where he never tired of relating his adventures in the Great Wild West.

Beyond Emporia *was* wild country. There were no settlements. The builders made them up as they went along—Saffordville, Elmdale, Cedar Point. Roving bands of Indians seemed to dislike the whole idea. They rarely killed, but they plundered and burned at random.

They were superstitious as well as resentful and refused to cross the tracks, or walk directly under telegraph wires, thus demonstrating their intellectual inferiority to the whites—who, very properly, refused to walk under ladders. The tribes, however, had no hesitation in crossing *under* the tracks, and so their migrations were funneled to those spots where the railroad built bridges. They often tore down telegraph wire, but it was one thing they didn't steal. So the linemen only had to put it back.

Two years before, in 1868, most of the local redskins had been cowed into an unwilling peace by Custer at the Battle of the Washita. But Santa Fe surveyors still had to work with escorts of fifteen carbined soldiers, who spent some of their time trying to avoid being run over by stampeding buffalo. One buffalo a day was usually enough to feed the entire party.

The line got to Newton and stopped. The company now had little more than 130 miles of track from Topeka out. To earn its land grant it had to be at the Kansas-Colorado state line by March 1, 1873. No one knew, to start with, just where the line was. Surveyors thought it might be about 340 miles west.

The extension to the state line would cost about $5,000,000. The road was making money, but saving up $5,000,000 out of the profits of a settlement-to-settlement road through new territory was a little too much for it. Money was getting tighter and prices were rising. Eastern capital didn't seem much interested. It began to look as though the Santa Fe might stop at Newton for a long time.

There was hardly a wilder place at which to stop. Cowboys, dry and cash-heavy after weeks on the trail, milled through saloons and bawdy houses; Mexican gamblers, overland from Santa Fe, resplendent in their silk shirts, slashed velvet breeches and crimson sashes. Cattle began to come up the trails from Texas to be loaded onto the cars. Newton boiled with business and sin.

Ministers held services in saloons, being rewarded with a drink and the privilege of taking up a collection from the faro and monte players. One such saloon preacher was the Reverend M. M. Haun, a tall Methodist. He preached regularly in the Golden Rule at 515 Main Street, using a beer barrel for a lectern. His sermon concerned the wages of sin, which, he intimated, would shortly be paid in full to most of his congregation. At the conclusion of the homily, two cowhands went through the crowd, hat in one hand, gun in the other, accepting offerings. Mr. Haun expressed his appreciation, politely refused a slug of raw whisky, and left.

He lived in the country most of his life and reared a large family.

His son, John E. Haun, was the Santa Fe station agent at Sedgewick for many years.

Free whisky by the barrel was set out at election time. At the first polling, eight men were shot dead and seventeen wounded. But the killing that cleaned up Newton was that of a Santa Fe man named Arthur Delaney, sometimes known as Mike McCluskie. He was a quiet Irishman, and, like most railroaders, on the side of the homefolks as against the evildoers, gamblers and scarlet women who flocked to prairie cattle towns.

On August 19, 1871, long after the Santa Fe got there, McCluskie remonstrated in a saloon with a wild Texan, Ed Baylor, who was conducting himself in a loud and disorderly fashion. Baylor pulled his gun—but McCluskie pulled quicker—and Baylor died "with a curse on his lips," says a Harvey County historian.

Hugh Anderson, leader of the Texas gang to which Baylor had belonged, swore vengeance, and with four other gang members, trapped McCluskie in a dance hall. In the battle, McCluskie died with his thousand-mile shirt—a railroad trademark comparable to a cowhand's boots—bullet-torn and bloody.

There now appeared on the scene a young man named Dennis Riley. He came into the dance hall with two .45s ready, kicked the door shut behind him and made a brief announcement. He was, he said, merely a poor consumptive boy beating his way west in the hope of reaching the healthful climate of Colorado. McCluskie had found him, half dead, in a Zulu car and had cared for him. So, now he would take care of the foul crew that had killed his friend.

Riley's guns spoke sharply, and five Texans, including Anderson, fell dead amid the screams of the girls and a short break in the continuous faro game. Riley held the hall at bay and quickly made his escape. He was never seen again. The better element, shocked at the wholesale slaying, ran the gamblers and the dance-hall girls out of town for a few weeks.

Santa Fe train crews kept Winchesters handy, and occasionally a train became a moving fort, exchanging shots with drunks and would-be-robbers as it rocked over the prairie.

The town council, in a spirit of civic pride, laid off a graveyard.

This, by ordinance, extended from the Santa Fe tracks for ten rods north, and from the city limits east to the Missouri River and west to the crest of the Rockies. It was quite a stretch of graveyard, but Newton never quite got around to using all of it. Some of its shooting, indeed, was in a spirit of play and included the bulleting of high silk hats worn by the effete Eastern tenderfeet who made the perilous trip west and got off to look the place over.

The Santa Fe had put on its first fast mail, manned mainly by engineers and firemen from the White Water Valley Division of the Big Four in Indiana. Many Santa Fe crews in early days came from Posey County, Indiana, though no one seems to know why. Anyway, the *Mail*, precursor of today's No. 7 and No. 8, went blasting and shrieking up and down between Topeka and Newton, 134 miles, in seven hours and twenty minutes.

In Topeka the annual report for the first full year of operation showed the road already building a reputation for reliability. Its eastbound expresses had missed only two connections with the Kansas Pacific. Although 33,598 passengers had been carried, not one had been hurt or killed. No employees were killed or injured. The year's worst wreck had been on a curve west of Burlingame where No. 4 had backed into a cow. Damage: $25, not including the cow, which was a total loss.

On the evening of January 23, 1872, No. 2 pulled into Topeka from the west, and from it stepped a tall, handsome fellow, with dundreary whiskers, clad in a combination of evening and Western dress. This was the Grand Duke Alexis, of Russia, homeward bound via New Orleans, from a bison hunt. He proceeded to the hotel, was wined and dined and the next day was dragged around town in a parade led by Major Tom Anderson, complete with sash aboard a white horse. Twelve special cops had been sworn in and decorated with tin stars, to keep a sharp watchout for bomb-throwers, the nihilists of St. Petersburg, as was well known, being quite capable of sending such disturbing characters to Topeka to pot the Duke. Nothing happened, however. The state legislators, who were in session, took the day off at full pay, and were editorially bawled out for their greed.

When they had nothing better to do, prairie philosophers in young towns along the track set their minds to grinding out laws for regulating the road on the theory that anyone could run a railroad better than railroad men. Teams still shied at engines, people were scared nearly out of their lives at grade crossings and complained that bells, whistles and engine exhausts kept them awake nights. After a time some of the new laws began to irritate railroaders. The station agent at Florence wrote to a Newton paper suggesting a law to end all laws:

"In case a horse gets scared at an engine the engineer shall take the engine apart as quickly as possible and conceal the parts in a nearby ditch until the horse has passed."

Meantime, small farmers called nesters by the cattlemen were pushing slowly west, putting up fences, breaking the sod, forcing the cattle drives farther from midwestern markets. They followed the railroad which carried them, their tools, stock and furniture out from Kansas City, Independence and St. Louis. These emigrants did their share of Indian fighting and grimly rebuilt fences the buffalo tramped down—but many a settler saw his first crop pounded out of sight by the thundering herds. There were antelope, rabbits and prairie chicken to eat, and coyotes to be shot.

In 1873 Mrs. J. F. Glidden, who lived near Chicago, started something that had a profound effect on the cattle business and cattle drives. She was a flower lover and the dogs that rooted in her garden annoyed her. She complained to her husband and he invented bob wire, often referred to by Easterners who don't know better as barbed wire. Within five years thousands of miles of it crisscrossed the plains and surrounded the sod and timber shacks of the nesters who were breaking up the open range.

A hundred pounds of it cost twenty dollars at first; in a few years the same amount cost $180 and trainloads of it were shipped West while cattle barons and cowhands cursed.

The Santa Fe trusted everybody. Agents at little way stations and sidings weren't bonded and often collected three or four thousand dollars in freight charges, sleeping with the cash and a couple of guns under their pillows until they could turn the money over to the conductor of an eastbound train for delivery at Topeka. Company records show that under this honor system the line never lost a cent.

The Santa Fe moved settlers west in boxcars and coaches. There was a rule that if a settler's car had livestock aboard, an attendant would be carried free. This led to the practice of a westing family holding out a couple of chickens when it sold out in the east, loading them solemnly in with the plow, chairs, stove and bedding and letting Father or one of the boys ride in the boxcar while the rest of the family rode in the coaches.

Moving settlers were always called Zulu, but no one knows why. For a time they were also known as Zebras. Zulu shippers always wanted their car coupled just back of the engine, where it would ride with fewer jerks, and those who put out a jug of fortyrod usually got the preferred place. Brakemen went along, chalking "Zulu-Jug" or "Zulu-No Jug" on the car sides as a guide to the switchman who made up the train. Anything could be shipped in Zulus, except a piano; the road drew the line at that.

The cattle drives up the long trails brought other things besides gunplay and hard drinking to the prairies. One of them was hymn-singing, which was early discovered to act as a sedative to nervous longhorns.

Since the Santa Fe depended a great deal on cattle business, it dealt tenderly with the cowmen and listened when they complained that the trains often stampeded their herds. This was serious, because a stampeding herd could work off beef tonnage at a fast clip. The best way to keep steers calm was to sing to them, and the best sort of singing soon was found to be hymns, which, in many cases, had a soporific effect unintended by their authors and composers.

The Santa Fe issued orders to its engineers and trainmen: a sharp lookout was to be kept for trail herds up ahead. When one was sighted, speed was to be increased and passengers were asked to refrain from shooting out the windows. Upon approaching the herd, steam would be shut off and the train allowed to drift silently past the beef critters.

This was the origin of the stories, told by Eastern dudes, of cowhands on the plains bawling "The Old Rugged Cross," and "Rock of Ages" as the trains hummed by; it won for the cowpokes a reputation undeserved by such profane fellows, of being converts of missionaries who, at the time, infested the plains.

Impressed passengers in the cars, train crews reported, often commented on the piety of cowhands and made vows to lead purer lives—a vow frequently forgotten at the next town, when off-duty cowmen, by their riotous conduct in saloons, dispelled the notion that they were sincerely converted.

Meantime the line surged west along the Arkansas River bottoms, with $5,000,000 found, somehow, for construction. This stretch had been surveyed by Captain John Ellinwood and Albert Alonzo Robinson.

Robinson was hired away from the St. Joseph & Denver City Road by Tom Peter. It was one of the best investments the Santa Fe ever made. Before he left the system, years later, to become president of the old Mexican Central, Robinson had fought many a battle and had built 5,000 important miles for the Santa Fe. He was a Vermonter, worked his way through the University of Michigan, learned to be an engineer and started out with the St. Joe & Denver only two years before the Santa Fe got him. He became successively chief engineer, vice-president and general manager.

The line running to Newton and west toward Dodge cut off the trail herds from Abilene and the cow towns to the north along the first transcontinental track. Tom Peter, prospecting around, figured that the infiltrating nesters soon would staple their wire far enough west across the plains to cut off the trail herds from Newton, too. It didn't happen for some years, but Peter took no chances and surveyed a branch line twenty-seven miles southwest down to the village of Wichita, where the herds might be intercepted. He went to New York with his idea and told the directors about it. They said no.

Peter came back west, got some friends together and built the branch himself. The directors then saw the light and leased the line from him and his associates for thirty-five percent of the gross earnings.

The western extension plan, was, for a time, to run a short line from Wichita to form a string across the great northward bow the Arkansas River made from Hutchinson around to the present location of Kinsley. Today a bowstring line cuts off the river bend between these two towns. But the plan was abandoned for the time being and the line run around north of the bend, where construction was easier. The land was relatively flat, miles of ties were laid virtually on the prairie. There were few settlements outside of Great Bend and stations were infrequent.

J. D. (Pete) Criley, who had built much of the Kansas Pacific line to Denver, now tackled the Santa Fe from Newton to the Colorado line. He managed to get down a mile a day, except on Mondays. Half a mile on Mondays was considered good. Hangovers. Day-after-payday 500 yards of new track still was the usual stint. But still, unless that track was built to the Colorado line before the deadline, the land grant would be lost—2,000,000 acres spread over a 300-mile strip of Kansas. It was May 1, 1872—ten months to go—271 miles of track across a wilderness—if the surveyors were right.

Pete got his gangs together and started grading. A few days later the track gangs began work. The grade was into Hutchinson, near the Arkansas River, by June 14th; track was down ten days later. Iron was spiked into Great Bend July 15th and, on July 20th, forty-six cars of cattle rolled east—to provide a little cash for more iron and more graders.

Criley's gangs were racing now. Then hard luck hit. July 23rd a prairie gale blew three cars off the track at Raymond. Six days later the westbound construction train was held up at Ellinwood. The crew beat off the robbers with wrenches, shovels and hammers and laid out two desperadoes, Roy Spencer and Jack Reynolds. August 3rd, a westbound passenger train was stuck up near Great Bend by three gunmen. Conductor Wyman uncoupled the engine, raced ahead to Raymond, got a posse together, backed the engine down to the train—and captured the robbers.

Tracks went on. At Pawnee Rock, Criley had laid sixty-five miles in thirty days. On August 8th, ten miles west of Larned, the record of his Irish, Swedes, Germans, Confederate and Union veterans, was ninety-nine miles in sixty-nine days. In October he was laying three miles of track a day; Thanksgiving Day saw more than 300 miles down in 230 days. That was the day they arrived at what the railroad's surveyor said was the Kansas-Colorado line, and here a tent community—State Line City—went up, as the graders arrived. The track got there December 22nd. Criley and Robinson had a drink and shook hands.

Just at dusk that day, a young surveyor hammered a stake into the prairie and nailed a board to it. Men from the track crew, homing wearily to bunk tents, looked at it and grinned. The eastern end of the board read "Kansas"; the western, "Colorado."

"Home for Christmas, boys," yelled Pete. "Work train leaves in the morning."

Tools were dropped. The few remaining rails were piled and the ties heaped on the frozen sod. The men gathered in their tents, drinking toasts and singing "The Man Who Attended O'Reilley's Bar," "Muldoon's Picnic" and "I Miss You, Nettie Moore."

Pete strode to his own tent, shucked off his warm, sheepskin-lined greatcoat, tossed it and his weatherbeaten old hat into a corner and turned in with a sigh of content.

Early next morning the whistle of the easting work train, crammed with men, aroused him. He smiled drowsily and turned over, only dimly aware of the ever-present Kansas wind outside, which had subsided to a petulant murmur. It touched the thin gray walls of his tent lightly. They quivered, strained a little at the stakes. Criley burrowed deeper into the warmth of his blankets—once again he slept.

Hours later he was awakened by Robinson, who ushered in a tall, bearded fellow with a notebook sticking out of his hip pocket.

"Pete!"

"Yes, what's the matter, Rob?"

"Bad news, Pete."

"Whisky all gone?"

"Worse than that. We need track—four miles of it."

"How? State Line's right outside. That's our limit."

"You don't understand, Pete. This man's a government surveyor and he says the line's four miles west," explained Robinson.

"My eye! It's right here," said Criley, kicking aside his blankets and reaching for his clothes. He knew, despite his protests, that Robinson must be right—Robinson and the government man . . .

"Government says the line's west, Pete," continued Robinson, "and the government'll take the word of its own men when it comes to proving up for the land grant—not ours. We'll have to build to the government stakes."

"Build! What with? We're damn near out of ties and track material. Most of the boys have gone home. *You* try getting a crew just before Christmas!"

"Well," rejoined Robinson, "We'll have to, somehow."

"OK, Rob—let's go!" Criley, fully dressed now, reached for his coat, jammed his hat onto his head and led the way.

He managed to collect a few men, told them to strike the tents of State Line City and move it, with teams, four miles west.

"This man"—indicating the surveyor—"will tell you where the state line is. Hurry—and you'll have a place to celebrate Christmas in yet!"

Robinson, meanwhile, had wired east for a work train. When it arrived, he and Criley started back down the track, wiring ahead to station agents to assemble what men they could. There was no new material and no chance to get any.

"Only one thing to do, Rob," said Pete.

"Tear up sidings?"

"Sure, four miles of them. And we'd better hustle—there's usually a blizzard in this country before Christmas."

A blizzard could stop track laying—and lose the land grant. The drifts could build up fast, when the wind died a little, and the stark cold came down from the Rockies. Then the ties, rails, spikes and everything else would disappear until spring. There would be politicians only too glad to demand that the road forfeit its land.

So they hustled—and finally they had a small crew, a few teams and a trainload of material. West they went again, to State Line City, now sitting far out on the prairie.

Track went down with a short break for Christmas—and another to recover from it.

Criley, talking to Robinson near end-of-track in the dusk of December 28th, looked at the black clouds piling up ahead.

"Looks like that blizzard is coming," he said. "Better tell the boys to make sure the tents are fast."

As Robinson turned, a shout went up from the track crew.

"Come on over here, Pete, and drive the last one," yelled old Mike O'Brien, the foreman.

Criley hefted a spike maul, whammed it down. Three swift strokes sank the spike to the last tie. There were no more ties; no more rails.

"How far're we over the government line, Mike?" he asked.

"Five yards," said Mike, pointing with a grubby finger to the stake the government surveyor had hammered into the sod.

"Enough, boys. Good work. Just in time, too—there's a grandfather of a blizzard coming tonight. . . ."

He walked back to the scarred boxcar as the first white flakes flew by on the wind. The operator was blowing on his fingers to keep them warm. Pete wrote out a message with a flourish.

To T. J. Peter, Gen. Mgr., Topeka, Kas.
We send you greetings on completion of the road to the state line. Beyond us lie fertile valleys that invite us forward, and broad plains die away in the distance dotted with mingling herds of bison and cattle, awaiting a further advance. The mountains signal us from their lofty crests and, still beyond, the Pacific shouts, Amen!

Signed: Pete Criley.

Back in Topeka the next morning, Tom Peter smiled as he read the message. Later that day he sent a reply to State Line City, the operator bringing it to Criley's tent through the swirling blizzard. It read:

We clasp hands with you over the timely and successful completion of our road to state line and heartily share your good wishes for the future.

It was national news. Up in Washington, Pennsylvania, the *Reporter* told its readers that the completion of the line "opens up 30,000 homesteads of 160 acres apiece . . . Mr. Lo retreats and civilization advances . . ."

A few hours after the track had been laid into Colorado, Peter Tellin throttled the first train across the line. After that everybody had a Christmas drink and fried buffalo steaks on the fireman's coal scoop—which was the way most enginemen got their lunches in those days.

Tellin had started with the line back in '68 as a member of a grading crew, a few months after he had arrived in America from Sweden. By 1870 he was foreman of a tracklaying gang north of Emporia, and quit to take up firing in June, 1870. In October, 1872, the engineer of a stock train from Newton to Emporia fell ill and the trainmaster told Peter to run the engine—giving him a section hand for a fireman. Neither of them knew much about his job, and they had to call on the conductor to keep up steam. The skipper wasn't much good, either, and Pete had to run the kettle, watch the water and do most of the firing himself.

At Emporia, tired and disgusted, he formally resigned from the road but came back when he was promoted to engineer, with the promise of a good fireman, who, Tellin thoughtfully added, ought also to be a good shot with a Winchester to ward off headlight-busting cowhands and other perils of the prairie.

The Santa Fe from Atchison to State Line now was 470.5 miles long. A few days later Governor Harvey, of Kansas, rode out, inspected the line, talked with the government surveyor—and approved the land grant. State Line City was rechristened Sargent—after M. L. Sargent, the road's general freight agent.

But there were some who thought it ought to have been named Criley. Years later, a Santa Fe historian complained: "He saved the Santa Fe millions, yet no station bears his name. There are towns all the way from the Kaw to Coolidge named for Santa Fe directors and other brass collars. But it was old Pete Criley who built the road, and set a record for speedy work. . . ."

The land grant was safe, but back along the line, there had been trouble, big and small. Through the coal lands around Carbondale, traffic became heavy in 1871—and so did the rain. People even complained of too much rain, practically an unheard-of thing in Kansas. The track, which was laid on gumbo, started to sink out of sight. Piling on more gumbo merely made it worse. Nobody quite knew what to do until an English section foreman who had worked on British roads, suggested digging out the gumbo, burning it and putting it back. This worked. Crews gathered up coal slack from the mines, burned the clay and so reballasted the track. This was the first use of burned ballast in America.

The Santa Fe learned other things too, as it went along. At Ellsworth, Kansas, the Kansas Pacific made arrangements with a bank to finance cattlemen while their herds were waiting shipment. Competition being what it was, the Santa Fe, after it got to Great Bend, copied this service and put $50,000 into a Great Bend bank for loans. The bank promptly folded and after that the line picked its bankers with greater care.

Running trains still came under the head of perilous business. Standard engine equipment included two Winchesters and 100 rounds of ammunition. West of Dodge there was a stand of Winchesters in the baggage car and, for long periods, soldiers guarded all stations against roving bands of thieving Indians.

"Uncle George" Nettleton was superintendent of the line west; the Redskins were on a rampage and Uncle George lived up to the growing tradition that the Santa Fe was a human railroad; he gave orders that all trains must stop and pick up tramps, prospectors and strays seen along the tracks, and take them to the safety of the nearest station, whether they could pay fare or not. Nettleton made such an impression that, when Tom Peter quit, after cleaning up in some coal-mine deals around Osage, Uncle George got his job.

There still were no train orders, and smoke-and-headlight operation remained the rule. Stations often were lined with buffalo hides against winter blizzards. Here and there was a trackside eating house, the buffalo meat piled outside. Guests cut off their own steaks and carried them in to the cook to be fried.

Around Syracuse, the cattle country defeated a colony of settlers who had come in and tried to raise crops. They failed, after two years, and the Santa Fe offered to take them back East, free. Fifteen families accepted, tearing down their buildings and loading their lumber for shipment "back home." The rest stuck and, in a year or two, won.

But all of the building of the Santa Fe hadn't been westward. Ever since the line, back in '68, had started south for Emporia instead of north for Atchison, people in the latter town had been good and sore. Here was a railroad calling itself Atchison, Topeka & Santa Fe—and it seemed to be ignoring Atchison altogether.

Colonel Holliday pointed out that, for the time being, it was also ignoring Santa Fe. He promised that as soon as the Carbondale coal business put a little money into the company's treasury, Atchison would get track. He kept his word.

Late in 1871, work started from both ends of the new line. John Fagan, who had run a construction train south of Topeka, took Engine No. 7 and ran it to Atchison, from Topeka, to Lawrence over the Kansas Pacific; from Lawrence to Leavenworth over what is now the Union Pacific, and from Leavenworth to Atchison over the Missouri Pacific. Crews built steadily toward each other and met two miles west of Grasshopper Falls—later changed to Valley Falls. Nobody in Kansas wanted to be reminded of grasshoppers.

The first Santa Fe train rolled up the line from Topeka on April 24, 1872, and Atchison celebrated.

But in Topeka there wasn't much celebrating, for, barring a few passengers, the road's main source of revenue came from hauling coal from Carbondale. The payroll was often late and the wives of enginemen and train and track crews used to watch the evening freight roll in, every car of coal meant $10 to the line, and half a dozen meant that everybody would get paid, at least in part!

The Santa Fe's engineers and stockholders, however, had little time to spend on the eastern end of the road. Out West, all hell was busting loose at Dodge City, and, just over the horizon, the first rumblings of the panic of '73 began to spell trouble.

CHAPTER FIVE

INTO THE ROCKIES

FINDING CAPITAL, trying to sell land to get a little cash, hunting for almost non-existent freight and passengers weren't the Santa Fe's only troubles in the evil days of '73. The line west of Dodge was hardly worth running trains over. The thirty-three miles to Granada, where the line ran out of track, might as well have been on the moon. If the road could have gone on to Trinidad, Colorado, it could have picked up some lumber, coal and ore for eastbound hauls, and made a few dollars freighting machinery and supplies west for the miners now flocking into the Rockies.

But there was no money for new construction; there was hardly enough to maintain the road between Topeka and Dodge. In September, with the panic in full swing, Jay Cooke & Company and the Northern Pacific crashed, scaring the investors away from railroad securities for months. Five thousand businesses went into bankruptcy. The Santa Fe hung on grimly. Station agents and conductors funneled their meager cash back east to Topeka. Most of it was reloaded into Jim Moore's pay car and started west again to pay section hands, operators, engineers and other employees. The car was often late—but it always showed up eventually.

Moore, who was paymaster, had an old coach fixed with sleeping quarters and a modest arsenal, loaded aboard his sacked cash and half a dozen armed guards and went rolling over the prairies behind a fast oo 00 type engine. Engines then were, and still are, described by railroaders by symbols. The oo 00 (4-4-0) class engines have a four-wheeled truck in front. A 00 OOO 00 type would be 4-6-4, six driving wheels and four wheel trucks ahead and behind.

The pay car's coming was wired ahead and its arrival at a plains station announced by a dozen blasts of the whistle. Men came running from everywhere, no matter what the hour, and were paid in gold and silver while the two armed guards stood by with Winchesters. Payment in cash got too dangerous in 1873 and the men were paid by check. This had its drawbacks, because most of the checks were cashed in saloons, with the inevitable results. Still, it was better than taking a chance on having the car held up and looted. One lost carload of pay-money could almost have wrecked the road.

It was the custom of train crews to run without lights out of Dodge, stop on the prairie out of gun range and light up the oil headlight and car lamps. This was the only safe system. A favorite sport of Dodge citizens was shooting out headlights and, as the gunmen were usually drunk, railroaders took as few chances as possible.

If this wasn't enough to make an engineer earn his $3.25 a day—12:01 A.M. to 12:01 P.M.—the Indians usually could be counted on to raid the line or burn lonely stations. If it wasn't Indians, it was buffalo herds or prairie fires. The fires swept before the wind over huge areas and were bitterly denounced by pioneer editors who blamed them for plagues, deserts, hard times, the prevalence of sin and grasshoppers. Engine sparks undoubtedly set many fires and the Santa Fe countered with spark-arresters, which sometimes worked.

New engines of the 4-4-0 type were hauling trains, but engineers were ordered not to run faster than a mile in three minutes on varnish strings or in four minutes on freight drags. These speeds might be exceeded only to get away from menacing Indians or to beat buffalo herds to a crossing. The engines could make surprising speed, but had a tractive value of only 7,900 pounds. They cost only about $7,000.

There were no vestibules on passenger cars. Conductors and

brakemen leaped from one lurching coach to the next. There were no lavatories. Coal stoves more or less heated the cars in winter, fighting against the blasts that blew in through windows shot out by eager hunters aboard the trains. Before 1873 you brought your own lunch; in that year crude eating houses were established here and there along the track.

There was no track fence; it was cheaper to pay for the occasional cows killed. Engineers tried not to hit them, because this might derail the train, but with headlights making only a dim glow for a few score feet, it was hard to see track obstructions at night. When cattle were sighted, the train slowed, the fireman dropped his shovel, picked up a pike-pole—standard engine equipment—and ran ahead to prod the longhorns off the track. There was a sort of gentlemen's agreement among the road, settlers and cattlemen: the road would pay half the appraised value of all stock killed. This arrangement was borrowed from the Union Pacific, which was having the same trouble farther north.

The panic went on. As it deepened, Henry Strong came to the Santa Fe as president. He was born in Glasgow, Scotland, son of the American Consul-General there. He became a lawyer and was working for the Burlington when the Santa Fe hired him away. Strong took over the road May 22, 1873, steered it for a year, and was replaced by Thomas Nickerson, a Massachusetts financier.

The roads had a hard time. Nicknames changed. The Kansas Pacific became the Keep Poor. The Santa Fe was the Jerkwater Line—because train crews, when the water got low, often had to stop by a creek, form a bucket brigade and jerk water from the stream to fill the tender tank. That wasn't the end of the trouble, either. In those days water was pumped into the boiler from the tank by a gadget that worked off the engine's driving mechanism. If an engine stood idle too long the water in the boiler might fall to a dangerous level. There was no way to get more water in except by running the engine.

In a case like this, the thing to do was jack up the drivers a little, grease the track with mutton tallow and spin the wheels without moving the hog, until enough water had been pumped into the boiler to cover the crown sheet.

This was the origin of the slip track, used by railroads to break in new engines, which may be run at moderate speeds without moving very far.

When G. M. Hoover and J. G. McDonald put up the tent that grew into one of the wildest towns of the plains, they called it Buffalo City. This singularly uninspired name was objected to by the post office, which already was wrestling with half a dozen Buffalo Cities, Creeks, Hills, Rivers and Villes. The post office changed the name to Dodge City, after Fort Dodge, five miles away. Buffalo hunters were cleaning up $100 a day around these parts, and the place grew rapidly, sure of the coming of the Santa Fe.

Through the dusty streets, into and out of the saloons and deadfalls, the tanned cowhands wandered, living according to legend, on navy plug and fortyrod, with a whirl at the tiger or monte for dessert.

The drawling Texans wore flannel shirts, with the gaudy handkerchiefs loosely knotted about the neck, and butternut pants tucked into long boots. They affected sombreros, wider than those worn by the Mexican gamblers, which were black and flat-topped. Most trail-hands carried two guns and were handy on the draw, although tales of their marksmanship are usually fanciful. They didn't have to be good marksmen: most of the fighting was at less than ten feet, and the quickest gunman had the edge over the more accurate, but slower shooter.

You could get a fight with a trail-hand any time by asking him his right name—or by calling him a cowboy. Cowboys were inventions of Eastern fiction writers and bore little resemblance to the genuine cattle puncher of the Chisholm and other Western trails.

The longhorns came up the trail by the thousand and the tens of thousand and were sent east in what were sometimes called "livestock palace cars." The last act is recorded in verse 362 of the Chisholm Trail, where a cowhand sings:

So we loaded 'em up on the Santa Fe cars
And said farewell to the old Two-Bars . . .
Come a-ty-yi-ippy ippi-ay-ippi-ay
Come a-ty-yi-ippi-ippi-ay.

Tracks across the plains and the wire of the settlers barred the way, farther and farther west, to the trail herds from the Red River, the Canadian and the Pecos. Up north the cow towns of Abilene, Hays City and Ellsworth were dying slowly as Newton, Wichita, Great Bend and Dodge took their places.

So the Santa Fe came to Dodge, the passengers shooting at buffalo, antelope, prairie chickens and disgusted Indians from the car windows. All over the roll of the prairie for miles around hunters kept up a steady barrage and the bullteams hauled the hides, hindquarters and tongues to the railroad.

It was a master stock country. From the train the rolling hills stretched to the far horizon, an empire of lush grass over which the buffalo ranged free and the antelopes ran springfooted, light as the cloud shadows that raced across the prairie before the western wind, full of zing and snap from the snowpeaks of the Rockies.

From the hills at dusk the valleys reflected the light like a looking glass and in the stillness the creeks flowed from the north and south, down to the swift-running Arkansas, hurrying eastward between low, broad banks.

Romantically, perhaps it was too bad the buffalo had to go. But historically and economically, it was inevitable. The prairies never could have been settled as long as seventy-five million huge grass-eaters moved freely over them. Cattle drives would have been stalled and stampeded. The road itself could not have been operated successfully if trains were forced to stop or inch their way through herds which no fence ever built could stop.

Buffalo lore and legend have centered around Dodge. The town lies at the intersection of the one hundredth meridian with the Arkansas River. That was the northwest corner of the old boundary between Spain and the United States, between Old Mexico and the United States and finally between the Texas Republic and the

United States. For some years after the railroad got there on September 19, 1872, the buffalo kept hunters, settlers and the road itself, alive.

The Indians, who hunted with bows and arrows and spears, rarely killed more than the natural increase of prairie game. They resented the coming of the whites naturally, as then it was red against white and finally both red and white against the buffalo. The buffalo lost out first; ten years after the railroad got to Dodge, they were almost gone. Dodge records show that, around that place alone, more than three million were killed.

In the winter of '72-'73 Charlie Rath and Bob Wright shipped 200,000 hides over the Santa Fe, along with 200 cases of tongues and hindquarters, which were frozen stiff on the ground and hurried east to New York and Chicago restaurants. There was a stockpile of 40,000 hides beside the track most of the time, worth around $100,000. Shipments grew with the years: in '73 a quarter of a million were shipped, along with about 800 tons of meat. In '74 the hide total was 442,289. Buildings at Dodge and other towns were lined and sheathed with hides.

Settlers followed the hunters, picking up bones. It took 100 bleached skeletons to make a ton, and, for this hard work, under the Kansas sun, the collectors got $8 when they delivered the bones, often miles across the prairie, to the railroad. It was $8 more than they would have received if there had been no railroad, and it kept many of them alive in the tough winters. Many a pioneer family stuck it out on "bone money." The bones, of course, were shipped east and ground into fertilizer.

The situation produced some remarkable characters. There was "Brick" Bond, who lived on the plains for three years straight, had from five to fifteen skinners working for him and claimed to have shot more buffalo than any man alive. Two hundred thousand in four years was his record. His skinners staked out the hides to dry, then later loaded them onto wagons for the bull teams to haul to Dodge. They were worth from $1 to $3 apiece.

Brick's record was challenged by Tom Nickson, who claimed he killed 140 buffalo in forty minutes, and 2,173 in thirty-five days.

And there was Prairie Dog Dave who, in addition to killing his thousands, once shot an albino buffalo for which Charlie Rath gave him $1,000. Where is that skin today? You may hunt long and diligently in Kansas in 1945 without finding a single skull or robe. Yet between 1868 and 1888 more than thirty-one million buffalo died there.

Dodge was a settlement of frame houses and business blocks, mostly with flat roofs upon which were mounted barrels full of water—an early form of sprinkler system. The theory was when a fire burned through the roof the water would spill down and put out the blaze. A childish trust in this theory by several settlers resulted in loss of their homes.

Dodge always claimed a large floating population and could have floated it on hard liquor without trouble. Although it had a bad reputation, records list only fourteen men shot the first year. The place had a very modest Boot Hill compared with Newton's River-to-the-Rockies graveyard.

One of the social leaders of the town was Moses Waters, an Irish saloonkeeper, who made so much money that he imported a stableful of blooded horses from England, along with an English hostler to look after them. Horses and hostler were shipped out on a Santa Fe stock train, the hostler looking upon the whole affair as a crass aping of the British aristocracy by the upstarts of the prairies.

As the town grew, it drew bad women and gamblers not only from the East but from the cow towns to the north—they came down across the prairie in hired Concord rigs and riding horses, hitting the old Santa Fe Trail at Great Bend and following it along the river. Cowboys came in from the South; settlers traded there from fifty miles around. The place soon got to be a battleground among the whites, who forgot their quarrels only long enough to combine against the Indians. Marshals and town officers usually sided with the gambling and red-light interests against the transients. There were no courts within fifty miles and no one had the patience to wait for a court, even if there had been one.

Even soldiers from Fort Dodge weren't safe, and Colonel Richard

I. Dodge, in command, wrote bitter letters to Governor Thomas Osborn in Topeka about "foul and cold-blooded murders" in the town. He pointed out that, as the government was spending thousands of dollars to protect the whites against the Indians, the state might reasonably spend a few dollars to protect the soldiers against the white civilians. The Colonel's opinion of the bad men of Dodge was that they formed "a foe ten thousand times more bloody and brutal than the Indians."

The Governor, writing in reply on June 4, 1873, gave Colonel Dodge "authority to arrest and hold, subject to orders of the civil authorities, all persons notoriously guilty of a violation of the criminal law," but urged the soldier to exercise this power "only in extreme cases."

Colonel Dodge soon found occasion to arrest two men accused of murder, but wrote the Governor that in doing so he probably was exceeding his authority as a soldier, and had acted "simply as a citizen obeying the chief magistrate of his state."

Some of the Dodge City hoodlums, however, didn't care for being arrested by the Colonel, even in his capacity as a citizen. Two of them sued him for $5,300. Governor Osborn backed him up and, with the help of the United States district attorney, the case was quashed.

As in many another town—and willynilly—the Santa Fe tracks became the dividing line. South of the tracks was the section good folks didn't go to after dark. Later a mayor once drew a line down the middle of the tracks and banished the red-light crowd south of it. This invasion of inalienable rights brought in gunmen from Las Vegas, Denver and Newton, and the Santa Fe depot, for a time, became a fort sheltering train crews from the bullets. Many a car and engine rolled eastward from Dodge with bullet holes here and there.

The better element finally gained the upper hand, and it wasn't long until marshals were dumping drunks into an old hand-dug well fifteen feet deep, to cool off. This was the town's first jail and it was kept full, partly by the efforts of two men named Ed and Bat Masterson. The Masterson boys had had a grading sub-contract for the Santa Fe through Dodge and, after the line was built, they became peace officers.

To get ahead of the story a little: when Ford County was organized around Dodge, Bat Masterson, in 1877, became its first sheriff. Brother Ed was a Dodge City marshal, along with the redoubtable Bill Tilghman and others. Ed was shot one afternoon by a rowdy Texan, Curly Wagner, who had come to town with the Walker gang and was raising hell in the Green Front saloon. Ed asked Wagner for his gun and Wagner pumped two bullets into Ed's body, setting his clothes afire.

Bat told Ed to crawl away and get help and then shot it out with the gang, getting its leader and his brother's murderer, who "died that night in awful agony," according to Dodge City historians. Then Bat set out to help his brother—and found him sprawled lifeless across the Santa Fe tracks. Bat looked at the body for a moment, put his gun away and, sitting down beside the body, cried like a baby.

Later, Bat went to work for the Santa Fe; we shall meet him again out beyond Cañon City, Colorado, in one of the great railroad wars of all time.

The man who decided to make the Santa Fe the dividing line in Dodge was Mayor Webster. He also was the man who staged the only bullfight ever held in Kansas. Doc Barton, a pioneer trailsman, supplied two mean old longhorns and the event was advertised far and near. Hell broke loose. The governor stormed. The Society for the Prevention of Cruelty to Animals protested. Federal officials in Washington forbade the match. Webster calmly wired all of them that Dodge City had seceded from the United States for the day—and the fight went on.

Unlike Garden City, Topeka, Hutchinson, Emporia and other Kansas towns, Dodge was laid out with comparatively narrow streets. This was because no one thought the place would outlive a temporary end-of-steel cattle shipping existence. There were too many other dying cow towns around to encourage any permanent city building. To criticizing visitors, Dodge citizens used to say:

"Our streets are wide enough for two bull teams to pass. When there are no more bull teams, there will be no more Dodge."

But as the buffalo died, and the cattle drives dwindled, the settlers kept Dodge alive. The bull teamers were wrong.

If it had trouble on the west end, things weren't running too smoothly on the east end for the Santa Fe. In the early '70s the Topeka City Directory had a paragraph reading: "We can boast of having within our walls one Chapman, who came here penniless and was compelled to pawn his trunk for board, but was able to leave here in a short period with a cool $125,000 in his pocket."

That would be G. C. Chapman, a typical railroad promoter, one of the breed who made it tough for railroad builders. The Santa Fe had to clean up after him. He talked various settlements and counties into voting him bonds to build a road called the Kansas Midland. This pike started out from Kansas City and ran to De Soto—twenty-four miles. It used Missouri Pacific tracks to Lawrence, fifteen miles, and then built twenty-six miles to Topeka.

Chapman finished the road, cashed in his bonds, left many material bills unpaid and lit out for Ohio. Here he built a line from Chillicothe to Columbus and cleaned up again. Last heard, he was living high in Venice, Italy.

Only one train, a mixed, ran on the Kansas Midland. It soon became a headache to everyone, including the Santa Fe, which was dickering around to get a connection into Kansas City. The Santa Fe was attempting to arrange a merger, but the Midland's assets never were the same from day to day. Old Hi Diggins was the conductor and lived in hell. Constables and sheriffs all along the line were continually attaching parts of its train for unpaid material bills. The procedure was for the constable to flag Diggins to a stop, cut off a flatcar or a boxcar, run it onto the siding, chain it fast and then let the train proceed.

When Conductor Diggins had collected a few dollars in fares he paid the constable and removed the marooned cars. But the process slowed up the Midland's train and it hardly ever made connections with the Santa Fe. It was no streamlined flyer to start with. In '74 the Santa Fe tired of the whole thing, and one night a crew from the line and one from the Midland just swapped trains. This put Santa Fe equipment on the Midland, where it could not legally be seized for debt. This solved the problem until the Santa Fe could take over the whole line in the spring of '75.

It wasn't much to take over. Heavy rains usually put it out of commission for days and the train was often marooned. Santa Fe paid off the debt and gradually worked the road into shape. Even then it was a gamble because there still was a lot of argument whether Kansas City, Westport, St. Joseph, Independence, Lawrence, St. Louis or Leavenworth was going to be the big rail crossroads at the Missouri. One road even saved ten miles by missing Kansas City altogether, a decision its builders afterwards regretted.

Out on the western end the panic eased a little, but in '74 the grasshoppers came. Crops, orchards, grass, trees were ruined overnight. What the grasshoppers didn't get, the prairie fires did. Trains were stalled because the drivewheels slipped on the crushed bodies of the insects and Master Mechanic H. V. Faries wired brushes ahead of the wheels to clear the rails. Faries also did something about fires started by sparks. He put a bonnet on the stacks of the Hinckley locomotives.

It worked. It blew smoke and cinders back into the cab and along the cars and, on one run, from Topeka to Emporia, a $2.10-a-day fireman reported in with half his hair burned off. He recovered on a Sunday, which was a day off and no work had to be done outside of cleaning up the roundhouse and polishing brasswork. Firemen often had their clothes off two or three times a month.

These working conditions were not peculiar to railroads; they were normal everywhere. In fact, railroaders had then, as now, the best jobs in their districts. There were plenty of twelve- and fourteen-hour-a-day jobs, with no Sundays off, and many a family was raised on twelve or fifteen dollars a week. Times were hard, jobs were scarce and everyone—railroad managers and workmen—just did the best they could until the sun shone again.

It looked as if that might never happen. There were times in '74 when the Santa Fe came near disaster. The line ran from Atchison and Topeka out to Granada, with branches to Wichita and El

Dorado. But there were few people and fewer tons for it to carry. Farmers almost starved; scores of them hitched up lean, gaunt bull teams and drove fifty, seventy, 100 miles into the settlements looking for food. Old trinkets and family heirlooms, brought years before from the East, were taken from trunks and sold to get a little money for coffee, sugar and flour. The salaries of all Santa Fe employees were cut twenty per cent.

In 1874, too, the Santa Fe hired its first woman employee. She was Mrs. Caroline Anderson, and she went to work as a clerk in the general office in Topeka. First thing that happened, her salary was cut with all the others. In 1945 the company had 6,900 women employees.

Santa Fe hauled in despairing settlers free, and out on the withered, ruined prairie were signs: Railroad station, five miles—food and water. In Boston and New York, financiers shook their heads. Kansas was finished. Investors put their gold coins away in safe-deposit boxes. They knew better than to put cash into a railroad across a desert.

But Santa Fe men never gave up. They couldn't—they had to live. . . . Building over the Colorado line had entitled the road to about 3,000,000 acres of land—or what had been land before the fires and grasshoppers. The road got title to this in 1873. According to the original land grant, the line was to receive every odd-numbered section for ten miles on each side of its track. But in Eastern Kansas, which was pretty well settled, much of this land wasn't available. The law, therefore, gave the road what was called "in lieu" lands farther west. Eventually this worked out to half the land on a strip forty miles wide from Emporia nearly out to Kinsley and, from this point, half of a twenty-mile strip as far as Colorado. It was nearly all in the Arkansas River Valley, and in normal years it was fertile and would produce great crops—provided the grasshoppers didn't eat them.

But the land was worth nothing until the railroad reached it. It had been there for years and nobody wanted it. What value it had in '73 and the next few years depended on the fact that the road provided reasonably cheap and fast transportation, not only for crops, but for food and supplies to keep the settlers going. The government, in fact, made a profit from the deal almost from the start. It took no chances, but the railroad did.

The government still held half the land along the track and, once the railroad started operating, the price of this property went up sharply. Furthermore, the land started paying taxes. In addition, the road had to haul government freight, soldiers and officials for half rates, and mail at reduced charges. Over the years it was a one-sided bargain and there should be a statue somewhere to the genius who invented it for the government. It was a moneymaker for the national treasury from the beginning.

But bargain or no, the land was the one big asset the Santa Fe had in those depression, insect-ridden years. It looked a hopeless task to sell it, or even to get people to settle on it, but the Santa Fe could do nothing else but try. It did. It managed somehow to borrow $1.25 an acre on the land and took the $3,500,000 this produced and poured it into rebuilding the rapidly disintegrating track. It saved a few dollars to start a land department.

Heading this department was D. L. Lakin, an Alabaman who had first come to Kansas as a representative of some Southerners who had bought land there. He was a friend of Colonel Holliday and had put some of his own money into the Santa Fe. In the spring of 1870 he set out in a covered wagon, far across the plains, to survey, classify and plan for the colonization of the great valley through which the road would run. He had a compass man and a flagman to help him, a few guards armed with the customary Winchesters, and some trade goods that he hoped might stave off the Arapahoes, Cheyennes and Comanches.

The fabulous part that the Santa Fe and other railroads played in development of the West is often forgotten. Before the rails ran, sixty years of migration by foot, bull team and horse had sifted only a few thousand people into a territory about half the size of the United States. Then came the railroad and in its first few weeks of operation sometimes doubled and trebled the population of great areas.

In 1865, Kansas had a population of 136,000 and its per capita tax was $1.60. In 1870, with the Santa Fe about a year old, taxes had risen to $2.22 and the state debt was up. Five years later taxes had dropped to $1.37 and, in 1877, after eight years of expansion, there were 700,000 people in the state and taxes were down to $1.12. Moreover, the state was completely solvent and had in its treasury more than enough to pay off all its debts.

The story of the Arkansas Valley, from Hutchinson, Kansas, up to Pueblo, Colorado—a typical Santa Fe development—is similar. The valley, before the railroad came, had 2,019 people along its thousand miles of fertility. In 1876 it had 45,868; in '77 it had 67,450. In 1872 its tilled acreage was 7,000. Five years later the figure was 600,000 acres under crop. It was a development, that, for speed never has been equaled anywhere on earth.

Getting a little ahead of the story: in one year—1877—the Larned, Kansas, land office parceled out 600,000 acres to more than 5,000 settlers. The Wichita office handed out 400,000 acres to thirty-five hundred pioneer farmers. The land had been there, waiting, for years. Anyone could have had it. No one wanted it. There was no way to make a living on it without cheap, certain and reasonably speedy transportation. The market would not absorb the old high freight charges; the settlers could not possibly afford to buy goods wagoned slowly out from the east—freights were higher than the cost of the goods in the first place.

The railroad changed all this almost overnight. Stagecoaches and freight wagons retreated as the track went west. They could not compete. The stages charged around twenty cents a mile; the railroad might charge five or seven cents, which seems high today, but it was cheap enough to bring life to wastelands. Stages made a few miles a day; trains made twenty miles an hour. People could not exist as farmers along a stage line; they could prosper within a few miles of railroad track.

Even the promise of a railroad was enough to start a boom. As often as it blueprinted a town along its pathway, the road found one waiting for it when it arrived.

Slowly the panic passed. Prospectors were filtering into the Colorado canyons, opening up silver mines, gold mines. Settlers were starting to people the prairies again, led from many parts of the world by the land department, as we shall shortly see. Money was a little easier. If the Santa Fe could get into the Colorado mining country, it might be able to make a few dollars freighting supplies back and forth. And there was a strange new character abroad: the train-tourist. Maybe he could be developed.

The track went down past historic Cimarron.

There are two Cimarrons in this story, and they should be kept distinct. Cimarron, Kansas, is eighteen miles west of Dodge City and named for the Cimarron crossing of the Arkansas River. It was near the spot where the old trail sent out a southwestern branch which led through the sandhills, crossed Cimarron River and joined the main line of the old highway near Wagon Mound and Fort Union in New Mexico. The actual eastern fork was at Ingalls Station, seven miles west of the Cimarron.

The New Mexico Cimarron also is on the old trail, but it is about seventeen miles west of the present Santa Fe track along the Canadian River, thirty-two miles south of Raton. The trail here runs along the western foot of the southern thrust of the Raton Mountains; Cimarron is on a creek of the same name, which flows southeast into the Canadian River.

The pronunciation puts the accent on the last syllable. The name is Spanish and means wild, or unruly.

From Dodge City to Granada, Colorado, was 130 miles of nothing much. It hardly paid to run trains over it. Halfway there was Jerry O'Loughlin's layout. This was a twenty by twenty-four dugout, roofed with rough lumber, and did duty as a sort of pre-Harvey House. Fred, himself, would have reviled the place in the brief, harsh terms for which he became famous, but the passengers piled off and ate buffalo steaks at a dollar a throw, with some beans and a few dried apples and coffee thrown in. It was a wild stretch, and the rule was that when the winds blew the trains ran. The water was pumped by windmills and a few calm days could stall everything.

The Santa Fe bestirred itself after months of enforced inaction. Men and materials were assembled and rolled out to Granada. In

May, 1875, President Thomas Nickerson and some of the directors went out to the end of the track and there Mr. Nickerson, after some speechmaking, drove a golden spike in the first rail of the extension west. The 133-mile stretch meant a lot to Pueblo and Southeastern Colorado, and a reporter from the Pueblo *Chieftain* was there to describe the scene. Oldtimers describe him as wearing a cowboy hat over city clothes and smoking a corncob with great nonchalance during the ceremonies. After the spike was in, he stepped to the telegraph office and handed the operator a story:

"The directors of the Santa Fe have arrived and their engine is branded 'Pueblo.' President Nickerson has driven the golden spike and building will commence at once. Everything is lovely and the goose hangs high."

"That'll be $9.70, young feller," said the operator, counting the words. "Want to cut out that about the goose?"

"Send it intact," ordered the reporter loftily.

There was no wire to Pueblo. The *Chieftain* got the message via Topeka, to which it was sent over Santa Fe wire; thence to Denver over a Union Pacific wire; and then down to Pueblo over an old government line.

A day later the terriers were laying track on the new grade that was heading west to Las Animas and West Las Animas.

The Santa Fe's graders and tracklayers ate heartily from supplies brought into their camp by a young hunter with light hair and keen blue eyes. He had a price list, a copy of which has been preserved: young beef, five cents a pound; big deer, $2.50; goat $1; dressed sheep, $1.50; wild turkey, fifty cents.

The youngster, who was seventeen, had little trouble in shooting his big deer and wild turkey. He had inherited his skill from his uncle—Kit Carson—after whom he had been named.

To build from West Las Animas to Pueblo, the Colorado & New Mexico Railroad had been incorporated July 5, 1873—but the track had got to Granada, Colorado, July 4th. The C. & N. M., with the Pueblo & Salt Lake and the Arkansas Valley, were now merged into the Pueblo & Arkansas Valley, a Santa Fe subsidiary.

At West Las Animas, the Santa Fe, P. & A. V. and the Kansas

Pacific came into collision: the prize was the line on to Pueblo. The fight had started in Bent County, Colorado, where, on Tuesday, December 15, 1874, an election was held to vote bonds for the Santa Fe. Whisky and gunmen were rushed down from Denver, which favored the Kansas Pacific, and the election went against the bonds. The Bent County people, angry, held another election March 16, 1875, and passed the bond issue of $150,000.

Then the K.P. rushed men and teams to West Las Animas and started grading furiously toward Pueblo on the survey line of the Santa Fe. Where the two lines crossed, there were battles between grading and surveying crews. The Santa Fe sent out a call for help, and Pueblo, which favored the line against Gould, sent armed posses to seize and hold strategic points in the line. The K.P. relied on a plat of its proposed line, as evidence in an injunction suit. The Santa Fe showed that this line was located, in reality, on the north side of the Arkansas; the Santa Fe was building up the south bank. The K.P. then paralleled the S.F. for twenty-five miles from West Las Animas to Timpas Creek, and there, beside the Santa Fe, the town of La Junta was born. But the K.P. couldn't get enough business and the track was finally torn up.

The K.P. which paralleled the S.F. from Topeka by building along the Kansas River, to the north; it sought to stop the Santa Fe from getting to Pueblo by dropping south and building up the Arkansas ahead of the Santa Fe.

And it had lost the race.

CHAPTER SIX

THE PRAIRIE BLOOMS

A RAILROAD TODAY hauls passengers one way and hopes they'll come back the same way. Back in the '70s the Santa Fe hauled them one way—west—and hoped they'd stay put. If they wanted to be hauled back, it was because they had gone broke in a drought, a grasshopper plague or from various other troubles. They had to be carried free, along with their household goods and breaking plows. This, in turn, meant that the returning pilgrims went back home to Ohio, Pennsylvania or Indiana, spreading horrendous stories of life in the Cottonwood and Arkansas Valleys—which didn't help sell any of the 3,000,000 acres of land the Santa Fe had for sale.

To sell this property the road hired D. L. Lakin soon after its founding, and made him its land commissioner. Lakin did sell some land, but if it wasn't grasshoppers it was drought, and if it was neither, it was buffalo stampedes or cattle drives trampling down the first cash corn crop. He did his best, but he became ill and resigned. A. E. Touzalin, an Englishman who was serving as general passenger agent, took over the job for two years and then quit to go to the Burlington. The work then was undertaken by Colonel A. S. Johnson, a native Kansan, the son of a missionary. It was under his twenty-year administration that the great land settlement projects of the Santa Fe were carried out. He served until midsummer, 1890. The department was abolished eight years later, its work accomplished.

But you can still buy hundreds of square miles of land from the Santa Fe for a few nickels an acre, or lease it for a penny or two an acre a year. It's no great bargain at those prices, either—in case you still believe in those "enormously-valuable-land-grants myths."

After Lakin and his parties had surveyed, staked out and made descriptions of the property, the land department started out to sell it. It got lists of prospective buyers from Emigrant Aid Societies and other organizations and printed bales of descriptive literature. It wasn't just a case of selling land; it had to stay sold and become productive to make any money for the road. The literature told the truth and discouraged buyers who didn't seem to have the stuff in them to make good.

There were no stenographers or typists then and all the "direct-mail" advertising was handwritten. Competition was keen, because the Burlington and the Union Pacific were land-heavy too, and trying to get some cash out of it. The Santa Fe had little money to spare, so brains and ingenuity had to take the place of dollars.

A small army of agents went into action, mainly on a commission basis. Reduced fares were offered homeseekers. Special trains were run and buyers offered eleven years to pay at low-interest rates. Agents circulated through Eastern states, organizing parties of land-hungry families and dry-nursing them out into the valleys along the Santa Fe route. But this didn't get the country settled fast enough, and somebody suddenly thought about Europe.

Books about Kansas and the Santa Fe lands were printed in German, Dutch, Swedish, French, Danish and Russian and given wide circulation abroad. The result was that several foreign colonies were set up along the line.

At Ellinwood, the Germania Colony was founded in 1873 by families from Germany, Austria and Switzerland. At Great Bend was the Gnadenthal Colony—a German-Russian settlement on Walnut Creek. More Germans from Westphalia, Hanover and Oldenburg settled around Offerle and Spearville, farther west. Pawnee Rock was founded by Swedes in 1874 and grew to be about 360 square miles in area.

The British aristocracy, including some members of Queen Victoria's family, invested in the Western Land & Cattle Company, which bought seventy-two square miles of Chase County for $150,-

000 and used the land to fatten cattle from the trail before shipping them to market.

There were thousands of farmers in Europe, however, who didn't read books but who wanted a new start in a new country. Touzalin, then head of the land department puzzled over how to get in touch with these people in Russia, France, Germany and England and then ran into Carl B. Schmidt. Schmidt was a German who had come to Kansas when he was twenty-one, had prospered and was then running an agricultural implement store in Topeka. He had, it turned out, spent much of his spare time writing to friends in Germany, telling them what a swell place Kansas was. This had created a small, pent-up demand for Kansas land. Touzalin made Schmidt general foreign colonization agent.

This was at a time, remember, when anyone who wanted to settle in the United States just took a boat from Hamburg, Leghorn or Liverpool and walked ashore in Boston, Philadelphia or New York. That was all there was to it; the welcome mat was out for one and all.

After Touzalin quit, Colonel Johnson kept Schmidt on. This naturally started a battle between the Touzalin-Burlington and Johnson-Santa Fe forces, with the former fighting to get European farmers up into Nebraska and the latter battling to get them for Kansas. The fight came to a head over a curious sect of people called Mennonites, who turned out to be the best assets the grain country ever acquired.

They were curious mainly in that they just wanted to be let alone and were willing to haul out and go traveling any time people interfered with them. They believed in adult baptism, the simple life and getting along with the neighbors without resort to bloodshed. They were also crackerjack farmers and colonists. A few thousand of them settled on its lands would be a prize for any railroad. Johnson put Schmidt to work capturing Mennonites.

They were an ancient sect, getting their name from Menno Simonis, a former Catholic priest who organized them in South Holland. Because they wouldn't fight or conform to medieval religious rules, they were forced out of Holland and into Germany, where they fared little better. So they sent out scouts to search for places where they might live in peace. Some came to America and won an invitation from William Penn.

And that is how the first American Mennonite colonies started.

Other scouts got a bid from Catherine II of Russia, a German girl herself, who thought it wouldn't do her South Russian subjects any harm to learn a little good farming. Catherine promised each Mennonite family 175 acres of land, no military service and only nominal taxes. Four hundred families took her at her word, moved to the Crimea and did right well for themselves—and the Crimea—for a hundred years.

But in 1870 a new Czar, Alexander, got tough, broke Catherine's promises and the Mennonites decided to hitch and haul. Some American Mennonites already had moved from Pennsylvania and Illinois into Kansas, and these paved the way for the first migrations from Russia.

In Kansas, meanwhile, was a man named Cornelius Jansen, busily picking out land for the newcomers. Jansen, himself a Mennonite, had been Prussian consul at Berdiansk, Russia, near the Mennonite colony, and had been tossed out by Alexander for sticking up for his fellow-religionists. He came to Kansas and selected about 100,-000 acres of land in Marion, McPherson, Harvey and Reno Counties.

News of all this got to St. Petersburg and the Czar hurriedly tried to interest the Mennonites in some free land along the Amur River, in Far Eastern Russia, alleging it was as good as Kansas. They weren't interested and, although returning scouts told of droughts and grasshoppers between Topeka and Great Bend, the people decided to take a chance.

In September, 1874, some 1,900 Mennonites arrived in New York with $2,000,000 in gold drafts. Agents for several railroads met them, looking with interest at the sturdy, solemn-faced new settlers. Men and boys were dressed alike, with wide hats, sober coats and long tight trousers. Women were clad in long-sleeved, high-necked bodices and wide skirts that swept the ground. The little girls in exact duplicates of their mothers' dresses, peered shyly from beneath brims of poke bonnets. They wore only dark colors and neither men nor women used buttons, preferring hooks and eyes. The hair of men and boys was long, and the men wore heavy beards.

With them they brought no gewgaws. There was not a musical instrument in the party; not a rug; not an easy chair. And, of course, no mirrors.

One of their leaders approached the Santa Fe agent. "We are the Amish," he said. "Where is Kansas?"

Some fast work on the part of the Santa Fe boys got them aboard a train for Topeka, where they arrived September 23rd. They were housed in a new factory, into which, only a few machines had been moved. Governor Osborn held a reception for them at the State House and they started a small boom in the town. It was after the panic. Prices were low, cash was scarce and the immigrants had money to spend.

The Santa Fe had chartered a Red Star liner to bring over the colonists' equipment and household goods from Berdiansk to Philadelphia. It came out on a special train, along with small armies of agents for other roads, all trying to lure the new settlers away to Nebraska, Iowa or Missouri. The Santa Fe met all offers. It cut rates and land prices. It promised to haul building material free for a year. It handed out passes to ministers and scouts. Finally the Mennonites had one objection left.

They went to Carl Schmidt and wanted assurance that Kansas would exempt them from military service. Schmidt took a deep breath—and promised. He made good, too. The legislature amended the law to read that any member of a religious sect which forbade bearing of arms might be exempt from service if he made an affidavit before May 1st each year. This law satisfied the colonists. Schmidt translated it into German and sent copies to the remaining Mennonites in Russia. It started more families on their way—and gave Kansas an edge.

It has since been calculated that, what with cuts in the price of its land, free services and general benevolence the Santa Fe made no profit at all on the sale of around 100,000 acres to the Mennonites. But it did set up colonies of hardworking, thrifty farmers who, in later years, built a heavy freight business for the road.

They did more than that. They popularized the growing of hard red Turkey wheat in the United States. This wheat has meant millions of dollars to the country. It was not, however, introduced in this country by the Mennonites. French settlers had been growing it for some time in Marion County, Kansas, but with little luck because the mills couldn't handle it. There was, in fact, little wheat grown in Kansas, which was looked upon as a corn state.

Twenty-five bushels of this seed wheat were brought along with the new settlers. A Mennonite pioneer, Bernhard Warkentin, put up a small waterpower mill on the Little Arkansas near Halstead in Harvey County at about the time mills were changing over from burrs to rollers. The rollers would handle the hard wheat and in a few years Kansas had become a top hard-wheat state in which Mennonites and other settlers, as well as the Santa Fe, prospered.

Besides the hard wheat, the Mennonites, being a tree-loving people, brought the mulberry, the wild olive and the apricot. The mulberry was valuable for its fruit and for hedges and fuel. Also they hoped to develop the silkworm but didn't.

They first settled in small replicas of the villages they had left in Russia. Houses were of sod or lumber, or a combination of the two. Several acres of shade trees and orchard surrounded the individual homes. There was a schoolhouse in the village center, which did duty also as a church. This almost communal life didn't last long and there is today little trace of the Mennonite towns that once dotted the prairie. There is no trace at all of the famous "long furrows" they turned with breaking plows straight across the land from one settlement to another to guide travelers. Some of the furrows were twenty miles long.

So they lived and worked in Kansas and, when strangers asked the secret of their farming successes, they gravely replied: "We plow the dew under—morning and evening."

They won the respect of their fellow-settlers in the Sunflower State, and twenty years after they came, the Lawrence *Record* wrote of them:

Through all the changes that these years have brought, the Mennonites have neither turned to the right hand nor to the left. They abided and toiled in Marion, McPherson and Harvey Counties. Within the same space of time smart Americans of the Kansas vintage have engineered booms in California, opened mines in the mountains of Colorado and New Mexico, helped rear the magic cities of Seattle and Portland, called with lusty voice for the opening of Indian lands.

But the Mennonites went on tilling their 100,000 acres of land bought of the Santa Fe Railroad, building houses, barns, granaries, setting out orchards and forest trees and raising stock. Day after day the Mennonites came in with their wheat. The Farmers' Alliance holds its secret noiseless session and nothing breaks the silence save the chuck of the Mennonites' wheat-laden wagons. The wild-eyed orator incites hearers to boycott the press and asks them to appeal to the arbitrament of arms—but the Mennonite keeps coming in with wheat. While the dung-hill statesman explains how the government robs the masses—the Mennonite comes in with wheat.

With settlement well under way, passengers taking No. 1 Mail & Express out to the front on the west end found track gangs and grading crews shoving the line along the north bank of the Arkansas River toward Pueblo, Colorado.

In the blizzard of '74, the road from Dodge to Granada was blocked for twenty-four days, which was a break for the Honorable Zebulon Kidwell. Mr. Kidwell, as a government transportation expert, had reported to a railroad commission in Washington on February 21, 1856, on the possibilities of operating trains across the plains. His conclusion was that from the midwest to the foothills of the Rockies, about 800 miles, trains would be stopped by storms in November and could not be "relieved" until the following May. He added: "To talk of doing business in the winter season on a road through such a region—though every conductor were a Kit Carson and every passenger a Frémont—would seem to be idle and preposterous."

Of a route farther to the south, the experts were equally pessimistic. Even old Senator Thomas H. Benton of Missouri said the Arizona and New Mexico deserts over which the Santa Fe later built, were so desolate "that even a wolf could not make his living." Regardless of the wolves' troubles, the railroad did. And if few passengers today are Fremonts, fewer conductors are Kit Carsons.

The winter blizzards and the droughts and grasshopper plagues of summer did not daunt the incoming settlers. Landseeking parties came from all over the east. A typical one gathered 1,400 homesteaders at Topeka, where they were met by Colonel Johnson and our friend Major Tom Anderson, now with the Santa Fe and convinced Colonel Holliday had been right in his large claims for the future of the Santa Fe.

The homeseekers were dined, bedded down, and next morning taken on a special train which ran slowly, so that its passengers could have a good look at the country. Settlements stopped west of Peace, a Quaker village northwest of Hutchinson, Kansas, now called Sterling. Beyond Peace, anyone who wished could get off and choose his acreage. "Land-exploring tickets" were good anywhere up to Kinsley. All a pilgrim had to do was point out the land he fancied and it was checked off on the map.

Some of the towns along the line, especially the cattle-shipping points, did not welcome settlers, who ran fences, plowed the sod and generally interfered with the wild, free life of the trail. You could get yourself shot at here and there by letting it be known you were a nester, a barbed-wire salesman or a manufacturer of posthole diggers. But this antipathy to settlers could be a blessing in disguise to land agents once in a while. It was Agent D. N. Heizer, later Mayor of Colorado Springs, who discovered this.

He had taken a party out to Great Bend and was showing the people around, north of there. It was raining, for a change, and it took four horses to drag a democrat wagon through the mud—a circumstance Mr. Heizer used to discredit those stories of Kansas droughts. Some of the land-lookers had been worrying about droughts, but that evening Mr. Heizer had a worry of his own. He found that a dentist in his party was trying to lure about forty of the landseekers away from Great Bend and up to Dodge, hoping to work them into a nucleus of some dental business.

Heizer had no interest in land around Dodge, and after arguing his case for Great Bend without result finally, in despair wired his friend, Mayor Dick Colly, at Dodge: "Homesteaders on way. Please show every courtesy and attention." Dick, he figured, would understand.

The dentist and his following pulled out for Dodge on No. 3 in the morning and, on arriving there, were met by a reception committee headed by Mayor Colly and Marshal Ed Masterson—Ed cheerfully unwitting of the fate in store for him three weeks later when he was shot to death. Today he was just helping out the boys. The truculent dentist having announced himself as head man of the party, Ed patted him over and found a gun. It would have been difficult not to have found a gun on anybody in Western Kansas—but this one was concealed, a misdemeanor in Dodge, where folks were required, by the mores of the times, to display their weapons openly. The dentist was thereupon arrested and locked up.

The remaining forty homesteaders then found themselves the main topic of talk at a mass meeting of cowhands and other stern characters at which the word lynching was freely bandied about.

This was enough for them. A spokesman told the meeting that he and his fellow pilgrims had decided that land around Great Bend was much better than around Dodge, and when did No. 2 go east? The mass meeting then dissolved, the tooth jerker was fined $10 and the whole party trekked back to Great Bend where Mr. Heizer met them with simulated astonishment. He sold them 60,000 acres north of town where homesteaders were not only safe but welcome.

Town boosters were called "boomers" in those days, although later the word, especially among railroaders, came to have the meaning of a transient worker, as against the "home guard." Every settlement had its boomers, usually led by the mayor and local clergy, who were fond of inviting pilgrims into church, Sundays, and putting in a few words about the climate, social advantages and general fertility. Sometimes the boomers were a trifle too enthusiastic, because in the drought years of '74 and '75 the Santa Fe had hauled huge tonnages free to save its settlers. During two springs the road also handed out thousands of bushels of seed grain, free, to its farmers—most of them repaying the loan after a good crop a year or two later. Crops came back in '75 with 80,000,000 bushels of corn and 13,000,000 bushels of wheat. Kansas was on her way.

In several single years since then, Kansas has produced more wheat than all of Canada. It has at various times produced more than one-fifth of the national supply. And most of this has been hauled by the Santa Fe.

For years there had been argument which town would become the great river terminal, but by the '70s Kansas City seemed to have won. The Santa Fe got there October 1, 1875, by a merger or two and the leasing of the Kansas City, Topeka & Western—itself the result of more mergers. Once on the river and with terminal facilities, the Santa Fe ventured no farther east for years.

Soon after it had its line operating to Kansas City, the Santa Fe ran a special train between that town and the capital at Topeka. The train carried early editions of the *Kansas City Times* and brought back copy for the paper from the *Times* legislative correspondents. Just before the session opened, a *Times* reporter scooped his rivals and got an advance copy of the governor's speech, which was important, for some forgotten reason. Not trusting the speech to the wire, the newspaperman hopped the eastbound special just as it was steaming out of Topeka. The governor's secretary discovered the plot and wired the cops at Lawrence to stop the train, take off the reporter and rescue the message.

The cops got the wire just as the special highballed through. Commandeering a switch engine they set out in pursuit, but the special was too fast for the switcher and at De Soto they stopped and telegraphed ahead to Kansas City. The reporter, a resourceful man named Pangborn, himself stopped the train on the city's outskirts, jumped off and raced to his office in a livery hack. More cops met the train at the terminal—but they had lost the race.

"The Santa Fe produced a hardy breed of railroaders and this race provided the sort of excitement in which they seemed to revel. Many a thriller was to be staged on the Santa Fe in future years."

Conductor John H. Bender was working his train west of Dodge one evening when he came to a large, rough character named Bill Evans.

"Ticket, please!"

"Here's my ticket. Pass on!" growled Bill, drawing a .45.

Bender said nothing, finished collecting his tickets, went to the baggage car, got a Winchester and came back. He stuck the muzzle of the rifle coldly against Bill's neck; and pulled the cord. The train slowed.

"You're riding on an expired ticket, Bill," he said. "Get off!"

Bill tramped five miles to Cimarron—and always bought a ticket after that.

Dodge didn't really get going as a cow town until some time after the Santa Fe came. Some of the cattle drives still stopped at Great Bend, to the eastward, and it was only when the settlers started to bust sod and string wire west of the Bend that Dodge came into its own.

A traveler in '74 described Dodge as just a row of frame buildings north of the Santa Fe track. The rest was vacant lots covered with buffalo hides staked down against the wind. East of town there were miles of bones, white on the prairie, with separate piles of skulls. The Dodge House was the hotel. Jake Shaefer, later billiard champion of the world, was running a saloon. The town was dead, dry and dusty all day and only livened up after supper when the hunters came in and the girls came out. For long periods the trains stopped and wyed at Dodge. Westward, the Indians tore up track, burned bridges, looted way stations.

But the line crept on to Pueblo. Train service started from Kansas City to the western front on March 1, 1874, and a day or so later, from Atchison, too. Even before this, in the summer of '73, more than 6,000 tourists had visited the Rockies, many of them to end-of-steel on the Santa Fe and then by stage into Pueblo and Trinidad.

The Colorado extension looked like a natural. In the mountains there was unlimited timber—the Santa Fe had floated down thousands of ties on the Arkansas, and Kansas settlers were in the market for lumber. Around Trinidad there was coal. Ranches were producing sheep, hides, wool and cattle. Across the main range of the Rockies there was a mining boom getting under way and miners and prospectors were calling for food, household goods, equipment and supplies. There was a two-way freight haul—and what looked like the beginning of a two-way tourist business.

The Santa Fe got out a magazine called *The Rocky Mountain Tourist and San Juan Guide*. It was aimed at settlers, miners, silver and gold hunters and tourists. The road proudly hailed itself as "The land hunters', buffalo hunters' and gold hunters' road." No. 1 became the Pueblo Mail & Express and made the run from the Missouri River to Pueblo in thirty-one hours—buffalo and cattle herds permitting.

Avery Turner, who was to go far with the Santa Fe, became the first yardmaster at Pueblo. He had a four-wheel switcher, the Vulcan, with a four-wheel tender. If not more than eight cars of freight showed up, the train was "abandoned for the day." The passenger train was a four-car affair seldom carrying more than ten or fifteen passengers of whom a third probably were deadheads. Brakemen and conductors coaled the engine—a ooOO—by carrying fuel up a board in 100-pound boxes and dumping it into the tender. This was known as steamboating. Conductors got $60 a month. Brakemen drew $45 and often doubled as wire-taps—slang for operators.

Brakemen also helped passengers get cinders out of their eyes. Standard treatment was to insert a flaxseed under the eyelid and let the cinder sleep itself out. Another early trick was to fish for the cinder with a loop of horsehair, and many oldtime conductors, before the days of sealed windows and air conditioning, used to pluck horsehairs from the lapels or shoulders of passengers' coats to make cinder loops.

In later years, Santa Fe conductors carried sticks of chewing gum which they handed to cinder-in-the-eye victims who were instructed to chew one end, roll it to a point and then touch the cinder with the tapered end. They were permitted to retain the rest of the gum, either for chewing or eye relief.

Meanwhile Kansas was settling up and quieting down. There came a time when the road could advertise it was "free from bad hills and bad Indians." The Indians were being rounded up and packed off to reservations. On November 4, 1876, seventy-six squaws, braves and papooses of the Sioux tribe passed through Topeka on a train. Led by Spotted Dog, Red Tail and Fast Bear, they attracted attention when they descended to eat at the Harvey House. A Topeka reporter wrote that "They didn't know how to behave themselves," and added:

"Some of the ladies at the depot considered it a great honor to grasp these dusky murderers of the plains by the hand."

It still was a moot point whether Sheridan was right.

For a while after the Pueblo extension started to operate, the road construction crews went back along its length, rerailing with heavier steel, building better bridges, putting up permanent stations and running miles of fence. In a year the line spent $340,000 for improvements.

The road now was a bridgeline between the various Eastern lines ending at the river and the Denver & Rio Grande, which ran north from Pueblo to Denver—and proposed building south to the Mexican border and beyond. As a bridge, the road proved profitable, netting $1,200,000 in 1876. In 1877 it ran a branch line down the Walnut Valley, thirty-one miles to Eldorado. After that, there seemed little need to expand farther east or west.

The temporary lethargy was roused on November 1, 1877, when William Barstow Strong joined the road as general manager and linked forces with Chief Engineer A. A. Robinson. They made a fighting team—and there was a fight waiting for them. Strong was a rugged Vermonter who started railroading as a station agent at Milton, Wisconsin. He worked his way up with several roads, and, like many a Santa Fe'er, came to the line from the Burlington, where he had been general superintendent.

Thomas Nickerson still presided. His first assignment for Strong was for him to go west and lay the groundwork far in advance of the front through the mountains and down into New Mexico. This progress was made possible partly by a ten strike engineered by

Colonel Johnson of the land department. In '76 the Colonel got together a great exhibit of Kansas products and sent it east to the Centennial Exposition at Philadelphia. It got a lot of attention and a lot of newspaper space, mainly because it flatly contradicted the notion, spread through the east, that Kansas was a desert overrun by grasshoppers and bad men.

Following up the exhibit with pamphlets, pictures and lectures, the Santa Fe started new land rushes to Kansas in '77 and '78. By the end of '78 it had sold 850,000 acres of land for around $4,000,000. But it had spent huge sums in chartering steamers, running special trains, sending colonizing agents to western Europe and Russia, cutting rates on lumber, household goods, farm equipment and in maintaining an army of agents and distributing thousands of descriptive bulletins. But the groundwork had been laid for some good, solid, lasting business. What the line was after was a permanent, prosperous population along its route.

To get emigrants and more miners out to the western end, the company kept publishing *The San Juan Guide*, later adding *The Rocky Mountain Tourist* full of engravings of Colorado scenery and boosts for the climate. In the Rockies more than 4,500 silver mines were flourishing. The Santa Fe cut No. 1's time from Kansas City to Pueblo to twenty-eight hours. Ten years before, it had taken two or three months by the old trail.

Emigrants rode out from Kansas City to the mountains for $20. A whole carload of household goods and livestock, with an attendant, were hauled to Pueblo in sixty hours for $100. The trip was about 634 miles.

But once off the Santa Fe the going became expensive. The narrow gauge Denver & Rio Grande charged $25 for the 175-mile run to Del Norte. Barlow & Sanderson stages got $40 for the 214 mile jaunt from Trinidad, Colorado, to Santa Fe, New Mexico—meals extra.

Out on the western end the Santa Fe was in a pocket. To the west of Pueblo the way to treasure was barred by the main range of the Rockies. To the south the way to trade at Santa Fe was grimly held by a lateral range the Spaniards called the Sangre

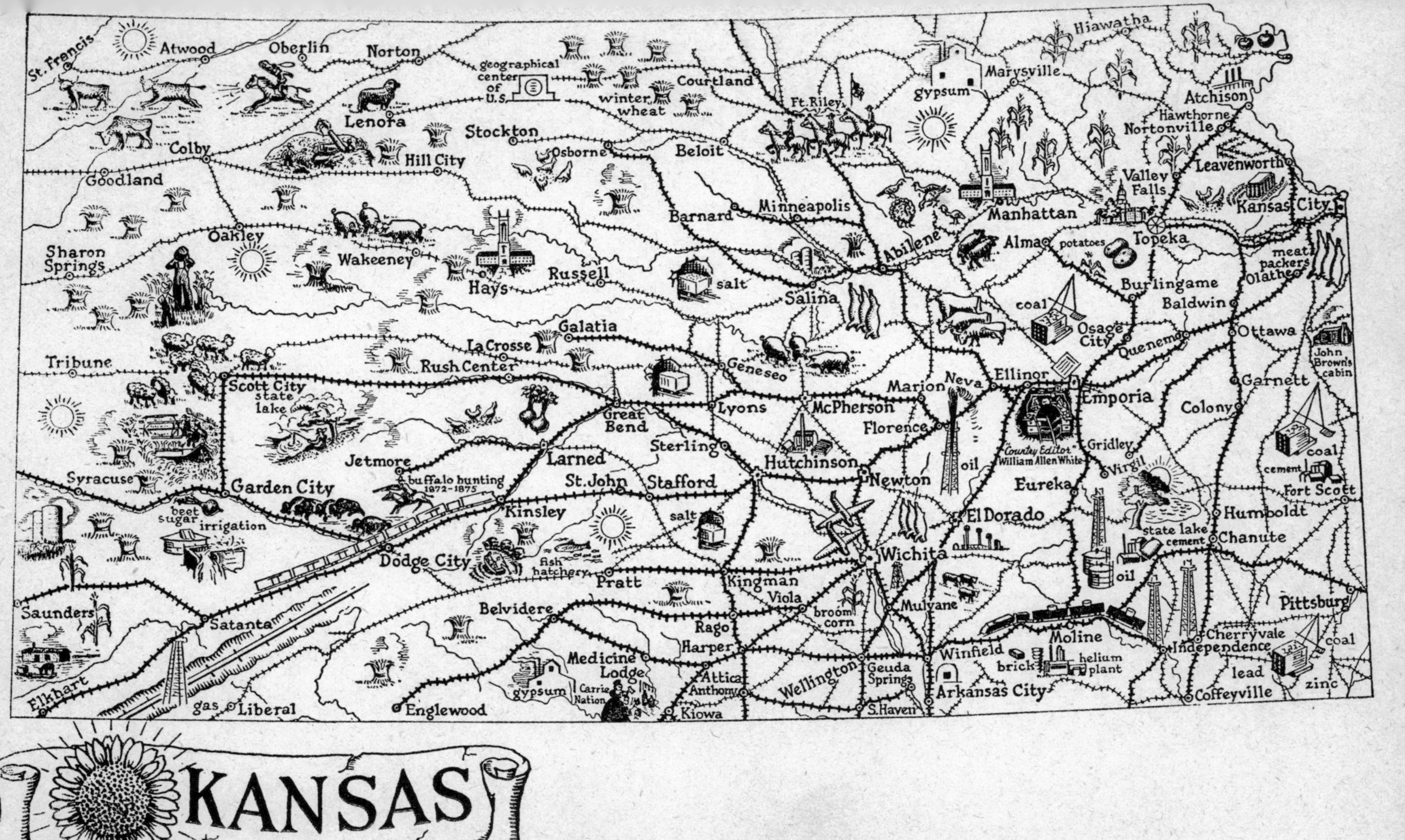
KANSAS
St. Francis
Atwood
Oberlin
Norton
geographical center of U.S.
Courtland
winter wheat
Lenora
Stockton
Hill City
Osborne
Beloit
Colby
Goodland
Barnard
Minneapolis
Oakley
Wakeeney
Hays
Russell
salt
Salina
Sharon Springs
Galatia
La Crosse
Rush Center
Geneseo
Tribune
Scott City
state lake
Great Bend
Lyons
McPherson
Marion
Neva
Ellinor
Emporia
Jetmore
Larned
Sterling
Hutchinson
Florence
Newton
Syracuse
Garden City
buffalo hunting 1872-1875
St. John
Stafford
Kinsley
beet sugar
irrigation
Dodge City
fish hatchery
Pratt
Kingman
Viola
broom corn
Wichita
Mulvane
El Dorado
Eureka
oil
"Country Editor" William Allen White
Saunders
Satanta
Belvidere
Rago
Harper
Medicine Lodge
Attica
Anthony
Wellington
Geuda Springs
S. Haven
Winfield
Arkansas City
brick
Moline
helium plant
gypsum
Carrie Nation
Elkhart
gas
Liberal
Englewood
Kiowa
Ft. Riley
gypsum
Marysville
Hiawatha
Atchison
Hawthorne
Nortonville
Valley Falls
Leavenworth
Kansas City
Manhattan
Abilene
Alma
potatoes
Topeka
meat packers
Olathe
Burlingame
Baldwin
coal
Osage City
Quenemo
Ottawa
John Brown's cabin
Garnett
Colony
Gridley
Virgil
coal
cement
Fort Scott
Humboldt
state lake
cement
Chanute
oil
Pittsburg
Cherryvale
Independence
coal
lead
zinc
Coffeyville

de Cristo and the old trappers called the Snowies. Apart from these barriers were two hardy opponents: General William J. Palmer and his narrow gauge Denver & Rio Grande, and Collis P. Huntington and his Southern Pacific. Both Palmer and Huntington were hard, resourceful fighters, but without them the task of climbing the mountains would have been tough to undertake. The Santa Fe's men, up to now, had had it fairly easy, following the gentle slopes of the Arkansas across Kansas and eastern Colorado.

The Denver & Rio Grande ran from Denver to Pueblo, but General Palmer, a Civil War veteran who took a personal pride in the line, hoped to extend it north to intersect the Northern Pacific and the Great Northern, and south to El Paso connecting with the Mexican Central into Mexico City. This seemed like a sound plan. As a bridge line, the road would cut across five or six east-west transcontinentals and thereby garner a lot of short-haul business.

Palmer naturally felt that his Colorado-owned line ought to have the rich and growing mining business. He organized to bar the Santa Fe from building up the deep, narrow canyon of the Arkansas, the one gateway into the mountain country that is now known as the Royal Gorge.

To the south, across Raton Mountain, ran the old Santa Fe Trail and along it still rumbled the wagons, using a toll road owned by an old frontiersman named Dick Wootton. This branch of the trail left the Santa Fe track at Otero, swung southwest through Trinidad and then up over the great lava heap of the mountain and then down to Las Vegas, New Mexico. The mountain flattened out about thirty-five miles to the east and the logical route would have followed this lower country. By taking the hill route, however, the Santa Fe got to Trinidad and the coal mines around that part of the country.

Otero was named for Don Miguel Otero, the last of the Spanish Santa Fe traders. It was renamed La Junta—The Junction—and surveys headed for Raton. But to get into New Mexico required permission of the territorial legislature—and, it began to appear—the Southern Pacific. General Manager Strong boarded a coach at

La Junta and rolled down over the old trail to Santa Fe. There were homeric battles ahead.

If there was war looming in the Rockies, there was revolution back along the line. It had been planned and won in a few short years, by a little Englishman with a mustache and goatee, whose name would, in the future, be more familiar to millions of people than those of any railroad builders.

He was Frederick Henry Harvey—and some enthusiasts called him the Civilizer of the West.

C H A P T E R S E V E N

THE COMING OF FRED HARVEY

FREDERICK HENRY HARVEY was the son of a Scottish-English couple, born in London, June 27, 1835. In 1850, when young Cyrus Holliday was getting ready to become a Pennsylvania lawyer, Fred Harvey left home. He had $10 and a ticket from Liverpool to New York on a sailing ship. A few days after landing he got a job in the Smith & McNeill restaurant and bar at 229 Washington Street. He started at the bottom. The pay was $2 a week and meals.

Out of this, somehow, the fifteen-year-old lad managed to buy a ship ticket to New Orleans, where he fought and won a bout with yellow fever. After this he got another restaurant job and, in 1855, with a few saved dollars, went to St. Louis, found a partner and opened an eating place of his own. It was successful.

Four years later he had met, wooed and wedded pretty Barbara Sarah Mattas, a Bohemian girl born in Prague in 1842. She was his partner, Sally, for many years. The young couple ran into hard times. The war between the states wrecked the restaurant business and Harvey got a job on a river packet running to St. Joseph, Missouri. This led, in 1862, to a position on the Hannibal and St. Joseph Railroad—known, according to the custom of the time, as the Horrible and Slow Jolting.

The road was rolling the mail into St. Joe from the East and Harvey worked on the first mail cars. He set up a home in Leavenworth, Kansas and here the family made its permanent residence for many years. Two children were born and died. Five more were born and lived. They were Ford, Byron, Sibyl, Minnie and Marie.

It was rough riding on the fast mail trains of those days, and young Fred soon quit to go to work for the Burlington; he rose to be Western freight agent. His growing family increased his expenses and he took on a sideline, soliciting advertising for the Leavenworth *Times & Conservative,* making as much as $3,000 in one year. His travels as a freight agent, among other things, forced him to eat at railroad lunch stands and he soon had a fine case of dyspepsia.

In the days of stage lines passengers had to depend on roadside eating places, much as many bus passengers must today. When the first long-distance trains ran, there were few beaneries and they were all notorious. So were "railroad pie" and sandwiches and coffee. Travelers didn't complain much; what was the use? They didn't tip, either. "I'll never be back," was the thought. They got little service. "He'll never be back," said the waiter.

Early eating houses along the railroad were privately operated. They were filthy, and the food was terrible. Often, their owners were in cahoots with train crews. The charge was four bits, in advance. No sooner had the customer paid and started to eat, than the bell rang, the whistle blew and the passenger had to dash back aboard his train, most of his meal uneaten. The beanery then paid off the train crew at a dime a passenger and waited for the next victims.

This sort of thing so irked Harvey that he determined to change it. He knew something about the restaurant business and, in 1875, he got a partner, Jeff Rice. They opened two eating houses, in Hugo and Wallace, Kansas. After a few months, Harvey decided that Rice didn't come up to his standards and the two split, whacking up the cash. Fred then tried to interest the Burlington in his idea of co-operation between himself and a railroad to provide decent food for travelers. The Burlington couldn't see it.

So he went to Charles F. Morse, superintendent of the Santa Fe; he had known Morse when Morse worked on the Burlington. The superintendent, who liked good food too, thought the idea had possibilities, and gave Harvey a green board.

With the money he had out of the Rice deal Harvey bought out a small eating place run by Peter Kline in the old Topeka depot and office building. That was the first Harvey House. The Santa Fe put up the space, some materials and supplies; Harvey put up his experience and ideas.

This was the start of an association that, for years, depended on a handshake and a spoken agreement based on "Whatever is fair and right." The arrangement would hold yet, except for the fact that government rules demanded written agreements.

Harvey closed down the Topeka eating house for two days, scrubbed it thoroughly, got fresh tablecloths and napkins, polished the silver and laid in a better grade of food. Then he opened up and, within a few weeks, was doing a capacity business, not only with rail crews and passengers, but with Topeka home folks. Both the Santa Fe and Harvey decided the experiment was a success.

They decided to branch out. There was a rundown hotel at Florence, down the line. Fred and the Santa Fe took it over as a combined hotel and restaurant. Harvey had about $10,000, a considerable sum for those days. He put in $5,370 in cash and got a handshake promise from Morse he'd get it back later. He did.

Mr. and Mrs. Harvey then picked up new furniture, beds, mattresses, linen, silver and cooking equipment. It was sensational in Florence, a hamlet of about 100 people. The furniture was mainly heavy walnut and most of it is around Eastern Kansas yet. The silver came from England, the linen from Ireland. The chef came from Chicago.

Fred went up and enticed him away from the Palmer House for $5,000 a year, which made him easily the wealthiest man in Florence. This chef let himself go. He became a sort of dream-boy to the farmers. He paid $1.50 a dozen for prairie chickens, six bits for a dozen quail, a dime a pound for butter, and equally high prices for vegetables and fruit.

The meals at the Florence House soon became famous, and travelers started stopping at the place overnight, if they could get there. This, in turn, brought business to the Santa Fe because, in that country, it was the only road on which people could get anything decent to eat, plus Harvey service.

While all this was going on, Harvey still was working for the

Burlington as a traveling agent. He quit in 1882. On May 28, 1893, a verbal agreement gave him control of all hotels and restaurants on the Santa Fe system. . . . When he died in 1901, he and the system owned and operated fifteen hotels, forty-seven restaurants, thirty dining cars and a San Francisco Bay ferry.

He has been given credit by some hearty eaters for "civilizing the West." Doubtless he helped, but some of the honors should go to the famous Harvey Girls, who took a demure decorum into the wild places. Most of them married well-to-do Westerners and carried into their homes the culinary niceties and social poise that distinguished Harvey House staffs.

The Santa Fe got its Harvey Girls by running ads in newspapers all over the East and Middle West. These called for "Young women of good character, attractive and intelligent, 18 to 30." No experience was necessary, but the good character requirement meant what it said. In most places the girls were under the stern eye of a matron, slept in dormitories and had to be in by ten o'clock, except on special occasions.

The girls promised, when signing, not to marry for a year, but love often found a way. Harvey accepted the frequent weddings philosophically and often staged parties for the newlyweds. The experience was that if a girl got through her first six months at Dodge City or Las Vegas or Albuquerque unwed she—and Harvey—were pretty safe for three or four years. Harvey always congratulated a girl who got through her first half year without an engagement ring.

Many teachers, wearying of the schoolroom and yearning for the wild, free life of the West—advertised in some Santa Fe literature of the period as "unrestrained by the crass stupidities of boiled-shirt civilization"—became Miss Harveys. They were not extra welcome, usually being unwilling to conform to the strict discipline and the direction of the matron.

The standard uniform included black shoes and stockings, a plain black dress with an "Elsie collar," and a black bow. The hair had to be plainly done and ornamented only with a white ribbon neatly tied. The hours usually were regular, but in cases of delayed trains the staff was expected to work any hours to get the passengers fed. For all this the starting wage was $17.50 a month, plus tips, board and sleeping quarters, which was generous for the day. Most passengers left tips, and, as each girl waited on eight or ten people several times a day, her income was ample. Most girls saved considerable money.

Waitresses usually married well, many of them becoming brides of Santa Fe engineers, conductors and station agents. It has been estimated that about 5,000 girls, of good character, attractive and intelligent, became wives as the result of acquaintanceships struck up in Harvey dining rooms and lunch counters.

There is a Western legend that more than 4,000 babies were christened Fred or Harvey or both, after these marriages, but there is no proof of this, and the original story was an invention of the late Elbert Hubbard.

In addition to the certified waitresses, there were hundreds of amateurs who, unable to pass the strict Harvey tests for neatness, poise and morality, struck out boldly on their own and got jobs in frontier restaurants by claiming to be Harvey Girls. The behavior of some of these brought no sheen to the Harvey escutcheon, but nothing could be done about it. It was one of the penalties of success.

So was a great deal of the poetry written about Harvey Houses and Harvey Girls. An early specimen was produced in 1895, by J. C. Davis, of Devore, California, described by the editor who printed his poem as "possessed of the Divine afflatus." Mr. Davis wrote:

Harvey Houses, don't you savvy; clean across the old Mojave,
On the Santa Fe they've strung 'em like a string of Indian beads,
We all couldn't eat without 'em but the slickest things about 'em,
Is the Harvey skirts that hustle up the feeds.

At first, Harvey meals were a straight four bits, but less at lunch counters where there was not the same variety of food. For fifty cents you got all you wanted of the finest eatables money could buy, including thick steaks for breakfast, with eggs atop if desired. These, with a platter of hashed brown potatoes formed a firm foundation for the ensuing six-high stack of pan-sized wheat cakes with maple syrup, topped off with apple pie and coffee.

Indeed, a Santa Fe traveler today might request such a breakfast in a Harvey diner, and get it, without being made to feel for an instant that he was at all queer in his eating habits. He would not get it for four bits, though.

A curiosity of eating at a Harvey House during a train stop was that the eaters always felt they had plenty of time and might toy leisurely with their food. This was the result of a formula and some split-second timing. It started on the train miles away, when a brakeman went through the cars finding out how many passengers wanted breakfast at the next meal stop, and whether they wanted dining-room or lunch-counter service. This information was wired ahead.

A mile from the station the engineer blew a signal and an immaculate attendant stepped outside the restaurant and bonged a gong once. This was the signal for the waitresses to place the first course on the tables under the inspecting eye of the headwaitress, who was known as the "wagon boss." As the train stopped the gong bonged several times and the passengers dashed for the tables. They had to be decently dressed, and for those without coats Mr. Harvey provided sober alpaca jackets in assorted sizes. These had to be donned by coatless patrons, the waitresses being under strict orders to ignore occasional boors who made scenes and demanded their rights.

Meanwhile the steaks were smoking in the kitchen and the platters of ham and eggs were sizzling. Having seated themselves and decorously eaten their mush or fruit, the patrons were asked whether they preferred coffee, tea, iced tea or milk. The waitress then fiddled with the cup before each patron and went away. Then there appeared the "drink girl," who magically poured the patron's preferred drink without even asking.

This was accomplished by a cup-code. If the waitress left the cup right side up in its saucer, that meant coffee. Upside down meant hot tea. Upside down but tilted against the saucer meant iced tea. Upside down, away from the saucer meant milk. Patrons who changed the positions of their cups were out of luck.

In most places the manager himself bore aloft the huge platters of sizzling steaks, forking them out with a lavish hand. Or, for lunch and dinner, it might be pork chops, roast beef or mutton. Harvey maintained, and the company still maintains in the mid-forties, experts in Kansas City and Chicago to pounce on the best cuts, and some of them became so expert they could look at a white-face on the hoof and tell his weight and tenderness to a pound and degree.

But whatever the entree was at lunch or dinner, it was not what the passenger had had yesterday or would have tomorrow. Menus were sent out from headquarters in four-day batches, so that if chicken hash was the main dish the first day out, something else would be offered at similar meals for the next three days. No Harvey patron ever complained of monotony. Or much of anything else.

Once in a while there was a kick, however. In the fall of 1897 a traveler named Jones dined at La Junta and, spurning the steaks, demanded beans. Under the Harvey rule, he got beans, but was charged the price of the regular meal.

He protested that beans were worth only a dime, but the manager held out for six bits, the standard price of a meal at the time. The customer went away sore and in a few hours the House got a collect wire and paid eighty-five cents to learn that Mr. Jones was still sore. Hours later it got another wire from San Francisco and paid $2.25 to learn Mr. Jones' sentiment and several days afterward it paid $5.67 to be apprised from Mexico City that: "I still think you charged me too much for those beans. Jones."

Mr. Harvey, a man of principle, paid the charges but refused to alter his rules.

The coming of a Harvey House to a Western town was not always regarded by local restaurant men as a direct gift from heaven. Since the House was part of the railroad it got all its supplies freight-free and its food almost always was of a much better grade and variety than the local product. This meant that it was able to serve better and fresher food in more attractive surroundings for lower prices than the home-town folks. And, in turn, it drew trade not only from train crews and passengers but from townspeople.

The result was that in some places the restaurant owners banded together to make it tough for Harvey. Since both the Santa Fe and Fred wished to keep on good terms with the home folks, they stressed that the restaurants at the depots were for the convenience of passengers and employees primarily. But in practice the houses were open to anyone with a few dimes—and a coat.

Mr. Harvey's right to enforce his no-coat-no-eat order was the subject of some long and bitter litigation in Oklahoma. There, Chairman Campbell Russell of the State Corporation Commission was refused a meal in the Harvey House at Purcell when he refused to don a coat, stoutly maintaining that coat-wearing was against Sooner custom. The case went up to the State Supreme Court which, after long deliberation, upheld Mr. Harvey and chided Mr. Russell.

The court pointed out that were Mr. Harvey ordered to admit people without coats he might be confronted by people without shirts, or even in breechclouts. Civilization, the judge hinted, was on a fairly precarious basis in Oklahoma as it was, and any civilizing influences should be warmly encouraged.

The only place where the coat rule was not insisted upon was Santa Fe, where the informal spirit of the artists and writers who flocked there, together with the traditions left by the caballeros, made it largely ignored, even in La Fonda, the luxury hotel. What law could not do in Oklahoma, custom accomplished in New Mexico.

There was for a long time another Harvey rule. Any child who was served in a high chair ate for half price. This rule was taken advantage of by many thrifty parents, who managed to get some extraordinarily large children into the chairs. Often, the kids themselves protested and some of the larger ones overbalanced in their rage. When prices went up after 1918 adults had to pay $1 for a meal, but kids still ate for six bits, frequently consuming more than the $1 customers.

Train crews were given coupons entitling them to eat for half price which, in early days, meant a four-course meal equal to any served in Delmonico's, for a quarter. In most Western towns these coupons became a sort of secondary currency and were accepted for all sorts of purchases "uptown." With a few of them a townie could give a banquet at the Harvey House for a couple of dollars.

The first trains over the plains had conditioned settlers to beware and back away at the sound of a bell, and so, when the first Harvey Houses were opened there was some confusion. Soon after the bell-ringer at Lakin, Kansas, had taken his stance at the entrance to the eating place one noon, a farmer came sneaking in through the kitchen, beaming.

"He warned me away from the front door," said the settler, "but I came in the back, anyway." He was given an alpaca coat and served with the best in the house.

In early days, and for many years, Harvey often led the grand march at the Friday-night dances, at which the matron stood at the door collecting tickets, inspecting patrons for neatness and sobriety and indicating the basket in which they were required to deposit shootin' irons and edged weapons.

Cowpokes occasionally made trouble, desiring to show off by riding ponies into dining rooms and firing off pistols to astonish pilgrims aboard trains. Sometimes they demanded to be fed coatless. When the Castaneda was opened at Las Vegas, New Mexico, in 1882, some cowhands and their foreman rode into the dining room, shot off a few bottlenecks and demanded food in loud and profane language.

Mr. Harvey, who was present, maintained his dapper serenity, stepped forward and raised a white hand. "Gentlemen," he said, "ladies dine here. No swearing or foul language is permitted. You must leave quietly at once." The cowhands, shamed, walked their horses out of the room, being careful that the screen door did not slam, and their foreman later apologized for them. Mr. Harvey, never a man to hold a grudge, set the men up to a fine lunch and would accept no payment, though insisting that his guests wear coats.

A regrettable episode occurred in El Vaquero in Dodge City in the '20s when Mayor "Big Bill" Thompson of Chicago led some cowhands into the dining rooms and demanded that they be fed coatless. Mr. Thompson was a forbidding figure in those days, having recently dared King George the Fifth of England to fight barefisted with him in the Chicago Stadium—a challenge prudently ignored by the monarch—and so the cowhands got their lunch, though cringing a little under the scornful glances of the Harvey Girls.

Harvey himself was a small, compact, wiry man, and usually nervous. He made no attempt to alter the eating habits of the Americans, which he often regarded as queer, but held, himself, to the English custom. He ate a light breakfast of toast and tea, a heavy meal at noon, a light tea with lemon, at four o'clock and a high tea with meat at seven. He retired at eleven, company or not, although always pointing out to remaining guests where food and drink of high quality might be obtained in the larder of his Leavenworth home.

He disliked written agreements, holding them a sign that the contracting parties did not trust each other. He explained that when a gentleman dealt with gentlemen no writing was needed. For years he bought coffee by the carload without ever asking the price. In buying or selling, "Whatever is fair" was his code.

The coffee, incidentally, always tasted the same—and does yet, no matter where it is drunk, East or West. Years ago Harvey had the water at each of his houses analyzed and then prepared special blends and formulas so that the product would be uniform whether made from Lake Michigan water or from the Arkansas, Pecos, Rio Grande or Canadian Rivers.

Until Harvey changed it, it was railroad custom to feed passengers local products. Out of Chicago they got lake whitefish and Illinois corn; out of California they got seafood and fruit. Harvey reversed this with the aid of fast refrigerator cars often run at the head end of passenger trains. When a Chicagoan got aboard the California Limited he found a menu featuring West Coast fruit and specialties. Eastbound Coasters discovered Kansas City steaks and Chicago mutton chops while crossing the Mojave Desert.

Dining car stewards were encouraged to take a personal interest in their cars, as managers did in their dining rooms and hotels. For years, Bill Gardner, steward on the Kansas City-Chicago run, handed out a special "1001 Dressing," an improvement on the usual Thousand Island mixture. To those patrons who liked it Mr. Gardner presented a personal card with the recipe. Harvey loved this sort of thing—he would just as soon people liked to ride with Mr. Gardner as with himself. The Santa Fe got the benefit anyway.

Harvey and the railway agreed early that profit from their joint dining-car service would have to be indirect. No railroad ever made a profit from its diners except in Europe, where they were run if they paid and taken off if they didn't, regardless of the length of the run. The Santa Fe's profit had to come from increased passenger travel and from more freight business from shippers who liked Santa Fe-Harvey service. No one ever has figured out how much extra business stemmed from Fred Harvey, but it was well worthwhile. The deficits were charged up to advertising.

Some of the houses lost money, too, although the service never was cut. One hotel along the line made a continuous loss of $1,000 a month. A new manager, out for a record, sliced this to $500 by skimping on the food, and felt pretty proud until Fred came around and heard about it. Mr. Harvey discharged the man, later repenting and placing him in another hotel. The house went back to losing its customary $1,000 a month and everybody was satisfied.

The guiding principle of the organization was "Maintenance of service regardless of cost." This was no empty phrase. Here is the menu for the regular seventy-five-cent dinner aboard a Santa Fe express westbound across Kansas in 1888:

BLUE POINTS ON SHELL

ENGLISH PEAS AU GRATIN

FILETS OF WHITEFISH, MADEIRA SAUCE

POTATOES FRANCAISE

YOUNG CAPON, HOLLANDAISE SAUCE

ROAST SIRLOIN OF BEEF AU JUS — PORK WITH APPLESAUCE

TURKEY STUFFED — CRANBERRY SAUCE

MASHED POTATOES — BOILED SWEET POTATOES — ELGIN SUGAR CORN

MARROWFAT PEAS — ASPARAGUS, CREAM SAUCE

SALMI OF DUCK — QUEEN OLIVES

BAKED VEAL PIE ENGLISH STYLE

CHARLOTTE OF PEACHES, COGNAC SAUCE

PRAIRIE CHICKEN, CURRANT JELLY

SUGAR CURED HAM PICKLED LAMB'S TONGUE
LOBSTER SALAD AU MAYONNAISE
BEETS
CELERY FRENCH SLAW
APPLE PIE COLD CUSTARD A LA CHANTILLY MINCE PIE
ASSORTED CAKES BANANAS NEW YORK ICE CREAM
ORANGES CATAWBA WINE JELLY GRAPES
EDAM AND ROQUEFORT CHEESE
BENT'S WATER CRACKERS FRENCH COFFEE

Wednesday Nov. 14, 1888 *Meals 75 cents*

To maintain the standard, Harvey and his supervisors were always making "unscheduled" inspection trips, but usually these were tipped off by friendly telegraph operators. Supervisors were identified by code words such as "Potatoes due Pueblo Tuesday" which apprised manager and wagon boss that an inspector was coming. There is a legend that Harvey once came home unexpectedly from a European tour and started right out in the hope of catching the boys and girls unaware. But sounders all along the line chattered the news that "Big load brass just arrived from Europe due your station Thursday."

Mr. Harvey, on arrival, found everything bright and shining—as indeed it would have been anyway. Brightness and shininess were invariable in Harvey Houses. The tablecloths had to be immaculate, the silver polished, the crockery gleaming in the lowliest plains town no less than in Chicago or Kansas City.

This high standard applied also to the Harvey Girls who, in 1906 inspired S. E. Kiser, a sweet singer of the prairies to write:

Oh, the pretty Harvey Girl beside my chair,
A fairer maiden I shall never see,
She was winsome, she was neat, she was gloriously sweet,
And she certainly was very good to me.

One of the standards forbade passengers to be made to feel they must gulp their food or miss their train. It was the boast of the Santa Fe that no Harvey patron ever missed a train, and of the house managers that no one ever got indigestion from bolting his meals. Managers were drilled to announce in calm, soothing tones, that there was plenty of time and that ample notice of the train's departure would be given. It was, too. No passenger ever felt hurried, or left hungry.

Even if the train crew, as sometimes happened, forgot to wire ahead, the managers knew pretty well how many meals they'd have to serve. They found out from experience that ninety percent of a trainload would descend for breakfast; forty percent would have lunch and sixty percent would eat dinner. These averages hold fairly well on diners to this day in peace time, but during the war lunch and dinner percentages were higher.

Harvey's flair for showmanship cropped out when a temporary eating establishment was opened in Holbrook, Arizona, soon after the line got there in 1884. The restaurant actually consisted of five old boxcars, sunbaked and with peeling paint. People got off the train and shuddered—outside. But inside they oh'd and ah'd. The cars were crisp and clean, painted in gaudy Indian colors. The tables were set as in the Astor, with the customary spotless Irish linen, English silver, crystal and imported crockery. There were great pitchers of ice water and bouquets of fresh flowers from California.

It was good psychology. Every traveler who stopped to eat went on to advertise: "Well, at Holbrook there are those five dingy old boxcars—but inside . . ."

From these old cars and the wooden hotels in Kansas and Colorado the Santa Fe along about the turn of the century began to develop a style of its own, with good architects doing the designing. The new architecture combined the old Spanish with the native Indian in what came to be known as Santa Fe style. The first example was the Alvarado at Albuquerque; perhaps the best is at La Fonda in Santa Fe.

Most of the credit for the new architecture and styling of the interiors went to Mary E. J. Colter, a foremost American architect and interior decorator who spent years in the Southwest and became an authority on its art.

Millions of dollars have gone into hotels and restaurants along the route, two of the best known being the Bright Angel Lodge and

El Tovar at Grand Canyon rim. These two represent an investment of nearly half a million dollars. At one time a solid trainload of water was hauled to the rim every day from Williams, Arizona, to supply guests. But the most fabulous hostelry was the old Montezuma Hotel and Sanitarium.

This was built at Montezuma Hot Springs, six miles up Gallinas Creek from Las Vegas, New Mexico, and a special branch line ran to it. It was a millionaire's dream, and wealthy and titled people from all over the world vacationed there. The boast was that no canned food ever was served in the place. Special refrigerator cars were kept busy hauling fresh meats, fish, fruits and vegetables for the guests. Harvey even had a contract with a tribe of Yaqui Indians down near Guaymas on the Mexican Gulf of California to supply live green turtles and sea celery. The turtles were shipped up in tank cars and kept in a pool at Las Vegas to fatten until needed. In winter, Mexico supplied out-of-season fruits and vegetables. The Montezuma isn't operating any more, but in its day it was tops in luxury in the Rockies.

Two more achievements were the reformation of news butchers on trains and a revival of Indian arts and crafts among desert tribes of the Southwest. When Harvey took over the news concession on the Santa Fe it was pretty bad. The butchers sold cheap, dirty books, bad candy and cheap cigars. Harvey cleaned up the men, called them train vendors, and gave them good, standard literature, fresh candy and respectable tobacco, with a humidor to keep it in.

The first "good book" the news agents offered travelers was chosen by Frank Clough, still with the news department in 1945. It was *David Harum* and only 100 copies were ordered. They went fast and 1,000 more were ordered. These were snapped up too. The sales record was held for years by Gene Stratton Porter's *Michael O'Halloran*, of which 17,500 copies were sold. Book publishers keep tab on Harvey sales sometimes to guide them in print orders.

Indians along the line were encouraged to weave rugs and blankets and fashion silver-and-turquoise rings, bracelets, necklaces and buttons, to be sold through Harvey stores and museums. Many of the Pueblo people still make a living this way, with Harvey experts supervising their work to make sure the standard is kept up.

In addition to its food-purchasing department, every Harvey manager is a purchasing agent. He keeps track of food production in his territory and if there is a fine crop of melons somewhere or peaches in some other section of the country, all the managers are notified, a bulk purchase is made and the products shipped to all houses direct. Beside this the concern operates poultry or dairy ranches, or both, at Newton, Kansas; Las Vegas, New Mexico; and Del Rio, Arizona, where there is a huge turkey farm.

When the new Union Depot was opened in Kansas City, Harvey branched out into a new line with drug and novelty stores. These stores, surprisingly, put in a full stock of expensive perfumes, equal to that of any Fifth Avenue shop. "Everybody" said that of course travelers wouldn't stop to buy gewgaws and luxury items at a railroad station, but "everybody" was wrong. The stores were a success from the start. Later similar ones were opened in the Union Station, Chicago; in Cleveland and St. Louis, where the Santa Fe does not operate, and in the Union Station in Los Angeles.

After Harvey's death his son, Ford, became president and carried on the tradition of the concern as a family institution operated to conform with personal standards set up by the founder. Upon Ford Harvey's death in 1928, he was succeeded by his brother Byron, who, in 1945, still was the guiding spirit in the enterprise. In the mid-forties two of Byron's sons were vice-presidents, and the concern still was a family affair, with no stock owned by outsiders.

Back in the thirties the Harvey system was serving 15,000,000 meals a year—and insisting that they should be real meals. During one checkup it was revealed that a manager had carved 156 steaks out of his meat supply. He was sternly rebuked by a supervisor and warned that that was fifteen steaks too many.

Just before the Second World War the Santa Fe and Harvey prided themselves that they could easily feed a city of 30,000 people. Within a year they were doubling that figure.

Through the years speed and more speed had put many Harvey Houses out of business as more and more trains ran through without stopping and dining cars took care of travel appetites. But the old houses paid off when the war came. They were quickly refurnished and put into service to feed sailors, soldiers and other fighters. Troops descended from trains without cook-cars three times a day between Chicago and the West Coast.

Hundreds of Harvey workers went to war—but scores of old Harvey Girls came out of retirement and donned white uniforms again. Many, who had married well, hadn't worked for years, but the old skill was there just the same. Where there weren't enough ex-Girls, volunteers manned the trays and ranges.

Later in the Second War, the system on the Santa Fe could, and usually did, feed 6,703 passengers at one sitting, and offer 969 rooms to travelers in sixteen hotels, ranging from the big 147-room La Fonda at Santa Fe and the 142-room Bright Angel Lodge, to the nineteen-room Havasu at Seligman, Arizona, and the twenty-nine-room Casa del Desierto at Barstow on the Mojave Desert.

The biggest food center was in the Union Station at Kansas City, where 380 lunch-counter patrons and 145 diners often were fed at once, with waiting lines for vacant seats. The smallest lunch counter was a twenty-four-seater at Galveston, Texas.

Sixty-five hundred people were working for Harvey during the war, and they weren't enough. Self-service restaurants had to be opened for Santa Fe employees at Barstow, Needles, Seligman and other places.

Plans for handling masses of troops and for huge increases in passengers were made long before Pearl Harbor, and during the war some remarkable records were set. For one thing, travelers became sandwich-happy. Two hundred news agents handed out more than half a million sandwiches a month and 150,000 bottles of milk along with them. On one trip the Scout used up more than 4,400 sandwiches, and new plants to turn them out on assembly lines were set up in eight places: Chicago, Kansas City, Newton, Clovis, Albuquerque, Gallup, Williams and Los Angeles.

The milk record went to pieces when thousands of Mexicans were imported for track labor. They came in over the Santa Fe from south of the border and Fred Harvey fed them as they rolled. They wanted milk and they got it. One immigrant train drank 7,000 bottles and yelled for more.

The System served over 30,000,000 meals in 1943, about 8,000,000 of which were served to the armed forces. Tons of food were purchased and fed to the travelers and included 512,000 pounds of coffee, enough for 20,480,000 cups; 662,000 pounds of butter; 1,117,000 gallons of milk and cream; 1,250,061 pounds of sugar; 2,423,400 pounds of flour; 4,616,400 pounds of potatoes; 956,840 pounds of fish; 2,493,595 pounds of poultry; 5,172,835 pounds of meat and 1,408,184 dozen eggs.

In a national advertising campaign the Harvey system invented what it thought was a mythical character—Private Pringle. It used the private as a basis for explaining why customers couldn't just stroll into a dining car as of yore and have a steward and two waiters ready with a large steak and trimmings. It turned out, however, that there was a real Private Pringle—Murray T.—who wrote from Africa that he liked the ads fine, had been made a corporal, and would Mr. Harvey please get him Lana Turner for a dinner companion upon his return. The Harvey system promised to do its best.

The Santa Fe's wartime dining cars suddenly found their business up more than 200 percent. On eighty cars 106 crews got up early and went to bed late to feed endless streams of travelers. It was normal for one thirty-six-seat diner on such trains as the *Scout* or the *Ranger* to feed 350 people at a meal, which meant ten thirty-minute sittings. At one notable breakfast on the *Scout*, the fry-cook fried 1,004 eggs in one pan. Fifty or sixty dozen eggs at breakfast became just a breeze for galley crews.

But, true to Harvey tradition, no diner, no eating house ever served a cold-storage egg.

The intrusion of such a gastronomic atrocity between a host and his guest, Fred Harvey always held, was an unpardonable breach of the laws of hospitality.

CHAPTER EIGHT

HEADED FOR TROUBLE

NO MAN ALIVE TODAY can boast of building 5,000 miles of railroad. Few ever could. The greatest builder of them all was Albert Alonzo Robinson. With him, spiking steel across deserts, up flinty defiles, down fertile river valleys, over the plains and through timber tangles, most of the way, there marched five other men.

The rail route over which you ride so easily today, was, in the first place, tramped over and climbed over and crawled over, and sometimes fought over, by a special breed of Americans—railroad builders. They had many characteristics in common—they were young men and they liked life in the open. Mainly, they were self-educated; they cared little for money and were highly individualistic. They thrived on obstacles and loved a fight, whether against a snow-capped lava mountain, a quick-sanded stream or a war party of Cheyennes. Nearly all of them were New Englanders of way-back stock.

They were, too, almost fanatically honest. They were hired to run a line for a railroad from here to there, by the best route, and that is where they ran it. They were sometimes offered bribes to swing this way or that, or threatened with a swift end for holding to the line across a range. But they laughed grimly and stayed loyal to the road—and most of them stayed poor, too.

In the Santa Fe's fighting years, six men led the battle front westward and southward. Their monuments today, aside from 5,000 miles of shining tracks from the prairies over the mountains and deserts to the western sea, are the nameboards on stations in little towns: Strong City, Kansas; Barstow, California; Kingman and Holbrook, Arizona; Coleman, Texas; Morley, Colorado; Robinson, New Mexico.

When the Santa Fe started battling in Southeastern Colorado in '78, William Barstow Strong, general manager, was just past forty. Robinson, his chief engineer, was thirty-three. Kingman, Morley and Holbrook, his locating engineers, were all under forty. Dick Coleman, who built the grade and laid the track, was a kid of twenty-two. It was a young man's game.

Head of the Santa Fe's Big Six was Strong, born in Brownington, Vermont, May 16, 1837. His people moved out to Beloit, Wisconsin, and, his schooling finished at eighteen, he got a job as station agent and operator in Milton, Wisconsin. From there he climbed the railroad ladder with the Milwaukee, the Northwestern, the Burlington, the Michigan Central, the "Q" again. He was general superintendent of the Q when the Santa Fe hired him November 1, 1877. A few months later he was made a director, and, at forty-four, became president. From bottom to top had taken him twenty-six years.

Strong was a big man physically. He worked all hours, knew everyone, strode about the line shaking hands with switchmen, dispatchers, freight crews and clerks. He was, for all his heartiness, a shy man, talking little, keeping his good deeds under cover. Besides building his railroad he founded and built reading rooms, clubhouses and a hospital association for his fellow-employees. And he helped to expand the Harvey House system.

When Strong joined the Santa Fe it operated 786 miles of track —618 from Topeka to Pueblo; sixty-six jerky, leased miles from Topeka to Kansas City, and a few branches in Eastern Kansas. He fought the road through, often against the judgment of the directors, to Chicago, Los Angeles, San Diego, Denver, Galveston, El Paso and Guaymas, Mexico. By September, 1889, the line had more than 7,000 miles in operation. This figures out at about a mile and a half a day for 142 months straight—good railroad construction in any language.

Strong's good right hand was a man who had come to the Santa Fe six and a half years ahead of him as an assistant engineer, when the line was about 100 miles long. This was Albert Alonzo Robinson, and he was a Vermonter too, from South Reading, where he was born October 21, 1844. He got his first surveying job on the Great Lakes for the government, working summers to earn money to go to school winters. His father was a carpenter, teacher and farmer. After his death, the boy took over and ran the family farm near Janesville, Wisconsin. His first job with the Santa Fe started April 1, 1871, after a spell with the old St. Joseph & Denver City as an axman in a survey crew. Tom Peter, swearer extraordinary, prohibitionist and pioneer builder of the Santa Fe hired him as an assistant on the line down to Osage City and Emporia.

In twenty-two years Robinson built 5074.1 miles of line which puts him near the top of the list of world champion builders. When he left to take over construction of the Mexican Central, the Santa Fe was the greatest rail system in the world. Before that, he had not only built lines west, but had put through the extension from Kansas City to Chicago by building 350 miles of new track, rebuilding 100 miles of rundown purchased track and throwing huge and expensive bridges over both the Missouri and the Mississippi.

He was a good business man besides being a first-rate engineer. He operated the Mexican Central for years with a silver intake and a gold output and made money. When he joined Central, stock sold for a nickel; its bonds for fifty. When he retired, the stock was up to fifty; the bonds to eighty.

With Robinson and Strong, for various periods, were three locators: Henry Randolph Holbrook, William Raymond Morley and Lewis Kingman. These three among them were responsible for the Santa Fe spending around $50,000,000—and there never was a hint that a dime had been misspent. The road did most of its own construction, went where it pleased and paid as it went.

Holbrook started his rail career with General Palmer on the Union Pacific surveys in '62 after a boyhood in Connecticut. He joined the Santa Fe and worked with Morley and Kingman for years, later retiring to Pueblo, where he built the famous twenty-five-mile Holbrook irrigation ditch.

Morley was perhaps the most spectacular of the three. He and

Kingman first met on surveys in New Mexico in '71 and when, in '77, Kingman was broke and jobless, Morley induced him to come with the Santa Fe. Morley had a reputation of being a good friend—and a good hater; an out-of-doors man whose written reports often looked like hentracks; a man who could locate a line through wild country better than most rail pioneers.

It fell to Morley to break the news to Santa Fe directors that Colonel Holliday's dream of a main stem through Santa Fe must be abandoned. His surveys showed that the line would have to run to the south, over Glorieta Pass and down through Galisteo, later called Lamy, unless the directors wanted to spend millions getting over more mountains into and out of the old capital. There wasn't enough business in Santa Fe, Morley pointed out, to justify the expense.

There had been some argument whether the road should go to Santa Fe even over a branch.

"There's no real reason for going over there," Robinson told Morley and Kingman one evening in Las Vegas. "I doubt if the freight ever will be enough to make the line pay. Of course, there's the territorial capital. . . ."

"That's true," said Morley, tamping his pipe. "But you know, Rob, it was the Colonel's dream, Santa Fe. He was always talking about it, back there in Topeka, the old timers tell me. He'd be pretty sad if . . ."

Robinson looked into the fire for a minute.

"You're right, Ray," he agreed. "We'll build to Santa Fe, even if it isn't on the main stem. It isn't often anyone has the satisfaction of making a dream come true."

Morley and Robinson talked it all over later, driving around New Mexico in a buckboard. Morley made the report; Robinson backed him. In Topeka there was disappointment and questioning. Morley had an independent survey made by a man anxious to have the main stem run through Santa Fe, and this report agreed with Morley's. So the stem veered south and a branch went up to the old transmountain trail town.

After his work in Raton Pass and in Royal Gorge—where we'll meet him and the others later—Strong gave Morley a gold-mounted rifle as a token of thanks and respect. Morley loved the gun and took it everywhere with him. A few years later, at a desert camp down in Mexico . . .

Kingman was a Bay Stater, born at North Bridgewater, February 26, 1845. He got his first railroad job shoveling snow for a survey party on a branch of the old Lowell Railroad in 1863. He came west a few years later, worked for the then Atlantic & Pacific, became surveyor-general of New Mexico, ran lines on the fabulous Maxwell Grant and, at Morley's suggestion, started with the Santa Fe at Pueblo, July 3, 1877.

Morley and Kingman lived with their families at Cimarron, New Mexico, and surveyed much of the line in those parts, working in snow and rain, heat and mountain blizzard through untamed country. They were to make a dramatic meeting one night in Raton Pass in the race to win and hold that place against the Denver & Rio Grande. We'll meet them again up there.

Kingman, without college training, was a typical railroad planner, kindly, persistent, a lover of solitude, never happier than when around a campfire at night or fighting his way across rugged territory to find a route for steel.

After the surveyors and locators came Richard R. Coleman, the grader and tracklayer, the blaster of mountains and tamer of wild rivers. He was a Pennsylvania boy and only fifteen when he went to work as a back flagman for Captain John Ellinwood, surveying the line between Florence and Emporia, Kansas. In those days, and for years afterward, he worked armed to the teeth, and his crews seldom were without soldier escort to blast away at marauding Indians. Dick himself carried a Henry carbine, relic of the Civil War, and two .36 Colt revolvers. At twenty, thus armed, he was bossing gangs laying track through Indian Territory.

Coleman built thousands of miles for the Santa Fe, including the line across Raton and other western passes. Occasionally, in early days, towns or counties ahead of the front would grade and bridge a right of way, as a sort of welcome offering. Pueblo County did this in '70 for the Kansas Pacific, which seemed to be headed that way at the moment. The K. P. however, ignored the whole thing, and the county, a bit miffed, offered the grade and bridges to Mr. Coleman, who was happy to accommodate them with Santa Fe track.

Locating and construction men often had to fight off crews from rival lines seeking to invade the territory. There was no national umpire, or any way of enforcing his decisions if there had been one. First come, first served, Rob Roy's dictum ruled: that he may take who has the power, and he may hold who can.

When Santa Fe, Union Pacific or the Rio Grande built into new territory the road considered the surrounding country as its own and prepared to fight to the end to keep out rivals. It had to—or go broke. There was no Interstate Commerce Commission to decide whether a second road was necessary "in the public interest," to regulate freight and passenger rates or to protect a pioneer road against a rival.

It was the old law of tooth and claw, and a railroad fought—or died. The plains and mountains were littered with the old abandoned grades and rusty iron of roads that didn't fight—or fought and lost. To expect to win the West without casualties was like expecting to fight Indians without anyone getting killed or wounded.

For the locators and constructors however, life was not all hard. There were frequent celebrations as track reached new settlements, or the first train came in, or a new branch was opened. Then the boys ahead of the front would come back on horseback or in wagons and the steel gang would lay off a day and help the townsfolk "whoop it up." The first train in always brought excursionists and usually two boxcars full of keg beer with cakes of ice atop, if anyone could find the ice.

As the train stopped the excursionists would pile off and shake hands with the townsfolk and the boys would roll out the kegs and knock in their heads. Waterboys with tin dippers stationed themselves at the kegs and ladled out the brew to all comers with washtubs, pails, old teapots and jugs. After a while, some bigwig in a boiled shirt, tubular pants, a Prince Albert coat and a gilded log chain across his ample stomach, would be hoisted to a tabletop and encouraged to sound off. The speech was always about the advance of civilization, usually depicted as riding the cowcatcher of the

Charles C. Burr No. 78, a 4-6-0 Taunton with old Larry O'Brien at the throttle.

In the twenty years from 1870 to 1890 there were hundreds of these celebrations from the Missouri to the Pacific—the happy throng often going direct from the beer kegs to the polls to elect state legislators hot for passing laws to make railroad operation wellnigh impossible.

A typical celebration was at Pueblo, where the first train arrived March 1, 1876, after some skullduggery in which "Denver Whiskey" played a part, according to the *Colorado Chieftain.* The Santa Fe, it seemed, had beaten the Kansas Pacific into Pueblo, despite those Denver scalawags. The Denver-Pueblo war was a typical city battle of the period. The *Chieftain* blacked up page one with a headline: "Three Cheers and a Tiger for the A. T. & S. F. R. R." The editorial said:

"The suspense in which our citizens have lived for several years past is at an end. We have arrived at a fruition of our hopes. The first engine and train are arriving. Our people have good reason to kill the fatted calf and rejoice with exceeding gladness."

The real show came off March 7th, and a day before the *Chieftain* predicted: "It is proposed to let go all holds . . . The biggest jubilee ever held in the Rocky Mountain Region. We propose to make Rome howl. Look out for the locomotive!!!"

On March 7th there was "eating, drinking and general rejoicing." Two excursion trains from Kansas were due in but were held up by snow. Two locomotives and a snowplow went into the ditch at Spearville, Kansas, but new engines were coupled on to haul the 700 excursionists west. They got in the next morning with both trains coupled together, and Engine No. 45, *Colorado Springs* (Baldwin) and No. 32, *Kansas* (Mason) blasting and whistling to wake the echoes. Ordnance Sergeant McCarthy from Fort Lyon loosed off a twelve-pounder Napoleon gun from the bluff. The Nineteenth Infantry band, sent over by General C. H. Smith from the fort played martial music and all agreed that "it compared favorably with the far-famed bands of European armies."

The excursionists got off amid cheers, led by Major Tom Anderson, the Old Scoffer of the Wakarusa picnic, but now "the gentlemanly general passenger agent of the Santa Fe." Every home in town had been opened and each visitor got a ticket telling him where to go for food, bed and entertainment.

Del Norte, San Juan, Colorado Springs and Denver sent down delegations—the Denver boys being a bit tongue-in-check. The Odd Fellows Lodge paraded a miniature locomotive carried by four boys. The *Chieftain* had a float carrying compositors at work and a small press in operation. This was drawn by four large white horses and a story of the parade was composed and printed on route. A little later a banquet "embraced every delicacy known to earth or water in the animal, fowl, fruit or vegetable kingdoms." Soon "The seductive wine made its appearance and the flow of soul now commenced in earnest."

This meant the speechmaking which went on for three hours as civilization advanced toward Pueblo and the Arkansas Valley on the cowcatchers of the locomotives *Colorado Springs* (No. 45) and *Kansas* (No. 32) of the oo00 type. The reporter for the paper gave up at last. "There are times," he wrote, "when the soul is too full for writing—the flowing periods refuse to marshal themselves in line. Such a fate has visited us now."

Christmas and Fourth of July were great days in Western towns back yonder—but the biggest of all was the day the first train arrived.

The locators and engineers watched these whoopee celebrations with ironic eye and went on to crawl up mountains and down, freeze on icy passes, scorch in desert heat, fight their way through heavy timber and try to figure out some way to get across 100 miles of wilderness on easy grades without too many curves and within easy distance of fuel and water—with maybe a ton or two of freight to keep the road operating after it was built.

There was little machinery then, and cutting, filling and tracklaying had to be done mainly by muscle. It was usually cheaper to go around a hill than through it—and from the train window today you may see in many places the old grade leaving the present track to loop around a knob through which your train now wheels deep in a rock cut. In the '70s, hacking that cut by black powder and pick and shovel might have bankrupted the road.

Railroads commonly follow river valleys when they can, leaving them to twist up mountain creeks to headwaters; then over the pass and down to the headwaters of another creek and so down into another valley. The great Arkansas Valley is a highway for the Santa Fe, and so are the Brazos, the Canadian, the Red, the Pecos, the Colorado, the Little Colorado, the Cimarron and a dozen other rivers.

Riding a train through hilly or mountain country, it is easy to imagine a great many of the curves are unnecessary. Often it would have seemed miles shorter and much simpler to have built a bridge from calk to calk of a long loop of a canyon than to have built around. Passengers often wonder about these curves and loops—and usually there is someone on the lounge car to explain it.

"You see," he says, "the railroads got so much valuable land for each mile they built, so they built as many miles as possible."

When railroad men, especially surveyors and locators, hear this, they usually go back and have a good stiff drink.

If railroads had been organized in the first place merely to get grants of land—which, in those days, was practically worthless, anyway—there might have been some excuse for curving lines all over the country. But since a railroad is operated to move weight, it has to be designed to move this weight in the most efficient and least expensive way. Every unneeded curve in the line means added expense, added time, added wear and tear on track and rolling stock. In the past twenty years railroads have spent millions taking out curves for this very reason—but there had to be more curves in early days to enable the low-powered locomotives to operate.

In the heyday of railroad building the locators were told to find a route from Alpha, Kansas to Omega, Colorado, by way of Epsilon, where there was a coal mine, and Sigma, where there was a farm center that might produce some freight. They were told also what the "ruling grade" might be; this grade had to fit the power of the engines assigned to the section. Motive power could haul just so much economically and that decided the maximum slope of grades. Engine construction also decided how tight curves could be made.

Now, if a locator came to two settlements, Delta and Beta, five miles apart, he could do it on a map with a ruler. But a contour map showed that Beta was 1,850 feet higher than Delta and a straight line would mean about a seven percent grade, which no engine in those days—and few in these—could climb. The locator was held to a 3.5 percent grade, which meant he could not slant his line upward more than 184.8 feet in a mile. To climb 1,850 feet he would have a line ten miles long, and that meant curves. In a mountain country, plotting curves usually was quite a trick. Especially if the estimate didn't allow for much rock work.

Here is a typical estimate, by Ray Morley, of the cost of constructing a mountain line in 1875. This particular stretch ran "from the mouth of Antelope Creek at Sagauche River, up canyons, over North Cochetopa Pass and down Cochetopa Creek to Wales Ranch."

Distance: Miles—26
Sidings: Six of ¼ mile—1.5 miles: Total 27.5 miles

205,129 cubic yards earthwork @ 20-68/100¢	$ 42,425.95
105,257 ” ” rock @ 99-20/100¢	104,416.90
30,292 ” ” loose rock @ 64-10/100¢	19,422.90
2,704 Second class masonry @ $4	10,816.00
150′ wooden trestle, 15′ high or under @ $8	1,200.00
45′ ” ” 20′ ” ” @ $10	450.00
Grubbing and clearing	1,100.00
Wooden boxes for culverts	1,075.00
Moving loose rock and retaining wall	5,000.00
Total @ $7,150.26 per mi. for 26 miles	185,906.75
27.5 miles of ties at 2640 per mile—72,600 @ 20¢	14,250.00
27.5 miles #56 iron, spikes, splices, etc., at $45.50	125,125.00
12 complete switches at $160	1,920.00
4 watertanks with windmills at $1,900	7,600.00
26 miles tracklaying @ $450	11,700.00
Engineering and contingencies 10%	34,677.17
Total cost	$381,178.92

Total average per mile: $14,671.11
Maximum grades 170′ per mile tangent
" curves 15° per 100′

Curvature might be reduced to 12° for, say $30,000 additional.
W. R. Morley.

That was the cost of building a few miles of mountain road. Today, with heavy steel, telegraph and power lines, a Central Traffic Control system and other speed and safety contrivances, the cost might be three times that. But $381,000 was a lot of money to ask directors to spend in '75 for a line that probably wouldn't produce $10 worth of revenue to the mile and which would be expensive to operate in the bargain.

While many early roads built into settled country, the Santa Fe plan usually was to build through potentially rich but undeveloped territory and hang on until the country caught up with it. This proved sound in the long run—but there were some breathless moments over balance sheets while the country was catching up.

Besides the best location for the line, the engineers also had to find water for the engines, and, if it was too hard, as it often was, some means of softening it before it could be used in boilers. They had to be on the lookout for a timber supply for ties and buildings and for some source of possible revenue from farms, mines or pioneer industries.

Many early rail wars started because a rival road tried to build, or did build into territory where there was hardly enough business to keep one line alive. When a rival road paralleled the pioneer line, there wasn't enough business for either, and so there were rate wars and general hell-raising and sometimes violence. The roads had to fight to keep operating. It was uneconomic and deplored by all right-thinkers sitting behind mahogany desks in New York or Boston—who never had the job of running a railroad against competition that stopped at nothing.

To hold its territory, the Santa Fe ran out feeder lines through Kansas, not only to bring in more freight but to discourage rival roads. A shoestring line, without branches, was open temptation for another line to invade the country, cross and recross the original line and siphon away tonnage. This strategy always was resisted by the pioneer line and often led to furious battles. It was not uncommon for Road No. 1 to wait until its rival had graded a right of way across it, and then spot a few cars at the crossing, man them with armed guards and defy the rival road to lay track. It never stopped the rival permanently, but often it delayed things long enough so that the managers of both roads could get together and work out a traffic agreement, to avoid a rate war that might ruin them both.

Locators and surveyors had, besides the tough field work, a great deal of paper work and figuring to do. Some of this was done around campfires at night, or in dusty board shacks beside the right of way. Data for a line fifty miles long might fill 100 pages of this book. There had to be, in addition to thousands of calculations, estimates of the availability of timber for ties, rock for ballasting and fills, water for engines, snow and spring rain that might wash out the track. . . . Locating a railroad was something more than a cross-country stroll.

The Santa Fe's decision to build into the Rockies was the result of long surveys by Ray Morley and Lewis Kingman—also an enthusiastic report by Colonel Holliday. Holliday at the time had become president of the Excelsior Coke & Gas Company at Topeka, and in June, 1878, made a trip into the Del Norte and Lake City mining districts and around the San Juan country of southwestern Colorado.

"If the miners can have quick and cheap modes of shipping out their ore," he wrote to President Thomas Nickerson of the road, "and shipping in their supplies, the business of that country will immediately assume such enormous proportions as to startle both of us." He urged that "our road" be built into the San Juan country.

A survey already had been made in the fall of '78 by Morley. He wrote to General Manager Robinson from his home in Cimarron on January 5, 1879, but he was not so enthusiastic as Holliday.

"An immediate extension of your road as far as the South Arkansas might pay, but if dependent on local traffic for support, I doubt the policy of extending it farther until the mining districts mentioned have had more time to prove their capacity for creating traffic . . ." he wrote.

On May 14, 1879, Robinson wrote to President Nickerson about the project. He favored a southerly route between the San Juan country and the Elk Mountains.

"This route," he wrote, "enters and controls a country free from competition by the Union Pacific or its branches. It is a country undoubtedly as rich, if not the richest, in precious metals as any country on this continent. This region will give permanent and profitable employment to a railroad long after the Leadville bubble has burst . . ."

Robinson urged that the Santa Fe seize and hold the route over Marshall Pass. The Denver Southern Pacific had a survey party working in the pass already. The suggestion seems to have been forgotten as the war in the Rockies became a battle for life, with hard-boiled trigger-happy armies facing each other.

It was to be a desperate knock-down-and-drag-out, a free for all with crews racing through wild canyons to spike track ahead of their enemies, and grim-faced gunmen standing guard in rock forts along the right of way.

It was like that in the Rockies in '78.

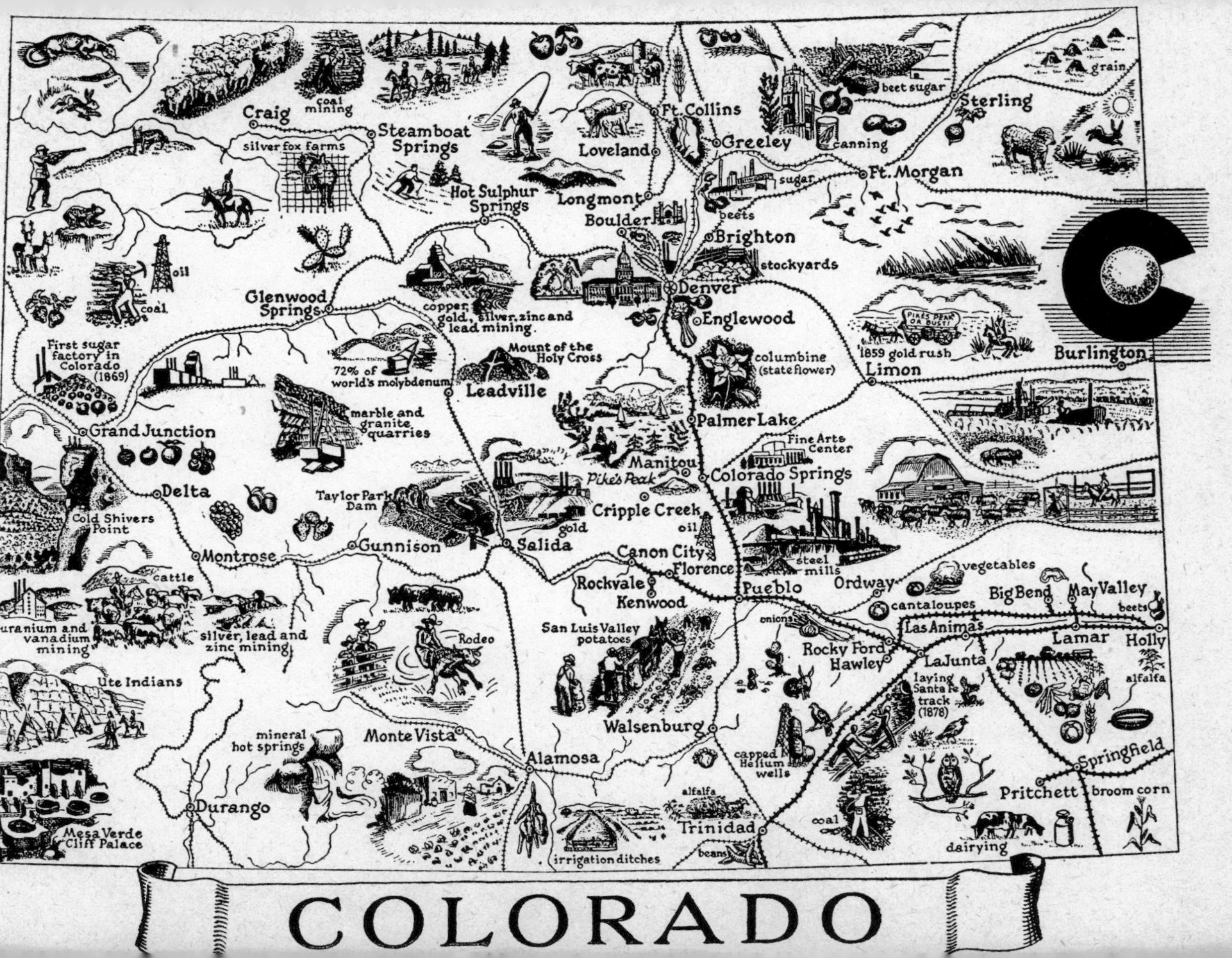

Craig
coal mining
Steamboat Springs
silver fox farms
Hot Sulphur Springs
Loveland
Longmont
Boulder
Ft. Collins
Greeley
sugar
beets
beet sugar
canning
Sterling
grain
Ft. Morgan
Brighton
stockyards
Denver
Englewood
oil
coal
Glenwood Springs
copper, gold, silver, zinc and lead mining.
Mount of the Holy Cross
Leadville
72% of world's molybdenum
First sugar factory in Colorado (1869)
Grand Junction
marble and granite quarries
PIKES PEAK OR BUST
1859 gold rush
Limon
Burlington
columbine (state flower)
Palmer Lake
Fine Arts Center
Manitou
Colorado Springs
Pike's Peak
Cripple Creek
gold
oil
Salida
Taylor Park Dam
Delta
Cold Shivers Point
Gunnison
Montrose
Canon City
Florence
Rockvale
Kenwood
Pueblo
steel mills
Ordway
vegetables
cantaloupes
Big Bend
May Valley
beets
Las Animas
Lamar
Holly
alfalfa
cattle
uranium and vanadium mining
silver, lead and zinc mining
Rodeo
San Luis Valley potatoes
onions
Rocky Ford
Hawley
La Junta
laying Santa Fe track (1878)
Ute Indians
mineral hot springs
Monte Vista
Alamosa
Walsenburg
capped Helium wells
Springfield
Pritchett
broom corn
Durango
Mesa Verde Cliff Palace
alfalfa
Trinidad
irrigation ditches
beans
coal
dairying
COLORADO

CHAPTER NINE

"SEIZE AND HOLD THAT PASS!"

OUT FROM GRANADA, COLORADO, the Santa Fe fought its way through historic country. Granada itself was once a great cattle depot where herds from the south reached the river and were turned over to the northern herders. Twenty-six miles west was old Fort Lyon, where a regiment of soldiers was kept to protect traders against Indians, and sometimes did. Eight miles beyond the fort, the line made its first crossing of the Purgatoire River—which it would cross again at Trinidad.

The Spaniards called the stream El Rio de las Animas Perdidas—River of Lost Souls. The French changed this to Purgatoire, and the American traders and trappers, scorning such outlandish names, translated this to Picketwire—which is its local name today.

At Las Animas, Colorado, the rail crews from the East had their first view of Pike's Peak—as had Lieutenant Zebulon Pike seventy years before. Kit Carson had lived here, and into town from the west rolled the old stage coach in which Horace Greeley had toured the wilderness in '59, cogitating on how best to express his deathless line. When the Santa Fe went through to Las Vegas, the coach's eight horses were unhitched for the last time and the vehicle was placed on exhibition, to be viewed with sentimental awe by young men who had taken Mr. Greeley's advice.

A few miles beyond Las Animas was Bent's Fort, where the trail crossed the Arkansas River. Not many years before, south of the river had been Mexico; north, the United States, where travelers came under the protection of American troops.

La Junta, which the Spaniards pronounced La Hoonta, and the railroaders called and still call La Hunta, had been founded by three traders, just about the time the Santa Fe started to build south from Topeka; but they had grown tired of waiting for the line and had moved on to Trinidad. And here, at La Junta, the road building east from Pueblo met the crews building west from Granada. At 10:15 on the night of February 28, 1876, the headlight of the engine *Newton* peered dimly from the east and her bell and whistle echoed the yells of about twenty welcomers on the board platform in front of the boxcar depot. Soon there were excursions from Kansas and Colorado, and celebrations for a week.

Records of the time show what it cost to build the line. Grading and bridging ran from $1,500 to $3,000 a mile. Rails, bolts, splices and so forth ran to $4,250 a mile. Ties were 35 and 40 cents each, floated down the Arkansas to the track crews. Water tanks with accompanying windmills, were $1,900. A mile of track could be laid for $350, excepting on Mondays and day-after-payday, when the customary lassitude set in.

It was usual, to start with, to spike only every third tie. This resulted in frequent engine derailments, but the locomotives were muscled and screwjacked back onto the track by all hands and passengers, at no added cost to the company. After the track had settled a bit, crews went back over the line, sledging in extra spikes and trueing up the gauge and alignment.

From Dodge west was still wild railroading. It was 265 miles to Pueblo and there were only eight towns—as they were flatteringly described—all the way: Lakin, Kansas and Granada, Las Animas, West Las Animas, La Junta, Rocky Ford, Napiesta and Chico, Colorado. All water was supplied by windmills, and no wind or too much could stop trains. There were four trains daily each way, except on dead-calm or stormy days. In September, 1878, the train register at Las Animas recorded: "No. 31 delayed—heavy wind."

In Southeastern Colorado the narrow-gauge Denver & Rio Grande and the standard Santa Fe had built themselves into a corner that was to be, for months, the Bloody Angle of the long railroad war that raged up and down the West for years.

Both lines were in Pueblo, the Rio Grande from the north, the

Santa Fe from the east. Barring the way west, were the Rockies; south the Sangre de Cristo Range. There was only one feasible way west—up through the canyon of the Arkansas, thirty feet wide

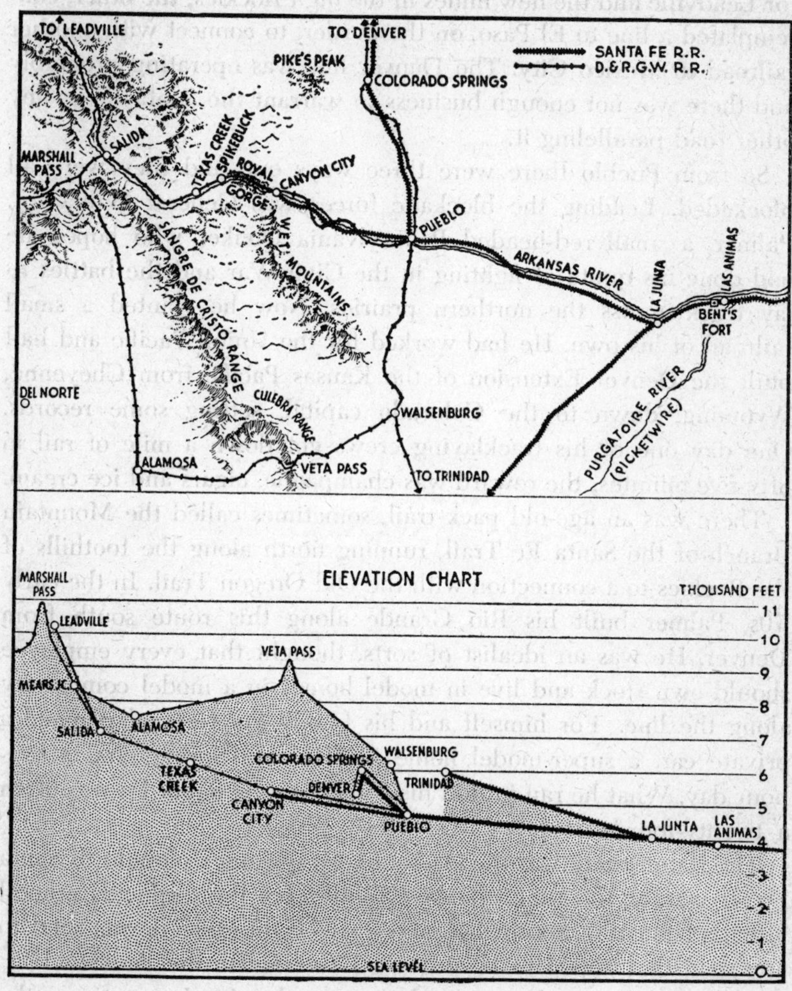

The Fight for the Royal Gorge

in places and leading to more passes. The best way south was over Raton Mountain, south of Trinidad, across which wound the Santa Fe Trail, which, in turn, followed an ancient path worn by the Utes.

North the road to Denver led along the Eastern foothills of the Rockies—and here the Rio Grande ran. It, too, had started westward toward the canyon and south toward Raton. One way it was headed for Leadville and the new mines in the high Rockies; the other, contemplated a line to El Paso, on the border, to connect with another railroad to Mexico City. The Denver line was operating profitably and there was not enough business to warrant the Santa Fe or any other road paralleling it.

So from Pueblo there were three ways out—and they were all blockaded. Leading the blockade forces was General William J. Palmer, a small red-headed Pennsylvania Quaker who hoped he had done his quota of fighting in the Civil War and the battles to lay track across the northern prairies. Now he wanted a small railroad of his own. He had worked for the Union Pacific and had built the Denver Extension of the Kansas Pacific from Cheyenne, Wyoming, down to the Colorado capital, setting some records. One day one of his tracklaying crews got down a mile of rail in fifty-five minutes; the reward was champagne, cigars and ice cream.

There was an age-old pack trail, sometimes called the Mountain Branch of the Santa Fe Trail, running north along the foothills of the Rockies to a connection with the Old Oregon Trail. In the early '70s, Palmer built his Rio Grande along this route south from Denver. He was an idealist of sorts, thought that every employee should own stock and live in model homes in a model community along the line. For himself and his family the General planned a private car, a super-model home in Colorado Springs and a five-hour day. What he ran into in his wars with the Santa Fe was often a twenty-four-hour day.

The Raton route was the classic highway from Colorado to Santa Fe. It was, at the time, the best route from the coalfields around Trinidad into the Southwest, and on to California. It was vital to any road that hoped to keep going westward to the Pacific.

Today, of course, there are other routes, but in pioneer times, the pull of tradition was strong, and Raton, on the old trail, pulled railroad builders like a magnet.

The Rio Grande-Santa Fe collision at Pueblo meant that someone had to do something. General Manager Strong decided that the Santa Fe should be the first to go south over the mountains and down to Santa Fe. This meant a charter from the Yankee-hating New Mexican legislature.

Gathering up Don Miguel Otero, Strong boarded a Barlow & Sanderson stage, headed down through Las Vegas and up to the capital—running there, head-on into the Southern Pacific, which looked on everything in the Southwest as its private preserve, as the Rio Grande looked on everything in Colorado.

Through Espee influence, it was whispered around the capital, a bill called the California Act had just been passed. This law, designed to keep railroads out of New Mexico, demanded among other things that the Santa Fe would have to raise in cash one-tenth of the cost of its New Mexico extension before it could start work. The Santa Fe was short of cash and such a law would block construction.

Don Miguel, nosing around, discovered the New Mexicans saying they didn't want a damyankee railroad in their territory anyway. But he found also that the California Act hadn't yet gone into effect; a general incorporation act still was basic law, and the Santa Fe could work under it. Acting fast, Strong and his local lawyers—who would accept damyankee money—organized the New Mexico & Southern Pacific Railroad to build from Raton Pass to the Arizona line. Then, for good measure, they slipped through a law exempting railroads from taxes for six years—and sent a wire to Colonel Holliday in Topeka, telling him his dream might be coming true, and to be sure to tell Major Tom Anderson, the old scoffer.

Strong climbed back aboard the stage and set out behind eight horses for Pueblo. There he found President Nickerson and the Boston directors of the system none too anxious to go ahead. Nickerson pointed out, with truth, that the whole Santa Fe Trail freighting business amounted only to $2,000,000 a year and the railroad could haul all of it in a week.

Seventy years later, one Santa Fe freight could move twice that business from Santa Fe to Chicago in two days at one cent a ton a mile.

Nickerson and the directors said, too, that the country through which the line was routed wouldn't produce much freight, and fewer passengers. Strong countered with a prophecy about the Colorado coal and ore business, which he thought would bring in enough cash to finance the Santa Fe extension. They fought it out during the winter, and finally, a few weeks after New Year's in '78, Nickerson told Strong, "You can have $20,000. No more. Go ahead and make surveys from La Junta—but no construction. Remember—$20,000."

Twenty thousand dollars wouldn't build even two miles of the mountain road.

Strong strode over to Robinson's engineering shack beside the track.

"We're going ahead, Rob. We have only $20,000—but once we get started they can't stop us," he said. "Let's get going!"

"Okay."

"Get started for Raton right away," continued Strong. "Dicker with Wootton for his road—but get in there and hold that pass. I'll write Kingman at Cimarron and you notify Ray Morley at Pueblo."

Robinson, shrugging into his greatcoat, glanced at the calendar. It was February 26th—and it would be cold up on Raton Mountain over which the old trail lifted just ten feet short of 8,000.

During the months of argument between the Santa Fe's directors and its engineers the Rio Grande had snaked down through the Southern Colorado mountains and into the San Luis Valley. It had headed for the coal town of Trinidad, which badly needed it—and then stopped at El Moro, four miles away. Rio Grande directors owned a townsite at El Moro and wished to profit from it. They did—at the expense of victory in Raton Pass, it turned out later. The Trinidados, who could see the smoke of Rio Grande engines and hear the whistles and the clank of couplers on still nights, were good and sore. They grew sorer when business houses started to move away over to the new townsite and so make more profits for the Rio Grande owners.

The Rio Grande had, in '76 and '77 built a line from Elmore over

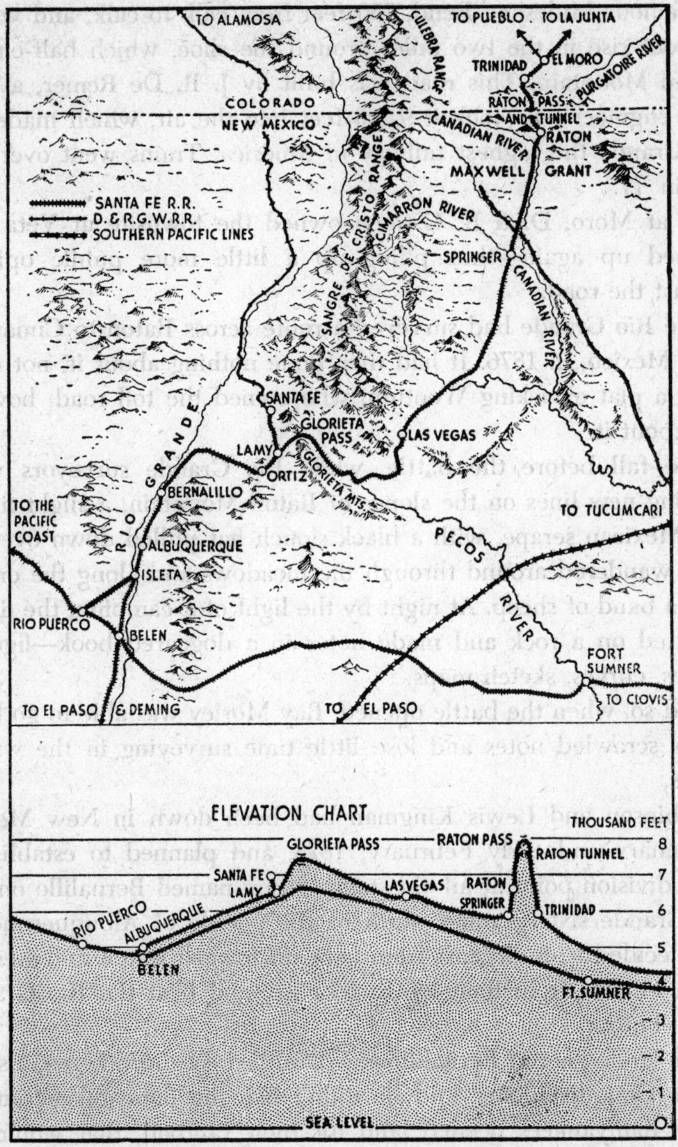

Across Raton Pass and Down Through New Mexico

Veta Pass and down to Alamosa and Fort Garland. This line made the famous Muleshoe Bend, 750 feet from calk to calk, and with a 400-foot rise in the two miles around the shoe, which half-circled Dump Mountain. This road was built by J. R. De Remer, a first-class engineer who took it 9,300 feet into the air, which made the Rio Grande the highest railway in America. Trains went over this line in '77.

As at Moro, D. & R. G. men owned the townsite at Veta and cleaned up again—thus piling up a little more public opinion against the road.

The Rio Grande had surveyed a route across Raton to Cimarron, New Mexico, in 1876. It had then done nothing about it, not even filing a plat or asking Wootton, who owned the toll road, how he felt about it.

The fall before the battle, while Rio Grande surveyors were running new lines on the slopes of Raton Mountain, a slight figure in a Mexican serape, with a black slouch hat pulled down over his eyes, wandered around through the meadows and along the creeks with a band of sheep. At night by the light of a campfire, the figure squatted on a rock and made notes in a dogeared book—figures, grades, curves, sketch maps.

And so, when the battle opened, Ray Morley was able to go back to his scrawled notes and lose little time surveying in the winter snows.

Robinson and Lewis Kingman had been down in New Mexico in January and early February, 1878, and planned to establish a main division point at an old stage station named Bernalillo on the Rio Grande sixteen miles north of the pueblo of Albuquerque. It was decided to build east from here up toward Raton and west to Santa Fe and from there on to El Paso, and beat the Rio Grande to the border.

The landowner at Bernalillo was Don Jose Leandro Perea, a scion of the Conquistadores, and he didn't like the damyankees either. If the damyankees needed land for their railroad, that would be $425 an acre—and it made no difference if for leagues around $25 would buy any acre you might pick.

"Okay, Senor," said Robinson, and went on down to Albuquerque where, not far from the old settlement and alongside his platted line, he bought all the land he needed for a handful of trade dollars.

And that is why, today, passengers on the *Chief* buy Indian trinkets and Navajo blankets from the squaws at Albuquerque instead of at Bernalillo.

While Robinson, in the chill pre-spring of '78, headed for Pueblo, the frog was laid at La Junta for the Santa Fe extension, which was to leave the Pueblo line here and swing southwest along the old trail through Trinidad and then head up the pass. At Pueblo, Robinson met bearded, tousle-headed Ray Morley and told him of Strong's plans.

As they talked, another Santa Fe stalwart was hurrying north to join them. It was Kingman. He and his family had wintered at Cimarron and, when he got the message from Strong ordering him to go to Raton to help win and hold the pass, he went into action. He commandeered a government telegraph repair wagon, bribed the driver and galloped up the trail. By daybreak they'd made fifty miles. Changing teams, they picked up Mexican laborers here and there and, by five o'clock on March 1st, had crossed the mountain on the toll road and were four miles down on the Colorado side. Here they camped for the night—and Robinson and Morley, racing up to Wootton's toll house in a pole buggy, saw their campfires far up the canyon.

To go back a little: Santa Fe and Rio Grande telegraph lines connected and the two concerns broke each other's codes and read each other's wires. The Rio Grande, getting wind of the Santa Fe plan, quickly organized a crew of graders, called in J. A. McMurtrie and J. R. De Remer, two of its best engineers, and held them ready at Pueblo for a dash into the pass.

Robinson and Morley, ears buried in coat collars, boarded a Rio Grande train at Pueblo, headed for El Moro. Morley strolled through the next car and then came back to Robinson.

"Who d'you think's up forward, Rob?"

"Not General Palmer?"

"Worse than that—McMurtrie and De Remer."

"They spot you?" asked Robinson.

"No, talking too busily. Better let them get off first at El Moro. They're headed for the pass too, unless I miss my guess."

"Funny, they'd be alone. But there's no grading gang on the train."

"Probably coming up on a work train later."

The narrow-gauge squealed around the tight curves and coughed heavily on the grades. It was nightfall when the cars jolted to a stop at El Moro. De Remer and McMurtrie piled out and headed for the hotel while Robinson and Morley watched. Following at a safe distance, the Santa Fe'ers saw the Rio Granders register for their rooms, yawn and go upstairs. Robinson grinned at Morley.

"Come on, Ray. Where's the livery stable?"

They hired a buggy and a team and drove off in the darkness through Trinidad and up the old trail toward "Uncle Dick" Wootton's toll house and hotel. It was ten o'clock and, as they drove, far up on the mountain, they saw the glow of Kingman's campfires in the cold, still air.

"That Lew, d'you suppose," asked Robinson.

"Hope so. If it is, we've won. If not . . . Well, can't take any chances. Might be a party of freighters."

They stopped the buggy at the chain across the road, turned the team into the corral and went in to find Uncle Dick getting ready for bed.

Richens Lacy Wootton was the son of a Mecklenburg County, Virginia, planter. He was born May 6, 1816, and at twenty struck out alone for Independence, Missouri, and joined a wagon train. He never went east again. He became a trader, Indian fighter, scout for Fremont, friend of Kit Carson, rancher, sheepman and toll-road owner. Indian fighting, although he did some, he considered nonsense.

"Leave the tribes alone and they'll kill each other off faster than the soldiers can do it," he used to say.

Dick made his first big money in '52. He got together a band of 8,900 sheep and drove them from Taos to the Sacramento Valley in 107 days. There he sold out to the hungry Forty Niners and came back in thirty-eight days with $50,000 in gold, and gold drafts in his saddle bags. After some ranching and trading around in Denver and Pueblo, both of which he helped to found, he bethought himself of some social security for his old age and decided on a toll road over Raton Mountain.

Getting franchises from the territorial legislatures of Colorado and New Mexico, he hacked, blasted, cut and filled about twenty-seven miles of highway from Trinidad on the north to the Red River on the south. He put up a home and hotel on the north slope, slung a chain across the road and did a thriving business.

Raton Pass was not used by all traders. Many of them took the Cimarron cutoff which enabled them, westbound, to miss the mountains by veering southwest above Dodge City and going down along the Cimarron on what now is the route of a branch line from Dodge to Boise City in the Oklahoma panhandle, and then on across northeastern New Mexico to Fort Union and Wagon Mound. But at the time the Rio Grande and the Santa Fe reached the country, a north-south leg of the trail used the pass. Barlow & Sanderson stages used the route and so did sheep and cattle herders, miners and traders.

Everything on feet paid toll except Indians, posses after horse thieves and occasional Mexicans. The Utes never had paid to cross their own mountains and didn't propose to start. The possemen usually were hellbent with rifle and rope and stopped for nothing. Once in a while Uncle Dick menaced Mexicans with an old army carbine and collected, and occasionally the Indians would leave a blanket or a deer skin.

The hotel was a favorite stopping place for the freighting teams and an open house for youngsters from Trinidad and El Moro, who held dances there every week. One was going on when Robinson and Morley opened the door and walked in. Wootton was just going to his room. They called him back. A few swift sentences told the story. Uncle Dick grew philosophical.

"Well," he said, "I guess I'll have to get out of the way of the locomotive."

"The Santa Fe will do right by you," assured Robinson.

After the line was built Strong and Robinson one day met Dick's son, Dick, Jr., in Trinidad. Strong asked the youngster if he thought $50,000 in cash would be about right for his father's road. "Let's go up and ask him," replied the boy.

At the toll house the old man shook his head.

"No," he said, "I don't want that much money in a lump. I'll tell you—you give me and my family a lifetime pass and $25 a month in groceries, and we'll call it square."

They shook on it. This agreement was kept until 1916, with Uncle Dick's widow getting the pass and the cash after his death in 1893. In 1925 the Santa Fe doubled the payment; in 1930 it increased it again, to $75. After Mrs. Wootton's death, an invalid daughter, Miss Fidelis, got $25 a month during her lifetime. Dick died at seventy-seven, having fathered five sons and five daughters.

As Robinson and Morley had driven up to Wootton's they had paralleled two surveys from El Moro and Trinidad up to the foot of the pass. But above Uncle Dick's place there was only one road—and two railroads wanted to go over it. Even as the engineers talked with Dick a messenger arrived on horseback from Trinidad. He had been sent by friendly townsfolk who, still mad at the Rio Grande, wanted to help the Santa Fe.

"They told me to tell you, Mr. Robinson, that General Palmer is onto your game and he's got a gang of men coming up here first thing in the morning to start grading. McMurtrie and De Remer are down in the hotel this minute."

Robinson and Morley exchanged grins.

To the messenger, Robinson said, "Thanks. It was good of you to come, and of the folks down there to send you. You've helped us save the pass. . . . Ray, let's get busy. Uncle Dick, are there any men around who would work for us for a day or two?"

They roused out the sleeping freighters and talked to a few of the boys up from Trinidad for the dance. Uncle Dick tackled them all.

"Want to make a few dollars working for the railroad?"

"What railroad? If it's the Rio Grande . . ."

"It's the Santa Fe."

"Give me a shovel, Uncle Dick."

Shovels and lanterns were handed out. Dick flung open the door and the cold night air rushed in. In the darkness at 2 A.M. the little party set off up the hill. The campfires had died out now. The lanterns went flickering slowly up the winding road; boots clumped hollowly on the plank bridges over tumbling Raton Creek.

"Wait for me," chirped sixty-two-year-old Uncle Dick. "I'm coming too."

At 4 A.M., still in the darkness, Morley said, "This'll do. One of you boys go on up where you see that red spot of campfire and find out if there's a Lewis Kingman there. If there is, tell him Robinson and Morley say to start grading now."

The boy struck off up the hill. The others stood, breathing heavily in the sharp cold air. Dick Wootton handed his lantern to a freighter and grabbed a shovel. The dirt flew. Others followed his example.

Raton Pass was the Santa Fe's by right of prior construction.

They all paused a minute and shook hands in the yellow lantern light. Morley laid out a rough line by guess and by God—they had no instruments—and a rough grade was shoveled up. High on the hill a campfire flared suddenly and in a few minutes the messenger came running down the mountainside.

"It's Mr. Kingman, all right. He told me to tell you he is grading right where the tunnel is going to be."

The two crews had been working less than thirty minutes when one of the shovelers, straightening up, looked down into the valley. Pinpoints of light flickered there and a few shouts came up on the dawn breeze.

"Must be the Rio Grande boys," chuckled Morley. "Well, we beat 'em to it."

"We sure did," said Uncle Dick, "and by twenty minutes." He wiped the sweat from his tanned old face, and smiled too.

Leaving their temporary graders to keep shoveling, Morley and Robinson went back down the hill and, near where Gallinas Creek meets Raton Creek, they found McMurtrie and De Remer, with a grade crew. The sky was paling over the peaks and the men moved dimly in the gray, misty dawn.

The four were old acquaintances, but there was an edge to their voices. One or two of the Rio Grande men were armed.

"You think you've beaten us, Morley," said De Remer.

"Uh-huh."

"Well, maybe you have—and maybe not. This isn't the only pass over the hill," retorted De Remer. "Maybe we know a better one."

"That so?"

"Hell, Ray, we had this country surveyed before you boys ever got west of Dodge," broke in McMurtrie. "There's a better line up Gallinas Canyon and down Dillon Canyon on the south side. Little longer, but the grade's better."

"I know about that, Mac. It's about ten feet lower—and seven miles longer. You can have it. We'll keep this one."

"Suit yourself. We're going up Gallinas. See you in Las Vegas. There'll be a D. & R. G. train waiting when you get in."

He swung on his heel and, with De Remer, started his crew grading on a line up Gallinas Creek, which veered off to the westward. But their hearts didn't seem to be in the work. Morley and Robinson watched them for a little while and then went to Uncle Dick's for breakfast. Kingman came striding down the mountain from his work 7,500 feet up, and there was a reunion. Robinson wrote a wire and sent it by messenger down to El Moro, not caring whether the Rio Grande read it or not. It was to Strong and it said to tell President Nickerson that Raton Pass was won.

Kingman got up instruments and chain men and ran his lines up the hill. Meanwhile, Strong started crews grading westward from La Junta down the new cutoff. May 1, 1878, saw miles of track down and, on September 15th, Trinidad was reached. Material which previously had to be freighted into the pass from Pueblo, now could be brought within a few miles of the work. There had been grading up into the canyon from May on and all that summer work proceeded at the top, where approaches were blasted for the tunnel.

At Trinidad the plains were ending and the mountains looked

ahead. Trail and track had climbed more than 5,000 feet from the Eastern Kansas prairies, 600 miles away. This was volcano country, with great lava masses and coal beds. To the south the trailsmen and the railroaders looked at Raton Mesa's northern tip, where Fisher's Peak rose 9,600 feet into the clear sky. The track swung around the peak, headed south up Purgatoire River and then up North Raton Creek, and so to the summit.

Track got to the Colorado-New Mexico line, just north of the tunnel, on November 1, 1878. It became evident it might be months before the bore was driven. The thing to do was to get stuff around to the south side and open a heading there too.

"Better go over the top, Rob."

"Okay, Mr. Strong."

They put Kingman and Morley to work running a shoofly switchback up over the mountain, nearly 8,000 feet in the air. Its grades ran to six percent; its curves to sixteen degrees. Once over the hump it ran on a 4.9 percent grade down to Willow Springs, soon to be renamed Raton. The line was laid with fifty-six-pound rail spiked to pine ties on the tangents, oak ties on the curves. "Uncle Avery" Turner, who had been boss back in La Junta, had charge of the material train laying track up the hill. The old eight-wheel engines could haul only thirty-three tons a trip—considerably less than one boxcar load today. It took a lot of trips to get ties and steel to the front.

About December 1, 1878, the last spike went in and Uncle Avery rode the first engine over the switchback and down into New Mexico—the first man ever to enter the territory on a locomotive. With the line now operating down to Willow Springs, material, powder and men could be shipped up to the south portal of the tunnel. The headings met—out the traditional fraction of an inch—at 3:35 on the afternoon of July 7, 1879.

After the switchback was built, the job of hauling heavy loads over it proved too much for the oo00 engines and the Santa Fe wired the Baldwin Locomotive Works for the most powerful engine on earth—and hurry. Not long after, it was shipped west in parts, being too heavy for a lot of pile bridges and wooden trestles. It weighed sixty-five tons.

This engine was the famous "Uncle Dick," named for Wootton. It was numbered 2403 and assigned to the New Mexico and Southern Pacific section of the Santa Fe. Originally it carried a 1,000-gallon saddle tank slung across the boiler, to give it more tractive power.

Officially the "Uncle Dick" was a consolidated type 2-8-0 with cylinders twenty by twenty-six and its eight drive-wheels were forty-two inches in diameter. Up a 3.5 grade it could haul 258½ tons. As a coal burner it proved to be twice as powerful as any former engine, though using less coal. Until crews learned how to run it, it was a bad track-jumper. Later the "Uncle Dick" was rebuilt to a conventional 2-8-0 type with tender.

From the top of the switchback, Uncle Avery looked down the southern slope into New Mexico. The Territory was a little bigger than Colorado. Some of it had been part of the Texas Republic; some, part of Mexico. Now it was to become part of the new empire of the Southwest, joined to the rest of the country by steel, waking to the blast of locomotives and the swift rush of laden cars.

From Raton Mountain the waters divided. To the north they flowed to join the Arkansas, which the Santa Fe had followed from Hutchinson, Kansas, out to west of La Junta. Rail and trail left the river at almost the same spot, swinging southwest and then south. From La Junta down to Glorieta Pass it was 270 miles by the trail route.

To the east, Uncle Avery saw the bulk of Bartlett Mesa, to the west the snowcaps of the Culebra range of the Rockies. At the foot of the hill lay Willow Springs underneath the sharp rise of Goat Hill. The old stage station soon would change its name to Raton—and be known forever after to railroaders as Rat-*oon.*

Away to the southward the plains rolled and in the haze Red River Peak loomed. The old trail had hugged the foot of the peak and then swung away southwest through Cimarron. The railroad would take a more southerly course, leaving the trail near present-day Otero and following the Canadian River's easier grades.

After the tunnel was finished and the switchback abandoned the "Uncle Dick" often hauled the passenger train from Trinidad to Las Vegas and, in 1880, with the saddle tank taken off, handled the *De Luxe* from La Junta to Santa Fe—298 miles.

This *De Luxe Express* had three cars: a combination coach with one end for ladies and the other for smokers, the two being unidentical in the '80s; a baggage-express-mail car; and a nifty number the Santa Fe had brought from the Intercolonial Railway of Canada. This car was lined with hardwood panels and furnished with huge chairs upholstered in red plush from which tourists might view the wonders of the Rockies. These chairs were on casters, and up in Canada they had worked all right. But around the mountains' ten-degree curves they had skidded all over the car and after one trip the casters were taken off. A few weeks later a sleeping car was added.

So that was one battle the Santa Fe had fought and won—though it had cost a trifle more than the $20,000 President Nickerson had allowed Strong. And $20,000 wouldn't have gone far in the new war into which the Santa Fe and Rio Grande flung their forces—a war for a rock canyon 2,000 feet high, a few score yards long and ten yards wide.

Before this new war should be over, there would be fortresses in the Rockies, a state bitterly divided, a snowstorm of court records, orders, injunctions and decisions, armored trains racing to capture stations, private armies grimly ready to fight each other—battle and sudden death.

CHAPTER TEN

GUNS IN ROYAL GORGE

IN THE RATON PASS BATTLE the Denver & Rio Grande had made two mistakes, and lost. First, General Palmer and his partner, ex-Governor Alexander C. Hunt, made people in Trinidad sore by promising to run the track there and then stopping four miles short, at El Moro, where they owned the townsite. Second, although the concern had surveyed the pass route it had filed no plats or profiles. The route was open to whoever got there first.

The first mistake had resulted in Santa Fe engineers being tipped off by the Trinidados concerning Rio Grande plans; the second had left it without a legal leg to stand on, if it had wanted to fight in the courts for right of way over the mountain.

The pass fight might have been a lesson to the Rio Grande—but it wasn't. The "Baby Road," two months later, made the same mistake—and this time the battle was longer, bloodier and more bitter. Courts and gunmen couldn't finish it; business men had to.

There had been silver strikes in the Leadville country, north and west of Pueblo and across the Rockies in the fall of '77. Up there amid the peaks was a score of new settlements, all yelling for supplies and a way to get their ore out cheaply. There was only one pass through the mountains, the narrow, rock-walled Royal Gorge, and in this gorge there was—maybe—room for one railroad.

The Rio Grande had surveyed through the gorge in '71, when Engineer J. A. McMurtrie had staked a line from half a mile west of Canon City to about three and one-fifth miles above the gorge. With McMurtrie was Ray Morley, now locating for the Santa Fe and therefore on the other side. Most of the Morley-McMurtrie stakes, in '78, were still there. But in Denver there was no plat of any proposed construction. The gorge, like the pass, was open to anyone.

Cañon City lay just below the defile and, like many another town, had been promised a connection with the Rio Grande. In 1872 the line started up toward the place and quit at Labran, eight miles away. The Cañonites were fit to be tied. They had to freight everything back and forth and the high cost of doing business was slowly killing the town. In the spring of '74 they voted a bond issue to encourage the Rio Grande to lay track into the city—and on July 6th the road advanced.

It advanced to three quarters of a mile from the city and stopped again, claiming it had done what it was legally required to do. The Cañonites got madder still. They were just waiting for another road to come and give them what the Rio Grande wouldn't. "My own little road," as General Palmer affectionately called the narrow gauge, now went helling off to the south and, as we have seen, built over Veta Pass and down to Fort Garland and Alamosa, Colorado, southwest of the Sangre de Cristo range. The directors had townsites down that way too.

Leadville and Cañon City tried to get the Santa Fe to parallel the Rio Grande up from Pueblo and through the gorge into the new diggings. On April 10, 1878, the Santa Fe announced it would build. Palmer countered at once. It was a declaration of war.

McMurtrie and De Remer were at Moro, having given up the grading in Gallinas Canyon north of Raton Pass. Palmer flashed McMurtrie a cipher wire ordering him at once to rush a crew to the end of track east of Cañon City and build through the gorge with all speed. The General charged later that Santa Fe operators got hold of this wire, decoded it and sent the word along to Robinson. This is probably true; both roads copied each other's messages and broke each other's codes. Anyway, by April 18, McMurtrie had a force ready.

Meanwhile, Robinson at Pueblo tried to charter a special train over the Rio Grande for Cañon City. At that time the roads still exchanged courtesies and the request was normal. It was refused. On April 19th it was war. Robinson wired Ray Morley, who was back at La Junta, to come on, fast. Morley coupled the engine of a work train to a caboose—there wasn't even a sidetrack at La Junta—and made the sixty-four miles to Pueblo in two hours, getting in about three in the morning.

The legend is that Morley aroused the D. & R. G. agent and demanded an engine to take him to Cañon City. This probably wasn't so. Morley was well known in Pueblo; he had worked for the Rio Grande; the Rio Grande people were on the alert for a Santa Fe move into the canyon. The story goes on that Morley was refused the engine, hired a livery nag and rode at full speed the forty-three miles to Cañon City, arriving at dawn (after the horse had dropped dead) having run the rest of the way afoot.

The truth seems to be that Morley went to a livery stable in Pueblo, hired a two-horse rig and driver and drove to the canyon settlement, arriving for breakfast. His friends say that he certainly wasn't the kind of man to ride a horse to death. The dead horse story probably stems from an experience of Meredith Jones, another Santa Fe engineer who got to Pueblo with reinforcements on April 22nd. They hired a rig from the same stable and made the journey in about eight hours, with time out for dinner at a Halfway House. On this trip, a horse did drop dead, from too many oats at the rest stop, and Jones and his men hoofed it the last few miles into Cañon City. The two stories, as stories often do, probably have become intermingled.

As Morley arrived at Cañon City a D. & R. G. work train was rolling up from Pueblo, with engineers, surveyors and a grading crew. Morley heard about this. He was without men or tools but then remembered that not only were Cañon City people friendly, but that James McClelland, a Scots-American hardware dealer who favored the Santa Fe, had a stock of tools. He got hold of McClelland, explained the situation and, grabbing a new shovel from the display rack, hiked on up to the mouth of the gorge and started to work.

McClelland quickly organized a working party and arming its

members with shovels, started them in wagons after Morley—thoughtfully handing out a few single-action Colt .44s, just in case. As the wagons left town, the Rio Grande crews, under McMurtrie and De Remer, came in and started following the Santa Fe graders up the valley. In the mouth of the gorge, Morley got McClelland's party to work and that was the situation when the Rio Grande crew arrived. There was some gun flourishing and hot words, but McMurtrie and Morley were old friends and quieted the hotheads.

Both sides, however, foreseeing trouble, started gangs building rock forts at spots overlooking strategic points in the canyon, in order, if necessary, to protect their workmen. Morley, with an army now swelled to about 150 Cañonites, kept on working. McMurtrie got *his* gangs to work, too.

Meanwhile a court battle that was to split Colorado into two factions for months, got going. A county judge gave the Santa Fe an injunction ordering the Rio Grande to stop work. A sheriff's deputy rushed this up the canyon and served it. McMurtrie called off his men at three o'clock in the afternoon of April 20th. But he left behind him, provisioned and armed, a score of guards holding the rock forts he had erected.

Morley came back down to Pueblo that night and was told by a citizen that the Rio Grande had just received a shipment of guns. Waiting until after dark, Morley slipped into the baggage room, pulled the firing pins, stowed them in a dark corner and slipped out again. That would put him one up on McMurtrie and De Remer if it came to a showdown.

It didn't—yet. Injunctions, writs, court orders, briefs and decisions began to fly daily. One morning a judge enjoined both roads from working in the canyon, and that afternoon lifted the ban against the Santa Fe, leaving things as they were. The *Pueblo Chieftain's* headlines flared: SANTA FE WINS POINT FROM PALMER LINE—RIO GRANDE VICTOR IN NEW SUIT—GUN BATTLE FEARED IN CANYON—RIO GRANDE ARMY BARS GORGE TO SANTA FE CREWS. . . . They did, too, and a judge held the D. & R. G. in contempt.

The war was now going full blast in the canyon, in the courts and in the newspapers, which printed vivid accounts of bloody battles that never happened, and which history-hunting writers have since printed as gospel. The *Gazette* and the *Rocky Mountain News* in Denver battled for the Rio Grande; the *Cañon City Record*, the *Pueblo Chieftain* and the *Denver Tribune* took the side of the Santa Fe. The editors let go all holds and denounced railroad builders and courts impartially.

Robinson, Morley and their surveyors ran a line up through the narrow canyon, clinging to rocks, blasting out a narrow path to work ahead on. At one point, where the gorge slivered to thirty feet, Morley turned to his chief and said, "This'll puzzle you, Mr. Robinson. We have to have a bridge here, but I'm darned if I know where you're going to put the footings."

Robinson looked at the swirling Arkansas at his feet, and then up to the towering tip of the chasm 2,000 feet above.

"Well," he said, "maybe we'll get an idea. . . ."

They ran the survey through, reaching the mouth of the Little Arkansas May 10th and Leadville June 18th. There was joy in Leadville when they got there but the camp learned, to its sorrow, that a survey isn't a railroad.

Meanwhile in the canyon Santa Fe grading crews battled it out with Rio Grande gunmen. Rocks rolled down from the heights. Bridges were burned. Rio Grande gangs raided Santa Fe camps and tossed tools into the rushing Arkansas. The newly laid grade was shot out with black powder or buried beneath tons of rock brought down by charges of dynamite. Survey stakes were pulled up and reset in the wrong places. Hell popped.

Rio Grande agents circulated among Santa Fe workers, offering four bits a day more. The Santa Fe went after its lured-away graders, promising them another four bits to return. De Remer took a party up into the gorge and built new forts on the heights. Some of them are still there.

A Santa Fe special rolled into Pueblo, commanded by William Barclay Masterson, and disgorged 100 prairie bad men, some minus coats and hats, but all remarkably well gunned. The Masterson army enwagoned itself and proceeded to the canyon with no little fanfare—and some sour comment from the Denver papers, which demanded to know, editorially, how long Colorado was going to stand for this sort of thing. Mr. Masterson, interviewed, responded briefly that it was going to last until the war was settled one way or the other.

The rowdy members of Masterson's party found plenty of diversion in Pueblo, and it was difficult to keep them at the front. Pueblo at the time boasted the largest gambling house in the country. It was a huge building on the main street and, according to Herbert Asbury's *Sucker's Progress* it contained "six faro banks, four roulette wheels, one Hieronymus bowl, four tables for hazard and craps, two for stud poker, two for draw poker, one for short faro, one for vingt-et-un and one for high suit." In the rear were two more gambling rooms, for daily drawings of policy and keno. There were a bar and lunch counter, and upstairs was a lodging house. Once a railroad worker or a gunman got into the place, he never came out again until he was broke, for the place never closed. Fifty men worked three shifts a day to keep it operating. When a Santa Fe guard or tracklayer did go broke, he got a brass check, good for a night's lodging, a drink or a meal, and then went back to work. Under these circumstances, building a railroad and fighting a war at the same time called for unending patience and fortitude.

The crux of the fight was the short, narrow, one-line section through the gorge. Beyond the gorge, twenty miles from Cañon City, there was room for three or four grades. Back in June, 1877, the Santa Fe had surveyed and staked a line in the narrows and had filed a plat which had been accepted by the general land office and the Department of the Interior. This tied up the gorge and left the Rio Grande, as it had been left on Raton, without much basis for its claims.

On April 16th, Lewis Kingman, on Raton, had noted the Rio Grande crews moving out of Gallinas and had flashed a message to Robinson to be on the alert. By April 22nd, Santa Fe crews were grading from Pueblo up toward Cañon City. A pony express service was organized to maintain contact between Manager Strong and the front—the Santa Fe wasn't trusting the wires any more. Robinson and Morley soon had 100 men working in the gorge, then 200, then 300—100 lured away from the Rio Grande. Palmer lured some of them back. The Santa Fe put up barracks for its army and hauled in supplies from Kansas. As one side or the other seized a strategic spot in the canyon, trenches were dug or stone redoubts put up and platoons of gunmen installed.

The Rio Grande wasn't helped by public sentiment. Many of its fighters were arrested and started back east by sheriffs' posses and city marshals. In court the Rio Grande was denied an injunction; the Santa Fe had won a round. In the canyon it was boss—but up above, west of the twentieth milepost in the Texas Creek country, Rio Grande crews were busy surveying and grading.

The next court battle won the Rio Grande the right to build in the canyon—provided it didn't interfere with construction or operation of the rival line. Since there was room for only one track, this looked like a good trick if the Rio Grande could do it. An amendment to the court order, however, allowed the Rio Grande to use Santa Fe track where the gorge was too narrow for both lines. All this meant very little. The fight shifted to the valley above the gorge, where both roads feverishly graded parallel routes, with armed men patrolling the rights of way.

Back to the courts they went, with the Rio Grande asking an injunction against the Santa Fe from grading west of the canyon. This time Palmer outsmarted his opponent: he *had* filed a plat; the Santa Fe hadn't. Santa Fe countered by projecting a line up the San Luis Valley and into territory north and west of Denver, which Palmer considered Rio Grande territory. It was intended as a diversion. New lawsuits tangled things further.

The upper Arkansas Valley became a battleground. Surveyors guarded by tough gunmen from Bat Masterson's army ran lines across their rival's grades. More forts were built and manned. Both companies let contracts calling for track to Leadville by April 1, 1879. The same contractor held contracts from both lines at the same time, and switched men back and forth. A muleskinner could work for the D. & R. G. in the morning and for the A. T. & S. F. in the afternoon—and frequently did, depending on who paid higher wages.

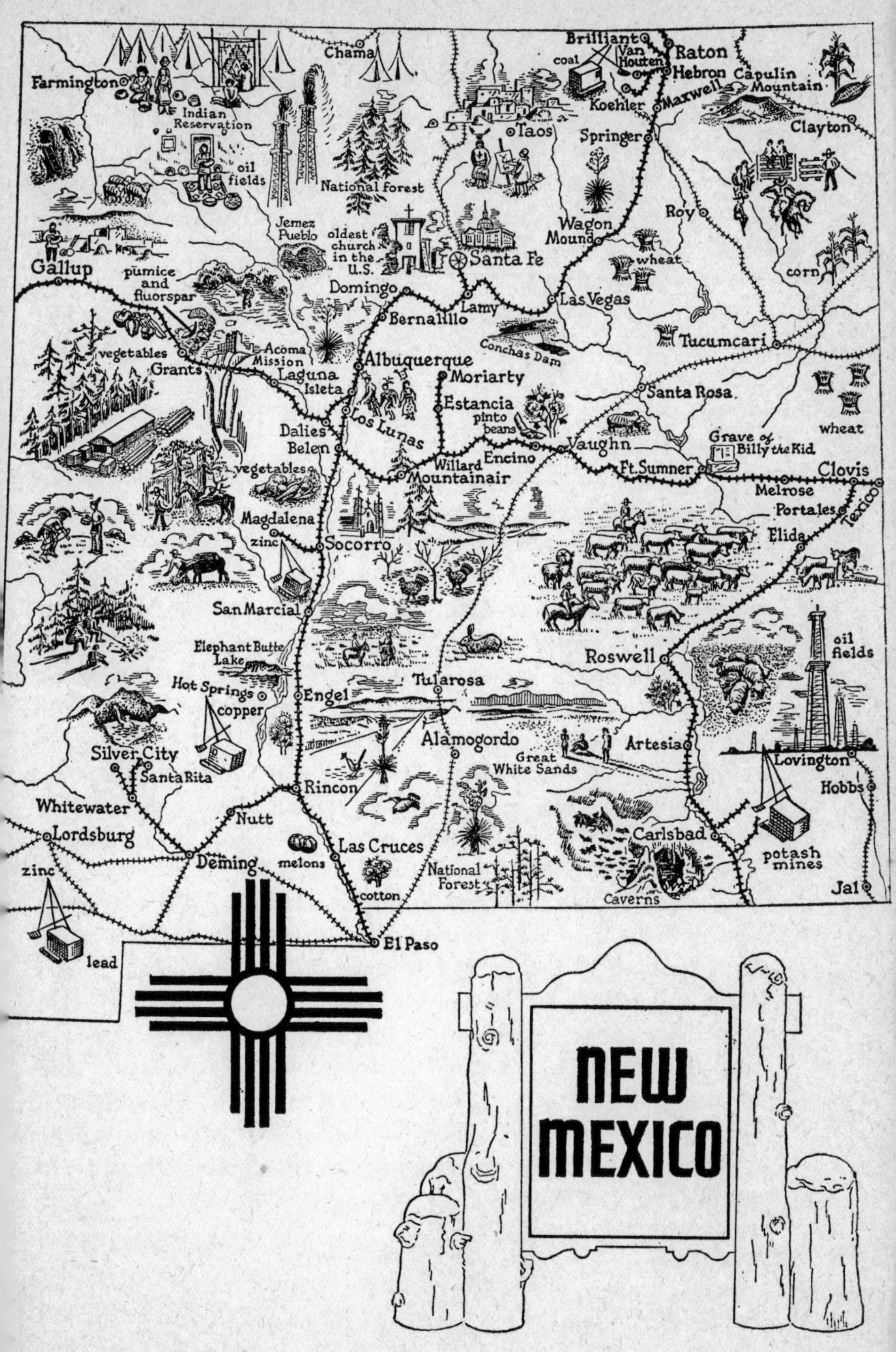

Farmington
Indian Reservation
oil fields
Chama
National forest
Brilliant
coal
Van Houten
Raton
Hebron
Capulin Mountain
Maxwell
Koehler
Taos
Springer
Clayton
Jemez Pueblo
oldest church in the U.S.
Santa Fe
Wagon Mound
Roy
wheat
corn
Gallup
pumice and fluorspar
Domingo
Lamy
Las Vegas
Bernalillo
Conchas Dam
Tucumcari
vegetables
Grants
Acoma Mission
Laguna
Isleta
Albuquerque
Moriarty
Estancia
pinto beans
Santa Rosa
Los Lunas
Dalies
Belen
wheat
Vaughn
Encino
Willard
Mountainair
Grave of Billy the Kid
Ft. Sumner
Clovis
Melrose
Portales
Texico
Elida
vegetables
Magdalena
zinc
Socorro
San Marcial
Elephant Butte Lake
Roswell
oil fields
Hot Springs
copper
Engel
Tularosa
Alamogordo
Artesia
Great White Sands
Silver City
Santa Rita
Lovington
Hobbs
Rincon
Whitewater
Nutt
Lordsburg
Carlsbad
Las Cruces
potash mines
zinc
Deming
melons
National Forest
cotton
Caverns
Jal
El Paso
lead
NEW MEXICO

Prospectors in the hills were lured into construction gangs. Mexicans were brought up from south of the Sangre de Cristos. The dirt flew—and then suddenly the whole fight collapsed. Financiers, tired of the battle, arranged a lease of the Rio Grande system to the Santa Fe. Everyone shook hands—but it was calm before storm.

Santa Fe said at once that the lease included the grade to Leadville; Palmer and Hunt insisted it didn't. Palmer and Hunt said the Santa Fe had agreed to abandon its projected parallel line from Cañon City and Pueblo to Denver. The Santa Fe denied it. They returned to the courts in a flurry of appeals, denials, charges and countercharges. Palmer handed over the baby railroad to the Santa Fe December 13th, 1878, and Santa Fe operation started next day.

The Santa Fe now commanded a track from Pueblo to Cañon City and used it to rush men and material up to the gorge, where it continued building. Rio Grande crews built a rock barrier at the twentieth milepost and manned it with riflemen.

Back to court. A decree stopped both companies from working. A commission was appointed to examine the whole affair and offer a compromise. Meanwhile a heavy snow stopped freighting into Leadville and other camps. These had filled up in anticipation of the railroad, and there wasn't enough food to go around. Leadville went on two-thirds rations; food prices skyrocketed. Citizens of the town worked up a rage similar to those of the Cañonites and Trinidados, blaming the Rio Grande for preventing construction of the Santa Fe line.

The courts rolled ponderously on. One set aside verdicts of another; appeals held up decisions; new motions snarled an already unsnarlable tangle.

As soon as the Santa Fe started operating the leased line it became apparent that Strong's plan was to build up to Pueblo at the expense of Denver. The idea was to use the Santa Fe from Kansas City to freight out supplies and then distribute these northward along the narrow gauge toward Denver. This was a reversal of traffic flow, which had come to Denver over the Union Pacific and the Kansas Pacific and then spread southward down the Palmer road. Obviously a continuation of the old routing would have robbed the Santa Fe of heavy westbound tonnage from Kansas City to Pueblo. To divert tonnage to its own route the Santa Fe raised rates on southbound tonnage out of Denver; lowered them on northbound shipments out of Pueblo. Denver commission houses and wholesalers roared.

Then suddenly in March, 1879, Palmer charged that the Santa Fe had callously broken the lease and demanded his road back. His general manager, D. C. Dodge, started to assemble an army to recapture the line at guns' point. War flared. Rio Granders besieged Santa Fe'ers in the baggage room at Colorado Springs. The defenders loosed off a volley and the attackers retired. Trains proceeded at irregular schedules, filled with armed men, rolling through stations where D. & R. G. platoons lay in wait. Stations became armed forts. In the midst of this a court order decided the Rio Grande had a prior right to the gorge.

Palmer organized another force to storm and recapture the narrow canyon. On June 9th Santa Fe wires were cut. Battles between Santa Fe and Rio Grande men raged up and down the line. The Santa Fe appealed to Governor Pitkin to send troops. Pitkin mobilized the state guard at Denver and told sheriffs in Colorado Springs and Pueblo to assemble and arm posses and be ready for a fight. This meant, in effect, arming friends of the Santa Fe.

Meanwhile Ray Morley got arms and ammunition from the East. Bat Masterson came up with a platoon of gunmen and held the fort. Robinson designed and built the famous bridge by running girders across the gorge from one wall to the other and hanging the span from it. The battle continued in the newspapers. The *Denver Rocky Mountain News* roared that the Santa Fe was "riotous, disorderly and insurrectionary." The *Chieftain* yelled that the Rio Grande was worse. But track went ahead over the bridge and up the gorge and, on May 7, 1879, the Santa Fe ran the first train through to end of track.

This was an excursion carrying 200 people. The *Denver Tribune*, which had a reporter along, said the road was "the most stupendous achievement of railway engineering over nature's efforts to obstruct the pathway of commerce." Some of the passengers feared the vibration of the locomotive would bring down the rock walls, but they stood firm. The train backed down to Pueblo—and the war went on. Another court reversed the decision that the Rio Grande had a prior right to the canyon.

De Remer held the fort at Spike Buck camp on the Arkansas above the canyon. This fort was of rock, fifteen feet square and four feet high. East of it, De Remer built a stone wall from the river to the canyon wall, manned it with gunmen and dared the Santa Fe to come on. Track gangs reached the deadline June 16th, ten days after the embattled De Remer had written Robinson to get out of the canyon or take the consequences. The Santa Fe contractor ordered his men to tear down the wall and go on laying ties. De Remer ordered up a battery of gunmen. Ray Morley came up swiftly.

De Remer stood dramatically on his wall, crying, "Thus far shalt thou come and no farther!"

"By what authority do you stop us?" asked Morley, hand on Colt.

"By the decisions of the court—and these fifty men back of me," announced the Rio Grande chief.

Morley grinned and ran his hand through his tousled hair. They were old friends, even if they were on opposite sides.

"Okay," he said. "We don't want a battle and a lot of men killed. You win—for the present."

A federal court now handed down a decision in the fight of the Rio Grande to break the lease. It was against the Santa Fe, which was ordered to stop operating the narrow-gauge line. The chips were down. A court order directed sheriffs of counties through which the road ran to seize the property by force if necessary. In East Denver posses smashed down the doors of the Santa Fe offices, marched in and took possession. Roundhouses were seized with locomotives in them. Armed men boarded trains, threw off Santa Fe crews and made forts of the cars. In Denver an armored train bristling with guns, was made up, filled with Rio Granders and sent south.

In Pueblo a Santa Fe squad, armed to the teeth, garrisoned the depot and defied the sheriff. He wired the governor for help and got none. The sheriff organized new posses and, after a pitched battle, overcame the Santa Fe forces and captured the dispatchers' office. Another armed train, captained by ex-Governor Hunt, was made up at Pueblo and chugged north, seizing stations along the way, shanghai-ing agents and holding them captive on the train, which had 200 gunmen as a mobile army. In this dramatic running battle—the only one of its kind ever fought in America—two Santa Fe men were killed and two wounded.

The train pulled into a small mountainside town and slammed to a stop. Two gunmen swung off, .44s ready and ran for the depot as the agent crashed the door shut. They beat on the panels with gunbutts, shouting hoarsely, "Better come out, Santa Fe, while the comin's good!"

"Go to hell!"

Shots crashed through the door. The window glass shattered by a bullet from the train, tinkled to the platform.

"If you're not out in one minute, you'll never get out alive!" shouted the leader of the gunmen.

Most of the agents surrendered; one or two shot it out—and died at their posts.

The train went on, blasting through the Rockies, the captured agents held under guns in the baggage car.

Out at Cañon City, the agent, expecting the attack, fortified his depot with heavy timbers. He and other Santa Fe'ers defended it with revolvers and Winchesters until they ran out of ammunition. Then they surrendered.

At Colorado Springs the southboard train under General Palmer captured the depot with the help of Sheriff Becker. A company of state cavalry stood by "preserving law and order," while the battle raged.

More court actions followed, and then, on June 14th, the Rio Grande suddenly went into the hands of a receiver and the Palmer-Hunt armies got ready for still another battle. The captured depot at Pueblo was built into a log fort and heavily garrisoned. Street fighting broke out and Rio Grande men were attacked if they were venturous enough to emerge from the fort.

A court settled the newest war on June 23rd by ordering the Rio Grande to return to the Santa Fe all the seized property.

And, in the midst of all this turmoil, the advertising department back in Topeka was calmly going ahead selling the gorge as a tourist attraction—not mentioning there might be a war thrown in for added excitement. One advertisement read: "The famous Arkansas Canyon—deeper than the Well of Democritus—for sale on easy terms in quantities to suit all purchasers."

Under the court ruling the Santa Fe now got back the narrow gauge and peace seemed near. The *Chieftain* celebrated with a seven-deck head:

HURRAH!

LET THE EAGLE SCREAM!

Bring Forth the Big Gun and Make Her Howl!

CROW, PROUD BIRD!

And Now Again, with Vim, Vigor and Vitriol!

SCREECH UNTIL YOU WAKE UP THE LAVA BEDS OF HELL!

At 12:45 today the D. & R. G. depot and everything was peacefully turned over to the A. T. & S. F. Co.

Cultural elements were sadly lacking on both rail armies and the Santa Fe's forces, getting from $3 to $10 a day and living high in hotels, were in no mood to be philosophical when Jim Moore's pay car was late. There was considerable payroll padding too. These padded payrolls came to Engineer Robinson, who worked upstairs in a stone fortress at Pueblo with two loaded revolvers on his desk. One day a mob of gunmen gathered outside the office, demanding their pay—which some of them hadn't earned. Robinson faced the angry 400 from the top of an outside stairway.

"You men will be paid tomorrow—those who have pay coming—no more and no less than you've earned." He had his hand on his gun butt.

The mob yelled. A bullet chipped the stone wall. The engineer didn't falter.

"You won't gain anything by killing me," he shouted. "I've got the payroll and unless I sign it none of you gets a cent."

The soberer of them saw the point and called off the reckless members of the mob. Robinson, gun in each hand, marched to his hotel, which was quickly surrounded by policemen. The mob, muttering and swearing, dispersed. Its members were paid off at the bank, which was heavily guarded, the next morning.

The situation late in the summer was that the Santa Fe had tracked twenty-three miles of line from Cañon City to De Remer's Wall. Beyond that the Rio Grande had built eight miles of narrow-gauge road, with no connection at either end. Above this eight miles of line was a Santa Fe fort, and west of this again the Santa Fe had graded a line to Leadville and promised the road would —the courts willing—be open by October 1st.

The D. & R. G. receivership lasted until September, 1879, when the Santa Fe announced it was locating a standard-gauge line paralleling the Rio Grande from Pueblo to Denver. Jay Gould—whose slogan was that he didn't build railroads, he bought them —bought into the Rio Grande, which thereupon announced it would build southward parallel to the Santa Fe into New Mexico. It became obvious that if all the new construction went in, everybody would go broke.

In December, Santa Fe, Union Pacific and Kansas Pacific worked out a freight agreement. Denver again was to be the main distributing point. The business men were getting together. The gunmen started drifting back to Dodge City, Great Bend and Newton to go buffalo hunting and cowpoking again.

What courts couldn't do, business men did. They argued through the winter and on March 27, 1880 announced an agreement. The Rio Grande was to pay the Santa Fe $1,400,000 for all construction west of Cañon City and the Santa Fe promised to abandon, for ten years anyway, its plan to build to Leadville or Denver. The D. & R. G. went back into the canyon, making a triumphant march of it, led by the bunting-hung engine De Remer. Construction restarted and the Rio Grande ran its first train into Leadville in July, 1880. Orators announced that civilization had advanced to the crest of the Great Divide.

The legal and business agreement, for the record, was this: Besides the cash payment for the canyon line, the Rio Grande agreed not to build to El Paso or St. Louis and the Santa Fe would stay out of Denver and Leadville, stopping at Pueblo, where eastbound freight from the Leadville country would be split fifty-fifty with another road. The lease was canceled, the receiver discharged.

So ended the greatest rail war in history. The D. & R. G. went back to peaceful operation of the narrow gauge. The Santa Fe went on pushing its line south and west through New Mexico.

Back along the line at Kansas, in the spring of '79, in the middle of the war, the Santa Fe had bought two new Consolidation locomotives from Baldwin. They were numbered 33 and 34 and were the largest narrow gauge engines ever built. After the Rio Grande got its road back. No. 33 was sold to it and No. 34 was dismantled, hauled back to the Topeka shops and rewheeled to standard gauge. It was renumbered and *H. M. S. Pinafore* being popular at the time, was named *Little Buttercup*. For years it was the most popular and best-known engine on the road: it hauled Jim Moore's pay car.

In the same spring an extra freight ran into a washout near Cimarron, Kansas. His train stalled, Conductor Charles Watlington set out down the track to warn No. 4, rolling east. No. 4's smoke whipped away in the storm and her whistle came faintly across the plains. Charlie hurried along, watching the dim headlight flicker through the rain. He waved his red lantern, but the engineer didn't see it and kept highballing. Mr. Watlington threw the lantern at the cab as the engine sped past, but that failed too. The train wheeled along, headed for disaster.

Charlie, beside the track, pulled his single-action Colt .44 and, like a lightning flash, shot out the air hose between the last two passenger cars and stopped the train. The passengers, apprised of their narrow escape, subscribed for a silver-plated lantern as a gift to the quick-thinking conductor. This set a precedent and for years heroic conductors were usually rewarded with silver-plated lanterns, suitably inscribed with their names, the date and the details of their heroism. This pleasant custom of late years has fallen into disuse.

The engine which Mr. Watlington stopped, was the old No. 14, the *Sioux* an oo00 type. Like some others, she had fenders over her drivers so that in rainy weather, when the track sank, the wheels would not throw mud and water into the engineer's face, or muddy up the boiler and paint. She had no driver brakes, and the engineer stopped by hoisting her over with a Johnson bar.

This pleasant custom also has disappeared.

About this time, railroading in the west began to develop a technique and railroad men invented a story that they were paid only for hauling full cars of freight. Many a brakeman or engineer, coming home to the little woman at Dodge or Hutchinson from Jim Moore's pay car—via The Exchange or the Cowboys' Rest—told his waiting wife, "Not much money this time, Honey. Been working mostly on empties."

As an antidote to war, there was the wedding of Mr. Lee Charles Gillen and Miss Ida Wickham. Mr. Gillen was station agent at Rocky Ford, Colorado. Miss Wickham was the daughter of Ma Wickham, who ran the boarding house there. The pair hired a minister to come over from Las Animas and perform the ceremony February 2, 1881. The minister was due on No. 1 at 11 A.M. and Ma Wickham prepared an enormous feast of chicken, steer meat and fixin's. Just before the hour set, the operator at the depot came running up with the news that a bridge over the Picketwire had gone out and that No. 1 was held at La Junta.

It looked as though all was lost, but the operator hurried back to his key, got the minister on the wire through the La Junta operator and had him make inquiries of a lawyer. This was done and, coming back to the depot, the minister wired Rocky Ford that a wedding by telegraph would be legal and in conformity with the revised statutes of Colorado.

So Mr. Gillen and Miss Wickham were married in the depot and the operators all up and down the line listened in and clicked out congratulations and 73s after it was over. Ma Wickham's blowout went on as scheduled.

It was a great triumph, and to the Gillens, at least it seemed greater than the Royal Gorge.

CHAPTER ELEVEN

UNLOCKING AN EMPIRE

THIS CHAPTER describes the building of the three earliest routes by which Santa Fe passengers and freight could reach the Pacific Coast from the midwest—but not "Santa Fe All the Way."

Route 1—Out to Albuquerque and Deming, New Mexico (Santa Fe); Deming to Coast points (Southern Pacific).

Route 2—Via Albuquerque and Isleta, New Mexico to the Colorado River at Needles, California (Santa Fe); Needles to Coast points (Southern Pacific).

Route 3—Via Albuquerque to Deming (Santa Fe); Deming to Benson, Arizona (Southern Pacific); Benson to Guaymas, Mexico, via Nogales and Hermosillo (Santa Fe).

While the Royal Gorge battles were going on, the Santa Fe was heading steadily west and south toward the city of Santa Fe, its original objective in '69. As the track was spiked, mile upon mile, a new plan began to mature in the minds of Strong, Robinson, Morley, Kingman and the men financing the building of the system. They would help create a new empire—following the old, tried Santa Fe pattern of pioneering into a territory and waiting for it to grow up around the track. That plan had always succeeded.

At this time the territories of Arizona and New Mexico were almost uncharted. Maps showed a score of mountain ranges that weren't in the right locations. Rivers were miles out of place, settlements marked where none existed.

Before they could plan a railroad, Robinson and his locators practically had to make their own maps. After this the plan began to emerge. The Santa Fe had built one empire in Kansas; now it was planning to build another in Northwestern Mexico.

For some twenty years there had been a feeling in the South and West that American settlers should move down into Sonora and the Gulf Country around Guaymas and that, when enough of them had settled there, they should organize as an American republic, after the Texas pattern, and later be annexed to the United States. This scheme was known to Robinson, as to most other Westerners of the period, and he made plans to help it along. On November 28, 1878, he wrote to Manager William Barstow Strong: "Construction of a road along the thirty-second parallel will bring to the front adventurers who will persistently work for and finally succeed in obtaining another Texas from the territory of Old Mexico. This will open the route to Guaymas on the Gulf of California and will call for another line to the Pacific which can be built by the Santa Fe."

Some idea of the empire-building possibilities of those days may be gained from the history of the old Maxwell Grant, which was just one man's private empire. For sixty-two miles the Santa Fe runs along what was the southeastern boundary of this great tract, starting one and one half miles south of Starkville, north of Raton Mountain in Colorado, down to about the location of Springer, New Mexico. The grant lay along the Red River, was three times as large as Rhode Island. No one knew for years what its size was, but on April 18, 1887, the United States Circuit Court for the Colorado District meticulously announced that it contained 1,714,764.94 acres, which gave its owner a certain amount of elbow room.

This grant came originally from Mexico and was held by Carlos Beaubien and Guadalupe Miranda. They sold it in 1864 to Lucien Benjamin Maxwell, who married Senorita Luz Miranda and fathered nine children. Maxwell was born in Kaskaskia, Illinois, came west, trapped, scouted with Kit Carson, fought with Fremont, sheepherded for years on the Cimarroncito—and suddenly struck it rich by driving a band of sheep into Sacramento Valley for sale to the miners. From this time on Fate would not let him lose. He gambled heavily, and won. He bought race horses and won. He speculated in land and won. He flung away money on every conceivable kind of vehicle and scores of blooded horses. He bought the Beaubien-Miranda grant and put up an enormous castle near Kit Carson's in Cimarron. It's still there, most of it.

This house, when the Santa Fe surveyed through, already had been abandoned. It had two huge dining rooms, one for men, one for women. It was a free hotel, dance hall, gambling resort and hole-up for everyone within 100 miles. Maxwell rode about the countryside, up and down the trail, in a great thoroughbrace Concord coach drawn by eight galloping horses. He was having the time of his life when gold was discovered on Cimarron Creek on his property. It broke him.

He tried to keep it secret but failed. Prospectors, gamblers, prostitutes and hangers-on flocked in and squatted. There was a welter of claim-jumpings and legal battles. Maxwell, sick and tired of it all, sold out to an English syndicate for $1,250,000. Part of this money he put into the Texas & Pacific and lost. Part went into a Santa Fe bank. He became its president and its notes featured his portrait, smoking a big cigar. But all his schemes failed finally; he died in '76 at Fort Sumner in poverty.

He had been king of a great deal more than he could survey and the discovery of still new riches, ironically, ruined him.

While the Santa Fe ran its lines down the edge of the old grant, heading southwest, the Southern Pacific had been building east from the Coast, getting to Yuma April 29, 1877. A year later Southern Pacific, Texas & Pacific and Santa Fe all were surveying routes in Southwestern New Mexico, Southern Arizona and Northern Mexico. The empire-building urge was strong.

There now developed a race between the Espee and the Santa Fe, building east and west. Obviously, the more track each road could own and control, the better off it would be. The Espee was tracking from Yuma to El Paso, where Texas, New Mexico and the Republic of Mexico meet on the Rio Grande. Meanwhile, the Santa Fe was tracking south, to reach Las Vegas, New Mexico, July 1, 1879, and roll in the first passenger train three days later.

Dan Daley throttled the first train into Las Vegas; Charlie Brooks was conductor. The usual celebration, combined with a Fourth-of-July shindig, went on. Freedom shrieked and civilization came to Las Vegas. There were two grand balls, one in the Exchange Hotel in Old Town, the other in Close & Patterson's dance hall near the tracks and not far from the site of La Castenada, the present Harvey House. Close & Patterson's displayed a large sign over the bar reading: "Everybody entertained in the best possible manner."

This dance hall became famous in February, 1882, when all its girls were baptized one Sunday in the presence of male and female missionaries sent out by the American Home Missionary Society to convert New Mexicans and given the freedom of the hall by its proprietors. The ceremony was reported in the *Daily Optic* for February 7th, which headlined: THE MILLENNIUM HAS COME!! The *Optic* recorded the names of some of the saved girls as Sadie, Big Hattie, Lazy Liz, Nervous Jessie and Careless Ida. A gambler named French Pete also was baptized and the *Optic's* reporter left early to avoid a like fate, which would have made him late for the next edition.

Conductor Charlie Brooks, basking in the limelight, resigned to open a first-class saloon, tapping an entire barrel of the finest Kentucky Bourbon on opening night. Soon afterward Mr. Brooks was attacked by inflammatory rheumatism and sent by the Santa Fe to recuperate at the Hot Springs near by. Here he died in a few weeks, with a kindly word for the railroad which had cared for him despite his back-sliding into the liquor business.

On the evening of July 23, 1879, a sturdily built man with striking blue eyes and a short beard climbed aboard the Santa Fe Express at Kansas City, took off his clothes and went to bed in the Pullman. Three days later he got off at Las Vegas and went in a hired rig up the creek to the Old Adobe House, a forerunnner of the fabulous Montezuma Hotel. The Adobe House was run by W. Scott Moore, a former Santa Fe freight conductor, who knew his guest and welcomed him as "Mr. James."

Jesse James, then regarded throughout the Southwest as a victim of Unionist brutality during the war between the states, was seeking a peaceful life. He spent a month inquiring about the sheep business and other opportunities, but could find nothing to suit him and his family. He took the train home in August—to meet death three years later at the hands of Charles and Robert Ford, a "foul deed" that drew widespread condemnation.*

Early in the '80's the Santa Fe bought the Old Adobe House and the Hot Springs, built a six-mile spur to them and put up the luxurious Montezuma Hot Springs Hotel and Sanitarium. This burned a year or two later, was rebuilt, burned once more and was rebuilt as the Phoenix, but is no longer operated. The original mecca for the gentry and nobility from all over the world was opened April 7, 1882, with Colonel W. G. Dickinson of Topeka as toastmaster at a formal banquet. Prof. Helm's Fourth Cavalry Orchestra played for the fourteen dances. All guests, under the watchful eye of Fred Harvey, wore coats and conducted themselves with the greatest decorum.

Before this, from July 7 to 15, 1880, General Grant and Mrs. Grant, traveling by Santa Fe, were guests at the old hotel where, the *Optic* reported, in a burst of phrase-coinage, champagne flowed like water. The General, occasionally a firm teetotaler, drank only the healthful waters of the Springs. At the close of his visit he spoke briefly, saying, "I have never been given a better time, nor have I enjoyed myself more at any place in the world than right here at Las Vegas."

President and Mrs. Rutherford B. Hayes, with General William Tecumseh Sherman and others, took a Santa Fe special train from Santa Fe for Kansas City in October, and on the 29th stopped at Las Vegas, where the Don Miguel Rifles formed a guard of honor on the platform, and a demijohn of the mineral waters was placed aboard the train. Restrained by custom from praising a commercial product, Mr. Hayes made no public comment.

The new hotel, well advertised by the Santa Fe, soon became popular with the mighty and elegant who had money. Two of the first guests were the British Marquis of Lorne and his bride, who was the Princess Louise, a daughter of Queen Victoria. The Prin-

* Refers to the famous ballad commemorating the shooting of Jesse James.

cess, bound by no custom, announced her health much improved by taking the waters.

In the Spring of '82, Captain Manners, a British army officer, arrived with his wife and created a problem by announcing he wished to live on the grounds in a tent, in the manner of the wild, free trappers and hunters of the region. Since the Santa Fe had recently spent a great deal of money fixing up the hotel, this request was not very flattering to it or to Mr. Harvey, who had been at great pains to assemble large supplies of expensive and exotic foods. Mr. Harvey, indeed, spoke to the officer, saying, "Captain Manners, while it is true we are *in* the wilds, we are not *of* them."

He relented later and directed the pitching of the tent, cautioning the Captain only to preserve the sanitary conventions of American civilization. The gentleman assented readily, and made frequent trips between the hotel and the tent. Some years later, in England, he became Duke of Rutland and his wife gave birth to a baby afterward well known as Lady Diana Manners, the actress. The Duke attributed neither event to the healthful mineral waters of the Springs.

As the surveys went south from Raton it became apparent that the decision not to go through Santa Fe had been right. The road would have to be located south and get to the old capital by a branch, 18.1 miles long. Reasons for the decision not to build through Santa Fe were several:

It was no longer a good business center—a few boxcars a month could handle its freight business. It would be better to cross the Glorietas and go down the Rio Grande Valley, which was building up fast. There was timber in the Glorietas and coal at Cerrillos, and the line should go through these sections. There was a political angle too: the road depended on public good will and, to many a New Mexican, it still was a damyankee venture. If it failed in its promise to give the Rio Grande settler centers of transportation they had enough votes to elect legislators who would pass laws to make operation difficult.

So Kingman surveyed a route over Glorieta Pass, down through Bernalillo and so on to Albuquerque and beyond. Engineers, graders and track crews having crossed Raton with a switchback at 7,720 feet, now licked Glorieta at 7,421 and dropped down into the valley through Lamy, named for the first American archbishop of Santa Fe. The road wound down Galisteo Creek and hit the river at Santo Domingo, to follow it down to Albuquerque and Isleta, and later to the Mexican border at El Paso. This line was prosperous. It operated 1,168 miles of good rail. Its gross earnings in 1879 were $6,381,442.

About fifty miles south and west of Las Vegas the line again ran through historic country where the Spaniards ruled for 300 years. In this country when Coronado came there were more than seventy Indian cities. To make them easier to dominate, dons and priests tried to reduce the number of these pueblos and brought on a rebellion that lasted twelve years, until the 'dobe cities were reduced to about a score—which is roughly their number today.

Three miles northwest of the track near Rowe, New Mexico, as the line went through, lay Pecos. This town, known to the pueblo people as Cicuye, once boasted two four-story apartment houses with five hundred rooms to a floor, many other buildings and a population of 20,000. In 1617 the Jemez tribesmen built a four-towered cathedral, a convent and several schools.

By the middle of the 1840's plague, war and revolt against the Spanish had made this a city of the dead, with only seventeen survivors. The sacred fire which had burned on the altar for 300 years, flickered and went out.

The track climbed to the summit of the Glorietas, getting over through a thirty-foot cut and farther on the engineers found grim reminders of the bitter battle of Apache Canyon, where Union and Confederate troops fought to a truce after nine hours of slaughter in 1862.

At Cañon City, five miles beyond the summit, the line was on the old trail again. Here there was a stopping place, with hotel, saloons and warehouses. Only twelve miles away, to the northwest, lay Santa Fe. The line got there February 9, 1880, and on that Monday at 11 A.M. a parade started from the west side of the old plaza. It was led by the Ninth Cavalry Band and included

General Edward Hatch and his staff, citizens afoot and in carriages, legislators from the capitol and students from St. Michael's College, carrying American flags. The parade marched to the depot where speeches were made, civilization advanced to the end of the Santa Fe trail and silver spikes driven into an oak tie by General Hatch, Chief Justice L. Bradford Prince, County Commissioner Staab and General Lew ("Ben Hur") Wallace.

The students then ranged themselves along the platform and waved the flags. One band was stationed on each side of the track, playing military airs. The train, with Uncle Avery on the platform of the last car highballing it in, rolled into the depot, having been backed up from Lamy by two locomotives, the *A. G. Greely*, a oo00 Baldwin, and the *Marion*, a oo000 Taunton. There was no wye at Santa Fe to turn a train.

This train wiped out the old Santa Fe Trail forever. No more would the bull teams, mule wagons and ridden ponies make the long trip back over the mountains and plains to the Missouri. The last dusty Barlow & Sanderson stage had come in from the East. From Kansas City to Santa Fe were 860.1 miles of continuous Santa Fe track. Colonel Holliday's dream had come true, in essence, and back in Topeka when the news arrived, Major Tom Anderson slapped his thigh and roared, "Well, he made it, but darned if I ever thought he would."

It was less than ten years since the Wakarusa picnic.

For two months, from February 9 to April 10, 1880, Santa Fe was end of track. Then it became just an end-of-branch city and Albuquerque was the terminal until the road reached San Marcial on September 10th.

Robinson and Kingman rushed the line ahead toward a junction with the Espee. There was money in the treasury. The road had paid its first modest dividend in August, 1879. The New Mexico division was making money; within three years of the day Avery Turner took the first train over Raton Summit the stockholders had made 164 percent on the money spent on the southern extension.

Down through San Marcial the line went, and on, seventy-six miles to Rincon. Here it branched, the southern leg heading for

El Paso, the western for Deming, New Mexico. At this point, on March 8, 1881, Santa Fe and Southern Pacific steel were connected for the first time—but not the last. Another stage coachline went out of operation.

Dick Coleman, who had built the Santa Fe line, drove a silver spike, in the traditional manner. So did A. C. Longstreet of the Southern Pacific. Engineer O'Neil of the Santa Fe cracked the throttle of the *C. C. Jackson* and she wheeled slowly over the connection. Now there was a steel trail from Kansas City to the Pacific over the Southern route.

About 9:45 on the evening of March 17, 1881, a switcher backed eight cars into a platform track at Kansas City and chugged away. A few minutes later, Engine 85, the Santa Fe, coupled on. There were two express cars, a baggage car, three coaches and two sleepers. One sleeper, the Santa Fe, was in charge of Conductor E. C. Fox; the other, Las Vegas, was in charge of Conductor Pat Kelly. Train Conductor J. F. George looked at his big silver watch and at 10:15 gave the hogger a highball. The whistle blew and the bell rang.

"All aboard for California!" yelled Conductor George.

Twelve bystanders, down to watch the first train leave Kansas City for the Pacific Coast, gave a mighty cheer.

The Santa Fe now made another attempt to get to the Coast over its own track. . . . In 1866, with General John C. Fremont at its head, the Atlantic & Pacific Railroad got a charter to build from Springfield, Missouri, out to the Canadian River, through Albuquerque and along the thirty-fifth parallel to the Pacific. By January 31, 1880, it had built just 34.4 miles of track in fourteen years. But it had a survey from Vinita, Indian Territory (Oklahoma) to San Francisco. It still held the thirty-fifth parallel route and the right to connect with the Southern Pacific at the eastern boundary of California, near where California, Nevada and Arizona met at the Colorado River.

Railroads in early days were projected to run roughly along parallels of latitude. Thus the thirty-fifth parallel route would take the line through Amarillo, Texas; Oklahoma City; Albuquerque, New Mexico; Flagstaff, Arizona and reach the Pacific just north of Santa Barbara, California. The thirty-second parallel route would start south of Fort Worth, Texas, miss Oklahoma and run along the New Mexico-Mexico line, cut across Arizona near Tucson and then skirt the southern edge of California to San Diego.

In 1880 the St. Louis & San Francisco road, also headed for the Coast, was as far west as Wichita, Kansas. It owned seven-eighths of Atlantic & Pacific stock. The 'Frisco and Santa Fe now took over the A. & P.—what there was of it—and proceeded to build west from Isleta on the Rio Grande twelve miles south of Albuquerque.

In Kansas, a short connection between Sedgwick, on the 'Frisco, and Halstead on the Santa Fe, gave the 'Frisco a continuous line from St. Louis to Isleta, through running rights over the Santa Fe track. This was done early in 1880 and in March of that year the extension to the Colorado River was started by Holbrook, who wagoned gangs and supplies 180 miles west of Albuquerque to Querino Canyon. Two and a half miles of track were laid in the canyon, to hold it against any rival road.

Work went ahead fast and by February 13, 1881, track was down to Fort Wingate, 128.3 miles west of Albuquerque. The *Mail & Express* made the run in eleven hours, fifty minutes. By September 24th the line reached Holbrook, named for the engineer, and went west about two miles a day.

Building was held up for six months while a bridge over Canyon Diablo was built. This canyon, twenty-six miles west of Winslow, Arizona, took fifteen months to span with an iron bridge, said to be capable of carrying thirty times the weight of any train that could run over it. It was started long before the track reached it, parts of the bridge being freighted across the desert from railhead and put together on the ground. It cost more than $250,000 and was 560 feet long and 225.5 feet above the canyon bed.

At the time, tracklayers and graders were getting $2.25 a day, spikers and iron men $2.50. They had just had a raise. So had General Manager Strong, who became president August 1, 1881, succeeding President T. Jefferson Coolidge.

Running down the Rio Puerco, from Gallup, the track crossed from New Mexico to Arizona through a canyon 6,000 feet high. This boundary is peculiar in that it does not follow any Greenwich meridian. Officially it is the thirty-second meridian west of Washington, D. C. This meridian was established at a time when the government was trying to set up a new system of measurement, with the Naval Observatory at the capital as the starting point. The

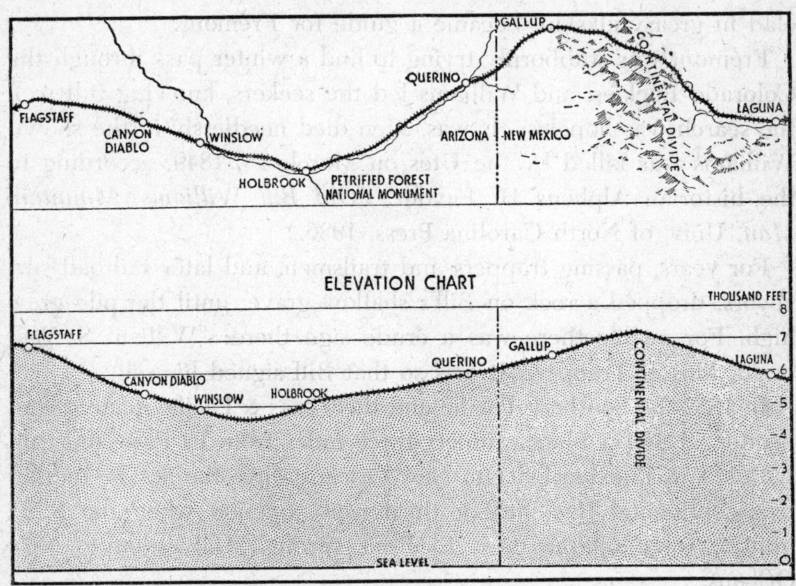

The Route Across Arizona

thirty-second meridian is three miles west of the 109th Greenwich meridian. The Washington meridian idea soon died—but the state line is there forever as a reminder.

South of Williams, Arizona, towers the great 9,600-foot volcanic cone of Bill Williams Mountain. Bill for years tramped the old Santa Fe Trail "knowing every foot of the way from the States to California." He was a lank, craggy, wisp of a man, who had started out in the Missouri bottoms as a rambling Methodist preacher. A girl laughed in his face when he wanted to marry her, and he took off on a shambling horse into the Osage country to convert the tribesmen. They converted him.

He threw away his Bible and became a trapper, trailsman and guide. He knew Carson, Dick Wootton, Maxwell—and Frémont. He lived with the Utes and became one of them—a medicine man with two squaws. But when the Utes plotted against a white caravan, Bill sent his own people a warning. The Utes banished him and condemned him to death. He fled back along the trail, and so, clad in greasy elkskin, became a guide for Frémont.

Frémont was stubbornly trying to find a winter pass through the Colorado Rockies, and Williams led the seekers, knowing full well the search was hopeless. It was. Men died needlessly in the snows. Williams was killed by the Utes on March 14, 1849, according to the historian Alpheus H. Favour, (*Old Bill Williams, Mountain Man*, Univ. of North Carolina Press, 1936.)

For years, passing trappers and trailsmen, and later railroad surveyors, dropped a rock on Bill's shallow grave, until the pile grew high. For awhile there was a crude sign there: "William S. Williams, Master Trapper." It was so that Bill signed himself.

In 1882 the Southern Pacific and the Texas & Pacific made a connection at Sierra Blanca, ninety-three miles from El Paso and this, with a T. & P. extension into New Orleans, gave the nation another transcontinental line. Still a third route opened when the S. P. built its own road east of El Paso, through Galveston, to New Orleans.

The Santa Fe-'Frisco plan for getting to the Coast over the A. & P. survey brought these roads into a new collision with the Espee, which seemed determined to keep competing railroads out of California. With Collis P. Huntington on the ground and Senator Leland Stanford in Washington, its word was pretty nearly law from the Oregon border to the Mexican line. Furthermore, it now was revealed that Huntington had quietly obtained control of the 'Frisco—which meant that the Santa Fe-'Frisco combination might build to the California line—but no farther.

The Southern Pacific, to maintain control of the new route, ran a line from Mojave, on its north-south California route, east to

Needles, to make a connection with the oncoming eastern road. To make it as tough as possible, Santa Fe men charged, the Southern Pacific insisted on a meeting at Needles, instead of at Topock, on the eastern bank of the river, and so forced the Santa Fe not only to build two miles of expensive track, but also to re-bridge the Colorado, a bad stream to fight. An early Southern Pacific bridge had gone out in a former flood.

But it had to be done and the Santa Fe did it. The last rail was laid to the crossing August 8, 1883. "Wild" trains were run over the river on the ninth and tenth. Superintendent F. W. Smith wired Topeka: "Everything is safe and strong to this date. The bridge is standing firm."

On August 21st there was service from east to west. Trains started from Albuquerque and Needles on time. The next evening the sleeping cars from San Francisco came in over the Espee and rolled east over the Santa Fe. Tuesday morning the first westbound sleepers rolled through, but coach passengers had to walk from train to train; all freight had to be transferred from cars of one road to those of another: Orders of the Southern Pacific.

A time card gave the running time of No. 1 from Albuquerque to Los Angeles, via Needles as thirty-five hours and five minutes; No. 2 on the eastbound trip took thirty-two hours, thirty minutes. This allowed plenty of time for catching up if the train was late. On August 26th the eastbound was delayed two hours forty-five minutes west of Peach Springs, but old No. 4, a lightweight passenger engine bought from the Chicago, St. Louis & Western, wheeled six cars into Albuquerque on time.

To wind up the story of this section of track for the time being, the "safe and Strong" bridge that was "standing firm" when the road opened, was washed out in the floods of 1884. Until it was repaired, passengers, freight, baggage and mail were ferried over the stream in flatboats.

If the Santa Fe had won its war to get through Royal Gorge in Colorado, it might have gone on to reach California by a route south of or through Salt Lake City. If the Southern Pacific hadn't rushed back east to Deming, New Mexico, the line would have continued on to the Coast. If the Santa Fe hadn't been blocked at the Colorado River it would have built on to a Pacific port. But it had been stopped three times, by Palmer, Huntington and Gould—just as it would have blocked them had it had a chance. That was the way railroading was played in those days.

Now, by the usual irony of things, the Santa Fe built into Mexico —and got to California. The Southern Pacific, snatching at the shadow of empire in Mexico, lost the substance of a rail monopoly in the enormously rich Golden State and acquired a vigorous rival in a field it had maintained as its private property.

The idea of creating another Texas in Mexico and opening a new short route to the Orient may seem far-fetched today, but in the '70s and '80s it seemed as natural as it now does to consider opening a new airline.

A railroad from the midwest to Guaymas on the Gulf of California, establishment of a deep-water port there and operation of a steamship line would easily have made true Colonel Holliday's vision of "the ships of the Santa Fe riding proudly in from the Orient." Guaymas is considerably nearer huge areas of the Orient than any California port.

Deming now came into the picture again. The original Deming was ten miles east of the present town, but when it was decided to make it the junction point between S. P. and Santa Fe, it was found there was no water there. So the place was picked up bodily and taken west to a site on the Rio Mimbres and reestablished. The town was named for Miss Deming, daughter of a sawmill man in Indiana, who married Charles Crocker, one of the hands. Mr. Crocker later became one of the "Big Four" and president of the Southern Pacific Railroad Company.

The original Santa Fe plan was to leave the main line at Deming, run southwest through New Mexico and the extreme southeastern corner of Arizona, across the border and continue through Hermosillo to the Gulf. This line would have followed Guadalupe Canyon up to the Fronteras; over the hump to Bacoachic on the Sonora River and thence down through Arispe to Hermosillo.

Ray Morley, roaming Sonora, found a better line almost due north from Hermosillo into Nogales. From there, on the border, a line could be run to connect with the Southern Pacific at Benson,

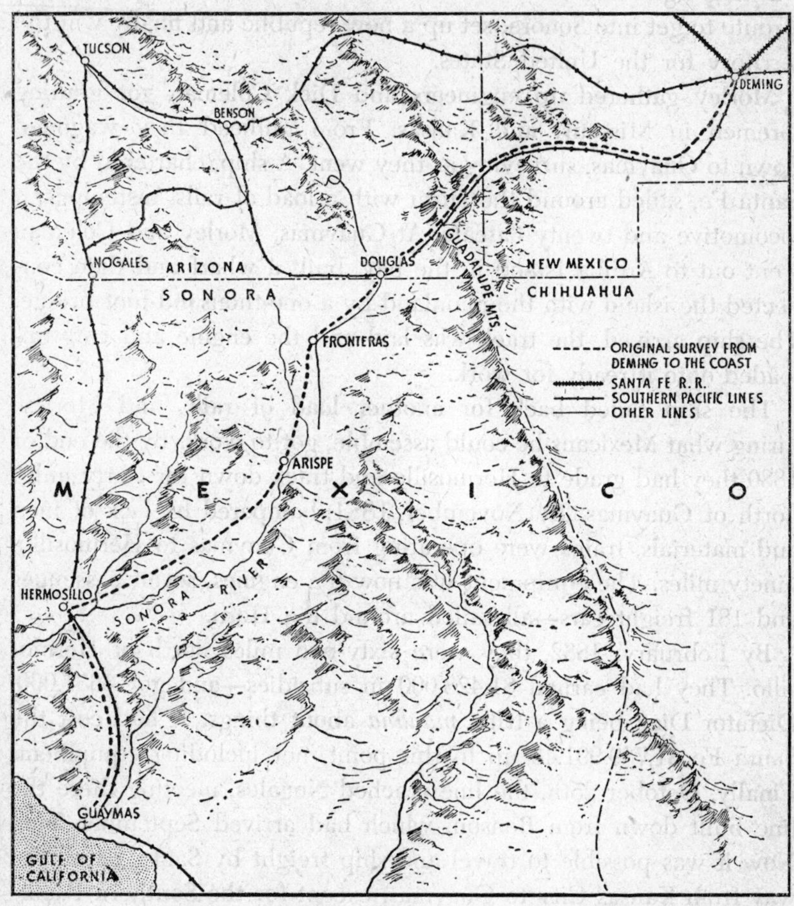

Early Attempts to Reach the Pacific Coast

Arizona, 176 miles west of Deming. From Benson it was 87.78 miles to Nogales, south from Nogales to Guaymas it was 262.41 miles more. This meant building 315.17 miles of new line.

Strong went down to Mexico City and talked to old Porfirio

Diaz, the dictator. They came to an agreement. The Santa Fe put up a cash bond and Diaz promised to pay a subsidy to help construction. It is curious now to recollect that by this agreement Diaz was helping to finance a railroad that many Americans planned as a route to get into Sonora, set up a new republic and finally win the territory for the United States.

Morley gathered up engineers and Dick Coleman got grading foremen in Missouri and Kansas. From railhead they wagoned down to Guaymas, surveying as they went. A ship, chartered by the Santa Fe, sailed around the Horn with a load of rails, fastenings, a locomotive and twenty flatcars. At Guaymas, Morley and Coleman went out to Ardilla Island in the bay, built a wharf and then connected the island with the mainland by a one-thousand-foot bridge. The ship arrived, the track was laid and the engine and cars unloaded onto it ready for work.

The ship sailed back for another load of rails, and Morley, hiring what Mexicans he could assemble, got to work. By the end of 1880 they had grade to Hermosillo and track down for thirty miles north of Guaymas. By November, 1881, hampered by lack of men and materials, trains were operating from Guaymas to Hermosillo, ninety miles. The equipment was now ten engines, seven passenger and 181 freight cars—all sailed around the Horn.

By February, 1882, they were sixty-two miles north of Hermosillo. They had earned $1,428,000 in subsidies—and got $651,000, Dictator Diaz being a trifle *mañana* about things. It had cost the Santa Fe $1,789,991.48 up to this point, not including equipment. Finally, October 25th, the line reached Nogales, meeting there the line built down from Benson, which had arrived September 26th. Now it was possible to travel and ship freight by Santa Fe all the way from Kansas City to Guaymas, except for the Southern Pacific link between Deming and Benson. The line proved profitable although the subsidy still suffered from *mañana*. By December 31, 1882, the Santa Fe had earned $2,570,530—and received $934,710.15.

To wrap up the Sonora adventure in one package: in 1884 the Santa Fe leased the Needles-Mojave line from the Southern Pacific, under an agreement to buy it when the Espee could furnish a clear title. The Santa Fe by then had built east from the South California coast, as we shall see in the next chapter. This lease gave it a line under its control from San Diego to Kansas City. Some years later there was a trade, and in it the Southern Pacific got the Guaymas line for the Needles line, later changing the junction point from Benson to farther west at Tucson.

Railroad opinion is that the Santa Fe got the better of the trade. The Guaymas line, mainly due to conditions in Mexico, has never made money; the death of the "Another Texas" scheme made it unimportant. The Needles line, on the other hand, now is part of the Santa Fe main stem.

In 1882 the Santa Fe again had reached tidewater on the Pacific but, as in the northern route, it still was at the mercy of the Southern Pacific, which controlled track over both routes (Deming-Benson and Needles-San Francisco-Los Angeles). At the Colorado River the Santa Fe was still 630 miles from San Francisco; 340 miles from Los Angeles; 435 from San Diego.

On the last lap of the Sonora Railway survey, Ray Morley and his engineers camped one hot fall evening near La Cruz, in Chihuahua. One of the men strolled over to Morley after supper, when the campfires burned brightly.

"I hear Mr. Strong gave you a gold-mounted Winchester for your work in the Royal Gorge fight, Ray," he said.

"That's right, I'm proud of it too. Like to see it?"

"Sure would."

Morley reached under the canvas of an ambulance in which he carried his gear. He grasped the rifle by its muzzle and pulled it out. There was the crack of a shot in the still desert air.

Near the shining track he helped to build, in Las Vegas, New Mexico, there is a monument to Ray Morley.

CHAPTER TWELVE

CALIFORNIA, HERE WE COME!

UNCLE AVERY TURNER came near to having a monument to himself in Las Vegas, too. He was skippering an eastbound freight over the Glorietas one winter night with an engine-runner known as Pawnee Charlie. Charlie was handling the throttle of No. 81, a big oo000 Taunton named *Arthur Sewell.* He had had a nip or two and was letting her swing the curves as much as she pleased, her flanges screaming and threatening to climb the high rail and head off into the canyon.

There was a polite mail clerk aboard and, after the train built up to around fifty-five on an eight-degree curve, he buttonholed Uncle Avery and asked: "Pardon me, but where does Charlie think we're going?"

"That," replied Turner, clutching a stanchion, "depends on how we've lived."

The wild ride continued for some miles, but the board was out against him at Bernal and, by instinct, he slammed to a stop. Turner hopped down, ran to the engine, climbed aboard, clipped Charlie on the chin, lowered him from the cab, dragged him to the baggage car and told the mail clerk to watch him. Then Uncle Avery took the 81 the rest of the way into Las Vegas.

It was the thoughtless inebriety of such men as Pawnee Charlie that caused the passage of Rule 10 which, becoming a nationwide Rule G, has made all railroad men and women teetotalers while on duty in the United States and its possessions.

Back along the line things had been stirring too. There were new

Kansas branches: 30.6 miles from McPherson to Lyons; 23.3 miles from Wellington to Caldwell; 56.6 miles from Burlingame to Manhattan—a joint track with Union Pacific; a thirty-seven-mile stub to Rockvale and the coal fields from Pueblo. In July, 1881, the line was graded and tracked from Rincon, New Mexico, fifty-eight miles to the Texas border, and then on twenty miles to El Paso.

Dick Coleman's crews were kept busy building feeder branches, mainly in the swiftly developing Kansas territory. This was not only to get business, but to open up new territory before competitors could strike steel across it. The Mop, the Q and the 'Frisco were quick to build into any likely section the Santa Fe didn't have ironed down. The river still was the great dividing line between east and west, and no one was sure yet whether Kansas City or Chicago would become the great interchange point.

All through the eighties the Santa Fe kept running emigrant trains west. They were gay affairs with guitars, violins and an occasional bass horn playing "O Susanna," which had been the great trek song of the Oregon Trail wagoners. The pilgrims went singing and rocking across the prairies behind the diamond stackers, sixteen cars of youngsters and oldsters with carpet bags and canvas, rope-tied bundles, out to start new lives in a new country. At Kansas City they bought straw mattresses and food in paper sacks. The car seats were wooden and at night pulled together to make beds. Four people to a section was the rule. Strangers got together, pooled food supplies and while the girls cooked, the men got off at the stops and rustled firewood for the big cooking range at one end of the car. Often, people who had never heard of each other at Kansas City had formed little settlement groups before the train got to Great Bend, and took up land together.

In 1882 the Santa Fe got into a battle typical of the sort of scrap roads often encountered. This one was fought and won by Dick Coleman, then resident engineer at Newton, Kansas, against some over-enthusiastic real-estate boomers out in Harvey County. The Santa Fe ran through the county and paid more than half the taxes. The boomers tried to float bonds to entice two rival roads to build through the territory, more to inflate realty prices than for any other reason. Since the Santa Fe knew there wasn't enough business for two lines, let alone three, and since it would have to pay for about sixty percent of the bond issue, it saw no reason why it should vote to tax itself to encourage rivals.

Coleman got on the job and found that while Newton might vote favorably on the bonds, the smaller towns of Sedgwick, Burrton and Halstead wouldn't. They weren't on the proposed new lines—even on paper. So, on election day, Dick solved the problem by commandeering two work trains, loading them with angry anti-bondites from the three towns and rolling them to Newton to let Nature take her course. The bond issue lost heavily. The farmers—and the Santa Fe saved themselves some taxes. The farmers were with the road not only for this reason; they had seen the value of their lands, because of the Santa Fe, increase about 400 percent in five years. During '82 the old Atlantic & Pacific line, now controlled by the Santa Fe, was pushed west from Vinita, Indian Territory, to Tulsa, sixty-four miles. By the end of the year the road was operating about 2,620 miles of track, of which 1,700 miles were steel main line. It had no floating debt and was making its bond and stock interest; it owned 348 locomotives and around 10,000 freight and passenger cars. It was leasing sixteen roads which it had, mainly, built under local corporations and would later absorb. Actually, it owned and operated under its own name only 470.58 miles of track.

While track was going west, it also was headed south, as Colonel Holliday had predicted. In 1880 the Santa Fe had bought the Kansas City, Lawrence & Southern Kansas system which had 365 miles of track between Lawrence, Coffeyville, Wellington and Harper. By the end of '84 this had been linked with the Santa Fe at Emporia, and new branches had increased the length to 506 miles. Two years later track was going south through Indian Territory, headed for Fort Worth and Denison, Texas. From Kiowa a southwestern branch led into the Panhandle cattle country. The Santa Fe was on its way to the Gulf.

Now we have to wheel out to California and lay some more track. Out in the mountains they were talking about an engineer and

CALIFORNIA
Crescent City
lumbering
Mt. Shasta
Eureka
copper mining
Lassen Peak only active volcano in U.S.
Redding
world's tallest tree (redwood 364 ft. high)
Red Bluff
stock raising
Chico
farming center since 1840
International Latitude Observatory at Ukiah
Oroville
gold mining
Pony Express
Yuba City
Marysville
Home of Luther Burbank's experiments
Sutter's Mill
Santa Rosa
wine
Placerville
Sacramento
eggs
rice
Richmond
Vallejo
Ferry Point
Pittsburg
figs
potatoes
Berkeley
Oakland
walnuts
Stockton
Yosemite National Park
San Francisco
Oakdale
Lick Observatory
Riverbank
San Jose
El Portal
Merced
plums
Santa Cruz
world's largest dried and canned fruit center
Hammond
Belmont
giant sequoias
Monterey
Piedra
Mt. Whitney
Carmel
lettuce
Fresno
Calwa
Minkler
wine
figs
Laton
Cutler
Lanare
highest point in the U.S. (14,496 ft.)
Mission of San Carlos Borromeo
Hanford
Visalia
Wyeth
lowest point in the U.S. (279.8 ft. below sea level)
artichokes
oil
cotton
Corcoran
Stoil
Jovista
Badwater
Alpaugh
hay
Ducor
mineral soda works
Death Valley
San Luis Obispo
Oil Jc.
Oil City
Landco
potatoes
Bakersfield
Kern Jc.
Taft
Magunden
Arvin
cement
Mojave
Mission
borax mining
Barstow
Santa Barbara
Ventura
oranges
N
Hollywood
Needles
W
Los Angeles
Pasadena
San Bernardino
Cadiz
Redondo Beach
Redlands
olives
San Pedro
Olinda
Fullerton
Riverside
Long Beach
Corona
San Jacinto
Rice
Orange
Atwood
E
Santa Ana
Elsinore
peppers
Indio
gypsum
melons
San Juan Capistrano
Fallbrook
dates
Blythe
Oceanside
Ripley
Escondido
citrus fruits
S
avocados
celery
San Diego
tomatoes
lettuce
cotton
old Spanish Lighthouse
National City
El Centro
Calexico

a fireman on an Arizona division who got religion at a meeting of the American Home Missionary Society and decided to trust their lives to Providence. They were rolling a freight down the divide and yelling and arguing about how far Heaven would go to protect the two converts.

As the old *Tarantula,* with wheels about the size of trade dollars, steamed past Riordan, just east of the Arizona summit, the fireman released the tender brake and, insisting that his faith in the Lord was greater than that of the hogger, dared him to show lack of faith by strongarming the brake. The Almighty, he said, would handle the drag down to Flagstaff, a drop of 415 feet in about six miles. They were hitting sixty around the curves when a brakeman came climbing over the coal and clubbed the brake, which was strictly against orders. He then presented the conductor's compliments to tallowpot and hoghead and informed them that they would have to pay out a round sum for sliding flats onto the wheels. In those days crews were fined $1 an inch for flat wheels, but were rewarded with a $5 bonus for discovering and reporting cracked wheels.

Such an incident of course could not happen nowadays, when all trains are equipped with the Westinghouse brake, with the K-2 triple valve, by which a trainman may stop a train no matter what the whim of the engineer.

The connection with the Southern Pacific at Needles, on the California side of the Colorado River, had proved disappointing. From the west, the Espee diverted traffic from the coast either over its own line through El Paso, or through Ogden, Utah, and across the Union Pacific bridge to Council Bluffs, Iowa, and thence to Chicago. The Mojave-Needles line, which the Espee had rushed east to bar the Santa Fe from California, supposed to feed into the Santa Fe, became almost worthless. The Santa Fe couldn't stop at Needles, which was becoming a dead end; it couldn't go back; to parallel the Southern Pacific across profitless desert seemed equally hopeless. It had promised its stockholders it was going to the Coast and it had to make good.

If the Santa Fe gave up, the Espee would grab the old Atlantic

& Pacific in which, through Jay Gould, it already had an interest. With a junction at Vinita with the 'Frisco it would have a through route to St. Louis. That might be the finish of the Santa Fe as a transcontinental, leaving it as a mere bridge line between Kansas City and some New Mexico or Arizona point on the Southern Pacific.

On the other hand, by running a track from Needles to San Francisco, the Santa Fe would have a coast terminal. But this would cost $38,000,000—and there just wasn't that much money.

Life was fairly fantastic at Needles for two or three years after the Santa Fe got there. There were two trains each day, the westbound getting in for breakfast, the eastbound for supper at a saloon-restaurant operated by Stackpole & Lincoln. This place was a lunch counter on one side and a bar room on the other, and railroad piecards were good at either spot. A great many railroaders in those days drank their meals, to the dismay of Fred Harvey, who appeared in 1887, took over and changed all that.

The bar was closed and the lunch counter cleaned up. This met with the wholehearted approval of the local saloonkeepers who presented Mr. Harvey with a holograph testimonial, lauding him for abolishing unfair competition.

The restaurant keepers of Needles took an opposite view and were loud in their complaints of Mr. Harvey's unfair practice of serving fresh eggs, edible bacon and authentic coffee. Mr. Harvey, too, kept on for a while the colored waiters, judging the climate of the town unsuited for the delicately nurtured Harvey Girls, as indeed it was.

The colored boys, probably appalled by the local scenery and lack of usable weather, were very religious and met all trains lined up on the wooden platform singing "His Precious Name." They were in demand whenever trainmen got killed, there being no minister in the place for some years. In '86 several sections of No. 51 hauled by such doughty hogheads as Blackie White, John Coons, Emmet Hodgdon and Windy Colcord came through, headed for a G.A.R. convention in San Francisco. The road, as a gesture, had organized a band of Mojave Indian squaws and taught them to play jews harps. They were assembled on the platform under Agent Jim Baylis and his office boy, Charles Battye and offered "Marching Through Georgia" as each train came in. The like of it has never been heard since.

Mojave braves, even then, were great shovelers and were taken out on work trains for this onerous duty, clad only in undershirts and gee-strings. The Indians, it turned out, thought being allowed to shovel was a great privilege granted them by the pale-faces who owned the fire wagons, but the road did not make this discovery until after it had started paying the redmen and it was then too late to change. Permission to shovel, and payment for it into the bargain, had become a Mojave tradition that endures to this day.

As we have seen, the Coast line dilemma was worked out on paper in 1884 when the Santa Fe leased the Needles-Mojave line from the Espee, with trackage rights into San Francisco, and an agreement to buy the line for $30,000 a mile when the Espee could give a clear title. With this lease the Santa Fe now could run 170 miles west of Needles to Waterman and then build a line seventy-eight miles long to San Bernardino, over Cajon Pass. This plan now was carried out, with Waterman changed to Barstow, Strong's middle name.

Up to now the Santa Fe had been stopped three times from building track to the Coast: at Royal Gorge, Colorado; at Deming, New Mexico; and at Needles. It had, it is true, a coast line from the Espee track at Benson, Arizona, down through Nogales to Guaymas on the Gulf. But the Espee could block that at any time by canceling trackage rights from Deming to Benson. So one more time the Santa Fe would fight for a coast outlet and this time it would follow the pathway of many another sturdy pioneer.

It would go around the Horn.

On the bright morning of October 11, 1880, a brisk young man of thirty-two, who had been railroading since he was seventeen, walked down the gangplank of the Pacific Coast Steamship Company's weekly steamer from San Francisco, the *Orizaba.* He took a rig to the Pico House and later in the day rented an office in the

Reed & Hubbell Building near Sixth and G Streets, in San Diego. A painter lettered the door: California Southern Railroad Company. Jos. O. Osgood—Chief Engineer.

This represented the fifth or sixth time the San Diegans had been promised a railroad, and they were pretty blase about it. There were no brass bands or speeches. They came fifty months later.

In 1845, when San Diego still was in Mexico, the San Diego & Gila, Atlantic & Pacific Railroad was organized to build to Yuma, Arizona. It never got started, possibly weighed down by its own name. In 1856 a survey was made for a road over Warner Pass to Yuma, and 10,000 acres of land around San Diego was offered to a road for building east. The war stopped the plan. In 1867 General John C. Frémont organized the Memphis, El Paso & Pacific. It collapsed in 1870. In 1873 the Texas & Pacific graded ten miles of road east of the city—and the Jay-Cooke-Northern Pacific crash stopped that.

In 1878 San Diego appealed to Jay Gould to build a line. Mr. Gould replied, "I don't build roads; I buy them." In 1880 the city got back 4,500 of the 10,000-acre grant that it had given away for a road that never got anywhere, gave the grant to the Santa Fe—and got its railroad. The first train rolled in November 17, 1885. It had taken the San Diegans just forty years.

South of San Francisco, there is one good natural harbor on the California Coast—at San Diego Bay. By all the rules, the great Southern gateway should be here, but fate, accident and politics have conspired through the years to make San Pedro, 150 miles north, the principal harbor, although it is largely the product of Los Angeles enterprise. But in 1880 no sane man would have built a road to San Pedro, which had very little compared with the great natural haven to the south. Besides, San Diego was 400 miles nearer Chicago by the southern route than was San Francisco.

So the San Diegans put up $25,410 in cash 17,355¾ acres of land and 485⅔ city lots. This included about half of the famous old Rancho de la Nacional, just south of town. There was considerable waterfront, too. The old Nacional land was used for the Santa Fe's first office building and the place named National City.

Joe Osgood quickly organized four locating and surveying crews and by March, 1881, the construction gangs were at work. The four-masted British ship *Trafalgar* dropped her hook into the bay

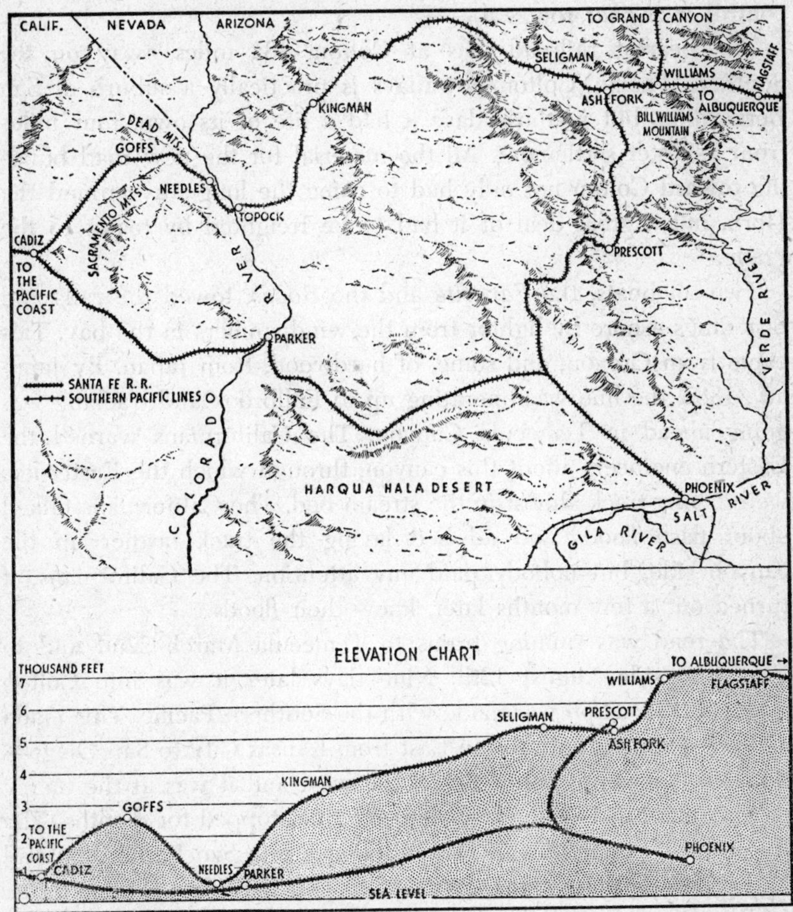

Into California at Last

100 days from Antwerp, with her holds full of Belgian and German rails. These rails were laid on a wharf the Santa Fe had built and onto them was unloaded the first engine No. 4, which was fired up

and given to Engineman John Xavier Zander to haul the construction train. The first conductor was J. H. McNeil. The *Trafalgar* sailed away and more railroad came month by month around the Horn. Jay Gould, Collis Huntington and General Palmer had no control over *that* route.

The nearest railroad was at Colton, 132 miles away on the Southern Pacific. Colton nowadays is practically a suburb of San Bernardino, but in those days it had a life of its own, four miles from its sister settlement. All the material for the new road building toward Colton not only had to come the long way around the Horn, but a great deal of it had to be freighted by teams to the grade.

Two towboats, the *Favorite* and the *Rover*, towed the rails and fastenings ashore by lighter from the windjammers in the bay. Ties came from Oregon, and some, of hardwood, from Japan. By January, 1882, the line was operating up to Fallbrook and tracking was going ahead in Temecula Canyon. The Californians warned the Eastern engineers about this canyon, through which the Easterners were laying track almost in the stream bed. The Californians talked about flash floods and advised laying the track farther up the canyon side, but nobody paid any attention. The Californians, it turned out a few months later, knew their floods.

The road was running trains to Temecula March 22nd and to East Riverside August 12th. Nine days later it was into Colton where a connection was made with the Southern Pacific. This made another through route to the East from Kansas City to San Diego—but still it was not Santa Fe all the way, and it was at the mercy of the Southern Pacific. At Colton the line stopped for months. The Espee disliked the idea of its continuance into San Bernardino and up over Cajon Pass and the desert, to join the other Santa Fe line at Barstow and, at last, give the rival line its own through route.

Besides legal obstacles, the Southern Pacific's trump card was a crossing frog—an arrangement of steel track by which one line may cross another at grade. This frog which became famous throughout Southern California, was designed by Ben F. Levet, a Santa Fe engineer, and put together at the National City shops.

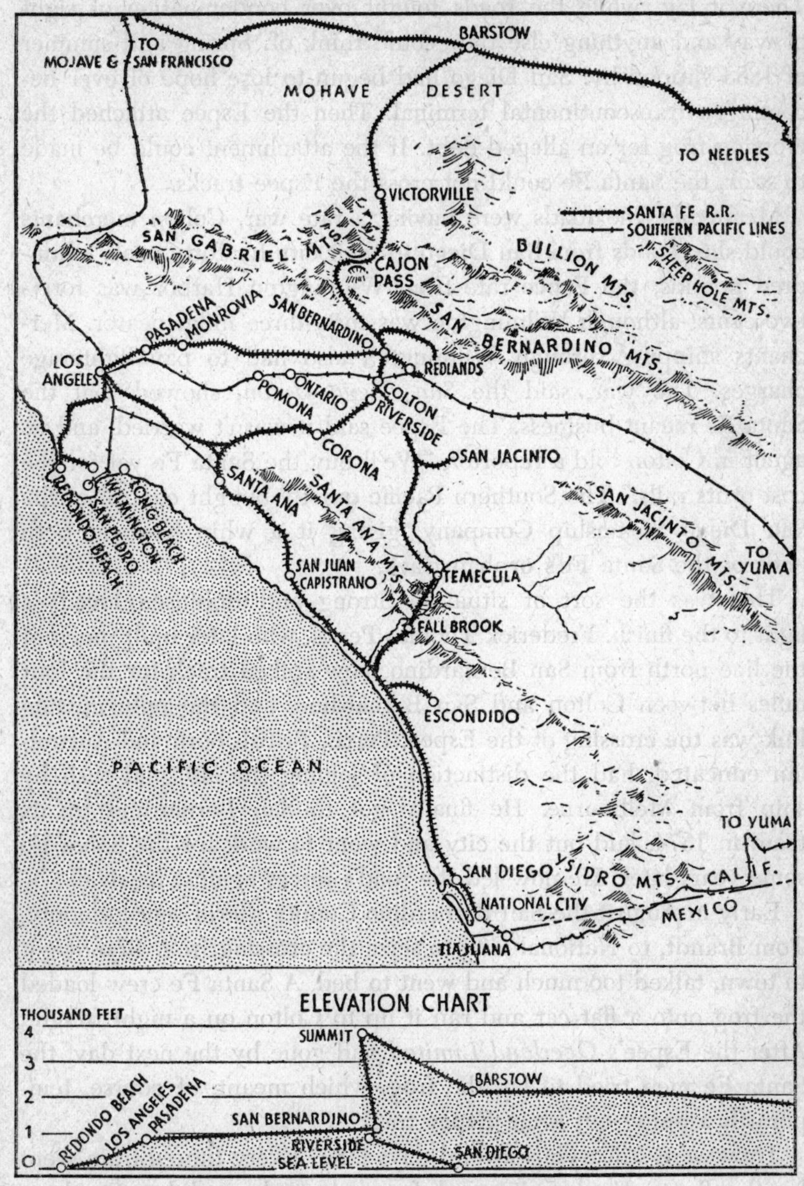

Illustrating the Battles in California

There it lay, while the roads fought over condemnation of right of way and anything else they could think of. Spring and summer of 1883 slipped by. San Diego had begun to lose hope of ever becoming a transcontinental terminal. Then the Espee attached the crossing frog for an alleged debt. If the attachment could be made to stick, the Santa Fe could not cross the Espee tracks.

Meanwhile the roads were having a rate war. Colton merchants could ship goods from San Diego to their city for forty cents a hundred pounds; the Espee rate from Wilmington Harbor was forty-two cents, although Wilmington was forty-three miles nearer. Merchants shipping through Wilmington also had to pay lighterage charges. The war, said the *San Diego Union*, showed that the Santa Fe meant business. The Espee said it wasn't worried, and its agent in Colton told a reporter, "We'll buy the Santa Fe yet for the cost of its rails." The Southern Pacific quietly bought control of the San Diego Steamship Company, giving it a whip hand at both ends of the Santa Fe's orphan track.

This was the sort of situation Strong and Robinson loved—a fight to the finish. Frederick Thomas Perris, who later built much of the line north from San Bernardino, now spiked track for the four miles between Colton and San Bernardino, and the only missing link was the crossing of the Espee. Perris, British born and Australian educated, had the distinction of joining the '49 gold rush by ship from Melbourne. He finally got to San Bernardino by ox team in 1874, laid out the city and went to work for the Santa Fe some years later. He now led the road's forces against its rival.

Early in August the San Bernardino County sheriff sent a deputy, Tom Brandt, to National City to seize the crossing frog. Brandt got to town, talked too much and went to bed. A Santa Fe crew loaded the frog onto a flat car and ran it up to Colton on a night freight. After the Espee's *Overland Limited* had gone by the next day, the Santa Fe men tried to lay the frog, which meant, of course, temporarily ripping out some Espee track.

They were still trying several days later. Every time a train went by the Santa Fe crew moved forward—and so did a Southern Pacific switch engine. The engine rolled forth and back across the point of intersection and everybody exchanged compliments. San Bernardino citizens raged. An angry mass meeting at the courthouse said unkind things about the Espee. The Espee countered with a charge that the Santa Fe wouldn't pay for the right to cross its track. The case went to court. Two locomotives guarded the track, withdrawing just long enough to permit regular trains to go by.

On August 9th Superintendent J. N. Victor of the Santa Fe had his gang ready again. The usual ten-wheeler steamed up. Citizens rang the firebell. The sheriff organized an armed posse and menaced the engine crew. Finally the engine wheeled away and the Santa Fe crew, with some citizen volunteers, broke the track, laid the frog and reconnected the rails. By September 4th track was ready to San Bernardino and the first passenger train from San Diego with Fred Perris at the throttle tooted triumphantly for the boxcar depot September 16th. The *San Bernardino Index* said that "An elegant little depot was being built." For a few weeks all was well.

But in February it rained. And rained. And rained. Miles of the line through Temecula Canyon went out, as the Easterners had been told it would. Bridges and ties were swept out to sea and ships reported them 100 miles offshore. It began to look as though the railroad that had come around the Horn was headed back over the same route. There was no track left between Oceanside and Temecula. There was also no money in the treasury to rebuild the road right away; San Diego had no rail service for nine months. Then the line raised $250,000 for repairs. The canyon route, though, was abandoned finally and a new line run up the coast through San Juan Capistrano and Santa Ana. All that remains of the canyon line today is a stub from Fallbrook Junction to Fallbrook. The bridges as built let the floods flow over them, not under them.

Meanwhile the Santa Fe still had the problem of getting from San Bernardino over the hill to the end of its westbound trackage at Needles, 248 miles away. It still had no control over the Espee line from Needles to Mojave, over which its business was forced to travel, when it could get any. Gould and Huntington worked against Strong. Strong fought back. Despite the cost, he forced the

Espee to lease him the line by threatening to parallel it. This lease was signed August 20, 1884, but the first Santa Fe locomotive didn't roll over the line until September 29th. This gave the system one more link of controlled line to the coast—but still it hadn't the through line it needed.

It was hard for the pilgrims, rolling up the long hill from the Colorado River to believe that California was more than one-fifth forest. Away on all sides stretched the desert, baking in the sun. The rainfall, trainmen told them, was less than six inches a year. There were date palms and New Washingtonia palms from the Colorado desert at Needles, but they were tricks of irrigation.

Southwest of Needles the Sacramento mountains lay stark and grim, and at their feet, the low, brush-and-sand roofed hovels of the Mojaves. The Mojaves were a branch of the Yuman people and their tribal name meant Three Peaks, which Francisco Garces, traveling through in 1771, had called the Needles.

The Indians lived miserably. The cactus and the Colorado gave them a livelihood. From the cactus spines they made fishhooks, combs and needles. From this same cactus, out on the desert, they got drinking water, but whether they admired its brilliant purples, yellows, reds and pinks when the rain and sun brought out its bloom, no one knew. Some cactus supplied fruit, some edible seeds.

The line ran up between the Sacramento and the Dead Mountains, thirty-one miles from Needles to just east of Goffs. The mountains looked forbidding, but in them were gold, silver and copper, and brave, sunburned men fought the hills for treasure.

The train went on, over a stark, silent plain, bordered by ragged canyon-cleft mountains. It was hard to imagine this dead, burned land having rains so heavy that the resulting freshets carried along huge boulders, but the boulders were there in the dry gullies to prove it.

This desert was volcanic country—and new. There had been lava flows where the train now wheeled, only 500 years before Columbus landed. In the *playas*—saucerlike depressions in the desert—were beds of glistening salt and gypsum. All around were the mountains—the Iron Range, the Sheep Hole, Marble, Bullion and Calico ranges.

It was a dead frightening country to people accustomed to friendly forests and singing rivers and the grass plains of Kansas. It was a country to get over, not to settle in.

Along this stretch of track the Santa Fe inherited perhaps the strangest string of station and siding names in America. Back in Arizona the line had such exotics as Chino, Pan and Manila; in New Mexico it had Suwanee, Optimo and Alaska. Now it got Hector, Nebo, Troy, Pisgah, Argos, Klondike, Siberia, Bagdad, Amboy, Bolo, Cadiz, Siam, Homer, Java, Ibis . . . They're still there, too.

With the Needles-Mojave line under control, the Santa Fe planned a line from Waterman seventy-eight miles long over Cajon Pass to San Bernardino. This, at last, would give it a route from Kansas City to the Coast. Waterman was renamed Barstow after a while, and work went ahead. Surveys had been made for the canyon route in 1881 and that winter some clearing and grading were done. Then nothing much happened for three years, but in 1885 work was resumed. From the south end Mexican gangs went to work under the general direction of Perris, who engineered the line.

Through the pass and down into San Bernardino, the Santa Fe again was on the old trail. Father Garces, Kit Carson, Jedediah Smith, had tramped the pathway which from 1833 to 1848 had been on the Santa Fe Trail up from the Coast. In the '40s the historic San Bernardino Rancho of the Lugos, containing 40,000 acres, was a stopping place. In March, 1851, 500 Mormon emigrants left Salt Lake under Captain Jefferson Hunt, marched down to the old Spanish trail and from there southward to the valley, arriving June 24th. They bought the Lugos ranch for $77,000—but in 1857, the scheme for the fabulous state of Deseret having failed, most of them went back to Salt Lake, leaving a prosperous three-year-old town to carry on.

Up the hill from the north end twenty-two Chinese gangs toiled, grubbing out cuts with hand tools, building the grade with dirt and rocks carried in baskets. They learned from the Indians to make fires of manzanita roots, how to mix pinon nuts with their rice—and how to leave alone the occasional brown bear who ambled by to eat the manzanita berries.

The first railroad survey in the Cajon Pass country was made in 1853 in Owens Valley across the Sierras, by Lieutenant R. S. Williamson, a government engineer, who said the only way to get down into the valley from the desert rim was through a 3.4 mile tunnel through a hogback in West Cajon. This tunnel was actually started in 1875 by backers of a railroad from Santa Monica to Independence, aimed to tap a mining boom in the Panamints. About a mile of the bore was dug—whereupon the boom collapsed and work stopped.

When the Santa Fe surveyed the country this section of the tunnel was considered—but Fred Perris insisted that there was a railroad route through East Cajon where a simple cut would break through the rim and make tunneling unnecessary. This route was adopted and is the line used today.

Cajon Pass is unique in that it is not a pass through a mountain but between two mountain ranges and across an earthquake fault. To the east is the San Bernardino range; to the west the much older San Gabriels. The country to the east still is in the formative stage, while the San Gabriel range has more or less settled down. Cajon, incidentally, means box and is pronounced, roughly, K'hóne.

The last spike was driven in the pass in November and on the fourteenth of the month, the line was open. Now the Santa Fe had an owned or controlled route from the Midwest to San Diego, although it still had to deliver Los Angeles business to the Espee at Colton.

The first through train left San Diego for the East from the old D Street depot on the evening of November 16, 1885. A. D. Zander ran the locomotive and the conductor was Clarence Henderson. There was only one mail and express car and one passenger coach to handle. But there were fireworks, brass bands, speeches and a barbecue at San Bernardino when the first No. 2 pulled in. And more of the same when the first No. 1 halted two days later and then sped on to reach San Diego on the rainy morning of November 17th. It carried about sixty people, forty-five of whom had gone up to San Bernardino and ridden back "just for the hell of it." On November 26th, the first Pullman train came in, hauling a Missouri-Pacific sleeper.

The coming of the Santa Fe, the *San Diego Union* said editorially the day after the first train arrived, might well start "a period of moderate expansion" in Southern California. This turned out to be the champion understatement of the year.

There was plenty of room to build railroads in San Bernardino County. It was the largest county on earth, its 20,000 square miles making it almost as big as Massachusetts, Connecticut and Rhode Island combined. A dozen communities started to build roads, some under the wing of the Santa Fe, some independently. An early road was the Los Angeles & San Gabriel, which opened to Pasadena September 17, 1885, went on to the San Gabriel wash and there connected with a line from San Bernardino.

In all, eleven baby roads were built and finally connected into one. In their early days they had their troubles. The Los Angeles & San Gabriel, for example. It had been started by some Pasadenans, headed by J. F. Crank. This line, like the others, got no help from the Espee, over which its materials had to be shipped. Carloads of everything got lost all over the country, eventually showing up in El Paso or New Orleans. Everybody in Pasadena got mad and finally both Santa Fe and Southern Pacific showed interest in buying the line.

Crank went east to talk it over. Senator Stanford of the Southern Pacific invited him to Washington. President Strong of the Santa Fe sent him a bid to visit Boston. Mr. Crank, still good and sore, went to Boston and within an hour had sold the line to Strong. Strong quickly built another track to connect San Bernardino with Los Angeles, using what there was of the Crank line. That put the Santa Fe into Los Angeles from the river, on May 31, 1887. A new direct line via Riverside, Orange and Redondo was finished and opened August 12, 1888. This, with the new track from San Diego to Los Angeles now gave the Santa Fe two coast terminals.

A fierce rate war now started in earnest between the two rival roads. In 1886 the highest rate for a railroad ticket between the Coast and Missouri river points was $15. The Santa Fe cut it to $10; the Espee to $5. For one day at the climax of the fight, the fare was $1 flat. Visitors and emigrants—some of the former quickly became the latter—poured in in sixteen-car trains hauled by two engines. The boom was under way.

There had been a few good years back in the Midwest following the dry seasons that ended in 1881 leaving thousands of farmers bankrupt and most of the railroads hard pressed. Now in the grain belt people had money and thousands of them used it to buy tickets west and look at this California country about which such fabulous tales were being told. Many a Kansan, Iowan or Hoosier, riding out for $10 or $15, looked at the place, asked: "How long has this been going on?" and sped back, at $5 or so, to sell his farm and equipment, load up the wife and children and catch No. 1 for the Golden State while you still could bring out a family for $50 or so, not counting the fried chicken and jelly roll in the shoebox lunches.

Some of these families were almost stopped at the border by their womenfolk. The guileless Mojave Indians met all the trains at Needles, and sold the pilgrims little clay figures which, upon examination, were found to be anatomically perfect. There was, of course, a lot of wondering by the women just what sort of a place this California might be, if this sort of frankness went on right at her Eastern border. It might grow worse going west. For some miles west of Needles the desert was littered with the clay figures, which husbands had thrown away before the children admired them. The Mojaves, discovering this, sent out their squaws to harvest the souvenirs and for months sold the same figures over and over again to relays of tourists. This made them lazy and they have fashioned few such figures since.

Everything was ripe in Southern California for a boom. Wages were high and work plentiful. Fruit and vegetable growing were simple and profitable, and shipping costs, due to the freight-rate war, quite low. Money was easy and soon Midwestern real estate agents went around in the valleys, popeyed with the wonder of it all. People in Rotterdam, London, Paris, Berlin and Brussels heard about it and shipped money over for lots and orange groves, some of which actually existed.

As the last links of the Santa Fe were opened for travel the boom roared into high gear. In three spring months of '87 thirteen new townsites were staked out along the track. By fall, between Los Angeles and San Bernardino there were twenty-five cities in thirty-six miles—one city for every 2,600 yards of track. When all the land along the Santa Fe was filled up, the city founders went over to the paralleling Southern Pacific and founded eight more towns. Then more got going between the two tracks. That made thirty-six towns ranging from little 800-acre places like Lordsburg, up to big ones like Monrovia (eight square miles) and Azusa, 3,000 acres in extent.

Azusa, claimed by its promoters to be named for an Indian word meaning Paradise, was indignantly repudiated by the Mojaves who said it was a pale-face invention meaning it had everything from A to Z in the U.S.A. People stood in line for a day and a night to buy Azusa lots. Lines also formed for most of the other cities—including Chicago Park, located in the wash of the San Gabriel River and likely to go to sea on the first flood. From waiting in line it was only a step to hiring someone to wait for you, and hoboes riding the rods from far and near were delighted to get $5 a day for waiting, something they had practiced for years without remuneration.

The Santa Fe was embarrassed by strident requests from all the on-line-towns for depots, and from the towns a mile or so away for branch tracks. The depots had to be either neo-Gothic or California Spanish, and if the road had built them all it would have been pretty nearly solid depot all the way out to San Bernardino. The road contented itself with running Sunday excursions, making frequent stops to let off the faint hearts and realists who wanted to look at what they were buying.

Even that didn't always help them. Promoters bought barrels of oranges, shipped them out to the desert and attached them to

Joshua trees just before the prospective buyers showed up over the horizon. "Look," said the promoters, "If this is the way oranges will grow *without* irrigation, you can just imagine what they'll do when we get water onto this tract!" People bought desert land miles from anywhere for $1,000 an acre—and some of them resold a day or two later for $1,500. Many buyers never saw the land they bought. They saw a map and hauled out the double eagles and greenbacks. Those who didn't hang on too long or have any fussy ideas about sales ethics cleaned up.

A promoter named Simon Homber bought some land more than forty miles north of Los Angeles, on the edge of the desert, for twenty-five cents an acre, which was more than it was worth. He cut this into lots at fourteen to the acre, which figured out at about one and three quarters cents a lot. He sold these lots at from $100 to $250, calling his town Border City—it bordered on the desert, didn't it? The $250 lots were right in the business district, naturally, on the corner of Main and California Streets. There is no record that a single buyer ever saw the property, all the advertising and selling being done in the East by mail.

A similar fraud three miles away put Manchester on the map. This was to be an industrial city—though what industry no one ever asked. Manchester cost its promoters $40 cash and sold to people in England, Denmark, Holland, Sweden and goggle-eyed sections of the United States for more than $50,000, cut up into 25 x 100 foot lots fronting on forty-foot streets. If it seems incredible that people would buy land they never saw in cities that never existed, remember that millons of shares of mining stock have been sold to people who never saw a mine.

Many towns went broke and moved in, buildings and all, with prosperous neighbors that wouldn't go broke until next week. Pomona woke up one morning to find La Verne coming across the city limits in half a dozen wagons and it wasn't two hours until the La Verne addition to Pomona was set up and open for business with hotel, barbershop, four bungalows and a real-estate office.

The City of Carlton was platted and got a hotel, restaurant, ten homes and a bank so fast that no one discovered until they were all operating that there was no water in the place and every drink had to be hauled five miles. Carlton died of thirst. Promoters of four cities along the Santa Fe got mad when the line wouldn't build $100,000 'dobe depots for them and stop all its trains and threatened to go over and locate along the Espee instead—which was just what the Espee was afraid of. Promoters over there were making the same sort of threat.

The boom brought many strange colonies to Southern California. Rialto, west of San Bernardino was settled by a party of men-only-Methodists from Halstead, Kansas, who bought 30,000 acres and, in the fall, brought out their wives and children to live in a tent city. This settlement survived the crash.

So did Whittier, named for the poet, founded in 1877 by the Society of Friends. It was the first Quaker colony on the Coast, a quiet little place in the Puente Hills.

Corona, on the other hand, was laid out as a circle city, with a driveway around it "on which gentlemen may drive their fast horses," the literature said. This circle later became an automobile racetrack until, in 1916, Bob Burman and two others were killed there. After that there were no more races.

Just before the boom got under way Etiwanda, named for a Michigan Indian chief, boasted that it had the first electric lights in California: Three arc lamps were run from a waterpower dynamo. They sputtered first on December 11, 1882.

Santa Ana perhaps labored under the most curious name in California: El Dulce Nombre de Jesus de los Temblores—The Sweet Name of Jesus of the Earthquakes. That name was quickly hushed up by the first land developers.

In 1889 the boom crashed—but out of it, in the long run, came thousands of acres of flourishing farms and orchards and valleys, bright with trim, prosperous, little towns. The little towns flash by us as we head east on No. 2.

Got some track building to do now, east of the river.

CHAPTER THIRTEEN

THE INVASION OF CHICAGO

IN THE MID-'80s a new vice-president of the system who wanted to learn something about railroading was told: "You'd better take a trip with Paymaster Jim Moore in the pay car." The vice-president went out to Topeka and soon they were ready to wheel west behind the *Little Buttercup*, Mr. Moore cussing out a Kansas railroad contractor who insisted on paying his graders and tracklayers partly in scrip, good only at certain stores. These stores overcharged the workmen and then contractor and merchants split up. It was a fairly common practice, although there wasn't much of it on the Santa Fe which, under Dick Coleman, built most of its own track.

"Gets the railroads a bad name," growled Mr. Moore. "They aren't to blame, but people think they are. . . . Let's roll." The conductor gave the hogger a highball and the *Little Buttercup* sounded off and steamed west. At each stop the boys climbed aboard while Jim, with a couple of armed guards in the background, paid them off in gold, silver and paper.

In the '80s the great trail herds were still plodding up the long plains pathways to Lakin and Las Animas, Dodge, Hutchinson and Great Bend, where they had to swim the Arkansas to get to the cars on the north bank. The agent at Lakin was feuding with the cowpokes because they persisted in riding their horses into the depot in winter to warm up around the potbellied stove. At that, the horses' manners were usually better than the cowhands'. . . .

Out near Spearville, Kansas, an express messenger named Harry Brown had been held up on No. 3 by the O'Rourke gang, with no bad effects except that the bad men had become greatly annoyed because Harry, quick on the trigger, had fired a couple of shots during the attempted robbery. This happened to be the bandits' signal to make the getaway, and the two guarding the engine crew ran to their horses and galloped off. The engineer, supposing it was all over, opened her wide and two robbers caught in the mailcar had to hit the grit at thirty miles an hour.

Day or two later the agent at Spearville got a scrawled note: "If you can't play sportsmanlike, we ain't going to give no warning in the future. We'll just start shooting. We'll blow the messenger's head off and get to business regardless. Signed: O'Rourke."

But Santa Fe engine crews, taking no chances, fired off their Winchesters at suspicious horsemen alongside the track as usual. It was, for years, considered unhealthy to try to hold up a Santa Fe drag.

As the pay car headed southwest Jim Moore recalled: "Had a funny thing happen down in El Paso in the spring of '84, soon after the road got there. Lost an engine."

That was the famous missing 196. She was a three-year-old oo00 type, a Hinkley. She got caught in a flash flood on the Rio Grande and simply disappeared in the quicksand. Soundings were made down to sixty feet where she went out of sight, but with no luck. Two years later, some Mexicans digging a ditch on the other side of the river and a mile away from where the 196 disappeared, came across her. She was excavated, taken apart, flatcarred to the Topeka shops, rebuilt and put back as a road engine.

In the pay car there was some new literature from the advertising department. It seemed the best way to the Colorado Wonderland was "by the Santa Fe, whose cars are Oriental chariots riding as smoothly as Venus in her palace sleeper drawn by sparrows down the railway track to Olympus . . ."

"Darn near makes you blush," said Mr. Moore.

At Kinsley, Kansas, a trainload of emigrants was stalled on January 23, 1886, in heavy snow. The passengers got off, trudged uptown and were fed free at the Harvey House. Superintendent H. R. Nickerson came over from Dodge on a sleigh and the Kinsley people put on a banquet for the travelers, who were having wonderful entertainment they hadn't planned on. The president of a one-horse pike in Massachusetts went around lecturing all the railroaders on how to handle trains in blizzards but no one took offense.

Some of the passengers borrowed the shop of the town paper and turned out the *B-B-Blizzard*, with full accounts of the incident and personals about the little girl in Car 56 making eyes at the tall soldier going out to Fort Wingate. A collection was taken up for Conductor Louis J. La Mere, who passed the time sleeping fitfully on a table in the depot waiting room. He accepted with a modest speech and was later given the customary silver-plated lantern with an illuminated scroll describing his deportment in the affair, the whole costing above $25 and the scroll bearing the signatures of seventy-four passengers.

At Sawyer, Kansas, J. W. Chamberlin of the Land Department came aboard the pay car for dinner and told the new vice-president that the town was named for an old joke—or maybe for a man named Sawyer. According to the original story, there was a meeting of settlers when the Santa Fe came through, to name the place. The argument grew hot, so Mrs. A. R. Mack, a pioneer, said she would tell a story to get everyone back in a good humor. She told the one about the brakeman coming through a chair car just as the train emerged from a tunnel, calling the next stop: "Sawyer! Sawyer!" A girl was being kissed by a young man. "I don't care if you did—we're married anyway," she retorted, with a toss of her head.

So the settlers compromised on the name of Sawyer for the new town. And to this day there are people who believe the story.

There were, drawled Mr. Moore, as the car pulled out, fewer deadheads riding trains nowadays. There had been a ruling cutting down the number of free passes; they used to be issued to practically anyone who asked. Bill Nye, the humorist, and his family lost theirs, numbered Q-035. Mr. Nye wrote pitiful letters to Santa Fe officials at Topeka, seeking some sinecure in which he could pose as an employee and thus rate a pass. One letter read: "I

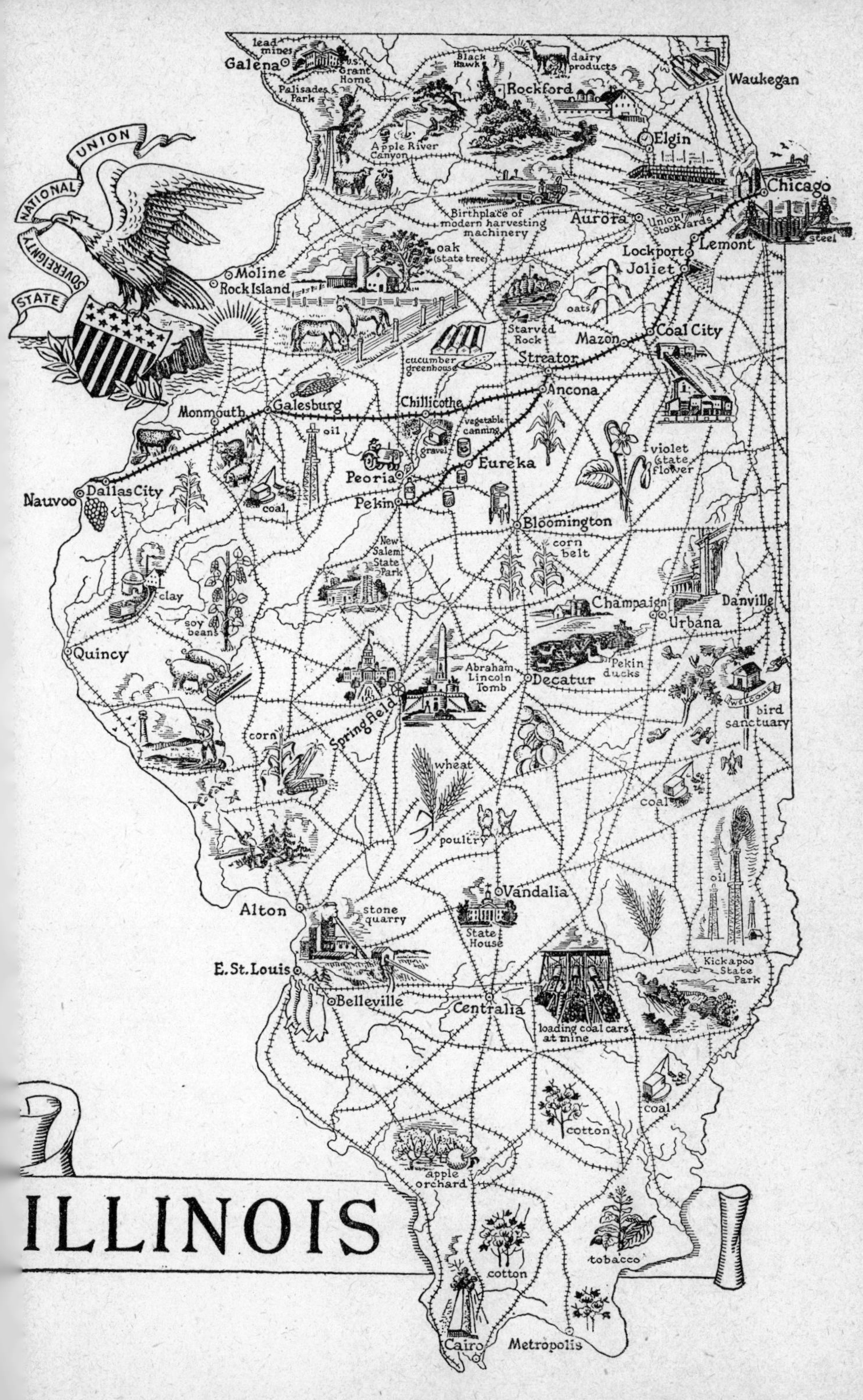

lead mines
Galena
U.S. Grant Home
Palisades Park
Black Hawk
Rockford
dairy products
Waukegan
Apple River Canyon
Elgin
NATIONAL UNION
STATE SOVEREIGNTY
Chicago
Birthplace of modern harvesting machinery
Aurora
Union Stock Yards
steel
Lemont
Lockport
Joliet
oak (state tree)
Moline
Rock Island
oats
Starved Rock
Mazon
Coal City
cucumber greenhouse
Streator
Ancona
Monmouth
Galesburg
Chillicothe
oil
vegetable canning
gravel
Eureka
violet (state flower)
Peoria
Pekin
Nauvoo
Dallas City
coal
Bloomington
New Salem State Park
corn belt
clay
soy beans
Champaign
Urbana
Danville
Quincy
Abraham Lincoln Tomb
Decatur
Pekin ducks
Springfield
welcome
bird sanctuary
corn
wheat
coal
poultry
oil
Vandalia
Alton
stone quarry
State House
E. St. Louis
Kickapoo State Park
Belleville
Centralia
loading coal cars at mine
coal
cotton
apple orchard
ILLINOIS
tobacco
cotton
Cairo
Metropolis

could become an Immigration Influencer for your road." The Santa Fe had to refuse, however. It had several already.

Out past Albuquerque they rolled, Mr. Moore telling how, when the road arrived in 1880 there were only a few old boxcars on a sidetrack and no buildings at all on the new townsite. The new town was two miles from Old Albuquerque, and it cost fifty cents on a buckboard to travel between the two. The new town had a few tents and the first merchants dug holes in the ground to keep their stock, which mainly sold on a barrelhead at "two bits" a shot, either whisky or beer. Lots were for sale at $10 each and there were a few takers. Everybody thought the new town would be at Isleta, some miles down the track. Now, as the vice-president rolled in with Jim Moore, here was quite a town and no more $10 lots.

"You can still buy $10 lots at Isleta, though," said Moore.

Out at Needles the Mojave Indians gathered around the depot with the little clay figures, as usual, to sell to the passengers on the *Oh-va-quath.* That was their name for the passenger train; it meant yellow houses—yellow being the color of the first cars.

The vice-president heard from engineers and conductors about old locating fights, when two roads were racing to get a grade established. A favorite trick was to wait until your rival had a line surveyed, and then run your own line back and forth across it every few miles. This was likely to turn up a place or two where your rival hadn't legally acquired a right of way—in which case you got your own right of way as suddenly as possible to block the first line by enjoining him from crossing you.

As the train rolled along, the paymaster pointed out all sorts of locomotives—the high-wheeled Hinkleys and assorted other oo00-types from Manchester, Brooks and Pittsburgh plants. The old diamond stack was pretty well universal. The first locomotive the road ever built came out of its shops in Topeka in '81. This was the second No. 1 and named the *C. K. Holliday* as the first had been, back in '69. It was the familiar oo00 type with 17″ by 28″ cylinders, weighing thirty-nine tons. The second No. 2 was a sister, named the *William B. Strong.* Both these engines had six-inch air pumps, driver brakes and coal-burning equipment. Second No. 3 came out in 1882 and was named the *T. C. Wheeler.* It was the last Santa Fe engine to bear a name.

"Kind of a pity they stopped naming them," mused Moore. "Not much romance in just a number. The engine crews like to think their engine belongs to them; they take a personal interest in her and get to know all her quirks. We've got about two hundred fifty operating now, and I guess it won't be long before the boys will just have to take any old coffeepot that's assigned them."

In 1886 and 1887 the road bought a fleet of oo00 and oo000 engines from the Schenectady works and one experimental locomotive from the same makers. This had one of the first oo00o wheel arrangements and a double cab that later came to be called a Mother Hubbard. The engine wasn't very successful and was rebuilt into a oo00. About the same time a oo0000 locomotive was ordered, but never finished. Some of the old locomotives gave sixty years or more of service, and it was common at Golden and Diamond Jubilees in Kansas towns for fifty- and sixty-year-old motive power to be exhibited alongside modern equipment.

Some of the early engines had injectors and some didn't—just old-fashioned pumps. The water cars were just two wooden tanks bolted down to a flat car and equipped with a rubber hose. The alkali water was bad and good water had to be hauled long distances. Alkali was hard on boilers which had to be cleaned frequently and traditionally leaked like sieves. There were no crummies on freight drags and the crew hung out in a boxcar, sitting on sacks of beans, flour or coffee. There was no telegraph over long stretches. On some trains a cord was unwound from a reel on the roof of the last car and led forward to the engine bell. If the train broke in two the bell rang, alarming all hands, who dashed out and strongarmed the brakes.

On some of the first three-car trains over the mountains there were notices asking passengers not to get off and pick flowers while the train was in motion. There was little around except buffalo grass and cactus anyway, and it was felt that as long as travelers weren't asked to get out and push they should be satisfied to sit quietly and not go helling off over the countryside.

By the time the vice-president was back in Topeka he knew something about railroading on the old Santa Fe.

"Thanks, Jim," he said. "Come and see me in Chicago some time. That new Chicago line from Kansas City is worth riding over. The boys made quite a record building it."

They had.

Construction of the Kansas City-Chicago track in the mid-'80s still stands as something to shoot at in railroading. In nine months Santa Fe engineers and crews located, surveyed, graded and ironed about 350 miles of new line; about 100 miles more was rebuilt almost from the grassroots and five big bridges were thrown across major rivers, to say nothing of scores of smaller ones totaling, in all, about nine miles of bridge.

Four men worked together to plan and execute this swift thrust of Santa Fe steel into Chicago from the Missouri. They were William Barstow Strong, then president; Albert A. Robinson, chief engineer; Octave Chanute, a bridge designer who later became a famous aviator; and J. F. Wallace the resident engineer, who, years ahead, was to become chief engineer for the Panama Canal. Maybe we should include Dick Coleman, who bossed construction crews on the long track.

It had become apparent that the Santa Fe would have to build to Chicago or be content to remain a bridge line. There were already four roads operating between lakes and river and not only were they all making money, but three of them were invading Santa Fe territory. They were the Rock Island, the Missouri-Pacific and the 'Frisco. To Strong and Robinson they seemed almost as menacing as the Border Ruffians against whom Colonel Holliday had fought nearly twenty years before.

The weakness of the Santa Fe position was this: farmers and other shippers in this territory, to get their products to the lakes, had to ship first to Kansas City and then transfer to another road to get to Chicago—which was slow and costly. Obviously, if east-of-the Missouri roads built into Western territory, they could offer one-road shipment all the way, which meant saving of time and money. In fact, the invaders already had started to do this.

The Union Pacific, with an Eastern terminal at Council Bluffs, Iowa, was up against the same problem. It found itself being paralleled across Nebraska, by Chicago roads, but because of lack of ready cash and other reasons, it was unable to build an eastern extension; it remained a bridge line.

The Santa Fe, luckily, had and could raise money for its invasion of the East. Robinson took a ruler and drew a straight line between Kansas City and Chicago. That was what he wanted, and he almost got it by warning all his locators not to plan any curves they couldn't account for. This line, if run, would have passed nearly through Keokuk and about ten miles south of Galesburg, Illinois. In the end, as we shall see, it missed Keokuk and ran through Galesburg.

This airline—which even today gives the Santa Fe the shortest and fastest route between the Missouri and the Lake—was partly the result of Western rail tradition, which was to build first and then locate towns along the track afterward. In the East the more usual plan was to connect already established towns which lengthened the line between terminals but provided more local business.

In the Santa Fe case the straight line proved profitable because most of its traffic was through-haul, anyway—and other roads had to base their tariffs on Santa Fe mileage, although having to haul passengers and freight more miles between Chicago and Kansas City.

There were, at first, three plans: buy the Chicago & Alton; run an airline stem all the way; buy the Chicago & St. Louis, from Chicago to Pekin, Illinois, and use about 100 miles of it, from Chicago to Ancona, as part of the new line. The Chicago & St. Louis would have to be rebuilt, but that could be done. The third plan was finally adopted.

The Chicago & St. Louis, known as the Hinckley Road, was the brainchild of Francis C. Hinckley, a Chicago promoter. It had fair grades and curves, but was in the two-streaks-of-rust class. It had been projected about the same time as the original Santa Fe, gone broke a couple of times and finally ambled into the old frame depot on 23rd Street in Chicago in 1884. Its equipment was shaky and by the time workmen had its track fixed on one end the other was falling apart. When the Santa Fe got it, its payrolls were five months behind and most of its employees, who came along on the deal, started to eat regularly again.

Later in 1885 Robinson went to C. F. Morse of the Kansas City stockyards, swore him to secrecy and gave him a check for several thousand dollars. Morse went to St. Louis and placed this check in a bank. This bank then redeposited the check in a bank in Keokuk, Iowa, payable to B. F. Booker. By this means it was hoped no one would get wise to the Santa Fe's plans—or know that Mr. Booker was a Santa Fe engineer from Topeka.

Booker and J. W. Snow, his assistant, went to St. Louis and bought twelve sets of surveying instruments from the Alloe Instrument Company, paying by check on the Keokuk bank. Then they returned to Keokuk, opened a modest office without a name on the door, and hired eight locating engineers. These men also were sworn to secrecy, told to hire crews and go out and survey the new line. They were to talk to no one, especially newspaper reporters, and to make reports on blank paper or hotel stationery.

This secrecy lasted until December, 1886, when the Santa Fe, having got a head start, came out into the open and established construction offices in Kansas City and Chicago. Chanute started designing his bridges to cross the Mississippi, at Keokuk, the Grand at Dean Lake, the Missouri at Sibley and the Illinois at Chillicothe. There was to be a fifth bridge—over the Des Moines River—but that came later when the road decided to miss Keokuk and cross the Mississippi at Fort Madison instead. By crossing at Keokuk the line would have missed the Des Moines River, which joins the main stream there.

After all plans had been made and the line surveyed, construction started in March, 1887, when the frost left the ground. The location crossed thirteen other roads, some at grade, some by over- and underpasses. These intersections with other lines made construction simple. Material was delivered at half a dozen places at the same time and soon 7,000 men were at work. Soon after building started, Galesburg citizens got together and offered twenty acres of ground for a depot and yards, as well as a right of way through the town if the line would swing north. It did.

Fort Madison outbid Keokuk, and the line again was veered north to run through it. The records show that both Galesburg and Fort Madison profited handsomely from their investments in the Santa Fe by immediate booms and increased property values. Galesburg, its citizens said, got a creek straightened for nothing; the cost to the Santa Fe was about twice the value of the land the town had given the road.

Construction was started by a grading crew that distinguished itself the first morning by getting arrested. This was at Knoxville, Illinois, a few miles out of Galesburg. It was an argument over relocation of a state highway, and a justice of the peace and a company lawyer had it straightened out quickly.

The five big bridges were engineering feats. They were all problem spans with treacherous rivers to conquer. They were built at record speed and partly in bitter winter weather. There were almost two miles of construction in them: the Illinois bridge ran to 1,438 feet; the Mississippi, 2,963; the Missouri, 4,053; the Grand, 458 and the Des Moines 900. Incidentally, if it had gone through Keokuk, the road might have leased a river bridge there owned by Andrew Carnegie; he was asking $20,000 a year for its use.

The Mississippi bridge was finished in December, and the last spike on the new road was hammered in at 6 P.M. in the dark murk of December 31st just six hours ahead of the deadline. This was near Medill, Missouri. The big Missouri bridge, where work had been hampered by weather and ice, was finished February 11, 1888, although a work train crept over a falsework on January 26th.

Meanwhile, the Santa Fe had spent nearly $13,000,000 on real estate and construction inside Chicago and had on order a fleet of new electric-lighted vestibule trains. It was going after the Chicago-Kansas City business in a big way, with speed and luxury as its attractions. It had, to start with, much the shortest line between the cities. And now, for the first time, it owned or controlled its own track from the lakes to the Pacific, which no other road did. It could offer through rates and through service.

MISSOURI
UNITED WE STAND DIVIDED WE FALL
SALUS POPULI SUPREMA LEX ESTO
cereal mills
Maryville
wheat
Trenton
corn
Kirksville
Medill
Baring
La Plata
gravel
St. Joseph
tobacco
Chillicothe
Bucklin
Marceline
Macon
Hannibal
coal
Gower
Plattsburg
Lathrop
Lawson
Norborne
Carrollton
Bosworth
Huck Finn and Tom Sawyer
Moberly
clay
Spring house (c. 1801) Daniel Boone Homestead
Richmond
Hardin
Henrietta
Marshall
University of Mo.
Mexico
Independence
Kansas City
Stock Yards
hay
Columbia
Fulton
St. Charles
University City
St. Louis
Sedalia
STATE FAIR
Jefferson City
corncob pipes
beer
Clayton
Clinton
Bagnell Dam
silica barites
Crystal City
Lake of the Ozarks
Rolla
St. Genevieve
Nevada
lead
Bolduc House (ca. 1785)
Flat River
iron
cement plants, sawmills, etc.
Lebanon
zinc
Cape Girardeau
Carthage
Springfield
Missouri mule
Joplin
caves
Charleston
Neosho
Poplar Bluff
cotton
lumber
Kennett
Caruthersville

And, more than anything, it had won its counter-invasion of Chicago territory and saved itself from the impending disaster of invasion by its Eastern rivals.

It is interesting to note the complexity of building a new line by a summary of the various corporations by which the Santa Fe got from Kansas City to Chicago. Started out of the Chicago depot, it operated from Dearborn Station to 49th Street over the tracks of the Chicago & Western Indiana; then over former Grand Trunk trackage to South Central Park Avenue, now Corwith; and then over about 100 miles of line it bought and rebuilt from the Chicago & St. Louis, to Ancona.

From Ancona it was Santa Fe track to the east end of the Mississippi River Bridge, which was built by the Mississippi River Railroad & Toll Bridge Company, owned by the Santa Fe. From the west end to the Iowa-Missouri line, construction was by the Chicago, California & Santa Fe Company of Iowa; from the line to the east end of the Missouri River Bridge at Sibley, it was Santa Fe again, but the bridge was built by the Sibley Bridge Company. Then from Sibley to Big Blue Junction, Missouri, once more it was Santa Fe; from the junction the road had trackage rights into the Union Station over the Kansas City Belt Line Railway.

The new vestibuled trains started out for Kansas City in April, 1888. The first one left Chicago on the evening of Sunday, the 28th. Thereafter there were morning and evening runs each day, each way. Running time was cut from fifteen hours to thirteen hours, forty-five minutes.

The new trains were the longest vestibuled jobs in the world, 600 feet from pilot to rear platform. The consist was mail car, baggage car, second-class coach, two first-class coaches, a parlor-smoker, a diner and two sleeping cars. With girder construction and collision posts, the new stock was collapse-proof and braced against telescoping. The conductor could set the brakes by pulling a cord anywhere in the train. A dynamo in the baggage car charged batteries under each car for electric lights—but the old oil lanterns were in place, just in case. And also, just in case the new steam-heating system failed, there were Baker coalheaters too.

The day coaches were finished in carved mahogany, with maroon and old-gold plush upholstery and each had a men's and women's room. The parlor car was in antique oak, with golden-brown ottomans, sofas and wicker settees finished with glace-silk plush. The two sixty-nine-foot sleepers were in Louis XV style, with all inside and outside hardware, even the brake handles, in solid bronze. This car was done in French oak and mahogany, with peacock-blue upholstery.

The diner was finished in hand-carved French oak, had sections for private parties and offered such delights as roast veal, chicken halibut, sweetbreads and spring lamb on the regular Fred Harvey $1 dinner with five kinds of wine available.

In the late '80s competition for passenger traffic led to some all-time highs in "inducements." The Santa Fe lost one party going from Iowa to California when a competing road offered a private car and free beer all the way. The Santa Fe countered with an offer of one free ticket for every four purchased and suggested taking along a clergyman as chaplain at half fare. But the beer won.

It was customary to charge full rates for a ticket and promise a rebate when the stub was turned in at the passenger's destination. In Iowa, one Santa Fe agent gathered up travelers by driving through the countryside around Cedar Rapids in a buckboard with two kegs of beer roped on. Being a teetotaler himself, he invariably got back to the office with two empty kegs and several carloads of homeseekers.

One part of an agent's job in those days was tacking up travel advertisements on fence posts and convincing Iowa farmers that they'd do much better in Kansas or California.

Passengers were having a swell time but out on the west end there was trouble, not only for management but for crews. The old Rio Grande fight had broken out again. The Santa Fe was finding it hard to get its traffic over the D. & R. G. line north of Pueblo. Strong didn't compromise this time. He promptly built 116 miles of new standard-gauge track from Pueblo to Denver, paralleling the Rio Grande, and from Pueblo ran a little extension to Cañon City, scene of the battles of 1880. In Denver he bought the Denver

Circle Railroad, an eight-mile belt track, for $800,000 and got a firm grip on terminal facilities and the freight business of northern Colorado.

Just before midnight on May 13, 1888, train No. 7 pulled out of Pueblo headed north for Colorado Springs. Conductor Ammon gave the highball to Engineer Bill Cowan—and that was the start of one of the weirdest rail dramas of the West. Ahead of No. 7 was No. 31, a mixed train which No. 7 had orders to pass at the Springs. At the south end of the Springs yards, the freight stopped and did some switching. The caboose and four cars were left out on the main stem with brakes set while the engine and the rest of the train went into a siding to pick up some more boxcars. The caboose and one freight car were equipped with handbrakes; the other three cars had air-brakes. The five cars and their contents made a fantastically perfect setup for what followed.

In the caboose were two passengers, drinking. They quarreled and one knifed the other to death. The murderer suddenly sober, quickly jumped from the death car and, seeing that the crew was half a mile away, loosened the handbrakes and bled the air. The cars started to roll back down the thirteen-mile grade to Fountain. The murdered man's body rolled slowly from side to side of the caboose, under the flickering light of the lantern hanging from the ceiling. The murderer ran swiftly from the right of way and disappeared, sure that the wreck would hide his crime.

The five cars gathered speed down the grade, flanges screaming around the curves. Faster and faster . . . No fiction writer could have loaded the string with more potential disaster. One car held 3,000 gallons of naphtha; the next, nine tons of giant powder; the third ten tons of hardware and steel rods; the fourth a few tons of tiling. The runaway train was a perfect projectile.

At Fountain, No. 7 had stopped. It was a moonlight night and off to the northwest the white pile of Pike's Peak shone coldly in the clear spring air. It was 2:39 A.M.

Engineer Bill Cowan of No. 7, oiling around, heard the runaway screaming down the track and yelled to his fireman to jump. Conductor Ammon heard it too, but before he could get his passengers out the flying cars had crashed into his train at seventy miles an hour. The caboose climbed the engine and fell apart, tossing out the body of the murdered man. The oil tank burst, and the oil, flowing over the engine, caught fire. Flames leaped along the train and licked at the passenger cars. Cowan, by their light, suddenly saw something that chilled his blood. One of the blazing boxcars had a red "Explosives" card tacked to it.

Cowan ran to Ammon and together they managed to get the passengers out, although some of them were injured. Then they cleared the town of excited people, awakened by the crash. Everyone was made to lie down in a newly dug ditch. The bodies of two passengers—and of the murdered man—were laid behind a sandpile. Then started the grim, nerve-racking wait.

Ten minutes passed. The flames ate into the siding of the powder car. Fifteen minutes. Twenty. Women were screaming with tension, men gnawing their hands—waiting, crouched in the ditch. At 3:15—thirty-five minutes after the crash—18,000 pounds of giant powder let go with a roar that rocked the mountains. A fourteen-car work train on a siding simply disintegrated. Tiling and hardware shot through the air. A large bolt hit a woman on the head, killing her instantly. But all the others, crouched in the ditch, were safe. Of the village of Fountain, little remained.

Where the powder car had been was nothing except a thirty-foot hole fifteen feet deep. No. 7's engine was a mass of twisted junk, still flaming. In Colorado Springs, thirteen miles away, every window went out, including $3,000 worth of plate-glass store fronts. Chimneys crashed in Pueblo, thirty-four miles to the south. La Junta, ninety miles away, shook with the blast. It was the most spectacular disaster Colorado had ever known.

An inquiry absolved the crew of No. 31 and the Santa Fe, and blamed the murderer. He, with half a dozen deaths on his soul, escaped.

Back in the midwest Fate was now stacking the cards against the Santa Fe. Just as the road had invested millions in new track and terminals and spent money generously for the finest equipment it could buy, crop failures cut into its revenues. In 1884 Kansas had produced 40,000,000 bushels of wheat; in 1887 the crop was less than 10,000,000. The corn crop dropped in the same years from 191,000,000 to 76,000,000 bushels.

With less grain to haul, freight and passenger rates dropped too, as competition for the lowered tonnage grew fiercer. In '84 the road averaged 1.9 cents for hauling a ton a mile; in 1888 it got only 1.25 cents. Fares were heavily cut and about one tenth of all passengers rode on passes, before the Interstate Commerce Act frowned on the practice.

Passage of this Act and the setting up of the Interstate Commerce Commission in '87 was of little help. Before the Commission came, the roads had been trying to stop cutthroat competition by means of pools and traffic agreements, and with some success. The Commerce Act forbade such agreements and substituted political control of the roads for business control. This meant that the roads were regulated largely by men who knew little or nothing about railroading.

No sooner had the Commission been set up than court decisions robbed it of its power. The result was that neither business nor government had any authority. Confusion became chaos.

In 1888, with the Chicago line operating, more trouble came. Heavy rains damaged long sections of track and at one time the line was blocked in thirteen places. As if this wasn't enough, the engineers of several Midwest lines now went on a long, bitter strike.

Strong fought bravely for the road he had built across the mountains, over the desert, through canyons, over rivers and down into the lush valleys of the Pacific Coast. He was now accused of "overexpansion," and it seemed useless for him to argue the truth—that the Santa Fe had been forced to expand or die. A railroad had to go forward or back; it couldn't stand still—and Strong and Robinson were not men to retreat.

On September 6, 1889, Strong resigned as president and was quickly succeeded by Allen Manvel, although most Santa Fe men would have preferred Robinson. Manvel had started in '59 as a $40-a-month clerk for the Rock Island and had come up the hard way. He was a shrewd, frugal, kindly man who worked fourteen hours a day and expected others to follow his example. Gradually he won the respect and affection of the people who worked for him.

He came in facing huge losses for the 1888 operation. The Chicago line had lost $441,555; the Sonora line, $335,914; the California extension $1,578,404; other lines like amounts. But still, a dividend of five and a quarter per cent had been paid in '88, following six per cent for 1881 to 1886 and six and a quarter in 1887. In 1889 the losses grew but there was hope in Kansas. The crops were better, the through line to Chicago was getting its share of the business. Manvel lumped thirty-seven bond issues into two, reorganized finances, cut costs, went after new tonnage and passengers.

There was hope again. The debt burden wasn't quite so heavy. In May, 1890, it seemed good business to buy the 1329.47 mile line of the 'Frisco for $22,511,687.50 and thus get into St. Louis. Out in the West the Colorado Midland was bought which gave the Santa Fe a new line from Colorado Springs to Glenwood Springs and a connection with the Rio Grande's line to Salt Lake City. There was renewed talk of a Santa Fe outlet west from Salt Lake to the California coast and some complaining that, having struggled out of the effect of one over-expansion era, the system was heading into another.

With the big troubles came little ones. Out on the desert passengers were complaining about the Navajos, Hopis, Apaches and the Mojaves, scores of whom the line was using as track laborers. Trackmen were hard to come by, being unable to stand the heat, mostly, and the track had to be kept up somehow.

The Indians were not clean, they were not loyal, and for most work they were pretty useless—but how they could shovel! They pried up bigger shovelfuls of dirt and heaved them farther and more accurately than any Paleface ever could, and they loved doing it. They would get out after quitting time and go on shoveling—often in the wrong places—just for the hell of it. Why the steam shovel ever had to be invented, many a desert track foreman will never know.

IOWA
OUR LIBERTIES WE PRIZE AND OUR RIGHTS WE WILL MAINTAIN
Estherville
Spencer
Hawarden
Le Mars
meat packing
Cherokee
Storm Lake
Sioux City
popcorn center of the U.S.
Onawa
apple center
Council Bluffs
Glenwood
Red Oak
seeds plants
Shenandoah
nursery stock
The Mormon Trail
State Flower
Bedford
Creston
Atlantic
Greenfield
Peru
Home of the Delicious apple
Carroll
Perry
brick tile
Des Moines
WAC.
Boone
Ames
Algona
rye
Eagle Grove
gypsum
Ft. Dodge
beets
oats
Mason City
cement tile
Charles City
Bily Clock Exhibit
Little Brown Church
Decorah
fish hatchery
Oelwein
Cedar Falls
Waterloo
Webster City
vegetable canning
Marshalltown
Tama Indian Reservation
Grinnell
Newton
Knoxville
Oskaloosa
Chariton
Albia
coal
Centerville
Ottumwa
meat packing
Fairfield
Dubuque
Balanced Rock
Cedar Rapids
onions
Clinton
Iowa City
Davenport
Muscatine
Washington
26 ft. 10 in
Burlington
Fort Madison
Keokuk

The famous "fake strike" of some Santa Fe telegraphers took place October 16, 1892. Under an agreement, operators all over the system had been given pay increases, and accepted them, with the exception of men on the Gulf lines. They started a strike October 15th, but men all over the rest of the system, having accepted the raise, stayed at work.

H. N. Barker, an operator at Dodge City, Kansas, thought it would be fun to order a general strike. He tapped out a fake message "as a joke on the manager," he explained later. It read:

"All dispatchers and operators: In view of the fact that the Gulf Colorado and Santa Fe is controlled by the Santa Fe road, I therefore declare a strike on the entire system to take effect at 1 A.M. Monday, October 17th. See that no telegraphing is done, no tickets sold. D. G. Ramsey, Grand Chief."

This false message was flashed over the eastern but not the western end of the system and at 10 A.M. the operators walked out. Barker, frightened, sent out a message from Dodge saying the strike order was a "fraud." No one believed him.

Operators now took the first message as genuine, the second as fake. Santa Fe officials who had been promoted from operators went back to the keys. Then "Grand Chief" Ramsey denounced the strike in a message to all operators and demanded that Barker be arrested. Operators went back to work at 8 P.M. and the wheels started to turn again. Fifty train crews lying idle at Argentine and Kansas City through lack of orders, went back to their jobs.

Barker never was arrested, and as new battles loomed ahead he and his fake were quickly forgotten.

CHAPTER FOURTEEN

NORTH FROM THE GULF

AFTER THE CIVIL WAR, Houston became the rail center of Texas. From here four lines radiated: the Galveston, Houston & Henderson went southeast about fifty miles to Galveston; The Houston & Texas Central ran a few miles north; The Texas and New Orleans ran a short distance east, and the Buffalo Bayou, Brazos & Colorado Railroad & Navigation line ran west from Harrisburg, near Houston for eighty miles. There was no rail connection between Texas and other states. The only way to get into Texas, except by foot or horsepower, was by rail to New Orleans, then by steamer to Galveston and then by rail to Houston. This made it hard to build railroads because everything—ties, bolts, nuts, rail cars and locomotives—had to be sailed in on free-deck schooners and the cost was high.

Galveston took a romantic pride in its position on a pirate isle and named its hotel after Jean Lafitte—but cotton put the town on the map. In the late '60s nearly all Texas cotton moved down to Galveston by rail or wagon. From there it was shipped out in the vessels that brought in practically all Texas imports, save a little tonnage hauled in by wagon across the east and north borders of the state. Cotton shipping demanded big tonnages of bagging and ties, and stocks of these were accumulated by Galveston merchants for sale at crop time.

Galveston was the richest city in the state and naturally her rivals —principally Houston—tried to get her trade away from her. Houston and Harris County found a means in the "Yellow Jack" epidemics that, every few years or so, hit the Gulf Coast. State law gave counties the right to quarantine against people and goods from sections hit by the plague and this was used to bar Galvestonians and their freight from Houston.

Since the only feasible way for Galveston to distribute her stocks of bagging, ties and other things needed by cotton planters was by the Galveston, Houston & Henderson to Houston, it soon occurred to Houston merchants that if, at the strategic moment, they ordered a quarantine against Galveston, the Gulf City would be unable to supply the planters' needs, and thus Houston, which had prudently laid in stocks, would be able to sell them at a good profit. No sooner thought than done.

Year after year, just as the cotton croppers needed bagging and ties, someone in Houston would discover a case of yellow fever in Galveston, a quarantine would be ordered and armed guards stationed on the trail and railroad leading up from the Coast. After Houston had sold her stocks to the plantations, the quarantine would lift—but Galveston would be stuck with huge tonnages of goods she could not sell. The Gulf merchants and bankers grew tired of it and talked of raising an army, taking it north along the railroad to the Harris County line and shotgunning their way to Houston.

This never actually happened. What did happen, was that Albert Somerville, Henry Rosenberg, C. R. Hughes, John Sealy and some other Galveston leaders called a mass meeting in the spring of 1873. Galveston's warehouses and compresses were chock-a-block and she was still the largest and richest city in Texas. The only storm cloud ahead was the almost certainty that, at the vital moment, Harris County and Houston would clamp down a quarantine again.

"Gentlemen," said John Sealy, "As Texans, that is something we are not going to stand for another year if we can help it."

"Give me a hundred veterans and some guns and ammunition," spoke up a Conferedate major, "and we'll get your freight into Houston for you."

"That might work, Major, and it might not," said Sealy. "But I have a way that will work, permanently."

"What's that?" shouted someone from the back row.

"We built one railroad out of Galveston—The Galveston, Houston & Henderson—and now Harris County blocks that any time it sees fit. Let's build another road, missing Harris County, and ship our goods over it without interference."

"We put up money for the Houston & Texas Central, too," objected another merchant. "What happened? It started from Houston and instead of coming here it has gone to Denison."

"Our new road," said Sealy, "will be under our control and it will start from right here. I'll subscribe for sixty shares."

"Put down the First National Bank for fifty," said J. M. Brown.

". . . and Union Marine & Fire Insurance for the same," chimed in President Isaac Dyer.

"I'll put down the Southern Cotton Press for 150," came back John Sealy.

The Galveston Wharf Company topped him with 200 and a county commissioner suggested an election to raise $500,000 for the project.

On May 28th a charter was obtained for the new line and a promise of a land grant helped the plans along. The name chosen was the Gulf, Colorado & Santa Fe although the line had no connection with the original Santa Fe. But there still was magic in the name.

Citizens subscribed $750,000; Galveston County put up half a million more. General Braxton Bragg, a hardhitting, black-whiskered Confederate brigadier who didn't like damyankees, was hired as chief engineer, somewhat to his surprise. He accepted the job and quickly got together a staff mainly composed of ex-majors, colonels and lieutenants.

The plan was to go north to Fort Worth, missing Houston and Harris County and finally reach Santa Fe. The Galveston, Harrisburg & San Antonio was building west toward San Antonio and with the Houston & Texas Central at Brenham, and the International & Great Northern at Navasota, the Gulf had places to go.

TEXAS
wheat
Etter
Borger
Canadian
carbon black
Skellytown
Pampa
Heaton
White Deer
Coltexo
Panhandle
Helium tanks
Amarillo
Dumas Jc.
Canyon
Hereford
potatoes
cotton
Tulia
Farwell
sugar beets
Plainview
cotton
Floydada
Lubbock Jc.
Seagraves Jc.
Doud Jc.
Crosbyton
Crosbyton Jc.
Bledsoe
Lubbock Slaton
Slaton Jc.
Hamlin
Seagraves
Lamesa
Snyder
P. & S.F.
Sweetwater
Tuscola
Midland
potash
Sterling City
El Paso
Guadalupe Peak highest point in state
Odessa
International Bridge
Pecos
San Angelo
Rodeo
cantaloupes
Eden
Menard
Ft. Stockton
Sonora
McDonald Observatory
Alpine
Paisano
natural gas
Texas Longhorn
quicksilver mine
(almost extinct)
Angora goats
Presidio
watch tower
Eagle Pass

Wichita Falls
Dennison
Gainesville
Paris
seeds
onions
Texarkana
Sherman
sorghum
coal
Denton
Greenville
Live Stock Exchange
Cotton Exchange
Mineral Wells
Dallas
lumber
Marshall
Weatherford
Ft. Worth
Terrell
Fashion Center
East Texas oil field
Longview
Cresson
oil tanks
Ennis
world's largest
Carthage
Cleburne
Tyler
Waxahachie
pecans
Corsicana
pecans
Palestine
Center
Brownwood
Mexia
Nacogdoches
Waco
Browning Room (Baylor)
Lufkin
Lometa
Temple
Jasper
limestone
oil
Kirbyville
mesquite tree
Milano
observation tower
"Big Thicket"
Taylor
Montgomery
Conroe
Silsbee
Somerville
pecans
Navasota
Cleveland
Austin
cotton
Beaumont
wild turkeys
Rosenberg
Houston
Port Arthur
Mission San Juan
Eagle Lake
Sealy
oil tanks
High Island
Sam Houston
Dar Jc.
Rayner
Alvin
Texas City
Garwood
Thompsons
Galveston
San Antonio
sulphur
Eldridge
Cane Jc.
The Alamo
state flower
salt
magnesium
"turkey trot"
Matagorda
Victoria
salt
grove of palms
Corpus Christi
cock fight
citrus fruits
McAllen
Harlingen
San Benito
Brownsville

If it could make these three connections, Galveston wouldn't have to do any more worrying about Houston.

On May 1, 1875, about 200 people gathered at 37th and Mechanic Streets in Galveston. The men, mostly mustached and with full beards, came dressed in broadcloth, with pegtopped pants, heavy silk cravats and new bowler hats. A few women in tight bodices, wide, pleated skirts and parasols, were given seats. Mayor Fulton and Alderman Ogle were there. So were most of the bankers and merchants.

At one o'clock a train of wagons came rolling down the street, filled with picks, shovels, wheelbarrows and plows. It lined up, the teamsters lolling on their seats to listen to the oratory. Everyone made speeches and the ladies became a bit bored. One or two of them moved over to the long tables where lavish refreshments had been set out. The mayor noticed the movement and took the hint. He motioned to Henry Rosenberg, the banker. Guy M. Bryan, who had been speaker in the lower house of the state legislature, wound up his speech with a prediction that "the Texas-Santa Fe will be a highway for the grain of the west, the wealth of the Pacific, the minerals of the far-off mountains of Colorado . . ."

Banker Rosenberg heaved up a shovelful of dirt and handed on the shovel to the Mayor. Everyone heaved dirt, and the ladies were gallantly allowed to take part. The perspiring gentlemen dug small shovelfuls of sand and passed them to the ladies who took them in gloved hands and daintily tossed them onto the growing pile. Then everyone filled up on crackers, champagne and cheese.

That was the way railroads got started in those days, though in the cruder North the boys stuck to soda biscuits, roast ham, beer and whisky.

As earlier in the mountains there had been the Bix Six, now there came into fame the Big Five—the men who drove the Gulf Line to success. It was one of the very few Texas roads that never went into receivership. These five men were: George Sealy, an Irish-Pennsylvanian from the Wyoming Valley, one of ten children born to immigrant parents. He worked his way through school and his first job was as station agent for the Lackawanna at Kingston,

Pennsylvania. He learned as he earned, and in 1857, at twenty-two, joined his brother John, who was working for the cotton and mercantile firm of Ball, Hutchings & Company. He opposed slavery, but when the war started, joined the Southern army as a private, refused to take pay and took care of his own expenses.

After the war he went back into the cotton and banking business and in '77, when the road was down and almost out, rescued it, raised cash and in four years had extended it to Fort Worth, Dallas and San Angelo. He got it back on a cash basis and afterward became one of the inventors of the commission form of city government. He had saved Galveston in '72 when years of carpetbagging rule had nearly ruined it.

A genial man, he used to slip out of his little red-brick bank and stroll, big cigar in his mouth, down to Reinke's Cafe where the cotton brokers congregated. He was very democratic and was always buying drinks for chance acquaintances.

Braxton Bragg was a North Carolinian who was credited with a major share of the Confederate victories at Shiloh and Chickamauga, and once commanded the Army of the Tennessee. He lost to Grant at Chattanooga and later surrendered to Johnston at Dalton, Ga. His weakness was his inability to follow up a victory. He was a dark, bearded man, with the awkwardness of Lincoln. He was a strict disciplinarian, even in his civil work. A good, two-fisted drinker, he frowned on men who couldn't handle their liquor.

Major J. P. Fresenius, who took over when Bragg quit, was a Frankforter from Germany. He had worked on several Southern roads and surveyed the Gulf line to Brenham. He built the bay bridge that withstood many storms until the concrete viaduct was constructed. There is a station named for him on the Montgomery branch.

Bernard Moore Temple, a Virginian, was wounded at Second Manasses, recovered, was wounded again, taken prisoner at Marie's Heights and sent to a Northern prison, from which he was released to walk home to the family plantation, Berclair, near Fredericksburg. Temple, Texas, is named for him, and in Goliad County there is a station on another road named for the plantation.

Walter Justin Sherman was an Ohioan, who had worked as an engineer for seven other roads before he started with the Gulf. He was a literary man and left many volumes of writings, mainly on engineering subjects.

General Bragg, since July, 1874, had been making surveys and planning the causeway across the bay to the mainland. His work mainly consisted of planning the first 125 miles of the line; he resigned in June, 1875, and was succeeded by his assistant, Major Fresenius.

It was in June of 1875 that grading for the new road started on the mainland and worked slowly north. It took two years to put forty miles of track in operation. Money was hard to get. In 1878 the road got twenty miles farther, to Richmond, and stopped. Again there was no money—not even to buy equipment, and without equipment there was no way to get business. The line went into bankruptcy, but not receivership. It owed George Sealy $250,000. He bought it at the foreclosure sale for $200,000.

The first rails, as they had for the California line at San Diego, came into Galveston Harbor on windjammers from England. The California-Southern had come around the Horn; the Texas Santa Fe came around Florida Cape.

The road proved again how profitable it was for states to offer public lands as an inducement to build railroads. Texas had leagues of land for sale in section-blocks at fifty cents an acre—in counties without a rail line. But after the railroad came the state asked from two to five dollars an acre. By giving away land worth fifty cents an acre, the state profited from a dollar and a half to four dollars and a half an acre in the land it still held for sale to private buyers.

The Gulf Line, as a matter of record, had great difficulty in locating any land for itself. Most of the acreage along its route had already been taken up and it had to go far afield into West Texas to find any vacant territory. It finally sold 3,554,560 acres of land for $211,168 net. Huge areas were sold for five cents an acre, which disposes once more of the legend that railroads got "immensely valuable lands" from which they reaped enormous profits. At the low figure of $10,000 a mile, the Gulf's land grant would build just about twenty miles of track.

The people of Texas profited greatly from the railroads. Before they came into operation, hauling charges were twenty cents a ton a mile, and the average daily haul, twenty miles. The first roads cut this cost in half and multiplied the speed five or six times. At the same time they cut in half the stagecoach fare of a dime a mile for

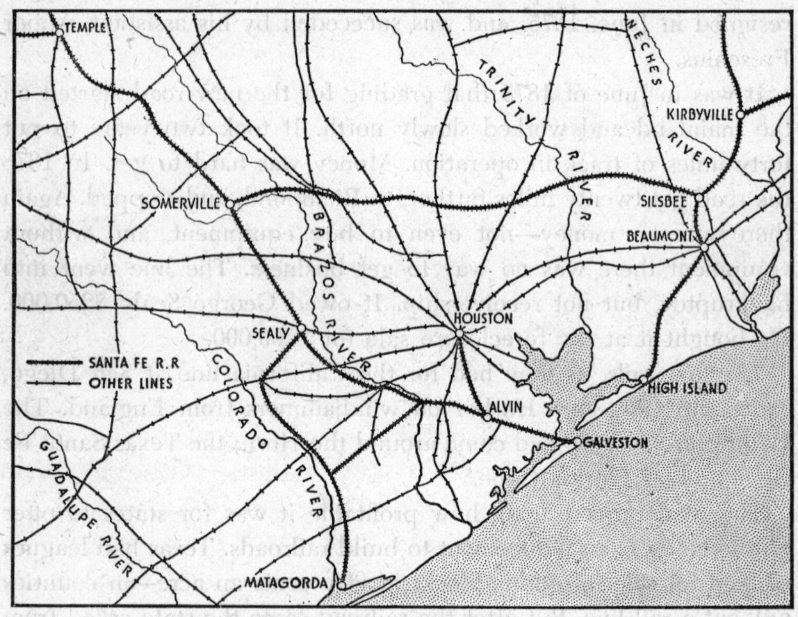

Down to the Gulf of Mexico

passengers, whom they carried at twenty miles an hour instead of six.

The sale of the road to Sealy included an agreement that he and his associates would build an additional 200 miles of track. The reorganized concern then elected George's brother, John, as president, and work went ahead again. By August there were sixty-three miles of rail from Richmond to Brenham and within the year the road got to Belton, another 100 miles. Belton was anxious for the division point, but it was decided to lay out a new town at Temple, a few miles east.

Fort Worth was reached late in 1881, and by May, 1882, the line had gone west to Lampasas. There were now 361.66 miles of track. Then again work stopped. The road, as had been promised, had bypassed Houston, but the trade of that city was important and, as the quarantine had been permanently lifted, the Gulf got trackage rights into the city over the International & Great Northern from Arcola, nineteen miles southwest. This operated until 1883, when a new line was built from Alvin direct to Houston, a distance of twenty-five miles.

The Gulf also was extending into the "piney woods" section of East Texas. It bought the Central & Montgomery in 1882 and, by using this as a link between Navasota and Montgomery, finally reached Conroe, north of Houston, by September 1, 1885. There, once more, it stopped. It was still a long way from the piney woods.

Meanwhile, the northern Santa Fe was building south through Indian Territory, headed for Texas. Gould and the Katy controlled most of the north-south traffic. The Gulf with no outlet to the north, had to take what was left, and engage in the usual money-losing rate battles. George Sealy got his stockholders together in Galveston and told them they should sell their road to the older Santa Fe.

"Okay," said the stockholders, "we'll leave it up to you, personally, George." They handed him their stock and agreed to accept whatever arrangements he made.

The final sale was at $8,000 a mile, paid in Santa Fe stock, with some assumption of debt. The Santa Fe would build south to Purcell, Oklahoma; the Gulf north to that point; in addition, the Gulf was to build northeast to Paris and run a branch from Cleburne to Weatherford. It is a tribute to Galvestonians that, when bad crops and bad business cut Gulf revenues so that it couldn't pay for this construction, Sealy and his fellow stockholders put up the money and carried out the agreement.

Under the bargain, the Gulf was faced with the job of building three hundred miles of track within a year and two months. No right of way had been secured, there were no rails, ties or material on hand; there were not even surveys. One April evening in Galveston, General Manager Webster Snyder called in Walter Justin Sherman, his chief engineer:

"Can you build 300 miles of track by June 15, 1887?" he asked.

"Where?" queried Sherman.

"Up to Purcell, out to Paris and Weatherford," replied Snyder.

Sherman fiddled, as engineers will, with his slide rule.

"Do we have any iron?"

"Not a yard."

"How about surveys? Any ties ordered? Anybody think about getting a work force together? We'll need engineers, contractors, grading machinery. . . . The way some people demand track you'd think you just rub an Aladdin's Lamp—and there it is."

"Well, Walter," said Snyder, "you're right, of course, and I must admit nothing's been done—but still, can you get that 300 miles of track built on time?"

"I'm writing a book."

"I know. But after all, you can do that later. Do we get track?"

Sherman sighed, then banged the desk, and slid his rule shut. "Okay, you get track. Darned if I know how—but I'll lay it some way. . . . Now I'll get out of here and get to work."

Surveyors went north that night and rails and ties were ordered. Crews of husky Negroes were assembled under white bosses. More than three months slipped by in organization and, with 250 days left to go, there was still the 300 miles of track to lay.

First, fifty engineers, a few hundred men and a score of teams buckled down. The number gradually increased until a hundred engineers, 5,000 men and 2,000 teams were spiking track in Texas faster than it ever had been laid before. The old Union Pacific race with the Central Pacific began to look pretty slow.

At seven in the morning when the whistle blew, the material men gave the crews a mile of track. After lunch at 1 o'clock the crews got another mile. When they had laid two miles they were through for the day.

The Santa Fe boys in the north heard of the speed and started a race. Every day the two tracks, south and northbound, were four miles closer together. To spur on his men, Sherman stood by the track at quitting time with a bucket of whisky, ladling it out with a dipper to the sweating workers.

The construction engineer, feeling sorry for the boys on the picks and shovels and wheelbarrows in the heat of the summer, split their ten-hour working day to give them a two-hour siesta at noon. He gave up this philanthropy when the men announced that they'd rather work through and take the hour morning and evening.

Down on the Galveston Bay Bridge, Sherman noticed something that didn't seem right to his economical Ohio soul. The teredos were eating away the piling every three years, and as this meant 5,000 expensive new red-cedar piles, Sherman made tests and found that teredos would eat elm piles just as heartily. Elm cost only a fraction of what the road had been paying for cedar piling. The teredos ate elm after that—and liked it.

Most of the Negroes working on the line were from the Brazos swamps and unused to the higher, drier climate, along the route north. They also brought along with them their local customs and the democratic processes they had acquired to a limited degree in the war between the states. So, everytime one of them died, an election was held to decide whether to bury him in the right of way or send the body back home to the swamps. Some of these elections had to be held two or three times with the body buried and taken up, and buried again, as voters wavered from one side to the other—and work stopped.

Meanwhile track was coming south from the Arkansas City end, but not fast enough to beat the deadline the government had set for completion of the line.

To connect with the Gulf Line, the Santa Fe got a Federal charter to cross Indian Territory south from Arkansas City, Kansas, to a junction at a then unnamed spot that later was to become Purcell. Crews started grading and tracklaying in '86, and the Salt Fork was bridged at White Eagle, Oklahoma, in September. Trains operated between Arkansas City and Ponca—the first name of White Eagle—a distance of thirty-one miles, by November 29th. The Cimarron was reached and bridged at Lawrie, Oklahoma, February 5, 1887. The line got to Deer Creek three days later. It was just end-of-track, but later, as Guthrie, it became famous. The first houses in Guthrie, Edmond and Oklahoma City—then just Oklahoma—were built of old ties by Colonel J. W. F. Hughes, of Topeka, who was roadmaster.

The Santa Fe, under its Federal charter, had to have track to Purcell and a connection south by April 20, 1887. It began to look as though this could not be accomplished, and the government prepared to take steps to cancel the charter. A writ was issued at Muskogee and given to a United States marshal to serve. Colonel Hughes got wind of this move and wired Chief Engineer Robinson in Topeka. Robinson sent his chief clerk, C. H. Curtis, to see what could be done.

Curtis got a locomotive and a bunk car at Arkansas City and started down the line, picking up station agents and operators along the way. This left the track deserted. The car, full of agents, was sidetracked north of Purcell and extra gangs put on to complete the track. Five hundred men and more than 200 teams sweated to get ties and steel down. Meanwhile the marshal was riding up and down the track to the north trying to find someone upon whom to serve the writ. He failed, riding a tired horse into Purcell a few hours after northbound and southbound crews had made the junction 106 miles north of the Texas line at 5:05 on the afternoon of April 26, 1887. Sherman dippered out two buckets of whisky and called it a day. He had set a new tracklaying record.

Near Fort Worth there is a station named Justin, in his honor.

With everything safe, Curtis started his agents and operators north again and strolled over to meet the marshal.

"What seems to be the trouble, marshal?" he asked.

The marshal explained that, inasmuch as the line had not been finished in time, he would be obliged to serve a writ of canceling the charter.

"But the line is finished," insisted Curtis. "See for yourself."

The marshal scratched his head. "Guess you're right," he admitted. Nothing more was heard of the cancellation move.

With a junction complete, through trains started operating between Galveston and Arkansas City and so on north to Kansas City, June 18, 1887. Both Guthrie and Purcell, merely a few rough shacks for railroad workers, were named for Santa Fe stockholders, Judge John Guthrie and E. B. Purcell.

The coming of the original Santa Fe to Texas started a new wave of enthusiasm for railroad building. Cities began offering cash bonuses for a line. Weatherford had put up $15,000 and got a forty-two mile branch from Cleburne; Paris put up $10,000, Ladonia the same; Honey Grove, $12,500; Farmersville, $15,000. The road got to Honey Grove in the spring of '87, and to Paris a few weeks later. Weatherford was reached in the fall.

While the cities and counties, through businessmen and working people helped railroads along, the Texas legislature passed some of the weirdest laws in a nation noted for weird railroad legislation. At one time the legislature even started designing locomotives and the law required engines to be equipped with ash pans and to carry bells weighing not less than sixty pounds.

Another law once provided that all trains must stop five minutes at each "wayside station." As these were about five miles apart this meant that, traveling over 100 miles of track, passengers would be held up a total of an hour and forty minutes even on "through" trains.

If a railroad man died away from home in Texas, his family was out of luck. The law forbade the shipment of the body home for burial unless full fare was paid. On the other hand if the man died in Louisiana, New Mexico, New York or Oregon, the body came home free, as a courtesy of the railroads. It was "moving in interstate commerce," and Texas couldn't regulate it.

The Atchison, Topeka & Santa Fe does not, legally, own a mile of railroad in Texas. That would be against the law. The law is that all Texas trackage must be owned by Texas corporations, and that the main office of each road must be located on its line in Texas. That is why, when entering Texas from any direction, all the roads change names and, in theory, ownerships.

The headquarters of the Panhandle & Santa Fe are at Amarillo; of the Gulf, Colorado & Santa Fe at Galveston. The principal officers must live in Texas, but the president need not. In 1944 only one railroad president, in fact, lived in the state.

In 1866 it became a law that every passenger train must carry a car for "freedmen." This was the origin of the Jim Crow car.

The Lampasas Line went on west from Lampasas, and down through Ballinger and San Angelo. This was great stock country and for years the Santa Fe shipped thousands of cattle, sheep and horses from this branch.

Arrival of the Santa Fe in San Angelo from Ballinger, October 1, 1888, touched off another celebration. A parade started under Grand Marshal S. W. Titus and included artillery, bells, a sixteen-piece band and blue-uniformed infantrymen from Fort Concho. This parade, fortified by Texans fresh out of the Grey Mule saloon, included three ladies riding side-saddle, a horde of assistant marshals wearing white-silk sashes and top hats, and hook-and-ladder and hose companies of firemen.

The parade marched down Chadbourne, Concho, Oakes, Harris and Beauregard Streets and then ambled up to Miles Grove on the banks of the North Concho for a barbecue at which sixty beeves and two hundred sheep were roasted and eaten. Former Governor Frank Lubbock, after whom Lubbock was named, formally welcomed civilization to San Angelo, which had, at that time, the slogan "The End of the Rainbow." The Santa Fe, on its part, gave away souvenir tin cups and free water, thus displacing the town's former water supply, a Mexican with *agua fria* at a dime a barrel.

There was a ball that night. The ladies came in grand array and the society reporter for *The Standard* wrote that the floor "presented a charming spectacle of arms and shoulders whiter than parian marble, and figures more beautiful than ever haunted the dreams of Phidias, undulated in the rapturous waltz. The frow-frow of silks and satins, and the heavy swish of velvets were lightened by the graceful purity of white lawns. There were but few dress coats—the Texan scorns the spike-tail. The ladies all wore skirts of dancing length, but none were en-train."

The belle of the evening was Miss Josie Taylor "in pink satin with lace trimmings, carrying a *corsage de flor natural*"—which could have meant a bunch of wild flowers.

That was the way Texas towns greeted railroads in the '80s.

In later years Santa Fe Park and four school playgrounds in San Angelo were gifts of the system. Around 1910 citizens put up a bonus of $40,000 for construction of a line from San Angelo to Sterling City. This scheme lagged and the Santa Fe planned to build the line itself, inheriting the bonus. President Ripley felt that, inasmuch as the system had planned the line before the bonus was raised, the money should be returned to the city. It was, and a committee bought about forty acres of riverfront land plus one block adjacent to each of four city schools, for playgrounds. There still was $10,000 left, and this was put into an endowment fund to help pay for the upkeep of the park spaces.

While it was building south from Arkansas City to meet the northbound Gulf Line at Purcell, the Santa Fe also was invading the Panhandle, farther west. The Southern Kansas Railroad had reached the border of Indian Territory near Shattuck late in '86 and now the line built southwest to Canadian and Panhandle City, about 100 miles. Ten years later it built on to Amarillo, which it had been reaching over a leased line of the Fort Worth & Denver City from Washburn. Amarillo had been made headquarters of the Panhandle & Santa Fe on November 9, 1899. In 1890 there were just 482 people in Amarillo; it has almost 50,000 in 1945.

One of the strangest trains ever operated on the Gulf Lines was the Yellow Jack Special. Late in October, 1898, Colonel L. J. Polk, general manager of the lines, got a tip that state health authorities were going to establish a yellow-fever quarantine against Galveston at midnight on Saturday.

Since this would tie up the road's business, the Colonel coupled a car to a yard engine and set off along the line at 5 P.M. Saturday to establish offices elsewhere. He left word that office records and more than a hundred employees were to be shipped after him that evening; the workers were to bring along their families.

Word of the quarantine spread around Galveston and the Yellow Jack Special was mobbed at the depot by thousands of people trying to escape. There was room, however, for only 300 passengers, and this space was taken by employees and their families; a baggage car carried the records; the train pulled out at nine o'clock, headed for nowhere.

An hour later it stopped at Alvin, to be met by a shotgun squad that ordered it to keep moving. The train backed down, the engine took water outside the city limits and then the Special steamed through the town nonstop, with the shotgunners waving her on. Their tempers hadn't been soothed by a query flung at them by a passenger: "Who the hell would want to stop at Alvin, anyway?"

The train sped on through the night, stopping at Brenham next morning for breakfast and at Temple for lunch. No passengers were allowed off at either place and coffee and sandwiches were poked at them through the windows. The Special rolled on to Cleburne—and there a surprise was in store for them. Instead of being scared to death, citizens of the town turned out with a band, an entertainment committee and offers of rooms in private homes for the office workers and their families. For three weeks Cleburne was headquarters for the Texas Santa Fe, then the quarantine was lifted and everybody went back to Galveston—to untangle a freight jam. Sixty-nine ships rode at anchor in the harbor, awaiting cargo.

Another passenger train holdup on the Santa Fe took place at Coleman Junction in 1899. A train stopped at the lonely Texas point one fall night to take water and a band of gunmen stuck up the crew at the head end.

R. E. Buchanan, claim agent for the road and affectionately known as Colonel Buck, was on the last car and, hearing shots, leaned out from the platform to see what was going on. One glance told him. He pulled his .45 and sent two bullets toward the bandits, dropped to the cinders and shot again, ran a few feet and

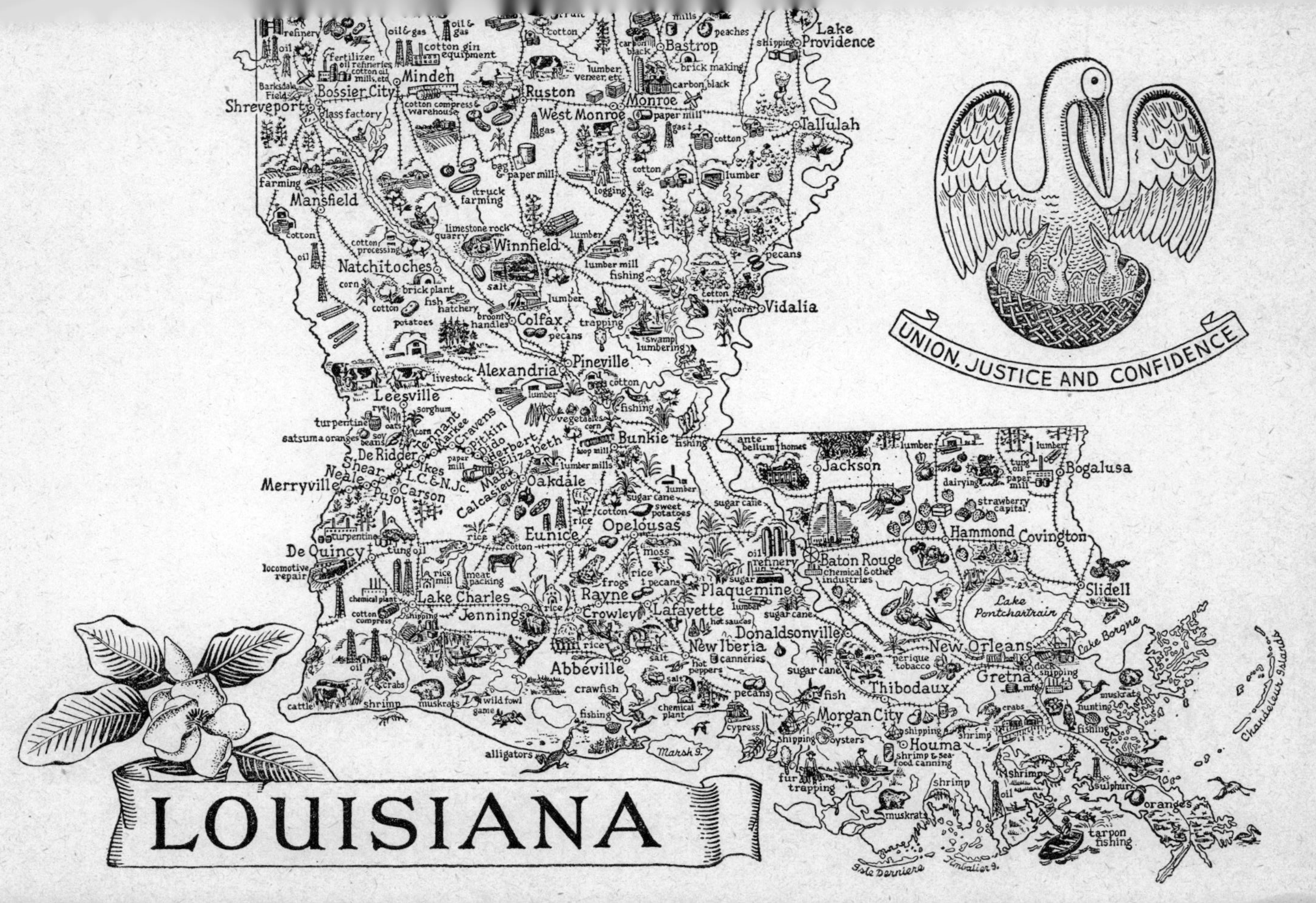
LOUISIANA
UNION, JUSTICE AND CONFIDENCE
Shreveport
Bossier City
Minden
Ruston
West Monroe
Monroe
Bastrop
Lake Providence
Tallulah
Mansfield
Natchitoches
Winnfield
Colfax
Vidalia
Alexandria
Pineville
Leesville
Bunkie
De Ridder
Merryville
Neale
Shear
Pujo
Carson
Ikes
L.C.&N.Jc.
Oakdale
Elizabeth
Herbert
Dido
Pitkin
Cravens
Markee
Tennant
Mabel
Calcasieu
De Quincy
Lake Charles
Jennings
Eunice
Opelousas
Rayne
Crowley
Lafayette
Abbeville
New Iberia
Plaquemine
Donaldsonville
Baton Rouge
Jackson
Bogalusa
Hammond
Covington
Slidell
New Orleans
Gretna
Thibodaux
Morgan City
Houma
Lake Pontchartrain
Lake Borgne
Chandeleur Islands
Isle Dernière
Timbalier I.
Marsh I.
Barksdale Field
refinery
oil
fertilizer
oil refineries
cotton oil mills, etc.
oil & gas
cotton gin equipment
glass factory
cotton compress & warehouse
lumber, veneer, etc.
carbon black
brick making
peaches
shipping
paper mill
gas
cotton
lumber
farming
truck farming
bag & paper mill
logging
limestone rock quarry
lumber mill
fishing
pecans
cotton processing
corn
brick plant
fish hatchery
salt
broom handles
trapping
swamp lumbering
potatoes
livestock
vegetables
turpentine
rye
sorghum
oats
soy beans
satsuma oranges
hoop mill
lumber mills
ante-bellum homes
dairying
tung oil
strawberry capital
sugar cane
sweet potatoes
rice
moss
oil refinery
chemical & other industries
tung oil
rice mill
meat packing
frogs
hot sauces
sugar
chemical plant
cotton compress
locomotive repair
perique tobacco
dock
canneries
hot peppers
crawfish
wild fowl
game
muskrats
crabs
shrimp
cattle
alligators
cypress
oysters
shrimp & sea-food canning
fur trapping
hunting
sulphur
oranges
tarpon fishing

fired a third time. Six shots from different places convinced the robbers they were up against a posse.

Colonel Buck, out of ammunition, roved through the cars, borrowed a revolver from a new groom—whose bride refused to let him join in the fray—and opened up again. One bandit was badly wounded and the rest fled, taking nothing. The sheriff easily traced the gang by the blood of the wounded member, and all of the robbers went to jail, it is remembered by H. E. Everheart of San Angelo, who was working for the road at the time.

At 7 A.M. September 8, 1900, No. 1 on the Gulf & Interstate, hauled by Engine No. 4, left Beaumont, Texas, headed for Port Bolivar, where it was due at 11:10 A.M. That was the day the great hurricane blew in, flooded Galveston Island, drowned scores and piled up a huge property damage. No. 1 fought its way along the coast, rocking in the gale, until the waves began to wash out the right of way ahead of it. It got to within eleven miles of Bolivar, with the waves washing high against the cars. Here a terrific gust blew the first passenger car off the track and rolled it 500 feet across the country. The engine and tender sank in the sand. The few passengers managed to get out and find shelter until the storm abated.

The wind and waves piled sand over the wrecked train. That just about sank the G & I too. The road had no money to rescue its equipment and there it stayed on High Island. Thirty miles of right of way and track were gone. For nearly three years the owners battled to get money enough to rehabilitate it—and eventually did. Beaumont and Galveston citizens chipped in $20,000 between them. The line was rebuilt and a crew went out and managed to get the engine, tender, day coach and baggage car back onto the rails, repaired and under steam again.

This train now went back to Beaumont, running wild. There the cars were repainted and put into shape and the train made a fresh start, leaving Beaumont at 7:10 A.M. The road offered to honor tickets of the passengers marooned three years before and several accepted. The train, with Dan Collins at the throttle and John

Woodfin firing, got to Port Bolivar at 11:10 A.M. September 24, 1903—three years, sixteen days late.

Various versions of this story have appeared, with the train's lateness ranging from two years and seven months to eight years. The truth was ferreted out from newspaper files at the Galveston Public Library by Mr. John G. Fitzhugh, a Texas authority on railroad history.

CHAPTER FIFTEEN

OKLAHOMA!

INDIAN TERRITORY originally contained about 69,600 square miles, most of them fertile, great stretches being some of the best grazing lands on earth. The first opening of about 2,000,000 acres was on April 22, 1889. The second, of Sac, Fox and Pottawatomie lands was on September 22, 1891. The Cherokee Strip was not opened until September, 1893.

The Strip or Outlet was a rectangle about 150 miles long and sixty wide. It was bounded on the north by Kansas, on the south by lands of the Cheyennes and Arapahoes (known as Old Oklahoma), and on the west by No Man's land out beyond the 100th meridian, and by the Texas Panhandle. It was watered by the Canadian, Cimarron and Salt Fork of the Arkansas.

In 1889 Congress offered the Cherokees $1.25 an acre for this tract of about 9,000 square miles, but the cattlemen who were leasing the territory offered the Indians $3 an acre and the Cherokees naturally refused the federal offer. President Benjamin Harrison thereupon ordered all cattle out of the Strip by October 1, 1890—depriving the Indians of their income and forcing the cattlemen to find new pastures. The move was political—to force the Indians' acceptance of the government offer.

The Cherokees held out for a time but finally sold at around $1.40 an acre—losing $1.60 because of the political jugglery at Washington.

In 1889, the Santa Fe ran north and south across the entire tract and Oklahoma City, then simply Oklahoma, consisted of the depot, a section house, a water tank, the home of the agent and three or four small buildings. The whole layout wasn't worth $10,000.

Away on all sides of the new land, rolled the rich brown prairie, here and there spotted with timber. By Presidential proclamation, huge sweeps of this land would belong, after noon on April 22, 1889, to those who could "enter and occupy it." Settlers were supposed to stake out and occupy 160 acres, but groups of merchants both from Texas and Kansas prepared plats for townsites, including one at Oklahoma.

This stratagem became known, and naturally when the rush opened the 40,000 settlers fought desperately either to get homesteads on the sites chosen for future towns, or to get as near to these sites as possible.

Although the Indians were legally owners of thousands of fertile square miles, watered by fine rivers, they never had a chance against the expansionist drive of the whites.

Parties of land-hungry men went raiding into the territory and were repulsed by soldiers. "Boomers" and "movers" tried again and again to take up land, filtering down from Kansas and up from Texas along the Santa Fe track. Newspapers, manufacturers, packing houses and wholesalers put on the pressure for purchase of the Indian lands by the government and opening of them to settlement. This pressure finally got too strong for Washington and the first opening of lands south of the Strip was ordered.

Best known of the Open-Oklahoma-to-Settlement boosters was Captain David L. Payne of Harvey County, Kansas. He was related to Davy Crockett and Daniel Boone. He rode one of the first Santa Fe trains into Emporia in '70, tramped to the site of North Wichita and located a claim near by. He left a year later and located on the northeast quarter of section six in Newton Township, later receiving a patent signed by General-President U. S. Grant.

Payne dug two wells, from one of which the first Santa Fe engines got their water in Newton. In '79 he started organizing colonies to settle in Indian Territory, but was stopped by the federal government. He continued his efforts for five years and was getting together another band of Kansans in Wellington for a new invasion.

OKLAHOMA
state park
Boise City
wheat
Buffalo
wheat
Alva
Cherokee
Medford
Blackwell
Tonkawa
Newkirk
Ponca City
lead
zinc
Bartlesville
oil
Miami
Vinita
oil
Pawhuska
Waynoka
Carmen
Aline
wheat
Woodward
Shattuck
Enid
flour mill
Perry
Pawnee
Osage Jc.
Collinsville
Will Rogers Memorial
Claremore
Tulsa
oil
Stillwater
Drumright
Sapulpa
Cushing
Bristow
Thomas
gypsum
Guthrie
oil
Muskogee
lime kiln
cotton
Custer City
Arapaho
Clinton
Hammon
El Reno
Davenport
oil
Okmulgee
corn
Oklahoma City
Anadarko
Chickasha
Shawnee
Elk City
Norman
Tecumseh
Seminole
Wewoka
Purcell
cement plant
Byars
Ada
McAlester
coal
Lone Wolf
building in which Geronimo was held captive
Mangum
Lindsay
Paul's Valley
Fort Sill
cotton
Altus
Lawton
Frederick
Duncan
corn
Atoka
Healdton
Ringling
Ardmore
Durant
cotton
Hugo
lumber

At breakfast in the Hotel De Barnard, on the morning of November 28, 1884, as he was making plans with other leaders of the invading force, he fell over dead. His photograph is on the wall of the State House in Oklahoma City to this day.

In the same year of 1884, H. L. Marvin, Chief Engineer of the Kansas Southern, a Santa Fe subsidiary, had surveyed three lines down through Indian Territory. One was through Enid, Kingfisher and Chickasha; the second from Arkansas City to Gainesville, Texas, via Guthrie and Oklahoma City; the third south from Coffeyville, Kansas, through Tulsa. The first was rejected as "too far west," and the last because the country was too hilly. Mr. Marvin reported that "there is nothing on the route except the settlement of Tulsa, two miles from the Arkansas River. The location is not suitable for a large town . . ."

Oil changed all that, later. The Santa Fe didn't get to Tulsa for twenty-one years.

These lands which were open for settlement were the ones upon which a dozen Indian tribes had been moved after the Civil War. In that war, the Indians in the South had joined the Confederacy and, after it was over, they received scant consideration from the North. The whole affair of the moving of the tribes from their homes and farms, and the subsequent dispossession of the new lands in Indian Territory is a disgraceful phase of the settlement of the west by whites.

To get to the lands first opened south of the Strip, settlers from the north had to cross the Outlet. The best way was by the new Santa Fe line from Arkansas City—the line built to join the Gulf track coming north from Galveston. This line was opened June 12, 1887, twenty-two months before the land rush.

In September of that year it opened another line from Kiowa, farther west, down to Higgins, Texas, and, by December, trains were running to Panhandle City. The road, therefore, was operating in Indian Territory, two years before the first rush and six years before the Strip was opened in 1893.

The Santa Fe carried settlers both over its eastern line and the Panhandle line, which entered the Strip south of Kiowa and headed for Amarillo. This line is now part of the Belen Cutoff. It rejoins the main passenger track at Dalies, just west of Belen, New Mexico.

In the summer of '87, before the land opening, Santa Fe trains started operating back and forth across the Territory. From these, a few days before the rush, "Sooners" tried to descend with the idea of hiding out in the timber and thus getting a head start on the milling thousands who were lined up back of the line—a scratch in the earth made by an army bayonet.

Soldiers and deputies patrolled around stations, keeping passengers aboard. Boxcars full of raw lumber, hardware, furniture, farm implements, however, were allowed entry, and stood in long rows on hastily built sidetracks, fifteen to thirty miles inside the border.

General Merritt, in charge of the rush, was headquartered in a private car fifteen miles inside the new free territory, and with him was Captain D. F. Stiles of the Tenth Infantry, assigned to keep order. They watched the line through telescopes and, congratulating themselves on their success in checkmating "Soonerism," figured it would take the first settlers, on the fastest horses, about ninety minutes to reach Oklahoma.

At noon an army bugle blew the signal at the line; another one blew at the Santa Fe's private car and General Merritt and Captain Stiles, just sitting down to lunch, laid aside their 'scopes to tackle buffalo steaks, soda bread and black coffee. They had hardly got down the first mouthfuls when the astonished bugler beat on the car door, saluted swiftly and announced: "General, sir, here they come!"

The "Sooners" had won, after all.

The prairie grass was alive with them, crawling out of ditches, dropping from trees, squirming from beneath freight cars, racing to get in their stakes.

Before 12:15 a dozen men from the Seminole Land & Town Company, having made fifteen miles from the border in fifteen minutes —in theory—were staking out a townsite around the Santa Fe depot, and settlers already were unloading freight cars into wagons. At 12:40 more than forty tents were up, and one settler was busily driving a stake in the center of the Santa Fe tracks and defying the agent and soldier-guards.

For the opening the Santa Fe assembled all the spare equipment, freight and passengers, it could find. It ran eleven trains from the north, carrying 1,000 people apiece. The Gulf Line sent up six trains, just as jammed. On the day of the rush the southbound trains from Arkansas City, Kansas, were halted at Orlando, just north of the border—about fifty miles north of Oklahoma City and twenty miles north of the Cimarron River, where Guthrie is today. The northbound train, from Texas, was held at Purcell, on the South Canadian River, thirty-three miles south of Oklahoma City.

At 2:05 a crowded Santa Fe train pulled into the Oklahoma station, unloading several hundred people, some of whom crawled out of windows and hammered stakes into land already claimed by the "Sooners" and townsite planners. One woman had ready a placard reading "Soldier's Widow's Land."

She hammered a stake into the prairie with the back of a hand-ax and nailed the sign to it. Two men, who had already staked the location, glowered angrily, but the words on the sign deterred them from violence. Captain Stiles strode by.

"Sorry, Ma'am," he said, taking in the situation, "but this site is already staked."

The woman defied him and the original locators muttered something about the law.

"Look, Ma'am," argued the Captain, "I'm a soldier and I'll help a soldier's widow. I'll find you another site. Come with me."

He found her a vacant site a few blocks away, but still on the newly laid out main street. She refused it—and another—and another, that the gallant Captain found for her. Finally he gave it up as hopeless—and the angry land-rusher eventually wound up three miles out of town on the prairie through her own stubbornness.

Procrastination was a thief of land, that day.

At 3:00 P.M. the Santa Fe train from Kansas pulled in and everything was done all over again. As its passengers tumbled madly out, hammers and stakes ready, the town had been organized by the Oklahoma Colony and voting begun for Mayor and City Clerk.

About 400 people voted at this election, and then other land and colonization concerns started to hold *their* own elections and most of the new settlers voted at these too, and at one time there were several sets of officials. Six thousand people slept on the prairie that night. By the next morning two more Santa Fe trains had brought in hundreds of new settlers and more had arrived by buggy, wagon, bicycle and afoot.

The townsite by this time was such a tangled web of conflicting claims that a mass meeting decided to abandon the whole thing and start over. This led to more confusion and for a week Captain Stiles and George Merritt tried to straighten things out. Some sort of order was finally created and by Saturday night Oklahoma City was organized with a mayor and other officials at a dollar a year. Five thousand people swarmed around the depot, a sort of community center, and sang the Doxology.

Up to this time, and through the Sunday following, no one had been shot. Most of the people were strangers and, with both hands busy driving stakes, had little time for frontier amenities. As they grew to know each other, however, this state of affairs was remedied and Boot Hill got a start. Stiles, keeping guard of the trains that rolled in, confiscated all the liquor he could find but a lot of it slipped by the guards. Despite this, a week later more than 1,000 buildings were up and the Santa Fe was hauling in lumber by the trainload.

Stiles' work was good enough to inspire the "better element" to order for him a gold-headed cane, and $300 was rushed up to Kansas City to buy it. The captain and twenty-five troopers frequently battled mobs of claim jumpers. At one historic brawl, they met and defeated 500 armed men who were bent on running off everyone else and holding the townsite for themselves.

At Guthrie, before the rush, the Santa Fe had an operator named Thompson, who became a "Sooner." He not only staked out a quarter section for himself, but applied for the postmastership of Guthrie. A boarding house was operated in the railroad section shack and Thompson, a man of imagination, got his fiancee down from Kansas to cook for the hands. The young lady at once established residence and got ready to stake a claim for herself next to that of her boy-friend.

So there was Thompson, with 320 acres within reach and a couple of town lots to boot . . . When the rush started, the lure of the land overcame the operator and he left his post to inspect his land. He found his claim jumped and several large, menacing men on guard with Winchesters.

The incident unnerved Thompson and, with his angry fiancee, he went back to work—so upset that he forgot a train order to hold a southbound passenger for a northbound livestock extra. The passenger stopped and chugged on again—to meet the stock train just south of town. Cars, cattle and passengers were scattered, but no one was killed. The line was tied up for a day while thousands of settlers clamored for food, water, household goods and baggage they had shipped in from the south.

The Santa Fe fired Thompson. His town lots proved to be in the middle of Main Street. His girl-friend quit and went back to Kansas.

Before the rush there were only three settlements in the section: Oklahoma (now Oklahoma City); Lisbon (now Kingfisher); and Guthrie. Five sidetracks spaced out along the line were the only places trains could pass. The night of the rush the Santa Fe shipped in trainloads of food, tanks of drinking water and flatcars stacked high with lumber. Some of the water in the new territory, the settlers soon found, was full of salt or gypsum and unfit to drink.

The Santa Fe had had little notice of the rush and sidetracks from Newton on the north to Fort Worth on the south were jammed with cars full of settlers' effects. Strings of boxcars at Arkansas City and Wichita were loaded with baggage, waiting to go south. F. J. Best, who became the first Oklahoma agent of the Santa Fe, took three clerks into Guthrie to handle the business; they could find no place to sleep, no food. Finally some soldiers gave them some bread, beans and sowbelly. They ate, and then, dogtired, slept under a tarpaulin on a pile of shavings.

The road soon had to come to the settlers' rescue. Despite the abundance of game in the country, most of the people were hungry. The Santa Fe not only sent in food trains, but bought tons of seeds and distributed them to the new farmers at cost, on unsecured notes. Contradicting the usual yarn that most of the rushers were gamblers and ne'er-do-wells, Mr. Best later said that more than ninety-five per cent of the notes were ultimately paid in full.

Trouble started some time after the land opened when a man named McCabe toured through the south spreading the notion among Negroes that the government would give them forty acres and a mule if they'd just emigrate to Oklahoma. Suddenly colored families by the hundred stampeded northbound trains. The Negroes arrived, penniless, in struggling little Oklahoma settlements in such numbers that the Santa Fe finally sent an agent down to hire colored preachers to preach against "goin' no'th." This dammed the flood and the Southerners eventually did start growing cotton in the new territory.

While the Oklahoma drama was being played, things were happening around the system.

Benjamin F. Spaulding was station agent at Waynoka on the Panhandle Line, the year before the Strip opened. He was working extra as operator one winter night, when a motherly old soul got off the train in a snowstorm and wanted to go to the hotel, a quarter of a mile away. There was no bus or livery rig in sight, so Ben, himself, piloted the lady up the track through the storm and saw her to the hotel. She beamed on him and said, "Thank you. Once again I have enjoyed Santa Fe courtesy." The landlord, however, gave Ben a wry look.

The lady was Carry Nation.

In the late '80s you didn't need money to buy a railroad. Communities were so anxious to get track that they banded together in community enterprises, voted bonds and subsidies and figured to pay off out of profits. Hardly a dollar was put up in cash to build the McPherson, Texas & Gulf, which became part of the Santa Fe. This line was invented by J. P. Usher, who had been in Lincoln's Cabinet. He died, but McPherson citizens got a charter and surveys were run in 1885 between McPherson and Kingman. The U. P., which had a line from McPherson south to Hutchinson, was interested in the McP. T. & G., but had quit service over the Hutchinson end. The McPhersonites thereupon went ahead and got towns and counties to vote bonds and subsidies for construction toward the Kansas-Indian Territory border.

In May, 1890, the U. P. started service over Rock Island tracks between McPherson and Hutchinson, but stopped after a few months and did not use its charter to build a parallel line. Charles Collins and G. A. Walkup of Hutchinson then talked the U. P. out of this charter to build from Hutchinson to Kingman. They had reorganized the line as the Hutchinson, Oklahoma & Gulf and now they went to work. Farmers gave rights of way freely. If they refused, the road went around their land. Lifetime passes were handed out for land needed. Grading and tracking contractors were paid in subsidy bonds. In turn they put up these bonds and right-of-way deeds as collateral for the material they bought to build the road. Engines and cars were leased for construction work and freight was delivered by other roads "on the cuff," there being considerable competition for the privilege, between the U. P. and the Rock Island, both of which hoped to get business from the new road.

The line proceeded south until one day it was found there were only sixty days left to build twenty-three miles to the south line of Reno County and so make good the bond contract. It was raining hard and work went on, in the mud, with the rails sinking under the weight of the engine. The day before the bond-limit expired, the crews still were a mile north of the line and fresh out of track and ties. So they went back along the track and, in time-honored fashion, tore up sidings, rushed the material south and built over the county line a few minutes before midnight of the last day. The spur had drained the resources of the builders and there was another reorganization.

The road changed names again and became the Hutchinson & Southern. Most of the original organizers had dropped out, leaving E. E. Wise and E. St. John of Chicago, owners of the line. It was a year of bad crops. Mortgages were being foreclosed everywhere. The Populist movement was roaring through the granger country and anything labeled Kansas sent cold chills up financiers' spines.

So Wise and St. John sold their bonds, paid off contractors, who paid off material and freight bills—and the Chicagoans found themselves with a thirty-two-mile railroad, free of debt—a unique railroad position, then or since.

The road put in good equipment and gave good service, but the times were against it. It linked finally with the U. P. and, with more subsidies, was continued south to the Kansas-Territory line, reaching there June 2, 1890. A change in U. P. management cast it adrift again and it struggled on until 1899, when the Santa Fe took it over. It became part of the South Central Kansas network.

Railroad building in the Texas and Oklahoma cattle country into which the Santa Fe tracked was often dangerous. The half-wild herds were unused to seeing unmounted men and often charged track crews. Since it was pretty hard to mount graders and tracklayers on horseback while they built a railroad, cowboys were hired to ride guard along the right of way and turn the charging cattle aside.

Even after the road started operating there were minor troubles.

Santa Fe station agents were always neat and clean and would stand for no one dirtying up their depots. In September, 1890, when Irving G. Thompson was agent at Collinsville, Indian Territory, a deputy sheriff caught a cattle rustler and brought him into the waiting room, the floor of which had just been scrubbed, while the deputy sent a wire to the sheriff. The rustler grabbed the officer's gun and Mr. Thompson grabbed the rustler and unarmed him. The deputy, a headstrong fellow, demanded his gun, announcing he was going to kill the rustler then and there.

"And dirty up my clean floor?" roared Mr. Thompson He made the deputy take his prisoner outside. Then he restored the gun to its owner, cautioning the deputy to do his shooting, if any, off railroad property.

The Populist movement, which made railroad financing hard in Kansas, had a curious minor effect too. In the early '80s there was a lot of British capital in the Santa Fe and, as a gesture of friendship to these stockholders, the road had a map prepared of North America. The lower half showed the Santa Fe system and the upper half, Canada, was covered by a British lion, couchant. As a further gesture of friendship, the road cast thousands of brass and iron paperweights in the form of the lion-at-ease. Carloads of these were made ready for distribution.

This all came to the notice of Populist leaders in Oklahoma and Kansas and they laid off revolutionizing the country long enough to pass stinging resolutions about it. They were all 100% Americans and wanted no British interference with anything in the Midwest. The Santa Fe prudently warehoused the paperweights and stored away the maps. At various times a few score of the souvenirs would be shipped around to station agents for their own use, and some of them still may be found in out-of-the-way depots and general offices. Tons of the brass ones, however, were melted down and used for journal bearings.

In 1888 a Santa Fe worker was killed in a boiler explosion at Wichita, and his widow was much troubled over a suitable motto for his headstone. Someone at the depot suggested that, taking the cause of death into account, she might do worse than adopt the state motto of Kansas. So she did.

The motto is, *Ad astra, Per aspera*—Through trouble to the stars.

Early in November, 1889, an editor of the *New York World* had an idea. He had been reading the works of M. Jules Verne, French novelist whose heroes were always flying off to the moon on rocket ships or going to the North Pole in submarines. His latest was *Around the World in Eighty Days* and its hero was Phineas Fogg, a melancholy and silent Englishman who made the trip on a bet, seldom speaking during the elapsed time, except to order fresh elephants, bribe black gangs on liners or charter special trains. The *World* man crooked his finger at Miss Nellie Bly, his girl reporter, and said:

"Nellie, how fast can you go around the world?"

"Seventy-five days, Sir!" replied Nellie, who also had been reading M. Verne.

In twelve hours she had drawn expense money, packed a bag and was off.

She managed to beat Mr. Fogg's record from the start and landed in San Francisco, January 21, 1890, five days ahead of the Fogg schedule, but just even with her promise to her editor. There was only one way to beat that promise—and the Santa Fe provided a special train.

This was a one-Pullman-and-baggage-car affair, and it raced east over some rough track in midwinter, with division superintendents riding with time cards and watches out most of the way. R. M. Bacheller, Assistant General Freight and Passenger Agent at Albuquerque had charge of the train, aboard which were nine people. Orders were the train had right of way over everything and speed limits were off. Enginemen could let out the Taunton and Schenectady engines all they wanted.

Crews became interested in the race. Engines were changed at Needles in one minute, and the time wired ahead to Seligman, where the boys made the change again in forty-five seconds. Some remarkable change records were made, La Junta claiming forty-two seconds, with an engine ready on the track ahead of a crossover, so that, as the old engine uncoupled and rolled onto the opposite track, the new one backed down and coupled on. There was little time for thorough air testing.

The run was clocked at sixty-nine hours for the 2,577 miles, San Francisco to Chicago, an average of thirty-seven and one-third miles an hour. It was the first race across the country—though later the Santa Fe was to become famous for such races against time. The fastest division was from La Junta, Colorado, to Coolidge, on the race track with 86.2 miles in eighty minutes. Winslow to Gallup, an upgrade for 128 miles with a water stop was run in 127 minutes. T. M. Hamill was the hoghead of this division and at Gallup he ran his Taunton off onto a sidetrack, headed for the roundhouse when one of the truck wheels rolled off and the engine stopped suddenly. If it had happened a few minutes before, there would have been no record—and maybe no Nellie Bly. Miss Bly, as the train stopped, had darted forward to the engine and handed Mr. Hamill a quart of Mumm's Extra Dry, as a souvenir. After the truck wheel had fallen off, the champagne was found intact and Mr. Hamill was absolved of all responsibility.

Nellie had been feasted and greeted all over the world, and had a drawing room full of gifts from Rajahs and Princes. Among these were a pet monkey and a box of rhinestones—and around a curve in the Glorietas these got mixed up. All but two were recovered and the theory was the monkey ate those. The animal was unwell the rest of the trip.

Out on the prairies, where the hoggers let the engines roll, the speed was recorded by Superintendent H. U. Mudge, who clocked short bursts at eighty, seventy-eight, eighty-five and one mile at ninety. Mr. Mudge looked up from his watch and told Miss Bly it might be unfortunate if the train left the track, as it might wreck a farmhouse somewhere. Crowds watched the train go by scores of depots, the Santa Fe's public relations department having judiciously sent word ahead of its coming. It arrived at Kansas City five hours ahead of schedule and took it easy into Chicago, having plenty of time to make the connection there.

Miss Bly turned up at the *World* a little over seventy-two days after she'd started out and was asked by the city editor where the heck she'd been all this time. Miss Bly smiled, wrote her story and turned in her expense account, listing the Mumm's Extra Dry under "miscellaneous."

CHAPTER SIXTEEN

SLOW! ROUGH TRACK!

IN LITTLE MORE than twenty years, from 1869 to 1890, the Santa Fe had grown to be the greatest railroad in the world. It owned or controlled track from Chicago to the Gulf of Mexico, the Gulf of California, the South Pacific Coast at San Diego and Los Angeles, and to Denver. It bought the Colorado Midland in September, 1890, and got a line over the mountains westward from its track at Colorado Springs, through Leadville and Aspen to Rifle Creek and Grand Junction, where it connected with the Rio Grande Western and so was in position to get to Salt Lake if it wanted to. The Midland cost $4,405,500 in stock and about $1,900,000 in cash.

It was bought to save the Denver & Santa Fe, a standard-gauge road paralleling the Rio Grande from Pueblo to Denver. This had been built by Strong, but the Rio Grande got most of the business and the line was in a bad way. The Midland made a connection with the Denver & Rio Grande Western at Grand Junction, and thus was able to divert a great deal of traffic, including mining business, to the Santa Fe line into Denver, and south via Pueblo to the main Santa Fe east-west route.

On its face, the Midland deal looked to be sound, and its first year's operation netted $22,424.17, despite heavy construction work.

The Santa Fe also bought the 'Frisco in May, 1890, and its directors explained to their stockholders that the purpose was to relieve the system of "complications, embarrassments and restrictions" due to the joint ownership by the Santa Fe and the 'Frisco of the Atlantic & Pacific. This joint ownership controlled 815 miles of line from near

Albuquerque to Mojave, California. It was used by the 'Frisco as part of its St. Louis-California route.

By the purchase, the Santa Fe got a direct route into St. Louis, and from there into Paris, Texas, thereby obtaining a traffic advantage in a large portion of the Lone Star State.

The 'Frisco deal cost the Santa Fe $26,285,175 and by it the system acquired 1851.22 miles of new track. This purchase, however, increased the amount of capital stock per mile from $10,540.89 to $11,296.34, which meant that each mile of the consolidated system had to earn dividends on $755.45 more than before the merger.

But if anyone in the system thought he could now sit back and enjoy the results of tremendous years of sweat and battle, he was soon awakened. There was near disaster ahead.

In the mid-'80s, Gould and Huntington, having won control of half of the Atlantic & Pacific, planned a double play. Gould schemed to throw the Santa Fe, which was in financial trouble and which owned the other half of the A. & P., into bankruptcy and, when it was down, capture it and add it to his Missouri-Pacific system. Huntington wanted the A. & P. out of the way to relieve the Southern Pacific of the menace of Santa Fe competition in California.

The Santa Fe fought this plan and a reorganization in 1889 thwarted it. The Santa Fe, as we have seen, bought the 'Frisco and Midland roads and, under President Allen Manvel and Board Chairman George C. Magoun, got a fresh grip on the situation.

The system in 1890 was in good physical shape. In 1887 it had bought 157 new engines, 198 passenger and 3,108 freight cars; in 1888 it added 115 locomotives, 97 passenger and 5,664 freight cars and in 1889 still more equipment.

Eighty-nine had been a bad year and much of this new equipment was stored. The California boom collapsed; passenger business dwindled. Freight business was up a little, but rate-cutting, commissions and other practices gnawed into income. Freight rates were steadily dropping while labor and material costs rose. Railways got 1.17 cents for hauling a ton a mile in 1880; ten years later they were only getting .91 of a cent.

Things went from bad to worse, not only with the railroads but with the country as a whole. The roads fought doggedly on, but in 1892, for every dollar they made, ninety-five cents went for operating expenses and fixed charges. A five or six per cent drop in the revenue would put them into the red. Manvel and Magoun, both men of high reputation, kept things moving as best they could. There was to be a World's Fair in Chicago in '93—there would be passenger traffic and perhaps grain crops would be good and freight business pick up. But scalpers were making most of the profit on passenger fares, commission men and other middlemen were siphoning off much of the freight revenue.

In February, 1893, the Pennsylvania & Reading crashed and the panic was on.

The New York, Lake Erie & Western went down; so did the Northern Pacific system and the Union Pacific. More than 600 Western and Southern banks failed. Thirteen commercial houses out of a thousand went into receivership. The Santa Fe held out grimly and fought back. With rail empires crashing, the boys on the road had their troubles, too.

In May of '93, John Rain was wheeling engine 228, a little o0000 (2-8-0) built by Hinckley in 1882, between Arkansas City and Purcell on the Oklahoma Division when the tank went dry and the firemen had to knock the fire. The engine rolled to within a mile of a water tank and stuck. The engineer and his fireman uncoupled the 228 and tried to get her started with a pinch-bar, but failed. Then Rain saw a couple of cowboys out in the brush, hailed them and explained. The cowboys looped lassos over the pilot beam and, urging on their ponies, soon had the locomotive up to the water tank. Mr. Rain gave the boys a dollar to buy a feed of oats for their horses, but it was feared the men, instead, spent the money for strong drink.

The adage that troubles never come singly proved its truth again. In the summer of '93 pay frauds were discovered on the Chicago-Kansas City line; the company was being robbed of about $17,000 a month by means of padded payrolls. It was not a great amount, but it was another drop of water on the wheel of disaster.

The mood of the country was typified by Sockless Jerry Simpson,

CYRUS K. HOLLIDAY 1826-1900

FOUNDER OF THE ATCHISON, TOPEKA AND SANTA FE RAILWAY SYSTEM

On October 30, 1868, the first shovelful of earth was turned at Topeka, Kansas. Mounted on the seat of a livery hack, Colonel Holliday made a speech in which he envisioned a railroad that would extend to the Gulf of Mexico and the Pacific. His neighbors smiled tolerantly.

BO-O-A-RD!

FIRST TRAIN TO RUN ON THE SANTA FE. Reconstructed years later from the identical old cars in the Topeka shops. This train made the trip from Topeka to Burlingame, Kansas, twenty-six miles in two hours and thirty-five minutes. Service was opened September 18, 1869.

MOTIVE POWER FOR THE SANTA FE TRAIL—THEN AND NOW

FRED G. GURLEY. He saw the Santa Fe through the later war years. Became President of the System on July 31, 1944, succeeding Edward J. Engel. He came to the company on June 1, 1939, as Vice President from the Burlington, where in thirty-three years he had worked up from junior clerk to Assistant Vice President. In addition to being an outstanding executive, he is a specialist in motive power, and when he cannot be found in his Chicago office, it is a safe bet that he is out on the line, riding one of the big diesel electrics.

SANTA FE ENGINE #1. The Cyrus K. Holliday, decorated for a Brotherhood of Locomotive Firemen's outing. Mr. Holliday in silk hat. When W. W. Fagan began as the first Superintendent of the Santa Fe, his rolling stock consisted of one locomotive, one coach, twelve flat cars and a handcar.

(Courtesy W. E. Garner)

A FAR CRY FROM THE ENGINEERING PROBLEMS OF '68. *Above:* Cajon Pass, California. Altitude, 3,822 feet. *Below:* Diablo Canyon, Arizona. Depth, 222 feet, width, 531 feet.

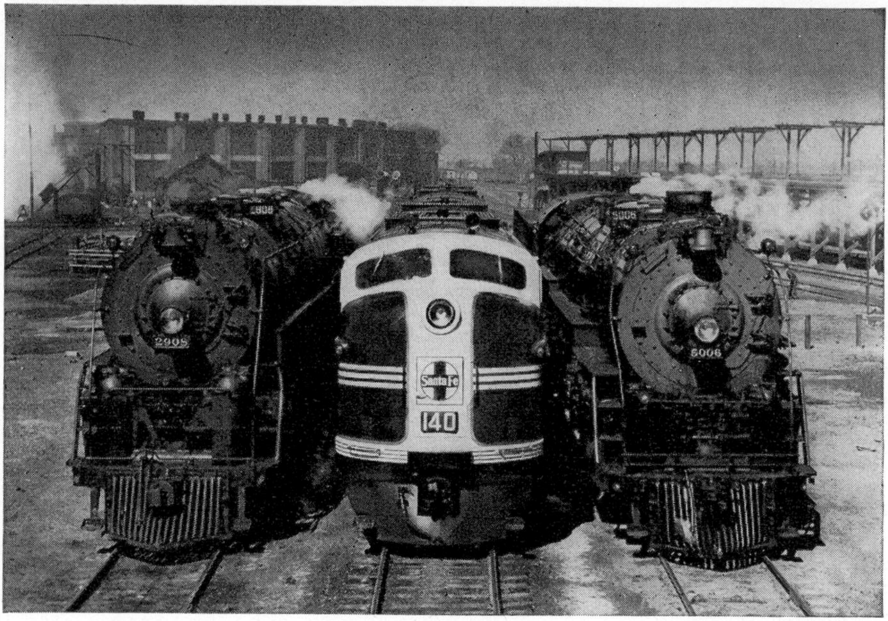

GROOMED AND READY FOR THE RUN

"Do you hear that whistle down the line? I figure that it's engine number forty-nine. She's the only one that'll sound that way—on the Atchison, Topeka and the Santa Fe." (Song from *The Harvey Girls.*)

(Copyright, 1945, by Leo Feist, Inc., N. Y.)

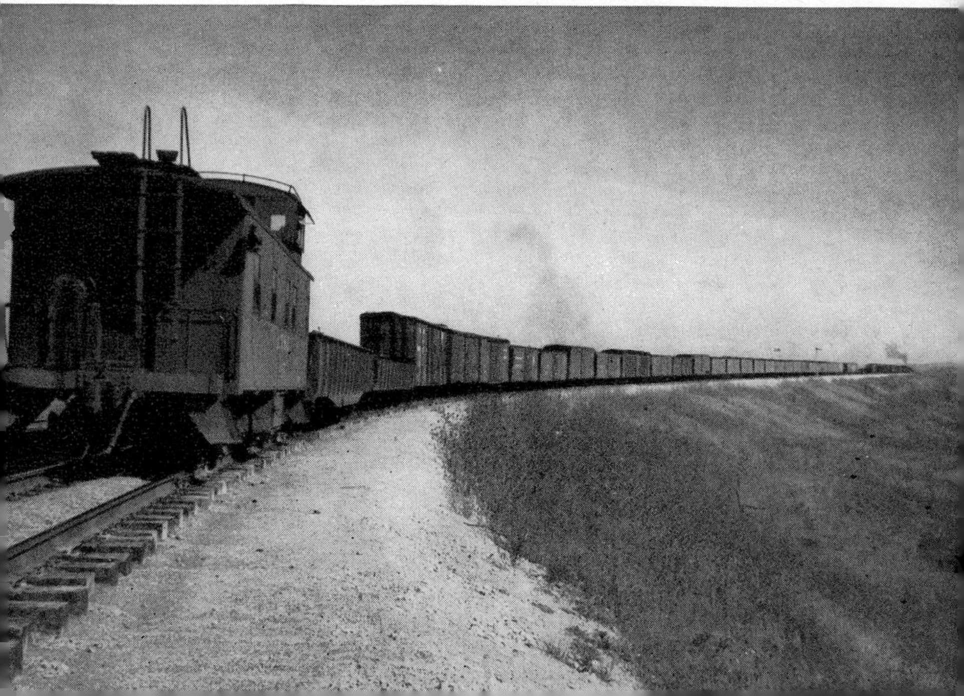

THE OLD TRAIL AND THE NEW. In the foreground the tracks made by the old caravans to Santa Fe, in the background the railroad. *Below:* San Francisco Street, Santa Fe, in the heyday of The Trail before the railroad came. (*Pictures, courtesy Kansas State Historical Society*)

DRILL, YOU TARRIERS, DRILL!

END OF RAIL THREE MILES EAST OF HUTCHINSON, KANSAS, IN 1872. The original photograph was taken by C. C. Hutchinson, founder of the town.

CONSTRUCTION PROBLEMS. Bridge 874 A, New Mexico.

Below: Laying culverts in high desert country, New Mexico.

A RESPITE FROM DEALING THEM OFF THE ARM. *Above:* Harvey Girls in patio at El Ortiz, Lamy, New Mexico. *Below:* Fred Harvey's chef, waitresses and Santo Domingo Indians.

A Modern Harvey House, Alvarado Hotel, Albuquerque.

HARVEY LUNCHROOM, COLORADO SPRINGS. TODAY.

HARVEY LUNCHROOM IN THE 80's.
(Courtesy L. W. Eastman, Winslow, Arizona)

LA FONDA. The Inn at the end of the Trail in the heart of old Santa Fe. *Below:* From an old drawing of La Fonda, otherwise the Exchange Hotel, at Santa Fe in the days of The Trail, before the railroad.

ACROSS THE PLAINS. These humble desert craft navigated the high country before the railroad and may still be seen on the lonely ranges.

Git Along Little Dogies
Come a Hi Yi Yippi I-Ay

FIRST DEPOT AT DODGE CITY *(Copyright J. Lee Knight, Topeka)*

FIRST BUILDING, DODGE CITY. This Sod House was owned by one Black Kelly, standing in the doorway. Original photograph taken by J. Lee Knight of Topeka in September, 1872.

(Courtesy J. B. Edwards, Abilene, Kansas)

INDIAN TRADING POST AT DIABLO CANYON. Photograph by Babbitt Brothers Trading Company, Flagstaff, Arizona. *(Courtesy H. R. Greer)*

IN SANTA FE COUNTRY. In the early days of railroad building in Arizona the U. S. Cavalry guarded the lines of transportation through the Apache regions.

The Tunstall-McSween store in Lincoln, New Mexico, headquarters of the McSween faction in the Lincoln County cattle war, in which Billy the Kid took a leading part. It was here that the Kid led a pitched battle in 1878 with the Murphy forces.

EARLY VIEW OF DODGE CITY. Building at left was a dance hall run by a gent named Jones, who may be seen in light clothing in front of the store.

THE OKLAHOMA LAND RUN. Guthrie, April 15, 1889, one week before "the strip" was opened for settlement. Tents in the background were those of soldiers stationed in the territory to prevent "sooner" encroachment.

Guthrie, twenty-one days after the run.

Guthrie, May 14th. This crowd is, for the most part, composed of Indians led by Chief Tohee, standing front center.

THE SANTA FE ENTERS SAN FRANCISCO VIA THE VALLEY ROAD. Celebrating the completion of the road to Fresno, October 5, 1896.

Inspecting progress, November 8, 1895. Among those aboard: J. D. Spreckels, Director, extreme left; Chief Engineer Storey, second from right.

DEATH VALLEY SCOTTY'S RECORD-MAKING RUN FROM LOS ANGELES TO CHICAGO IN 1905. This engine in charge of Conductor D. H. Rhoades and Engineer E. Sears made the run from Albuquerque to Las Vegas in three hours, eight minutes.

Engine #478 pulling the Scotty Special west of Grants, New Mexico. Engineer, Harry Rehder; Conductor, Dennis Dullea. Total time from Los Angeles to Chicago, forty-four hours, fifty-four minutes.

FRED HARVEY,
THE PROVIDER

He believed in offering the best food obtainable, in bounteous quantities, served by young ladies of impeccable character. He operated a system of hotels and restaurants unique in railroad history.

ALBERT ALONZO ROBINSON. "No man alive today can boast of building 5,000 miles of railroad. The greatest builder of them all was Robinson."

EDWARD P. RIPLEY

WILLIAM B. STOREY

THE FOUR PRESIDENTS OF THE SANTA FE FROM ITS RE-ORGANIZATION IN 1895 UP TO AUGUST, 1944.

SAMUEL T. BLEDSOE

EDWARD J. ENGEL

THE PETRIFIED FOREST, ARIZONA

AN INDIAN TRADING POST, ARIZONA

A NAVAJO WICKIUP, NEW MEXICO

"And I told Mr. Goldwyn . . ."

PULLMAN CAR STORIES—NOW, AND THEN

"It seems there was a farmer who had two daughters . . ."

Courteous Service in Pullman Palace Sleeping Cars
IN THE NINETIES

"Everything's up to date in Kansas City . . ."
(Copyright 1943 by Williamson Music, Inc., N. Y.)

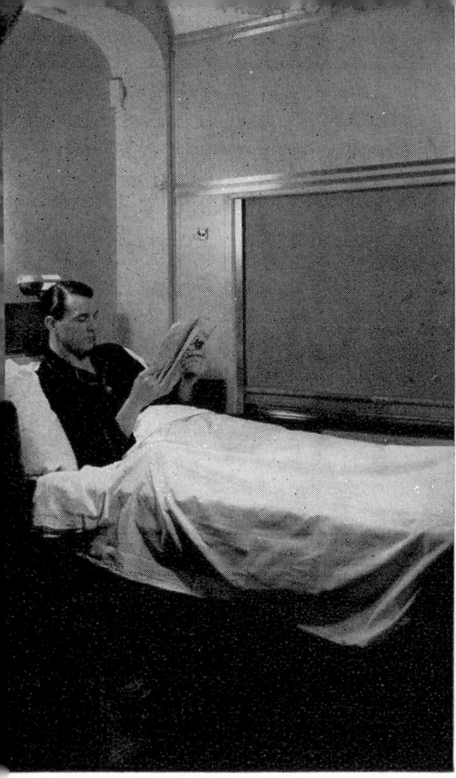

"HAPPY DAYS ARE HERE AGAIN . . ."
(Permission copyright owners, Advanced Music Corp., N. Y.)

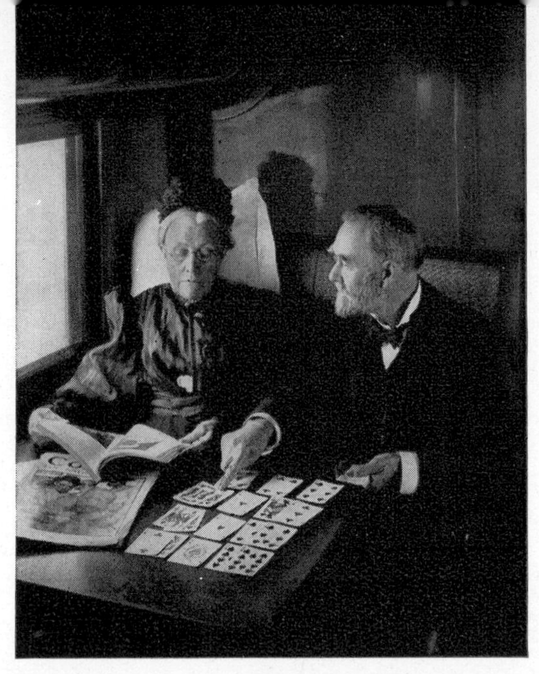

CALIFORNIA AND A WELL-EARNED REST.

AN OASIS IN THE DESERT

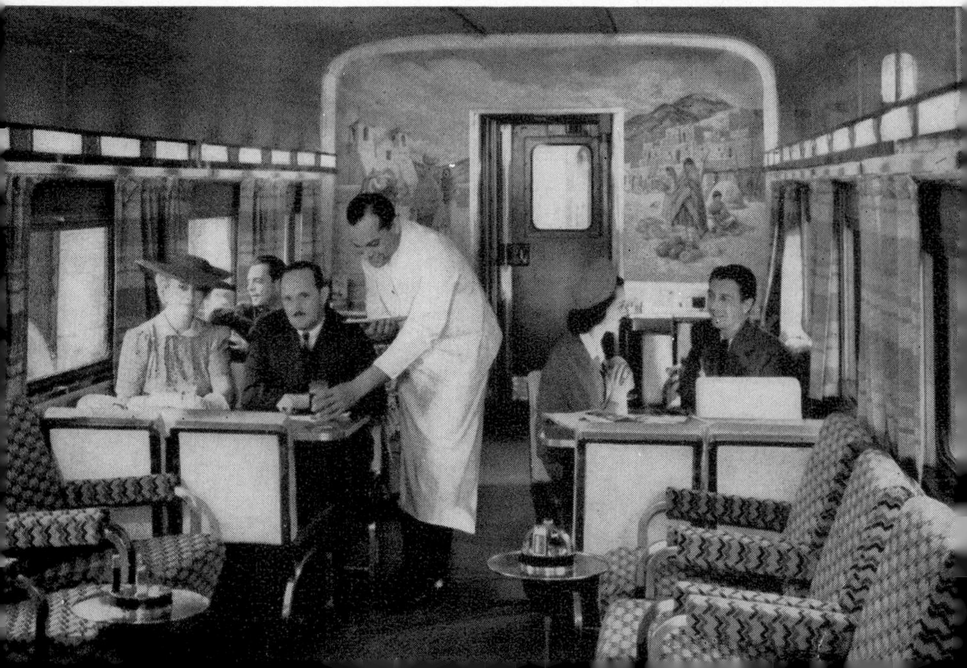

THE SANTA FE AT WAR

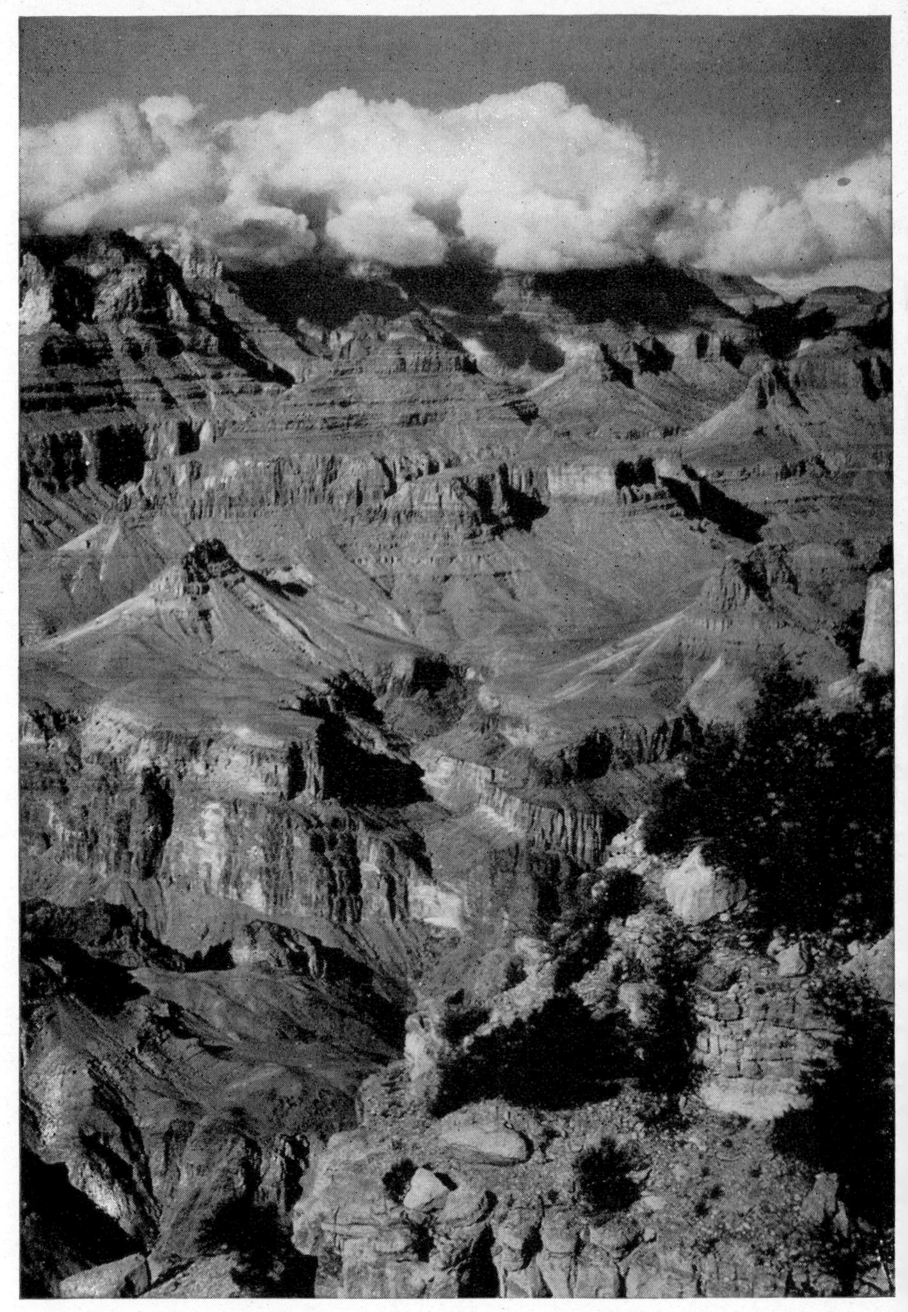

THE GRAND CANYON OF THE COLORADO

DEVELOPMENT OF THE LOCOMOTIVE. These pages are strictly for railroad fans.

1. 1881, Santa Fe locomotive #2, named the W. B. Strong.
2. 1878, named the Uncle Dick for old Dick Wootten, Consolidation—2-8-0 Type, built for mountain hauling.
3. 1900, Consolidation—2-8-0 Type.

1. 1902, The Decapod, 2-10-0, class 12 32/58 F 1.
2. 1904, passenger locomotive of Atlantic or 4-4-2 Type.
3. 1901, heavy-duty passenger-service locomotive 2-6-2 Type for level terrain.

1. 1904, 2-10-2 Type built for mountain hauling. Originally equipped with tandem compound cylinders.
2. 1913, Consolidation—2-8-0 Type freight locomotive.
3. 1914, Pacific, 4-6-0 Type, built for heavy passenger service.

1. 1919, 2-10-4 Type, for heavy freight service. First locomotive to have a four-wheel trailer.
2. 1937, 4-6-4 Type, high power oil-burning locomotive, hauls the Chief and other high-speed passenger trains between Chicago and La Junta.
3. 1923, Pacific, 4-6-2 Type, for heavy passenger service.

1. 1923, 4-8-2 Type. Used in passenger service over mountainous territory between La Junta and Los Angeles.
2. 1927, 2-10-2 Type, distinctive freight locomotive.
3. 1935, first diesel electric locomotive to power the Super Chief.

1. 1937, Diesel electric locomotive, used on the Super Chief, one of the Santa Fe's fleet of streamlined trains.
2. 1938, 4-8-4 Type. Built for heavy mountain passenger traffic.
3. 1941, 4-8-4 fast steam passenger locomotive used to haul the Chief between La Junta and Los Angeles.

1. 1928, 2-10-4 Type heavy-duty locomotive. Its tender carries 20,000 gallons of water and twenty-three tons of coal.
2. 1944, 4-8-4 Type, one of thirty oil burners. Capacity of its tender is 25,000 gallons of water, 7,000 gallons of oil.
3. 1939, 1,000-horsepower diesel electric switcher.

1. 1944, G. E. diesel electric switcher, weighs 44 tons.
2. 1945, 4,000-horsepower diesel electric which hauls the Super Chief.
3. 1945, The Santa Fe has eighty of these 5,400-horsepower diesel electric freight locomotives in operation.

in Congress from Kansas and by the indomitable Mary Ellen Lease, who went around the Midwest advocating "raising more hell and less corn." Groups of passengers argued about Populism, sixteen-to-one and the gold standard with conductors and brakemen, got carried past their destinations and then raised hell with the railroad for doing it.

The old war with the Espee and the Denver & Rio Grande flared again. The Santa Fe cut rates from Chicago to the Coast, the round trip from $85.50 to $55.50. The Espee slashed rates to the Chicago Fair. Before the fight was over, fares were down fifty per cent and the roads were losing money on every ticket.

The Colorado-Midland fought with the D. & R. G., one battle being waged over the opening of a swimming pool at Glenwood Springs. The Midland offered passengers $1 tickets from anywhere within forty miles; the paralleling Rio Grande made it fifty-five cents. The reductions see-sawed until the Midland made it free. The Rio Grande not only made it a trip for nothing, but threw in free tickets to the swimming pool. This performance was followed by another war for traffic between Denver and the Aspen-Glenwood Springs territory. The fare which started out at $12.85 got down to $1 flat. Nobody could make money that way.

In '93, J. W. Reinhart was chosen president to succeed Manvel and inherited a system made up of:

Atchison, Topeka & Santa Fe Rail Road Company
Gulf, Colorado & Santa Fe Railway Company
New Mexico & Arizona Railway Company
Sonora Railway Company, Limited
Southern California Railway Company
Southern Kansas Railway Company of Texas
Rio Grande & El Paso Railroad Company
St. Louis, Kansas City & Colorado Railroad
Wichita & Western Railway Company
Atlantic & Pacific Railroad Company
St. Louis & San Francisco Railway Company
Colorado Midland Railway Company

Reinhart was a youngster of forty-one with twenty-five years of experience, starting with a small line in Pennsylvania. He had joined the directorate of the Santa Fe in 1888, was made fourth vice-president and put in charge of the line's finances. At the end of the year, the 'Frisco still was being operated as a separate concern, and the Santa Fe went into receivership.

The hindsight boys got to work at once. The *London Economist*, representing British capital in the system, said that "Practically nothing that has been said by the road's officials in regard to the company's position is deserving of belief; it has, in fact, been wholly deceptive in its character, although perhaps this was not intentional." It added that "Mr. Reinhart has proved far from trustworthy."

Reinhart, a Western University of Pennsylvania graduate, had worked for several railroads and, in 1886, was general passenger ticket agent for the Lake Shore & Michigan Southern. He quit this line and set up as a railroad expert. After the Santa Fe hired him, in an effort to bring order out of chaos, he surveyed the road and worked out a plan to consolidate various units of the system. This won him the job of carrying out his own plans, and placed upon him a great deal of responsibility for what followed.

Although the Santa Fe, like other roads, was slashing rates right and left to get business, Reinhart, in May, 1893, gave out a statement that "It will be the policy of the road absolutely to maintain rates." In August, with earnings steadily declining, Reinhart announced that he "knew this depression was coming and prepared for it." Three weeks later he said the road was "financially easy" and denied rumors of impending bankruptcy.

On December 20th, George Magoun, whose character and experience had been a sheet anchor for the road, died—three days before the Santa Fe went into receivership. This was followed by a great deal of criticism of the line's financial management. The balance sheets began to be examined because, right up to the collapse, they had shown apparently sound, prosperous operation. One of the first things that turned up was the fact that the road had paid out $3,700,766.92 in illegal rebates—and that this payment, fantastically, was carried as an asset. Bad debts—one amounting to $305,843.59—still were on the books, although uncollectible.

Stephen Little, an independent accountant, reporting for the stockholders, blamed illegal payment of rebates, overstatements of income and other factors. He recommended writing down the line's assets by $10,250,000 as a starter. Reinhart replied that Little was wrong and that the income really was greater than the books showed. The *Commercial & Financial Chronicle* now took a hand and backed up Little, asserting his charges were true and accusing the line of "dealing dishonestly with its competitors."

A receiver's examination showed that during the Reinhart management the system had overstated its income by $7,285,620.51, and asserted that the annual statements had been fraudulent. Worn-out and discarded equipment worth nothing had been carried as assets valued at $1,201,050; income from bad investments, purely mythical, was listed as having actually been received. The *book* value of the line's assets was at least $10,250,000 more than it really was.

Reinhart made no specific reply to the receivers' charges. As investigations went on, the charges were proved true, and the president, instead of fighting, quit under fire, pleading ill health. He was later prosecuted by the Interstate Commerce Commission for granting illegal rebates, but was freed, because at the time of the rebates, he was not in charge of the road's operations.

Not everyone complained about the railroads, though. Some regarded them with respect and forebore to make trouble. In the fall of 1906, John Fitzhugh, later with the Gulf Lines at Galveston, was riding between Davis and Sulphur, over a short Oklahoma stub, now abandoned. It was a bright, sunny day and the windows were open. The conductor came through for the tickets in the freedmen's car and saw a colored woman and her baby. He walked back to chat with Mr. Fitzhugh and a few minutes later returned to the colored folks' car.

The baby was gone. "He done fell out th' window, Cap'n," said the mother. "Ah din' want to bother you white folks about it none!"

The skipper stopped the train, backed it slowly down the track—and a mile or two back found the baby playing happily in a sandpile.

The financial criticism, undeterred by this forgiving spirit on the part of a passenger, still was crying over spilled milk. So was the cry of "overexpansion" brought against the line. For that matter, the whole country had overexpanded—and the Chicago Fair was a triumphant celebration of that fact. Little called the California extension of the Santa Fe a "wretched road, running as it does through an alkaline desert." But he did not explain how else California could have been reached. Various branches were denounced as unnecessary—but nothing was said of the pleas and petitions from settlers living along these routes, for the building of the road, nor of the settlers themselves putting up the money to build the track. Rail critics shouted themselves hoarse about "watered stock."

There seems to be a widely held notion that "watered stock" was something issued by the railroads and that many railroad officials grew rich on it. The idea has been fostered by some politicians who blame "watered stock" for high freight rates, delayed trains, having to wait to get into a diner and a freight car jumping the track at Gene Autry, Texas.

When the railroads were first built across the plains, most counties and some settlements that were established ahead of the track wished the line to run through or to them. Since experience had proved that a railroad repaid its cost to the county several times over, and provided a sure source of future tax money, prairie settlers and city folks almost always voted bond issues to finance construction.

These bonds had to be sold somewhere. America, in those days, was a great debtor nation, and the pools of money were in Europe—England, Denmark, Germany, Holland. So the bonds eventually had to depend on European capital. This capital was controlled by slow, ponderous men with gold logging chains across their white waistcoats. They thought of America as a wilderness and questioned the chances of any railroad projected across country minus civilization and chock-a-block with wild Indians, wilder cowhands, buffalo and longhorns. From where they stood in Antwerp, Amsterdam or London, it looked like nonsense.

Naturally, the bonds sold at a discount. This meant that if Buffalo

County floated a $10,000 issue to help build an iron pike, it got only $5,000 cash and so, naturally, got only $5,000 worth of railroad for $10,000. The line often traded its stock for the bonds, and so likewise only got $5,000 worth of road for $10,000 worth of stock. Just how this could have been avoided—without abandoning all railroad expansion—no politician ever has explained.

The result was that, in time, the system had $1,000,000 worth of stocks and bonds covering only $500,000 worth of railroad—but they had to pay six or eight per cent on the face value, which meant that the European financiers were making twelve to sixteen per cent on their money. If anyone was to blame for watering railroad stock, it wasn't the railroads and it wasn't the counties and towns that put up their money to get railroads. Their whole interest lay in exactly the opposite direction.

As a matter of fact, hundreds of miles of Western railroad cost twice what they should have, simply because European, and a few Eastern financiers didn't have any faith in the West and charged exorbitant prices for the money they lent. The people who did have faith, and who taxed themselves and worked to build the roads had to bear an added burden—and in the end they were blamed for the sin of little faith committed by men, far away, who didn't know a switch key from a Johnson bar.

During the receivership, a reorganization plan was worked out by a committee from New York, London and Amsterdam, but the man to whom most credit is given was Victor Morawetz, the general counsel. He led the way in the rehabilitation of 9344.57 miles of railroad, with a capital of $102,000,000 and a staggering debt load of $233,595,247.74.

And on December 12, 1895, the new railway got a new president. He was Edward Payson Ripley—he is said to have read about his election in a newspaper while on a train en route to Chicago, a few days before he took office.

Ripley, who was to lead the Santa Fe for many years, and build international reputations both for himself and the system, was a Dorchester, Massachusetts boy, born there October 30, 1845. When the Santa Fe was just getting started in Topeka, young Ed Ripley was working for the Pennsylvania in the freight department. He quit when he was twenty-five and went to the Burlington as a clerk—and kept going right on up until he became general manager, in his early forties. In 1890 he left the Q to become vice-president in charge of traffic for the St. Paul, a post he held until he came to the Santa Fe as president.

His inheritance was a system that had just come out of receivership, and so needed not only a physical refurbishing, but the rebuilding among its people of the old Santa Fe spirit. Ripley, a man of enormous energy and great sentiment, set about these twin jobs with vigor.

Depression had followed the panic of '93, and the Santa Fe, along with most other roads, had earned only about sixty per cent of its fixed charges during the receivership. But times seemed to be brightening and, on December 10, 1895, the system was sold at what was then the biggest auction ever held anywhere on earth. The whole vast trackage of the Santa Fe went to Edward King, representing the reorganization committee.

The new owners, two days later, turned these assets over to a new corporation. The old Atchison, Topeka & Santa Fe Rail Road died; in its place came the Atchison, Topeka & Santa Fe Railway Company.

The sale was a dreary affair, conducted on the east side of the old Topeka depot on a wintry afternoon, by Judge J. B. Johnson, the master in chancery. President Ripley looked on for a while, and then walked away to spend the time in the railroad shops, getting acquainted. The crowd stood around, shivering, while the Judge read a long history of the system, its growth, decline, fall and resurrection. His voice gave out and W. H. Rossington took up the story. Various protests from banks and bondholders were read, for the record, and then King bid $60,000,000 for the property and its franchises—a nominal sum.

The auctioneer's gavel fell: "*Sold!*" he cried, hoarsely.

The crowd drifted away. A few officials rode over with Judge Johnson to the office of Judge Henry C. Caldwell of the Circuit Court for the District of Kansas. In the gathering darkness, Caldwell signed the papers at 6 P.M.—and Colonel Holliday's railroad company went out of business.

But only as far as operating a railroad was concerned. Up and down the long lines from Chicago to the Gulf, to the Pacific, over the prairies and through the mountains, the trains still ran, life went on, and the Harvey Girls followed the cup code as usual.

On December 12, 1895, the new company was granted its charter, with Colonel Holliday an incorporator, just as he had been of the old concern. He served for a while as a director. On July 1, 1896, he was made president of the old company, then in process of liquidation, and served until March 29, 1900—when he died. He was seventy-four years old.

The new concern started out with capital and bonded debt of $367,960,433.53. The receivership management had cut debts and fixed charges, started economies and built up business. Public confidence in the line, which had been pretty low when the crash came in '93, seemed to be coming back. Ripley's reputation played a great part in convincing investors that, from now on, there would be honest, vigorous management.

After the reorganization the Santa Fe lost both the Colorado-Midland and the 'Frisco. The Midland bondholders foreclosed and the stock was forfeited. The Santa Fe's investment in the 'Frisco was around $25,000,000. Ripley and his advisers looked over the situation. The line had proved unprofitable; its common stock was worthless. Some of its bonds had a value—and $5,633,000 worth of them, at par, were sold for $1,971,550. The two lines separated in the spring of 1896.

The St. Louis, Kansas City & Colorado, running from St. Louis, seventy miles to Union, Missouri, also was sold and eventually became part of the Rock Island's main St. Louis-Kansas City stem. In addition, a few unprofitable branches were given up—but increasing business soon put a stop to this, and modest expansion started again.

In 1897, with reorganization eighteen months behind it, the Santa Fe regrouped its lines. On May 3rd the old A. & P. line from Isleta to Needles was bought for $18,130,000. From Albuquerque east, fifty-six miles of the A. & P. in Indian Territory went to the 'Frisco, which had been the Santa Fe's partner in the Western venture. The Sonora Line that Strong and Robinson had built went to the Southern Pacific, giving it an outlet from Arizona down to Guaymas on the Gulf. The Espee, in turn, handed the Needles-Mojave line to the Santa Fe.

All this buying, selling and trading left the Santa Fe with its own through lines from Chicago to Denver, Los Angeles, San Diego, El Paso and Galveston. With more than 9,000 miles it still had the longest track in the world under one management. Readjustments cut this by June 30, 1898, to 6946.21 miles.

Out West another homeric railroad battle was beginning—a fight that was, at last, to get the Santa Fe to the Golden Gate over its own track. This was an old, old war. . . . Its cause was the railroad monopoly that Northern Californians asserted hampered the growth of business, held back development of farm lands and raised prices of a thousand kinds of things the great valley of the San Joaquin and the Bay cities had to have.

Bitterness against the railroad monopoly in Northern California boiled up when, in 1882, it was reported that Huntington and Gould had bought half the stock of the Atlantic & Pacific from the 'Frisco. The A. & P. had been jointly owned by the 'Frisco and the Santa Fe, and construction west from Isleta, New Mexico to Needles, had been, technically, by the A. & P. The Santa Fe planned to get to both Northern and Southern California over its own tracks and naturally expected the Gould-Huntington half of the A. & P. would do its best to block the move. Cities around the Golden Gate seethed again, as they had for years. On January 30, 1882, P. T. Dickinson, a San Francisco leader, wrote to Colonel H. C. Nutt, president of the A. & P., from 324 Pine Street. He said that the Southern Pacific was threatening to freight the California grain crop to the Gulf of Mexico for water shipment—and why? Because, wrote Mr. Dickinson, cheap coal came to California in windjammers as ballast and the windjammers then freighted away the grain. The Southern Pacific had recently acquired heavy interests in coal mines.

Furthermore, wrote Mr. Dickinson, the Huntington interests planned a steamship line from Guaymas, Mexico, to Hawaii, and the Orient—and this would rob San Francisco of that trade.

Other San Francisco citizens joined Anti-Monopoly Clubs. One, in the Sixth Ward, met at 417 Kearny Street every week and denounced robber barons. The *San Francisco Chronicle*, on February 3rd, said, "Turkey for the railroad and buzzard for the toiling and frugal yeomanry: that is the motto of the monopolists."

The Santa Fe forces fought as best they could. They had leased the connecting line the Espee built, from Mojave to Needles to keep them out of California. They finally got their own line to San Diego and Los Angeles in the mid-'80s. But they were still a long way from putting up any sort of fight for the rescue that San Francisco, Fresno, Stockton and other California cities were asking.

At one time Northern California had hoped for competition from the Union Pacific, which was seeking a coast outlet over the old Central Pacific. Huntington blocked this by leasing the Central Pacific and making it part of the Southern Pacific. He had once blocked the Santa Fe at the Colorado; now he blocked the Union Pacific at Ogden. On the Pacific Coast, from Tehachapi north to Portland, Oregon, the Espee ruled the rails.

There was, however, a crack in the Coast Line's armor. In 1890 Huntington and Stanford, five years a senator, had split, Huntington accusing Stanford of using the line for political advancement. Huntington got himself elected president and announced a policy change, omitting politics. It was more a promise than performance. The politics went on as usual and public opinion started to crystallize.

From time to time revolts against high rates and bad service had flared locally, but as these usually met with reprisals, they left things in worse state than before. Shippers tried politics at Sacramento and failed. Then they decided to try competition. For a time, Eastern goods were shipped from Atlantic ports around the Horn—

but from San Francisco to a valley town a few score miles away the rail freight often was higher than for the Horn voyage.

A new battle started in October, 1891, when a British windjammer sailed into the Golden Gate with a cargo consigned to A. Carpentier of San Francisco. This cargo had been shipped from New York—via Antwerp, Belgium, and for a good reason. Direct shipments from New York to San Francisco around the Horn must, under the law, be shipped in American bottoms—and the rates on these could, naturally, be raised by agreement between the rail monopolists and the shipping men. Shipping goods to Antwerp under a foreign flag, trans-shipping them for delivery to San Francisco, cost less than it did to send the goods 3,000 miles across America.

Then the United States Treasury Department clamped down on the merchants and said the New York-Antwerp-San Francisco run by foreign ships was illegal. Between October 16, 1891, and May 28, 1892, federal agents seized the cargoes of sixteen ships entering the Golden Gate. The savings by the Antwerp route as against the all-rail route had been about $4 a ton; this now was lost and it seemed that the railroad had scored a victory. But the shippers fought it through the courts, the test case being labeled: "United States of America versus 250 kegs of nails."

The nails won. A court held with the shippers.

But soon the merchants lost again. Congress at once amended the shipping laws to bar the overseas route, and Northern California started paying through the nose once more. It was the last straw, or nearly.

There was one more. The only competition for the railroad now could come from the Pacific Mail Steamship Company. This competition had been killed long before by a railroad combine which subsidized the company for $75,000 a month and then forced it to raise its freight rates to a point where it couldn't compete with the railroads. The subsidy had run to $14,000,000. This amount had to come out of the shippers' pockets and so, in effect, they were excess-taxed to set up a system for forcing them to pay higher freight rates, and kill off competition in transportation.

San Joaquin Valley people were especially hard hit. It cost more to ship goods to them the few miles from San Francisco to their towns, than it did to ship the same goods from North Atlantic ports to the Golden Gate. For example, it cost sixty-five cents to ship 100 pounds of canned goods from New York to San Francisco (3,000 miles) but it cost eighty-two cents to roll the same 100 pounds down to Bakersfield, only 350 miles away. Eastbound freight rates were so high that the Valley, capable of producing thousands of tons of food a season, shipped hardly any. Grocers fought bitterly.

One battle between farmers and the Espee has become famous as the Mussel Slough Massacre, in the northern end of the Valley. This resulted when the road hiked the price of land, which the farmers had started paying for at $2.25 and $2.50 an acre, to $30. In ten minutes seven men were dead and the tragedy spurred on organization of a competing valley road. The fight is well described in Frank Norris' novel *The Octopus*, and others as well. It now is almost forgotten that Dinuba, on the Visalia branch of the Santa Fe gets its name from this battle—Dinuba being a battleground in Ancient Greece.

At last the thing came to a head. San Francisco and the Valley would build a road of their own. Two score of San Francisco's leaders met at the Chamber of Commerce on January 22, 1895. Isaac Upham rose and said there ought to be a people's railroad from Stockton to Bakersfield, and that $350,000 was needed to start it. Somebody said that was a lot of money. Then Claus Spreckels, the sugar king, got the floor. Dan Meyer said to put down one per cent of all his real estate, and cash too. Three per cent, amended W. P. Belshaw.

"Gentlemen," said Mr. Spreckels, "you're not fighting a little concern. You're fighting a big one, a rich one, and one that will fight back. You talk of $350,000. That's nothing. Make it $3,000,000 and I'll put myself down for $50,000 right now."

"Make mine $5,000," said Thomas Brown. "Five thousand for me, too," chimed in George Fitch. "I'll put in $100,000, Dad," said

John D. Spreckels. Another son, Adolph B., matched his brother. Alvinza Howard and W. F. Whittier put up $50,000 each.

The San Francisco Savings Union gave $50,000; James D. Phelan, $25,000. Clubs made up small subscriptions—$50 to $500. Jim Flood pledged $25,000 and so did Joe Donohoe. There was hardly a well-known man in San Francisco who didn't chip in. The Hearst Estate was in for $25,000. In a month the total amounted to $2,248,000, and on February 20th, the San Francisco & San Joaquin Valley Railway was organized. Its directors were Claus Spreckels, W. F. Whittier, Charles Holbrook, John T. Doyle and E. F. Preston.

The little valley towns celebrated. Fresno, Stockton, Santa Clara, San Jose, Bakersfield, fired cannon, listened to bands, held torchlight parades, subscribed for stock, offered land for right of ways and depots. The railroad was coming—the people's railroad. Once again the old community spirit of America was working, as it had thirty years before on the Kansas prairies.

W. B. Storey, Jr., who had been assistant engineer for the Southern Pacific, was hired as chief engineer of the new line and went to work at once making surveys down the valley toward Bakersfield.

William Benson Storey was a native son, born in San Francisco on November 17, 1857, while it still was a gold-rush town. His family went to live in Colfax in the Sierra foothills, and he got his first railroad experience working around the old Central Pacific depot. He worked his way through school as a stake driver on a road being run from Oakland to Berkeley, where the state university had been set up. But he had only two years of college, and then went surveying up into Idaho, Utah and Wyoming for the Central Pacific. In 1883 he helped build the new Espee line along the Sacramento River from Redding and up past Mount Shasta and into the Klamath Valley. He built several score miles of line for the Southern Pacific—coming to the Valley Road as chief engineer. He was to go on to become president of the Santa Fe.

The great central valley of California runs from the slopes of Mount Shasta, down between the Coast Range and the Sierra

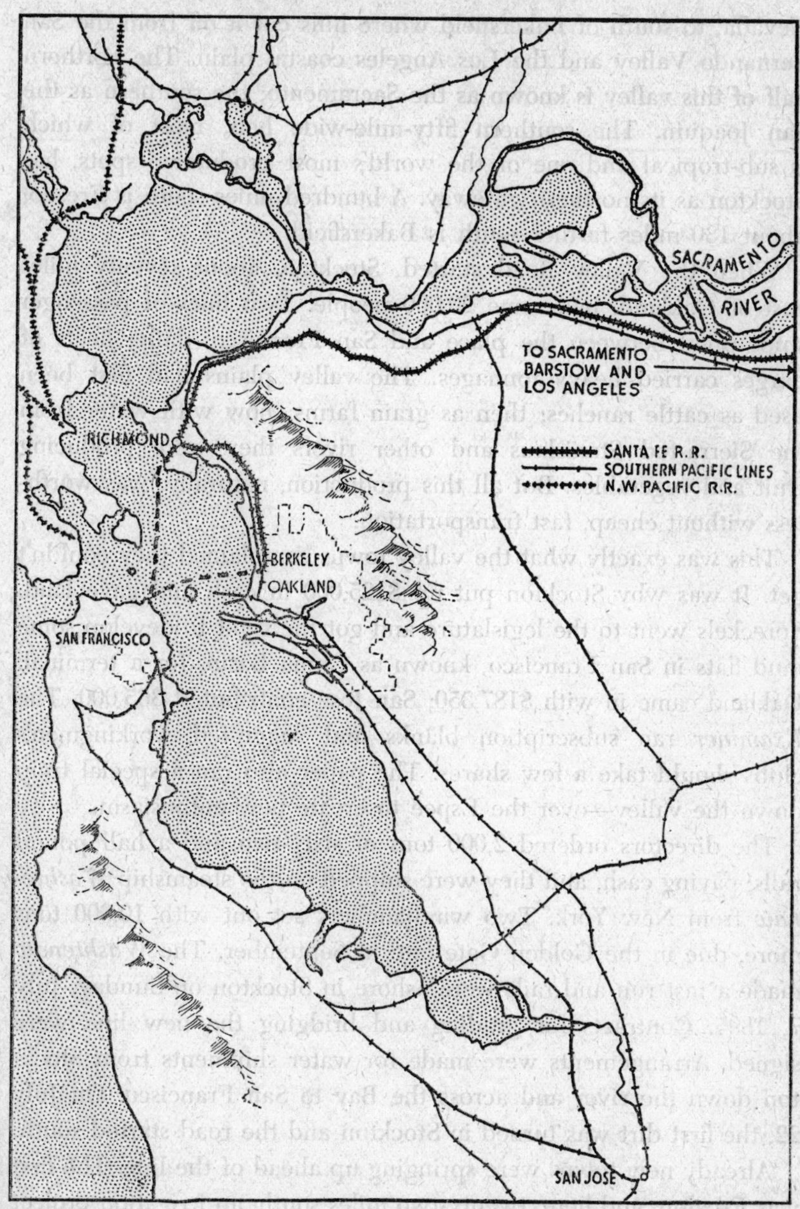

To Tidewater on San Francisco Bay

Nevada, to south of Bakersfield where hills cut it off from the San Fernando Valley and the Los Angeles coastal plain. The northern half of this valley is known as the Sacramento; the southern as the San Joaquin. The southern fifty-mile-wide half, most of which is sub-tropical and one of the world's most productive spots, has Stockton as its northern gateway. A hundred miles south is Fresno; about 130 miles farther south is Bakersfield.

When the Valley Road started, Stockton, about seventy miles east of Oakland, had some 20,000 people. Two lines of passenger ships plied between the place and San Francisco, daily; fleets of barges carried heavy tonnages. The valley plains had first been used as cattle ranches; then as grain farms; now with water from the Sierra-fed Stanislaus and other rivers they were producing fruit and vegetables. But all this production, naturally, was worthless without cheap, fast transportation.

This was exactly what the valley towns complained they couldn't get. It was why Stockton put up $125,000 in cash and gave land. Spreckels went to the legislature and got the right to develop some mud flats in San Francisco, known as China Basin, for a terminal. Oakland came in with $187,350; San Jose contributed $65,000. The *Examiner* ran subscription blanks and suggested workingmen's clubs should take a few shares. The paper also ran a special train down the valley—over the Espee to create new enthusiasm.

The directors ordered 2,000 tons of sixty-two and a half pound rails, paying cash, and they were shipped on the steamship *Washtenaw* from New York. Two windjammers set out with 10,000 tons more, due in the Golden Gate late in September. The *Washtenaw* made a fast run and rails were ashore in Stockton on Sunday, July 7, 1895. Contracts for grading and bridging the new line were signed. Arrangements were made for water shipments from Stockton down the river and across the Bay to San Francisco. On July 22, the first dirt was turned in Stockton and the road started south.

Already new towns were springing up ahead of the line. The first was Escalon, and here, twenty-two miles south, an irrigation project got started—now that there would be some chance for fruit growers to ship their produce and make a few dollars. The road built steadily south to Fresno, to which it was opened October 5, 1896.

The first train, with Engineer John Armstrong handling the 50, a oo00 Baldwin, ran to six new coaches and two combination passenger-baggage cars, painted yellow with silver and black lettering. The new engine, just out of the shops, quickly hit a mile-a-minute clip after leaving Stockton at 8:07 A.M. and made the twenty-one miles to Escalon in twenty-one minutes. She was decorated with ropes of flowers, red, white and blue, and yellow streamers, and her brasswork shone brightly.

The whole valley turned out to line the track and cheer as the first train went by. Frequent stops were made for people to inspect the cars and the engine. The train got to Fresno at 1:30 in the afternoon and the town went wild. Parades, bands, fireworks, speeches, banquets. Girls in white dresses with balloon sleeves rode in the procession, carrying banners reading: "Ready to ship on the Valley Road." Vineyards near by put up signs: "Ready to ship on the Valley Road," and small boys, equipped with wooden guns, raised hell, unmolested.

For months the favorite pastime of a score of thriving little towns was going down to the depot to see the *Emancipator* go through. That was what they called the Valley Line train in those days.

Hanford, thirty miles down the line from Fresno, was reached by the first train on Friday, May 21, 1897. It was September 9th when the line got to Visalia and, on May 27, 1898, it opened to Bakersfield. Although Storey had surveyed several routes across the Tehachapi Mountains, blocking the way south, all would have meant expensive construction—and the Espee had the shortest practicable line. So the Valley Road extended from Bakersfield to Kern Junction and there joined the Espee. The roads agreed to use the fifty-eight-mile line between Kern and Mojave as a bridge across the pass, rejoining the separate line of the Southern Pacific and the Santa Fe at Mojave.

The Kern Junction-Mojave connection gave the Valley Road—now the Santa Fe—a direct line from Chicago to Stockton. There it still was dependent upon water transportation to get to San Francisco.

From Stockton to the East Bay, across from San Francisco, presented problems: ten miles of tule swamp and two mountain ranges in the seventy-seven-mile route. The track was built across the swamp by steam shovels with clamshell buckets, which threw up an embankment, let it settle and threw up some more. There were slides and washouts, but Storey persevered and at last had a stable foundation for trains. Once in a while the dried tules in the roadbed caught fire, but ballast on top fixed that. It took five dredges, working twenty-two hours a day, a year to build the fill.

The Franklin Tunnel, through the tumbled, unstable coastal hills, also caused trouble, but was finally holed through in ground that moved constantly and had to be held back by costly masonry work. But the line went on and, by the summer of 1900, it was completed down to a deepwater terminal at Richmond.

On the sunny morning of July 6, 1900, the ferry, *Ocean Wave*, left her slip at the foot of Market Street at eight, to start the first direct Santa Fe service between San Francisco and Chicago. She was newly painted and scoured, her brass shone, and Captain Lauritzen, in a fresh blue uniform, stood on her bridge with his hand on the engine-room telegraph. The bell jangled and down below Engineer Edward Mahony opened the throttle. Two hundred and fifty people aboard cheered and 2,000 on the wharf cheered back.

Forty minutes later the *Ocean Wave* slid into the old Tiburon Ferry slip at Richmond, then the Santa Fe Terminal. Baggage was wheeled off and put into the baggage car of a six-car train which included three coaches, a mail car and a Pullman. Passengers climbed aboard. Conductor Anderson gave a highball to Engineer Comstock, who rang his bell and whistled. The *Ocean Wave* whistled back and rang her bell. Comstock opened his throttle and the 250, a oo000 built by Dickson, hauled the first train east, up through Franklin Tunnel, over the tule swamps and so to Stockton and down the valley.

Two hours later, the first local train got in from Stockton with fifty passengers who were taken to San Francisco on the *Ocean Wave.* The first No. 1 rolled in around 6:45 P.M., having been delayed along the route by crowds gathered to see her steam through the valley. Scores of little girls, dressed in white, appeared at various towns and pelted the train with flowers, and Conductor H. H. Sturgill and Engineer L. Baker hadn't the heart to run through without stopping.

A reporter for the *Richmond Daily Independent*, who interviewed passengers, wrote, "Treatment of the passengers by Santa Fe representatives was so entirely different from the service generally received that everybody was talking of it in wonder. It was a revelation to most of them."

First passengers from Chicago to San Francisco over the Santa Fe's own system landed at the Ferry Building in that city at 7:40 that evening.

To get into Oakland, the Santa Fe bought what there was of a narrow-gauge line, the California & Nevada, originally projected by "Borax" Smith to run to Bodie across the Sierra, and thence to Death Valley. There were 24.5 miles of this pike, and the Santa Fe used 11.32 miles of the right of way to get to Oakland. The line was re-christened the Oakland & East Side. The first train rolled into the city May 16, 1904.

The Valley Road, having achieved its purpose, was now sold to the Santa Fe, which paid the actual cost of construction and equipment, and started operating the line early in July, 1900. Storey stayed on as chief engineer, under James Dun, the system's chief engineer, whose favorite pastime was to climb into the cab of an old McQueen, set the throttle and bet the engineer in minutes and seconds the time they'd arrive at a station twenty miles away. He hardly ever lost.

CHAPTER SEVENTEEN

DOWN THROUGH ARIZONA

THE NEVER-ENDING WAR between the Santa Fe and its rivals brought on battles in the mountains and deserts of Arizona and the cool, misted forests of the Northern California valleys where the giant redwoods grow. The desert battle was the outgrowth of Arizona's early attempts to get a railroad into her copper country, centering around Jerome.

This project was backed by Territorial Governor F. A. Tritle, who had been appointed by President Chester A. Arthur. He was a typical politician and spent a great deal of time writing to railroad presidents for free passes for himself and his family. One of the presidents was Colonel H. C. Nutt, of the A. & P., which, in the early '80s, was jointly owned by the Santa Fe and the 'Frisco. Nutt and Tritle had been boyhood pals in Iowa, and Tritle used up a lot of energy trying to get the Colonel to build south from the main stem at Seligman or Ash Fork in Arizona, into the mining country and on to Prescott, then the territorial capital.

This scheme languished, so Arizona went along in the old way, by burro, stage and horse.

Before the railroad got to Prescott and the mining country, goods were freighted in wagon trains—a lead wagon and two or three trailers. From sixteen to twenty-four mules hauled this outfit and were commanded by a driver riding the "nigh mule," which was saddled. Reins gave place to a jerkline between rider and lead mules, and a few signals directed the animals which way to turn.

Each train's attendants carried revolvers and sawed-off shotguns

lumbering
Monument Valley
Grand Canyon
Boulder Dam
mining
Keet Seel, Navajo cliff dwelling
lumbering
Hopi Indian doorway
Painted Desert
Navajo weaver
Petrified Forest
Seligman
Williams
Kingman
Ash Fork
Flagstaff
Winslow
Holbrook
shopping center
Drake
Clarkdale
meteor crater
Entro
gold mine
Prescott
Blue Bell
Parker Dam
Parker
Congress
citrus fruits
McNary
Bouse
Matthie
Wickenburg
Salome
Vicksburg
Beardsley
forage crops
Glendale
Roosevelt Dam
copper mining
Tonto Nat'l Mon.
Litchfield
Buckeye
Phoenix
Mesa
Tempe
Miami
Globe
lettuce
cotton
citrus fruits
cantaloupes
Chandler
Florence
Coolidge Dam
dates
Gila Bend
Casa Grande
Thatcher
Clifton
Safford
Yuma
Somerton
Gila Monster
pipe organ cactus
copper mining
Mission San Xavier del Bac
Ajo
copper mining
Tucson
Papago Indian Reservation
Saguaro (state flower)
Tombstone
Tumacacori Mission Nat'l Mon.
copper mining
Bisbee
Douglas
Nogales

against road agents or Apaches. Bells tinkled on the lead mules, to aprise approaching trains, so that one or the other could get out of the way on a siding of the one-track mountain trail.

Phoenix, which didn't get going until 1870, was named by Lord Darrel Duppa, an English remittance man who had a few acres of land forty miles south of Prescott on the Agua Fria. In those days many titled British families packed off their younger sons to "the colonies"—the United States being regarded as only temporarily lost to the crown. Some of these young men did very well in cattle and mines, but others simply lived on the monthly money order from England. Duppa was one of the latter.

He spoke English, French, Spanish, Latin, Greek and Italian, and during his lean periods—approximately twenty-five days a month —he was maintained by miners and cattlemen as a cultural curiosity the like of which did not exist between the Rio Grande and the Colorado. Duppa got drunk at a meeting of Phoenix settlers gathered to name the new town and, after listening to various dull suggestions, delivered an oration, the gist of which was that, as the new metropolis would rise upon the ashes of a dead aboriginal civilization, the only possible name was Phoenix. This was considered a very tony name and unanimously adopted, just prior to the establishment of Mike's Brewery on Washington Street, around which the city grew. It was a town mostly of adobe, its streets lined with fruit and cottonwood trees.

To this city, Governor Tritle in 1884 planned to build a road from Prescott. Colonel Nutt still wouldn't build south from the main east-west line, so Tritle abandoned him to his fate and planned a junction at Phoenix with the Southern Pacific, operating as the Maricopa & Phoenix. On May 10, 1884, Tritle's road, the Central Arizona, was organized and application made to the legislature for a charter.

At the same time the Southern Pacific asked for a charter to link Phoenix and Prescott by building north—which would have meant parallel lines again. The charters came up in the legislature, affectionately known as the Thieving Thirteenth. The Tritle road's charter promptly disappeared and Representative DeForest Todd was accused of having stolen it. The road's backers organized a posse to recover the papers by force, and Mr. Todd took refuge in a hospital, getting a doctor to announce that if annoyed or disturbed, he might die. The posse didn't believe it but was unwilling to take a chance.

So while Mr. Todd lay in the hospital with the charter under his pillow, a substitute was quickly written and passed a few hours before the legislature quit. There was a joker in it, however: it required a referendum of county taxpayers to make it legal. . . . Injunctions and delays held up this election for four years—and that scheme was dead.

In June, 1885, a Minnesota syndicate made another try. It organized the Arizona Central—a reverse of the name of the Tritle Road—to build a narrow gauge from Prescott north to a connection with the main line of the Atlantic & Pacific at Seligman. A week later a New York syndicate took over and reorganized the Central Arizona to build a standard-gauge line on the same route—and the shooting started.

T. S. Bullock, a local promoter connected with the Arizona Central, got a kind word from Colonel Nutt of the Atlantic & Pacific and started surveying, prudently importing a score of trigger-happy guards to defend his stakes. The Central Arizona did the same. The two crews zigzagged back and forth across each other's lines and there were gun battles in the hills and canyons.

Stockmen in the country didn't want either line, which they were afraid would break up their holdings and encourage miners to come in. They didn't want miners staking claims all over the pasture land, either. So now there was a three-way war going on—with the inevitable result. The rival roads got together to oppose the stockmen. On July 16, 1885, the Arizona Central and the Central Arizona were merged as the Prescott & Arizona Central. Bullock held control and went ahead with construction.

A year later it still was being built. Ranchers drove cattle across its grade and stampeded work camps at night with volleys of shots. Grade stakes disappeared; tie piles mysteriously caught fire; track material vanished. But the line staggered on, laid on the grassroots, winding around every knoll to save excavation or filling. Bullock bought some old forty-pound rail from the Atlantic & Pacific and finally got his track finished January 1, 1887. The first train, he announced with pride, would run the next day.

That night the road's two locomotives were captured, run out on the plains and wrecked. Colonel Nutt lent Bullock an engine and the first train managed to get south from Seligman to Prescott. It was a fantastic railroad. Trainmen and passengers usually had to get off half a dozen times and fix track before the train could roll on. Fares were a dime a mile and freight rates sky high. But the road started a small mining boom and made money, though Bullock himself became unpopular because of the bad service and high charges.

This growing unpopularity led, five years later, to the entry of the Santa Fe. On August 17, 1892, the first spike for the Santa Fe, Prescott & Phoenix line was driven at Ash Fork and the line started south over a survey made by Major G. W. Vaughn. It was the beginning of the end for the Bullock road.

In April, 1893, graders, making a cut near Iron Springs, discovered gold, and there was trouble. Many of them quit to stake claims and construction almost halted for a while. The find petered out, however, and the men straggled back to work. Track got to Prescott April 24th, and two days later the first passenger train rolled in from the north. The link between Ash Fork and Prescott was 57.1 miles. The Bullock line gave up three months later.

The Peavine, as the Santa Fe, Prescott and Phoenix soon was known, was the brainchild of Frank M. Murphy, a State of Mainer, who fought for the line in order to open up the mining country south of the Santa Fe track in Arizona. Most of it—in fact, most of the track in Northern Arizona was built by two men, both from New York: Major Vaughn and William Abiel Drake. Vaughn was from Perry, Drake from Franklin. Both had college educations and got their starts as assistant engineers, Vaughn on the Winona & St. Peter in Minnesota, Drake on the New York & Oswego Midland. Vaughn was chief engineer of the Santa Fe, Prescott & Phoenix from 1892 to 1895, when Drake took his place. Drake had built the Denver line for the Santa Fe, from Pueblo, north.

Murphy reached Arizona in '77 and inevitably got into the mining game. He made a fortune and, in '95, sold his Congress Mine to "Diamond Joe" Reynolds. United Verde Mine was beginning to come in, and Murphy and Reynolds organized to build a line from the Santa Fe to Prescott to carry ore and supplies. Just at this moment Reynolds died. It was six years later before Murphy got a franchise from the legislature to build the Santa Fe, Prescott & Phoenix. One backer of this line was Dexter M. Ferry, the seed man.

The road was pushed south from Prescott by Drake and Vaughn, but it was a costly proposition through the mountains and some of the miles ran up to $40,000. The panic of 1893 almost wrecked the road, but Murphy's reputation was good enough to save it, with the help of the Prescott National Bank, which was organized for the specific purpose of keeping the line out of bankruptcy.

The road went south to Phoenix, 136.6 miles, reaching there March 13, 1895. There was some right-of-way trouble at the city limits. The tracklayers, waiting until midnight, speedily built the line into town and ran a locomotive over it before the law could stop them. The trouble was quickly forgotten, and Tom Fitch, a golden-voiced orator who made a specialty of welcoming new railroads anywhere in Arizona, did the honors. Plenty of giant powder was touched off, and the town's brass band played.

The present Peavine, straightened a little and regraded in many places through some of the most spectacular country in the West, runs south from Ash Fork through scrub spruce and cedar, with plenty of range grass, then goes into Prescott a mile above sea level and climbs for nine miles over the pass at Prieta. Then it drops down a thirteen-mile grade into the historic Skull Valley and goes on to Wickenburg through rough range country. South of this again the line winds through Hassayampa Canyon and out into the Salt River Valley, irrigated from the backwater of the Roosevelt Dam.

The most spectacular scenery, though, is on the mining branches, from Drake up to Clarkdale and from Entro up through Humboldt to Blue Bell. The Clarkdale branch follows the Verde River through a deep canyon of tinted rocks and into a land of prehistoric cliff dwellings.

When the state capital was moved from Prescott to Phoenix, there was no line between the two places. Travel was by stage over the rough Black Canyon Road for nearly 140 miles. Members of the Fifteenth Legislature, scorning such primitive vehicles, proudly donned high silk hats as a badge of office, took the train to Seligman, went to Los Angeles over the Santa Fe and came back to Phoenix over the Espee—a round trip of about 1,100 miles, at the taxpayers' expense. This legislature was known thereafter as "The Fancy Fifteenth."

Now another Santa Fe-Southern Pacific fight started. This was the triangle battle—the triangle being this: the Northeast corner is at Belen, New Mexico, from which the Santa Fe runs west 634.3 miles to Cadiz on the desert, seventy miles west of Needles in California. The Southeast corner is at Rincon, on the El Paso line about 147.1 miles south of Belen, from which a branch runs southwest to meet the Espee at Deming. This connection gave the Santa Fe its first route to California. The Santa Fe idea now was to build from Deming northwest to Phoenix, then over the Santa Fe, Prescott & Phoenix to Wickenburg and from there east to the Colorado, crossing the river at Parker and so on to Cadiz to meet the main line between Mojave and Needles.

This new line, around two sides of a triangle would have added about 200 miles to the route, but it would have missed all the mountain work on the northern stretch and would have added an economical freight line.

The Santa Fe organized the Phoenix & Eastern, August 31, 1901, and started surveying east. Apparently to block it, the Espee organized the Arizona Eastern soon after grading started for the Santa Fe in 1904. Harriman, now heading the Espee, fought as hard as usual. The Santa Fe got to Winkleman on the Gila, September 28, 1904, and went on later to Christmas on the Southwestern edge of the San Carlos Indian Reservation. Here it stopped.

In a canyon east of Phoenix, the Santa Fe and the Espee fought a battle reminiscent of the Rio Grande-Santa Fe fight in the Royal

Gorge—only this time there was room for two lines. The Santa Fe had located deep in the canyon. The Espee crews came along—although their track was nowhere near—and started grading a line 100 feet higher up the rock walls. Huge blasts were set off and no sooner had the Santa Fe crews leveled a grade than from above would come tumbling hundreds of tons of rocks to ruin it.

The Santa Fe workmen soon realized that drastic action would have to be taken if they ever hoped to complete the job, so one night they stormed up the cliff and attacked the Espee blasters. In April, the court ordered the Southern Pacific out of the canyon. Two weeks later another court sent the graders back, after a promise that they would not again interfere with Santa Fe construction.

The next day, however, the blasting began anew and the battle raged for weeks until a compromise was reached. Three years later the Santa Fe sold the road to the Espee. It still ends at Christmas with the link to Deming uncompleted.

The Wickenburg-Cadiz cutoff now is the main line between Phoenix and California. This was built by the Arizona & California Railway, which got to Salome from Wickenburg, July 10, 1905.

Salome, fifty-five miles west of Wickenburg, was named for Mrs. Grace Salome Pratt, who lived near by. It is famous as the home of the late Dick Wick Hall, editor of the *Salome Sun*, creator of a frog that never learned to swim and of the town's slogan: "Where She Danced". Hall founded the place a year before the railroad got there.

Salome is a trading center for Happy Valley and for the Harqua Hala gold mine, the Glory Hole and other desert shafts. The road reached Parker on the Colorado River, June 17, 1907. It was not until the summer of 1908, however, that the bridge was opened. Then, for the first time, through Santa Fe trains began running between Phoenix and the Coast.

As they grow older, railroads tend to get flatter, straighter and shorter. There is a good illustration of this on the Peavine. Originally the line around Rock Butte was twenty-six miles long, climbed a hill and had forty bridges and some twelve degree curves. A new line was run through Hell's Canyon in 1902. This cut out three miles of track, thirty bridges, more than seven complete circles of curvature, 421.4 feet of elevation and 977 feet of up and down grade. The maximum grade on the old line was three per cent, on the new route, half of that.

This meant a saving of motive power and maintenance of $30,000 a year to the road. It also meant resetting the mile posts all down the line and changing the passenger fares and freight tariffs between Ash Fork and Phoenix. Because changing tariffs is a complicated job, most railroads wait until their various cutoffs total a few miles, and then make the change. This is why every road, almost, has a short mile or two in it. Otherwise all the mileposts west and south of a cutoff would have to be changed. Mileage in this country is almost always measured west and south, because the country got started in its northeast corner and its great migrations were south and west.

The "merit system" for employees went into effect in 1898 and for years worked satisfactorily. Only now and then there was some confusion, as in the case of General Manager J. J. Frey's trip between Chicago and Shopton, Iowa, when an engineer received ten merits for making up time. Frey wired from Shopton to the division superintendent making the recommendation, and said, "at times the train went seventy miles an hour."

The telegrapher who filed the wire told the engineer who was about to leave Shopton with Frey's private car. This eager employee decided that if speed would do it, ten merits were as good as his. He opened his engine wide as they pulled out, and Mr. Frey got the wildest ride of his life. This time he promptly recommended ten *de*merit marks for the engineer, who realized then that such speed in a forty-five-mile zone was entirely out of order.

Railroads were seldom co-operative when one wanted to build across another at a grade. In '98, near Plattsburg, Missouri, Trainmaster Robins of the Santa Fe sat in a caboose several days and nights to prevent the Kansas City & Northern Connecting Railroad from laying a frog across Santa Fe tracks, for some forgotten reason. When things were settled and the K. C. & N. C. finally crossed, there was quite a dip in its track and the pilot of the engine caught under the Santa Fe rail. This was fixed, for a while by the crews greasing a heavy oak plank and sliding the pilot over it.

There are some famous depots—Waterloo in London, Grand Central in New York, Dearborn Street in Chicago, Gare du Nord, Paris and Howrah in Calcutta—but the depot that was to be known around the world, by more millions of people than any other, was opened in Los Angeles, Saturday, July 29, 1893, in the middle of a national panic. It was called "La Grande" and stood at Santa Fe Avenue and First Street for forty years, until people got to calling it, affectionately, the "Old Santa Fe Depot."

Union depots have cost many millions, but the old Santa Fe station cost only $50,000. It was of Moorish design "with modifications" which included an inside trim of Oregon pine and California redwood, with separate lunchrooms for ladies and gentlemen. There was an adjoining park with a walk laid out in the shape of the famous "kite track" that made a figure eight with San Bernardino as its center and was a favorite excursion trip.

The drinking fountains ran icewater and in each waiting room, carved in Flagstaff sandstone, was the motto: "East or West, Santa Fe Is Best."

"The ladies' waiting room," said the *Evening Express*, "is more like a ladies' boudoir." You entered through "portieres of Persian fabric" treading on Brussels carpets and there were cushioned seats near a bay window. There was also an alcove, that W. H. Hoff, the depot master, and a great wag, said would be reserved for girls who were eloping over the Santa Fe, a favorite marital method of the time. Fifty-two trains arrived at and left the depot each day.

When the depot was formally opened, 5,000 people heard speeches by General Manager K. H. Wade, Governor Eli Murray of San Diego, Senator White, and the local bench, bar and clergy.

Then Meyer Mendelsohn opened the ticket window and sold H. W. Whilhouse ticket No. 6250 for a trip around the Kite. Baggage Agent H. Isaacs, pressed by the *Express* reporter, admitted that the year before, he had handled 297,000 pieces of baggage "without the loss or detention of a single piece." The Railway News Company opened up and started selling postcards showing large ocean-going vessels sailing up Los Angeles River, with delighted tourists picking oranges from palm trees along the bank.

This station, years ahead, was to become familiar to millions of people, most of whom couldn't understand English. It served, almost weekly, as a movie set, its nameboard covered by one reading "Des Moines" or "Rose Prairie" or "Hot Springs." At any moment a movie company was likely to descend upon Mr. Mendelsohn and commandeer a locomotive or a couple of Pullmans. Practically every known star either swung aboard, got off a sleeper, or waved from the rear platform of the departing *California Limited* or *Navajo.*

Santa Fe's first *Chicago Limited* left Los Angeles Thursday, October 31, 1895, at 9 P.M. and at 10:40 P.M. was reported lost without a trace east of San Bernardino. It was finally found by a rescue party in a hack from Cropley's Livery Stable & Feed Barns which, luckily, were holding out in San Bernardino against the competition of the railroad.

No. 2 had pulled out of San Bernardino at 10:25 with Engineer Lumsden handling a nine-car train which included five new Pullmans. There was a heavy mist and, between Irvington and Keenbrook, about ten miles north of San Berdoo, the train was heading for Cajon Pass at thirty-five miles an hour. Suddenly a huge shape loomed up at a grade crossing, and the engineer and fireman, thinking it was another train, jumped—without waiting to shut off the steam or apply the air. The train rushed on into the fog, out of control, crashed briefly into a small wagonload of wood stalled on the crossing, and kept going. The Mexican driver and his team were unhurt.

The train ran about a mile and a half and stopped on a grade.

Engineer Lumsden had a broken leg, but the fireman was uninjured. He started back down the track, while the train crew, a bit mystified by the unmanned engine, set out the usual flags and torpedoes. The fireman finally got back to San Bernardino and told the trainmaster what had happened. A new fireman and engineer were taken out to the stalled train, they got up steam and, three hours late, went on up the hill.

Nobody now remembers Sol Barth of Arizona. The legend goes that he once claimed the Grand Canyon—and everything else in Northern Arizona from the Little Colorado to the Big Sandy. To Mr. Barth, the canyon was simply a nuisance—it prevented him from visiting his domain on the north side more often. He seldom went near there—it annoyed him. It was, to a man raised on the Russian steppes, a thoroughly disorderly piece of territory.

Tovarish Barth was born in Russia in 1842 and came to the United States at the age of thirteen. Three years later he crossed the plains with the Mormons, helping them push the cumbersome two-wheeled carts in which they rolled their belongings. He followed the trail to San Bernardino, California, where there was an early colony of Latter Day Saints. He remained two years and then went back to Arizona which he had noticed and liked on his trip west. This was in 1860; he was eighteen. He got to trading with the Indians and at one time had a mail contract between Fort Whipple and Santa Fe. His Indian business was successful and, as the story has it, he finally managed to "trade" the Navajos out of Grand Canyon and about 1,000,000 acres around it. On part of his holdings he established the town of St. Johns, which he gave to the Mormons for a settlement. He served in the Arizona legislature during the eleventh and nineteenth terms and, when the Santa Fe was surveying across New Mexico and Arizona, accompanied Kingman, Holbrook and others on their locating trips.

The Canyon itself is 217 miles long, from four to eighteen wide and a mile deep. It has small mountain ranges in it, and the Colorado River at the bottom is fed by scores of side canyons. From a train across the West today, travelers see thousands of small gullies, steep-sided, sandy-bottomed and dry except for short periods after heavy rains. Any one of these channels, some two feet wide, some 200, is a Grand Canyon in miniature. All it needs is time and opportunity. The Grand Canyon probably got started from a small gully. Water dug it, and water is still digging it, helped by the rocks and sand the hundred-yard river carries along with it.

More than two and a half million people have looked into the Canyon, getting to the rim by foot, horseback, autos, bus and train. The sightseeing started with one of Coronado's lieutenants, Garcia Lopez de Cardenas, who was led to the rim by the Hopis, along with his party of a dozen early come tourists, and stayed four days trying to find a way down. Finally he gave up.

The canyon sides are in a succession of steps, from 300 to 500 feet high, with steep rock walls between. The rocks vary from red to white and buff to pale green, and the colors change under varying conditions of sunshine and moonlight. The huge, eroded rocks jutting up from the canyon sides are known as temples, and most of them are named for religious leaders—Vishnu, Buddha, Zoroaster, Ra, Horus, Wotan, Brahma, Osiris, and so forth.

The Canyon area is said to be, for those who can read the signs, the best geological history of America, going back at least 20,000,000 years, and probably much longer. There are three main trails going down into the gorge—Kaibab, Hermit and Bright Angel, of which the latter is most used. At the river, the elevation is still 2,500 feet above sea level. The first white man to make a boat trip through the Canyon was Major J. W. Powell, who started from Green River, Wyoming, May 24, 1869, with two small boats and got through safely.

The Canyon had been a tourist attraction before the rails got there, with Ripley and the advertising department promoting it as one of the world's major wonders. The line to the Canyon was not built by the Santa Fe.

Most of the line from Williams, Arizona, to the rim was built by Chicago investors in copper mines around Anita, forty-five miles north of Williams. They opened the road in April, 1900, and by July, 1901, had eight more miles finished. This left an eleven-mile gap to the rim. The company, then the Santa Fe & Grand Canyon, failed; the Santa Fe took it over and completed the line, which is a little less than sixty-four miles long. Before this, travel to the rim was by stage from Williams or Ash Fork, but now through Pullmans were operated during the summer months.

The Valley War had hardly ended before the two old rivals, the Santa Fe and the Southern Pacific, found themselves heading into another battle. This time the rich timber country north of San Francisco was the prize. This is a land of hills and canyons, heavy rainfall and untracked wilderness, full of redwood groves. The Espee started to build north, through Willits, and to the Eel River, along which it ran surveys.

The Santa Fe started at the other end by buying a line that ran south from Eureka, on Humboldt Bay, far to the north 38.5 miles south to Shiveley. The Espee line ended twenty-seven miles above Willits, where it hit the Eel River. This left a gap of 105 miles, and another race seemed inevitable. Storey, new chief engineer of the Eastern lines, was sent out to his home state from Topeka to see what could be done. He reported that two roads through the country would mean failure for both; there just wasn't that much business.

There were already nine small roads involved in the route. The line south started with the Eureka & Klamath River Railroad, from Trinidad north of Eureka to Samoa, a lumber-mill suburb of Eureka. Then came the San Francisco & Northwestern, from Arcata, also north of Eureka, to Shiveley.

From the south came the San Francisco & North Pacific from Tiburon, on the north side of the Gate to Ukiah, and from Ukiah to Sherwood, the California Northwestern, a lumber road. Minor roads had stretches between north and south railheads, mainly used for timber hauling. The Espee had left the California Northwestern track at Willits and built north to Eel River.

The two rivals saw the light, got together at last and, on January 8, 1907, formed the Northwestern Pacific on a fifty-fifty basis; took over the nine roads and built the line together.

The northward drive into the timber of Northern California, and to the coast at Eureka just south of the Oregon border, was a job calling for engineering ingenuity. The country itself was so new, geologically, it wouldn't stay put. Torrential winter rains not only washed out fills and made the grade soggy, but the rivers rose twenty-five or thirty feet overnight and so the grade had to go in well above highwater mark in the canyons.

There was no way to get into the country except by wagon roads. Trucks broke down on the brutal trails hacked out of the timber. All bridges had to be of steel, with heavy cutwaters upstream to fend off the 100-foot redwood logs that came rushing down in the floods. Most of the men and equipment had to be taken to Eureka on steamers from San Francisco or Puget Sound, then south for some distance on a railway, and then by trail or track through the forest to the line of survey. In one 103-mile stretch there were thirty tunnels to be holed through. In one mile there were three bores; the longest run without a tunnel was 10.5 miles. When the tunnels were bored, they wouldn't stay bored in the unstable hills, which were constantly shifting, though imperceptibly to the naked eye.

Much of the work was done by shovel and wheelbarrow. In some places teams were taken in. For sixty-five miles the line ran along the Eel River, which was a mild description of its course. North of Willits the line ran in the canyon of Outlet Creek for twenty-seven miles, crossing the stream twelve times.

Work on the Northwestern Pacific went along slowly because of the tough country and the hard job of getting material to the men. Only 39.52 miles were built in 1912; 24.95 in 1913; 29.1 in 1914. The road was finally opened through from Sausalito to Trinidad on July 1, 1915. Operations just about earned the fixed charges, and that was all. This now gave the Santa Fe a roundabout route from Chicago almost to the Oregon border, with a ferry link from East San Francisco Bay to Sausalito.

The last great battle between the Southern Pacific and the Santa Fe roared along for three and a half years. The Santa Fe won it—but the Southern Pacific profited greatly too—and the public got another demonstration of the fact that competition not only results in better service, but profits the competitors.

During the depression around 1933 both systems fought bitterly for a diminishing amount of passenger business. Passengers dwindled to a trickle; train service suffered; two years later things were in such shape that something had to be done. The Santa Fe stepped out with streamlined trains hauled by diesel-electric engines, between Los Angeles and San Diego. It had plans too, for a fast bus-streamliner service between Los Angeles and San Francisco. It went to the state railroad commission and asked the right to operate intrastate buses in California. The Santa Fe had the right to operate interstate, but not intrastate. The Southern Pacific and its Pacific Greyhound affiliate had practically an intrastate monopoly.

The Southern Pacific fought hard and the battle went on month after month. The Santa Fe managed to line up scores of chambers of commerce, civic clubs, county boards and city councils on its side, and finally on April 18, 1938 the railroad commission gave the victory to the Santa Fe. The commission's decision said that the public interest "needed the salutary influence and driving force of a solidly-financed, widespread and coordinated competitive bus-rail service." It predicted that "millions of potential passengers" would patronize the new service.

The Southern Pacific fought on in the State Supreme Court but the battle was lost. Both roads put on new, fast, luxurious streamliners that at once created new business. The Santa Fe started its famous coordinated service—air-conditioned buses between Los Angeles and Bakersfield, Golden Gate streamliners between Bakersfield and Oakland, buses between Oakland and downtown San Francisco, where it built a new modern bus terminal.

The result was that both carriers attracted new crowds of passengers and made money. The new services and equipment proved a godsend when the war came and the routes between San Diego, Los Angeles and San Francisco became some of the most heavily-traveled in the country.

Getting political candidates over the road sometimes proved quite a chore to the Santa Fe. Mr. William Jennings Bryan, particularly, was a trial, being unwilling to stop talking in time to allow his special trains to make schedules. On one of his numerous

Presidential campaign tours through Kansas he was accompanied by Trainmaster H. R. Lake. The special was on a fast schedule, with stops at Emporia, Ottawa, Argentine and Kansas City. Mr. Bryan lingered so long orating to the crowds that the train was always at least ten minutes late in starting—until Mr. Lake conceived the idea of getting the candidate onto the back platform and letting him talk from there. Then, at starting time, Mr. Lake simply highballed the engineer and they pulled out, Mr. Bryan still talking to the receding crowd. . . . Sometimes he was talking when they pulled into the next town.

Getting babies over the road wasn't always easy, either. There is a legend that a Santa Fe conductor in Kansas, in the '80s, found a hungry infant on his train. There was no milk aboard, so the skipper stopped out on the plains, sent a brakeman to milk a cow and then started up again.

There are stories of such kindhearted and resourceful conductors by the score, but engineers are not far behind. Joe M. Gerard, who throttled on the Cleburne, Texas—Purcell, Oklahoma run for more than forty years, was known down in that country as Santa Claus. The run in early days was through a poor country of settlers living in tents, dugouts and log houses.

It was Joe's custom to gather up things he thought the settlers might need and toss them from the cab as he wheeled by. Folks tipped him off when a new baby arrived, and Joe came through with pins, diapers, blankets and other necessities. In time, people all along the line gave him things they thought his trackside settlers could use and he operated a regular distribution system.

In 1938 he started the custom of dressing up as Santa Claus, loading the cab with gifts and candy and tossing them to scores of kids who lined the track for miles. The train became known as the *Santa Claus Special* and, as the years passed, more and more people gave Joe gifts to pass along. Mr. Gerard retired in 1944.

The present Santa Fe trademark was invented by J. J. Byrne who, in 1897, was passenger traffic manager at Los Angeles. The line had had several trademarks, none very satisfactory. In 1897 the current one looked like a bar of soap and carried the words "Santa Fe Route." This annoyed Paul Morton, vice-president in charge of traffic because, he pointed out, Santa Fe is Spanish and route is French. Mr. Morton, a stickler for correctness, said this was a "bilingual mess."

He called into conference George T. Nicholson, W. J. Black and J. J. Byrne, all of the passenger department, and asked for ideas. Mr. Byrne being from the West, had a silver dollar and, with this, drew a circle. He put this in a square and then drew a cross inside the circle. The idea of the cross, he said, came from Holy Faith—a translation of Santa Fe. This trademark was adopted and became permanent, the accent being omitted from the "e".

Accent or not, Santa Fe has two pronunciations which were illustrated several times a year by poems sent in by pleased customers. One was by Mrs. Mary A. Ryan, of Trenton, New Jersey:

The smoothest road from lakes to sea,
By far the best is Santa Fe.

And Homer E. Kellam of San Fernando, California, wound up a four-line stanza with:

If you're headed for Chicago, or the 'Frisco Bay
The most pleasant way to travel, is the good old Santa Fe.

There are other examples partial to the Santa Fe, the varying pronunciations of "Fe" giving them wide latitude. Thus the author of "Cayce Jones"—often misspelled "Casey"—rhymed it with "be:"

The fireman said: 'What can they be?'
He said The Southern Pacific and the Santa Fe

Very few of the poets cared about geography, and some of the odes took the line far afield. In 1912, Mrs. E. M. Summers, of Clovis, New Mexico, sang:

Speed away, speed away, on the Santa Fe,
To the Northland far away, to the land of ice and snow,
'Tis nice, I know, to see the home of the Eskimo,
So speed away, speed away on the Santa Fe.

The road itself tried to guide pronunciation with "Santa Fe All the Way," but millions of people still say Santa Fee.

The Santa Fe, starting with Nellie Bly, had hurried several people from the coast to Chicago to set new rail records. Nellie made it from San Francisco to Chicago in sixty-nine hours.

In 1895, B. P. Cheney, Jr., a Santa Fe director, with a party, rolled from Colton, near San Bernardino, to Chicago, in seventy-nine hours and two minutes. No records were set and washouts held the train back; the run is remembered mainly because later it turned up in fiction form in "Captains Courageous," by Rudyard Kipling.

In '99, Collis P. Huntington, president of the Southern Pacific, took a party in two special cars and a coach from Pueblo, Colorado, to Chicago over the Santa Fe. Since Mr. Huntington had what almost amounted to a phobia against traveling by night, no records were set.

On March 27, 1900, A. R. Peacock of the Carnegie Steel & Iron Company, decided he would treat a small group of friends to a special run. The train consist was a special Pullman and a combination buffet-smoking-baggage car. It left Los Angeles at 10 A.M. and rolled into Dearborn Street Station fifty-seven hours, fifty-six minutes later for a new record. Short spurts were records at seventy-five miles an hour. This record stood until 1903, when H. P. Howe, of the Engineering Company of America made a trip from New York to Los Angeles in eighty-three hours twenty-one minutes.

The Santa Fe handled this special out of Dearborn Street Station —just one hotel car and a coach—at 10:17 A.M. August 5th, and got to La Grande Station in Los Angeles at 1:06 P.M., August 7th. The time was fifty-two hours, forty-nine minutes, and the average speed forty-two and eight-tenths miles an hour. Everyone thought that that was a record which would stand for a long time.

But just before noon on Saturday, July 8, 1905, a heavily built man topped by a Stetson, walked into the office of J. J. Byrne, general passenger agent, in the Conservative Life Building in Los Angeles.

"I'm Walter Scott, of Death Valley," he announced. "Can you put me into Chicago in forty-six hours?"

"I guess so," said Mr. Byrne, never a man to lose his aplomb.

"How much?" Mr. Scott riffled through a handful of $1000-bills.

"Fifty-five hundred dollars," replied Mr. Byrne. "Have you any suggestions about a name for the train?"

"Yes," said Mr. Scott, "call her the *Coyote Special.* And how soon can we get going?"

"You be at the depot at 12:30 next Sunday afternoon. We'll start at one."

The *Coyote Special* backed into La Grande Station shortly before leaving time. The train consist was the baggage car 210, the diner, 1407, and a Pullman-observation car, *Muskegon.* The engine was the 442, a Baldwin ten-wheeler oo000, a six-year-old with John Finlay, a big Scotsman, at the throttle. A crowd had gathered, and exactly at 12:47 a limousine drove up with Mr. and Mrs. Scott. The wife, a pretty girl with dark hair and eyes, went to the Pullman where Charles E. Van Loan, a writer, and Frank Newton Holman, a Santa Fe representative, awaited her. Mr. Van Loan already was typing a story for the newspapers.

Mr. Scott climbed on the engine, shook hands with the engineer and fireman, mounted the tender, made a short speech to the crowd, climbed down and boarded the car. At one o'clock Conductor George Simpson highballed and the special slid out of the station and was soon well on its way east.

From there on crowds lined the track night and day to see the special go by. At San Bernardino a helper engine was coupled on for the run up Cajon Pass. Near the top, instead of stopping to take off the helper, a brakeman climbed back and uncoupled the engine. The helper then sped ahead and ran into a siding. The switch was thrown instantly and the *Coyote* roared on without stopping. This was the first time this stratagem ever had been attempted.

Walter Scott was born in Covington, Kentucky. He came to Northern Nevada in his teens and rode the range, trailed cattle and served as a water boy for a government survey party in Death Valley. He toured the country and the world with Buffalo Bill, as a rider, for twelve years, and then, with Arthur Johnson a Chicago millionaire, established himself in Grapevine Canyon, above Death Valley. His fantastic life and apparently endless wealth brought him a lot of publicity and the nickname of Death Valley Scotty. He loved the spectacular, and speed was a mania with him.

Fast engine changes were made everywhere on the trip, eighty seconds being considered slow. On the run to Barstow, Finlay ran between mileposts 44 and 43 in thirty-nine seconds—ninety-six miles an hour. Over a twisting track near Needles, Fred Jackson took the 1010, a big, high-wheeled prairie engine, around the curves at sixty-five miles an hour, and a dinner the passengers were just sitting down to went on the floor. Too bad, because Chef Geyer had done himself proud.

The menu started with caviar sandwiches (Mr. Scott regarding canapes as dude food), and iced consomme. It went on through porterhouse steak and broiled squab to ice cream and coffee.

The special rolled on, day and night, with Mr. Van Loan dropping off dispatches frequently for the Associated Press. The ride was front-page news all over the country and, as the special ate up miles and set new records, interest mounted.

A few miles before the end of each division, Mr. Scott would make his way through the baggage car, climb recklessly onto the tender and slide down into the cab to hand out twenty-dollar gold pieces to engineer, fireman and division superintendent, who usually rode the head end.

For the Santa Fe race track east of La Junta the road used the 536, an Atlantic type oo0Oo balanced compound. This was changed at Syracuse for the 531, which Scotty rode into Dodge. At Dodge, exhilarated by the speed, which averaged sixty-seven miles an hour, Mr. Scott sent a telegram to President Theodore Roosevelt. It read: "An American cowboy is coming east on special train faster than any cowpuncher ever rode before stop how much shall I beat the record query."

Mr. Roosevelt, apparently unable to hit upon an answer, did not reply.

The time piled up records everywhere, ending with running 2.8 miles between Cameron and Surrey, in Illinois, in ninety-five seconds, at a rate of 106 miles an hour, and set a world record. The engineer was Charles Losee, a veteran of the line, who wheeled the *Coyote* from Fort Madison to Chillicothe, 105 miles in 101 minutes. The engine was the 510.

At 11:54 A.M., on July 11th, the special pulled into Dearborn Street. It had taken just forty-four hours, forty-five minutes to travel the 2,267 miles from Los Angeles. Nineteen engines and eight engine crews had been used on the trip. Of the engines, two were Rhode Island ten-wheelers; one was a Baldwin ten-wheeler; there were four Baldwin Prairies, three Baldwin Pacifics and nine Baldwin Atlantics.

Mr. and Mrs. Scott returned home a few days later without fanfare, on the *California Limited.*

In Northern Texas lay *El Llano Estacado*—the staked plain. The tract is 3,000 to 4,000 feet high, and everybody knew it was no good for anything except cattle—maybe. There was Amarillo, and in 1890 it had 482 people. There were about forty counties which now came to be known as the South Plains and, in thirty-three of them, in the same year, there were 4,477 people scattered over the 40,000 square miles. The Santa Fe bought and built into this country—which was no damn good, everybody knew that—and by 1930 Amarillo had 43,182 people; 7,000,000 acres were producing from fifty to seventy million bushels of grain every year and there were 305,270 people living there. Cotton was just getting started and, within a few years, it was coming out of the South Plains at the rate of 1,000,000 bales a year.

That is what a railroad did to a country everybody knew was good for nothing except stock—maybe.

The road went down from Canyon, west of Amarillo, toward the Gulf, and got to Plainview, fifty-seven miles south, in 1907. In 1907 there was a panic, and it took two years to get to Lubbock, forty-six miles farther. In 1909, if East Texas wanted to ship anything over the Santa Fe to the West Coast, it had to send it north through Fort Worth to Guthrie, Oklahoma, and then west to Kiowa and so over the main line. From Galveston to Los Angeles was 2,161 miles. But the Santa Fe, to get business, had to set its rates at those of shorter competing lines. It hauled thousands of tons of freight millions of miles for nothing.

The thing to do was to build a cutoff from the end-of-track at Coleman, west of Brownwood, northwest in an airline to Lubbock, and there join the line up to Amarillo on the main Santa Fe stem. This 205-mile link would put Galveston within 1,578 miles of Los Angeles, get rid of 583 miles of line around two sides of a triangle and put the Santa Fe on a better competitive basis.

Meredith Jones, whom we met in the Royal Gorge fight, started running a line. It went straight through Sweetwater—and every town in West Texas started yelling for it. Abilene was especially vociferous, and Governor Tom Cameron and the politicians, anxious for votes, brought pressure on Ripley and James Dun, his engineer, to divert the line through fifty settlements, no matter how crooked the track became. Jones worked soberly ahead up along the airline all through 1907—and then the national panic stopped everything.

Everything, but the politicians. When construction was resumed, they formed the Roscoe, Snyder & Pacific and located a long, wavy line in the general direction of the straight Santa Fe survey. This meant that the Santa Fe survey crossed the R. S. & P. every few miles—and every crossing meant a new political fight. At Sweetwater, the T. & P. held up construction and Dun beat the game by building an overhead crossing. The line got started again in 1909 and was opened December 1, 1911, to Canyon.

This still left a small triangle, and to cut it off a line was built from Lubbock to Farwell by Joseph Weidel. This saved 192 miles on the western route and was in operation March 1, 1914.

Down in the cattle country eight miles east of Coleman, at the Southern end of the new cutoff, was a small, neat Texas town minding its own business. It was named Satanta, after an Indian chief who had foregone scalping the palefaces and was thus honored for his consideration and courtesy. When the town grew to post-office size, one old cattleman sent back its name to Washington for registration.

A fifth-assistant postmaster glanced at the crabbed handwriting. "Satanta! No such name. Ignorant old cowpokes. Must mean Santa Anna."

So Santa Anna it is.

If Spencerian handwriting was an unknown quantity to the cattlemen, so was a train in the 1900's. This state of affairs showed up when the Canyon-Plainview branch was built. At one town, hundreds of people drove in from miles around on horseback, and in buggies, surreys, farm wagons and buckboards to see the first train arrive. The engine came in, blowing its whistle and ringing its bell—sixty pounds, brass, as provided for the peace and dignity of the commonwealth by the revised statutes of the State of Texas.

All the animals at once hightailed it over the plains, dragging along a tangled mass of men, women and children. Luckily, no one was injured, and if first-train arrivals were fraught with danger, so was grading and tracklaying. Workmen went armed against coyotes, rattlesnakes, badgers and bobcats, and usually a few guards with 30.30 Winchesters patrolled the new grade, where rattlers liked to sun themselves.

If the track crews weren't fighting weather or varmints or indignant landowners, they were battling each other. The same branch line, from Canyon to Plainview, was the scene of the still-remembered duel between Spike Maul George and Oklahoma Slim.

Most of the work on this branch was done by hoboes, supplied by labor contractors in Kansas City and Fort Worth. They were tough hombres, and the toughest was George, who not only claimed the spiking championship of the world but boasted that he'd licked every foreman who fired him. George stood six feet six, weighed 240 pounds and was teamed with Slim, who was even taller, but not as hefty. They got the lead spikers' jobs and spiked furiously against each other, winning the approval of Doc, the rangy Alabamian foreman, a mild-mannered man with hard gray eyes and straw-colored hair. Doc's life, however, was marred by the jeers of the 'boes concerning what might happen to him if he dared fire Slim or George. His authority was at stake.

One evening, George, seeing he could not beat Slim at track-spiking, challenged him to a duel with mauls. This duel was fought the same night behind the work train, the contestants battling for two hours and forty minutes before an admiring audience which applauded the thudding of the steel mauls against tough brown bodies. Neither fighter seemed to gain any advantage, but as time went on both weakened visibly. They were swinging slowly at each other, panting furiously, almost all in, when Doc strolled over.

He grabbed away their weapons, tossed them aside and with his thumb pointed to the timekeeper's car.

"Go get it, boys!" he ordered.

The champion spike maulers of the world obeyed sullenly. The 'boes shifted uneasily and looked at Doc with new respect. As for Doc, he had lost two good track builders—but he had once and for all established his authority over his gangs.

He was the one foreman who could fire champion spike maulers —and not get licked for it.

CHAPTER EIGHTEEN

MR. RIPLEY FIGHTS IT THROUGH

THE OLD WESTERN TRAILS pioneered by the Kaws, Hopis, Arapahoes, Cheyennes, Piutes, Navajos and a score of other Indian tribes were thrown together into the old Santa Fe trail, by Coronado, Father Serra and the traders and hunters who followed them. Coronado had left the trail with less than 1,000 miles of mountain and prairie track, including various cutoffs and branches.

Then had come Holliday with his dream of making an iron track out of the old trail; and Tom Peter had ridden the trail from the Kaw to the Rio Grande and had returned to Topeka to report that the buffalo lived on the land and the Indians lived on the buffalo—and both were fat; and where buffalo and Indians might prosper, so might white men and steel track.

Then Peter had started to build the road, and men like William B. Strong, Edward P. Ripley, A. A. Robinson, Ray Morley, Richard Coleman. W. B. Storey, Henry Holbrook, Lewis Kingman, G. W. Vaughn, Walter Justin Sherman, William A. Drake, Gen. Braxton Bragg and E. B. Purcell and a dozen others had continued to build it piecemeal, scorning the soft spots, the padded chairs and mahogany desks in New York, Amsterdam, London, Boston and Chicago, until they had track spiked down from the Lakes to the Gulf, and from sea to sea—the Atlantic at Galveston to the Pacific at the Golden Gate and the South California Coast.

Of them all, Strong was in many ways the greatest. He spent a dozen years with the system, ramming it westward, fighting through the Rockies, taking it down over the passes to the Southwest. He bought the Rio Grande and fought to hold it, and lost out to timid directors. He battled to make the Santa Fe strong and independent. He took the line into El Paso and down through Mexico to Guaymas. He joined with the 'Frisco to push track over the desert to the Colorado and then on to the Pacific. He went south through Indian Territory and lined up with the Gulf Lines to get to the Mexican Coast. He surged eastward from Kansas City to Chicago—and when he was through, there were 7,000 miles of track.

Strong built. And then the country went broke and the Santa Fe with it. Victor Morawetz took the shattered lines and put them in shape financially, but they still were merely a collection of railroads. Ripley took them and made a system—a system with a heart and soul, that callboys at Ash Fork, freight clerks in Newton, hoggers on the mountain division, vice-presidents in Chicago and operators at lonely Texas stations all thought of as their own railroad.

Ripley took the lines when they had 6445.40 miles and a gross income of $30,000,000. Within twenty years he had more than 11,000 miles of main stem earning $126,000,000 gross a year. But more than that, he had 75,000 Americans working for the road, and pulling for it. They were for the system because it was for them; and it was for them because of Ripley.

One of Ripley's first orders was that anyone working for the Santa Fe couldn't work for anyone else. It had to be "Santa Fe all the Way." He was against hiring men away from other roads, preferring to develop and promote his own men.

The president of a rival line once wrote him, asking him to hire an executive of his own road. Ripley wrote back: "We prefer to promote our own men and I would advise you, respectfully, to find a place in your own organization for a man who has served you faithfully and well."

No sooner had he organized the road into a unit than Ripley started to advertise it. Thomas Moran, a famous artist of the nineties had made a painting of the Grand Canyon, then reached by stages over a seventy-mile route from Williams or Ash Fork. Ripley bought the painting, had it lithographed and mounted in gilt frames and distributed by the thousand. Schools, homes, stations, hotels and offices all over the country hung it on their walls. Copies of the picture are still being used.

The Santa Fe then, and after it started trains to the rim in 1901, took artists to the old Hopi House by the score and let them paint to their hearts' content, buying the best results. Half the Canyon paintings in America today—and in Europe too—are the result of this art subsidy.

Ripley was always making trips over the system, and his tall, massive body, with its big head and great chin and nose were familiar to nearly everyone along the line. He was of athletic build, with clear gray eyes which could not see very well, although he hated to wear glasses. He cared little for dress and was equally at home in caboose or private car.

Perhaps his earliest inspection trip was the one which was made to launch his safety-first campaign—the pioneer of the country. Enlargement of the system-wide hospital organization was the first direct result of this tour. This organization was planned not only to care for the injured, but the sick as well.

But for all the safety-first crusades, nature still caused accidents. In June, 1903, the Kaw and Missouri Rivers overflowed around Kansas City and washed out the roadbed around Nineteenth and Liberty Streets. A big pipe from the old Holly Street reservoir on a near-by hill three hundred feet higher than the tracks, passed under this bit of road and an engine going over broke it. The reservoir let go. Millions of gallons of water boiled up and four 135-ton Baldwin locomotives and two Pullman cars just disappeared. Where they had been was a pit forty feet deep covering more than an acre. Another coach, out in the Argentine yards, sank in the flood and was discovered months later on an island ten miles below Kansas City.

Sixteen of the seventeen river bridges went out in this flood, the Missouri Pacific saving its span by holding it down with fifteen locomotives and a score of loaded coal gondolas.

Ripley started the pension system so that every employee at sixty-five was (and is) assured a comfortable old age.

The reading rooms and clubhouses all over the road are another

Ripley monument. They are open to employees and their families, providing books, magazines, newspapers, baths and sleeping quarters, and even, at Needles, a plunge.

At the clubs there are entertainments and lectures, concerts, glee clubs and bands. Before the war, traveling troupes provided much of the entertainment; these included world travelers, scientists and well-known singers, all sent out by the road on "the Santa Fe circuit."

These pension plans, safety-first campaigns, clubhouses and other innovations, Ripley believed to be "enlightened self-interest." He added to them by subsidizing Railroad Young Men's Christian Associations at many points along the line, and by cutting prices of meals at Harvey Houses to the no-profit point for employees. "We want better men, and we are willing to spend money to make them better and happier," he wrote in explanation.

He fought government ownership and advocated allowing the railroads to work out plans to improve service by traffic agreements, which were and are forbidden by law. Years ago he pointed out that every night five trains of various railroads ran each way between Chicago and Kansas City, six between Chicago and Omaha, six between Chicago and the Twin Cities, five between Kansas City and St. Louis—and that normally half the equipment could easily handle the traffic. The government, he declared, forced the roads to this expensive and uneconomic operation—and then accused them of waste and mismanagement.

He acquired a substantial amount of preferred stock and his salary for seven years was $75,000 a year. On his seventieth birthday he was erroneously reported to have been raised to $100,000 annually—which would have been the highest pay of any railroad president in the country. There were the usual cries of anguish, and the *Topeka Capital* announced that "Now it's possible for farmers and shippers to understand Mr. Ripley's incessant complaints that they don't cough up high enough rates." They were coughing up less than a cent a ton-mile.

Ripley was one of the first corporation heads to cultivate public relations with stockholders. In 1915 letters were sent to the company's 45,000 stockholders asking them to make suggestions for better management of the railroad and for criticism of existing methods.

According to the *Topeka State Journal*, only once in twenty years had a stockholder outside the official family been present at a meeting. A South Dakota farmer, passing through Topeka, stopped to attend a meeting. He voted his stock and made a speech. "I just wanted to see how the job is done," the farmer said. "I'm satisfied."

Ripley once bought half a railroad for $1. This was the Kansas Southwestern from Arkansas City to Anthony, and he bought it on his theory that depressions are the time to expand and invest. The Kansas Public Utility Commission had ordered $150,000 spent on the road and the owners objected. W. B. Biddle, the receiver, offered the line to Ripley. It was half owned by the 'Frisco.

"I'll name a price, give or take," said Ripley.

"Okay," replied Biddle.

"One dollar."

"Sold!"

Ripley was also responsible for starting operation of the *California Limited*, for years the crack train to the Coast. It was all Pullman and you had to buy a ticket. No passes were allowed, and even Ripley, when he rode it, paid fare, just as everyone else did. In the summer, as many as seven sections, each consisting of eleven sleepers, pulled out of Dearborn Station within half an hour every day—all full. At one memorable time no fewer than forty-five of these trains were operating over the road simultaneously, twenty-two westbound and twenty-three eastbound, over the three-day running time. This set a record never afterward approached for one train. Each train on its long run used a minimum of fifteen engines and fifteen train crews. For more than ten years, the *California Limited* was the star limited train of the world.

In the course of his Santa Fe career, Ripley was engaged in the usual battles with politicians. One of the most famous was with Theodore Roosevelt and concerned a rebate, which was forbidden by the law. T. R. tried to make capital of it. His investigators snooping around, discovered that in 1908 the Grand Canyon Lime and

Cement Company had shipped 384 cars of lime from Nelson, Arizona to Los Angeles, at $3.50 a ton. En route, some of the lime had been lost and the shipper put in a claim for a rebate. They got $400 from the Santa Fe claim agent. The Department of Justice descended on the road and it was fined $330,000. Ripley fought the decision, carried the case to the Supreme Court and won—and that was the end of a political fight to make capital out of a standard railroad practice.

Railroading had its small ironies for Ripley, too.

A tie is a slab of wood, preferably hard, about eight feet long, eight inches wide and six inches thick. It takes about 3,000 of them to support a mile of main-line track and from three to twenty years for them to become unserviceable, depending on climate, treatment, variety of wood and the amount of pounding they get from locomotives. Steel ties have been tried and discarded. Longitudinal ties have been tried too; they don't work. The old cross tie still carries the track.

Years ago a Midwestern road had an idea. Catalpa wood grew fast and made good ties. The Santa Fe planted rows of catalpas along its track and invented a rolling sawmill that would run on rails and work as it went along. The trees all died the first hard winter.

The Santa Fe got its early ties from Colorado forests, floating them down the Arkansas. In 1907 it needed hardwood and, since it was cheap to ship by freighter, it sent E. O. Faulkner half around the world looking for tie timber. The result was that the Santa Fe bought a million oak trees a year from Japan until 1912. In 1908 it started shipping in 125,000 *ohia* ties a year from Hawaii. Then it had an idea.

North of San Diego the system bought some thousands of acres, planted eucalyptus trees and sat back to wait for fifteen years to harvest the timber. The trees grew all right, but the only trouble was the wood wouldn't hold spikes well enough. So Rancho Santa Fe, as the timber tract was called, became a country estate development, and still is. A lot of the Australian eucalyptus trees in

California stem from the Santa Fe experiment. Many farmers and orchardists planted them for commercial use.

But if the Santa Fe was out of luck with its eucalyptus forest at Rancho Santa Fe, luck turned her other cheek at Santa Fe Springs, twelve miles south of Los Angeles. The road opened its line through here August 11, 1888, platted some land and planned a hotel. Lots were offered for $200 apiece, with few buyers. The boom collapsed and the land lay idle for years.

Every once in a while, some hopeful concern drilled for oil, but with no luck. A few acres were sold here and there for dairying and citrus production. Then, in the early '20s, Los Angeles Pioneer Oil Company sank a hole—and struck oil. It had taken since 1865, when the first well was sunk, to find it.

Soon more than 500 wells were producing, and the place became the largest oil-shipping point in California—supplying, incidentally, much locomotive oil for the road.

Tramping across the Topeka yards one day in 1905, President Ripley saw a new little shack, and, looking inside, saw a man sitting there doing nothing. He was, apparently, blind. Ripley passed on without comment. But when he got back to his office he called Shop Superintendent John Purcell and asked him about the man.

"That's Bill Hazen," said Purcell. "He used to be our blacksmith foreman. Eyes went back on him, so I tried him at several different jobs but there was nothing he could handle—so I just built him a shack and made him a supervisor."

"Supervisor of what?" queried Ripley.

"Oh—just a supervisor," stammered Purcell with some embarrassment. "The boys all like him—they bring him to work and take him home at night. And we only pay him $3 a day. . . . He's been a faithful employee—you wouldn't want to fire him, would you?"

"No, of course not," said Ripley. "But still, there will be other cases, and, after all . . . Well, keep him on . . ."

Ripley thought a lot about the matter. On December 12, 1906, the Santa Fe Pension Plan was born. It provided for old or incapacitated employees like Bill Hazen. Timekeepers all over the system began checking ages of the men, and in many cases got short answers. Some of the workers feared that the road was getting ready to discharge the oldtimers!

Because of this fear, some of the men began lying about their ages, and when two of the oldest of them, Owen Callaghan and Peter Cart were asked to state their ages, they shouted, "Sure we're thirty-five, each of us," and went on vigorously digging a ditch.

"Too bad," grinned the timekeeper, "you're thirty years too young to retire on a swell pension."

"Faith and begorra," said Owen shaking his grizzled head. "Me mother always told me the divil loves a liar. . . ."

The plan, as finally set up, gave every employee with fifteen years service a monthly pension ranging from $20 to $75 or more when he reached the age of sixty-five, or when he became unable to work, regardless of age. In the thirty years that followed, the road paid out $11,279,000 in pensions, without any contribution from employees. Then the government stepped in and stopped it.

Instead, a retirement plan was invented in which employees were forced to contribute part of their wages to match contributions from the railroad. Costs skyrocketed, both to workers—who had paid nothing before—and to the railroad. Pensioners got very little more under the new arrangement than they had in the past.

The company's pension roll for 1936 totaled $1,156,218 and, recent figures show, would have amounted in 1944 to $1,930,884. This is the amount the company would have paid out under its own plan.

Under the governmental retirement plan, however, the railroad paid out in 1944 $5,651,095 in retirement taxes and the employees paid out an equal amount. Under the government plan, the average monthly pension in 1944 was $72.54; under the company's plan it would have been $60.28.

The figures show that the huge increases in costs have not been reflected in a proportionate increase to beneficiaries of the system.

However, the federal plan was advantageous to the employee in one respect. He could now move from one railroad to another without losing his pension rights. But its operating costs were added to the deductions made from the workman's wages; under the private plan these costs came out of the line's operating income.

Ripley, although he organized the Santa Fe's pension system, did not believe in retirement. When he was seventy-two, two years over the limit, he told a reporter "No man should retire. The Lord made man for work and the Lord should set the quitting time."

The federal retirement act caused the abandonment of the Santa Fe's death-benefit system, under which dependents got lump sums ranging from $250 to $3,000, depending upon the length of time deceased had served, and rates of their pay. The Santa Fe deducted nothing from salaries and paid all costs. Payments to survivors, under the federal plan, have been consistently less than under the old Santa Fe arrangement. Many oldtimers on the road still maintain that the federal plan wiped out several hundred dollars they had "invested" by reason of years of service—which didn't count when the government took over.

Ripley was an open-door executive and so, in 1906, he was not surprised when Albert MacRae, a stenographer for Vice-President Kendrick, came into his office hopping mad. He was waving some papers and Ripley asked what the trouble was.

"Well, some of the people working for this road don't seem to know what it's all about," he stormed. This agent out at Blankville, for example. That's a competitive point for the Gulf Lines and the Texas & Pacific."

"What's he doing?" asked Ripley.

"What's he *doing*! Well, he doesn't know that the Gulf Lines are part of the Santa Fe system—so he's routing traffic over the Texas and Pacific. He's a friend of the T. & P. agent . . ." continued MacRae.

". . . who'll probably be the last man to tell him the truth," smiled Ripley. "Well, what do you think we should do?"

"There ought to be some way we could make all of our employees familiar with the Santa Fe and what it's doing and trying to do. Maybe a monthly magazine. . . ."

"Excellent idea," said Ripley. "Ask Mr. Kendrick if he can spare you—and go ahead and produce the magazine."

And a few weeks later the Santa Fe magazine started. It has never missed an issue since. The early numbers carried warnings against cigarettes, strong drink, loan sharks and other menaces of the day. Soon, however, it developed into a clearing house of information on operating subjects, plus news of the people working all over the system. Frequent articles had to do with Santa Fe history and were very helpful in letting every employee know "what it was all about." The book has a high rating among employee magazines, a circulation around 80,000 a month and is distributed free.

The only complaint against it is that it is so interesting it gets read on company time, instead of being taken home.

In the late '80s Arthur E. Stillwell, an insurance man and real-estate promoter, became interested in Fairmount Park, an amusement resort some miles outside Kansas City. At the opening of the place the promoter hired William Jennings Bryan to make the dedication speech. It was the first time Mr. Bryan had been paid for such work, which he had hitherto considered a privilege—and it opened new vistas. From then on he always charged for oratory.

Despite its auspicious start, however, the park was hard to get to and Stillwell organized the Air Line Railroad to Independence, Kansas, with a stop at Fairmount. This was a success and led him, a few years later, to organize a new direct road from Kansas City to the Gulf, known as the Kansas City, Pittsburg & Gulf. It used the old Air Line trackage to get out of Kansas City.

Stillwell was the son of a jeweler in Rochester, New York. He believed in dreams, visions, hunches, and certain small fairies he called "Brownies," who appeared at various crises and offered advice and suggestions. During the organization of the Kansas City, Pittsburg and Gulf, the plan had been to go to Galveston, but the Brownies appeared one night and counseled against it.

"Instead," Stillwell recounted, "they located a city site for me on the north side of Sabine Lake, Texas, and advised me to make that the terminal, christening it after myself: Port Arthur. I found out that the site was not at all suitable, but I followed my Brownies' advice, anyway."

He went south and laid out Port Arthur, with the help of Dutch capital, American investors being a bit shy of the location, which was renowned for mosquitoes and seemed about the last place to start a new deep-water port. The road, however, was rushed through and put into operation, seemingly with success. It cut 114 miles from the former route.

Then Stillwell got into a fight for control with John W. (Bet-a-Million) Gates and, when it was over, the founder was out. Gates then reorganized the line as the Kansas City Southern. In '99 Stillwell was broke, blaming Wall Street financiers who, he said, were determined not to allow common, everyday citizens to control railroads anywhere.

A sidelight on the man's character is that after he had lost the fight with Gates he read, casually, a line of George Ade's: "It's a man's own fault if he wears sideburns." The line haunted him and that night he consulted his Brownies, who held with Mr. Ade. The next day Stillwell shaved off his whiskers.

But many people still believed in him and, on February 10, 1900, they gave a banquet for him at the Midland Hotel in Kansas City. At the start of the affair he regarded it as a farewell party and in this mood, got up to make a swan-song speech. Then the Brownies came. He listened an instant, standing silent, and then announced suddenly in confident tones:

"I have designed a railroad that will be 1,600 miles long but will bring the Pacific Ocean 400 miles nearer Kansas City, and Kansas City 1,600 miles nearer Central and South America."

This was the idea that gave birth to the Kansas City, Mexico & Orient Railway. The plan was to build almost in a direct line down through Kansas, Oklahoma and Texas, then across the Rio Grande and down through Chihuahua and Sinaloa to Topolobampo. This port is south of Guaymas, on the Gulf of California to which the Santa Fe had run the Sonora system from Texas, later trading it to the Southern Pacific for the Mojave-Needles line. Topolobampo once was the site of a Mexican socialist colony. It lies on a land-locked, deep-water harbor about eighteen miles from the open Gulf and is the port of entry into a huge fertile area that has never been fully developed to this day. Behind this land are largely worked mineral deposits on both sides of the Sierra Madre. Lieutenant George Dewey, later Admiral and the Hero of Manila Bay, first surveyed the harbor in '73. According to his report, there were seventeen feet of water over the bar at low tide and the place was ripe for development.

The Stillwell plan was sound, and still is. The route is much the shortest from the Midwest to New Zealand, Samoa, Hawaii, Australia and Southeast Asian ports; it runs through a potentially wealthy territory. But like almost every other project in which he led, it was dogged by disaster. Whether in the future it will be revived and put into operation depends on many things—our relations with Mexico, for one. The Mexican government owns the line south of the border and this almost precludes a joint operation by American and Mexican interests. The sad experience of the Southern Pacific with the Sonora line isn't any inducement to American railroaders to try to operate any lines in Mexico.

Anyway, Stillwell went to Mexico City and talked to Dictator Porfirio Diaz about the project. Governors of nine Midwest states wired the old Mexican Chief that Stillwell was coming, and backed his plan. Diaz offered a subsidy of $5,000 a mile for the road and Stillwell returned to raise capital.

Work got under way after awhile on three sections—northeast and southwest from Chihuahua, when the Orient met the Mexican Central; and north from Topolobampo. Seventy-six miles from deep water northeast to Fuerte finally were put into operation. On the northern stretches Pancho Villa did some grading, using twelve teams and 200 peons. He and Stillwell disliked each other—Stillwell saying that Villa was a "dirty, greasy fellow." In one of the revolutions, Pancho led his men up into the mountains of Chihuahua and blew up one of Stillwell's silver mines, apparently for personal spite.

Although Stillwell took credit for letting his Brownies invent the Orient, the idea really had been started back in '92 by the Populists, who had visioned a line from Canada to the Pacific. About this time

Canadian Mormons had gone to Topolobampo, set up a colony and, by carrying earth in baskets, had actually graded a few miles of line northward toward the border. They had been stopped by lack of money and the project slumbered. . . .

If you ask anyone to name the nearest Pacific port in North America to Kansas City, you will seldom get a correct answer. But if you take a pin and a piece of string and put the pin in the map at Kansas City and draw a circle, you'll find that the nearest port is Topolobampo, on the Gulf of Mexico—that is, if you have a map that even shows Topolobampo. But forty years ago Topolobampo was a name to conjure with. And Stillwell conjured more than $8,000,000 out of English investors and more than $12,000,000 out of Americans, with it.

The Orient Line, as surveyed, called for 1,034 miles of track in the United States, and 595 in Mexico, a total of 1,629. Construction went ahead slowly as money trickled in from stock subscriptions. A contract was signed with the Hamburg-America Line for freighters and liners to operate between Topolobampo and Pacific islands in the Orient. Revolts and revolutions in Mexico stopped work. Diaz left hurriedly for Paris, and the new administration was unfriendly.

In 1912 three construction concerns filed claims against the road and asked for receivers. At that time the line had 988 miles in operation, the longest stretch being from Wichita, Kansas, to Granada, Texas. It was making expenses and a little more. In Mexico there was a stretch of 287 miles both ways from Chihuahua and 105 miles in from the Gulf to La Junta, in the mountains.

In 1928 the Santa Fe bought the system, with the main stem from Wichita to Alpine, Texas. Alpine, with an elevation of 4,484 feet, was the gateway to the Davis Mountains and known as the Roof Garden of Texas.

Under the receivership not much was done, and on January 1, 1918, the line, along with all the rest, was taken over by the railroad administration for war operation. After the war it was returned to the receivers.

The Santa Fe then sold the Mexican mileage of the Orient to

B. F. Johnson, a millionaire land and sugar operator, getting for the 289 miles $650,000 in cash and mortgage bonds for $900,000. In 1940 the Mexican government took over the road as it did other foreign property, including oil wells, and blandly proposed to ignore the mortgage which it had inherited. However, after some negotiations, President Lazaro Cardenas agreed to pay ten per cent of the sum, and so the Santa Fe eventually got $740,000 for the trackage, or about $2,560 a mile.

When the Second World War opened a few months later, the American Army became interested in the old line, which still offered the shortest rail haul between the Midwest and much of the Pacific and Southeast Asia. Nothing came of the scheme, because 215 mountain miles of track would have had to be built out of scarce materials, and a great deal of construction work done at Topolobampo.

Santa Fe track mileage from Kansas City to San Francisco in 1944 was 2,096 and to Los Angeles it amounted to 1,776 miles. The K. C. M. & O. Line, Kansas City to Topolobampo as surveyed, was 1,629 miles. From Chicago to Topolobampo was 2,080 miles. Chicago to San Francisco, 2,547; Chicago to Los Angeles, 2,227.

Given Mexican co-operation—including American operation of the route—the line could be useful if any great trade developed between America and Australia, the Pacific islands and the Orient. It would save 400 miles of rail haul, but the saving in time—a day or so—would be more than offset by extra ship time. Still, for heavy freight where the time element is unimportant, it might prove economical.

This line with the Sierra gap built, could open up a new empire in Northwestern Mexico, as other lines have opened up and developed empires in our own Southwest. During the Second World War, hundreds of American railroad men went down into Mexico to help run the roads there, which were in bad shape, physically and financially; thousands of Mexicans came north of the border and learned railroading from Americans. Now, with the war ended, there are all the ingredients for expansion—assuming a stable agreement between Mexicans and Americans.

C H A P T E R N I N E T E E N

THE COMING OF THE DIESELS

HISTORY'S GREATEST engineering mistake probably was the decision to make four feet eight and one half inches the standard railroad gauge. The decision, according to railroad legend, was a compromise arrived at in the English Parliament in the late '80s by arbitrarily taking the width of Roman chariot wheels and making that the standard. The wheel marks still were visible in some parts of England.

Two exceptions to the universal gauge are the Russian five-foot gauge and the Japanese three-foot-six-inch width and various gauges in Australia and India. Most of the civilized world uses the standard, however, and on this continent you may load a boxcar with coffee in Guatemala and roll it up to Churchill on Hudson Bay, or Prince Rupert in British Columbia.

Many engineers agree that a six-foot gauge would have been more economical. It would have meant shorter trains and increased speed limits. Also it would have made heavier motive power possible. Locomotives today are limited in breadth and height and, to some extent, in length. A wider gauge would have allowed them to be built more compactly.

Despite the problem of balancing an engine nine feet wide on a track little more than half that, and operating this machine around curves in safety, some remarkable power plants have been built for the railroads. Of late years the concentration has been on brute power, with economy of fuel, and speed has been left to take care of itself. Speed today is not limited by the ability to build fast locomotives, but by safety factors. Engine builders could produce 300-mile-an-hour engines tomorrow—if anyone could make track to hold them at that speed. Even if the track would stand up, there always is the ultimate limiting factor in railroad speed: centrifugal force. As speed is built up, the curves must be made flatter and flatter, and banked more steeply, but there is a limit even to this.

Every time a railroad radically increases the speed of its crack trains, it has to spend more on track work than it does on the new train.

When, early in 1935, the Santa Fe decided to set up a new fast schedule between Chicago and California, it started a track-improvement program. First, it spent $1,827,000 for 140 miles of new 112-pound steel. It laid out $1,500,000 for straightening curves; $700,000 for superelevating curves and reballasting miles of track for high-speed operation. That made a minimum total of more than $4,000,000 before a fast wheel turned, and didn't count improvements to the signal system and the laying out of new schedules.

Meanwhile, the Electro-Motive Corporation, a General Motors subsidiary, was building a $360,000 diesel-electric locomotive in its La Grange, Illinois, shops. This engine, rated at 3,600 horsepower, was built in two units and looked very little like the sleek, silver streamliners of today. It was taken out onto the road and tested on mountains and deserts, under all kinds of weather until the bugs were worked out. Then, in October, it was given a test run, hauling a nine-car Pullman standard train from Chicago to Los Angeles.

When this train, the *Super Chief*, started from Dearborn Station, the Santa Fe's Los Angeles-to-Chicago record still stood at Scotty's mark—forty-four hours, fifty-four minutes, set in 1905. The *Chief*, the fastest long-distance train in the West, made the run in fifty-five hours.

The locomotive hauled her train over the course in thirty-nine hours and thirty-four minutes, beating the Scott special's time by five hours, twenty minutes. Later a run was made in thirty-six hours, forty-nine minutes.

This engine definitely set the Santa Fe in line to use more and more diesel-electric power, which was not only more economical to operate, but much easier to track, safer at high speeds and would, eventually, do away with expensive water installations, especially on desert stretches. The locomotive was 127 feet long, weighed 240 tons, had a standard top speed of ninety-eight miles an hour and was gaily painted in cobalt and saratoga blue, olive and scarlet. Its Winton diesels weighed twenty pounds to one horsepower.

At 7:15 P.M. May 12, 1936, the first *Super Chief* left Dearborn Station, having been christened with California champagne by Mrs. Bartlett Cormack, daughter of President and Mrs. Bledsoe, of Beverly Hills. It was not a streamliner—just a Pullman standard train. It landed its passengers, including President Bledsoe, Mr. and Mrs. Eddie Cantor and two daughters, and Miss Eleanor Powell, the dancer, in Los Angeles at 8:59 A.M., May 14th—one business day out of Chicago—and one minute ahead of schedule.

Miss Powell made most of the trip in white-silk pajamas and many of the passengers, upon detraining at Los Angeles, were sadly behind in their studies of the application of the two-cycle diesel engine to train operation.

On the westbound trip the train had got up to 102 miles an hour, between Joliet and Shopton, Illinois; and had made the Chicago-La Junta stretch, most of it uphill in 892 minutes for the 992 miles. On the first eastbound trip, the train reeled off 321 miles on the "race track" east of La Junta at eighty-one miles an hour, its carded schedule. It rolled into Dearborn Street thirty-nine hours, thirty-eight minutes out of Los Angeles.

This was quite an improvement over the first Santa Fe *De Luxe*, which was a six-car luxury train carrying only seventy people. There were two all-drawing-room cars, a compartment, an observation, a clubcar and a diner. The diner had the first air-cooling and washing installation, and the train carried a lady's maid, a barber, a manicurist, hairdresser, shower and tub baths, electric curling irons, stereoscopic views, a fiction library and wire bulletins. The extra fare was $25 and the time sixty-three hours for the 2,267-mile run. Up to then, the time had been sixty-eight and a half hours.

This train first left Chicago on Thursday, December 12, 1911. Bud Fisher, the cartoonist, was aboard. A few days later a cartoon appeared in which Mutt asked Jeff why the Santa Fe ran through so many graveyards. Jeff explained that those weren't gravestones—just milestones.

In those days a uniformed flower boy met the *De Luxe* and the *California Limited* westbound at Summit, California, atop Cajon Pass. . . . Men and women passengers got bouquets of carnations, roses, violets and other flowers, and at one time there were free souvenir wallets of alligator hide, lettered in gold and bearing a picture of the train.

For years very few improvements were made in dining cars, the basic patents for which had been taken out by George M. Pullman in 1865. In 1925 Byron S. Harvey invented a new two-car unit for the Santa Fe. This was run at the head end of the train and included a diner and a club lounge, with bath, barber shop and soda fountain. There were also sleeping quarters and shower bath for the crew. The galley was the full width of the car and located at the forward end so that passengers did not have to pass it. The diner, seating forty-two, was finished in maple with black inlays and passengers waited for seats comfortably in the lounge until the steward called them. The car was patented by the Harvey system and for years ran on the *California Limited.*

While it was speeding up its passenger trains, the road also was building some tremendous freight power. In 1911, its shops both at Topeka and San Bernardino were erecting locomotives that, until the next batch came out, were always the largest in the world. Two monsters were built from four o 0000 (2-8-0) engines, producing a couple of o 0000 0000 (2-8-8-0) Mallets. These followed two big engines for passenger service, built by Baldwin with the curious wheel arrangement of oo00 000 0 (4-4-6-2). These operated under road numbers 1398 and 1399. They were used for six years and then rebuilt into two simple oo000o (4-6-2) engines. In the same year Baldwin brought out two huge Mallets with o0000 0000o (2-8-8-2) wheels. A few years later the Santa Fe rebuilt these into four o0000o (2-8-2) types.

The fight for size and power in engines reached a peak in 1911 when Topeka shops built ten Mallets with a o 00000 00000 o (2-10-10-2) wheel arrangement. They were the largest the world had ever seen, exerted a tractive effort of 111,600 pounds. They were not very successful and later were rebuilt into twenty o 00000 o (2-10-2) engines. But this wasn't quite the end.

In 1915 the Santa Fe locomotive department asked Baldwin to design a quadruplex double compound Mallet, with a wheel arrangement o 0000 0000 0000 0000 o (2-8-8-8-8-2). This monster was to have four pairs of cylinders, and five foot drivers. The boiler was to have a flexible joint in its middle and the engine was to have two cabs, one in front and the other far behind, back of the firebox. This little number was to weigh 442½ tons and have a tractive effort of 200,000 pounds. It never was built, and the coming, a few years later, of improved power plants and finally the diesel-electric locomotives, made it seem old-fashioned and inefficient.

In 1929 the Santa Fe with Universal Air Lines and the New York Central, pioneered a train-plane service across the country. Passengers left New York on the *Southwestern Limited* for Cleveland. At Cleveland they boarded planes and were flown to Garden City, Kansas. They were picked up by No. 3, the *California Limited*, and wheeled to Los Angeles. Eastbound the same stages were operated. The trip took three nights and two days. The arrangement lasted only until night flying became a commonplace, and faster planes made changes unnecessary.

A passenger on the first flight was Mrs. Mabel Walker Willebrandt, counsel for Universal Aviation Corporation. She carried a bottle of Atlantic Ocean water from Mayor Jimmie Walker of New York, to Mayor Cryer of Los Angeles, who is said to have handed it to a policeman to pour into the Pacific, thus completing the ceremony. There is no record that the cop ever carried out his orders.

The first war and its aftermath discouraged any great advances in train equipment or operation until, as we have seen, about 1936, when the first *Super Chief* came out. While this standard train was in operation, the Santa Fe and the Edward G. Budd Manufacturing Company were designing and building a new streamliner that was to be the last word in speed and luxury. The Electro-Motive Corporation produced a new power plant of 3,600 horsepower rated at 107 miles an hour.

The train as a unit, was 856 feet 11¾ inches long and the consist included a mail-storage-post-office car, a bar-lounge-barber-shop car, four full sleepers and a sleeper-observation car besides the diner. The cars were named after Indian pueblos: Isleta, Laguna, Acoma, Cochiti, Oraibi, Taos and Navajo. Loaded, the train carried 104 passengers and had berths for twelve train-crew members and eight postal clerks.

The power plant was unique in many ways. It consisted of four 900-horsepower diesel motors generating a current to operate eight electric traction motors directly connected to truck axles. Any one of the diesel plants could be cut out en route for repairs, and the train would operate on the remaining three. The motors were controlled by telegraph from the cab, the impulses sent by throttle-lever movements actuating an electro-pneumatic device that set motor-speed at any desired point.

The plant also hollered for help if anything went wrong. In case of low oil pressure, overheating or other mechanical failure, a gong rang and colored lights indicated the trouble. Furthermore, the gong kept ringing and the lights continued to flash until the trouble was fixed or the engine shut down. Technically, the diesel motors were each twelve cylinder V-type, two cycle machines with cylinders of eight-inch bore and ten-inch stroke, operating on a seven bearing crankshaft through drop-forged connecting rods and aluminum pistons. At 750 revolutions each motor delivered 900 horsepower. The traction motors operated on 600 volts D.C. Operating weight of the locomotive was 284 tons.

The train was of conventional Pullman arrangement, but sheathed in stainless steel; it was made up of separate coaches, without the articulation of two or more cars that was an earlier practice in streamliners. Cars could be cut in and out of the train at will. About 120 different firms contributed to the passenger equipment, which was decorated inside by Paul F. Cret, a Philadelphia architect; S. B. McDonald, a Chicago designer and decorator, and Roger W. Birdseye, advertising manager of the Santa Fe. A great deal of hardwood was used for decorative effect. The train immediately became popular.

It made its first westbound run May 18, 1937, and then went on a weekly schedule. On February 22, 1938, a second *Super Chief* came out. This also was a nine-car unit. The sleepers were built by Pullman; the club, baggage, dining and lounge cars by Budd. The motive power was similar to that of the first *Super Chief*. Having used up all the easy names on its first train, the Santa Fe labeled its second string of streamlined sleeping cars, San Acacia, Chimayo, Talwiwi, Tchirege, Agathla, Awarobi, Tsankawi, Tyuonyi, Puye—probably the strangest assortment of names ever attached to trains.

With these two trains the Santa Fe now had twice-a-week streamliner service between Chicago and the Coast. *El Capitan's* five-car trains operating on the same schedule as the *Super Chiefs'* and offering chaircars, lunch counters, newsstands and various services—were soon added, giving the road thirteen streamliners—the largest fleet in the world.

The new diesel-electrics proving successful in passenger service, the Santa Fe now started a program of replacing much of its steam freight power with the same sort of engine. Electro-Motive again went to work and in February, 1938, a new 5,400-horsepower hog rolled west on a test run across the rivers, over Kansas and down the old familiar track through New Mexico and Arizona.

From his Laying Star Ranch, high in the Lukaichukai Range of Arizona, old Chief Chee Dodge drove his big chidee—which was the Navajo word for automobile—down to Gallup, to see about his lambs. Every spring he shipped lambs to the clustered steel and brick hogans of the palefaces, as did his fellow Navajos. In Gallup he climbed up nimbly, despite his eighty years, to see Mr. Tom Young. Mr. Young sat in a swivel chair with padded arm rests—a white-collar guy, puffing a two-fer cigar—and looked out of his comfortably heated little room through broad windows. Behind him was the faint rhythmic purr of machinery.

Yes, said Mr. Young, it was true what the Chief had heard over the Wind-that-talks about the new lightning wagon the Santa Fe was using to zip the Navajos' lambs to market at a speed to make their wool uncurl and stand on end. Chief Dodge, who had seen the first fire wagons chug into Gallup more than sixty years before, told Mr. Young that he would like to see this new lightning wagon that would haul 100 carloads of lamb or wool to market at seventy-five miles an hour.

"You're sitting in it right now, Chief," said Mr. Young, smoking his big cigar and cocking a polished shoe against an airbrake pipe. "You are in the control room of the lightning wagon, as you say in the Navajo tongue. In the talk of the palefaces, it is the Jeep and it has the strength of 5,400 wild mustangs."

Then Mr. Young opened the door into the motor compartment of the great new locomotive and the roar of the 5,400 mustangs rushed into the little steel cabin. The old Chief listened to the beat of sixty-four cylinders and then climbed down the steel ladder and looked up and down the 193 feet of the Jeep's blue-and-yellow length. Into this steel corral he estimated you might pack 100 ponies, but no more. He talked briefly with Chief Many Goats and Chief Deer Leader who said that the palefaces were certainly great medicine men and could perhaps make 5,400 mustangs gallop at seventy-five miles an hour with 100 cars of lambs.

Then Mr. Young blew in his rear brakeman with five short blasts of the airhorn, acknowledged a highball with two short ones, set his bell a-ringing and poured mud into the Jeep's vitals. The roar lifted up and up as the sixty-four cylinders spun four generators which turned sixteen motors, which twirled thirty-two wheels. The Jeep slid away, trailing 3,100 tons of airplane parts and general cargo, headed for Arizona and the West Coast. The speedometer needle moved up smoothly until it registered seventy-six miles an hour. John Morris, in charge of diesel power for the Santa Fe said this would do for the time being and Mr. Young cut her down a notch and puffed away on his cigar.

The mighty Jeep, the world's first diesel-electric freight engine, was making her first commercial run with a fancy drag of sixty-six carloads of heavy freight. She had started from the Argentine yards at Kansas City and her destination was Los Angeles. She demonstrated conclusively that all the things which the Santa Fe had said of her were true: she was one of the strongest things on earth on wheels and not only could she start more freight cars moving than any other engine, but she could move more of them uphill than any other power plant operating on high-speed freight schedules.

No. 100—its official railway title—was more than a locomotive. It was, said enthusiasts, the beginning of the end of steam traction on the Santa Fe. There will be steam engines operating for many years yet, but not many more will be built. Few steam switchers will, from now on, come from the erection shops. The big, high-speed, heavy-duty, national transportation job is being taken over by a prime mover that is more efficient, cheaper to run, faster, and will eventually be cheaper to build.

At one stroke, No. 100 could cut fast freight time from Chicago to the Pacific Coast from six to four, or even three days, any time such a schedule was set up. It could start a heavy load faster, swing down the long mountain grades more swiftly, maintain better speed and cut time by eliminating stops. Hauling a train from the Great Lakes to the West Coast by steam required nine engines in 1938, which had to make thirty-five stops for fuel and water. No. 100 went right through with five brief fuel stops.

Freight movement was comparatively slow in this country because freight trains spent a lot of time "in the hole" on sidings waiting for faster passenger drags to go by. Progressive railroaders like E. J. Engel, president of the Santa Fe, had been working toward a so-called one-speed railroad, over which everything would move at about the same schedule—and a fast schedule at that. This would eliminate much delay because freights would run as second sections to crack passenger schedules, as some of the hot-shot merchandise trains already were running.

The fastest runs in America for some years were made by trains with diesel-electric power. Westerners grinned at the bragging Easterners when they boasted of sixteen- and eighteen-hour trains between New York and Chicago, about 950 miles. The Santa Fe's *Super Chief* made the 992-mile run from Chicago to La Junta, Colorado, in fifteen and a half hours and lifted itself 4,059 feet in the air to boot.

Millions of Americans felt, and still feel affection for the old steam-locomotive and its traditional brave engineer up there on his narrow seat, half frozen in winter, half boiled in summer. The white plumes of steam, the billowing of black smoke, the whistle and the bell, the flash and whirl of connecting rods—all these combined to make something heroic and romantic. That is, they did for the layman; for the motive-power department they added up mainly to a continuous headache.

On the other hand, the diesel-electric looked like a steel box sliding along—no steam plumes, no whirling machinery, no chugging—and the air horn didn't sound like the old chime whistle.

But if you put the old steamer up against a modern motor, the old clanker couldn't compete. It was, in the '40s, a little cheaper to build—but mass-production methods were whittling down that advantage. Locomotives like No. 100 and its fifty sisters on the Santa Fe, hauled 5,000 tons of freight in 100 cars 500 miles without a stop. They moved a ton a mile for one-twenty-fifth of a cent for fuel.

Another advantage the diesel-electric had: it ran continuously over long periods. If anything in the steam engine failed, the train stopped. In a motor, if one section went sour, the other three hauled the train while repairs were being made. A steam locomotive was available for duty only about one-third of the time, although on some of the new jobs an availability of sixty per cent was claimed. A diesel-electric was ready for action ninety-five per cent of the time. One of them sped the Santa Fe's *Super Chief* between Chicago and Los Angeles, 2,225 miles each way, for a solid year—and was late only twice because of engine trouble.

You sat comfortably in the control cabin of the Jeep, looking out over her streamlined nose as the steel ribbons slid beneath her, and Kansas and Oklahoma, Texas and New Mexico flowed by. Ahead of you were broad, sloping safety glass windows like those in your car. The familiar wipers had a slot in them for spreading glycerin over the glass in winter.

Across from you sat Jack Burke, who had run engines over every foot of Santa Fe track. He worked from a softly padded swivel chair, watching indicators and gauges. Jack didn't make mistakes—but if he did, lights would flash and bells would ring. A needle on an illuminated dial told him how to set his throttle; lamps warned him if his drivewheels slipped, if he had a hotbox, if he exceeded predetermined speed. He had to keep his foot on a deadman's pedal or the train stopped.

The cabin was heated by hot-water radiators and insulated against the roar of the motors so that when, from the fireman's seat, you called across "Clear board!" Jack acknowledged the green signal ahead with a conversational "Clear board!"

Around the streamlined prow of the cabin was a steel ridge. That's an "anti-climber" and it was there so that if the Jeep hit a cow or a car at seventy-five miles an hour nothing would fly up to break the windows and injure the crew.

All along the track, as No. 100 rolled by, the folks turned out to watch it and wave at it. School kids lined up in the little towns, and Jack slowed her down and yanked at the air-horn cord and set the bell ringing. Where highway paralleled track, automobiles full of people rolled bumper to bumper, pacing the train, waving and shouting. At the stops businessmen, ranchers, high-school kids, co-eds and mothers with babies climbed the Jeep's steel sides and wormed past her thundering motors. All along the track, camera fans crouched to get pictures; at night the flashlights went off in quick succession, lighting up the interior of the darkened cab.

At every stop the boys climbed up and asked questions about cylinder bore and scavenger ports and torque and how many miles to the gallon. Merchants wanted to know how much it would cost for this big hauler to get goods to them from the East, fruit from the Coast. Sheepmen and cattlemen figured that, with her easy stops and starts, livestock would arrive at market in better shape. Section foremen grinned and said this baby wouldn't pound track to pieces the way the hammering Mallets did.

Most of the millions who rode streamliners called them "diesel trains," but they were really electric trains carrying their own power plants, diesel driven. The 1944 locomotives represented a transition stage: in future the power may be all diesel, or it may be all electric, if someone invents a method of picking radio power out of the air. The old trollywire method of getting power was good where traffic was heavy, as on the Pennsylvania between New York and Washington. On long western runs, the Milwaukee road's 600-odd miles of trollies across the ranges built thirty years ago, and the Great Northern's short trolly stretch over the Cascades, probably never will be extended. The rolling power-plant system has definitely shown itself to be better.

You wondered, perhaps, why the engineers didn't drive direct from the diesels through a clutch, as in your car. Well, they would —if they could find a clutch that would work and stand up. The electric generators and motors were in there because they would start a train from a standstill and a diesel motor wouldn't, any more than the gas motor could start your car without using the clutch. The engineers didn't like all the added expense, weight and complication of electric generators and motors, but they hadn't yet found a way to eliminate them. If any one can invent a way of doing this he may die rich. Some day, someone will do it.

The diesel-electric revolution in freight moving was the work of three men, backed by a fourth. It started in 1922 when Charles F. Kettering of General Motors worked out a two-cycle diesel in the General Motors Research Laboratories and in Kettering's yacht, the *Olive K.* The result was a new engine first exhibited at the Century of Progress Exposition at Chicago in 1933. It was small enough to fit into railroad space limitations and powerful enough to haul a heavy cargo fast.

The new diesel-electric trains that followed were products of the work of practical railroaders, electricians and automobile men. Harold L. Hamilton, now president of Electro Motive Corporation, the General Motors subsidiary that builds most of the diesel jobs, probably should be known as the "Daddy of the Diesels." "H.L." was born in Northern California and, at twenty, was firing on the Sacramento division of the Southern Pacific. He tried professional baseball with the old Pacific Coast League, but came back to his first love and was a boomer fireman and engineer all over the country, from the Western Pacific to the Florida East Coast. He learned what it took to get trains over the track—and wondered if there wasn't a better way.

Finally, Hamilton quit and went to selling motor trucks for White. Along in 1922 he was Western sales manager with headquarters at Denver, with the old idea of motorizing the railroad still gnawing at him. Union Pacific and General Electric had played around with gas-electric rail cars, but never had gone very far. Some of the motor-truck boys had tried flanging truck wheels to run on rails, but this hadn't worked well either. Hamilton hired a part-time draftsman out of his savings, and, by and by he had a gas-electric car of his own, on paper. He took the plans and pounded New York pavements for nine months, raising $50,000 to build the car. It worked. He sold it and built another. Thus Electro Motive was born in Cleveland, Ohio.

When Kettering developed his small diesel, General Motors took over the old Winton Company and Hamilton's concern. Hamilton resigned, but the pull was too strong, and he was soon back, running his old outfit.

The engineering end of No. 100 came from Dick Dilworth, who, like Hamilton, learned his profession the hard way. Neither ever went to college. Dilworth was a Seattle boy, son of a Puget Sound tugboat skipper—and he learned about gas engines in the Philippines, making them run on gin when gas prices went too high. He gained much experience building power plants all over the country and in Mexico, worked for General Electric and finally joined Hamilton in Electro Motive as chief engineer.

Hamilton and Dilworth between them built gas-electric railcars from 1923 to 1930. When Kettering gave them the new diesel they just lifted out the gas engine and dropped in the new one.

Then General Motors sent in Frank H. Prescott from its Delco plant to apply mass-production methods to the new motive power. Prescott is from Muskegon, Michigan, and a graduate of Michigan State. An electrical engineer, he was regarded in the automotive industry as a manufacturing wizard. At Electro Motive's plant at La Grange, near Chicago, the Prescott system brought in material at one end and rolled locomotives out at the other under their own power on an adaptation of an automobile production line. No. 100 represented only about four hours of work for the plant.

Hamilton, Dilworth and Prescott started shooting at 600-horsepower, fifty-mile-an-hour switchers and 6,000-horsepower passenger engines that would make 117 miles an hour. In 1944 there were more that 1,000 switchers operating, along with about 150 of the passenger swifts. Baldwin and American Locomotive were building them, too.

For years, back in the minds of Hamilton and his associates was the idea of a freight diesel-electric. Moving freight always was a problem for the railroads. Trains were slow and had to switch in and out of the main line to let the varnish strings go by. Engines had to be refueled and rewatered frequently. Heavy power pounded the track out of line; an engine packed along eighty tons of water; even the best locomotive had to get slack in a long string of cars and jerk them, one by one, to a start, causing drawbar breakage and long delays.

So, when they could get a day off from making switchers and passenger engines, Hamilton, Dilworth and Prescott planned a freight diesel-electric and finally built an experimental engine. They ran this all over the country, without fanfare, in good weather and bad, 83,000 miles over twenty railroads, up heavy grades and down them, with overloads and at excess speeds. Finally they were $1,000,000 in the hole—but they had a locomotive that would outpull anything else on wheels—and they knew what was right about it, and where the bugs were. They ran the experiment into the shop and used it as a model for No. 100. They demonstrated No. 100 to the Santa Fe and she sold herself in jig time. There wasn't any argument—the big Jeep out-performed the best steam power the road had, at much less expense of operation.

Hamilton, as an old railroad engineer, remembered that one railroad headache was getting a heavy train down a mountain grade. The only way was to use the brakes, run slowly and stop every few miles to let the red-hot brake shoes and wheels cool off. This wore out thousands of brake shoes and ruined wheels, which flaked off.

Going downhill was slower and more expensive than going up. Hamilton told Dilworth something ought to be done about it.

And something was. In the control cab of the Jeep, Jack Burke was letting her down the steep western grade of Cajon Pass toward San Bernardino, California. There wasn't a brake on, but the heavy locomotive and her string of cars rolled steadily downward at twenty-three miles an hour. She picked up a little on the steeper dips and in front of Jack a light flashed as the speed topped twenty-five. Jack steadied her down with a touch of the air and then released the brakes again. You looked back around the curves and not a wheel was smoking. At the foot of the hill you laid your hand against a wheel—it was cool as a mint julep. And that never had happened before on any train coming down Cajon Pass grade.

The secret was the dynamic brake. You set your speed at the top of a hill, flipped a switch and your motors became generators. The drag held back the train. The dynamic brake had been used on the Milwaukee since 1910, but on this trolly operation the power generated downhill was fed back into the line and used to haul an upcoming train. In diesel-electric operation the problem was to get rid of the power. This was done by turning it into heat and spilling it over the roof.

This irked Dick Dilworth because an engineer hates anything inefficient. On the Jeep's run from Chicago to the Coast she generated more than 5,200 horsepower—and wasted it over the prairies and ranges. Some day someone will find a way to use that power—maybe to refrigerate a fruit train.

As the automobile industry slowly took over part of the job of supplying motive power to railroads, it was interesting to see the difference in methods. Each steam locomotive was a bit of a prima donna; roads built them in small batches, seldom more than twenty or twenty-five at a time. Each road had its own ideas and so one standard design could not be used. The diesel-electric builders stuck to one master design, as automobile builders did, and made only minor changes to suit the whims of various roads.

If you wanted to build a jeep you first placed sixteen pairs of forty-inch wheels on a track. Then you put sixteen electric motors above them and geared the motors to the axles. Then you added your generators to make power and four 1,350-horsepower V-12 diesel motors to run the generators. You added an electric system, air and water lines, controls, lights, brakes—and even toilet facilities. Then you enclosed the result in a steel box, put a control cab at each end and cut the thing into four sections, so it would take sharp curves and make continuous running possible, even with one or two motors out of service. Then you had a locomotive 193 feet long, about ten wide and fourteen high.

No. 100 brought her freight drag to a stop in the Santa Fe yards in Los Angeles, fifty-five hours out from Argentine, Kansas. John Morris said her speed average was 32.5 miles an hour—which was limited speed a few years ago. Her fuel cost was twenty-five cents a mile. And not a worn brake shoe or flaked wheel on the train, although she came down eighty-three miles of mountain grades faster than any freight trains before—except runaways.

Jack Burke took his foot from the deadman's pedal, straightened his tie, flicked a bit of dust from his suit and leaned back in his swivel chair. He grinned, and said, "Some engine, Brother!"

CHAPTER TWENTY

TALES ALONG THE TRACK

RAILROAD MEN, from callboys to president, run up against a lot of curious people—some of whom make their hair stand on end, some of whom provoke a laugh or a tear. . . .

When state legislators spit on their hands and proceed to make laws about railroads no one can predict what is going to happen. In 1909, for example, the Illinois legislature almost passed a law giving towns the right to decide what kind of motive power might be used by railroads passing through them. . . . Just what would have occurred if this had become a law and Galesburg had decided on electric motors, Streator on gasoline power and Joliet on steam engines, no one knows.

Texas always liked to have a finger in the railroad pie and, in 1910, passed a law that all stations must be named according to their post offices, that all engines must have ashpans, and that all members of volunteer fire departments must be carried free.

Three years later Kansas forbade the Santa Fe to make "surprise tests" of signals in order to find out if its employees were obeying them. The only purpose of these tests, the legislature ruled was "to deceive engineers."

While Kansas and some other states passed some curious regulatory laws in past days, there was never a Kansas law to the effect that "If two trains meet on a single track both shall stop and neither shall proceed until the other has passed." This story keeps going around, but Miss Louise McNeal, State Librarian of Kansas, says that repeated searches through revised statutes have failed to turn up anything.

The truth probably is that a bill about trains on a single track was introduced, got space in the newspapers and then failed of passage. A hurried reading of such an item might lead a careless historian to report the passage of a law instead of the introduction of a bill.

Things legislatures couldn't think of to annoy railroads, some strange private characters could. In 1918 when the Santa Fe was building from Caney, Kansas to Fairfax, Oklahoma, it was blocked in Osage county by William Easley, a farmer who wouldn't sell the road a right of way. When the road condemned the land, the resourceful Mr. Easley announced that he had planted 153 quarts of nitroglycerine along the route of survey. He was arrested and held for $25,000 bail.

After a day or two in jail, Mr. Easley laughed and said it was all a joke—there wasn't any nitroglycerine.

"Maybe there is, and maybe there isn't," decided the grading contractor. He was in no mood to take a chance on it, so he made Easley plow up the right of way himself, using Easley's team and plow. . . . Sure enough, there wasn't any nitro, it turned out.

That was trouble—but there were laughs, too. Down on the Gulf Lines in Texas in 1917 a circus was being moved. The train was waiting in a siding for a passenger when three elephants managed to get their trunks, unnoticed, into the tender tank, and used all the water in giving themselves a shower. The train stalled and there was nothing to do—except uncouple the engine and make the elephants tow it three miles down the track to a water tower. This was done, Santa Fe annals record, "under the direction of a Hindu mahout named O'Reilly."

Life could twist from comedy to tragedy overnight and back to comedy again. In the summer of 1916, Conductor M. A. McNeil stopped his fifty-car freight in Valley Center, Kansas, twelve miles north of Wichita and found out what petticoat government meant.

Valley Center had an all-woman government at the time—Kansas always being willing to try anything once—and so Conductor McNeil found himself and his crew arrested by Mrs. Goodrich, the City Marshal, on a complaint signed by Miss Avis Francis, the

Mayor. He was taken before Mrs. Ridenour, the Judge, and fined $5 for block crossing. After that trains proceeded through Valley Center without stopping.

A few days later, just as Santa Fe folks had stopped grinning over that, on Saturday evening, September 25, 1916, a freight train kicked a tank car into a siding at Ardmore, Oklahoma.

Ardmore was a prosperous little town of 12,000, where whites, blacks and Indians made a living from cattle and oil, in a rich country. It was hot, and Ardmore went to church on Sunday and to business on Monday without a thought of the tank car, which had been consigned by the Victor Gasoline Company of Cushing to the Ardmore Refining Company, and was filled with 10,090 gallons of volatile casinghead gas.

At noon, Monday, a switchman heard a curious whistling noise coming from the car, and told the yardmaster. The refinery was immediately notified, and, after lunch, sent a man over. He didn't know much about it, but he climbed onto the car, unscrewed the domecap and threw it open. This was at 2:13 P.M. Two minutes later, forty-eight people were dead, more than 500 were injured and most of the town lay in ruins.

The gas, expanded by the heat, had flowed out of the car when the dome was opened, and spread over the ground. A chance spark ignited it—and the flash and roar were seen and heard twenty miles away. Heavy as the life-toll was, it would have been more if the yardmaster hadn't taken the precaution, during the lunch hour, of posting guards at crossings near by, and warning people away. Streets were tangled masses of bricks, wires, glass and timber; fire licked through the ruins; survivors fought grimly to dig out buried victims and twisted bodies.

After the wreckage had been cleared, five inquiries started: by the railroad, the Bureau of Explosives, the Railroad Commission, the State Fire Marshal and the Carter County Grand Jury. While these were going on, Ardmorites were suffering for lack of compensation to pay hospital and burial bills and reconstruction expenses.

The Santa Fe's legal department looked into the affair and decided the system was not to blame. But Counsel Samuel T.

Bledsoe felt that there was a moral obligation to help now, instead of letting the victims wait for months until blame could be placed. He went to President Ripley and made a suggestion. Ripley agreed with him and, on October 4th, Mayor Van Mullen of Ardmore got this wire:

> During its entire life, the Santa Fe has never declined to pay any just claim, and in the face of this terrible calamity which has overtaken the people of Ardmore, I am not disposed to await the judgment of the courts. I therefore propose that careful investigation of claims for death, personal injury and property damage be entered upon by a committee of your citizens and that a statement be prepared and submitted to us with a view to prompt adjustment of such claims, in cash, upon a reasonable basis. Mr. F. G. Pettibone, our general manager, will see you soon about details.

This stand saved scores of Ardmorites from ruin—and many others from losing anything that they might have won in court to the shysters who flocked into town. At a main intersection a billboard was put up, with a Santa Fe emblem in the middle, flanked by the names of Ripley and Pettibone. Underneath were the words:

"Great is the Santa Fe: One corporation with a soul!"

The Citizens' Committee, under Mayor Van Mullen, went over every claim, except a few from people who insisted on going to court. Awards were made, and the Santa Fe finally paid out more than $1,000,000 to over 2,000 persons. Only one citizen who had been offered $1,250 for an injury was dissatisfied. He took his case to court. The court awarded him $1,000.

The tank car, ironically, was almost undamaged—and in it still were 5,000 gallons of gas.

Ripley had been good to Oklahoma once before. In 1912 the state had been financially badly off, and it had appealed for help. The Santa Fe paid $80,000 in taxes in advance, and to top that off, paid Oklahoma counties another $320,000 to keep them afloat.

Christmas time, 1916, came around and, with it, many things for Ripley's attention: editorials and letters from Ardmore, thanking the system for its action after the explosion; and the usual number of problems. One was from four-year-old Miss Clara McIntyre of Chicago:

> "Dear Mr. Ripley," she wrote, "I am going to Los Angeles on the *California Limited* tomorrow, and I shall miss my Christmas tree. Please, Mr. Ripley, can I have a Christmas tree?"

She had one, in the lounge car—and every passenger found a small electric candle in his window, that Christmas Eve.

There were two other adventures with oil and gasoline in 1917. In March—again at Ardmore—a trackside tank of fuel oil was fired by lightning. F. A. Redmond, the manager of the oil concern, flagged down a train of empty tankcars and by running a pipe from the bottom of the flaming tank, saved about 100,000 of the 123,000 gallons in the car.

In October of that year, at Kiowa, two gasoline cars were derailed and began to leak. A fast thinker quickly sold gasoline to passing motorists at a dime a gallon—which salvaged a few dollars.

There were, of course, through the years, the usual number of people who wanted to use the Santa Fe without paying for it. Thousands of hoboes rode free, clinging to the rods, huddling in the "blind baggage" and on the roofs of cars. Among them it was considered a feat to "hold down" fast passenger trains for two or three divisions. Many of them were killed every year. So were hundreds of trespassers, whose surviving relatives often sued the road—and collected, too. When trespassers were arrested, for their own safety, juries and courts seldom would convict them.

It got to a point, where, in 1910, a Chicago factory turned out a gadget for the use of hoboes. It consisted of three steel rods and a flanged wheel. This was supposed to be attached to a bicycle—which could then be used by tourists to wheel up and down the railroads to vacation spots—and if the fast mail ran them down, they could always sue. A mail-order house actually sold 5,000 of the "adapters," and in several cases where the users were injured, suits were brought against the line. None was successful, though.

In 1911, to save money, Banka A. Meyer of Lawrence, Kansas, expressed himself, collect, from Lawrence to Galveston, Texas, in a large crate, which also contained a supply of food and water. He got as far as Fort Worth, Texas, where his water ran out. He was caught when he left the express car to quench his thirst. Nothing much happened to him and he became a sort of local hero.

In 1910, walkers—later to be known as pedestrians—were in high favor in the United States, and had rights and privileges. One of the most famous was Edward Payson Weston, who spent most of his waking hours walking about the country, cheered on by crowds, entertained by chambers of commerce, and emulated by thousands of people organized into clubs.

In January, 1910, Mr. Weston wrote to President Ripley inquiring whether he might use the Santa Fe's right of way to walk from Los Angeles to Chicago. Rival lines have charged that Mr. Weston chose the Santa Fe because his given names were the same as its president's. Mr. Weston denied this and said that the roadbed, grades and curves were superior for his purpose to those of any other road.

Mr. Ripley not only assented to the scheme, but provided Mr. Weston with a gasoline handcar and a crew to tote his belongings, and the right, in emergencies, to flag down a passenger train or two, to obtain food. Thus fortified, Mr. Weston set out from Los Angeles La Grande Depot in February. He was seventy-one at the time; the Santa Fe was going on forty-two.

Crowds greeted him all the way, and marching clubs often paced him through the towns. Mr. Weston was rather a publicity seeker and several times complained at the meagerness of the welcoming throngs. He was pacified by being permitted to address groups of Santa Fe workers in roundhouses and repair shops along the route. In his lectures he always warned against the evils of cardplaying, dice throwing, strong drink and cigarette smoking.

Once he stopped the *California Limited* in the Glorieta Mountains and demanded food. The steward, mindful of Fred Harvey traditions, gave him two cold roast-beef sandwiches, with lettuce and mayonnaise, a wedge of chocolate cake and a glass of healthful, pure water. Mr. Weston remarked on the excellence of the food, drained the glass, handed it back to the steward, warned him against the dangers of strong drink and proceeded on his way.

He made a side trip to Grand Canyon and then marched on over the hills and down across the plains, attended by the faithful gas car, admiring crowds and bales of publicity. Crossing Illinois he inquired as to the arrangements for welcoming him in Chicago, and learned that the Gem of the Prairie was giving him number two billing beneath a graft scandal. This so angered him that he refused to go into the city. He walked around it, heading east through Indiana. He arrived in New York May 2nd—ninety walking-days out from the Coast, to be welcomed by Mayor William J. Gaynor and 15,000 cheerers. His feet, he maintained, didn't even hurt!

At various times religion overtakes people who have cheated the road and they make restitution. The total runs into hundreds of dollars a year. The cash restorers invariably mention their conversion and frequently announce that they are praying for Divine guidance for station agents, the president or the system itself.

In 1913, a Twin Falls, Idaho, citizen who had fooled a Santa Fe conductor in Kansas into underestimating the age of his child, thus saving $14.30 in fare, got religion. "I fooled your conductor," he wrote, "but none of us can fool the Greatest Conductor of us all." He sent along the $14.30.

Fred Horton, a train dispatcher at Arkansas City, Kansas, became converted to Christianity in the spring of 1908, and soon after, "tried to figure out what I could do to help my fellow men." He found a hillside parallel with the track, three miles north of the depot. Obtaining the owner's permission, he built a huge text of stones:

"CHRIST DIED FOR THE UNGODLY—Rom. 5-6"

The letters were sixteen feet high and twelve feet wide. Working, often by moonlight, Mr. Horton finished the job in seven months, and for years afterward, spent many weekends repairing the 400,000 pounds of stone that went into the text, which has been seen by scores of thousands of travelers.

In 1910, Ed Johnson, a farmer near Talmadge, Kansas, ordered two forty-foot stock cars and when they arrived, loaded three sows in each and consigned them to Kansas City. He told the train crew that the Lord had appeared to him in a dream, announcing that the three sows in each car would increase bountifully on the trip and that the cars would be jampacked with hog by the time they got to the Argentine yards.

The crew, much impressed, permitted Mr. Johnson to sit in the cupola of the caboose to watch the miracle. At Emporia, a yard crew built up the sides of the cars with boards, but the Lord, Mr. Johnson told his freight crew, "couldn't get the hogs in." He thereupon unloaded the animals, sold them and went home.

Under the postal laws, the Santa Fe had to haul mail, including parcel post, at a very low rate. Ripley fumed at this and, in the summer of 1911, found a case that showed up the unfairness.

A shipment of 11,000 pounds of condensed milk was posted from Deming to Silver City, New Mexico, a distance of fifty miles, the Santa Fe hauling the shipment too, from the Silver City depot to the post office. For all this service, the system collected $2.50. At postal rates the fee would have been $120.

Mr. Taft, apprised of this and other glaring injustices, announced publicly: "We're stealing from the railroads, that's what we're doing."

Early in 1939, the Reverend L. C. Vermillion of the Journeycake Memorial Baptist Church in Dewey, Oklahoma, wrote to the Santa Fe to say that his parishioners used the whistle of No. 212, the *Tulsan* streamliner, as a call to morning prayer. He wrote:

"It seems to me that the whistle of the *Tulsan* is saying, in soft, mellow, but brilliant tones: 'Pray! Pray!' "

Special efforts were made by the road to keep the northbound streamer, due through Dewey without stopping, on its carded time of 9:45 A.M.

Santa Fe train crews often have shown Christian charity far beyond the limits of duty. In 1938, aboard the eastbound *Scout*, a woman, poorly dressed and with two small children, gave birth to another baby west of Barstow, California. The train crew helped, and, discovering that the kids had only one change of clothing, washed and ironed these; so at Barstow the young mother was taken off with reasonably clean and neat children. She was sent to a hospital—where it was found that all she had was a ticket to Philadelphia, $1.39 in cash and the address of her husband in that city.

The crew, as the days passed, kept track of the case. A wire was sent to the husband in which the woman's plight was explained. He replied: "Cannot help. Wife away from home in California fifteen months."

The Barstow boys said little about the man, but what they said wasn't nice. They dug down and got together a fund of $178 for the mother, and when she could travel, put her back on a train for the east.

Babies by the dozen have been born on Santa Fe trains and were often named for the train or the car. There are Kansas girls named Santa and Fe. In 1913 a baby girl was born to Mr. and Mrs. Chester B. Ford of Chicago on No. 6, west of Fort Madison. The conductor, a diffident man, hesitated to suggest a name, but when pressed, said that Airdrie, the name of the Pullman in which the child had been born, might be nice.

Mr. Ford dissented and the little girl was named Miss Mary Santa Fe Ford. Passengers and crew chipped in $16.80 as a birthday gift.

At 11 P.M., October 5, 1944, James Michael Rajacich, a young Santa Fe employee at San Bernardino, got off the eastbound *California Limited* at Kansas City to buy a package of cigarettes—and created an uproar that lasted until 9:40 A.M. the next day, spreading to Chicago. Mr. Rajacich was going to Hibbing, Michigan, to spend a vacation with his mother, and he was taking along his son Jimmie. Jimmie was ten months old and traveled in a basket.

Cigarette hunting being what it was in the fall of '44, Mr. Rajacich missed his train and the baby went on alone through the night.

Well, not quite alone. He had a train conductor, two brakemen, a Pullman conductor, a porter, a dining-car crew and sixteen carloads of passengers looking after him. The train was flagged down at Henrietta, Missouri, so that the baby's formula, telegraphed there from Kansas City, could be put aboard. Conductor R. W. Harrison made up the formula, feeding young Jimmie at three and six A.M., according to instructions. A porter stood by all night and, at Joliet, announced that no diaper changes had been necessary.

The *Limited* was met at Dearborn Street Station by a crowd of several thousand, two police patrol wagons, two squads of detectives, five reporters and cameramen.

When the father turned up on the *Ranger*, two hours later, he nearly got arrested for kidnapping, and had a time proving he was on the level. He proved also that a satchel containing $2,500 worth of bonds which his son was gripping, was his.

Santa Fe people, too, are usually willing to entertain passengers to the best of their ability.

On the Rio Grande division in New Mexico there is a branch from Whitewater into the mining country and at Hanover Junction it splits into a V. One leg of this runs around a mountain to Hanover and Fierro; the other leg runs to Santa Rita, on the other side of the hill. In 1907 the train ran up one leg, backed down to the junction and then ran up the other leg. J. B. Briscoe, in 1945, division superintendent at Amarillo, was agent at both Hanover and Santa Rita. He was given a horse and after doing his work with the train at Hanover, rode across the mountain on a shortcut trail to meet the train again at Santa Rita.

This considerably mystified the passengers, especially as Conductor Bob Ward told them that the agent was twins. Ward and Briscoe even worked up a feud between the brothers, Mr. Briscoe playing both roles.

Nor were railroaders at a loss when trains were delayed. On July 8, 1910, No. 10 from Los Angeles was stopped at Seligman, Arizona, by a washout, and passengers heard they would be held up two or three days. Fred Harvey served meals, and Agent Langworthy waxed the floor of the reading room and announced a dance. He found a piano and a violin and provided music.

The second day, sightseeing trips were arranged, with the yard engine hauling flat cars around to local points of interest. That evening, Division Foreman Armentage gave a free lecture on "Life in India," and followed it the next afternoon with one for the children, titled "In Darkest Africa," getting his material from the Santa Fe library.

The line, which had fought plenty of its own wars, once got itself involved in a foreign war too. This was on May 8 and 9, 1911, when the El Paso yards became a battleground between opposing Mexican armies. The *insurrectos* attacked Ciudad Juarez, across the river, and bullets flew thick on the American side.

The Mexican National Railways rolled fourteen of its big Mallets over the American side for safety and spotted them along the river track. They made a bullet-proof barrier, and the Santa Fe spotted a string of reefers in front of its depot for a similar purpose. Bullets thudded against the locomotives and cars, and one drove into the Harvey House bar, which maintained its usual dignity. The war ended when Juarez surrendered. The only Santa Fe casualty was a teal duck, one of the denizens of the Stores Department's private zoo.

Ripley had taken the Santa Fe when it was broke, run down and disheartened and made a railroad out of it. The age rule caught up with him and he retired January 1, 1920. It was a tragedy to a man who had held, through the years, that no man should retire until he dropped—and Ripley died five weeks later.

He was succeeded by William B. Storey, who had started with the road back in the battle-days of the Valley Line in California and had gone on to become chief engineer and then vice president of the system. Storey served for more than thirteen years, retiring May 2, 1933. After his retirement, Samuel Thomas Bledsoe streamlined the road and to a great extent set the pattern for the sort of system it became in the '40s.

Bledsoe was a Kentuckian, born in Clinton County, May 12, 1868. He studied law at the University of Texas, taught school from 1885 to 1889 and put in his evenings studying more law. After being admitted to the bar at Sherman, Texas, he moved to Ardmore, Oklahoma, and later to Guthrie and Oklahoma City. His first Santa Fe job was as local attorney at Ardmore in '95, when he was twenty-seven. Then he went up rapidly through the legal department to become president, May 2, 1933, when Ripley retired under the age rules.

Under Bledsoe, who took over in a depression period, the Santa Fe carried on the Ripley policy of expanding during hard times. He built a fleet of streamliners, ten for transcontinental runs, five for local services. The first run of the *Super Chief* was a present on his sixty-eighth birthday and he and Mrs. Bledsoe made the trip.

Then he went into the highway transportation field, putting the system into the bus business in fourteen states and starting the co-ordinated bus-streamliner service between Los Angeles and San Francisco, via Bakersfield. Similar co-ordinated service for freight was started in Kansas.

To round out the system, Bledsoe completed the 112-mile line between Las Animas, Colorado and Boise City, Oklahoma, which started operation February 1, 1937. This cutoff opened a new route from Texas ports into Colorado. Later in the same month he bought the Fort Worth and Rio Grande Railway, a 215-mile line that now is part of the southern division of the Gulf Lines.

A friendly person, Bledsoe took a family interest in the lives of hundreds of Santa Fe men and women, and was a heavy—but unknown—contributor to the various charitable funds along the line. He died at his Chicago home early in the morning of March 8, 1939.

One day in November, 1900, Ripley had needed a stenographer and called for one. A young man of twenty-six, who had been working in another office of the line, was sent in.

"You sent for me, Mr. Ripley?"

"Yes," replied the president. "I need a good stenographer. What's your name?"

"Ed Engel, sir."

"All right—let's get to work."

After Bledsoe's death, Edward J. Engel—who had been a stenographer for Ripley back in 1900—was elected president. His people had come to Pennsylvania from Holland in the 1700s and their sons and daughters had moved west to Ohio where Engel was born, in Havana, June 28, 1874. He went to school in Havana and Republic and then took a business course at Sandusky. On March 23, 1899, he started working for the Santa Fe—and never stopped until July 31, 1944, when he retired. He became president March 28, 1939.

Engel was a railroader above everything; he had a wide knowledge of finances, operating methods, traffic and most other branches of the business. A quiet, dignified gentleman, he knew thousands of railroaders from Chicago to the Coast and the Gulf—and looked upon himself as one of them, with just a different title.

Under Engel, the Santa Fe, when the war struck, undertook to spend millions to increase the capacity of its system while operating under the heaviest load of its career. He headed the system until July 31, 1944, when he retired under the age rule, and was succeeded by Fred G. Gurley.

Gurley got his start with the Burlington, for which he worked thirty-three years and where he rose from a junior clerk at Sheridan, Wyoming, to become assistant vice-president. He joined the Santa Fe June 1, 1939, as a vice-president.

When Gurley couldn't be found in his office, the best place to look for him was up in the cab of a diesel-electric hog out on the line somewhere; he spent more time there than he ever did in his private car, first because he loved the big haulers, and second because, as he explained it, "I'd rather see where I'm going than where I've been." He was proud of the fact that his railway had the greatest pool of diesel-electric power in the world, developed largely under his guidance.

Gurley, a Sedalia, Missouri, boy, was only fifty-five when he took over the presidency, and he still had a great deal of his youthful drive and enthusiasm. Out along the lines he was on a first-name basis with thousands of his fellow-rails. He had their respect, too, because as a grizzled engineer on the *Chief* put it, "He knows what it's all about."

Although he had a good grasp of the intricate business of railroading, Gurley was, down at the bottom, an operating man, an authority on motive power, highspeed trains and the complicated job of running one of the busiest systems in the world.

Ripley, Storey and Bledsoe, Engel and Gurley built track and locomotives and millions of things that make a railroad—but they built something more. . . .

In September, 1944, a Chicago-Kansas City train stopped one night at Fort Madison, Iowa, and from it the conductor and a trainman carried Albert E. Stine, an Associated Press man of 4508 Broadway, Kansas City. A. E. Buckingham, the Santa Fe's agent at Fort Madison helped them and, as the train went on, saw Mr. Stine safely to the Sacred Heart Hospital and waited while the doctors examined the sick passenger.

The physicians came out with grave faces.

"He'll have to have a major operation. We'll need blood transfusions."

So Mr. Buckingham bared his arm and gave his blood. After that, he sent for Mrs. Stine, also a Kansas City newspaper worker. Next day he visited the hospital and brought along two other Santa Fe men, already rolling up their sleeves.

"You'll need some more blood for Mr. Stine—here it is," he said.

Railroading isn't all just running trains.

CHAPTER TWENTY-ONE

THE TRAIL THAT IS ALWAYS NEW

IN 1940, when the war effort got going, statisticians in the Office of Production Management figured a couple of minutes and announced the railroads were going to collapse. They figured some more and said the roads would be called on to move 46,000,000 carloads of freight in 1941—and added that the roads couldn't do it. The figure-sharks added columns and found that the roads had 600,000 fewer freight cars and 16,000 fewer locomotives than in 1929 and reached for the crying towels.

". . . and," someone else pointed out, "on top of everything else, the roads'll have to move two grain crops, because most of the 1940 tonnage still is in elevators and until it is moved there's no room for the new crop." This particularly interested the Santa Fe, which moves more grain than any other road.

Some of the young enthusiasts at Washington said the only thing was for the "gumment" to take over the roads right away. These theorists were restrained by older heads who remembered, with pain, what happened when the government took over the roads in 1918. After the politicians got through, it took railroad men ten years to restore the systems to good working order.

The Railroad Administration, in fact, gave the Santa Fe a check for $22,500,000 to pay for maintenance and improvement work the government should have done during the war years, but didn't. The line still has a photograph of the check.

Despite all the political prophecies of failure, no one on the railroads got very excited in the spring of '41. They knew that the

46,000,000 carloads the Office of Production Management figured on, wouldn't show up; that the figure, at most, would be 41,000,000. They knew they could move this load and have a car or two left over.

They knew these things because they worked with thousands of stockraisers, manufacturers, grain growers, lumbermen, steel-mill operators—shippers of everything from alum to zinc. These shippers, organized nationally, represented four out of every five tons of freight shipped around the country. For years before O.P.M. ever was thought of, this organization had been predicting, accurately, just what freight tonnage was going to be—and helping the Santa Fe and other roads to move it.

Without this organization, the wild Washington predictions of car shortages and railroad breakdowns would have caused a panic. Every shipper would have over-ordered cars; rushed to hoard materials—and jammed the works. But for eighteen years all the big shippers and most of the little ones had been relying on their own organization to get freight moved. They knew to within one per cent just what the job was, and they knew, too, that the roads probably could do it.

In the chill darkness of the great Argentine yards west of Kansas City, the signal lights winked amber, green and red, and the yellow reefers, red boxcars and dingy gondolas and flats came rolling in from out yonder. Beef and mutton from the mountains and plains, oranges from California, wheat from Oklahoma and the Panhandle, live chickens and frozen fruit, eggs and butter . . .

The long drag slowed to a stop. A diesel switcher clicked onto the caboose and hauled it away. Another crummy was snapped onto the end of the string. Three quarters of a mile away, at the head end, the big hog that had brought the train from La Junta was uncoupled and the 3919 backed down to couple on. It was a hotshot freight and no time was lost.

Four sections were rolling—almost 300 cars. The first section growled out past, just as the third section was pulling in from the West on the next track. The caboose was dimly lit with oil lamps. A coal-stove glowed cherry-red and the coffee pot was perking. Along the sides of the car were padded leather seats and thumbtacked above them were the inevitable chromos of leggy movie stars, without which no caboose from the Big Four to the Santa Fe is complete.

Outside, the conductor had been inspecting his train, seeing that the car-seals were unbroken, getting a clearance from the airbrake inspectors. He swung his electric lantern up and down. Highball! From the head end three-quarters of a mile away, the answer winked. Up there, the engineer eased back on the throttle of the big 3919, which coughed mildly, picked 'em up and started wheeling 'em out through the yards, rocking at the crossovers, out past the signal towers and over the switches, building speed. The string was soon roaring along over the high-speed track.

The conductor spread his paperwork on the tiny desk in a corner of the caboose under the lamp and went to work. "Good load tonight," he mused, "nearly 3,400 tons." The 3919 was rolling them faster, chasing the first section a mile ahead, and with the headlight of the third section chasing her, in turn, a mile behind.

All over the Western country that night, similar freights were pounding along, moving more tonnage faster than ever before. The railroad boys had less equipment to work with now than they had ten years before, and every car had to carry more, hit a faster pace and be loaded and unloaded more speedily; every locomotive had to wheel heavier tonnage on a tighter schedule.

In the second war there wasn't any car shortage to speak of; there were few jams at the ports as there were in 1918 and '19, when strings of loaded cars waited for weeks on sidetracks to be unloaded. As the traffic peaks passed each year, it became apparent that the prophets of gloom at Washington were wrong: the roads had done the job with a bit to spare—they could have rolled a few hundred more carloads a few more million miles if they'd had to.

The record today is that in 1944 the roads moved 300 per cent more freight than they did in 1929 with 600,000 fewer cars and 16,000 fewer locomotives. They did it partly by taking in their customers as partners, by good old American community effort.

The story goes back to 1918 when cars full of food, munitions and whatnot, were backed up hundreds of miles from ports. Cars were loaded in the West and Midwest and started out for New York, Boston or Norfolk, and rolled eastward faster than ships could handle the tonnage. The result was that thousands of boxes were used for storage instead of for transportation. It got so bad that Eastern firms with goods in transit sent out troubleshooters, loaded with cash, to prowl around Midwest yards, find missing cars and bribe train crews to couple them onto eastbound trains.

Under political control the mess went from bad to worse. When the war ended, every shipper was sore, the railroad plant was run down, the equipment was in bad shape, trains were slow and uncertain, and it sometimes took a month to move a freight car from the Midwest to either coast. Even when a car got to its destination, the cargo's owner, more often than not, let it sit on his sidetrack for awhile, paying a small demurrage fee because this was cheaper than putting the goods into a warehouse.

The result was that shippers and railroad men ran high blood pressures, and car shortages—some real and some conversational—were chronic. Manufacturers who failed to make deliveries on schedule blamed the roads. The roads growled back. Things got so bad that in 1922 the railroads and a few grain and lumber shippers decided to do something about it.

In those days, if the traffic manager of the Peerless Peanut Plant in Kansas City—an imaginary corporation—wanted a couple of cars on his sidetrack he went through a regular routine. He ordered four cars apiece from the Santa Fe, Burlington and Missouri Pacific—and a couple from the Rock Island, just to make sure. The general theory was that if you ordered fourteen cars from four roads you might get two from one road. Sometimes this worked—and sometimes the plant's traffic manager came to work to find fourteen cars spotted at his loading platform. This simply meant that other shippers—all of them over-ordering cars—went without; and that the roads were hauling thousands of empty cars back and forth for no good reason.

Even when cars did roll with freight, they rolled half empty and made only a few miles a day. In those days the average freight-car run was not much more than fifteen miles in twenty-four hours.

There was a high percentage of loss and breakage due to bad crating and careless handling. The roads blamed the shippers, the shippers blamed the roads and the air was full of snarls and yawps. Finally a few shippers calmed down long enough to call a meeting among themselves and some railroad freight-traffic men. When the thing started, both sides sat down and glared at each other for a while. This was in January, 1923.

Eventually some cool heads on both sides worked out a plan. The main idea was that the shippers would try to discover as far ahead as possible just how many of what sort of cars they would need, where and when. These estimates would be given to the roads and the latter would try to provide cars. There'd be no more ordering nine cars where one was needed; cars would be unloaded and loaded with neatness and dispatch; the roads would speed up freight schedules. They thought, if they tried, they might get thirty miles a day out of freight cars—and a few months later they did. In October, 1940, they were getting almost forty miles; and in August, 1941, they got nearly forty-seven. In 1944, it was about sixty miles.

There are now thirteen of these shippers' boards from border to border and coast to coast. Membership represents four out of every five tons of non-war freight shipped. A few years ago the thirteen regional boards organized into The National Association of Shippers Advisory Boards.

Membership in the regional boards is voluntary and members pay their own expenses, with some clerical help from the roads. Keystone of the system is a quarterly estimate of freight-car requirements. Each regional headquarters keeps a constant check on shippers in its district, through questionnaires, and so knows just how many cars, and of what kind, will be required in what places on what days. All these reports are consolidated and sent to the railroads, which thus have a clear picture of the situation.

To understand how the shippers and railroads work together, you might imagine patrons of a department store getting together and deciding, four times a year, just how many frocks, fur coats, pairs of stockings and lipsticks they were going to buy in the next three months. Each patron would get a questionnaire on which she would list her needs. A central organization would go through the cards and from them make a master list and give it to the store. The store would then go ahead and spot the necessary supply of furs in one department; the quota of coats in another, and so forth. Of course, the analogy isn't quite correct, because a shipper has a choice of only about a score of varied kinds of freight cars and a woman shopper needs a choice of about a hundred frocks, to be conservative. But the principle is the same.

When the war started, both Army and Navy took a leaf out of the shippers' book. It's a rule with them now that no car of freight ever is started out unless it can be unloaded at its destination. Today, the cars keep rolling.

What the shippers worked out and the Army and Navy adopted, helped the roads early in the war to move an average of 5,000 carloads of war stuff a day among 150 war plants, camps and projects all over the country—and to do this on top of moving 1,500,000 soldiers in six months on more than 3,000 special trains, plus the normal freight and passenger movement. Once the Santa Fe used fifty-five trains to move an army camp overnight.

One other thing cooperation between shippers and carriers has done: it has brought down freight rates to the lowest on earth. It now costs a shipper less than a cent to move a ton of freight a mile—the actual figure recently was 1,000 tons a mile for $9.73, which is about a tenth of what it costs to move goods by Chinese coolie.

In the old days you often had to split a train on a grade, take half of it over and then come back for the rest. Now the big hogs—5-6,000-horsepower engines—can ramble up hill and down dale with 5,000 tons without any trouble; and across flat territory like Iowa and Illinois, they travel at nearly sixty miles an hour. Often, before speed restrictions went on, ambitious engine-runners got 100-car trains up into the seventies on the straightaways, but they're more conservative today—and more freights stay on the track.

The caboose is a rolling home to its crew of conductor and two or three brakemen. Away from home, they live aboard, cooking on the potbellied stove, eating on a letdown table, sleeping on the lengthwise seats. Section Two's crew made itself comfortable in the car during the layovers between bringing in an eastbound train and taking out a westbounder.

While the 3919 was hauling her string across the rivers toward Kansas City, the 109, a blue-and-yellow diesel-electric freighter with 5,400 horses under her hood, was lugging her ninety-two-car drag of war material west from Winslow, Arizona, up past Canyon Diablo and over the hump west of Flagstaff. In the hot, sunflooded yards, the 3856 rolled through eastbound with a steady blast from her stub stack, hauling a string of yellow reefers full of fresh food, growling as she picked up speed for the long grade up to Gallup in New Mexico.

In her neat home, within earshot of the roar and clatter of the yards, Mrs. Pedro Martinez told Fred Gurley she had to have a washing machine. Mrs. Martinez' husband and two sons worked on the railroad, and Mrs. Martinez desired to keep them and five small children reasonably neat and clean. Fred Gurley said, well, just have a little patience and they would get a washing machine for Mrs. Martinez.

As president of the Santa Fe, keeping war freight and passengers moving was part of Mr. Gurley's job, and so was Mrs. Martinez' washing machine. The washing machine really was very important, because a railroad is just a lot of men and women and kids, and if they aren't happy, the whole thing can break down.

It had become commonplace to say that American railroads are "doing a magnificent job" in handling a war-load three, four or five times their normal capacity. The usual explanation was that the roads were running a lot more trains faster, and this, ironically enough, was correct.

But operating more trains, longer trains and faster trains over systems designed and powered to handle the modest business of pre-war years was quite a trick. When the war started, the roads were running out of ten years of depression and had no great incentive to do anything except keep trains running and not go into the red—or too far into the red.

No one yet knows how far you can stretch a railroad, because no railroad ever has been stretched to the limit. Most roads, especially the Western systems, could handle an even bigger load than they carried in the war years. Some roads carried from three to five times the load they carried in 1940—and they still had something in reserve.

The trouble with making a railroad do more work than it was built to perform is that there is no one big thing that can be done. Many little things had to be done at thousands of places—huge terminals and lonely desert sidings—and then make them all work in harmony.

The Santa Fe, for example, saved a little oil and a little manpower by abolishing a few thousand switch lamps and replacing them with red-and-green reflectors to pick up engine headlights. This saves some oil, and the lamp tenders who used to go around filling and cleaning lamps can now do something more useful.

At the other end a few dozen big diesel-electric freight haulers at almost half a million apiece, helped add a few freight cars to long drags. The road did not have to pump so much boiler water, and the new power made better time and spent more time hauling stuff and less time in the repair shop. The Santa Fe in 1945 had eighty of these engines working on the Western end. Some of them had been operating continuously for months.

Building bigger and more efficient steam power and then rerailing hundreds of miles with heavier steel to take the terrific pounding steam locomotives inflict on track 3, helped too; but that was just a start. Out on the long desert stretches, all this extra steam power may blow a million gallons of water up through smokestacks, and in that country the road had to spend a million or two for new dams and wells and pipelines to get more water, and then spend more money to treat the water so it wouldn't ruin boilers.

Water still was a problem in many parts of the Southwestern states—but new wells and pipelines plus greater use of diesel-electric power, helped solve it.

The Santa Fe has the largest privately owned communication system on earth, with telegraph, teletype and telephone reaching from Coast to Coast. In 1929 it started experiments with radiophones on trains, but although the apparatus worked well enough in a laboratory, it couldn't stand up to the tough, all-weather operating conditions on the line.

But experiments continued and, on June 4, 1944, the first radio-equipped freight train made a run from Bakersfield, California, to Chicago. This was a 3,500-ton Spud Special and it was operated by telephone between caboose and engine cab, instead of by the usual hand and whistle signals. In addition, the train was made up at Bakersfield and broken up at Chicago by radiophoned directions from yardmasters to yard crews. T. P. Brewster, the Santa Fe's veteran radio expert, had charge of the tests. A radio-equipped diesel switcher was used.

On the trip, engine and train crews talked to each other under all conditions, except once when the engine was in one tunnel and the caboose in another. All train business was done by telephone, with considerable saving in time.

Along with all their other war jobs, the roads had to do a trifle of passenger educating here and there. Thousands of people rode trains who had never been on one before, and Pullman porters began to tell of cases where upper-berth passengers took the ladder to bed with them, to be sure of getting down in the morning. There were cases, too, where traveling housewives started to make up their own berths in the morning, to the astonishment of veteran porters, who hadn't heard of such things since the fall of '78.

By doing many little things and a few big things to save a minute here and an hour there—and doing these things in the middle of a war—the road got an almost incredible amount of work out of its plant and still had something tucked away for emergencies.

Stops and starts slow up mass movement, especially of freight. In 1945, the Santa Fe was making thousands of fewer starts and stops than it was five years before. This was accomplished by a small box of tricks called a Centralized Traffic Control Board, known to railroaders as C.T.C. C.T.C. was operating trains in 1945 only on scattered divisions, but on these sections it was cutting as much as one-third from freight running time and adding up to eighty per cent to the capacity of single-track lines.

Rail passengers are familiar with the long, slow process of getting two trains past each other on a single track. Under the old system, a freight stopped at a station for orders telling it where to meet an oncoming train. Then it ambled out and down the pike until it came to a siding. The head brakeman climbed down, unlocked the switch, threw it and climbed back. Then the train proceeded slowly onto the siding and stopped again, so that the rear brakeman could climb down, reset the switch for mainline trains, and climb back again.

After the opposing train had gone by, the whole operation was repeated at the other end of the siding—and if the freight had lost only twenty minutes, that was a triumph.

By 1944, on single-track roads such as the Los Angeles-San Diego line, C.T.C. was making running meets for hundreds of trains. Switches were thrown and signals set from control points as much as seventy-five miles away by a dispatcher who sat in front of a board on which tiny lights painted him a picture of his entire division. By turning small handles, he either kept everything moving or cut waiting time to a minimum. Train crews never had to get down —unless they had to telephone the dispatcher. There were phones every few miles for emergencies.

Switches were being thrown by small, powerful motors alongside tracks, and the whole system was so interlocked that it was impossible to have collisions—unless the engineer deliberately overran his signals. Nor could crews forget to reset switches, as sometimes happened in the old days, with disastrous results.

It cost about $13,000 a mile to install C.T.C. systems, and they saved their cost in a short while. They were a godsend in wartime, because they made it possible for single-track lines almost to double their capacity, and made it unnecessary to double-track long stretches during a period of steel scarcity.

When the war started, the Santa Fe and other Western roads especially, were hogtied by state laws and union rules from operating very efficiently. Arizona had a law limiting freight trains to seventy cars, and passenger trains to fourteen. California had an excess-crew law that forced the roads to put a conductor and six brakemen on some eighty-five-car trains, although such trains were being handled by three men in almost all other states.

These laws and rules cut down the length of trains for more than 700 miles back from the West Coast to the border of New Mexico and Arizona. Consequently motive power and sidings were geared to these short trains. Suddenly, there was a vital need for longer, faster trains. The Interstate Commerce Commission set aside the car-limit law for the duration, but in California, long freights still have to carry three or four surplus men—except in cases of emergency—at a time when the manpower shortage is described as "critical."

With trains getting longer, faster and more numerous, hundreds of sidings had to be lengthened, dozens of freight yards had to be expanded overnight. At Barstow, California, for example, the Santa Fe had to blast down a mountain and dig a sort of Culebra Cut to get a dozen tracks in where only two ran before. It was a similar story at other division points, and on other roads. And all this construction had to be done while a terrific overload of war-freight and passenger business was kept moving without delay.

Those were some of the big things the roads had to do. It also did some little things that no one noticed: built acres of homes for new workers and provided quarters for hundreds of women workers. It had to build eating-places for crews, set up more hospital accommodations; find and develop sources for added millions of gallons of water.

It rebuilt long stretches of track to permit higher speeds—and incidentally make smoother riding. You can take a train around a two-degree curve with 3½ inch elevation at seventy miles an hour, maybe; if you relocate this curve and make it only one degree, you have a 100-mile-an-hour track. If you lengthen out switches to get away from those two sharp little curves from the main line onto a siding, you can run through sidings at forty miles an hour, instead of eighteen. If you can level out a grade, you can move more cars faster with the same power.

The Santa Fe, coming out of ten years of poor business none too prosperously, nevertheless used its own money to rebuild itself. It did this partly in self-defense. It knew that once it accepted a political dollar, the camel's nose would be inside the tent. Railroads were getting quite enough political regulation as it was; they wanted no more.

The ironic part of the whole thing was that government freight and government passengers, which formed the bulk of the overload, and which made necessary the spending of millions, were carried over long stretches at half the regular rates charged private shippers and civilian passengers. This was part of the agreement between the so-called Land Grant roads and the government—an arrangement that had built up millions of dollars of profit for the government and left the roads with huge tracts of almost worthless land. Thousands of square miles of this land in 1945 were worth only two bits an acre.

The war not only loaded the road with extra work, but it robbed it of thousands of experienced workers at the very time they were vitally needed. Common labor disappeared into war plants and the Army and Navy. In the West, thousands of Jap-American workers were whisked away suddenly into relocation camps. All this meant the hiring and training of new armies of workers, including hosts of women, and the importation of more than 10,000 Mexicans to take over track maintenance. They all had to be fed and housed, too.

Out in the Southwestern states where the road took on many Navajos, Mojaves and other tribesmen, timekeepers gave up trying to find out the names of the Indians. The braves were given arbitrary names like Bill Jim or Dick Harry. It worked all right. The Indians were good workers—until payday. There was no necessity for working after that, until their money was all gone.

Another job was making locomotives do more work. In the old days an engine ran a division, or about 100 miles, and stopped. Engines today are running many divisions without stopping for overhauls. The Santa Fe, in fact, runs the longest steam haul in the world—between Kansas City and the Coast—1,791 miles, with no change of engines. Some yard diesels have been running continuously for eighteen months without going to the shops for repairs.

War production means moving more food, for another thing. That means keeping refrigerator cars moving faster. One thing you can do is pre-cool these cars before loading them, so they'll use less ice and have to stop less frequently en route. So the Santa Fe built huge pre-cooling plants near food-producing centers, to blow blizzards through reefers and make ice-boxes out of them before fruit, vegetables and meat are loaded.

A few big things have doubled and tripled the capacity of the Santa Fe and other roads in the past three years—a few big things and a lot of little things—like Mrs. Martinez' washing machine and Fred Gurley hunting all over Arizona for it.

P. S. Mrs. Martinez got it, all right.

In the early 1940's, American railroads saved the country from defeat; in the mid-'40's, they made victory certain. Faced on two fronts by well-prepared, determined and efficient enemies, the United States could not have survived without its network of steel track, its concentration of steam, diesel and electric-motive power, its huge carrying capacity and an army of men and women that could, and did, shuttle men and material swiftly and surely where they were needed, when they were needed.

Our people could see with their own eyes how iron track, a few locomotives and a score or two of cars could bring swift prosperity into sweeps of wasteland, and they built the early roads, manned them and rose, many of them, to become superintendents and managers and presidents.

When he came into power, Hitler discarded time-tried methods, not only of government, but of mass-transportation. He scorned his railroads and fell in love with concrete and rubber.

He lived to rue the day. Concrete and rubber could not move tonnage fast enough and surely enough for him and his armies. Logistics defeated him. America, which had developed the cheapest, fastest and heftiest mass-transportation system on earth, had sense enough to stick to it. Without it there would have been no point to turning out billions of tons of planes, tanks, guns, ships, shells, cars, trucks, dynamite—and fighting men. These became useful only when transported somewhere with speed and efficiency.

Today, scores of communities exist mainly to keep railroads operating. No great city could keep going two weeks without track. In many places, the railroad, with its division point, its shops, its icing plant or fueling depot, is the major payroll contributor.

Keeping the railroads running still is America's No. 1 neighborhood enterprise. It was railroad communities, big and little, that saved the country when fury struck from east and west together in 1941.

For service in the war, the Santa Fe furloughed more than 12,000 of its employees, many of whom went into railway work in India, Burma, Italy, France, Africa and other spots—and found some queer old foreign kettles to run. The 710th, 713th, 758th, Railway Battalions were "Santa Fe outfits," and among their members was Kit Carson, grandson of Old Kit, who left his job in the Pueblo roundhouse to keep 'em running overseas.

In hundreds of cases Santa Fe firemen, brakemen, mechanics and clerks merely changed into olive-drab and went on doing the same jobs they'd been doing at Newton, Albuquerque, Chicago or San Bernardino—though taking chances with bombs, bayonets and bullets as their fathers and grandfathers had taken with buffaloes, bandits and blizzards.

In the midst of all this the Santa Fe looked ahead. It got ready to make the century-old dream of St. Louis for a direct line to the Pacific Coast come true. Late in 1945 the system was planning, subject to Interstate Commerce Commission approval, to open a new fast route from St. Louis to Kansas City, there connecting with the existing main line.

The plan was to acquire, with the Burlington System, the line of the Chicago & Alton between Kansas City and Mexico, Missouri, 163.3 miles; and from Mexico to St. Louis to operate over the Burlington for the 117 mile stretch. The Santa Fe proposed to operate into the Union Station at St. Louis. The new route would provide an alternative one-change passenger route from Atlantic to Pacific, with the break at St. Louis.

In June, 1945, another ambition was fulfilled when the Interstate Commerce Commission approved the Santa Fe's application to build a line a little more than two miles long into the City of Long Beach, California. This extension had long been desired both by the railroad and the city. It furnished a single line connection between Chicago and the only southern California port not then reached by Santa Fe rails. After the Commission's decision authorizing construction of the new line into Long Beach, an agreement was reached with the Southern Pacific and the Pacific Electric whereby under trackage and switching agreements the harbor and lines of railroad of the Harbor Commission would be reached over existing tracks of those lines thus rendering unnecessary the construction of new mileage. Long Beach Harbor, along with Los Angeles Harbor, promised to be of outstanding importance in the development of post-war traffic to the East.

This has been the story of one railroad, the Santa Fe. It started as a little prairie project in a Kansas frontier town. It fought for its life against the things the settlers battled, and, like most of them, it won. It took its steel track high into the snowpeaks of the Rockies, the Sierras, the Sangre de Cristos and the Glorietas, along the friendly Arkansas, the Rio Grande and the Brazos. It threw steel across the Mississippi and the Missouri, the Canadian and the Colorado, the Red and the Cimarron, the Illinois and the Des Moines.

It fought its way across blazing deserts through rock canyons and prairie hills to blue water on the Gulf and the Pacific and the Lakes. It planted towns on the plains and in the hills and peopled them with pioneers with the will to fight and live.

It lugged the necessities and the small luxuries of life to the grangers, and hauled their wheat, corn and cattle back to market. When they went broke in drought or grasshopper plague or Indian uprising, it hauled them and their plows, furniture and stock back to the settlements, free, so they could refit and go West to try again.

Settlers might quit, but the Santa Fe never quit.

It battled its way to the Pacific and the Gulf and the Rockies. It went broke and tried again—and won.

When the new war came it transformed itself overnight into a great steel shuttle between the rivers and the Lakes, the West Coast and the Texas shore, highballing ever-mounting tonnages at ever-increasing speed. While it did this, it managed, somehow, to build for itself and the nation a better, more efficient transportation machine so that no matter how tonnage figures mounted, no matter how many new thousands of people poured into its trains, there always was just a little leeway between what it had to do and what it could do. Demand raced with capacity.

Capacity always won—thanks to the men and women who built and operated the machine that rolled more tons more miles than they'd ever been rolled before.

As victory came to the nation the Santa Fe was able to take stock and found that it had met every demand made upon it during World War II. At war's end the picture was encouraging. The system was in good physical shape. During the war, despite the enormous overload its trains had carried, the plant had been improved, new facilities constructed, motive power built up and the financial position strengthened. There was a need for new rolling stock, but this was on order and in production. The system was set for a fast, profitable run through the peacetime years ahead.

The long string of silver cars slides out of Chicago, swinging the curves, swaying at the crossovers, and lines out on the arrowflight track to the Southwest. The firm, skillful hands of Octave Chanute lift her across the Illinois and the Grand, the Des Moines and the Mississippi and the Missouri. The old ferryman at Westport Landing leans silently on his long steering oar as she rushes along the Kaw, past the ghosts of the pioneers of long ago.

In the darkness, the erect figure of Colonel Holliday stands, his silvery beard windblown, left hand on his goldheaded cane. He lifts his high hat with a touch of fatherly pride and a smile of modest triumph as the train sings along the steel rail.

In the dusk, near Newton, the shadowy figure of Jesse Chisholm sits motionless on his painthorse beside his old trail, and over the wind the cowhands sing softly to the bedded herds from Oklahoma and the Canadian River.

Out across the plains the streamliner rolls in the white moonlight, through the empire of grass that became the granary for half the world, until she meets the flowing Arkansas and winds up the long, long valley with the water speeding swiftly past. Against the horizon clouds, bright in the sky-glow, the prairie-schooners lurch westward, whips snapping, trail songs booming, white canvas cracking in the lusty wind from the snowpeaks far ahead. A woman on a wagonseat behind a bull team tosses a calico poke-bonnet as the silver cars flash by.

Far across the prairie, galloping in company, Phil Sheridan and George Custer are riding with the feathered war-chiefs of the Cheyennes and the Pawnees, old scores forgotten now in the happy hunting grounds. The thunder of the buffalo herd drifts with the night breeze and the antelope race across the grasslands.

Beside the old trail to Santa Fe, are the ghosts of the prairie people, the mountain blasters, the desert conquerors. These were the people who manhandled track across the plains and through the grim passes beyond. Behind them the corn grew tall and golden and the wheat sprouted, greened and ripened. Ore cascaded down from mountain mines. Sheep drifted white in the high meadows. Over the hot, dead sand wastes, the water flowed like quicksilver, and in the desert the oases spread, green and lush and fruitful.

From the sod there lifted new homes and red barns and prim churches and white schoolhouses with the flag streaming in the western gale, and by the track chubby brown babies waved at the engine, and it sang to them and raised a white plume in answer. Across long stretches of the Western land, men and the railroads were comrades in battle, partners in prosperity.

Out across Kansas, the shades of the sodbusters and the trackspikers and muleskinners watch the silver string go by. At Dodge City Bat Masterson stands open-palmed in friendship, a grim smile lighting his bronzed face. Cimarron and Garden City, Lakin and

Syracuse—and old Pete Criley waving her across the state line into Colorado with his battered hat and an Irish shout. Out past Las Animas and the slight, tow-thatched figure of Kit Carson, blue eyes ashine in the moonlight. La Junta, and Bill Becknell's wagons outspanned beside the old trail, and his campfire glowing red.

She swings south now, leaving the Arkansas, greeting the Purgatoire briefly, blasting for the hill ahead. Trinidad, and Uncle Avery Turner peering at his big silver watch as the train rolls through. Into the Pass and up to where, on Raton Mountain, a dim company of brave ones waits—Ray Morley and Lew Kingman, Will Strong and Albert Robinson—and Uncle Dick Wootton to highball her over the top and down onto storied plains of New Mexico, down through the oaks and junipers and pines.

Down past Lucien Maxwell's great empire she roars, and across Cimarron Creek, with Henry Holbrook on the old trail, away over at the foot of the range, listening to her hum by in the valley silence. On past Wagon Mound and through the lush meadows the Spaniards called Las Vegas; up over the Glorieta Pass, racing with Pawnee Charlie's straining old Baldwin hauling a nine-car drag. Down the grade to Albuquerque and Isleta in the Rio Grande Valley, with Coronado's *caballeros* riding, riding, swords flashing in salute, and the wraiths of the gentle *padres* holding up thin brown fingers in blessing as they have done for centuries.

Over Rio Puerco and through the Pueblo country, climbing up to the Continental Divide, and over it to Gallup—and there's Arizona beyond. Down the long winding curves into the valley, and up still once more to top the Arizona summit above Flagstaff. Craggy Bill Williams in his elkhide suit waves from the mountain they named for him, and listens, as the train sounds die away, down the long slopes to the Colorado.

The silver cars roar across the bridge, and here's California. The morning sun wakes the desert and bakes the night chill from the air. The grim mountain rim to the north and west is etched with black shadows and the heatwaves dance between the cactus and greasewood. Ah Fong and Lin Wang built this track—but their spirits rest with their bones, far off in Kwang-tung beside the Pearl River.

Over the sun-scorched wasteland and down to the oasis at Barstow, beside the Mojave, and then south again for Cajon Pass, the nick in the desert rim and the ghosts of the Mormons marching, led by Jefferson Hunt, pushing their handcarts, singing of the Promised Land spread out below. Over the crest, with Fred Perris lifting a friendly hand, and the Mexican tracklayers whispering a *Vaya con Dios.*

Down the long, winding grade of the valley of San Bernardino, where the dons lived and loved on the spreading ranchos in the spacious days of long ago. Westward again and, on the last lap, through the orange groves and past the bright little cities, and the ghosts of the forgotten boom towns hidden amid the eucalyptus trees. Up the last hill to Pasadena and down the last long grade with the throttle closed and a touch of air steadying her. The chime of the whistle sings in triumph as she goes drifting down to the golden beaches and the Pacific's heave of blue at the end of the long trail, the old trail.

The trail that is always new.

APPENDIX I

WHO, WHEN AND WHERE

Chronology of the origin of the Santa Fe:

Fall of 1857—Cyrus Kurtz Holliday, pioneer and land-dealer of Topeka meets and becomes friends with Luther C. Challis, pioneer, merchant, banker and ferry operator of Atchison, when the two are members of the Kansas Territorial Legislature at Lawrence. They talk over construction of a railroad between Topeka and Atchison.

Sunday-Monday, January 30-31, 1859—Colonel Holliday writes a charter for The Atchison and Topeka Railroad Company, in a hotel in Lawrence. He introduces this as a bill in the legislature, Tuesday, February 1st; it is passed by the lower house, February 3rd and by the senate February 11th, and is signed by the governor the same day.

Saturday and Monday, September 15 and 17, 1860—The company is organized in the office of Luther C. Challis in Atchison by Peter T. Abell, Asaph Allen, Lorenzo D. Bird, Luther C. Challis, F. L. Crane, Milton C. Dickey, Samuel Dickson, George H. Fairchild, Wilson L. Gordon, George S. Hillyer, Cyrus K. Holliday, Jeremiah Murphy and Samuel C. Pomeroy.

September 17, 1860—The first board of directors and the first officers are elected. Directors are Peter T. Abell, L. D. Bird, L. C. Challis, F. L. Crane, M. C. Dickey, G. H. Fairchild, Cyrus K. Holliday, Joel Huntoon, S. C. Pomeroy, Edmund G. Ross, Jacob Safford, J. H. Stringfellow and R. H. Weightman. Officers are: C. K. Holliday, president; P. T. Abell, secretary; M. C. Dickey, treasurer.

March 3, 1863—A territorial law, setting aside 2,931,247.54 acres for the company, dependent on construction of a railroad, is passed. The land is deeded to the territory by the federal government and is not, directly, a federal gift.

August 7, 1868—The company is legally authorized to buy from the Leavenworth, Lawrence & Galveston Railroad 114,401.76 acres of the

Pottawatomie Indian Reservation in Eastern Kansas, for $1 an acre for resale to provide funds for construction, and as collateral for construction loans.

October 30, 1868—First dirt turned near bank of the Kaw River in Topeka. First construction is a pile bridge across the Kaw, to connect with the Kansas Pacific Railroad.

The first station on the line is at Pauline, six miles south and 243 feet above the starting point.

APPENDIX II

SANTA FE TOWN NAMES

The Santa Fe itself named a heavy percentage of the places through which it runs, largely because it got there before the settlements existed. Most of the names are Indian, Spanish or Santa Fe—that is, named for railroaders from switchmen to presidents. The Eastern end of the system runs to Indian names: Kansas City, Chicago, Topeka, Oklahoma City. Western and Southern divisions tend toward Spanish: Galveston, Presidio, El Paso, San Diego, Los Angeles, San Francisco.

Some names that sound Spanish aren't Spanish at all, but Indian or invented: Pasadena, Mojave, Yosemite, Satanta, Visalia, Dinuba, Placentia.

Wry sense of humor named Klondike, Siberia, Nome and other hot desert sidings. Names like Rome, Troy, Cadiz, Virgil, Ulysses do not denote any love of the classic; they're merely short names for short sidings, easy to remember and unlikely to be confused on train orders.

Foreign colonists are responsible for Exeter, Moscow, Canada, Anaheim. The last, in California, is a combination of Ana, the saint, and *heim*, German for home. It was a German colony, started with 1,165 acres of land bought for $2,320 in 1857.

Some names are mistakes: Santa Anna, Texas, was sent into the post office as Satanta, the name of an Indian chief; Washington thought the Texans couldn't spell. Milano, Texas, should have been Milam, for Ben Milam, a local landowner. Washington misread it. San Angelo has a curious history. Originally, it was Santa Angela, named for a Mother Superior of the Ursuline Convent in San Antonio. The post office, for some unknown reason, changed not only the name but the sex.

The system has three locations named for ships, and used to have four. Maine, Arizona; Algoa, Texas, named for a British ship blown ashore in the 1900 hurricane; and Ironsides, California, because the *USS Constitution* moored near there some years ago. Samoa, on Humboldt Bay in Northern California, also was named for a ship, but the Santa Fe no longer operates there. Besides Maine, other mementoes of the Spanish-American War are Guam, Manila, Luzon and Dewey—and in Oklahoma, Yewed, which is Dewey spelled backward.

Some towns have luck with their names and some don't. There are, for example, Antioch and Pittsburg, four miles apart on Upper San Francisco Bay. Antioch, meaning a desirable location on the water, was so named July 4, 1851, and still is. Pittsburg started out August 1, 1849 as The City of New York of the Pacific. In '52 the post office cut it to Junction. In '68 it became New York Landing; in '78, Cornwall; in '95 Black Diamond; in 1900, Diamond. In 1911 it became Pittsburg and has managed to resist change since. It probably has had more names than any town in the country.

Port Chicago, scene of a disastrous wartime explosion in 1944, originally was Bay Point, a lumber town remarkable for its municipal saloon, the profits from which paid for water, street lights, sewers and other public services.

Sentimental landholders, townsite platters and railroaders named many places. Shirley, California, is for the wife of a stenographer in the general manager's office. Lamanda Park in the same state is a combination of Leonard and Amanda Rose. Lenwood stems from Ellen Woods, wife of the founder. Visalia, California, comes from Nathaniel Vise and his wife, Thalia. Chanesa, Texas, is a combination of Charles, Nellie and Sarah, children of C. W. Kouns, once general manager. Edruvera came from Edwin, Ruth and Vera, children of a director of the old Orient Line. Floydada, Texas, is simply Floyd and Ada Price, made immortal.

Hodge, California, was named by Arthur Brisbane for two brothers who homesteaded near by. In the winter months the great editor lived on his alfalfa ranch here and the Santa Fe dispatched his daily newspaper columns from a telegraph station set up in a boxcar on a sidetrack.

Salome, Arizona, on the Parker-Cadiz cutoff west of Wickenburg, was named by Dick Wick Hall for Mrs. Grace Salome Pratt, who was postmistress for awhile. Mr. Hall, who founded the place in 1904, made it famous with the *Salome Sun* and the Salome frog, that never saw water. It was known for years as Salome, Where She Danced. The town is a trading center for the rich Happy Valley mining districts.

Incidentally, just west of Santa Fe track down the Pecos River near the Texas-New Mexico state line, is Langtry—which was *not* named for Lily Langtry. Judge Roy Bean, a local gavel-banger, won some fame by informing the Jersey Lily that he had named the town for her and to her death she believed it. The fact is that it was named some years prior to Judge Bean's advent into the region—for a section-foreman.

More than 200 place names on the system are those of officials, employees or members of their families, ranging from brakemen to presidents. Here are most of them:

Abbyville, Tex.	Wife of an official
Abell, Tex.	P. T. Abell, director, 1889-91
Alden, Kans.	Early-day official, 1881
Allantown, Ariz.	Allan Johnson, construction department
Allison, Tex.	Robert A. Allison, general manager
Alva, Okla.	Attorney
Angell, Ariz.	G. W. Angell, early-day superintendent
Anton, Tex.	J. F. Anton, superintendent
Archer, Cal.	W. Archer, first water service superintendent
Arntz, Ariz.	W. P. Arntz, trainmaster, Albuquerque division
Barnard, Kans.	J. F. Barnard, general manager, subsidiary
Barnhart, Tex.	William Barnhart, right-of-way agent
Barstow, Calif.	William Barstow Strong, president
Beal, Cal.	Amos M. Beal, superintendent, A&P
Bean, Cal.	S. L. Bean, mechanical superintendent
Bellemont, Ariz.	In honor of Miss Bella Smith, daughter of F. W. Smith, A&P general superintendent in early days
Belva, Okla.	Daughter of section foreman, 1894
Betts, Okla.	C. E. Betts, general auditor
Bissell, Cal.	W. A. Bissell, assistant traffic manager
Bledsoe, Tex.	Samuel T. Bledsoe, president
Booker, Tex.	B. F. Booker, early locating engineer
Briscoe, Tex.	J. B. Briscoe, division superintendent
Bucklin, Mo.	Major Bucklin, engineer, subsidiary
Butler, Cal.	J. E. Butler, chief dispatcher, 1910
Byrne, Tex.	John J. Byrne, assistant passenger-traffic manager
Chalender, Ariz.	George T. Chalender, motive-power superintendent, 1883
Challis, Tex.	Luther C. Challis, one of the founders
Chambers, Ariz.	Ed Chambers, vice-president
Chanesa, Tex.	For three children of C. W. Kouns, general manager, subsidiary
Chase, Kans.	An official
Cheney, Kans.	Benjamin P. Cheney, director, 1873-1894
Claus, Cal.	Claus Spreckels, president of the Valley Road
Clements, Kans.	Auditor H. C. Clements
Connell, Kans.	J. M. Connell, general passenger agent
Conrad, Okla.	Assistant general auditor
Coolidge, Kans.	T. Jefferson Coolidge, president

Copeland, Kans.	E. L. Copeland, secretary-treasurer
Courtney, Mo.	Right-of-way agent
Cruice, Ariz.	Fred P. Cruice, assistant general-freight agent
Cuyler, Tex.	T. De Witt Cuyler, director
Daze, Ariz.	William Daze, road foreman of engines in the '80s
Deerfield, Kans.	Early official
Denair, Cal.	John Denair, superintendent at Needles, Cal.
Dennison, Ariz.	Locating engineer
Doud, Tex.	Charles Doud, vice-president and auditor
Drake, Ariz.	W. A. Drake, chief engineer, A&P
Dunmoor, N. M.	Chief Engineer James Dun and wife, *née* Moore
Edelstein, Ill.	John Edelstein, an employee
Edgerton, Kans.	A contractor
Ellinwood, Kans.	Capt. J. R. Ellinwood, engineer
Engel, N. M.	E. J. Engel, president
Eppler, Tex.	H. R. Eppler, construction department
Etter, Tex.	W. K. Etter, vice-president
Farnsworth, Tex.	H. W. Farnsworth, director
Fells, Cal.	General Manager Wells (First letter changed to avoid confusion with another station)
Fields, Ariz.	Billy Fields, brakeman who lost arms in wreck here
Fishel, Cal.	H. L. Fishel, construction engineer
Fluhr, Cal.	C. G. Fluhr, division superintendent
Follett, Tex.	Locating engineer
Forbes, Cal.	Conductor John Forbes
Fox, N. M.	F. C. Fox, general manager
Franconia, Ariz.	Frank Smith, son of F. W. Smith, general superintendent, A&P
Galivan, Cal.	J. B. Galivan, trainmaster, Los Angeles
Gallup, N. M.	D. L. Gallup, auditor, A&P, later comptroller, New York
Gaylord, Tex.	G. L. Gaylord, director
Gilmore, Tex.	Pat Gilmore, assistant superintendent
Gish, Cal.	George Gish, train dispatcher, Los Angeles
Gleed, Ariz.	Charles S. Gleed, director
Gluck, Tex.	A. A. Luck, contractor (G added to avoid confusion)
Goodwin, Okla.	George L. Goodwin, assistant treasurer
Gower, Mo.	Division superintendent
Grants, N. M.	Grant Brothers, contractors
Gray, Kans.	A. D. Gray, assistant treasurer

Gregg, Cal.	Harry Gregory, agent at Fresno
Grier, N. M.	Maiden name of official's wife
Griffith, Ariz.	A clerk
Hagerman, N. M.	J. J. Hagerman, president Pecos Valley & North Eastern, later acquired by the Santa Fe
Harris, Ariz.	G. W. Harris, chief engineer
Hawes, Cal.	Dave Hawes, conductor
Heaton, Tex.	An assistant secretary
Heidenheimer, Tex.	S. Heidenheimer, director
Helendale, Cal.	Daughter of A. G. Wells, vice-president
Heman, Okla.	Conductor F. A. Heman, of first train out of Chicago
Hibbard, Ariz.	I. L. Hibbard, general manager
Hillard, Okla.	Director
Holbrook, Ariz.	H. R. Holbrook, engineer
Holliday, Kans.	C. K. Holliday, founder and president
Hunnewell, Kans.	Director
Huntoon, Tex.	Joel Huntoon, director
Hurley, N. M.	J. E. Hurley, general manager
Hutchinson, Kans.	C. C. Hutchinson, townsite owner
Jimgrey, Cal.	Chief dispatcher, Needles
Johnlane, Tex.	J. J. Lanem, traffic manager
Johnson, Kans.	A. S. Johnson, land commissioner
Juilliard, Tex.	A. D. Juilliard, director
Justin, Tex.	Walter Justin Sherman, engineer
Kaster, Ariz.	Chief surgeon
Keefe, Okla.	J. H. Keefe, vice-president
Kempner, Tex.	I. H. Kempner, director
Kenna, N. M.	E. D. Kenna, vice-president
Killeen, Tex.	Frank P. Killeen, official
Kingman, Ariz.	Lewis Kingman, engineer
Krum, Tex.	Chas. K. Krum, official
Lamont, Cal.	Thos. W. Lamont, director
Larson, Cal.	Office employee
Laura, Ill.	Daughter of a contractor
Lautz, Tex.	H. B. Lautz, general manager
Lehman, Tex.	Frank A. Lehman, general manager, Topeka
Lord, Tex.	H. C. Lord, president
Louise, Ariz.	Daughter of A. G. Wells, vice-president
Love, Ariz.	Engineer killed in First World War
Lucy, N. M.	Wife of Chief Engineer James Dun
Lupton, Ariz.	Geo. W. Lupton, assistant to vice-president

Machovec, Tex.	E. E. Machovec, mechanical superintendent
MacKie, Tex.	F. J. MacKie, assistant general manager.
Magoun, Tex.	George C. Magoun, director
Malott, Cal.	Chief clerk
Margaret, Tex.	Wife of director
McBride, Tex.	Assistant secretary
McClure, Okla.	Wife of a director
McConnico, Ariz.	Railroad builder
McInnis, Okla.	E. E. McInnis, general counsel
McKibben, Tex.	J. F. McKibben, auditor
McLellan, Ariz.	C. T. McLellan, superintendent, Eastern division
McVay, Ariz.	Driller of first well here
Merrick, Kans.	R. G. Merrick, assistant freight and traffic manager
Mertzon, Tex.	M. L. Mertz, treasurer
Morse, Tex.	C. A. Morse, chief engineer
Mulvane, Kans.	John Mulvane, contractor
Nelson, Ariz.	Fred Nelson, division superintendent
Nevin, Ariz.	W. G. Nevin, general manager
Nickerson, Kans.	Thomas Nickerson, president
Nortonville, Kans.	T. L. Norton, Jr., roadmaster
O'Donnell, Tex.	T. S. O'Donnell, contractor
Ogg, Tex.	O. J. Ogg, division superintendent
Opdyke, Tex.	Charles P. Opdyke, director
Otis, N. M.	J. E. Otis, director
Parker, Ariz.	Earl H. Parker, chief engineer
Partridge, Kans.	Maiden name of wife of official
Peabody, Kans.	F. H. Peabody, director
Perley, Tex.	I. E. Perley, director
Perris, Cal.	Fred T. Perris, engineer
Pettibone, Tex.	F. G. Pettibone, vice-president and general manager
Pierceville, Kans.	Charles W. Pierce, an official
Pomeroy, Tex.	S. C. Pomeroy, director
Pritchett, Colo.	Dr. Henry S. Pritchett, director
Read, Tex.	J. C. Read, purchasing agent
Rich, Cal.	Chief dispatcher, Needles
Ripley, Cal.	President E. P. Ripley
Robinson, N. M.	A. A. Robinson, chief engineer
Rogers, Tex.	John D. Rogers, director, GC&SF
Rosenberg, Tex.	Henry Rosenberg, president, GC&SF

Saltmarsh, Cal.	Col. S. M. Marsh, car accountant and World War I officer
Sanbron, Ariz.	Brakeman killed in First World War
Sawyer, Kans.	Warren Sawyer, official
Sealy, Tex.	George and John Sealy, directors of the GC&SF
Sears, Kans.	Thos. Sears, general superintendent, Missouri Division
Seligman, Ariz.	F. & W. Seligman. Boston bankers
Shaufler, Tex.	E. H. Shaufler, general manager, subsidiary
Shirley, Cal.	Wife of stenographer
Silsbee, Tex.	N. D. Silsbee, treasurer
Skeen, Tex.	J. B. Skeen, valuation engineer
Smyer, Tex.	Superintendent C. E. Smyer
Spearville, Kans.	Alden Spear, official
Spencer, Kans.	Geo. W. Spencer, contractor
Strohm, Okla.	C. B. Strohm, superintendent of transportation
Strong City, Kans.	Wm. B. Strong, president
Stuart, Cal.	E. B. Stuart, agent
Sutton, Kans.	Michael Sutton, attorney
Sylvester, Tex.	W. W. Sylvester, director, subsidiary
Sylvia, Kans.	Wife of President Robinson
Titley, Tex.	Bridge and building supervisor
Touzalin, Okla.	Director A. E. Touzalin
Trull, Cal.	W. B. Trull, agent
Tuttle, Cal.	R. H. Tutttle, superintendent at Fresno
Victorville, Cal.	J. N. Victor, constructor
Wall, Ariz.	H. S. Wall, mechanical superintendent
Wallis, Tex.	J. E. Wallis, director, GC&SF
Way, Kans.	M. E. Way, agent
Wellman, Tex.	A. O. Wellman, assistant treasurer
Wellsville, Kans.	D. L. Wells, engineer
Wilder, Kans.	Edward Wilder, secretary-treasurer
Willard, N. M.	Constructor
Williamsburg, Kans.	W. H. Schofield, constructor
Williamsfield, Ill.	Contractor
Winslow, Ariz.	General E. F. Winslow, president, subsidiary
Wylie, Tex.	W. D. Wylie, right-of-way agent, GC&SF

INDIAN NAMES AND MEANINGS

Mazon, Ill.	Nettle	Navasota, Tex.	Muddy water
Pontoosuc, Ill.	Boat landing	Alamota, Kans.	Indian chief

Chautauqua, Kans.	Clear water	Ponemah, Ill.	Heaven
Neosho Rapids, Kans.	Clear water	Tenaha, Tex.	Muddy water
Ottawa, Kans.	Trading place	Alki, Kans.	After awhile
Satanta, Kans.	Indian chief	Geuda Springs, Kans.	Healing waters
Topeka, Kans.	Potato field	Olathe, Kans.	Beautiful
Wichita, Kans.	Many lodges	Quenemo, Kans.	Indian chief
Atoka, N. M.	Indian chief	Tecumseh, Kans.	Indian chief
Ponca City, Okla.	Indian tribe	Wakarusa, Kans.	Deep river
Waynoka, Okla.	Good water	Taiban, N. M.	Three creeks
Zuni, N. M.	Long nails	Pecos, N. M.	Crooked
Moqui, Ariz.	Dead	Tonkawa, Okla.	Gathering place
Supai, Ariz.	Blue water	Acomita, N. M.	Little white rock
Hopi, Ariz.	Peaceful	Navajo, Ariz.	Cattle pool or area of cultivated land
Harcuvar, Ariz.	Sweet water	Cosnino, Ariz.	Indian tribe
Topock, Ariz.	Bridge	Willaha, Ariz.	Water hole
Tehachapi, Cal.	Oak land	Coconino, Ariz.	Little water
Cucamonga, Cal.	Many waters	Walapai, Ariz.	Pine tree folk
Chillicothe, Ill	Indian chief	Mojave, Cal.	Three hills
		Orosi, Cal.	Golden valley
		Pasadena, Cal.	Valley's crown

SPANISH NAMES AND MEANINGS

Most of the system's Spanish names are in Colorado, New Mexico, Arizona, California and Texas. Many of them, with their meanings, follow:

Acequia	Aqueduct	Chino	Chinese
La Junta	The junction	Saḅlon	Coarse sand
Belen	Bethlehem	Blanco	White
Isleta	Little island	Trigo	Wheat
Rio Puerco	Dirty river	Planada	Level ground
Ceniza	Lake	Escalon	Stepping stones
Laguna	Volcanic ash	Pinole	Corn meal
Pinto	Painted, spotted	Cerrito	Little hill
Canyon Diablo	Devil's Gorge	Roble	Oak
Corva	Ham-shaped	Las Animas	The spirits
Abra	A gorge	Trinidad	The Trinity
Puro	Pure	Algoso	Weedy
Doce	Twelve	Sandia	Watermelon
Agua Fria	Cold water	Rito	Ceremony

Cubero	A cooper	Cantara	A pitcher
Cheto	Spanish province	Puente	A bridge
Carrizo	Cat-tails	Yeso	Gypsum
Sereno	A night-watch	Culebra	A snake
Piñaveta	Pine woods or Piña, silver—Veta, vein	Tornero	Turner (for a Y)
		Lamesa	The tableland
		Paisano	Countryman
Del Rio	Of the river	Ocotillo	"Candle wood" frequently called a cactus
Prieta	Dark		
Flores	Flowers		
Aguila	Eagle	Casa Piedra	Rock house
Caliente	Hot	Peral	Pear orchard
Tosco	Clumsy	Venida	Arrival
Fresno	Ash tree	Mirador	Balcony
Madera	Timber	Trocha	Narrow path
Merced	Mercy	Seguro	Secure
Avena	Oats	Raton	Mouse
Tiburon	Shark	Fontana	Fountain, spring
Opaco	Opaque	Santa Fe	Holy Faith
Tulare	Tules	Rincon	A corner
Loma	A hill	Aliso	Alder
Del Rey	Of the king	El Toro	The bull
Antes	Before	Encinitas	Little oaks
Lerdo	Slow, heavy	Ladrillo	A brick
Saco	Sack	Prenda	A promise
Cajon	Box	Olinda (Port.)	Happy land
Tejon	Badger	Las Vegas	The meadows
Los Angeles	The angels	San Jacinto	St. Hyacinth
Redondo	Round	De Luz	Of the light
La Mirada	The view	Cimarron	Wild, unruly
Venta	A market	Carnero	Meat, usually sheep
Escondido	Hidden		
Linda vista	Lovely view	Bautista	Baptist
San Diego	St. James (of Alcala)	Siega	Harvest
		Gallinas	Chickens
Esperanza	Hope	Pedernal	Flint
Prado	Flat meadow	Portales	Porches
Val Verde	Green valley	Espuela	Spur
Arcilla	Clay	Tinaja	Water jar
Amarillo	Yellow	Perdiz	Partridge
Abajo	Below	Presidio	Military post
Alameda	Strolling place		

APPENDIX III

RAILROAD SLANG

Railroaders probably have produced more slang than the people of any other industry. Some of it has become part of the American language. An example is: *Wrong side of the tracks.* Even today, in some small towns, the tracks form a dividing line of social importance. This stems from the time new settlements were laid out on the plains. The first buildings invariably were saloons, dance halls and bawdy houses, strung along the tracks. Sober and God-fearing emigrants naturally established themselves away from such evil resorts and the line became a boundary. In some early settlements it was an actual boundary, by law.

The phrase was a switch on the old Erie Canal designation: *Wrong side of the locks.* Before railroads, canals often formed social lines.

The term *red-light district* is claimed by Dodge City, Kansas. One of the town's rowdiest resorts had a large pane of red glass in its door and settlers, moving in aboard Santa Fe trains often asked trainmen for advice. Conductors and brakemen, being honest and upright citizens, warned pilgrims against the dangers of Dodge. Trains usually arrived at night, and so the simplest way was to advise newcomers to watch for the red light—"and stay away from that district."

There are at least twenty slang words for *caboose*, which is actually a *way car. Caboose* itself is a corruption of a slang word—*calabozo*, as *hoosegow* is a corruption of *Juzgado. Highball*, meaning a go-ahead signal, has nothing to do with liquor; it dates back to the time when a ball was raised on a staff to indicate a clear track ahead.

Besides slang, there are many phrases peculiar to railroading. Trains do not leave, they *leave out*. They are not on time; they are *on the advertised.* A timetable is a *card* and trains are not scheduled, they are *carded.* Railroaders never say "A quarter to eight" or "Half past ten." It is always *seven-forty-five* or *ten-thirty*—or more likely a figure exact to the minute, which is a railroad rule. Trains usually are known by numbers, not by names. The *Chief* may be eastbound or westbound, but *No. 19* is always westbound and *No. 20* is always eastbound. Odd-numbered trains almost always are west- and southbound; even-numbered trains north- and eastbound.

In the old days conductors always were addressed as *Captain*, and many old-timers appreciate being so-called. The custom has broken down in recent years, along with the habit of calling Pullman porters *George*. From this there sprang, in pre-airconditioning days, a catch-phrase: Passengers struggling to open windows were advised to "Let George do it!"

Many roads have nicknames that are in general use. The St. Louis and San Francisco is the *Frisco*; the Chicago, Burlington & Quincy is the *Burlington*, or the *Q*; the Missouri, Kansas and Texas is the *Katy* and the Missouri Pacific is the *Mop*, while the Chicago, Indianapolis & Louisville is the *Monon*. The Espee, Cotton Belt, Big Four, Nickel Plate and others are familiar to travelers. The Santa Fe used to be the *Atchison*, but the term is little heard nowadays, although the road still is listed under that name on the New York Stock Exchange. The International & Great Northern once was widely known in Texas as the *Injun*, from its initials.

Many branch roads have local names. On the Santa Fe the line from Ash Fork to Prescott and Phoenix, Arizona, is the *Peavine*. The El Paso branch out of Albuquerque is the *Horned Toad*. The Rincon-Silver City-Santa Rita branch in New Mexico is the *Hi-line*.

Here is a short glossary of railroad slang, some of its words peculiar to the Santa Fe, some of it nationwide:

Age	Seniority; time in service
Air-monkey	Air-brake repairman
Alley	Clear track in a yard
Anchor them	Set hand brakes on still cars
Angel's seat	Cupola in caboose
Ape wagon, bouncer, buggy, cage, chariot, clown-wagon, crib, crummy, dog-house, hack, hay-wagon, hearse, louse-cage, monkey-house, parlor, palace	Caboose
Armstrong	Engine unequipped with automatic stoker
Baby lifter	Passenger brakeman
Baby loads	Partly loaded cars, unbraced

Baggage-buster	Baggageman
Bail in	Shovel in the coal
Bait can	Lunch basket
Balling the jack	Running fast
Barn	Roundhouse
Batter	To work an engine too hard
Battleship	A large locomotive
Beam	Signal light
Bearcat	Craneman
Beehive	Yard office
Behind the hounds	Late
Bell cow	Car foreman
Bell-timer	Locomotive fireman
Belly-robber	Boarding contractor
Bender	A track liner
Bending rail, rust or iron	Relining a switch
Bible	Labor agreement
Big crummy	Business car
Big 'E'	Engineer, member Brotherhood of Locomotive Engineers
Big hole	Emergency brake application
Big hook	Wrecking derrick
Big mundy	Sledge hammer
Big Noise	Agent
Big 'O' or Big 'Ox'	Conductor, member Order of Railway Conductors
Bill buster	Car clerk handling waybills
Binders	Hand brakes
Black diamonds	Company coal
Blackie, hoghead, hogger, pig-mauler, pigjockey, whistle-tuner	Locomotive engineer
Blazer	Journal box, packing on fire
Bleed a car	Drain the air reservoir
Bleeder	Air-brake valve
Block-head, donicker, groundhog, shack, pin, end man, squirrel	Brakeman
Blow smoke	To brag

Blow up	Quit a job suddenly
Blue printer	Division engineer bookman
Board	Fixed signal, usually referred to as slow, order, clear or red
Boil up	Launder
Bookkeeper	Flagman
Boomer	One who has worked for many roads
Boxcar	All-room Pullman
Brainless wonder	Any railroader considered a little queer
Brain-plate	Trainman's hat badge
Breeze	Compressed air
Bridge monkey	Bridge workers
Brownie box	Superintendent's car
Brownies	Disciplinary marks, as per Brown System
Bubble-board	Track level board
Buckle the balonies	Connect air hose
Bug	Telegraph instrument; or a lantern
Bug torch	Trainman's lantern
Bull cod	Knuckle lock
Bull engine, or bullgine	Locomotive
Bullfighters, chili pickers, cholos	Mexican laborers
Bull head, skipper, captain, brains, Car whacker, corn-doctor, grabber, ORCs	Conductor
Bullsnake	Yardmaster
Bull's nose	Freight car coupler
Bump	Displace a fellow-employee by exercising seniority
Bust a fusee	Light a fusee
Butterfly	Usually a switching move
Butterfly Boy	Roadmaster
Caboose bounce, or hop	Engine and caboose only
Calliope, galloper, hog, jack, kettle, skillet, pig	Locomotive
Can	Oil or water car
Car jockey, cinder cruncher, dolly-flap-	

per, cherry-picker, short-fielder, long-fielder, yard-goose	Switchman
Car peck	Car inspector
Carry a white feather	Steam from the safety valve
Carry dead men	Mishandle time
Carrying signals, markers, banners, the green	Displaying signals for a following section
Cat's claw	Spike puller
Chain gang	Construction, or extra gang
Chase the red	Go back from stopped train to protect it
Chew cinders	Engines do this when reversed and working steam while running
Chinaman; Chink	Car washer
Choker	Necktie
Choppy	Rough track
Cinder dick	Special officer
Cinder snapper	Passenger on observation platform, rear car
Civil engineer	Locomotive engineer out of a job
Clam diggers	Employees in San Francisco Bay area
Clean the clock, wipe the clock	Emergency air application
Clean the slate	Release the air
Clearance	Service letter
Clipping 'em off at the stack	Running fast
Close or open the gate	Close or open the switch
Club	Hickory stick to help set hand brakes
Club a car	Set the hand brake
Club job	Track where it's necessary to set hand brakes to prevent cars rolling downgrade
Clucks, calico	Girl clerks
Cock-loft	Caboose cupola
Consist	The makeup of a train
Cooler, reefer, freezer	Refrigerator car
Cooning the train	Going over the tops of cars
Corner	Strike a car not in the clear on a siding
Cornfield meet	Head-on collision
Cotter-key bender	Riptrack repairman
Couple the rubbers	Connect air hose
Cowboy pullman	Drovers' car

Cow cage, crate	Stock car
Cow catcher	Locomotive pilot
Cow punchers	Car inspectors
Crackerbox, glow-worm	Diesel streamliner
Cripple	Car needing repair
Crock	One pint
Crowning it	Coupling caboose on end of train
Crummies	Cabooses
Cupola, crow's nest	Observation tower in caboose
Cut	A few cars and an engine; several cars together
Dancing the carpet	Explaining to the boss
Dead freight	Non-perishable freight
Deadhead	Pass passenger; fireman's term for brakeman
Deadheading	Not doing one's work; working without union card
Deadhead's home	Smoking car
Dead man	Fictitious worker
Deck	Floor of locomotive cab or boxcar roofs
Decorate	Riding atop a freight train
Decorations	Signal devices on trains
Devil-claw	Young roadmaster
Diamond	A crossover
Diamond cracker, tallow-pot, greaseball, smoke agent, water warmer	Fireman
Diamond stackers	Old-fashioned locomotives with enlarged tops to the smoke funnels in diamond shape
Dicks	Special service officers
Die game	Stalling on a hill
Diesel	Fast
Dinger	Assistant yardmaster
Dirt stiffs	Grading gang
Dishonest	Either colorblind, or a drinker
Dispatcher's delight	Attentive telegraph operator
Division boomer	One of many jobs
Dog catchers	Men sent out to relieve crew caught by 16-hour law
Dogging	Lying down on the job
Dogleg	Curve in track to clear object between two tracks

Dolly	Switch stand
Doodlebug	Diesel-electric locomotive
Dope	Waste and oil for packing boxes; orders; instructions
Double gun	Working both injectors to supply boiler
Doubleheading	Two engines to one train; belonging to two unions
Double the hill	Cut train in half, take each section up separately
Down in the corner	Reverse lever full forward position
Down on the sand and beating her on the back	Sand on the rail, reverse lever full forward, throttle wide open
Drag	Slow freight train
Drawbar flagging	Leaning against the last car's drawbar to "protect" the train
Dream book	Cigaret papers
Drill crew	Yard crew
Drone cage	Private car
Drop	In switching, cutting off cars and allowing them to coast to their places
Dropper, hump rider	Yardmen who ride cars in hump yards
Drummer	Yard conductor
Dummies, greenbacks	Rerailing frogs
Dust the flues	Sanding flues of oil-burning locomotive
Dutch drop	When dropping cars, engine reverses and passes cars in opposite direction
Dynamiter	Triple valve that suddenly applies brakes
Elephant tracker	Special officer
Errand boy	Roadmaster
Espee	Southern Pacific Company
Eye	Signal
Family disturber	Pay car
Federal sheet	Arrival and departure record
Field, garden	Yard
Firefly	Trainmaster
Fireworks	Fusees
First reader	Conductor's train book
Flag	An assumed name
Flatwheel	An employee who limps
Flimsies	Way bills, train orders
Flying switch	A switching movement made without stopping
Fly light	Miss a meal

Fog	Smoke or steam from engine
Fog-gauge	Steam pressure indicator
Freeze the hub	Cool a heated journal
Frog	X-shaped track where one line crosses another
Fruiter; GFX	Green fruit train
Galloping rods; monkey motion	Valve gear of a locomotive
Galvanizer	Car inspector
Gandy dancers; snipes	Section laborers
G-bum	Habitual drinker (violating Rule G)
Go high	Go on tops of cars to relay signals
Getting the block	Giving clear track ahead
Glad hand	Submerged water-valve connection, or air or steam-hose coupling
Glass	Insulators
Glory	String of empties; death by accident
Gons	Gondolas, a type of open car
Grab iron	Hand hold on side of car
Grass	Cars of asparagus
Graveyard	Track for damaged or condemned equipment
Griever	Local chairman of labor union
Growlers	People moving belongings on freight cars
Groundhog	Air hose
Guns	Track-torpedoes
Gut, gut wagon	Air hose; air-hose repair wagon
Gyppo	Railroad contractor
Hand 'em up	Deliver orders
Hard joint	Rough coupling
Harness	Passenger trainmen's uniform
Hay	Overtime; sleep
Head floor lady	Chief clerk to agent
Heel	Braked cars on end of track
Herder	Man who couples and uncouples engines at end of run
Hi-daddy	Flying switch in which cars are cut off behind engine and switch thrown after engine has passed
Highball	Signal waved by hand or lamp in high, wide semicircle, meaning "proceed"; in early days ball was raised on trackside staff as signal
Highball artist, eagle eye	Engineer noted for fast running

Highballers	Mechanical wigwag signals on caboose
High iron; stem	Main line
Highliner	Main line fast passenger train
High wheeler	Passenger locomotive
Hit the grit	Fall or get kicked off a car
Hog	Locomotive
Hogback	Elevation in track
Hog law; dog law	Law providing all train crews must stop work after sixteen hours of continuous service
Hole	Side track
Home guard	Employee who stays with one road
Hopper	Open car which may be unloaded through bottom
Hoptoad	Derail
Horse her over	Reverse the engine
Hot box, stinker	Overheated journal
Hot car	Car to be given special attention
Hot shot	Fast train of any class
Hummer	One of outstanding ability
Hump	Artificial hill at end of classification yard over which cars are pushed and allowed to roll to various tracks
Humpback job	One on a peddler freight
Hump yard	Classification yard into which cars roll by gravity
Hut	Locomotive cab
Identy	Stub of ticket identification slip
In the corner	Throttle wide open
In the hole	On a siding
Irish Valentine	Traingram (comes in green envelope)
Iron skull	Boilermaker
Jack and a half	Overtime
Jack-block	Marker-lamp plugs on rear of train
Jackpot	Traffic congestion
Jam-buster	Assistant yardmaster
Jay rod	Clinker hook
Jeep	Diesel-electric freight engine
Jerk soup; jerk a drink	Take water from track pan while running
Jerk this by you	Drop this car
Jerkwater	Anything small or insignificant
Jerry	Section foreman
Jewel; setting jewels	Journal brass; putting in a new journal brass
Jigger	Full tonnage train of dead freight

Jim crow	Rail bender
Johnny ball	Insulator
Johnson bar	Hand operated reverse lever
Join the birds	Jump in a derailment
Juggler	Way freight crew member who loads and unloads less-than-carload freight at station stops
Juice	Air brakes
Jungle	Loafing place; a tramps' hangout
Keeley	Water can for hot or heated journals
Keep hot	Full pressure of steam
Kick	Act of cutting off cars and allowing them to roll into siding
Kicker	Triple valve that sticks and throws brakes into emergency application of air, sometimes by bump of train
Kick in the corner	Reverse lever full position forward
Kill an engine	Put fire out
King	Freight conductor; sometimes applied to yardmaster
King snipe	Section foreman
Kitty	Station cash fund
Knock the stack off	To work the engine hard
Knowledge box	Yardmaster's office
Knuckle buster	Monkey wrench
Ladder; lead	Main track of a yard from which each individual track leads off
Letters	Service certificates
Lever jerker	Interlocker leverman
Lid; ham	Telegraph department amateur
Lie by	Siding
Lightning slinger, brass pounder, op., wire tickler	Telegraph operator
Lincoln Pin (link and pin)	Narrow-gauge road
Liner	Passenger train
Little Jeff	The independent brake valve
Little space on the book	Credit
Lizard scorcher	The cook
Long fielder	Switchman who works farthest from engine
L.U.G.	Engine stored in good condition

Lung	Draft gear of a car
Lunger	Car with drawbar out
Main pin; Master mind	An official
Make a joint	To couple cars
Make a pass	To make a switch (of cars)
Markers	Rear end signals
Master maniac	Master mechanic
Master mechanic's blood	Valve oil
Mikados	Jap section boss prior to 1942
Mikes	Mikado type class engines
Modoc	Employees' train
Money hog	One who prefers runs on jobs with lots of overtime
Monkey	Brakeman on hump riding cars
Monkey suit	Passenger train employee's uniform
Monkey tail	Emergency air valve in caboose
Moonlight master maniac	Night roundhouse foreman
Mountain lion	Roadmaster
Mud	Fuel oil
Mud chicken	Surveyor
Mud hen; old soak	Saturated engine
Mud hop	Yard clerk
Mule	Boilermaker
Muskrats	Water service men
Nigger head	Steam exit on top of boiler from which pipes to injector, etc., issue
Nipper's guide	Fictitious track book
No bill	Non-union employee or car traveling without waybill
Non-air	Non-union railroad worker
Nose on	Couple on with head end of engine
Number dummy; number grabber	Yard or car clerk
Nurse	Hostler
Nut cracker	Automatic airbrake valve on engine
Nut splitter; nut busting	Machinist
Oil can	Tank car
Old alibi	Roadmaster

Old head	Veteran employee; stories or advice of old hand
Old hoss	Salvage freight
Old rail	Veteran railroad worker
Old Waterbury; turnip	Railroad watch
Old whiskers	Senior official
On the advertised	On time
On the grease	Slippery rail
On the peg	To have full boiler pressure
On the spot	Off duty
Orderboard	Signal at station warning engineer to get orders
Ornament	Stationmaster
O.S.	To report a train passing a station to the dispatcher
Outlawed	Applied to crew that has worked sixteen hours, limit allowed by law
Paddle	Semaphore signal; shovel
Package run	Local train
Palace of justice	Business car
Parlor maid; parlor shack	Hind flagman on freight
Parlor stinger	Flagman
Patting her on the back	Hooking up the reverse lever as speed is attained
Peck	Twenty minutes allowed for lunch
Peckerneck	Apprentice
Peddler	Local way-freight
Pie book	Meal ticket
Pig pen	Roundhouse
Pike	Railroad
Pin ahead and pick up two behind	Cut off engine and pick up three cars from siding, put two on the train and set the first one back on the siding
Pinch her down	Reduce speed prior to stop
Pin for home	Go home for the day
Pin head	Clerk; sometimes brakeman
Pink	Caution card; "rush" company telegram
Pin puller	Switchman riding engine to uncouple cars
Plug	Water crane; short passenger train
Plug 'em	To use emergency application of brakes
Plug-one	Horse train; in old days, the throttle; engineers were "plug pullers"
Poor guess	Dispatcher

Pops	Air-retainers
Possum belly	Tool box under caboose
Potato bug; pollywog	Motor train
Potbelly	Caboose stove
Pounding her	Working locomotive to capacity
Punch	Keep after material on order
Puncher	Request for reply to correspondence
Pure food sheet	Register
Pussy foot	Special officer
Put in a jewel	To put in a journal brass in a car
Putty	Steam
Rabbit	Derail
Race horse	General foreman
Railbird	Railroad employee
Raisin pickers	Employees at Fresno, California
Rat holes	Tunnels
Rattler	Freight train
Rawhider	Conductor, engineer or any official especially hard on men or equipment
Real estate	Poor coal
Red ball; dancy drag	Fast merchandise freight
Red board	Stop signal
Red onion	Railroad eatinghouse
Reefer	Refrigerator car
Reefer block	Train of reefers
Rent man	Roadmaster
Ribbons of rust	Main track
Ride the cushions	Ride passenger train
Ride the point	Ride farthest car being pushed by engine
Ride the rods	Ride freight train without paying
Ring master	Yardmaster
Rip track	Minor car repair track
Ritz	Harvey House
Robissary	Commissary car
Rock	Garnishment
Rocking chair, to get the,	To retire on pension
Rocking chair count	Any guesstimate
Rocking-chair job	Diesel switcher
Roof garden	Mallet locomotive or helper on a mountain job
Rule "G"	"Thou Shalt Not Drink"
Runty	Dwarf signal

Sacred ox	Mallet locomotive or helper on mountain job
Sandhouse; sandhouse dope	Rumors created by trainmen about future railroad plans
Sap	Ship soon as possible
Saw	Meeting of trains longer than available siding
Scissorbill	Uncomplimentary term
Scoop	Fireman's shovel on front and rear of switch engines
Seal grabber	Clerk who records number of seals on car
Sea shore	Sand
Secret works	Automatic airbrake application
Set in	Accept employment
Shave	Burn weeds on right of way
Shiner	Trainman's lantern
Shining time	Starting time
Shoo-fly	Temporary track around obstruction
Short flag	Drawbar flag
Short rail	Derail
Shorts	Cars left between stations
Shovel runner	Steam-shovel engineer
Show cars	Supply train
Shuffle the deck	To switch cars on house tracks at every station
Shunting boiler; goat	Switch engine
Side-door Pullman	Boxcar used by bum stealing a ride
Side swipe	Cars on two tracks coming together
"Siftin' through the dew"	Traveling at high speed
Skunk	Motor car with striped front
Slave driver	Yardmaster; any rawhide official
Slobber Bucket	Sometimes applied to locomotive at Amarillo
Slug	Heavy fire in locomotive firebox
Smoker	Locomotive
Smoking 'em; running on smoke orders	A method of getting from one station to another without orders, moving along slowly and watching for smoke of approaching train; dangerous but sometimes done in old days
Snake	Switchman
Snipe	Track laborer
Sniping outfit	Surfacing gang
Snoozer	Pullman car
Soft-bellies	Wooden frame cars
Soup jockey	Cook

Soup ticket	Short report thrown from train showing consist; Register check
Soup wagon	Creosote wagon
Spar	Pole used to shove cars into the clear when switching
Speedy	Callboy
Spike gun	Machine for driving spikes
Spike puller	Young roadmaster
Spot	To place a car or engine in designated position; also sleep on lunch period or rest on company time
Spotter	Man assigned to snoop around, checking up on men's conduct
Spurs	Tracks with switches at one end only
Squealer	Journal box hot from friction
Stab	Delay
Stake artist	Chainman in engineering department
Stake 'em by	To shove cars with a heavy pole provided for that purpose
Star gazers	Brakemen who fail to see signals
Stem	Main line
Stem winder	Climax type geared engine
Stick	Staff used on certain stretches of track to control block; carried by engine crews from one station to next
Stinker	Overheated journal box
Stopper puller	Member of crew who follows engine in switching
Strawberry patch	Rear end of a caboose by night
String	Several cars coupled together
Strings	Telegraph wires
Suck it by	Make a flying switch
Sunkink	Track out of line due to heat expansion
Switch shanty	Gossip
Symbol train	Fast freight
Take the hole	Take a siding
Taking her by the neck	An engine pulling a drag up a grade
Tallow pot	Fireman
Tank	Locomotive tender
Tank town	Small town where train stops for water; any very small town
Teddy	Sixteen-hour law

The joint	The coupling
Thousand-miler	Starched blue shirt worn by railroad men, especially boomers
Throttle fever	Desire to run engine
Throttle on gate	Throttle wide open
Throwed a wingding	Drunk on duty
Tie 'em down	Set hand brakes
Tin cans	Tank cars
Toad	Type of derail used on top of rail
Toepath	Running board
Token	Train order
To make a cut	To uncouple cars
To make a jerk	A running switch
Tongue	A drawbar
Toonerville	Local freight train
Top dresser drawer	Upper bunk in caboose
To pull out a lung	Pull the draft gear out of a car
To set a binder	To apply hand brakes
Tracer	Following movement of car or shipment by wire
Train line	Pipe that carries compressed air to operate air brakes
Tramp run	No destination train; picks up, sets out, clears
Travel hogger	Road foreman of engines
Traveling man	Traveling engineer or fireman
Try the wind	Test automatic airbrakes
Tumbling shaft	Reverse shaft on engine
Turn the pops up	Open retainers
Underground hog	Chief engineer
Up and down	Proceed
Upstairs man	Waiter who serves outside of diner
Varnish string	Passenger train
Varnish wagons, cars or string	Passenger coaches
Walking canes	Lining cars
Walk up against the gun	Go up stiff grade with injector on
War club	Electric lantern
Washout	Violent stop signal made with arms by day and lamp by night swung in wide, low semicircle across tracks
Water dogs	Water service repairmen
Westinghouse	Airbrake

Whale belly	Steel car or type of coal car
Whirley	Gas shovel
Whiskers	Age, seniority; the boss
Whiskers on rails	Frost
Whistle stop	Small town
White lead	Engine tied up in back tracks for future service
White rabbits	Derails
White rat	Train auditor
Whizz	Automatic air brakes
Wiggle	Drop a bunch of cars
Willie	Waybill for loaded car
Windcutter	Streamliner
Wing 'er	Set brakes on moving train
Wipe the clock	Emergency application of brakes
Wrench wringer	Pipe fitter
Wye	Tracks running off main line in "Y" for turning cars or engines where there is no turn table
Yard	System of tracks for storing cars or making up trains
Yard bull	Railroad detective
Yard goat	Switch engine
Yardless	Yardmaster
Yellowboard	Caution signal
Zulu; zebra	Emigrant outfit

APPENDIX IV

SANTA FE DEPARTMENTS

Executive Department—Board of Directors
Executive Committee—President
Vice-President—Executive Department
Vice-President—Operating Department
Vice-President—Traffic Department
Public Relations Department—*Santa Fe Magazine*
Transportation Department
Car Service Department
Telegraph Department
General Watch & Clock Inspector
Safety Department
Special Service
Personnel
Leases and Contracts
Director of Employment
Women's Service
Hospital Associations
Mechanical Department
Engineering Department
Signal Department
Timber Treating Department
Freight Traffic Department
Refrigerator Department
Live-Stock Department
Agricultural Department
Passenger Traffic Department
Express and Mail
Baggage Department
Advertising Department
Eating House and Dining Department–
Fred Harvey Management

Law Department
Claim Department
Accounting Department
Treasury Department (Secretary, Assistant Secretaries, Assistant Treasurers)
Comptroller
Commissioner of Taxes & Manager of Insurance
Retirement Bureau
Land Commissioner
Purchasing Department
Store Department—Stationer
Ice Department

NOTE—Superintendents of Special Service report to their respective general managers.

Freight Traffic Department industrial matters are handled by the respective freight traffic managers.

Baggage matters on AT&SF Ry are handled by General Baggage Agent, Topeka; on Coast Lines, by General Baggage, Express and Mail Agent, Los Angeles; on P&SF Ry by Traffic Manager; on GC&SF Ry by General Passenger Agent.

APPENDIX V

TRAINS

During the war, about 1,800 trains—most of them freights—moved over the Santa Fe every twenty-four hours. They ranged from cross-country streamliners between the Lakes and the Coast, down to mixed trains on branch lines, like No. 57 from White Deer to Skellytown in the Texas Panhandle, and No. 43, shuttling 26.8 miles from Socorro to Magdalena, New Mexico.

Here are some of the more important passenger trains operating early in 1945. As a rule, odd-numbered trains run west and south; even-numbered trains north and east.

NUMBER	NAME	ROUTE
1–2	The Scout	Chicago-Los Angeles
3–4	The California Limited	Chicago-Los Angeles
5–6	The Ranger	Chicago-Galveston, Texas
7–8	The Fast Mail	Chicago-Los Angeles
9–10	Centennial State	Kansas City-Denver
11	The Kansas Cityan (**)	Chicago-Oklahoma City
12	The Chicagoan (**)	Oklahoma City-Chicago
13–14	Local	Chicago-Pekin, Ill.
15	Texas Express	Newton-Galveston
16	Chicago Express	Galveston-Newton
17–18	The Super Chief (**)	Chicago-Los Angeles
19–20	The Chief	Chicago-Los Angeles
21–22	El Capitan (**)	Chicago-Los Angeles
23–24	The Grand Canyon Limited	Chicago-Los Angeles
61–63	The Golden Gate (**)	Bakersfield-Oakland (*)
62–64	The Golden Gate (**)	Oakland-Bakersfield (*)

(*) Co-ordinated with bus service, Los Angeles—Bakersfield and Oakland—San Francisco.

(**) Diesel streamliner.

71–73–77–79	The San Diegan (**)	San Diego-Los Angeles
72–74–76–78	The San Diegan (**)	Los Angeles-San Diego
211–212	The Tulsan (**)	Kansas City-Tulsa, Oklahoma

Following is a historical list of trains operated by the Santa Fe System from 1892 to 1938, with dates of inauguration and when discontinued, if they are not now operating.

1892 THE CALIFORNIA LIMITED Chicago-Los Angeles
Daily—Nov. 27, 1892 to May 3, 1896
1896 Discontinued from May 4, 1896 to Nov. 1896
1896 Resumed Chicago-Los Angeles
Twice Wkly (Wed. & Sat.)—Nov. 4, 1896 to May 31, 1897
1897 Discontinued from June, 1897 to Oct. 1897
1897 Resumed Chicago-Los Angeles
Twice Wkly (Wed. & Sat.)—Oct. 26, 1897 to Feb. 1898
1898 Tri. Wkly—Feb. 1898 to Mar. 1898
1898 Twice Wkly—Apr. 1898 to May 1898
1898 Discontinued from June, 1898 to Nov. 1898
1898 Resumed—Tri. Wkly—Nov. 2, 1898 to May 31, 1899
1899 Discontinued from June, 1899 to Nov. 1899
1899 Resumed
Tues.-Wed.-Thurs.-Sat.—Nov. 5, 1899 to June 1, 1900
1900 Discontinued from June, 1900 to Nov. 1900
1900 Resumed—Tri. Wkly—Nov. 7, 1900 to June 8, 1901
1901 Twice Wkly—June 9, 1901 to Nov. 2, 1901
1901 Dly—Nov. 3, 1901 to May 31, 1902
1902 Tri. Wkly—June 1, 1902 to Nov. 15, 1902
1902 Dly—Nov. 16, 1902 to June 3, 1903
1903 Twice Wkly—June 4, 1903 to Nov. 22, 1903
1903 Dly—Nov. 23, 1903 to June 18, 1904
1904 Twice Wkly—June 19, 1904 to Nov. 12, 1904
1904 Dly—Nov. 13, 1904 to June 3, 1905
1905 Twice Wkly—June 4, 1905 to Nov. 11, 1905
1905 Dly—Nov. 12, 1905 to Mar. 31, 1938

1905 LOS ANGELES EXPRESS—Dly Chicago-L.A.-San Francisco
Train schedules shown in Feb. 15, 1905, timetable. Not available prior to that date. Service discontinued Feb. 14, 1915.

1905 SAN FRANCISCO EXPRESS—Dly Chgo.-L.A.-San Francisco
Train schedules shown in Feb. 15, 1905, timetable. Not

available prior to that date. Service discontinued Feb. 14, 1915.

1905 CHICAGO EXPRESS—Dly San Francisco-L.A.-Chicago
Train schedules shown in Feb. 15, 1905, timetable. Not available prior to that date. Service discontinued Nov. 29, 1931.

1905 ATLANTIC EXPRESS—Dly Los Angeles-Chicago
Train schedules shown in Feb. 15, 1905, timetable. Not available prior to that date. Service discontinued Nov. 29, 1931.

1896 THE CALIFORNIA LIMITED Los Angeles-Chicago
Twice Wkly (Mon. & Thurs.)—Nov. 9, 1896 to May, 1897
1897 Discontinued from June, 1897 to Oct. 1897
1897 Resumed
Twice Wkly (Tues. & Fri.)—Oct. 26, 1897 to Feb. 1898
1898 Tri. Wkly—Feb. 1898 to Mar. 1898
1898 Twice Wkly—Apr. 1898 to May 1898
1898 Discontinued from June, 1898 to Nov. 1899
1899 Resumed—Sat.-Sun.-Tues.-Thurs.—Nov. 11, 1899 to June 1900
1900 Discontinued from June, 1900 to Nov. 1900
1900 Resumed—Tri. Wkly—Nov. 13, 1900 to June 1901
1901 Daily—Nov. 7, 1901 to June 1902
1902 Tri. Wkly—June, 1902 to Nov. 1902
1902 Daily—Nov. 1902 to June, 1903
1903 Twice Wkly—June, 1903 to Dec. 1903
1903 Daily—Dec. 3, 1903 to June, 1904
1904 Twice Wkly—June, 1904 to Nov. 1904
1904 Daily—Nov. 15, 1904 to June 1905
1905 Twice Wkly—June 1905 to Nov. 1905
1905 Daily—Nov. 1905 to Mar. 31, 1938
1938 Discontinued from Apr. 1, 1938 to May 24, 1938
1938 Resumed—Daily—May 25, 1938

1905 COLORADO EXPRESS Chicago-Denver
Train schedules shown in Feb. 15, 1905, timetable. Not available prior that date. Service discontinued Nov. 29, 1931.

1905 TEXAS EXPRESS Chicago-Galveston
Train schedules shown in Feb. 15, 1905, timetable. Not available prior that date. Service discontinued Aug. 31, 1932.

1905 CHICAGO EXPRESS Denver-Chicago
Train schedules shown in Feb. 15, 1905, timetable. Not available prior that date. Service discontinued Nov. 29, 1931.

1905 COLORADO FLYER Chicago-Denver
Train schedules shown in Feb. 15, 1905, timetable. Not available prior that date. Service discontinued Nov. 29, 1931.

1911 OVERLAND EXPRESS—Dly. San Fran.-L.A.-Chicago
Nov. 20, 1911. Serv. discont'd Jan. 15, 1916

1911 EASTERN EXPRESS—Dly. San Francisco-L.A.-Chicago
Nov. 20, 1911. Service discontinued Feb. 14, 1915

1911 TOURIST FLYER—Dly. Chicago-L.A.-San Francisco
Eastbound Nov. 20, 1911. Westbound Nov. 20, 1911
Service discontinued Oct. 15, 1915

1912 THE SAINT L.A.-San Francisco—Jan. 20, 1912
Service discontinued Dec. 31, 1918

1912 THE ANGEL San Francisco-L.A.—Jan. 20, 1912
Service discontinued Dec. 31, 1918

1912 THE DE LUXE—Tue. Only Chicago-L. A.
Eastbound Dec. 8, 1912. Westbound Dec. 12, 1911
Service discontinued May 1, 1917 (Eastbound) and Feb. 13, 1918 (Westbound)

1913 THE OIL FLYER Kansas City-Tulsa—Dec. 7, 1913

1915 SANTA FE EIGHT—Dly. San Francisco-L.A.-Chicago
Feb. 4, 1915. Service discontinued June 8, 1929

1915 THE MISSIONARY—Dly. Chicago-L.A.-San Francisco
Westbound Feb. 14, 1915. Service discont'd June 2, 1918

1915 THE OVERLAND—Dly. Chicago-L.A.-San Francisco
Westbound Feb. 14, 1915. Serv. discont'd Jan. 15, 1916

1915 CHICAGO FLYER—Dly. San Francisco-L.A.-Chicago
Eastbound Feb. 14, 1915. Service discont'd June 2, 1915

1915 THE NAVAJO—Dly. Chicago-Los Angeles
Eastbound Oct. 15, 1915. Westbound Oct. 15, 1915

1916 THE SCOUT—Dly. Chicago-Los Angeles
Eastbound Jan. 16, 1916. Westbound Jan. 16, 1916
Service discontinued Jan. 4, 1931

1916 THE RANGER Chicago-Galveston—Mar. 1, 1916

1920 SAN FRANCISCO LIMITED—Dly. Chicago-L.A.-San Fran.
Westbound Nov. 14, 1920. Serv. discont'd Apr. 30, 1921

1920 THE MISSIONARY—Dly. Chicago-L.A.-San Francisco
Eastbound Apr. 15, 1920. Westbound Apr. 15, 1920

Service discontinued Mar. 6, 1932 (Westbound)
Service discontinued May 10, 1936 (Eastbound)

1920 CHICAGO LIMITED—Dly. San Francisco-L.A.-Chicago
Nov. 14, 1920. Service discontinued Apr. 30, 1931 (Eastbound)

1926 THE CHIEF—Dly. Chicago-Los Angeles
Eastbound Nov. 14, 1926. Westbound Nov. 14, 1926

1927 THE ANTELOPE Kansas City-Brownwood—June 12, 1927

1929 THE HOPI—Dly. Los Angeles-Chicago—June 9, 1929
Service discontinued Mar. 6, 1932

1929 GRAND CANYON LIMITED Chicago-Los Angeles
Eastbound June 9, 1929. Westbound June 9, 1929

1932 FAST FIFTEEN Kansas City-Galveston—Sept. 1, 1932

1936 THE SCOUT (Service Resumed) Chicago-Los Angeles
Eastbound May 10, 1936. Westbound May 10, 1936

1936 THE SUPER CHIEF Chicago-Los Angeles
Eastbound May 15, 1936. Westbound May 12, 1936
Lv. Chgo. Tues. Only. Lv. L.A. Fri. Only

1938 THE SUPER CHIEF Chicago-Los Angeles
Eastbound Feb. 22, 1938. Westbound Feb. 22, 1938
Lv. Chgo. Tue. & Sat. Lv. L.A. Tue. & Fri.

1938 EL CAPITAN Chicago-Los Angeles
Eastbound Feb. 22, 1938. Westbound Feb. 22, 1938
Lv. Chgo. Tue. & Sat. Lv. L.A. Tue. & Fri.

1938 THE SAN DIEGAN Los Angeles-San Diego—Mar. 23, 1938

1938 THE CALIFORNIA LIMITED
Discontinued from Apr. 1, 1938 to May 21, 1938

1938 THE KANSAS CITYAN Chicago-Okla. City—Apr. 17, 1938

1938 THE CHICAGOAN Okla. City-Chicago—Apr. 17, 1938

1938 THE CALIFORNIA LIMITED
Resumed May 22, 1938—Daily

1938 THE GOLDEN STATE Bakersfield-Oakland—July 1, 1938

1940 THE TULSAN Chicago-Tulsa—Jan. 14, 1940

1940 CENTENNIAL STATE Kansas City-Denver—Oct. 27, 1940

APPENDIX VI

SOME SANTA FE FIRSTS

Use of chemicals in treating locomotive boiler water, 1902.
Four-wheel, trailer-trucks, locomotive, 1919.
Three hundred pound radial stay boiler, 1927.
Solid front and main bushing, 1923.
Floating bushing back end of main rod, 1920.
Large locomotive tenders, 1911.
Cast steel box type spark arresters, 1933.
All-steel way cars, 1927.
Rotary air valve in way cars, 1929.
Spray method of painting, 1921.
Integral-back cylinder heads, 1925.
Car-floor planing devices, 1931.
Sandblasting engine tanks and steel cars, 1911.
Nail and car-siding puller bars, 1910.
Round hole table grates, 1919.
New welding practices using oxy-acetylene machines, 1908-1916.
Axle-generated power for passenger cars, 1897.
Electrical markers on rear of all passenger trains, 1903.
Oil burning locomotives, 1894.
Ice-method of air washing and cooling on long-distance diners, 1911.
Fresh air damper controls, 1935.
Air delivery grilles in lower berths, controlled by occupant, 1935.
Long distance locomotive running.
Multiple unit 3600-h.p. diesel passenger locomotive, 1935.
Multiple unit 5400-h.p. freight locomotive, 1941.
Lidgerwood method of tire-turning on locomotives, 1931.
Inside steel finish, passenger cars, 1913.
Air jack for removing passenger car wheels, 1896.
First apprentice system for mechanical employees.

System-wide set of fire rules, fire roads in shop areas, water barrels at strategic spots.

Coast-to-Coast private communication system.

Double track or two-track line, Lakes to Coast.

Operation of own fleet of refrigerator cars.

In 1918 the Santa Fe, on its Valley Division in California, originated the present system of out-of-face welding of battered rail ends, to extend rail-life and provide smoother riding.

In addition, Fred G. Gurley, who became president of the system in 1944, was among the first to suggest application of the electric-grid brake to diesel locomotives. This brake, which relieves the locomotive and car wheel brakes on long downgrades, was first used on the Santa Fe.

APPENDIX VII

FINANCIAL

Original capitalization of the Santa Fe was $52,000, of which $5,200 was put up in cash by the thirteen incorporators. In 1944 the nominal capitalization of the system was $242,706,000 represented by 2,427,060 common shares with a par value of $100; plus 1,241,728 shares of $100 par value non-cumulative and non-redeemable $5 preferred stock, representing $124,172,800. The December, 1944, funded debt was $243,662,500.

This made a total of $610,541,300, assuming par value for both classes of stock. Total assets were more than a billion and a half dollars. Working capital in 1944 was nearly $51,000,000. Debt retirement in 1942 totaled $18,266,000; in 1943 it amounted to $33,647,249.

The present concern is fifty years old; it was incorporated in Kansas in 1895, following a reorganization of the original company. It maintains general offices in Chicago, New York and Topeka.

The system is first in mileage and in 1942 and most of 1944, fourth in revenues among American railroads. Omitting banks and insurance concerns, it is the ninth largest corporation in the country. Its gross intake for 1944—an abnormal war year—was around half a billion dollars. Normal years vary between $130,000,000 and $270,000,000, depending on crops and business conditions.

The system's stock exchange symbol is SF; its rating is that of the leader in its class. It has paid common dividends regularly since 1900, with three exceptions. Its $5 preferred dividends have been fully paid, except for three curtailments, since 1899. In 1933 $4 was paid; in 1938 $2.50 and in 1939 $3.50. Common dividends in 1929 were $10; they fell to nothing four years later; rose to $2 in 1934 and since 1942 have been at the rate of $6. There are more women than men stockholders.

Early in 1945 the Santa Fe owned 14,549 miles of main line track; it operated 15,105 miles. Its yard tracks totaled 5,700 owned miles;

5,991 operated miles. This gave a total of owned trackage of 20,249; of operated trackage: 21,096.

In financial parlance the Santa Fe is exceptionally self-contained. This means it depends upon its own territory for most of its business. Almost three-quarters of its normal tonnage originates on its own lines; almost sixty-five per cent of the tonnage terminates there. Main tonnage is in livestock, cotton, grain, petroleum products, citrus fruits and grapes, which make up two-thirds of the total haul. Normally, passenger business accounts for little more than one-tenth of gross income, although this rose to more than one-fifth in the war years of '43 and '44.

In 1899 the system had a gross income of $43,000,000. This was almost reached in nearly every single *month* in 1944. In 1944 the lines paid each month ten times as much taxes as they paid in the entire *year* of 1900. In other words, taxes increased more than 100 times in forty-four years.

In 1900 the system paid 30,000 employees $16,000,000 in wages and salaries. In 1944 it paid 60,000 almost $160,000,000. The average wage in 1900 was $544; in 1944 $2,900. In 1944 there were 64,000 employees, earning $185,000,000.

The peak of employment was reached in November, 1920, when the payroll carried 82,059 names. The average wage was $1,716 a year and the total wage bill for the year $134,907,063. From then the totals dropped until they hit low in the summer of 1938. Then, only 39,349 people got paychecks—but these averaged $1,925 for a total of $75,765,141. Low month was May, with only 33,613 workers. The war years stepped up employment, and would have stepped it up more if more men and women could have been hired. But it seemed unlikely that the 1920 figure ever would be topped again, as railroad operation became more and more automatic and concentrated in fewer control centers.

The road in 1940, a semi-depression year, earned $1.55 on its common stock. This figure rose in 1941 to $6.56; in '42 to $15.82; and in '43 to $29.44. For the fiscal year ending June 30, 1944, earnings per share dropped to $18.96, due to mounting taxation and increased operating costs. In 1944, while gross income increased ten per cent, net income was down twenty per cent, for the same reasons. The figures are for charter years, ending June 30th.

Common stock price hit a high in 1929 of 298⅝; three years later it touched a depression low of 17⅞. In 1940 a series of depression years had resulted in a high of only 25¼ and a low of 13. Since then there has been a steady rise, with a high of 83½ in 1944, a climb from the year's low of 53½.

Through Western Improvement Company, which it owns, the Santa Fe has extensive interests in timber, real estate, mining, oil and other enterprises, some of which it operates to supply its material needs.

Under Ripley, the system set up a rule that depression periods should be used to improve and rebuild track and equipment, and this rule still is followed as far as feasible. The expense of this progress is met from reserves, which are maintained at a high level. The result is that when business improves the system is well equipped to handle it without delay and can devote itself to tonnage hauling instead of repairs and improvements.

THE ATCHISON, TOPEKA AND SANTA FE RAILWAY SYSTEM

Funded debt outstanding excluding bonds in Treasury and Funded debt per mile

YEAR ENDING DECEMBER 31	FUNDED DEBT OUTSTANDING DECEMBER 31	OWNED MILEAGE DECEMBER 31	FUNDED DEBT PER MILE
1896	$160 186 050	6 457	$24 808
1897	171 327 500	7 026	24 384
1898	178 594 460	7 383	24 190
1899	181 420 210	7 652	23 709
1900	184 985 710	8 128	22 760
1901	195 925 710	8 519	23 000
1902	225 928 310	8 658	26 094
1903	229 385 250	9 093	25 226
1904	237 367 720	9 240	25 691
1905	265 644 520	9 423	28 191
1906	285 493 520	9 816	29 086
1907	306 024 370	9 946	30 769
1908	331 966 320	10 015	33 149
1909	290 974 070	10 121	28 750
1910	317 192 623	10 583	29 973
1911	328 204 820	10 608	30 939
1912	337 412 149	10 685	31 577
1913	314 790 149	10 790	29 175
1914	312 493 648	10 893	28 688
1915	307 190 921	11 069	27 751

THE ATCHISON, TOPEKA AND SANTA FE RAILWAY SYSTEM

Funded debt outstanding excluding bonds in Treasury and Funded debt per mile (Continued)

YEAR ENDING DECEMBER 31	FUNDED DEBT OUTSTANDING DECEMBER 31	OWNED MILEAGE DECEMBER 31	FUNDED DEBT PER MILE
1916	297 279 761	11 087	26 813
1917	287 969 989	11 297	25 490
1918	286 639 989	11 317	25 328
1919	285 553 458	11 407	25 034
1920	291 072 628	11 475	25 366
1921	289 888 269	11 509	25 188
1922	287 722 594	11 600	24 803
1923	275 958 984	11 608	23 773
1924	275 933 159	11 721	23 541
1925	275 906 992	11 845	23 293
1926	277 178 172	12 089	22 927
1927	277 125 920	12 127	22 853
1928	281 751 801	12 195	23 104
1929	311 575 201	12 923	24 110
1930	310 626 335	13 119	23 677
1931	309 698 182	13 260	23 355
1932	309 672 262	13 250	23 371
1933	309 664 262	13 117	23 608
1934	309 660 262	13 013	23 796
1935	309 653 262	12 939	23 931
1936	309 642 556	12 931	23 947
1937	322 870 636	13 217	24 429
1938	325 447 796	13 156	24 738
1939	332 127 036	13 124	25 307
1940	334 522 116	13 113	25 512
1941	323 230 750	13 069	24 734
1942	304 964 750	12 826	23 777
1943	271 317 500	12 813	21 175
1944	243 662 500	12 781	19 064

THE ATCHISON, TOPEKA AND SANTA FE RAILWAY SYSTEM

Common stock outstanding
Dividends and rate declared during each year

YEAR ENDING DECEMBER 31	COMMON STOCK OUTSTANDING DECEMBER 31	DIVIDENDS DECLARED DURING YEAR	RATE
1896	$101 955 500	$ –	–
1897	101 955 500	–	–
1898	101 955 500	–	–
1899	101 955 500	–	–
1900	101 955 500	–	–
1901	101 955 500	3 568 443	3½%
1902	101 955 500	4 078 220	4%
1903	101 955 500	4 078 220	4%
1904	101 955 500	4 078 220	4%
1905	101 955 500	4 078 220	4%
1906	102 709 500	4 605 448	4½%
1907	102 956 500	6 177 390	6%
1908	102 956 500	5 147 825	5%
1909	160 673 500	7 293 243	5½%
1910	165 518 500	9 898 980	6%
1911	169 325 500	10 044 795	6%
1912	173 403 500	10 235 445	6%
1913	194 486 500	11 085 000	6%
1914	196 467 500	11 745 420	6%
1915	209 749 500	12 093 945	6%
1916	216 577 500	12 813 750	6%
1917	220 455 500	16 486 403	7½%
1918	221 785 500	13 289 595	6%
1919	222 873 500	13 351 695	6%
1920	224 715 500	13 441 110	6%
1921	225 397 500	13 518 420	6%
1922	227 052 500	13 605 660	6%
1923	232 418 500	13 909 245	6%
1924	232 409 500	14 525 594	6¼%
1925	232 409 500	16 268 665	7%

THE ATCHISON, TOPEKA AND SANTA FE RAILWAY SYSTEM

Common stock outstanding
Dividends and rate declared during each year (Continued)

YEAR ENDING DECEMBER 31	COMMON STOCK OUTSTANDING DECEMBER 31	DIVIDENDS DECLARED DURING YEAR	RATE
1926	232 409 500	18 011 736	7¾%
1927	232 409 500	23 240 950	10%
1928	241 629 300	24 162 668	10%
1929	241 629 300	24 162 930	10%
1930	242 166 900	24 184 275	10%
1931	242 706 000	21 843 465	9%
1932	242 706 000	2 427 060	1%
1933	242 706 000	–	–
1934	242 706 000	4 854 120	2%
1935	242 706 000	4 854 120	2%
1936	242 706 000	4 854 120	2%
1937	242 706 000	4 854 120	2%
1938	242 706 000	–	–
1939	242 706 000	–	–
1940	242 706 000	2 427 060	1%
1941	242 706 000	7 281 180	3%
1942	242 706 000	15 775 890	6.5%
1943	242 706 000	14 562 360	6%
1944	242 706 000	14 562 360	6%

THE ATCHISON, TOPEKA AND SANTA FE RAILWAY SYSTEM

Preferred Stock Outstanding, Dividends and Rate Declared during each year

YEAR ENDING DECEMBER 31	PREFERRED STOCK OUTSTANDING DECEMBER 31	DIVIDENDS DECLARED DURING YEAR	RATE
1896	$104 999 530	$ –	–
1897	114 175 130	–	–
1898	114 165 700	1 141 657	1%
1899	114 165 700	3 139 557	2¾%
1900	114 173 800	5 708 690	5%
1901	114 173 800	5 708 690	5%
1902	114 173 800	5 708 690	5%
1903	114 173 800	5 708 690	5%
1904	114 173 800	5 708 690	5%
1905	114 173 800	5 708 690	5%
1906	114 173 800	5 708 690	5%
1907	114 173 800	5 708 690	5%
1908	114 173 800	5 708 690	5%
1909	114 173 800	5 708 690	5%
1910	114 173 800	5 708 690	5%
1911	114 173 800	5 708 690	5%
1912	114 173 800	5 708 690	5%
1913	114 173 800	5 708 690	5%
1914	114 173 800	5 708 690	5%
1915	124 173 700	5 958 684	5%
1916	124 173 700	6 208 685	5%
1917	124 173 700	6 208 685	5%
1918	124 173 700	6 208 685	5%
1919	124 173 700	6 208 685	5%
1920	124 173 700	6 208 685	5%
1921	124 173 700	6 208 685	5%
1922	124 173 700	6 208 685	5%
1923	124 173 700	6 208 685	5%
1924	124 172 800	6 208 640	5%
1925	124 172 800	6 208 640	5%

THE ATCHISON, TOPEKA AND SANTA FE RAILWAY SYSTEM

Preferred Stock Outstanding, Dividends and Rate Declared during each year (Continued)

YEAR ENDING DECEMBER 31	PREFERRED STOCK OUTSTANDING DECEMBER 31	DIVIDENDS DECLARED DURING YEAR	RATE
1926	124 172 800	6 208 640	5%
1927	124 172 800	6 208 640	5%
1928	124 172 800	6 208 640	5%
1929	124 172 800	6 208 640	5%
1930	124 172 800	6 208 640	5%
1931	124 172 800	6 208 640	5%
1932	124 172 800	6 208 640	5%
1933	124 172 800	5 960 294	4.8%
1934	124 172 800	6 208 640	5%
1935	124 172 800	6 208 640	5%
1936	124 172 800	6 208 640	5%
1937	124 172 800	6 208 640	5%
1938	124 172 800	1 241 728	1%
1939	124 172 800	6 208 640	5%
1940	124 172 800	6 208 640	5%
1941	124 172 800	6 208 640	5%
1942	124 172 800	6 208 640	5%
1943	124 172 800	6 208 640	5%
1944	124 172 800	6 208 640	5%

THE ATCHISON, TOPEKA AND SANTA FE RAILWAY SYSTEM

Investment in Road and Equipment and Material and Supplies and Net Railway Operating Income and Ratio of latter to former. Years ending December 31, 1896 to 1943 both inclusive.

YEAR ENDING DECEMBER 31	ROAD & EQUIPMENT* AND MATERIALS & SUPPLIES TOTAL	NET RAILWAY OPERATING INCOME	RATE OF RETURN ON INVESTMENT
1896	374 547 622 42	6 572 467 18	1.75
1897	391 081 523 83	7 470 472 94	1.91
1898	397 665 714 30	9 152 149 99	2.30
1899	401 658 162 68	14 104 529 88	3.51
1900	410 536 037 98	18 476 340 57	4.50
1901	426 145 587 45	22 691 175 45	5.32
1902	442 447 740 83	22 464 756 44	5.08
1903	451 879 972 31	23 410 298 47	5.18
1904	462 682 281 89	21 635 564 59	4.68
1905	474 289 414 19	22 866 266 83	4.82
1906	519 130 216 05	30 007 446 80	5.78
1907	555 532 907 03	28 024 455 26	5.04
1908	561 826 874 75	30 061 258 78	5.35
1909	574 983 473 23	33 144 173 92	5.76
1910	625 612 063 71	31 472 700 93	5.03
1911	632 018 849 72	30 465 424 03	4.82
1912	658 419 707 15	34 108 200 92	5.18
1913	680 355 903 66	32 695 232 01	4.81
1914	689 025 375 07	34 187 998 31	4.96
1915	699 890 309 15	37 915 128 20	5.42
1916	711 472 225 87	48 328 636 36	6.79
1917	732 549 685 80	47 219 419 57	6.45
1918	756 743 056 80	40 850 206 73	5.40
1919	777 719 984 96	38 035 650 57	4.89
1920	811 464 910 14	37 380 590 56	4.61

* Charge to Accounts 701 Road and Equipment Property and 702 Improvements on Leased Property including donated property credited to Account 702½B Donations and Grants.

THE ATCHISON, TOPEKA AND SANTA FE RAILWAY SYSTEM

Investment in Road and Equipment and Material and Supplies and Net Railway Operating Income and Ratio of latter to former. Years ending December 31, 1896 to 1943 both inclusive. (Continued)

YEAR ENDING DECEMBER 31	ROAD & EQUIPMENT* AND MATERIALS & SUPPLIES TOTAL	NET RAILWAY OPERATING INCOME	RATE OF RETURN ON INVESTMENT
1921	839 570 685 28	41 268 307 35	4.92
1922	854 510 383 62	40 003 402 02	4.68
1923	907 046 747 04	46 362 271 79	5.11
1924	950 249 627 84	47 283 278 92	4.98
1925	971 921 813 72	53 666 692 42	5.52
1926	1 007 499 507 95	66 078 881 03	6.56
1927	1 048 249 983 42	54 603 104 49	5.21
1928	1 077 045 874 73	55 332 525 98	5.14
1929	1 124 433 257 45	68 652 330 71	6.11
1930	1 166 266 808 50	44 876 466 42	3.85
1931	1 176 302 760 81	31 449 273 69	2.67
1932	1 174 631 133 40	17 659 793 45	1.50
1933	1 169 275 731 65	13 961 760 41	1.19
1934	1 156 038 334 21	15 229 318 58	1.32
1935	1 148 891 957 00	15 703 352 26	1.37
1936	1 153 954 285 97	18 501 903 57	1.60
1937	1 183 967 892 74	17 077 110 60	1.44
1938	1 183 127 270 02	18 026 118 09	1.52
1939	1 177 808 036 17	19 170 865 58	1.63
1940	1 186 169 036 41	24 017 624 55	2.02
1941	1 214 558 831 24	40 546 790 03	3.34
1942	1 221 655 075 52	83 547 609 35	6.84
1943	1 251 976 256 36	65 839 747 88	5.26
1944	1 307 110 060 71	60 178 927 59	4.60
Average	834 121 243 73	33 913 836 77	4.07

* Charge to Accounts 701 Road and Equipment Property and 702 Improvements on Leased Property including donated property credited to Account 702½B Donations and Grants.

APPENDI

CHRONOLOGICAL DEVELOPMENT OF TH

Year	Termini		Road Miles	Date Construction Company Incorporated	Originally Opened for Operation
	From	To			
(1)	(2)	(3)	(4)	(5)	(6)
1859			None	2-11-59	
1863			None	2-11-59	
1869	Topeka, Kans	Burlingame, Kans	26.67	2-11-59	9-23-6
1870	Burlingame, Kans	Emporia, Kans	33.65	2-11-59	7-25-7
1871	Emporia, Kans	Newton, Kans	73.60	2-11-59	7-17-7
1872	Atchison, Kans	Topeka, Kans	50.46	2-11-59	5-25-7
	Newton, Kans	Hutchinson, Kans	32.00	2-11-59	7-17-7
	Hutchinson, Kans	Great Bend, Kans	51.00	2-11-59	8-5-7
	Great Bend, Kans	Larned, Kans	22.00	2-11-59	8-12-7
	Larned, Kans	Dodge City, Kans	62.00	2-11-59	9-19-7
	Newton, Kans	Wichita, Kans	27.12	6-22-71	5-13-7
1873	Dodge City, Kans	Colo State Line	116.04	2-11-59	2-20-7
	Kansas State Line	Granada, Colo	10.83	7-5-73	7-7-7
1875	Lawrence, Kans	Corliss(De Soto Jct)	16.52	7-20-65	..-..-6
	Topeka, Kans	Lawrence, Kans	26.36	12-2-68	6-13-7
	Missouri St Line	Corliss, Kans	21.90	5-29-73	9-29-7
	KC Union Depot, Mo	Kans-Mo State Line	1.28	9-29-75	..-..-7
	Granada, Colo	Las Animas, Colo	54.62	3-24-75	9-13-7
1876	Las Animas, Colo	Pueblo, Colo	85.34	9-29-75	3-5-7
1877	Corliss, Kans (Cedar Jct)	Pleasant Hill, Mo	44.82	11-14-70	1-..-7
	Florence, Kans	Eldorado, Kans	29.32	3-10-77	8-1-7

VIII

ATCHISON TOPEKA AND SANTA FE RAILWAY SYSTEM

Name of Construction Company	Acquired by The AT&SF Ry Co (1)				Disposed of
	By Construction	By Lease Contract Control or Consolidation	Purchased or Merged	Reference Notes	A—Abandoned S—Sold *—Lease terminated #—Leased to others
(7)	(8)	(9)	(10)	(11)	(12)
Atchison & Topeka (Name changed—Nov. 24, 1863)					
Atchison, Topeka & Santa Fe					
Atchison, Topeka & Santa Fe	9-23-69			O	
Atchison, Topeka & Santa Fe	7-25-70			O	
Atchison, Topeka & Santa Fe	7-17-71			O	
Atchison, Topeka & Santa Fe	5-25-72			O	
Atchison, Topeka & Santa Fe	7-17-72			O	
Atchison, Topeka & Santa Fe	8-5-72			O	
Atchison, Topeka & Santa Fe	8-12-72			O	
Atchison, Topeka & Santa Fe	9-19-72			O	
Wichita & South Western		5-13-72	4-10-01	L	
Atchison, Topeka & Santa Fe	2-20-73			O	
Colorado & New Mexico		7-7-73	1-19-00	L	
St Louis, Lawrence & Denver		10-1-75	2-15-99	L	
Lawrence & Topeka		10-1-75	2-15-99	L	
Kansas Midland		10-1-75	2-15-99	L	
Kansas City, Topeka & Western		10-1-75	2-15-99	L	
Pueblo & Arkansas Val		9-13-75	1-19-00	L	
Pueblo & Arkansas Val		3-5-76	1-19-00	L	
St Louis, Lawrence & Denver		3-6-77		L	10-15-84(S)
Florence, El Dor & Wal Val		8-1-77	4-10-01	L	9-22-42(A)

CHRONOLOGICAL DEVELOPMENT OF TH[E]

Year	Termini		Road Miles	Date Construction Company Incorporated	Originally Opened for Operation
	From	To			
(1)	(2)	(3)	(4)	(5)	(6)
1878	La Junta, Colo	Trinidad, Colo	80.50	9-29-75	9-1-7
	Trinidad, Colo	New Mex State Line	15.69	9-12-78	12-7-7
	Denver and Rio Grande Ry Co (Leased 12-14-78; Dispossessed by D&R(				
	Denver, Colo	Colo. Springs, Colo	75.00	10-27-70	10-26-7
	Colo Sprgs, Colo	Pueblo, Colo	44.60	10-27-70	6-15-7
	Pueblo, Colo	Florence, Colo	32.80	10-27-70	10-31-7
	Coal Creek Jct, Colo	Coal Creek, Colo	2.60	10-27-70	..-..-7
	Florence, Colo	Canyon City, Colo	8.40	10-27-70	7-6-7
	Pueblo, Colo	Cucharas, Colo	43.00	10-27-70	2-22-7
	Cucharas, Colo	El Moro, Colo	43.70	10-27-70	4-20-7
	Cucharas, Colo	La Veta, Colo	21.60	10-27-70	..-..-7
	La Veta, Colo	Garland, Colo	28.60	10-27-70	7-..-7
	El Moro, Colo	Engleville, Colo	6.70	10-27-70	..-..-7
	Garland, Colo	Alamosa, Colo	30.60	10-27-70	..-..-7
1879	Emporia, Kans	Eureka, Kans	47.10	1-23-77	6-30-7
	Colo-New Mex St Ln	Las Vegas, N Mex	118.20	2-6-78	7-4-7
	Florence, Kans	Hillsboro, Kans	20.50	11-5-78	8-25-7
	Wichita, Kans	Mulvane, Kans	15.60	10-28-78	9-15-7
	Mulvane, Kans	Wellington, Kans	31.90	10-28-78	9-15-7
	Hillsboro, Kans	McPherson, Kans	26.80	11-5-78	9-29-7
	Mulvane, Kans	Winfield, Kans	22.70	10-28-78	9-29-7
	Eureka, Kans	So Ln Greenwood Co	16.60	1-23-77	10-10-7
	So Ln Greenwood Co	Howard, Kans	12.16	12-13-78	12-31-7
	Winfield, Kans	Arkansas City, Kans	13.00	10-28-78	12-31-7
	Canyon City, Colo	Texas Creek, Colo	22.30	9-12-78	7-14-7
1880	Las Vegas, N M	Galisteo(Lamy), N M	65.00	2-6-78	2-9-8
	Galisteo(Lamy), N M	Santa Fe, N M	18.00	2-6-78	2-16-8
	Lamy, N M	Albuquerque, N M	67.20	2-6-78	4-15-8
	McPherson, Kans	Lyons, Kans	30.60	11-5-78	6-1-8

TCHISON TOPEKA AND SANTA FE RAILWAY SYSTEM *(Continued)*

Name of Construction Company	Acquired by The AT&SF Ry Co (1)				Disposed of
	By Construction	By Lease Contract Control or Consolidation	Purchased or Merged	Reference Notes	A—Abandoned S—Sold *—Lease terminated #—Leased to others
(7)	(8)	(9)	(10)	(11)	(12)
eblo & Arkansas Val		9-1-78	1-19-00	L	
eblo & Arkansas Val		12-7-78	1-19-00	L	
11-79; Restored by U. S. Court 7-16-79; Receivership 8-14-79).					
enver & Rio Grande		12-14-78		L	8-14-79(*)
enver & Rio Grande		12-14-78		L	8-14-79(*)
enver & Rio Grande		12-14-78		L	8-14-79(*)
enver & Rio Grande		12-14-78		L	8-14-79(*)
enver & Rio Grande		12-14-78		L	8-14-79(*)
enver & Rio Grande		12-14-78		L	8-14-79(*)
enver & Rio Grande		12-14-78		L	8-14-79(*)
enver & Rio Grande		12-14-78		L	8-14-79(*)
enver & Rio Grande		12-14-78		L	8-14-79(*)
enver & Rio Grande		12-14-78		L	8-14-79(*)
enver & Rio Grande		12-14-78		L	8-14-79(*)
nsas City Emp & Southern		6-30-79	4-10-01	L	
w Mex & Southern Pacific		7-4-79	2-15-99	L	
arion & McPherson		8-25-79	4-10-01	L	
wley, Sumner & Fort Smith		9-15-79	4-10-01	L	
wley, Sumner & Fort Smith		9-15-79	4-10-01	L	
arion & McPherson		9-29-79	4-10-01	L	
wley, Sumner & Fort Smith		9-29-79	4-10-01	L	
ns City, Emp & Southern		10-10-79	4-10-01	L	
k & Chautauqua		12-31-79	4-10-01	L	
wley, Sumner & Fort Smith		12-31-79	4-10-01	L	
eblo & Arkansas Val		7-14-79		L	3-27-80(S)
w Mex & Southern Pacific		2-9-80	2-15-99	L	
w Mex & Southern Pacific		2-16-80	2-15-99	L	
w Mex & Southern Pacific		4-15-80	2-15-99	L	
arion & McPherson		6-1-80	4-10-01	L	

CHRONOLOGICAL DEVELOPMENT OF TH

Year	Termini		Road Miles	Date Construction Company Incorporated	Originally Opened for Operation
	From	To			
(1)	(2)	(3)	(4)	(5)	(6)
	Wellington, Kans	Caldwell, Kans	23.30	10-28-78	6-13-8
	Albuquerque, N M	San Marcial, N M	102.50	2-6-78	10-1-8
	Clelland, Colo	Rockvale, Colo	2.83	9-12-78	11-25-8
	Pueblo, Colo	MP 1+3082, Colo	1.56	9-12-78	11-25-8
	MP 1+3082, Colo	MP 24+3000 (Portland)	22.98	9-12-78	11-25-8
	Portland, Colo	Clelland, Colo	8.90	9-12-78	11-25-8
	Burlingame, Kans	Alma, Kans	34.23	9-3-72	8-1-8
	Alma, Kans	Manhattan, Kans	22.39	9-3-72	8-1-8
	Lawrence, Kans	Ottawa, Kans	27.10	2-12-58	1-1-6
	Ottawa, Kans	Richmond, Kans	14.90	2-12-58	12-26-6
	Olathe, Kans	Ottawa Jct, Kans	32.20	3-25-68	8-21-7
	Richmond, Kans	Thayer, Kans	66.60	2-12-58	12-26-7
	Thayer, Kans.	Cherryvale, Kans	15.70	2-12-58	7-17-7
	Cherryvale, Kans	Coffeyville, Kans	18.52	2-12-58	9-3-7
	Cherryvale, Kans	Independence, Kans	9.70	6-26-71	1-1-7
	Independence, Kans	Grenola, Kans	45.30	2-11-79	12-1-7
	Grenola, Kans	Wellington, Kans	58.80	2-11-79	4-1-8
	Wellington, Kans	Hunnewell, Kans	18.32	4-5-80	6-16-8
	Wellington, Kans	Harper, Kans	35.02	2-11-79	9-20-8
	Isleta, N M	Sandia, N M	64.17	7-27-66	12-22-8
	Sandia, N M	Rio Puerco, N M	9.05	7-27-66	12-22-8
	Rio Puerco, N M	Acoma (Anzac), N M	2.08	7-27-66	12-22-8
1881	San Marcial, N M	Rincon, N M	74.00	6-19-80	3-1-8
	Rincon, N M	Deming, N M	53.95	6-19-80	3-1-8
	Rincon, N M	Texas St Line, N M	56.35	4-18-81	7-1-8
	Tex-NM St Ln Tex	El Paso, Tex	20.15	10-28-80	7-1-8
	El Dorado, Kans	Douglas, Kans	24.27	3-10-77	8-1-8
	Lyons, Kans	E. Ln Barton Co, Kans	15.64	11-5-78	9-1-8
	E Ln Barton Co, Kans	Ellinwood, Kans	5.21	1-1-81	9-1-8

TCHISON TOPEKA AND SANTA FE RAILWAY SYSTEM *(Continued)*

Name of Construction Company	Acquired by The AT&SF Ry Co (1)				Disposed of
	By Construction	By Lease Contract Control or Consolidation	Purchased or Merged	Reference Notes	A—Abandoned S—Sold *—Lease terminated #—Leased to others
(7)	(8)	(9)	(10)	(11)	(12)
owley, Sumner & Fort Smith		6-13-80	4-10-01	L	10-31-18(A)
ew Mex & Southern Pacific		10-1-80	2-15-99	L	
ueblo & Arkansas Val		11-25-80	1-19 00	L	
ueblo & Arkansas Val		11-25-80	1-19-00	L	
ueblo & Arkansas Val		11-25-80	1-19-00	L	6-3-21(A)
ueblo & Arkansas Val		11-25-80	1-19-00	L	
an, Alma & Burlingame		8-1-80	4-1-99	J	
an, Alma & Burlingame		8-1-80	4-1-99	J	4-18-98(S)
'worth, Lawrence & Gal		12-15-80	2-15-99	C-1	
'worth, Lawrence & Gal		12-15-80	2-15-99	C-1	
ansas City & Santa Fe		12-15-80	2-15-99	C-1	
worth, Lawrence & Gal		12-15-80	2-15-99	C-1	
worth, Lawrence & Gal		12-15-80	2-15-99	C-1	
worth, Lawrence & Gal		12-15-80	2-15-99	C-1	
uthern Kansas		12-15-80	2-15-99	C-1	
uthern Kansas & Western		12-15-80	2-15-99	C-1	
uthern Kansas & Western		12-15-80	2-15-99	C-1	
mner County		12-15-80	2-15-99	C-1	
uthern Kansas & Western		12-15-80	2-15-99	C-1	
lantic & Pacific		12-22-80	7-1-02	C-2	
lantic & Pacific		12-22-80	7-1-02	C-2	11-..-13(A)
lantic & Pacific		12-22-80	7-1-02	C-2	
o Grande, Mex & Pacific		3-1-81	2-15-99	L	
o Grande, Mex & Pacific		3-1-81	2-15-99	L	
o Grande, Mex & Pacific		7-1-81	2-15-99	L	
o Grande & El Paso		7-1-81		L	
orence, El Dor & Wal Val		8-1-81	4-10-01	L	
arion & McPherson		9-1-81	4-10-01	L	
arion & McPherson Exten		9-1-81	4-10-01	L	

CHRONOLOGICAL DEVELOPMENT OF TH

Year	Termini		Road Miles	Date Construction Company Incorporated	Originally Opened for Operation
	From	To			
(1)	(2)	(3)	(4)	(5)	(6)
	Sedgwick, Kans	Halstead, Kans	8.89	12-6-80	12-31-8
	Burlington Jct, Kans	Burlington, Kans	41.40	2-4-70	4-1-7
	Anzac (Acoma), N M	Pinta, Ariz	117.00	7-27-66	7-1-8
1882	Dillon, N M	Dillon Canon (Blossburg), N M	3.47	1-16-82	1-1-8
	San Antonio, N M	Carthage, N M	9.64	1-16-82	4-1-8
	Las Vegas, N M	Hot Springs, N M	9.02	1-16-82	4-9-8
	Leavenworth, Kans	Meriden Jct, Kans	46.30	6-20-79	11-1-8
	Olathe, Kans	Waseca Jct (Holliday)	14.10	6-18-81	6-1-8
	Pinta, Ariz	Canyon Diablo, Ariz	112.00	7-27-66	7-1-8
	Canyon Diablo, Ariz	Yampai, Ariz	137.00	7-27-66	12-31-8
	Sonora System				
	Benson, Ariz	Nogales, Ariz	87.78	1-12-82	9-26-8
	Guaymas, Mex	Nogales, Mex	262.41	5-1-79	10-25-8
	Southern California Lines				
	National City, Cal	Fallbrook Jct, Cal	49.65	10-23-80	1-2-8
	Fallbrook Jct, Cal	Fallbrook, Cal	17.00	10-23-80	1-2-8
	Fallbrook, Cal	Temecula, Cal	10.72	10-23-80	3-22-8
	Temecula, Cal	Elsinore, Cal	14.80	10-23-80	8-21-8
	Elsinore, Cal	Perris, Cal	12.00	10-23-80	8-21-8
	Perris, Cal	Colton, Cal	21.70	10-23-80	8-21-8
1883	Yampai, Ariz	(Beg Colo (River C/L, Ariz	103.28	7-27-66	5-20-8
	Beg. Colo River Ln Chg, Ariz	E. E. Old Bridge, Ariz	9.72	7-27-66	5-20-8
	E. E. Old Brdg, Ariz	End Colo R Ln Ch, Cal	0.28	12-18-74	10-21-8
	End of Ln Ch, Cal	Needles, Cal	2.40	12-18-74	4-18-8
	Southern California Lines				
	Colton, Cal	San Bernardino, Cal	3.50	10-23-80	9-13-8

'CHISON TOPEKA AND SANTA FE RAILWAY SYSTEM *(Continued)*

Name of Construction Company	Acquired by The AT&SF Ry Co (1)				Disposed of
	By Construction	By Lease Contract Control or Consolidation	Purchased or Merged	Reference Notes	A—Abandoned S—Sold *—Lease terminated #—Leased to others
(7)	(8)	(9)	(10)	(11)	(12)
'vey County		12-31-81		L	12-15-95(A)
ıs City, Burl & Santa Fe		4-1-81	2-15-99	C-1	
ıntic & Pacific		7-1-81	7-1-02	C-2	
v Mexican		1-1-82	2-15-99	L	
v Mexican		4-1-82		L	2-20-96(A)
v Mexican		4-9-82	2-15-99	L	12-31-37(A)
orth, Topeka & S-Western		11-1-82		J	9-17-17(S)
sas City & Olathe		6-1-82	2-15-99	C-1	
ntic & Pacific		7-1-82	7-1-02	C-2	
ntic & Pacific		12-31-82	7-1-02	C-2	
' Mexico & Arizona		9-26-82		C-3	6-30-97(#)
ɒra, Ltd		10-25-82		C-3	6-30-97(#)
:ornia Southern		1-2-82	1-17-06	C-6	
:ornia Southern		1-2-82	1-17-06	C-6	
'ornia Southern		3-22-82		C-6	1-28-92(A)
'ornia Southern		8-21-82	1-17-06	C-6	2-1-35(A)
ornia Southern		8-21-82	1-17-06	C-6	2-15-27(A)
ornia Southern		8-21-82	1-17-06	C-6	
ıtic & Pacific		5-20-83	7-1-02	C-2	
ıtic & Pacific		5-20-83		C-2	1890(A)
ıern Pacific		10-21-83		C-4	1890(A)
ıern Pacific		10-21-83		C-5	
ɒrnia Southern		9-13-83	1-17-06	C-6	

CHRONOLOGICAL DEVELOPMENT OF TH

Year	Termini		Road Miles	Date Construction Company Incorporated	Originally Opened for Operation
	From	To			
(1)	(2)	(3)	(4)	(5)	(6)
1884	Nutt, N M	Lake Valley, N M	13.31	1-16-82	4-1-
	Deming, N M	Silver City, N M	46.55	3-23-82	7-1-
	Wichita, Kans	Kingman, Kans	44.93	5-17-83	10-1
	Chanute, Kans	Walnut, Kans	24.28	6-1-83	1-1
	Walnut, Kans	Girard, Kans	16.00	6-17-81	5-1
	Ottawa, Kans	Emporia, Kans	54.19	12-11-80	2-1
	Harper, Kans	Attica, Kans	11.46	7-1-84	11-10
	Needles, Cal	Barstow, Cal	170.53	12-18-74	4-16
	Barstow, Cal	Mojave, Cal	71.97	12-18-74	10-. .
1885	Socorro, N M	Magdalena, N M	27.34	1-16-82	1-1
	Attica, Kans	Kiowa, Kans	22.41	4-16-85	8-6
	Southern California Lines				
	San Bernardino, Cal	Barstow, Cal	80.73	1-10-82	11-15
1886	Douglas, Kans	Winfield, Kans	19.14	3-10-77	11-1
	Attica, Kans	Medicine Lodge, Kans	21.26	4-16-85	1-11
	Osage City, Kans	Quenemo, Kans	20.41	5-31-86	8-1
	Southern California Lines				
	Highgrove (Citro), Cal	Riverside, Cal	3.30	9-29-85	1-
	Riverside, Cal	Arlington, Cal	6.70	9-29-85	3-1
	Pekin, Ill	Pekin Jct, Ill	21.29	2-24-59	1-
	Streator Jct, Ill	Ancona, Ill	30.71	2-24-59	1-
	Mazon River, Ill	Ancona, Ill	28.00	2-24-59	5-2
	Chicago (Crawf'd Av)	Mazon Riv, Ill	60.16	5-15-82	1-
	Gulf, Colorado and Santa Fe Railway Company				
	Galveston, Tex	Arcola, Tex	42.15	6-6-73	[illegible]
	Arcola, Tex	Richmond, Tex	20.85	6-6-73	10-1
	Richmond, Tex	Sealy, Tex	31.20	4-19-79	12-3
	Sealy, Tex	Brenham, Tex	31.50	4-19-79	8-
	Brenham, Tex	Milano, Tex	48.10	4-19-79	11-

TCHISON TOPEKA AND SANTA FE RAILWAY SYSTEM *(Continued)*

Name of Construction Company	Acquired by The AT&SF Ry Co (1)				Disposed of
	By Construction	By Lease Contract Control or Consolidation	Purchased or Merged	Reference Notes	A—Abandoned S—Sold *—Lease terminated #—Leased to others
(7)	(8)	(9)	(10)	(11)	(12)
:w Mexican		4-1-84	2-15-99	L	12-1-34(A)
City, Deming & Pacific		7-1-84	2-15-99	L	
ichita & Western		10-1-84	12-31-98	J	
nsas Southern		1-1-84	2-15-99	C-1	
br, Topeka, Iola & Mem		1-1-84	2-15-99	C-1	
nsas City & Emporia		2-1-84	2-15-99	C-1	
rper & Western		11-10-84	2-15-99	C-1	
ithern Pacific		10-1-84		C-5	
ithern Pacific		10-1-84		C-5	
w Mexican		1-1-85	2-15-99	L	
ithern Kansas		8-6-85	2-15-99	C-1	
ifornia Southern		11-15-85	1-17-06	C-6	
rence, El Dor & Wal Val		11-1-86	4-10-01	L	
ithern Kansas		1-11-86	2-15-99	C-1	
cago, Kansas & Western		8-1-86	4-10-01	C-7	12-14-33(A)
er, Santa Ana & Los Ang		1-8-86	1-17-06	C-8	
er, Santa Ana & Los Ang		3-15-86	1-17-06	C-8	
cago, Pekin & S'western		12-15-86	6-1-00	C-14	
cago, Pekin & S'western		12-15-86	6-1-00	C-14	
cago, Pekin & S'western		12-15-86	6-1-00	C-14	
cago, St Louis & Western		12-15-86	6-1-00	C-14	
f, Colorado & Santa Fe		5-15-86		C-9	
:, Colorado & Santa Fe		5-15-86		C-9	
f, Colorado & Santa Fe		5-15-86		C-9	
:, Colorado & Santa Fe		5-15-86		C-9	
, Colorado & Santa Fe		5-15-86		C-9	

CHRONOLOGICAL DEVELOPMENT OF TH

Year	Termini From	Termini To	Road Miles	Date Construction Company Incorporated	Originally Opened for Operation
(1)	(2)	(3)	(4)	(5)	(6)
	Milano, Tex	Rogers, Tex	30.30	4-19-79	12-9
	Rogers, Tex	Temple, Tex	13.40	4-19-79	2-..
	Temple, Tex	Belton, Tex	8.20	4-19-79	3-1
	Temple, Tex	Valley Mills, Tex	41.00	4-19-79	8-31
	Valley Mills, Tex	Morgan, Tex	29.00	4-19-79	8-31
	Morgan, Tex	Kopperl, Tex	8.00	4-19-79	9-7
	Kopperl, Tex	Cleburne, Tex	22.00	4-19-79	10-21
	Cleburne, Tex	Ft Worth, Tex	28.00	4-19-79	12-8
	Belton, Tex	Lampasas, Tex	48.00	4-19-79	5-15
	Cleburne, Tex	Dallas, Tex	53.33	9-16-80	8-1
	Alvin, Tex	Houston, Tex	25.66	4-19-79	5-1
	Somerville, Tex	Navasota, Tex	28.60	4-19-79	6-1
	Navasota, Tex	Montgomery Jct, Tex	26.45	12-29-77	..-..
	Montgomery Jct, Tex	Montgomery, Tex	0.95	12-29-77	..-..
	Montgomery Jct, Tex	Conroe, Tex	17.59	4-19-79	9-
	Lampasas, Tex	Goldthwaite, Tex	36.00	4-19-79	9-
	Goldthwaite, Tex	Brownwood, Tex	35.00	4-19-79	12-3
	Brownwood, Tex	Coleman Jct, Tex	23.74	4-19-79	4-
	Coleman Jct, Tex	Coleman, Tex	6.26	4-19-79	4-
	Coleman Jct, Tex	Ballinger, Tex	37.50	4-19-79	4-
	Dallas Jct, Tex	Farmersville, Tex	36.60	4-19-79	11-
	Farmersville, Tex	Ladonia, Tex	30.50	4-19-79	12-3
	Ladonia, Tex	Honey Grove, Tex	11.80	4-19-79	12-3
	Ft Worth, Tex	Gainesville, Tex	64.40	4-19-79	12-3
1887	Howard, Kans	Moline, Kans	8.22	10-6-82	1-
	Denver Circle		9.67	11-16-80	2-1
	Pueblo, Colo	Denver, Colo	116.36	3-22-87	10-
	Wilder, Kans	Cummings Jct, Kans	46.19	10-24-85	11
	Kingman, Kans	Pratt, Kans	34.86	9-11-85	7-1

Name of Construction Company	Acquired by The AT&SF Ry Co (1)				Disposed of
	By Construction	By Lease Contract Control or Consolidation	Purchased or Merged	Reference Notes	A—Abandoned S—Sold *—Lease terminated #—Leased to others
(7)	(8)	(9)	(10)	(11)	(12)
ulf, Colorado & Santa Fe		5-15-86		C-9	
ulf, Colorado & Santa Fe		5-15-86		C-9	
ulf, Colorado & Santa Fe		5-15-86		C-9	
ulf, Colorado & Santa Fe		5-15-86		C-9	
ulf, Colorado & Santa Fe		5-15-86		C-9	
ulf, Colorado & Santa Fe		5-15-86		C-9	
ulf, Colorado & Santa Fe		5-15-86		C-9	
ulf, Colorado & Santa Fe		5-15-86		C-9	
ulf, Colorado & Santa Fe		5-15-86		C-9	
icago, Tex & Mex Central		5-15-86		C-9	
ulf, Colorado & Santa Fe		5-15-86		C-9	
ulf, Colorado & Santa Fe		5-15-86		C-9	
ntral & Montgomery		5-15-86		C-9	
ntral & Montgomery		5-15-86		C-9	
lf, Colorado & Santa Fe		5-15-86		C-9	
lf, Colorado & Santa Fe		5-15-86		C-9	
lf, Colorado & Santa Fe		5-15-86		C-9	
lf, Colorado & Santa Fe		5-15-86		C-9	
lf, Colorado & Santa Fe		5-15-86		C-9	
lf, Colorado & Santa Fe		8-1-86		C-9	
lf, Colorado & Santa Fe		11-1-86		C-9	
lf, Colorado & Santa Fe		12-31-86		C-9	
lf, Colorado & Santa Fe		12-31-86		C-9	7-10-38(A)
lf, Colorado & Santa Fe		12-31-86		C-9	
ıs City, Emp & Southern		1-1-87	4-10-01	L	
ıver Circle		6-3-87		L	5-..-98(A)
ıver & Santa Fe		10-1-87	1-19-00	L	
vorth, North'n & South'n		11-1-87	2-15-99	L	
gman, Pratt & Western		7-12-87	12-31-98	J	

CHRONOLOGICAL DEVELOPMENT OF TH

Year	Termini		Road Miles	Date Construction Company Incorporated	Originally Opened for Operation
	From	To			
(1)	(2)	(3)	(4)	(5)	(6)
	Pratt, Kans	W Ln Kiowa Co, Kans	44.85	9-11-85	7-12-
	Arkansas City, Kans	Purcell, Okla	154.48	4-16-85	6-12-
	Girard, Kans	Frontenac, Kans	12.39	4-16-85	6-12-
	Kiowa, Kans	Okla-Tex Ln	116.35	4-16-85	9-12-
	Hutchinson, Kans	Kinsley, Kans	84.43	5-31-86	1-1-
	Chanute, Kans	Longton, Kans	44.54	5-31-86	1-1-
	Independence, Kans	Havana, Kans	17.10	5-31-86	1-1-
	Havana, Kans	Cedarvale, Kans	38.73	5-31-86	1-1-
	Burlington, Kans	Gridley, Kans	11.05	5-31-86	5-1-
	Colony, Kans	Yates Center, Kans	25.10	5-31-86	8-1-
	Great Bend, Kans	Scott City, Kans	120.59	5-31-86	9-1-
	Scott City, Kans	Selkirk, Kans	35.23	5-31-86	9-1-
	Augusta, Kans	Mulvane, Kans	20.80	5-31-86	10-1-
	Benedict Jct, Kans	Virgil, Kans	30.19	5-31-86	10-1-
	Virgil, Kans	Madison Jct, Kans	10.92	5-31-86	10-1-
	Mulvane, Kans	Viola, Kans	21.00	5-31-86	10-1-
	Viola, Kans	E Ln Clark Co, Kans	117.03	5-31-86	10-1-
	E Ln Clark Co, Kans	Englewood, Kans	28.25	7-28-86	10-1
	Larned, Kans	Jetmore, Kans	46.80	5-31-86	10-1
	Bazar, Kans	Gladstone, Kans	6.57	5-31-86	10-1
	Gladstone, Kans	Ellinor, Kans	3.23	5-31-86	10-1
	Gladstone, Kans	Strong City, Kans	5.01	5-31-86	10-1
	Strong City, Kans	Neva(Evans), Kans	5.94	5-31-86	10-1
	Neva, Kans	Concordia, Kans	114.17	5-31-86	11-15
	Abilene, Kans	MP 10+390, Kans	10.19	5-31-86	11-15
	MP 10+390, Kans	Salina, Kans	10.57	5-31-86	11-15
	Abilene, Kans		1.95	5-31-86	11-15
	Little River, Kans	Holyrood, Kans	30.27	5-31-86	12-31
	Ancona, Ill	Mississippi River	136.85	12-4-86	12-17

TCHISON TOPEKA AND SANTA FE RAILWAY SYSTEM *(Continued)*

Name of Construction Company	Acquired by The AT&SF Ry Co (1)				Disposed of
	By Construction	By Lease Contract Control or Consolidation	Purchased or Merged	Reference Notes	A—Abandoned S—Sold *—Lease terminated #—Leased to others
(7)	(8)	(9)	(10)	(11)	(12)
ingman, Pratt & Western		7-12-87	12-31-98	J	12-10-95(A)
outhern Kansas		6-12-87	2-15-99	C-1	
uthern Kansas		6-12-87	2-15-99	C-1	
uthern Kansas		9-12-87	2-15-99	C-1	
icago, Kansas & Western		1-1-87	4-10-01	C-7	
icago, Kansas & Western		1-1-87	4-10-01	C-7	
icago, Kansas & Western		1-1-87	4-10-01	C-7	
icago, Kansas & Western		1-1-87	4-10-01	C-7	12-9-38(A)
icago, Kansas & Western		5-1-87	4-10-01	C-7	
icago, Kansas & Western		8-1-87	4-10-01	C-7	11-27-33(A)
icago, Kansas & Western		9-1-87	4-10-01	C-7	
icago, Kansas & Western		9-1-87	4-10-01	C-7	5-3-96(A)
icago, Kansas & Western		10-1-87	4-10-01	C-7	
icago, Kansas & Western		10-1-87	4-10-01	C-7	5-1-44(A)
icago, Kansas & Western		10-1-87	4-10-01	C-7	
icago, Kansas & Western		10-1-87	4-10-01	C-7	8-15-37(A)
icago, Kansas & Western		10-1-87	4-10-01	C-7	
uthern Kans & Panhandle		10-1-87	4-10-01	C-7	
icago, Kansas & Western		10-1-87	4-10-01	C-7	
icago, Kansas & Western		10-1-87	4-10-01	C-7	
icago, Kansas & Western		10-1-87	4-10-01	C-7	1899-1900(A)
icago, Kansas & Western		10-1-87	4-10-01	C-7	
icago, Kansas & Western		10-1-87	4-10-01	C-7	1900-01(A)
icago, Kansas & Western		11-15-87	4-10-01	C-7	
icago, Kansas & Western		11-15-87	4-10-01	C-7	7-1-16(A)
icago, Kansas & Western		11-15-87	4-10-01	C-7	1-8-35(A)
icago, Kansas & Western		11-15-87	4-10-01	C-7	
icago, Kansas & Western		12-31-87	4-10-01	C-7	
icago, Santa Fe & Calif		12-17-87	6-1-00	C-14	

CHRONOLOGICAL DEVELOPMENT OF TH

Year	Termini: From	Termini: To	Road Miles	Date Construction Company Incorporated	Originally Opened for Operation
(1)	(2)	(3)	(4)	(5)	(6)
	Mississippi Riv Brdg		0.61	10-23-86	12-17-
	Mississippi Riv Brdg	Iowa-Mo St Line	19.79	12-13-86	12-31-
	Iowa-Mo St Line	Sibley Brdg, Mo	173.18	12-13-86	12-31-
	St Louis, Mo	Union, Mo	55.24	12-20-84	18
	Bonner, Mo	Dripping Springs, Mo	1.70	12-20-84	18
	Panhandle and Santa Fe Railway Company				
	Okla-Tex Ln	Canadian, Tex	27.97	11-2-86	9-12-
	Canadian, Tex	Miami, Tex	22.24	11-2-86	11-15-
	Gulf Colorado and Santa Fe Railway Company				
	Ladonia, Tex	Paris, Tex	32.00	4-19-79	18
	Gainesville, Tex	Red River, Tex	6.90	4-19-79	6-12-
	Red River, Tex	Purcell, Okla	100.00	4-19-70	6-12-
	Cleburne, Tex	Weatherford, Tex	41.73	4-19-79	18
	Southern California Lines				
	Los Angeles, Cal	Pasadena, Cal	8.70	9-5-83	9-17-
	Pasadena, Cal	Olivewood, Cal	1.30	9-5-83	10-1-
	Olivewood, Cal	Lamanda Park, Cal	2.10	9-5-83	11-7-
	Lamanda Park, Cal	Duarte, Cal	7.80	9-5-83	11-5-
	Duarte, Cal	San Gabriel Riv, Cal	1.19	5-20-87	5-31-
	San Bernardino, Cal	San Gabriel Riv, Cal	38.88	5-20-87	5-31-
	Arlington, Cal	Rincon(Prado), Cal	12.80	5-20-87	6-27-
	Rincon(Prado), Cal	Orange, Cal	18.10	5-20-87	9-15-
	Orange, Cal	Santa Ana, Cal	2.03	5-20-87	9-15-
	Los Angeles, Cal	Redondo Jct, Cal (Ballona Jct)	2.00	5-20-87	9-23-
	Ballona Jct, Cal	Inglewood, Cal	9.72	5-20-87	9-23-
	Inglewood, Cal	Santa Monica Jct (Mesmer), Cal	2.79	5-20-87	9-23
	Santa Monica Jct, Cal	Pt Ballona, Cal	2.59	5-20-87	9-23

.TCHISON TOPEKA AND SANTA FE RAILWAY SYSTEM *(Continued)*

Name of Construction Company	Acquired by The AT&SF Ry Co (1)				Disposed of
	By Construction	By Lease Contract Control or Consolidation	Purchased or Merged	Reference Notes	A—Abandoned S—Sold *—Lease terminated #—Leased to others
(7)	(8)	(9)	(10)	(11)	(12)
iss Riv Rd & Toll Br		12-17-87	6-1-00	C-14	
hicago, Santa Fe & Calif of Iowa		12-31-87	6-1-00	C-14	
hicago, Santa Fe & Calif of Iowa		12-31-87	6-1-00	C-14	
Louis, Kans City & Colo		1887		C-10	12-14-99(S)
Louis, Kans City & Colo		1887		C-10	12-14-99(S)
outhern Kansas, of Texas		9-12-87		C-11	
outhern Kansas, of Texas		11-15-87		C-11	
ulf, Colorado & Santa Fe		1887		C-9	
ulf, Colorado & Santa Fe		6-12-87		C-9	
ulf, Colorado & Santa Fe		6-12-87		C-9	
ulf, Colorado & Santa Fe		1887		C-9	
os Ang & San Gabriel Val		5-31-87	1-17-06	C-12	
os Ang & San Gabriel Val		5-31-87	1-17-06	C-12	
os Ang & San Gabriel Val		5-31-87	1-17-06	C-12	
os Ang & San Gabriel Val		5-31-87	1-17-06	C-12	
alifornia Central		5-31-87	1-17-06	C-12	
alifornia Central		5-31-87	1-17-06	C-12	
alifornia Central		6-27-87	1-17-06	C-12	
alifornia Central		9-15-87	1-17-06	C-12	
alifornia Central		9-15-87	1-17-06	C-12	
alifornia Central		9-23-87	1-17-06	C-12	
alifornia Central		9-23-87	1-17-06	C-12	
alifornia Central		9-23-87		C-12	1902(S)
alifornia Central		9-23-87		C-12	6-13-92(A)

CHRONOLOGICAL DEVELOPMENT OF TH

Year	Termini From	To	Road Miles	Date Construction Company Incorporated	Originally Opened for Operation
(1)	(2)	(3)	(4)	(5)	(6)
	Santa Ana, Cal	San Juan Capistrano	34.82	5-20-87	11-30-8
	Escondido Jct, Cal	Escondido, Cal	21.30	5-20-87	12-31-8
	San Bernardino, Cal	Mentone, Cal	12.51	5-20-87	12-31-8
1888	Clelland, Colo	Canon City, Colo	6.83	9-12-78	1-1-8
	Rockvale, Colo	Kenwood, Colo	3.51	9-12-78	1-1-8
	Frontenac, Kans	Pittsburg, Kans	8.23	4-16-85	2-17-8
	Manchester, Kans	Barnard, Kans	43.24	5-31-86	1-1-8
	Concordia, Kans	Nebr St Ln, Kans	37.60	5-31-86	10-1-8
	St Joseph, Mo	Winthrop, Mo	18.91	8-8-87	1-7-8
	St Joseph, Mo	Henrietta, Mo	73.07	1-8-68	7-22-7
	Henrietta, Mo	No Lexington, Mo	3.16	1-8-68	7-22-7
	Missouri Riv Brdg		0.76	3-24-87	1-26-8
	Sibley Bridge, Mo	Big Blue Jct, Mo	20.10	12-13-86	1-26-8
	Ashland Ave, Chic, Ill	Crawford Ave, Chic, Ill	2.12	5-11-87	7-1-8
	Big Blue Jct, Mo	Kansas City, Mo	6.44	6-27-82	11-. .-8
	Panhandle and Santa Fe Railway Company				
	Miami, Tex	Panhandle City, Tex	50.20	11-2-86	1-15-8
	Gulf Colorado and Santa Fe Railway Company				
	Ballinger, Tex	San Angelo, Tex	35.24	4-19-79	10-1-8
	Southern California Lines				
	Inglewood, Cal	Redondo, Cal	10.77	4-23-88	4-16-8
	Perris, Cal	San Jacinto, Cal	19.44	5-20-87	4-30-8
	Redondo Jct, Cal	Orange, Cal	29.50	5-20-87	8-12-8
	San Juan Capistrano, Cal	Fallbrook Jct, Cal	14.67	5-20-87	8-12-
1890	Topock (near), Ariz	Beal, Cal	13.06	7-27-66	5-10-
	Atlantic and Pacific Railroad Co—Central Division				
	Seneca, Mo	Vinita, Okla	34.40	7-27-66	18
	Vinita, Okla	Tulsa, Okla	63.90	7-27-66	18

TCHISON TOPEKA AND SANTA FE RAILWAY SYSTEM *(Continued)*

Name of Construction Company	Acquired by The AT&SF Ry Co (1)				Disposed of
	By Construction	By Lease Contract Control or Consolidation	Purchased or Merged	Reference Notes	A—Abandoned S—Sold *—Lease terminated #—Leased to others
(7)	(8)	(9)	(10)	(11)	(12)
California Central		11-30-87	1-17-06	C-12	
California Central		12-31-87	1-17-06	C-12	
California Central		12-31-87	1-17-06	C-12	
Pueblo & Arkansas Val		1-1-88	1-19-00	L	
Pueblo & Arkansas Val		1-1-88	1-19-00	L	
outhern Kansas		2-17-88	2-15-99	C-1	
Chicago, Kansas & Western		1-1-88	4-10-01	C-7	
Chicago, Kansas & Western		1-1-88	4-10-01	C-7	
t Joseph, St Louis & Santa Fe		1-7-88	6-1-00	C-13	1900(A)
t Louis & St Joseph		1-31-88	6-1-00	C-13	
t Louis & St Joseph		1-31-88	6-1-00	C-13	3-31-30(A)
ibley Bridge Co.		1-26-88	6-1-00	C-14	
Chicago, Santa Fe & Calif of Iowa		1-26-88	6-1-00	C-14	
tch, Top & Santa Fe in Chi		7-1-88	3-6-02	C-14	
Kansas City Belt		1-26-88		C-15	2-23-10(S)
outhern Kansas of Texas		1-15-88		C-11	
Gulf, Colorado & Santa Fe		10-1-88		C-9	
Redondo Beach		4-16-88	1-17-06	C-12	
California Central		4-30-88	1-17-06	C-12	
California Central		8-12-88	1-17-06	C-12	
California Central		8-12-88	1-17-06	C-12	
tlantic & Pacific		5-10-90	7-1-02	C-2	
tlantic & Pacific		5-23-90		C-16	6-27-96(S)
tlantic & Pacific		5-23-90		C-16	6-27-96(S)

CHRONOLOGICAL DEVELOPMENT OF THE

Year	Termini: From	Termini: To	Road Miles	Date Construction Company Incorporated	Originally Opened for Operation
(1)	(2)	(3)	(4)	(5)	(6)
	Tulsa, Okla	Red Fork, Okla	4.00	7-27-66	188
	Red Fork, Okla	Sapulpa, Okla	10.15	7-27-66	188
	St Louis & San Francisco Railway Company				
	St Louis, Mo	Rolla, Mo	110.7	3-12-49	186
	Rolla, Mo	Lebanon, Mo	71.2	5-12-68	186
	Lebanon, Mo	Springfield, Mo	57.3	5-12-68	5-..-7
	Springfield, Mo	Pierce City, Mo	48.7	5-12-68	10-..-7
	Pierce City, Mo	Neosho, Mo	22.9	7-27-66	187
	Neosho, Mo	Seneca, Mo	15.48	7-27-66	187
	Pierce City, Mo	Carthage, Mo	26.3	4-13-72	187
	Carthage, Mo	Brownsville, Kans	20.0	4-12-72	187
	Brownsville, Kans	Oswego, Kans	27.0	3-19-75	187
	Oswego, Kans	New Albany, Kans	60.7	3-21-79	187
	New Albany, Kans	Wichita, Kans	83.4	3-21-79	188
	Monett, Mo	Mo-Ark St Ln, Mo	32.0	6-4-80	188
	Mo-Ark St Ln, Ark	Fayetteville, Ark	38.4	7-17-80	188
	Fayetteville, Ark	Fort Smith, Ark	63.1	9-10-76	188
	At Van Buren, Ark		1.0	3-23-85	188
	Fort Smith, Ark	Ark-Okla St Ln, Ark	9.0	9-10-76	188
	Ark-Okla St Ln, Okla	Red River, Okla	144.0	9-10-76	188
	Red River, Tex	Paris, Tex	16.47	7-28-81	1-..-8
	Springfield, Mo	Bolivar, Mo	38.79	3-3-84	188
	Springfield, Mo	Chadwick, Mo	34.86	6-10-82	188
	Springfield Connecting	Ry, Mo	3.18	12-31-86	1-1-8
	Oronogo Jct, Mo	Joplin, Mo	9.32	3-22-85	187
	Carbon, Mo	Carbon Mines, Mo	3.25		
	Granby, Mo	Granby Mines, Mo	1.50	7-27-66	187

.TCHISON TOPEKA AND SANTA FE RAILWAY SYSTEM *(Continued)*

Name of Construction Company	Acquired by The AT&SF Ry Co (1) By Construction	By Lease Contract Control or Consolidation	Purchased or Merged	Reference Notes	Disposed of A—Abandoned S—Sold *—Lease terminated #—Leased to others
(7)	(8)	(9)	(10)	(11)	(12)
tlantic & Pacific		5-23-90		C-16	6-27-96(S)
.tlantic & Pacific		5-23-90		C-16	6-27-96(S)
acific RR (S'west Branch)		5-23-90		C-16	6-27-96(S)
outh Pacific		5-23-90		C-16	6-27-96(S)
outh Pacific		5-23-90		C-16	6-27-96(S)
outh Pacific		5-23-90		C-16	6-27-96(S)
tlantic & Pacific		5-23-90		C-16	6-27-96(S)
tlantic & Pacific		5-23-90		C-16	6-27-96(S)
lemphis, Carthage & Northwestern (Mo)		5-23-90		C-16	6-27-96(S)
lemphis, Carthage & Northwestern (Mo) (Kans)		5-23-90		C-16	6-27-96(S)
lissouri & Western		5-23-90		C-16	6-27-96(S)
t Louis, Wichita & Western		5-23-90		C-16	6-27-96(S)
t Louis, Wichita & Western		5-23-90		C-16	6-27-96(S)
t Louis, Ark & Tex (Mo)		5-23-90		C-16	6-27-96(S)
t Louis, Ark & Tex (Ark)		5-23-90		C-16	6-27-96(S)
t Louis & San Francisco		5-23-90		C-16	6-27-96(S)
ort Smith & Van Buren		5-23-90		C-16	6-27-96(S)
t Louis & San Francisco		5-23-90		C-16	6-27-96(S)
t Louis & San Francisco		5-23-90		C-16	6-27-96(S)
aris & Great Northern		5-23-90		C-16	6-27-96(S)
pringfield & Northern		5-23-90		C-16	6-27-96(S)
pringfield & Southern		5-23-90		C-16	6-27-96(S)
pringfield Connecting		5-23-90		C-16	6-27-96(S)
lissouri & Western		5-23-90		C-16	6-27-96(S)
		5-23-90		C-16	6-27-96(S)
tlantic & Pacific		5-23-90		C-16	6-27-96(S)

CHRONOLOGICAL DEVELOPMENT OF THE

Year	Termini		Road Miles	Date Construction Company Incorporated	Originally Opened for Operation
	From	To			
(1)	(2)	(3)	(4)	(5)	(6)
	Pittsburg, Kans	Weir City, Kans	8.81	10-24-86	
	Girard, Kans	Galena, Kans	46.43	2-25-76	187
	Fayetteville, Ark	St Paul, Ark	33.29	9-6-86	188
	Jansen, Ark	Mansfield, Ark	18.34	3-28-87	10-..-8
	Cuba, Mo	Salem, Mo	40.50	1-17-71	187
	Goltra, Mo	Sligo, Mo	5.25	9-29-80	188
	Howes Station, Mo	Plank Iron Mines, Mo	5.50	1-17-71	187
	Bangert, Mo	Smiths Bank, Mo	2.75	10-3-87	187
	Beaumont Jct, Kans	Ark City & St Ln	61.86	3-27-74	188
	Arkansas City, Kans	Bluff City, Kans	48.85	3-27-74	188
	Bluff City, Kans	Anthony, Kans	10.50	3-27-74	188
	Hunnewell Branch, Kans		2.54		188
	Wichita, Kans	Ellsworth, Kans	107.20	2-8-86	188
	The Colorado Midland Railway Company				
	Colo Springs, Colo	Newcastle, Colo	233.91	11-23-83	10-15-8
	Aspen Jct, Colo	Aspen, Colo	18.40	11-23-83	10-15-8
	Cardiff, Colo	Spring Gulch, Colo	15.00	11-23-83	10-15-8
	Snowden, Colo	Arkansas Jct, Colo	6.60	11-15-88	1-..-8
	Rifle, Colo	Grand Jct, Colo	62.08	6-26-89	11-16-9
1891	Stewart Ave, Chic, Ill	Ashland Ave, Chic, Ill	3.18	5-11-87	11-18-9
	Southern California Lines				
	Highland Jct, Cal	Mentone, Cal	12.88	8-11-90	8-17-9
1892	*Southern California Lines*				
	Santa Monica Jct, Cal	Santa Monica, Cal	5.42	4-4-92	6-18-9
1893	Ash Fork, Ariz	Prescott, Ariz	58.81	5-27-91	4-28-9
1895	Prescott, Ariz	Phoenix, Ariz	136.66	5-27-91	3-14-9
1896	*Southern California Lines*				
	Elsinore Jct, Cal	Alberhill, Cal	7.76	12-6-95	7-1-9
	Casa Blanca, Cal	Prenda, Cal	2.04	6-27-92	189

ATCHISON TOPEKA AND SANTA FE RAILWAY SYSTEM *(Continued)*

Name of Construction Company	Acquired by The AT&SF Ry Co (1)				Disposed of
	By Construction	By Lease Contract Control or Consolidation	Purchased or Merged	Reference Notes	A—Abandoned S—Sold *—Lease terminated #—Leased to others
(7)	(8)	(9)	(10)	(11)	(12)
Pittsburg & Columbus		5-23-90		C-16	6-27-96(S)
Joplin		5-23-90		C-16	6-27-96(S)
Fayetteville & Little Rock		5-23-90		C-16	6-27-96(S)
Little Rock & Texas		5-23-90		C-16	6-27-96(S)
St Louis, Salem & Little Rock		5-23-90		C-16	6-27-96(S)
Sligo Furnace		5-23-90		C-16	6-27-96(S)
St Louis, Salem & Little Rock		5-23-90		C-16	6-27-96(S)
Dent & Phelps		5-23-90		C-16	6-27-96(S)
Kansas City & Southwestern		5-23-90		C-16	6-27-96(S)
Kansas City & Southwestern		5-23-90		C-16	6-27-96(S)
Kansas City & Southwestern		5-23-90		C-16	6-27-96(S)
L D Latham & Co, Cont'rs		5-23-90		C-16	1891(A)
Kansas Midland		5-23-90		C-16	6-27-96(S)
Colorado Midland		11-1-90		C-18	1896(S)
Colorado Midland		11-1-90		C-18	1896(S)
Colorado Midland		11-1-90		C-18	1896(S)
Aspen Short Line		11-1-90		C-18	1896(S)
Rio Grande Junction		11-16-90		C-18	1896(S)
Atch, Top & Santa Fe (Chi)		11-18-91	3-6-02	L	
San Bernardino & Eastern		8-17-91	1-17-06	C-17	
Santa Fe & Santa Monica		6-18-92		C-17	1902(S)
Santa Fe, Prescott & Phoenix		4-28-93		C-19	
Santa Fe, Prescott & Phoenix		3-14-95		C-19	
Elsinore, Pom & Los Angeles		7-1-96	1-17-06	C-17	
Southern California		1896	1-17-06	C-17	

CHRONOLOGICAL DEVELOPMENT OF TH

Year	Termini From	Termini To	Road Miles	Date Construction Company Incorporated	Originally Opened for Operation
(1)	(2)	(3)	(4)	(5)	(6)
1897	Whitewater, N M	San Jose, N M	14.60	3-13-91	189
	Gulf Colorado and Santa Fe Railway Company				
	Conroe, Tex	MP 102-Meriam, Tex	29.60	4-2-91	189
1898	Frontenac, Kans	Midway, Kans	1.73	4-16-85	189
	San Jose, N M	Santa Rita, N M	3.98	12-24-97	12-1-9
	Entro(P&E Jct), Ariz	Mayer, Ariz	26.40	9-14-97	10-15-9
	At Galveston, Tex		—	6-26-97	189
	Stockton, Cal	Fresno, Cal	123.44	2-26-95	8-21-9
	Fresno, Cal	Hanford, Cal	30.20	2-26-95	6-2-9
	Calwa, Cal	Visalia, Cal	43.80	2-26-95	9-10-9
	Hanford, Cal	Bakersfield, Cal	80.40	2-26-95	6-1-9
	Panhandle and Santa Fe Railway Company				
	Panhandle City, Tex	Washburn, Tex	14.72	12-10-87	188
	Washburn, Tex	Amarillo, Tex	14.04	5-26-73	188
1899	Braman, Okla	Tonkawa, Okla	16.75	6-2-99	8-17-9
	Kans-Okla St Ln	Bartlesville, Okla	18.50	6-14-93	8-1-9
	Bartlesville, Okla	Owasso, Okla	38.35	6-14-93	11-1-9
	Hanover, N M	Fierro, N M	6.66	5-1-99	12-1-9
	Hutchinson, Kans	Kingman, Kans	31.58	10-7-89	188
	Kingman, Kans	Harper, Kans	27.20	10-7-89	189
	Harper, Kans	Anthony, Kans	7.77	10-7-89	189
	Anthony, Kans	Kans-Okla St Line	13.13	10-7-89	189
	Kans-Okla St Line	Wakita, Okla	8.46	10-7-89	189
	Wakita, Okla	Medford, Okla	12.13	9-24-96	3-1-9
	Medford, Okla	Blackwell, Okla	26.61	9-24-96	3-1-9
	Blackwell, Okla	Ponca City, Okla	14.48	12-21-97	7-1-9
	Kans-Okla St Line	Braman, Okla	8.26	8-16-97	189
	Visalia, Cal	Corcoran, Cal	24.61	2-26-95	6-..-9
	Southern California Lines				

TCHISON TOPEKA AND SANTA FE RAILWAY SYSTEM *(Continued)*

Name of Construction Company	Acquired by The AT&SF Ry Co (1)				Disposed of
	By Construction	By Lease Contract Control or Consolidation	Purchased or Merged	Reference Notes	A—Abandoned S—Sold *—Lease terminated #—Leased to others
(7)	(8)	(9)	(10)	(11)	(12)
ver City & Northern		3-..-97	4-17-99	L	
xas, Louisiana & Eastern		7-26-97		C-9	
uthern Kansas		1898	2-15-99	L	
nta Rita		12-1-98	1-13-00	L	
escott & Eastern		10-15-98		C-19	
ion Pass Depot (Galv'n)		1898		C-26	
n Fran & San Joaquin Val		12-..-98	4-1-01	C-28	
n Fran & San Joaquin Val		12-..-98	4-1-01	C-28	
n Fran & San Joaquin Val		12-..-98	4-1-01	C-28	
n Fran & San Joaquin Val		12-..-98	4-1-01	C-28	
nhandle		4-20-98		C-20	4-12-08(A)
rt Worth & Denver City		4-20-98		C-21	4-12-08(*)
ckwell & Southern		8-17-99	1-26-00	L	
nsas, Oklahoma, Central		8-1-99	7-2-00	L	
& Southwestern		11-1-99	7-2-00	L	
oover		12-1-99	1-19-00	L	
tchinson & Southern		10-1-99	12-20-99	C-22	
tchinson & Southern		10-1-99	12-20-99	C-22	
tchinson & Southern		10-1-99	12-20-99	C-22	10-16-29(A)
tchinson & Southern		10-1-99	12-20-99	C-22	
tchinson & Southern		10-1-99	12-20-99	C-22	
lf		10-1-99	12-20-99	C-22	
f		10-1-99	12-20-99	C-22	
tchinson & Southern		10-1-99	12-20-99	C-22	
nsas & Southeastern		2-20-99	12-20-99	C-23	
Fran & San Joaquin Val		6-..-99	4-1-01	C-28	

CHRONOLOGICAL DEVELOPMENT OF TH

Year	Termini		Road Miles	Date Construction Company Incorporated	Originally Opene for Operation
	From	To			
(1)	(2)	(3)	(4)	(5)	(6)
	Richfield (Atwood)	Olinda, Cal	4.26	6-27-92	18
	Lake View Jct, Cal	Lake View, Cal	8.02	11-1-98	18
1900	Guthrie, Okla	Pawnee, Okla	71.58	7-24-99	6-1-
	At Beaumont, Tex	(Side track)	3.83	3-26-97	9-...
	Bakersfield, Cal	Kern Jct, Cal	2.40	2-26-95	7-1-
	Stockton, Cal	Ferry Pt, Cal	70.12	2-26-95	7-1-
	Gulf Colorado and Santa Fe Railway Company				
	Beaumont, Tex	Fords Bluff, Tex	25.73	3-21-93	7-1-
	Fords Bluff, Tex	Buna, Tex	9.50	..-..-..	18
	Buna, Tex	Kirbyville, Tex	15.99	3-21-93	5-1-
	Kirbyville, Tex	Roganville, Tex	11.45	3-21-93	18
1901	Seward, Okla	Cashion, Okla	10.60	1-9-00	8-..
	Arkansas City, Kans	Geuda Springs, Kans	5.98	8-27-85	18
	Geuda Springs, Kans	Bluff, Kans	42.87	8-27-85	18
	Bluff, Kans	Anthony, Kans	10.44	8-27-85	1
	Pecos, Tex	Tex-NM St Ln (Corral)	54.24	3-1-90	1-1
	Tex-NM St Line (Texico)	Cameo, N M	13.20	3-10-98	3-1
	Cameo, N M	Roswell, N M	100.00	3-10-98	3-1
	Roswell, N M	Carlsbad (Eddy), N M	74.87	8-27-90	10-6
	Carlsbad (Eddy), N M	NM-Tex St Ln (Corral)	35.00	8-27-90	1-13
	Williams, Ariz	Anita, Ariz	50.42	7-31-97	3-1
	Anita Jct, Ariz	Anita Camp, Ariz	2.89	7-31-97	3-1
	Anita Jct, Ariz	Grand Canyon, Ariz	13.14	7-31-97	7-1
	Gosford, Cal	Hazelton, Cal	30.27	3-17-00	12-23
	Panhandle and Santa Fe Railway Company				
	Amarillo, Tex	Tex-NM St Ln (Texico)	94.50	3-19-98	3-1
1902	Pawnee, Okla	Ralston, Okla	17.90	7-24-99	6-15
	Ripley, Okla	Cushing, Okla	10.93	7-24-99	6-15
	Avery, Okla	Quay, Okla	19.23	7-24-99	12-1

TCHISON TOPEKA AND SANTA FE RAILWAY SYSTEM *(Continued)*

Name of Construction Company	Acquired by The AT&SF Ry Co (1)				Disposed of
	By Construction	By Lease Contract Control or Consolidation	Purchased or Merged	Reference Notes	A—Abandoned S—Sold *—Lease terminated #—Leased to others
(7)	(8)	(9)	(10)	(11)	(12)
uthern California		1899	1-17-06	C-17	
rris & Lakeview		1899		C-24	2-15-37(A)
stern Oklahoma		6-1-00	6-20-07	L	
aumont Wharf & Terminal		10-9-00		C-26	
n Fran & San Joaquin Val		7-1-99	4-1-01	C-29	
n Fran & San Joaquin Val		7-1-00	4-1-01	C-28	
lf, Beaumont & Kans City		1900		C-25	
aumont Lumber Co		1900		C-25	
lf, Beaumont & Kans City		1900		C-25	
lf, Beaumont & Kans City		1900		C-25	
thrie & Western		8-..-00	6-20-07	L	4-5-34(A)
Louis, Kans, S'western		10-25-01		C-27	6-22-36(A)
Louis, Kans, S'western		10-25-01		C-27	
Louis, Kans, S'western		10-25-01		C-27	
cos River		1-24-01		C-30	
cos Val & Northeastern		1-24-01			7-1-08(A)
cos Val & Northeastern		1-24-01	2-1-12		
cos Val		1-24-01	2-1-12		
os Val		1-24-01	2-1-12		
ta Fe & Grand Canyon		7-18-01	12-31-42	C-32	
ta Fe & Grand Canyon		7-18-01	12-31-42	C-32	
ta Fe & Grand Canyon		7-18-01	12-31-42	C-32	
set		12-23-01		C-47	
os & Northern Texas		1-24-01		C-31	
tern Oklahoma		6-15-02	6-20-07	L	
tern Oklahoma		6-15-02	6-20-07	L	
tern Oklahoma		12-1-02	6-20-07	L	

CHRONOLOGICAL DEVELOPMENT OF TH

Year	Termini		Road Miles	Date Construction Company Incorporated	Originally Openec for Operation
	From	To			
(1)	(2)	(3)	(4)	(5)	(6)
	Goffs, Cal	Barnwell, Cal	29.44	11-26-92	9-15-
	Barnwell, Cal	Leastalk, Cal	8.34	10-30-95	19
	Leastalk, Cal	Ivanpah, Cal	7.66	10-30-95	19
	Gulf Colorado and Santa Fe Railway Company				
	Rayburn, Tex	Silsbee, Tex	50.00	6-6-73	8-1-
	Poland Jct, Ariz	MP 0+1142, Ariz	0.21	2-6-01	6-..
	MP 0+1142, Ariz	MP 1+3579, Ariz	1.47	2-6-01	6-..
	MP 1+3578, Ariz	Torres, Ariz	0.32	2-6-01	6-..
	Torres, Ariz	Poland, Ariz	5.95	2-6-01	6-..
	Mayer, Ariz	Blue Bell, Ariz	1.76	2-6-01	12-..
	Blue Bell, Ariz	Cordes, Ariz	2.70	2-6-01	12-..
	Cordes, Ariz	E of Middleton, Ariz	7.84	2-6-01	12-..
1903	Havana, Kans	Caney, Kans	5.39	4-4-03	10-24
	Newkirk, Okla	Kaw City, Okla	16.50	7-24-99	4-19
	Avery, Okla	Shawnee, Okla	43.00	7-24-99	7-1
	Shawnee, Okla	Tecumseh, Okla	4.00	7-24-99	11-1
	Kaw City, Okla	Ralston, Okla	26.00	7-24-99	12-1
	Esau Jct, Okla	Quay, Okla	14.50	7-24-99	12-1
	Kramer, Cal	Johannesburg, Cal	29.66	5-18-97	1-17
	Pauls Valley, Okla	Lindsay, Okla	23.80	7-13-99	12-..
	E. of Middleton, Ariz	N of Crown King, Ariz	2.67	2-6-01	11-..
	E. of Middleton, Ariz	N of Crown King, Ariz	6.73	2-6-01	11-..
	Phoenix, Ariz	Mesa, Ariz	14.00	8-31-01	6-1
	Gulf Colorado and Santa Fe Railway Company				
	Roganville, Tex	San Augustine, Tex	58.22	8-5-98	7-1
	Sealy, Tex	Eagle Lake Jct, Tex	17.70	3-10-98	1-.
	Eagle Lake Jct, Tex	Lakeside, Tex	0.75	1-26-70	1
	Lakeside, Tex	Wharton, Tex	24.85	3-10-98	1-.
	Wharton, Tex	Bay City, Tex	24.90	3-10-98	1-.

TCHISON TOPEKA AND SANTA FE RAILWAY SYSTEM *(Continued)*

Name of Construction Company	Acquired by The AT&SF Ry Co (1) By Construction	By Lease Contract Control or Consolidation	Purchased or Merged	Reference Notes	Disposed of A—Abandoned S—Sold *—Lease terminated #—Leased to others
(7)	(8)	(9)	(10)	(11)	(12)
vada Southern		7-1-02		L	9-13-23(A)
lifornia Eastern		7-1-02		L	5-3-21(A)
lifornia Eastern		7-1-02		L	1913(A)
lf, Colorado & Santa Fe		8-1-02		C-9	
dshaw Mountain		6-. .-02		C-33	
dshaw Mountain		6-. .-02		C-33	4-10-39(A)
dshaw Mountain		6-. .-02		C-33	6-12-33(A)
dshaw Mountain		6-. .-02		C-33	6-14-32(A)
dshaw Mountain		12-. .-02		C-33	
dshaw Mountain		12-. .-02		C-33	2-6-40(A)
dshaw Mountain		12-. .-02		C-33	12-12-32(A)
ntgomery County	10-24-03		10-24-03	O	
stern Oklahoma		4-19-03	6-20-07	L	
stern Oklahoma		7-1-03	6-20-07	L	
stern Oklahoma		11-1-03	6-20-07	L	
stern Oklahoma		12-1-03	6-20-07	L	
tern Oklahoma		12-1-03	6-20-07	L	
dsburg		5-1-03		L	12-30-33(A)
wa, Chick & Fort Smith		12-. .-03	6-20-07	L	
dshaw Mountain		11-. .-03		C-33	12-12-32(A)
dshaw Mountain		11-. .-03		C-33	7-18-26(A)
enix & Eastern		6-1-03		C-34	3-14-07(S)
f, Beaumont & Gt North'n		7-1-03		C-36	
e Belt		11-. .-03		C-35	
alo, Bayou, Brazos & Colo		11-. .-03		C-35	
e Belt		11-. .-03		C-35	
e Belt		11-. .-03		C-35	

CHRONOLOGICAL DEVELOPMENT OF TH

Year	Termini From	Termini To	Road Miles	Date Construction Company Incorporated	Originally Opened for Operation
(1)	(2)	(3)	(4)	(5)	(6)
	Bay City, Tex	Matagorda, Tex	21.40	3-10-98	1-. . -
	Raynor Jct, Tex	Calhoun, Tex	4.37	3-10-98	2-1-
	Eagle Lake Jct, Tex	Eagle Lake, Tex	1.07	3-10-98	7-. . -
	Northwestern Pacific Railroad Company				
	Alton, Cal	Camp Nine, Cal	15.13	2-26-69	Unkno
	Alton, Cal	Eureka, Cal	20.68	11-14-82	7-6-
	Alton, Cal	Burnells, Cal	1.68	11-14-82	7-6-
	Eureka, Cal	Arcata, Cal	9.00	3-5-00	7-1-
	Burnells, Cal	Carlotta, Cal	3.39	4-26-02	7-7-
1904	Tecumseh, Okla	Pauls Valley, Okla	49.52	7-24-99	2-1-
	Richmond, Cal	Oakland, Cal	11.48	3-6-02	5-16-
	Riverbank, Cal	Oakdale, Cal	6.30	6-24-04	12-19-
	N. of Cr. King, Ariz	Crown King, Ariz	6.00	2-6-01	5-. . -
	Mesa, Ariz	Winkelman, Ariz	81.26	8-31-01	9-28
	Hazelton, Cal	Maricopa, Cal	2.48	3-17-00	4-. . -
	Gulf Colorado and Santa Fe Railway Company				
	Bragg, Tex	Saratoga, Tex	9.49	6-6-73	1
	San Augustine, Tex	Center, Tex	19.56	8-5-98	1-1-
	Calhoun, Tex	Eldridge, Tex	3.86	3-10-98	1-. .
	Eldridge, Tex	Bonus, Tex	5.54	3-10-98	1-. .
	Boedecker Jct, Tex	Garwood, Tex	2.97	3-10-98	2-. .
1905	Owasso, Okla	Tulsa, Okla	11.03	12-12-95	5-1
	Matthie (A&C Jct), Ariz	Salome, Ariz	50.03	9-10-03	7-10
	Northwestern Pacific Railroad Company				
	E of Albion, Cal	Keene's Summit, Cal	11.63	5-26-91	1
	Albion, Cal	E of Albion, Cal	3.00	5-8-02	1
	Clearbrook Jct, Cal	Clearbrook, Cal	1.00	5-8-02	1
	Shively, Cal	Camp Nine, Cal	2.30	5-12-03	7-. .

TCHISON TOPEKA AND SANTA FE RAILWAY SYSTEM *(Continued)*

Name of Construction Company	Acquired by The AT&SF Ry Co (1)				Disposed of
	By Construction	By Lease Contract Control or Consolidation	Purchased or Merged	Reference Notes	A—Abandoned S—Sold *—Lease terminated #—Leased to others
(7)	(8)	(9)	(10)	(11)	(12)
ane Belt		11-. .-03		C-35	
ane Belt		11-. .-03		C-35	
ane Belt		11-. .-03		C-35	
cific Lumber		5-15-03		C-37	6-26-28(S)
l River & Eureka		5-14-03		C-37	6-26-28(S)
l River & Eureka		5-14-03		C-37	6-26-28(S)
lifornia & Northern		5-14-03		C-37	6-26-28(S)
lifornia Midland		7-7-03		C-37	6-26-28(S)
astern Oklahoma		2-1-04	6-20-07	L	
kland & East Side		5-16-04		L	
kdale, Western		12-19-04		L	
adshaw Mountain		5-. .-04		C-33	7-18-26(A)
oenix & Eastern		9-28-04		C-34	3-14-07(S)
nset		4-. .-04		C-47	
alf, Colorado & Santa Fe		1904		C-9	1-15-34(A)
alf, Beaumont & Gt North'n		1-1-04		C-9	
ane Belt		1-. .-04		C-35	
ane Belt		1-. .-04		C-35	9-16-40(A)
ane Belt		2-. .-04		C-35	
chison, Topeka & Santa Fe	5-1-05			O	
izona & California		7-10-05		C-38	
bion Lumber		1-1-05		C-37	6-26-28(S)
bion & Southeastern		1-1-05		C-37	6-26-28(S)
bion & Southeastern		1-1-05		C-37	6-26-28(S)
n Francisco & Northwestern		1905		C-37	6-26-28(S)

CHRONOLOGICAL DEVELOPMENT OF TH

Year	Termini		Road Miles	Date Incorporated	Originally Opened for Operation
	From	To			
(1)	(2)	(3)	(4)	(5)	(6)
	Keene's Summit, Cal	Wendling, Cal	8.26	3-25-03	19
1906	McConnico, Ariz	Chloride, Ariz	21.57	4-10-99	4-16-
	Reedley, Cal	Wahtoke, Cal	6.68	7-25-05	8-1-
	Davis, Okla	Sulphur, Okla	9.27	7-24-99	10-1-
	Guthrie, Okla	Enid, Okla	55.17	3-31-02	10-10-
	Blanton Jct, Okla	Hillsdale, Okla	10.71	3-31-02	2-1-
	Hillsdale, Okla	Okla-Kans St Ln, Okla	46.22	3-31-02	1-1-
	Gulf Colorado and	*Santa Fe Railway Company*			
	Kirbyville, Tex	DeRidder, La	39.00	11-11-04	8-1-
	Longview, Tex	Tallys(Camden), Tex	10.71	1-4-77	4-11-
	Tallys(Camden), Tex	Martins Creek, Tex	10.50	12-18-82	18
	Martins Creek, Tex	Carthage, Tex	15.21	10-3-87	3-17-
	Carthage, Tex	Gary, Tex	9.84	8-17-96	18
	Gary, Tex	Timpson, Tex	8.98	8-17-96	18
	Timpson, Tex	Grigsby, Tex	18.41	9-14-04	19
1907	Barnwell, Cal	Searchlight, Ariz	23.00	4-16-06	4-1-
	Salome, Ariz	Parker, Ariz	56.81	9-10-03	6-17-
	Okla-Kans St Ln, Kans	Kiowa, Kans	1.32	8-16-05	4-3-
	Kiowa, Kans	Gerlane, Kans	9.90	8-16-05	4-3-
	Gerlane, Kans	Medicine Lodge, Kans	8.88	8-16-05	4-3-
	Medicine Lodge, Kans	Belvidere Jct, Kans	30.51	8-16-05	4-3-
	Gulf Colorado and	*Santa Fe Railway Company*			
	DeRidder, La	Cravens, La	18.00	11-11-04	6-1-
	Panhandle and Santa Fe	*Railway Company*			
	Canyon, Tex	Plainview, Tex	57.30	3-19-98	2-18-
	Northwestern Pacific	*Railroad Company*			
	San Rafael, Cal	San Quentin, Cal	2.10	2-25-69	18

TCHISON TOPEKA AND SANTA FE RAILWAY SYSTEM *(Continued)*

Name of Construction Company	Acquired by The AT&SF Ry Co (1)				Disposed of
	By Construction	By lease Contract Control or Consolidation	Purchased or Merged	Reference Notes	A—Abandoned S—Sold *—Lease terminated #—Leased to others
(7)	(8)	(9)	(10)	(11)	(12)
›rt Bragg & Southeastern		1905		C-37	6-26-28(S)
·izona & Utah		1-6-06		L	7-1-33(A)
·esno County		8-1-06		L	
ıstern Oklahoma		10-1-06		L	12-15-38(A)
enver, Enid & Gulf		1-1-06	6-20-07	C-39	
enver, Enid & Gulf		1-1-06	6-20-07	C-39	
enver, Enid & Gulf		1-1-06	6-20-07	C-39	
sper & Eastern		8-1-06		C-9	
›ngview & Sabine Val		4-1-06		C-40	
alveston, Sabine & St Louis		4-1-06		C-40	
ɔx, Sabine Val & Northwest'n		4-1-06		C-40	
arshall Timpson & Sabine Pass		4-1-06		C-40	
arshall Timpson & Sabine Pass		4-1-06		C-40	10-26-33(A)
ɔxas & Gulf		4-1-06		C-40	10-26-33(A)
ırnwell & Searchlight		4-6-07		L	9-13-23(A)
·izona & California		6-17-07		C-38	
enver, Kansas & Gulf		4-3-07	6-20-07	C-39	
enver, Kansas & Gulf		4-3-07	6-20-07	C-39	11-1-42(A)
enver, Kansas & Gulf		4-3-07	6-20-07	C-39	9-30-23(A)
enver, Kansas & Gulf		4-3-07	6-20-07	C-39	
sper & Eastern		6-1-07		C-9	
·cos & Northern Texas		2-18-07		C-31	
n Rafael & San Quentin		1-8-07		C-41	6-26-28(S)

CHRONOLOGICAL DEVELOPMENT OF TH

Year	Termini From	Termini To	Road Miles	Date Incor-porated	Origi-nally Opened for Oper-ation
(1)	(2)	(3)	(4)	(5)	(6)
	Jct(Petaluma), Cal	Donahue, Cal	5.65	11-16-69	1870-7
	Sausalito, Cal	San Anselmo, Cal	10.03	12-19-71	11-1-7
	San Anselmo, Cal	Manor, Cal	2.22	12-19-71	11-1-7
	Fulton, Cal	Rio Campo, Cal	18.18	5-23-77	5-29-7
	Manor, Cal	Monte Rio, Cal	54.84	12-19-71	7-4-7
	Monte Rio, Cal	Duncan Mills, Cal	3.43	12-19-71	7-4-7
	San Anselmo, Cal	San Rafael, Cal	2.58	12-19-71	11-1-7
	San Rafael, Cal	Cloverdale, Cal	70.00	11-16-69	1870-8
	Tiburon, Cal	San Rafael, Cal	8.77	10-21-81	1882-8
	Duncan Mills, Cal	Cazadero, Cal	7.41	8-19-85	11-1-8
	Cloverdale, Cal	Ukiah, Cal	27.42	8-17-76	1888-8
	Ignacio, Cal	Spears Point, Cal	7.67	8-17-86	1888-8
	Spears Point, Cal	Glen Ellen, Cal	18.92	3-13-89	188
	Santa Rosa, Cal	Sebastopol, Cal	6.33	11-16-69	2-17-9
	Almonte, Cal	Mill Valley, Cal	1.74	9-6-89	4-22-9
	Samoa, Cal	Arcata, Cal	7.86	1-6-96	189
	Ukiah, Cal	Willits, Cal	25.55	3-17-98	3-4-0
	Arcata, Cal	Twenty-Five Jct, Cal	17.44	1-6-96	10-. .-0
	Willits, Cal	Sherwood, Cal	14.38	3-19-98	5-1-0
	Duncan Mills, Cal	Markham, Cal	2.98	12-19-71	Unknow
	Bridge, Cal	Willow Creek, Cal	4.49	12-19-71	Unknow
	Twenty-Five, Jct, Cal	Trinidad, Cal	2.34	1-8-07	6-22-0
1908	Butchel, Colo	Keesee, Colo	38.79	12-12-95	7-1-0
	Bristol, Colo	Kornman, Colo	16.97	12-12-95	7-1-0
	Las Animas, Colo	Waveland, Colo	2.26	12-12-95	7-1-0
	Texico, N M	Cameo, N M	19.02	10-30-02	7-1-0
	Clovis, N M	Belen, N M	240.11	10-30-02	7-1-0
	Belen, N M	Rio Puerco, N M	17.41	10-30-02	7-1-0

TCHISON TOPEKA AND SANTA FE RAILWAY SYSTEM *(Continued)*

Name of Construction Company	Acquired by The AT&SF Ry Co (1)				Disposed of
	By Construction	By lease Contract Control or Consolidation	Purchased or Merged	Reference Notes	A—Abandoned S—Sold *—Lease terminated #—Leased to others
(7)	(8)	(9)	(10)	(11)	(12)
n Francisco & North Pacific		1-8-07		C-41	6-26-28(S)
orth Pacific Coast		1-8-07		C-41	6-26-28(S)
orth Pacific Coast		1-8-07		C-41	6-26-28(S)
ilton & Guerneville		1-8-07		C-41	6-26-28(S)
orth Pacific Coast		1-8-07		C-41	6-26-28(S)
orth Pacific Coast		1-8-07		C-41	6-26-28(S)
orth Pacific Coast		1-8-07		C-41	6-26-28(S)
n Francisco & North Pacific		1-8-07		C-41	6-26-28(S)
n Francisco & San Rafael		1-8-07		C-41	6-26-28(S)
orth Western of Calif.		1-8-07		C-41	6-26-28(S)
overdale & Ukiah		1-8-07		C-41	6-26-28(S)
arin & Napa		1-8-07		C-41	6-26-28(S)
noma Valley		1-8-07		C-41	6-26-28(S)
n Francisco & North Pacific		1-8-07		C-41	6-26-28(S)
n Francisco, Tamalpais & Bolinas		1-8-07		C-41	6-26-28(S)
ureka & Klamath River		1-8-07		C-41	6-26-28(S)
alifornia, Northwestern		1-8-07		C-41	6-26-28(S)
ureka & Klamath River		1-8-07		C-41	6-26-28(S)
alifornia Northwestern		1-8-07		C-41	6-26-28(S)
orth Pacific Coast		1-8-07		C-41	6-26-28(S)
orth Pacific Coast		1-8-07		C-41	6-26-28(S)
orthwestern Pacific		6-22-07		C-41	6-26-28(S)
chison, Topeka & Santa Fe	7-1-08			O	
chison, Topeka & Santa Fe	7-1-08			O	
chison, Topeka & Santa Fe	7-1-08			O	
astern of New Mexico		7-1-08	2-1-12	L	
astern of New Mexico		7-1-08	2-1-12	L	
astern of New Mexico		7-1-08	2-1-12	L	

CHRONOLOGICAL DEVELOPMENT OF TH

Year	Termini From	Termini To	Road Miles	Date Incor-porated	Origi-nally Opened for Oper-ation
(1)	(2)	(3)	(4)	(5)	(6)
	Sandia, N M	Dalies, N M	3.56	10-30-02	7-1-
	Swink, Colo	Shelton Jct, Colo	5.24	1-17-06	7-1-
	Holly, Colo	Bristol, Colo	13.66	1-17-06	7-1-
	Rocky Ford, Colo	Fenton, Colo	3.42	1-26-06	7-1-
	Fenton, Colo	Shelton Jct, Colo	2.66	1-26-06	7-1-
	Shelton Jct, Colo	Butchel, Colo	9.98	1-26-06	7-1-
	Lamar, Colo	Keesee, Colo	13.16	1-26-06	7-1-
	Gulf Colorado and Santa Fe Railway Company				
	Cravens, La	Oakdale, La	24.40	11-11-04	2-9-
	Port Bolivar, Tex	Flake, Tex	6.00	5-19-94	5-1-
	Flake, Tex	High Island, Tex	20.71	5-19-94	3-15-
	High Island, Tex	Beaumont, Tex	44-17	5-19-94	3-15-
	Panhandle and Santa Fe Railway Company				
	Panhandle, Tex	Amarillo, Tex	24.66	11-2-86	4-12-
1909	Pentland, Cal	Taft, Cal	10.08	6-18-08	1-1-
	Taft, Cal	Fellows, Cal	4.78	6-18-08	1-1-
	Gulf Colorado and Santa Fe Railway Company				
	Gary, Tex	Center, Tex	21.31	9-14-04	19
	Miles, Tex	Paint Rock, Tex	16.49	4-2-09	12-27-
	Northwestern Pacific Railroad Company				
	Baltimore Park, Cal	Detour, Cal	1.40	1-8-07	5-11-
	Wendling, Cal	Christine, Cal	2.76	1-8-07	6-13-
	Rio Campo, Cal	Monte Rio, Cal	1.54	1-8-07	11-15-
1910	Richfield (Atwood), Cal	Fullerton, Cal	5.10	2-18-10	7-1-
	Garden City, Kans	Scott City, Kans	36.92	1-4-07	7-1-
	Ariz-Calif St Line	Cadiz, Cal	83.43	9-10-03	7-1-
	Gulf Colorado and Santa Fe Railway Company				

TCHISON TOPEKA AND SANTA FE RAILWAY SYSTEM *(Continued)*

Name of Construction Company	Acquired by The AT&SF Ry Co (1)				Disposed of
	By Con-struc-tion	By lease Contract Control or Consoli-dation	Pur-chased or Merged	Refer-ence Notes	A—Abandoned S—Sold *—Lease terminated #—Leased to others
(7)	(8)	(9)	(10)	(11)	(12)
astern of New Mexico		7-1-08	2-1-12	L	
olly & Swink	7-1-08		3-15-07	C-43	
olly & Swink	7-1-08		3-15-07	C-43	
:kansas Valley	7-1-08		3-16-07	C-43	12-31-15(A)
:kansas Valley	7-1-08		3-16-07	C-43	12-10-31(A)
:kansas Valley	7-1-08		3-16-07	C-43	
:kansas Valley	7-1-08		3-16-07	C-43	
sper & Eastern		2-9-08		C-9	
ulf & Inter-State of Texas		1-17-08		C-44	1-22-42(A)
ulf & Inter-State of Texas		1-17-08		C-44	1-22-42(A)
ulf & Inter-State of Texas		1-17-08		C-44	
uthern Kansas, Texas		4-12-08		C-42	
ınset, Western		1-1-09		C-45	
ınset, Western		1-1-09		C-45	12-30-38(A)
exas & Gulf		1909		C-40	
oncho, San Saba & Llano Val		12-27-09		C-44	4-16-37(A)
orthwestern Pacific		5-11-09		C-41	6-26-28(S)
orthwestern Pacific		6-13-09		C-41	6-26-28(S)
orthwestern Pacific		11-15-09		C-41	6-26-28(S)
ıllerton & Richfield		7-1-10		L	
arden City, Gulf & Northern		7-1-10		L	
rizona & California		7-1-10		C-38	

CHRONOLOGICAL DEVELOPMENT OF TH

Year	Termini: From	Termini: To	Road Miles	Date Incorporated	Originally Opened for Operation
(1)	(2)	(3)	(4)	(5)	(6)
	San Angelo, Tex	Sterling City, Tex	43.66	4-2-09	8-1-
	Panhandle and Santa Fe Railway Company				
	Plainview, Tex	Lubbock, Tex	46.23	3-19-98	1-9-
	Plainview, Tex	Floydada, Tex	26.75	3-19-98	5-1-
	Lubbock, Tex	Slaton, Tex	17.48	3-19-98	6-13-
	Slaton, Tex	Lamesa, Tex	53.35	3-19-98	10-1-
1911	Laton, Cal	Shilling, Cal	15.52	8-8-10	2-22-
	Wahtoke, Cal	Piedra, Cal	10.70	10-21-09	3-18-
	Fellows, Cal	Shale, Cal	2.25	6-18-08	4-20-
	Gulf Colorado and Santa Fe Railway Company				
	Lometa, Tex	Brady, Tex	66.00	6-6-73	9-11-
	Panhandle and Santa Fe Railway Company				
	Slaton Jct, Tex	Coleman, Tex	182.55	3-19-98	12-1-
	Sweetwater Jct, Tex	Sweetwater, Tex	3.12	3-19-98	12-1-
1912	Chloride Exten, Ariz		2.47	1-6-06	19
	Shilling, Cal	Lanare, Cal	2.05	8-8-10	19
	Gulf Colorado and Santa Fe Railway Company				
	Brady, Tex	Whiteland, Tex	10.94	6-6-73	2-25-
	Whiteland, Tex	Eden, Tex	21.24	6-6-73	1-1-
	Longview, Tex	Ore City, Tex	29.66	12-14-10	5-26-
1913	Dodge City, Kans	Elkhart, Kans	119.23	11-17-11	7-1-
	Cedar Glade, Ariz	Clarkdale, Ariz	38.44	11-17-11	2-1-
	At Raton, N M		0.18	6-26-05	19
	Raton, N M	Dillon, N M	3.23	6-26-05	19
	Dillon, N M	Clifton, N M	3.04	6-26-05	19
	Des Moines, N M	Clifton, N M	42.09	6-26-05	9-..-
	Clifton, N M	Preston, N M	6.53	6-26-05	9-..-
	Preston, N M	Koehler Jct, N M	7.24	6-26-05	7-..-

TCHISON TOPEKA AND SANTA FE RAILWAY SYSTEM *(Continued)*

Name of Construction Company	Acquired by The AT&SF Ry Co (1)				Disposed of
	By Construction	By lease Contract Control or Consolidation	Purchased or Merged	Reference Notes	A—Abandoned S—Sold *—Lease terminated #—Leased to others
(7)	(8)	(9)	(10)	(11)	(12)
oncho, San Saba & Llano Val		8-1-10		C-44	
ecos & Northern Texas		1-9-10		C-31	
ecos & Northern Texas		5-1-10		C-31	
ecos & Northern Texas		6-13-10		C-31	
ecos & Northern Texas		10-1-10		C-31	
aton & Western		2-22-11		L	
ings River		3-18-11		L	
unset Western		4-20-11		C-46	12-30-38(A)
ulf, Colorado & Santa Fe		9-11-11		C-9	
ecos & Northern Texas		12-1-11		C-31	
ecos & Northern Texas		12-1-11		C-31	
'estern Arizona		1912		L	7-1-33(A)
aton & Western		1912		L	
ulf, Colorado & Santa Fe		1-1-12		C-9	
ulf, Colorado & Santa Fe		1-1-12		C-9	
ort Bolivar Iron Ore		5-26-12		C-48	2-29-20(*)
odge City & Cimarron Val		7-1-13		L	
erde Valley		2-1-13	12-31-42	L	
Louis, Rocky Mt & Pacific		8-1-13		C-50	9-1-16(A)
Louis, Rocky Mt & Pacific		8-1-13		C-50	9-15-15(A)
Louis, Rocky Mt & Pacific		8-1-13		C-50	7-15-35(A)
Louis, Rocky Mt & Pacific		8-1-13		C-50	7-15-35(A)
Louis, Rocky Mt & Pacific		8-1-13		C-50	9-15-15(A)
Louis, Rocky Mt & Pacific		8-1-13	1-30-43	C-50	

CHRONOLOGICAL DEVELOPMENT OF TH

Year	Termini		Road Miles	Date Incor-porated	Origi-nally Opened for Oper-ation
	From	To			
(1)	(2)	(3)	(4)	(5)	(6)
	Koehler Jct, N M	Cimarron, N M	27.18	6-26-05	7-. .-C
	Cimarron, N M	Ute Park, N M	12.40	6-26-05	5-. .-C
	Koehler Jct, N M	Koehler, N M	3.47	6-26-05	19C
1914	Lehigh, Okla	Ada Jct, Okla	39.88	9-20-04	3-1-C
	Ada Jct, Okla	Byars, Okla	30.28	9-20-04	3-1-C
	Byars, Okla	Purcell, Okla	18.84	9-20-04	3-1-C
	Purcell, Okla	Chickasha, Okla	38.65	9-20-04	8-1-C
	O&C Jct, Okla	Chickasha, Okla	3.44	11-24-09	12-15-1
	Ada Jct, Okla	Ada, Okla	1.93	8-11-09	11-15-C
	Minkler, Cal	Wyeth, Cal	20.57	5-22-13	10-1-1
	Cutler, Cal	Exeter, Cal	20.98	5-22-13	10-1-1
	Redbank, Cal	Woodlake, Cal	2.16	5-22-13	10-1-1
	Panhandle and Santa Fe Railway Company				
	Lubbock Jct, Tex	Farwell, Tex	88.00	3-19-98	3-1-1
1915	Exeter, Cal	Lindsay, Cal	6.92	5-22-13	10-1-1
	Cushing, Okla	Pemeta, Okla	10.32	4-7-15	191
	Oilton, Okla	Jennings, Okla	8.00	4-7-15	1-12-1
	Panhandle and Santa Fe Railway Company				
	Lubbock Jct, Tex	Crosbyton, Tex	38.43	4-6-10	4-10-1
	Northwestern Pacific Railroad Company				
	Willits, Cal	Shively, Cal	105.69	1-8-07	7-1-1
1916	Pemeta, Okla	Oilton, Okla	5.90	4-7-15	1-1-1
	Frey Jct, Okla	Drumright, Okla	4.10	4-7-15	1-1-1
1918	Lindsay, Cal	Porterville, Cal	12.10	5-22-13	1-1-1
	Oil Jct, Cal	Ainrof, Cal	5.36	—	19C
	Treadwell, Cal	Porque, Cal	2.47	—	19C
	Panhandle and Santa Fe Railway Company				
	Lubbock, Tex	Seagraves, Tex	63.86	4-6-10	7-1-1
1919	Holyrood, Kans	Galatia, Kans	31.20	2-21-17	7-1-1

TCHISON TOPEKA AND SANTA FE RAILWAY SYSTEM *(Continued)*

Name of Construction Company	Acquired by The AT&SF Ry Co (1)				Disposed of
	By Con- struc- tion	By lease Contract Control or Consoli- dation	Pur- chased or Merged	Refer- ence Notes	A—Abandoned S—Sold *—Lease terminated #—Leased to others
(7)	(8)	(9)	(10)	(11)	(12)
Louis, Rocky Mt & Pacific		8-1-13		C-50	11-9-42(A)
Louis, Rocky Mt & Pacific		8-1-13		C-50	11-9-42(A)
Louis, Rocky Mt & Pacific		8-1-13	1-30-43	C-50	
lahoma Central		8-1-14		L	1-28-34(A)
lahoma Central		8-1-14	12-31-42	L	
lahoma Central		8-1-14		L	1-28-34(A)
lahoma Central		8-1-14		L	6-9-41(A)
ickasha Terminal		8-1-14		L	6-9-41(A)
a Terminal		8-1-14	12-31-42	L	
nkler Southern		10-1-14	12-31-42	L	
nkler Southern		10-1-14	12-31-42	L	
nkler Southern		10-1-14	12-31-42	L	
os & Northern Texas		3-1-14		C-31	
nkler Southern		10-1-15	12-31-42	L	
Fields & Santa Fe		5-7-15	6-30-41	C-49	
Fields & Santa Fe		5-7-15	6-30-41	C-49	6-16-34(A)
sbyton-Southplains		8-1-15		C-51	
thwestern Pacific		7-1-15		C-41	6-26-28(S)
Fields & Santa Fe		1-1-16	6-30-41	L	
Fields & Santa Fe		1-1-16		L	3-1-42(A)
nkler Southern		1-1-18	12-31-42	L	
thern Pacific		3-21-18	3-21-18	C-53	
thern Pacific		3-21-18	3-21-18	C-53	12-10-28(A)
th Plains & Santa Fe		7-1-18		C-52	
on County & Santa Fe		7-1-19	12-31-42	L	

CHRONOLOGICAL DEVELOPMENT OF TH

Year	Termini: From	Termini: To	Road Miles	Date Incor-porated	Origi-nally Opened for Oper-ation
(1)	(2)	(3)	(4)	(5)	(6)
1920	Porterville, Cal	Ducor, Cal	12.40	5-22-13	7-15-
	Oil Jct, Cal	Landco, Cal	2.82	5-22-13	7-15-
	Waynoka, Okla	Buffalo, Okla	51.44	7-18-19	7-1-
	Panhandle and Santa Fe Railway Company				
	Shattuck, Okla	Okla-Tex St Line	9.22	7-25-16	7-1
	Okla-Tex St Line	Spearman, Tex	75.42	7-25-16	7-1
1921	Rice, Cal	Blythe, Cal	41.42	12-30-14	11-1
	Blythe, Cal	Ripley, Cal	7.43	12-30-14	10-31
1922	Hammond, Cal	Belmont, Cal	16.88	4-4-14	8-1
1923	Hickman Jct, Okla	Naphtha, Okla	6.39	12-12-95	2-28
	De Noya Jct, Okla	De Noya, Okla	2.83	12-12-95	2-28
	Satanta, Kans	Manter, Kans	53.87	11-17-11	1-1
	Owen, Okla	Pawhuska, Okla	35.21	2-24-17	8-12
	Magunden, Cal	DiGiorgio, Cal }	16.75		7-14
	DiGiorgio, Cal	Arvin, Cal }			8-7
1924	Ellinor, Kans	Gladstone, Kans	4.08	3-21-22	5-5
	Bazar, Kans	Eldorado, Kans	37.86	3-21-22	5-5
	El Segundo, Cal	Wilmington, Cal	12.70	4-20-22	12-31
	Salina, Kans	Osborne, Kans	80.81	12-14-14	1-1
	Raton, N M	Carisbrooke, N M	3.86	2-9-05	12-1
	Carisbrooke, N M	Yankee, N M	3.13	2-9-05	12-1
	Carisbrooke, N M	Sugarite, N M	1.93	2-9-05	12-1
1925	Marland, Okla	Lio, Okla	9.86	12-12-95	1-1
	Kans-Okla St Line	Boise, Okla	39.60	1-12-25	12-
	Boise, Okla	Felt, Okla	19.22	1-12-25	12-
	Panhandle and Santa Fe Railway Company				
	Doud, Tex	Bledsoe, Tex	63.38	4-6-10	12-
	At Bledsoe, Tex		1.22	4-6-10	12-
1926	Torrance, N M	Willard, N M	35.52	12-7-00	8-

TCHISON TOPEKA AND SANTA FE RAILWAY SYSTEM *(Continued)*

Name of Construction Company	Acquired by The AT&SF Ry Co (1)				Disposed of
	By Construction	By lease Contract Control or Consolidation	Purchased or Merged	Reference Notes	A—Abandoned S—Sold *—Lease terminated #—Leased to others
(7)	(8)	(9)	(10)	(11)	(12)
nkler Southern		7-15-20	12-31-42	L	
nkler Southern		7-15-20	12-31-42	L	
ffalo Northwestern		7-1-20	6-30-41	L	
rth Texas & Santa Fe		7-1-20		C-52	
rth Texas & Santa Fe		7-1-20		C-52	
ifornia Southern		11-1-21	12-31-42	L	
ifornia Southern		11-1-21	12-31-42	L	
sno Interurban		4-17-22		C-56	
hison, Topeka & Santa Fe	2-28-23			O	3-26-39(A)
hison, Topeka & Santa Fe	2-28-23			O	3-26-39(A)
lge City & Cimarron Val		1-1-23		L	
ge County & Santa Fe		8-12-23	6-30-41	L	
		8-7-23	8-7-23	C-53	
thern Pacific		8-7-23	8-7-23	C-53	
Dorado & Santa Fe		5-5-24	12-31-42	L	
Dorado & Santa Fe		5-5-24	12-31-42	L	
ta Fe & Los Angeles Har		12-31-24	12-31-42	L	
na Northern		7-1-24	12-31-42	C-54	
a Fe, Raton & Eastern		1-1-24		C-55	12-1-42(A)
a Fe, Raton & Eastern		1-1-24		C-55	7-15-35(A)
a Fe, Raton & Eastern		1-1-24		C-55	12-1-42(A)
ison, Topeka & Santa Fe	1-1-25			O	6-23-42(A)
art & Santa Fe		12-1-25	12-31-42	L	
art & Santa Fe		12-1-25	12-31-42	L	9-6-42(A)
h Plains & Santa Fe		12-1-25		C-52	
h Plains & Santa Fe		12-1-25		C-52	10-6-42(A)
a Fe Central		6-1-26		L	1-3-29(A)

CHRONOLOGICAL DEVELOPMENT OF TH

Year	Termini From	Termini To	Road Miles	Date Incor-porated	Origi-nally Opened for Oper-ation
(1)	(2)	(3)	(4)	(5)	(6)
	Willard, N M	Moriarty, N M	30.35	12-7-00*	8-. .-
	Moriarty, N M	Stanley, N M	11.60	12-7-00	8-. .-
	Stanley, N M	Kennedy, N M	18.86	12-7-00	8-. .-
	Kennedy, N M	Santa Fe, N M	19.54	12-7-00	8-. .-
	Panhandle and Santa Fe Railway Company				
	Panhandle, Tex	Borger, Tex	31.16	11-2-86	10-16-
	Gulf Colorado and Santa Fe Railway Company				
	Ardmore, Okla	Wilson, Okla	20.00	1-8-13	10-1-
	Wilson, Okla	Ringling, Okla	9.98	1-8-13	7-. . .-
	Healdton Jct, Okla	Healdton, Okla	5.91	11-23-16	9-. .-
1927	Manter, Kans	Pritchett, Colo	55.81	11-17-11	2-1-
	Pawhuska, Okla	Osage Jct, Okla	26.81	2-24-17	7-1-
	At Porphyry, Cal		2.28	3-3-26	3-5-
	Porphyry, Cal	Alberhill, Cal	12.09	3-3-26	3-5-
	Panhandle and Santa Fe Railway Company				
	White Deer, Tex	Skellytown, Tex	10.40	11-2-86	10-15
1928	Wilkes, Kans	Mulvane, Kans	6.96	12-12-95	19
	Beardsley, Ariz	Griggs, Ariz	12.84	12-21-11	5-19
	Wichita, Kans	Wichita Jct, Kans	4.30	5-1-00	12-1
	Wichita Jct, Kans	Milton, Kans	27.12	5-1-00	11-13
	Milton, Kans	Anthony, Kans	27.98	5-1-00	4-1
	Anthony, Kans	Cherokee, Okla	32.65	5-1-00	4-1
	Cherokee, Okla	Carmen, Okla	13.39	5-1-00	4-1
	Carmen, Okla	Fairview, Okla	21.82	5-1-00	9-13
	Fairview, Okla	Longdale, Okla	11.55	5-1-00	7-1
	Longdale, Okla	Canton, Okla	6.37	5-1-00	9-22
	Canton, Okla	Oakwood, Okla	11.00	5-1-00	12-9
	Oakwood, Okla	Foley, Okla	21.00	5-1-00	7-6
	Ewing, Okla	Clinton, Okla	2.03	5-1-00	10-1

TCHISON TOPEKA AND SANTA FE RAILWAY SYSTEM *(Continued)*

Name of Construction Company	Acquired by The AT&SF Ry Co (1)				Disposed of
	By Construction	By lease Contract Control or Consolidation	Purchased or Merged	Reference Notes	A—Abandoned S—Sold *—Lease terminated #—Leased to others
(7)	(8)	(9)	(10)	(11)	(12)
nta Fe Central		6-1-26		L	
nta Fe Central		6-1-26		L	4-15-43(A)
nta Fe Central		6-1-26		L	6-3-39(A)
nta Fe Central		6-1-26		L	1-3-29(A)
nhandle & Santa Fe		10-16-26		C-42	
la, New Mex & Pacific		10-16-26		C-57	
la, New Mex & Pacific		10-16-26		C-57	
gling & Oil Fields		10-16-26		C-57	
dge City & Cimarron Val		2-1-27		L	
ge County & Santa Fe		7-1-27	6-30-41	L	
ona & Santa Fe		3-5-27	12-31-42	L	
ona & Santa Fe		3-5-27	12-31-42	L	
handle & Santa Fe		10-15-27		C-42	
hison, Topeka & Santa Fe	1928			O	
, Ariz & Santa Fe		5-19-28		L	
sas City, Mexico & Orient		10-19-28	6-30-41	C-60	
sas City, Mexico & Orient		10-19-28	6-30-41	C-60	
sas City, Mexico & Orient		10-19-28	6-30-41	C-60	
sas City, Mexico & Orient		10-19-28	6-30-41	C-60	9-19-42(A)
sas City, Mexico & Orient		10-19-28	6-30-41	C-60	
sas City, Mexico & Orient		10-19-28	6-30-41	C-60	
sas City, Mexico & Orient		10-19-28	6-30-41	C-60	
sas City, Mexico & Orient		10-19-28	6-30-41	C-60	
sas City, Mexico & Orient		10-19-28	6-30-41	C-60	
sas City, Mexico & Orient		10-19-28	6-30-41	C-60	
sas City, Mexico & Orient		10-19-28	6-30-41	C-60	

CHRONOLOGICAL DEVELOPMENT OF TH

Year	Termini From	Termini To	Road Miles	Date Incorporated	Originally Opened for Operation
(1)	(2)	(3)	(4)	(5)	(6)
	Clinton, Okla	Elmer, Okla	77.47	5-1-00	1-1-0
	Elmer, Okla	Okla-Tex St Line	1.92	5-1-00	12-1-0
	Panhandle and Santa Fe Railway Company				
	Clinton, Okla	Butler, Okla	21.50	11-10-08	3-21-1
	Butler, Okla	Strong City, Okla	30.00	11-10-08	10-18-1
	Strong City, Okla	Cheyenne, Okla	7.09	12-2-12	191
	Okla-Tex St Ln, Tex	Benjamin, Tex	70.69	7-20-99	12-..-0
	Benjamin, Tex	Sweetwater, Tex	89.91	7-20-99	12-..-0
	Sweetwater, Tex	San Angelo, Tex	77.03	7-20-99	6-..-0
	San Angelo, Tex	Girvin (Granada), Tex	132.10	7-20-99	3-7-1
	Girvin (Granada), Tex	Fort Stockton, Tex	32.12	7-20-99	11-17-1
	Ft Stockton, Tex	Alpine, Tex	62.71	7-20-99	6-30-1
	Central California Traction Company				
	Stockton, Cal	Lodi, Cal	16.00	8-7-05	9-2-
	Lodi Jct, Cal	Sacramento, Cal	39.27	8-7-05	9-1-1
1929	*Panhandle and Santa Fe Railway Company*				
	Cheyenne, Okla	Okla-Tex St Line	23.96	4-9-20	5-15-
	Pampa, Tex	Tex-Okla St Line	56.50	7-30-27	5-15-
1930	*Gulf Colorado and Santa Fe Railway Company*				
	Cane Jct, Tex	Guy (Sena Jct), Tex	17.79	3-10-98	6-22-
	Panhandle and Santa Fe Railway Company				
	Del Rio Jct, Tex	Sonora, Tex	64.95	7-20-99	7-1-
	Paisano, Tex	Presidio, Tex	72.44	7-20-99	11-1-
1931	Felt, Okla	Okla-NM St Line	11.42	1-12-25	11-15-
	Okla-NM St Ln, NM	Clayton, N M	12.25	1-12-25	11-15-
	Mt Dora, N M	Farley, N M	35.64	1-12-25	11-15-
	Boise City, Okla	Okla-Tex St Line (near Kerrick)	21.08	1-12-25	5-15-
	Gulf Colorado and Santa Fe Railway Company				

.TCHISON TOPEKA AND SANTA FE RAILWAY SYSTEM *(Continued)*

Name of Construction Company	Acquired by The AT&SF Ry Co (1) By Construction	By lease Contract Control or Consolidation	Purchased or Merged	Reference Notes	Disposed of A—Abandoned S—Sold *—Lease terminated #—Leased to others
(7)	(8)	(9)	(10)	(11)	(12)
ansas City, Mexico & Orient		10-19-28	6-30-41	C-60	
ansas City, Mexico & Orient		10-19-28	6-30-41	C-60	
linton & Oklahoma Western		1-1-28		C-58	
linton & Oklahoma Western		1-1-28		C-58	
heyenne Short Line		1-1-28		C-58	
ans City, Mex & Orient of Tex		10-19-28		C-61	
ans City, Mex & Orient of Tex		10-19-28		C-61	
ans City, Mex & Orient of Tex		10-19-28		C-61	
ans City, Mex & Orient of Tex		10-19-28		C-61	
ans City, Mex & Orient of Tex		10-19-28		C-61	
ans City, Mex & Orient of Tex		10-19-28		C-61	
entral California Traction		1-1-28		C-59	
entral California Traction		1-1-28		C-59	
linton & Oklahoma Western		5-15-29		C-58	
linton-Okla-Western of Tex		5-15-29		C-62	
ane Belt		6-22-30		C-63	
ans City, Mex & Orient of Tex		7-1-30		C-61	
ans City, Mex & Orient of Tex		11-1-30		C-61	
khart & Santa Fe		11-15-31		L	9-6-42(A)
khart & Santa Fe		11-15-31		L	9-6-42(A)
khart & Santa Fe		11-15-31		L	9-6-42(A)
khart & Santa Fe		5-15-31	12-31-42	L	

CHRONOLOGICAL DEVELOPMENT OF TH

Year	Termini From	Termini To	Road Miles	Date Incorporated	Originally Opened for Operation
(1)	(2)	(3)	(4)	(5)	(6)
	Guy, Tex	Thompsons, Tex	16.00	3-10-98	1-15
	Panhandle and Santa Fe Railway Company				
	Spearman, Tex	Morse, Tex	18.58	7-25-16	5-15
	Heaton Jct, Tex	Coltexo, Tex	8.24	7-30-27	2-15
	Amarillo, Tex	Tex-Okla St Line, Tex (near Kerrick)	100.50	11-1-30	5-15
1937	Boise City, Okla	Okla-Colo St Line	20.15	1-12-25	2-1
	Okla-Colo St Line	Las Animas Jct, Colo	90.33	11-17-11	2-1
	Gulf Colorado and Santa Fe Railway Company				
	Birds, Tex	Granbury, Tex	36.50	6-1-85	10-1
	Granbury, Tex	Dublin, Tex	49.60	6-1-85	3-1
	Dublin, Tex	Comanche, Tex	22.10	6-1-85	11-1C
	Comanche, Tex	Brownwood, Tex	30.60	6-1-85	7-1
	Brownwood, Tex	E Brady Jct, Tex	43.92	6-1-85	3-1
	E. Brady Jct, Tex	Brady, Tex	2.76	6-1-85	3-1
	Whiteland, Tex	Menard, Tex	27.48	6-1-85	2-2
1938	Ennis, Ariz	Bumstead, Ariz	5.31	12-21-11	4-1
1941	Bumstead, Ariz	Webb, Ariz	1.27	12-21-11	4-1

TCHISON TOPEKA AND SANTA FE RAILWAY SYSTEM *(Continued)*

Name of Construction Company	Acquired by The AT&SF Ry Co (1)				Disposed of
	By Con-struc-tion	By lease Contract Control or Consoli-dation	Pur-chased or Merged	Refer-ence Notes	A—Abandoned S—Sold *—Lease terminated #—Leased to others
(7)	(8)	(9)	(10)	(11)	(12)
ne Belt		1-15-31		C-63	
rth Texas & Santa Fe		5-15-31		C-52	
nton-Okla-Western of Tex		2-15-31		C-62	
rth Plains & Santa Fe		5-15-31		C-52	
khart & Santa Fe		2-1-37	12-31-42	L	
dge City & Cimarron Val		2-1-37		L	
rt Worth & Rio Grande		3-1-37		C-9	
rt Worth & Rio Grande		3-1-37		C-9	
rt Worth & Rio Grande		3-1-37		C-9	
rt Worth & Rio Grande		3-1-37		C-9	
rt Worth & Rio Grande		3-1-37		C-9	
rt Worth & Rio Grande		3-1-37		C-9	3-16-40(A)
t Worth & Rio Grande		3-1-37		C-9	
ifornia, Arizona & Santa Fe		4-14-38		L	
ifornia, Arizona & Santa Fe		4-11-41		L	

Chronological Development of
THE ATCHISON, TOPEKA AND SANTA FE RAILWAY SYSTEM

Notes referred to in Column (11) on preceding Pages of this Chart, giving explana tion of methods by which each branch of the railroad became a part of th Atchison System on the dates given in Columns (8) and (9):

(1) Properties acquired prior to December 12, 1895 were acquired in name c Atchison, Topeka and Santa Fe Railroad Company.

O — Constructed by the Atchison Company and operated from date in Col. (8) b the Atchison Company.

L — Operated by the Atchison, Topeka and Santa Fe Rd Co under lease from dat in Col. (9).

J — Jointly owned and operated by the AT&SF Rd Co with other carriers fro date in Col. (9).

C-1 Controlled by stock ownership, operated separately as the Southern Kans Ry System, from date in Col. (9) to May 1, 1888, then leased to the AT&S Rd Co.

C-2 Controlled by stock ownership, operated separately by Atlantic and Pacific R Co from date in Col. (9) until June 24, 1897, then by Santa Fe Pacific R Co till July 1, 1902.

C-3 Controlled by stock ownership, operated separately as the Sonora Syste from date in Col. (9) until leased to Southern Pacific. Sold to Southe Pacific on Dec. 27, 1911.

C-4 Leased by Atlantic and Pacific Rd Co from Southern Pacific from date Col. (9) till abandoned in 1890.

C-5 Leased by Atlantic and Pacific Rd Co from Southern Pacific from date in Co (9) till June 24, 1897, then by Santa Fe Pacific Rd Co till July 1, 1902, the by The AT&SF Ry Co.

C-6 Controlled by stock ownership, operated separately by the California Southe Rd Co from date in Col. (9) till Nov. 7, 1889, then by Southern Californ Ry Co till June 1, 1904, when property was leased to The AT&SF Ry Co.

C-7 Controlled by stock ownership, operated separately by The Chicago, Kans & Western Rd Co from date in Col. (9) till October 1, 1889, when it w leased to the AT&SF Rd. Co.

C-8 Controlled by stock ownership, operated separately by California Southe Rd Co from date in Col. (9) till May 20, 1887, then by the California Ce tral Ry Co. till Nov. 7, 1889, then by the Southern California Ry Co. till June 1904, when the property was leased to the AT&SF Ry Co.

C-9 Controlled by stock ownership from date in Col. (9) and operated separately to date by the Gulf, Colorado and Santa Fe Ry Co.

C-10 Controlled by Stock ownership, operated separately from 1887 till sold on December 14, 1899.

C-11 Controlled by stock ownership, operated separately by the Southern Kansas Ry Co of Texas from date in Col. (9) till June 5, 1914, when the name was changed to Panhandle and Santa Fe Ry Co, the present operating company.

C-12 Controlled by stock ownership, operated separately by California Central Ry Co from date in Col. (9) till Nov. 7, 1889, then by the Southern California Ry Co till June 1, 1904, when leased to The AT&SF Ry Co.

C-13 Controlled by stock ownership, operated separately by the St Joseph, St Louis and Santa Fe Ry Co (formerly St Joseph and Santa Fe Rd Co) from date in Col. (9) till January 1, 1890, when leased to AT&SF Rd Co.

C-14 Controlled by stock ownership, separately operated by the Chicago, Santa Fe and California Ry Co from date in Col. (9) till Sept. 30, 1889, when leased to AT&SF Rd Co.

C-15 Controlled by stock ownership, separately operated by the Kansas City Belt Ry Co. Jointly used by Santa Fe with other companies.

C-16 Controlled by stock ownership, separately operated by the St. Louis and San Francisco Ry Co from date in Col. (9) till sold under foreclosure on June 27, 1896.

C-17 Controlled by stock ownership, separately operated by the Southern California Ry Co from date in Col. (9) till June 1, 1904, when leased to the Santa Fe.

C-18 Controlled by stock ownership, separately operated by the Colorado Midland Ry Co from date in Col. (9) until sold in 1896.

C-19 Controlled by stock ownership, separately operated by The Santa Fe Prescott and Phoenix Ry Co from date in Col. (9) until December 29, 1911 when sold to the California Arizona and Santa Fe Ry Co and leased to The AT&SF Ry Co.

C-20 Controlled by stock ownership, operated separately by the Southern Kansas Ry Co of Texas under lease from date in Col. (9) till purchased by that company on January 1, 1900 and operated by that company till abandoned April 12, 1908.

C-21 Trackage rights only over tracks of Fort Worth and Denver City Ry Co from date in Col. (9) till April 12, 1908, when Southern Kansas Ry Co of Texas built from Panhandle to Amarillo.

C-22 Controlled by stock ownership, but operated as agent for The Hutchinson

Chronological Development of
THE ATCHISON, TOPEKA AND SANTA FE RAILWAY SYSTEM
(Continued)

Notes referred to in Column (11) on preceding Pages of this Chart, giving explana tion of methods by which each branch of the railroad became a part of th Atchison System on the dates given in Columns (8) and (9):

and Southern Ry Co from date in Col. (9) till December 20, 1899, whe purchased by The AT&SF Ry Co.

C-23 Controlled by stock ownership, separately operated by Receiver from date i Col. (9) till Feb. 20, 1899 when leased to The AT&SF Ry Co.

C-24 Controlled by stock ownership, operated as a switch track by the Southe California Ry Co from date in Col. (9) till Dec. 28, 1911 when it was pu chased by the CA&SF Ry Co and leased to The AT&SF Ry Co.

C-25 Controlled by stock ownership, operated separately by the Gulf Beaumo and Kansas City Ry Co from date in Col. (9) till July 1, 1914 when leased the Gulf Colorado and Santa Fe Ry Co.

C-26 Controlled by stock ownership, separately operated by the Gulf Colorado ar Santa Fe, as agent, from date in Col. (9).

C-27 Controlled by stock ownership and separately operated by The Kansas Sout western Ry Co from date in Col. (9).

C-28 Controlled by stock ownership and separately operated by The San Francis and San Joaquin Valley Ry Co from date in Col. (9) till purchased on Ap 1, 1901.

C-29 Controlled by stock ownership but separately operated under lease by tl Santa Fe Pacific Rd Co from date in Col. (9) till July 1, 1902.

C-30 Controlled by stock ownership but separately operated by The Pecos Riv Rd Co from date in Col. (9) till July 1, 1913 when leased to the Panhand and Santa Fe Ry Co.

C-31 Controlled by stock ownership but separately operated by The Pecos ar Northern Texas from date in Col. (9) till July 1, 1914 when leased to tl Panhandle and Santa Fe Ry Co.

C-32 Controlled by stock ownership, separately operated by The Grand Canyo Ry Co from date in Col. (9) till Jan. 1, 1924 when leased to The AT&S Ry Co.

C-33 Controlled by stock ownership, separately operated under lease by The San Fe Prescott and Phoenix Ry Co from date in Col. (9) till Jan. 2, 1912 wh sold to the California Arizona and Santa Fe Ry Co and leased to The AT&S Ry Co.

C-34 Controlled by stock ownership, separately operated under lease by The Santa Fe Prescott and Phoenix Ry Co from date in Col. (9) till sold to Southern Pacific March 14, 1907.

C-35 Controlled by stock ownership but separately operated by The Cane Belt Rd Co from date in Col. (9) till July 1, 1905 when leased to the Gulf Colorado and Santa Fe Ry Co.

C-36 Controlled by stock ownership but separately operated by the Gulf Beaumont and Kansas City Ry Co from date in Col. (9) till December 1, 1903 when leased to the Gulf Colorado and Santa Fe Ry Co.

C-37 Controlled by stock ownership (100% Santa Fe) but separately operated from date in Col. (9) by the San Francisco and Northwestern Ry Co till Jan. 8, 1907 when it was sold to the Northwestern Pacific Rd Co, which was controlled 50% by Santa Fe and 50% Southern Pacific. The property was separately operated by the Northwestern Pacific Rd Co from that date to June 26, 1928 when the Santa Fe sold its share to the Southern Pacific Co.

C-38 Controlled by stock ownership, separately operated by The Santa Fe Prescott and Phoenix Ry Co from date in Col. (9) till Dec. 28, 1911 when sold to the California Arizona and Santa Fe Ry Co and leased to The AT&SF Ry Co.

C-39 Controlled by stock ownership, but separately operated by The Denver Enid and Gulf Rd Co from date in Col. (9) till May 22, 1907 when sold to The Eastern Oklahoma Ry Co and leased to The AT&SF Ry Co.

C-40 Controlled by stock ownership but separately operated by The Texas and Gulf Ry Co from date in Col. (9) till June 30, 1914 when leased to the Gulf Colorado and Santa Fe Ry Co.

C-41 Controlled by stock ownership, jointly with Southern Pacific Co (50% each) and separately operated by the Northwestern Pacific Rd Co from date in Col. (9) till June 26, 1928 when the Santa Fe sold its share to the Southern Pacific Co.

C-42 Controlled by stock ownership from date in Col. (9) and separately operated by the Panhandle and Santa Fe Ry Co.

C-43 The uncompleted roads of The Holly and Swink Ry Co and The Arkansas Valley Ry Co were purchased by The AT&SF Ry Co on March 15th and March 16th, 1907, respectively, completed by The AT&SF Ry Co and placed in operation on July 1, 1908.

C-44 Controlled by stock ownership but separately operated from date in Col. (9) till July 1, 1914 when leased to the Gulf Colorado and Santa Fe Ry Co.

C-45 Controlled by stock ownership, 50% Santa Fe—50% Southern Pacific, and operated separately by Sunset Western Ry Co from date in Col. (9) until

Chronological Development of
THE ATCHISON, TOPEKA AND SANTA FE RAILWAY SYSTEM
(Continued)

Notes referred to in Column (11) on preceding Pages of this Chart, giving explana tion of methods by which each branch of the railroad became a part of the Atchison System on the dates given in Columns (8) and (9):

leased to Sunset Rd Co July 1, 1910 and operated under lease by the Sunse Rd Co from July 1, 1910 till March 20, 1912 when sold to Sunset Ry Co an operated since by that company.

C-46 Controlled by stock ownership, 50% Santa Fe—50% Southern Pacific, oper ated separately under lease by Sunset Rd Co from date in Col. (9) til March 20, 1912 when sold to Sunset Ry Co and operated since by tha company.

C-47 Controlled by stock ownership, 50% Santa Fe—50% Southern Pacific, oper ated separately by the Sunset Rd Co from date in Col. (9) till March 20 1912 when sold to Sunset Ry Co and operated since by that company.

C-48 Controlled by private parties but operated under a temporary agreement fron date in Col. (9) till July 1, 1913, leased to and operated by The Texas an Gulf Ry Co from July 1, 1913 till July 1, 1914 when leased to the Gulf Colorado and Santa Fe Ry Co.

C-49 Controlled by stock ownership but operated by The AT&SF Ry Co as agen from date in Col. (9) to Jan. 1, 1916 when leased to The AT&SF Ry Co Cushing to Pemeta acquired from Cushing Traction Co and Oilton to Jenning acquired from Oil Belt Terminal Co.

C-50 Acquired control under contract of purchase and possession taken on Augus 1, 1913, separately operated by St Louis Rocky Mountain and Pacific Ry Co Name was changed to Rocky Mountain and Santa Fe Ry Co on March 10 1915 and property was leased to The AT&SF Ry Co on July 1, 1915.

C-51 Controlled by stock ownership and separately operated from date in Col. (9 till August 17, 1916 when the name was changed to South Plains and Sant Fe Ry Co. It was leased to Panhandle and Santa Fe Ry Co July 1, 1917.

C-52 Controlled by stock ownership and operated under lease by Panhandle an Santa Fe Ry Co from date in Col. (9).

C-53 One-half interest in the line was purchased by The AT&SF Ry Co as of dat in Col. (9) and it is operated in alternate years by the Santa Fe and South ern Pacific. (Entire mileage shown).

C-54 Property purchased at Sheriff's sale on Feb. 7, 1924, deeded to The Salin and Santa Fe Ry Co (incorporated Feb. 23, 1924) and leased to The AT&S Ry Co on July 1, 1924.

C-55 Property purchased Jan. 1, 1924 by the Rocky Mountain and Santa Fe Ry Co and leased to The AT&SF Ry Co.

C-56 Controlled by stock ownership by Santa Fe Land Improvement Co. from 1922, but operated separately until May 15, 1926 when control passed to The AT&SF Ry Co and property was leased to that company.

C-57 Controlled by stock ownership of The Healdton and Santa Fe Ry Co from date in Col. (9) and leased to the Gulf Colorado and Santa Fe Ry Co.

C-58 Controlled by stock ownership of The Clinton and Oklahoma Rd Co (incorporated April 9, 1920) from date in Col. (9) and leased to the Panhandle and Santa Fe Ry Co.

C-59 Controlled by stock ownership, one-third each by Santa Fe, Southern Pacific and Western Pacific, and separately operated from date in Col. (9).

C-60 Controlled by stock ownership of The Kansas City Mexico and Orient Rd Co from date in Col. (9). It was separately operated by the Kansas City Mexico and Orient Rd Co till August 1, 1929 when property was leased to The AT&SF Ry Co.

C-61 Controlled by stock ownership of the Kansas City Mexico and Orient Ry Co of Texas from date in Col. (9). It was operated separately by the KCM&O Ry Co of Texas till August 1, 1929 when property was leased to the Panhandle and Santa Fe Ry Co.

C-62 Controlled by stock ownership of the Clinton-Oklahoma-Western Rd Co of Texas (incorporated July 30, 1927) from date in Col. (9) and leased to the Panhandle and Santa Fe Ry Co.

C-63 Controlled by stock ownership and leased to Gulf Colorado and Santa Fe Ry Co from date in Col. (9).

APPENDIX IX

SANTA FE PRESIDENTS

From the Santa Fe's inception down to the present 19 men have guided the destinies of the railroad.

The first president was Cyrus K. Holliday who served from September 17, 1860, until January 13, 1864. After the road was reorganized on December 12, 1895, he served a second term as president of the old company from July 1, 1896, until his death on March 29, 1900. The old company went out of existence on July 25, 1920, with the death of Charles S. Gleed, its last president.

For the most part, the Santa Fe's earlier leaders maintained their executive headquarters in either Boston or New York. Even Holliday spent much of his time in the East seeking assistance for his new-born infant, although his headquarters until the time of his death were at Topeka. The first Santa Fe president to make his headquarters in Chicago was Allen Manvel who served from September 6, 1889, until February 24, 1893. With the road's re-organization on December 12, 1895, Edward P. Ripley established executive offices in Chicago where they since have been located.

A chronological list of Santa Fe presidents of both the old and new companies, the period they served, and the location of their executive offices follows:

ATCHISON & TOPEKA RAILROAD

President	From—To	Location of Office
Cyrus K. Holliday	11-23-1863—9-17-1864	Topeka

ATCHISON, TOPEKA AND SANTA FE RAILROAD

President	From—To	Location of Office
Cyrus K. Holliday	11-23-1863—1-13-1864	Topeka
S. C. Pomery	1-13-1864—9- 2-1868	Topeka and New York
W. F. Nast	9- 2-1868—9-24-1868	New York
H. C. Lord	9-24-1868—2-17-1869	New York
Henry Keyes	2-17-1869—9-24-1870	Boston
Ginery Twitchell	10-10-1870—5-22-1873	Boston
Henry Strong	5-22-1873—5-28-1874	Boston
Thomas Nickerson	5-28-1874—5-13-1880	Boston
T. Jefferson Coolidge	5-13-1880—8- 1-1881	Boston
Wm. B. Strong	8- 1-1881—9- 6-1889	Boston
Allen Manvel	9- 6-1889—2-24-1893	Chicago
J. W. Reinhart	3- 7-1893—9- 1-1894	Boston and New York
D. B. Robinson (acting)	9- 1-1894—7- 1-1896	Chicago
Cyrus K. Holliday	7- 1-1896—3-29-1900	Topeka
Charles S. Gleed	11- 4-1900—7-25-1920	Topeka

THE ATCHISON, TOPEKA AND SANTA FE RAILWAY COMPANY

President	From—To	Location of Office
Edward P. Ripley	12-12-1895—1- 1-1920	Chicago
W. B. Storey	1- 1-1920—5- 2-1933	Chicago
S. T. Bledsoe	5- 2-1933—3- 8-1939	Chicago
E. J. Engel	3-28-1939—8- 1-1944	Chicago
F. G. Gurley	8- 1-1944—	Chicago

INDEX

"*A. G. Greely*," (Locomotive), 166
Abell, P. T., 31, 349, 353
Ade, George, 296
Air Line Railroad, 295
Alexis, Grand Duke, 53
Allen, Asaph, 349
Allison, Robert A., 353
Alloe Instrument Company, 203
American Home Missionary Society, 11, 27, 162, 179
American Locomotive Company, 313
American Settlement Company, The, 37
Ammon, Conductor, 207
Anderson, Conductor, 260
Anderson, Hugh, 52
Anderson, Major Tom, 21, 42, 45, 53, 120-121, 166
Anderson, Mrs. Caroline, 75
Angell, G. W., 353
Anthony, Susan B., 37
Anti-Monopoly Cheap Freight League, 17
Anton, J. F., 353
Archer, W., 353
Arizona & California Railway, 268
Arizona Central Railroad, 264
Arizona Eastern Railroad, 267
Arkansas Valley Railroad, 79
Armentage, Division Foreman, 325
Armijo, Manuel, 8
Armstrong, John, 259
Arntz, W. P., 353
Arthur, President Chester A., 262
"*Arthur Sewell*," (Locomotive), 176
Atchison Associates, 47
Atchison and Topeka Railroad Company, 11, 349
Atchison, Topeka and Santa Fe Railway System,
  Chronological development, 396-447
  Departments, 377-378
  Financial data, 386-395
  Some Santa Fe Firsts, 384-385
  Trains, 379-383
Atlantic & Great Western Railroad, 23
Atlantic & Pacific Railroad Company, 118, 167, 170, 178-179, 182, 242, 245, 251-252, 264
Aubrey, Francis Xavier, 10
Austin, Stephen F., 8

Bacheller, R. M. 240
Baker, L., 261
Baldwin Locomotive Works, 141, 157, 166, 259, 280, 282, 288, 303, 313

Baltimore & Ohio, 36
Barker, H. N., 211
Barnard, J. F., 353
Barney & Smith, 41
Barnhart, William, 353
Barth, Sol, 272
Bartling, Bill, 42
Barton, Doc, 72
Battye, Charles, 181
Baylis, Jim, 181
Baylor, Ed, 52
Beal, Amos M., 353
Bean, Judge Roy, 352
Bean, S. L., 353
Beaubien, Carlos, 160-161
Becker, Sheriff, 154
Becknell, W. H., Captain, 7, 49, 347
Belshaw, W. P., 255
Bender, John H., 91
Bent, William, 15
Benton, Senator Thomas H., 87
Best, F. J., 235
Betts, C. E., 353
Biddle, W. B., 290
"Big Four," the, 172
Bird, Lorenzo D., 349
Birdseye, Roger W., 305
Bissell, W. A., 353
Black, W. J., 278
Bledsoe, Samuel T., 302, 318-319, 326-328, 353
Blush, Dan, 10
Blush, Joe, 20
Bly, Nellie, 239-240, 279
Bond, "Brick," 69
Booker, B. F., 203, 353
Bragg, General Braxton, 214, 216-217, 286
Brandt, Tom, 186
Brewster, T. P., 338
Brisbane, Arthur, 352
Briscoe, J. B., 325, 353
Brooks, Charlie, 161
Brown, Harry, 196
Brown, J. M., 214
Brown, Thomas, 255
Bryan, Guy M., 215
Bryan, William Jennings, 274, 295
Buchanan, James, 28
Buchanan, R. E., 226-227
Buckingham, A. E., 329
Bucklin, Major, 353
Budd, Edward G., Manufacturing Company, 304
Buffalo Bayou, Brazos & Colorado Railroad and Navigation, 212
Buffalo Bill, see Cody, William Frederick
Bullock, T. S., 264
Burke, Jack, 309, 314
Burlington Railroad, see Chicago, Burlington & Quincy Railroad
Burman, Bob, 195
Burnside, General A. E., 35
Butler, J. E., 353
Butternut Boys, 9
Byrne, J. J., 277, 279, 353

"C. C. Jackson," (Locomotive), 167
"C. K. Holliday," (Locomotive), 40, 42, 199
Cabeza de Vaca, Alvar Nuñez, 5
Caldwell, Henry C., 250
California & Nevada Railroad, 261
"California Limited," (Train), 271, 282, 290, 303-304, 320-321, 324-325

California Northwestern Railroad, 274
California Southern Railroad Company, 182
Callaghan, Owen, 293
Cameron, Tom, 283
Cantor, Eddie, 302
"Captains Courageous," Kipling, 279
Cardenas, Garcia Lopez de, 273
Cardenas, Lazaro, 299
Carnegie, Andrew, 204
Carpentier, A., 254
Carson, Kit, 9, 15, 49, 127, 160, 189, 347
Carson, Kit (Grandson), 343
Carson, William, 16
Carson, William Kit, Jr., 16
Cart, Peter, 293
Castaño de Sosa, 5
"Cayce Jones," quote from, 278
Central & Montgomery Railroad, 219
Central Arizona Railroad, 263-264
Central Pacific Railroad, 10-11, 14, 16, 33, 220, 253, 256
Centralized Traffic Control Board, 338-339
Chalender, George T., 353
Challis, Luther 31, 33, 349, 353
Chamberlin, J. W., 198
Chambers, Ed, 353
Chanute, Octave, 201, 345
"Charles C. Burr," (Locomotive), 120
Chapman, G. C., 73
Chase, Enoch, 26
Chase, Salmon Portland, 14
Cheney, B. P., Jr., 279, 353
Chicago & Alton Railroad, 202
Chicago & Western Indiana Railroad, 205
Chicago, Burlington & Quincy Railroad, 81-82, 98, 115, 177, 250, 328, 333
Chicago, California & Santa Fe Company of Iowa, 205
"Chicago Limited," (Train), 271
Chicago, Milwaukee, St. Paul & Pacific Railroad Company, 115, 311, 314
Chicago, Rock Island & Pacific Railway, 201, 209, 237, 251, 333
Chicago, St. Louis & Western Railroad, 171, 202, 205
"Chief" (Train), 135, 301
Chillicothe & Omaha Airline Railroad, 16
Chisholm, Jesse, 49, 346
Chivington, Colonel, 15
Clements, H. C., 353
Clough, Frank, 110
Cody, William Frederick, 280
Colcord, Windy, 180
Coleman, Richard R., 115, 118, 167, 174, 177, 196, 201, 286
Colfax, Schuyler (Smiler), 14
Collins, Charles, 237
Collins, Dan, 227
Colly, Mayor Dick, 89
Colorado & New Mexico Railroad, 79
Colorado Midland Railway Company, 242, 245, 251
"Colorado Spring," (Locomotive), 120-121
Colter, Mary Elizabeth Jane, 109

Comstock, Engineer, 260
Conkling, Roscoe, 18
Connell, J. M., 353
Coolidge, T. Jefferson (President), 168, 353
Coons, John, 180
Copeland, E. L., 354
Cormack, Mrs. Bartlett, 302
Coronado, Francisco Vasquez, 5-6, 49, 165, 347, 273, 286
Cortez, Hernando, 2, 49
Cowan, Bill, 207
"Coyote Special," (Train), 280-282
Craft, Brit, 42
Crane, F. L., 349
Crank, J. F., 191
Crawford, Governor, 11
Cret, Paul F., 305
Criley, J. D., 40, 57-60, 347
Crocker, Charles, 11, 14, 172
Cruice, Fred P., 354
Cryer, Mayor, 304
Curtis, C. H., 222
Custer, George Armstrong, 16, 51, 346

Daley, Dan, 161
Davis, J. C., 101
Daze, William, 354
Death Valley Scotty, 279-281, 301
"De Luxe Express," (Train), 143, 302
Delaney, Arthur, 52
Deming, Miss, 172
Denair, John, 354
Denver & Rio Grande Western Railroad, 94, 118, 128, 132, 135, 137, 138, 140, 143, 144-157, 206, 242, 245
Denver & Santa Fe Railroad, 242
Denver Circle Railroad, 206-207
Denver Southern Pacific Railroad, 126
"De Remer," (Locomotive), 156
De Remer, J. R., 134-135, 138-139, 145-148, 153, 156
Dewey, George, 296
De Witt, T., 354
Diaz, Porfirio, 173-174, 297-298
Dickey, Milton C., 349
Dickinson, P. T., 252
Dickinson, Colonel W. G., 163
Dickson, Samuel, 349
Diggins, Hi, 73
Dilworth, Dick, 312-314
Dodge, Chief Chee, 306
Dodge, D. C., 152
Dodge, General G. M., 11
Dodge, Colonel Richard I., 70-71
Donohoe, Joe, 256
Doud, Charles, 354
Doyle, John T., 256
Drake, "Crazy Ed," 30
Drake, William Abiel, 265, 286, 354
Dugan, Al, 42
Dun, James, 261, 283, 354, 355
Duppa, Lord Darrel, 263
Durant, Thomas C., 11
Dyer, Isaac, 214

Easley, William, 317
Edelstein, John, 354
"El Capitan," (Train), 306
Electro-Motive Corporation, 301, 304-306, 311-312
Ellinwood, Cap't. John R., 12, 56, 118, 354

"Emancipator," (Train), 259
Engel, E. J., 308, 327-328, 354
Eppler, H. R., 354
Etter, W. K., 354
Eureka & Klamath River Railroad, 274
Evens, Bill, 91
Everheart, H. E., 227
Excelsior Coke & Gas Company, 125

Fagan, John, 63
Fagan, W. W., 42
Fairchild, George H., 349
Falkner, E. O., 291
Faries, H. V., 74
Farnsworth, H. W., 354
Fields, Billy, 354
Ferry, Dexter M., 266
Finlay, John, 280
Fishel, H. L., 354
Fisher, Bud, 302
Fisk, Jim, 13
Fitch, George, 255
Fitch, Tom, 266
Fitzhugh, John G., 228, 247
Fletcher, "Dandy Tom," 19
Flood, Jim, 256
Fluhr, C. G., 354
Forbes, John, 354
Ford, Chester B., 324
Ford, Charles, 163
Ford, Mary Santa Fe, 324
Ford, Robert, 163
Fort Worth & Denver City Railroad, 225
Forth Worth and Rio Grande Railroad, 327
Fox, E. C. (Conductor), 167
Fox, F. C., 354
Francis, Miss Avis, 317
Franklin Tunnel, The, 260
Frémont, General John C., 28, 136, 160, 167, 182
Fresenius, Major J. P., 216
Frey, J. J., 269
Frisco Railroad see St. Louis & San Francisco Railway Company, 168, 177, 245
Fulton, Mayor, 215

Galivan, J. B., 354
Gallup, D. L., 354
Galveston, Harrisburg & San Antonio, 214
Galveston, Houston & Henderson, 212-213
Galveston Wharf Company, The, 214
Garces, Father, 189
Gardner, Bill, 106
Gates, John W., 296
Gaylord, G. L., 354
Gaynor, William J., 322
"General A. E. Burnside," (Locomotive), 44
General Electric Company, 312
General Motors Corporation, 312
George, J. F. (Conductor), 167
Gerard, Joe M., 277
Geyer, Chef, 281
Gillen, Lee Charles, 158
Gilmore, Pat, 354
Gish, George, 354
Gleed, Charles S., 354
Glidden, Mrs. J. F., 54
Goodrich, Mrs., (City Marshal), 317

Goodwin, George L., 354
Gordon, Wilson L., 349
Gould, Jay, 13, 80, 156, 172, 180, 182, 184, 187, 219, 243, 252
Grand Trunk, 205
Grant, General U. S., 14, 163, 216, 230
Grant Brothers, 354
Gray, A. D., 354
Great Northern Railway Company, 95, 311
Great Northwestern Railroad, 115
Greeley, Horace, 18, 127
Gregory, Harry, 355
Gulf & Interstate Railroad, 227
Gulf, Colorado & Santa Fe Railway Company, 211, 214, 219, 221, 224-225, 231, 233, 245, 247, 287, 317
Gunn, Otis Berthoude, 34
Gurley, Fred, 328, 336, 342, 385
Guthrie, Judge John, 223

Hagerman, J. J., 355
Hall, Dick Wick, 268, 352
Hamburg-America Line, 298
Hamill, T. M., 240
Hamilton, Harold L., 311-312
Hannibal and St. Joseph Railroad, 97
Harriman, Ed, 13, 267
Harris, G. W., 355
Harrison, R. W., 324
Harvey, Byron, 111, 303
Harvey, Ford, 111
Harvey, Frederick Henry, 78, 96, 97-113, 163, 180, 206, 321, 325
Harvey, Governor, 61
Harvey House, 93, 97-113, 162, 197, 289, 326
Harvey Girls, 100, 112, 251
Hatch, General Edward, 166
Haun, John E., 52
Haun, Reverend M. M., 51-52
Hawes, Dave, 355
Hayes, President Rutherford B., 163
Hazen, Bill, 292
Hearst Estate, 256
Heidenheimer, S., 355
Heizer, D. N., 88
Helm, Professor, 163
Heman, F. A., 355
Henderson, Clarence, 190
Hibbard, I. L., 355
Hillyer, George S., 349
Hinckley, Francis C., 202
Hinckley Road, 202
Hitler, Adolf, 342
Hodgdon, Emmet, 180
Hogbin, D. E. "Jersey," 40
Holbrook, Charles, 256
Holbrook, Henry Randolph, 115, 116, 168, 272, 286, 347, 355
Holliday, Colonel Cyrus, 10-11, 12, 14, 15, 19, 21, 32, 36, 42, 49, 63, 76, 88, 97, 117, 125, 131, 166, 172, 178, 251, 286, 345, 349, 355
Holliday, David, 22
Holliday, Lillie, 27, 42
Holman, Frank Newton, 280
Homber, Simon, 194
Hoover, G. M., 67
Hopkins, Mark, 14
Horton, Fred, 322

Houston & Texas Central Railroad, 212, 214
Howard, Alvinza, 256
Howe, H. P., 279
Hughes, C. R., 215
Hughes, Colonel J. W. F., 222
Hunt, Alexander C., 144, 151, 154
Hunt, Captain Jefferson, 189, 347
Huntington, Collis P., 14, 95, 170-172, 184-185, 187, 243, 252, 253, 279
Huntoon, Joel, 31, 349, 355
Hurley, J. E., 355
Hutchinson, C. C., 355
Hutchinson & Southern Railroad, 237
Hutchinson, Oklahoma & Gulf Railroad, 237

Indianapolis & Cincinnati Railroad, 41
Interior, Department of, 149
International & Great Northern Railroad, 214, 219
Intercolonial Railway of Canada, 143
Interstate Commerce Commission, 209, 247, 340
Isaacs, H., 271

Jackson, Fred, 281
James, Jesse, 162
Jansen, Cornelius, 84
Jay Cooke & Company, 64, 182
"Jeep," (Locomotive), 307, 309, 313-314
Johnson, President A. J., 14-15
Johnson, Colonel A. S., 81, 83, 88, 94, 355
Johnson, Allan, 353
Johnson, Arthur, 280
Johnson, B. F., 299
Johnson, Ed, 323
Johnson, J. B., 250
Jones, Mary Dillon, 23
Jones, Meredith, 146, 283
"Joseph Nickerson," (Locomotive), 45
Judah, Theodore D., 14
Juilliard, A. D., 355

"Kansas," (Locomotive), 120-121
Kansas City & Northern Connecting Railroad, 270
Kansas City Belt Line Railway, 205
Kansas City, Lawrence & Southern Kansas, 178
Kansas City, Mexico & Orient Railway, 296-298
Kansas City, Pittsburg & Gulf Railroads, 295
Kansas City Southern Railway Company, 296
Kansas City, Topeka & Western Railroad, 90
Kansas Midland Railroad, 73
Kansas Pacific Railroad, 21, 22, 34, 36, 40, 42, 53, 63, 79-80, 118, 120, 130, 156, 350
Kansas Public Utility Commission, 290
Kansas Southwestern Railroad, 290
Katy see Missouri-Kansas-Texas Railroad
Kearny, Gen. Stephen W., 8-9, 49
Keefe, J. H., 355
Kellam, Homer E., 278
Kempner, I. H., 355

Kenna, E. D., 355
Kettering, Charles F., 311
Kettle, Chief Black, 15
Kelly, Pat, (Conductor), 167
Kendrick, Vice-President, 294
Keyes, Henry, 35, 47
Kidwell, Honorable Zebulon, 87
Killeen, Frank P., 355
King, Edward, 250
Kingman, Lewis, 115, 116, 125, 132, 134-135, 139, 141, 149, 159, 164, 166, 272, 286, 355
Kipling, Rudyard, 279
Kiser, S. E., 108
Kline, Peter, 98
Kouns, C. W., 352, 353
Kouns, Charles, 352
Kouns, Nellie, 352
Kouns, Sarah, 352
Krum, Chas., 355

Lackawanna Railroad, 215
Lafitte, Jean, 212
Lake, H. R., 277
Lake Shore & Michigan Southern Railroad, 246
Lakin, D. L., 76, 81
La Mere, Louis J., 198
Lamont, Thos. W., 355
Lane, James H., 32
Lanem, J. J., 355
Langtry, Lily, 352
Langworthy, (Agent), 325
Lauritzen, Captain, 260
Lautz, H. B., 355
Lease, Mary Ellen, 245
Leavenworth, Lawrence & Galveston Railroad, 349
Leavenworth, Pawnee & Western Railroad, 35
Lehman, Frank A., 355
Levet, Ben F., 184
Little, Stephen, 247
"Little Buttercup," (Locomotive), 157, 196
Longstreet, A. C., 167
Lord, Henry (President), 35, 47, 355
Los Angeles & San Gabriel Railroad, 191
Los Angeles Pioneer Oil Company, 292
Losee, Charles, 282
Lowell Railroad, 118
Lubbock, Frank, 224
Luck, A. A., 354
Lum, Reverend Samuel, 27
Lumsden, (Engineer), 271-272
Lupton, Geo., W., 355

Machovec, E. E., 356
Mack, Mrs. A. R., 198
Mackie, F. J., 356
MacRae, Albert, 294
Magoun, George C., 243-244, 246, 356
Mahony, Edward, 260
"Mail," (Train), 53
"Mail & Express," (Train), 168
Manners, Captain, 164
Manners, Lady Diana, 164
Manvel, Allen, 209, 243-244
Maricopa & Phoenix Railroad, 263
Marietta & Cincinnati Railroad, 36
"Marion," (Locomotive), 166
Marsh, S. M., 357
Marvin, H. L., 231

Martinez, Mrs. Pedro, 336, 342
Masterson, Bat, 71-72, 150, 152, 346
Masterson, Ed, 71-72, 89
Masterson, William Barclay, 148
Maxwell, Lucien Benjamin, 160, 347
McCabe, 236
McCarthy, Ordnance Sergeant, 120
McClelland, James, 146
McCluskie, Mike, 52
McDonald, J. G., 67
McDonald, S. B., 305
McInnis, E. E., 356
McIntyre, Clara, 320
McKibben, J. F., 356
McLellan, C. T., 356
McMurtrie, J. A., 135, 138-139, 144-147
McNeal, Louise, 316
McNeil, J. H., 184
McNeil, M. A., 317
McPherson, Texas & Gulf Railroad, 236
Mead, James R., 49
Memphis, El Paso & Pacific Railroad, 182
Mendelsohn, Meyer, 271
Mennonites, 84, 86-87
Merrick, R. G., 356
Merritt, General George, 232, 234
Mertz, M. L., 356
Mexican Central Railroad, 56, 95, 116
Mexican National Railways, 326
Meyer, Banka A., 321
Meyer, Dan, 255
Michigan Central Railroad, 115
Miles, General Nelson A., 15
Milwaukee Road see Chicago, Milwaukee, St. Paul & Pacific Railroad Company
Miranda, Guadalupe, 160
Miranda, Luz, 160
Missouri-Kansas-Texas Railroad, 34, 219
Mississippi River Railroad and Toll Bridge Company, 205
Missouri Pacific Railroad, 63, 73, 177, 191, 201, 243, 288, 333
Moore, Jim, 64, 155, 157, 196-200
Moore, W. Scott, 162
Moran, Thomas, 287
Morawetz, Victor, 249, 287
Morley, William Raymond, 115, 116, 123, 125, 132-134, 137-139, 141, 144-153, 159, 173-175, 286
Morris, John, 307, 315
Morse, C. A., 356
Morse, Charles F., 98, 203
Morton, Paul, 278
Mudge, H. U., 241
Mulvane, John, 356
Murphy, Frank M., 265-266
Murphy, Jeremiah, 349
Murray, Eli, 270
"*Muskegon*," (Observation Car), 280

Names, of Santa Fe towns, 351-359
Nation, Carry, 37, 236
National Association of Shippers Advisory Boards, 334
National Pacific Railroad, 46
"*Navajo*," (Train), 271
Nelson, Fred, 356
Nettleton, "Uncle George," 62

Nevin, W. G., 356
New England Emigrant Aid Society of Boston, 37
New Jersey Railroad, 36
New Mexico & Arizona Railway Company, 245
New Mexico & Southern Pacific Railroad, 131
New York & Oswego Midland Railroad, 265
New York Central System, 304
New York-Kansas League, The, 37
New York, Lake Erie & Western Railroad, 244
Nicholson, George T., 278
Nickerson, H. R., 197
Nickerson, Thomas, 79, 93, 125, 131, 140, 143, 356
Nickson, Tom, 69
Niles Machine Works, 41
Noble, Ed, 42
Northern Pacific Railway, 64, 95, 182, 244
Northwestern Pacific Railroad, 274
Northwestern Packet Line, 13
Norton, T. L., Jr., 356
Nutt, H. C., 252, 262, 264
Nye, Bill, 198

Oakland & East Side Line, 261
O'Brien, Larry, 120
O'Brien, Mike, 60
"Ocean Wave," (ferry), 260
Octagon Settlement Company, The, 37
O'Donnell, T. S., 356
Office of Production Management, 330
Ogg, O. J., 356
Ogle, Alderman, 215
Ohio & Mississippi Railroad, 40
Oklahoma Slim, 284
O'Loughlin, Jerry, 78
Oñate, Don Juan de, 6
O'Neil, Engineer, 167
Opdyke, Charles P., 356
"Orizaba," (steamer), 181
O'Rourke, Gang, 196
Osborn, Governor Thomas, 71, 85
Osgood, Joseph O., 182
Otero, Don Miguel, 95, 131
Otis, J. E., 356
"Overland Limited," (train), 186

Pacific Coast Steamship Company, 181
Pacific Mail Steamship Company, 254
Pacific Railway, 36
Padilla, Father Juan de, 5-6
Palmer, General William J., 95, 116, 130, 135, 144-145, 147, 150-151, 154, 184
Pangbor, Reporter, 90
Panhandle & Santa Fe, 224
Parker, Earl H., 356
Pawnee Charlie, 176, 347
Payne, Captain David L., 230
Peabody, F. H., 356
Peacock, A. R., 279
Penn, William, 84
Pennsylvania & Reading Railroad, 244
Pennsylvania Railroad, 250, 309
Perea, Don Jose Leandro, 134
Perley, I. E., 356

Perris, Frederick Thomas, 190, 347, 356
Peter, Rhody, 48
Peter, Thomas J., 12, 21, 34, 35, 41, 56, 60-61, 62, 116, 286
Pettibone, F. G., 319, 356
Phelan, James D., 256
Philadelphia, Wilmington & Baltimore Railroad, 36
Phoenix & Eastern Railroad, 267
Pierce, Charles W., 356
Pierce, President Franklin, 29, 229
Pike, Lieut. Zebulon, 127
Pitkin, Governor, 152
Pittsburgh & Erie Railroad, 23, 30
Polk, Colonel L. J., 225
Pomeroy, Samuel C., 31, 32, 33, 349, 356
Powell, Eleanor, 302
Powell, Major J. W., 273
Prairie Dog Dave, 70
Pratt, Mrs. Grace Salome, 268, 352
Pratt, James, 44
Prescott, Frank H., 312
Prescott & Arizona Central Railroad, 264
Prescott National Bank, 266
Preston, E. F., 256
Price, Ada, 352
Price, Floyd, 352
Prince, Chief Justice L., 166
Pringle, Murray T., 113
Prichett, Dr. Henry S., 356
Pueblo & Arkansas Valley Railroad, 79
Pueblo & Salt Lake Railroad, 79
Pullman, George M., 303
Purcell, E. B., 223, 286
Purcell, John, 292
Quincy Railroad see Chicago, Burlington & Quincy Railroad

Railroad Administration, 330
Railroad slang, 360-376
Railroad Young Men's Christian Association, 289
Railway News Company, The, 271
Rain, John, 244
Rajacich, James Michael, 324
Ramsey, D. G., 211
"*Ranger*," (Train), 325
Rath, Charlie, 69-70
Read, J. C., 356
Redmond, F. A., 320
Reinhart, J. W., 245-247
Reynolds, "Diamond Joe," 266
Reynolds, Jack, 57
Rice, Jeff, 98
Ridenour, Mrs. (Judge), 317
Riley, Dennis, 52
Rio Grande & El Paso Railroad Company, 245
Rio Grande Railroad see Denver & Rio Grande Western Railroad
Ripley, President Edward Payson, 225, 249-251, 273, 283, 286-290, 291-292, 294, 318-321, 323, 326-328, 356, 388
Robins, Trainmaster, 269
Robinson, Albert Alonzo, 34, 56, 57-60, 93, 114, 116, 125, 132, 134-135, 137, 138-139, 141, 145-149, 155, 159-160, 166, 201-203, 209, 222, 252, 286, 347, 356, 357
Rock Island Railroad see Chicago, Rock Island & Pacific Railway
Rogers, John D., 356

Roosevelt, Theodore, 281, 290
Roscoe, Snyder & Pacific Railroad, 283
Rose, Amanda, 352
Rose, Leonard, 352
Rosenberg, Henry, 213, 215, 356
Ross, Edmund G., 14-15, 17, 19, 21, 31, 49, 349
Rossington, W. H., 250
Russell, Campbell, 104
Ryan, Mary A., 278

Safford, Jacob, 349
St. John, E., 237
St. Joseph & Denver City Road, 56, 116
St. Louis & San Francisco Railway Company, 168, 177, 245
St. Louis, Kansas City & Colorado Railroad, 245, 251
St. Paul & Pacific Railway, 13
St. Vrain, Ceran, 15
San Diego & Gila, Atlantic & Pacific, 182
San Diego Steamship Company, 186
San Francisco & North Pacific Railroad, 274
San Francisco & Northwestern Railroad, 274
San Francisco & San Joaquin Valley Railway, 256, 258-259, 261
San Francisco de Santa Fe, 3
San Francisco Savings Union, 256
"*Santa Claus Special*," (Train), 277
Santa Fe & Grand Canyon, 274
"*Santa Fe Express*," (Train), 162
Santa Fe Pension Plan, 292-294
Santa Fe, Prescott & Phoenix Railroad, 265-267
Sargent, M. L., 45, 61
Sawyer, Warren, 357
Schmidt, Carl B., 83, 85
Schofield, W. H., 357
Scott, Walter, 279-281, 301
"*Scout*," (Train), 323
Sealy, George, 215, 217-219, 357
Sealy, John, 213, 216, 218, 357
Sears, Thos., 357
Seligman, F., 357
Seligman, W., 357
Seminole Land & Town Company, 232
Serra, Father, 286
Seymour, Horatio, 14
Shaefer, Jake, 91
Shaufler, E. H., 357
Sheridan, General Phil, 10-11, 346
Sherman, Walter Justin, 217, 220-222, 286, 355
Sherman, General William, 163
Sherwood, Lorenzo, 17, 18
Sibley Bridge Company, 205
Silsbee, N. D., 357
Simpson, George, 280
Simpson, Sockless Jerry, 37, 244
"*Sioux*," (Locomotive), 157
Skeen, J. B., 357
Slang, railroad, 360-376
Sloat, John Drake, 9
Smith, Bella, 353
Smith, "Borax," 261
Smith, General C. H., 120
Smith, F. W., 171, 353, 354
Smith, Frank, 354
Smith, Jedediah, 189
Smith, Uncle Billy, 30

Smyer, C. E., 357
Snow, J. W., 203
Snyder, Webster, 220
Somerville, Albert, 213
Sonora Railway Company, Limited, 245, 252, 296
Southern California Railway Company, 245
Southern Cotton Press, 214
Southern Kansas Railroad, 225, 231
Southern Kansas Railway Company of Texas, 245
Southern Pacific Company, 95, 131, 159, 161, 167, 170-174, 179, 184-185, 187-195, 243, 245, 252-253, 255-259, 263, 267-268, 274-275, 278-279, 296
"*Southwestern Limited*," (Train), 304
Spaulding, Benjamin F., 236
Spear, Alden, 357
Spencer, Geo. W., 357
Spencer, Roy, 57
Spike Maul George, 284
Sprague, Kate Chase, 14
Spreckels, Adolph B., 256
Spreckels, Claus, 255-256, 258, 353
Spreckels, John D., 255
Staab, County Commissioner, 166
Stanford, Leland, 14, 170, 191, 253
Stiles, Captain D. F., 232-233
Stillwell, Arthur E., 295-298
Stine, Albert E., 328-329
Storey, W. B., Jr., 256, 259, 261, 274, 286, 328
Stringfellow, J. H., 31, 349
Strohm, C. B., 357
Strong, William Barstow, 93, 95, 115, 130-131, 135, 138, 140-143, 149-151, 159-160, 168, 173-175, 181, 187, 191, 201, 206, 209, 242, 252, 286, 353, 357
Stuart, E. B., 357
Sturgill, H. H., 261
Summers, E. M., 278
"*Super Chief*," (Train), 301, 304, 306, 327
"*Super Chief II*," (Train), 306, 308
Sutton, Michael, 357
Sylvester, W. W., 357

"*T. C. Wheeler*," (Locomotive), 199
Taft, William Howard, 323
"*Tarantula*," (Locomotive), 179
Tellin, Peter, 61
Taylor, Miss Josie, 225
Temple, Bernard Moore, 216
Texas and New Orleans Railroad, 212
Texas & Pacific Railroad, 161, 170, 182, 283, 294
"*Thomas Nickerson*," (Locomotive), 45
"*Thomas Sherlock*," (Locomotive), 45
Thompson, Mayor "Big Bill," 105
Thompson, Irving G., 238
Thompson, (Operator), 234
Tilghman, Bill, 72
Titus, Grand Marshal S. W., 224
Todd, DeForest, 263-264
"*Tom Peter*," (Locomotive), 45
Touzalin, A. E., 81, 83, 357
Towns, Names of, 351-359

Treasury Department, 254
Tritle, F. A., 262
Trull, W. B., 357
Turner, Avery, 92, 141-142, 166, 176, 347
Tuttle, R. H., 357
Twitchell, Ginery, 50

"*Uncle Dick*," (Locomotive), 142
Union Marine & Fire Insurance, 214
Union Pacific Railroad, 9-10, 11-12, 16, 33, 50, 63, 66, 82, 116, 119, 126, 130, 156, 177-179, 202, 220, 236, 238, 244, 253, 312
Universal Air Lines, 304
Universal Aviation Corporation, 304
Upham, Isaac, 255
Usher, J. P., 236

Van Loan, Charles E., 280
Van Mullen, Mayor, 318
Vaughn, Major G. W., 265, 286
Vegetarian Settlement Company, 37
Vermillion, Reverend L. C., 323
Victor, J. N., 187, 357
Villa, Pancho, 297
Vise, Nathaniel, 352
Vise, Thalia, 352

Wade, Ben, 14
Wade, K. H., 270
Wagner, Curly, 72
Walker, Jimmie, 304
Walkup, G. A., 237
Wall, H. S., 357
Wallace, J. F., 201
Wallace, General Lew, 166
Wallis, J. E., 357
Ward, Bob, 325
Warkentin, Bernhard, 86
Waters, Moses, 70
Watlington, Charles, 157
Way, M. E., 357
Webster, Mayor, 72
Weidel, Joseph, 283
Weightman, Judge R. H., 31, 349
Wellman, A. O., 357
Wells, General Manager, 354
Wells, A. G., 355
Wells, D. L., 357
Western Improvement Company, 388
Weston, Edward Payson, 321
Whilhouse, H. W., 271
White, Blackie, 180
White, Senator, 270
Whittier, W. F., 256
Wichita & Western Railway Company, 245
Wickham, Ida, 158
Wickham, Ma, 158
Wilder, Edward, 357
Willebrandt, Mabel Walker, 304
"*William B. Strong*," (Locomotive), 199
Williams, Craggy Bill, 347
Williams, William S., 169-170
Williamson, Lieut. R. S., 190
Winona & St. Peter Railroad, 265
Winslow, E. F., 357
Wise, E. E., 237
Woodfin, John, 227
Woods, Ellen, 352
Wootton, Fidelis, 138

Wootton, Dick, Jr., 138
Wootton, "Uncle Dick," 6, 15, 95, 132, 134, 136, 140, 142, 347
Wright, Bob, 69
Wylie, W. D., 357
Wyman, (Conductor), 57

"Yellow Jack Special," (Train), 225
Young, Tom, 306

Zander, A. D., 190
Zander, John Xavier, 184

SANTA FE

Sacramento R.
SACRAMENTO
STOCKTON
SAN FRANCISCO
FRESNO
Colorado R.
DENVER
PUEBLO
SANTA FE
GRAND CANYON
BARSTOW
ALBUQUERQUE
LOS ANGELES
SAN DIEGO
PHOENIX
CARLSBAD
EL PASO
PRESIDIO
PACIFIC OCEAN
MEXICO
Smiley